D0122339

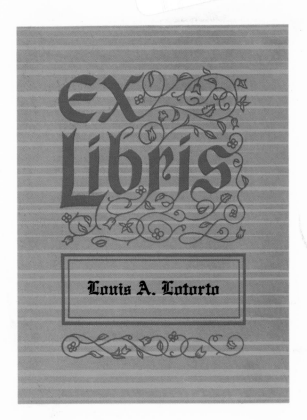

Ex Libris

Louis A. Lotorto

THE BEST PLAYS OF 1977–1978

THE
BURNS MANTLE
YEARBOOK

THE
BEST PLAYS
OF 1977-1978

EDITED BY OTIS L. GUERNSEY JR.

Illustrated with photographs and
with drawings by HIRSCHFELD

○ ○ ○ ○ ○ ○

DODD, MEAD & COMPANY
NEW YORK • TORONTO

Copyright © 1978 by Dodd, Mead & Company, Inc.

ISBN: 0-396-07637-8

Library of Congress Catalog Card Number 20-21432

Printed in the United States of America

"Getting Out": by Marsha Norman. Copyright © 1978 by Marsha Norman. Reprinted by permission of William Morris Agency, Inc. on behalf of the author. See CAUTION notice below. All inquiries should be addressed to: George Lane, William Morris Agency, Inc., 1350 Avenue of the Americas, New York, N.Y. 10019.

"The Gin Game": by D. L. Coburn. Copyright © 1977, 1978 by D. L. Coburn. Reprinted by permission of Flora Roberts, Inc. See CAUTION notice below. The complete play is published by Drama Book Specialists, 150 West 52nd Street, New York, N.Y. 10019. Inquiries concerning stock and amateur acting rights should be addressed to: Samuel French, Inc., 25 West 45th Street, New York, N.Y. 10036. All other inquiries should be addressed to the author's representative: Flora Roberts, Inc., 65 East 55th Street, New York, N.Y. 10022.

"A Life in the Theater": by David Mamet. Copyright © 1975, 1977 by David Mamet. Reprinted by permission of Grove Press, Inc. See CAUTION notice below. All inquiries should be addressed to the publisher: Grove Press, Inc., 196 West Houston Street, New York, N.Y. 10014.

"Chapter Two": by Neil Simon. Copyright © 1978 by Neil Simon. Reprinted by permission of Random House, Inc. See CAUTION notice below. All inquiries should be addressed to Random House, Inc. 201 East 50th Street, New York, N.Y. 10022.

"A Prayer for My Daughter": by Thomas Babe. Copyright © 1977 by Thomas Babe. Reprinted by permission of The Lantz Office Incorporated. See CAUTION notice below. All inquiries concerning stock and amateur acting rights should be addressed to: Samuel French, Inc., 25 West 45th Street, New York, N.Y. 10036. All other inquiries should be addressed to the author's representative: The Lantz Office Incorporated, 114 East 55th Street, New York, N.Y. 10022.

"Deathtrap": by Ira Levin. Copyright © 1978 by Ira Levin. Reprinted by permission of Howard Rosenstone & Company, Inc. See CAUTION notice below. All inquiries concerning amateur acting rights should be addressed to: Dramatists Play Service, Inc., 440 Park Avenue South, New York, N.Y. 10016. All other inquiries should be addressed to the author's representative: Howard Rosenstone & Company, Inc., 850 Seventh Avenue, New York, N.Y. 10019.

"Family Business": by Dick Goldberg. Copyright © 1976, 1978 by Dick Goldberg. Reprinted by permission of Brett Adams Limited. See CAUTION notice below. All inquiries should be addressed to the author's representative: Brett Adams Limited, 36 East 61st Street, New York, N.Y. 10021.

"The 5th of July": by Lanford Wilson. Copyright © 1978 by Lanford Wilson. Reprinted by permission of International Creative Management. See CAUTION notice below. The complete play is published by Hill and Wang, a division of Farrar, Straus and Giroux, Inc. Inquiries concerning amateur acting rights should be addressed to: Dramatists Play Service, Inc., 440 Park Avenue South, New York, N.Y. 10016. All other inquiries should be addressed to the author's agent: Bridget Aschenberg, International Creative Management, 40 West 57th Street, New York, N.Y. 10019.

"Da": by Hugh Leonard. Copyright © 1975 by Hugh Leonard. Reprinted by permission of Curtis Brown, Ltd. See CAUTION notice below. The complete play is published by Atheneum Publishers. All inquiries should be addressed to the author's representative: Gilbert Parker, Curtis Brown, Ltd., 575 Madison Avenue, New York, N.Y. 10022.

"Tribute": by Bernard Slade. Copyright © 1978 by Bernard Slade. Reprinted by permission of the author's agent. See CAUTION notice below. Inquiries concerning stock and amateur acting rights should be addressed to: Samuel French, Inc., 25 West 45th Street, New York, N.Y. 10036. All other inquiries should be addressed to the author's representative: Jack Hutto.

"The Best Little Whorehouse in Texas": book by Larry L. King and Peter Masterson; music and lyrics by Carol Hall. Produced by Universal Pictures. Copyright © 1978 by Larry L. King, Peter Masterson and Susannah Productions, Ltd. Lyrics copyright © 1977, 1978 by Daniel Music, Ltd., Shukat Music, a Division of The Shukat Company, Ltd. and MCA Music, a Division of MCA Inc. All rights reserved, including public performance for profit. Any copying, arranging or adapting of the lyrics contained herein without the written consent of the owners is an infringement of copyright. See CAUTION notice below. All inquiries concerning the use of the lyrics should be addressed to MCA Music, 445 Park Avenue, New York, N.Y. 10022. All other inquiries should be addressed to: The Sterling Lord Agency Inc., 660 Madison Avenue, New York, N.Y. 10021; Writers & Artists Agency, 162 West 56th Street, New York, N.Y. 10019; or The Shukat Company, Ltd., 25 Central Park West, New York, N.Y. 10023.

CAUTION: Professionals and amateurs are hereby warned that the above-mentioned plays, being fully protected under the Copyright Law of the United States of America, the British Commonwealth, including the Dominion of Canada, and all other countries of the Copyright Union, the Berne Convention, the Pan-American Copyright Convention and the Universal Copyright Convention, are subject to license and royalty. All rights including, but not limited to, reproduction in whole or in part by any process or method, professional use, amateur use, film, recitation, lecturing, public reading, recording, taping, radio and television broadcasting, and the rights of translation into foreign languages, are strictly reserved. Particular emphasis is laid on the matter of readings, permission for which must be obtained in writing from the author's representative or publisher, as the case may be with the instructions set forth above.

EDITOR'S NOTE

THE intensity of experimental production by scores of off-off-Broadway groups has been rising yearly. In 1977-78 the New York theater fairly seethed with showcase offerings, which our volume continues to record in a comprehensive listing of more than 800 entries prepared by Camille Croce (plus a comment on the season's highlights by one of its dramatists, Marion Fredi Towbin). On the surface of OOB, the boiling bubbles break into air, as experimental and professional production mingle with each other and criss-cross the invisible border into each other's territory. It is hard to define where the one leaves off and the other begins, but our Miss Croce has endeavored to do so in this 1977-78 *Best Plays* volume with expanded coverage of each of the borderline cases, with their Equity showcase agreements, "mini-contracts" and other near-professional-status symbols.

Our *Best Plays* series of theater yearbooks was first to give national recognition to the cross-country theater movement eleven years ago. Ella A. Malin's listing of professional regional productions, with full casts and credits of new-script premieres, is still by far the most complete, in this volume as, collectively, in the other ten. Miss Malin wishes particularly to acknowledge with thanks the help she gets from personnel in the regional theater offices in collecting the facts for her monumental record of theater activity from coast to coast, from the Gulf over into Canada.

Our section on "The Season Around the United States" also carries expanded summaries of events in Washington by David Richards, drama critic of the Washington *Star* and in Los Angeles by Ron Pennington, drama critic of the *Hollywood Reporter,* plus an outline of nationwide dinner theater highlights by Francine L. Trevens. And as an introduction to this section we again present the citations by the American Theater Critics Association of outstanding new scripts presented outside New York in 1977-78. This coverage includes capsule reviews of all the plays cited, plus a full-scale, Best Play-type synopsis of ATCA's principal selection. We note that the ATCA selections in last year's volume turned out to be something of a preview of this year's New York theater season. Four of the ATCA 1977 choices — *The Gin Game, A Life in the Theater, Family Business* and *A History of the American Film* — were produced in New York in 1978, two on Broadway and two off. The first named was the year's best American play and the first three are Best Plays in this volume. ATCA's principal 1977 selection, *And the Soul Shall Dance,* wasn't produced on the New York stage, but it was seen in New York in 1978 in a nationally-televised Public Service network special.

As we set down these notes about this year's *Best Plays* volume, it comes to mind that several other published collections of facts about various areas of theater appear at the end of each season like streams during snow-melt; but only *Best Plays* does it *all* and *has* done it all for decades. *The Best Plays of 1977-78* follows this precedent with a listing of *all* Broadway and off-Broadway shows (and only Best Plays runs complete off-Broadway information, while other publications including the New York *Times* have stopped trying even to categorize off-Broadway shows), plus an evaluation of it all by the editor in the critical perspective of a whole year. Our volume encompasses *all* important professional productions from the shores of the Pacific to the darkest Greenwich Village alley; *all* the major cast replacement data on New York shows, thanks to Stanley Green; *all* theater-related information from twelve months of play-publication lists and obituary pages, thanks to Rue Canvin; *all* the facts of long runs, awards great and small, and all the other details of a theater year collected, examined, checked and rechecked with essential and much-appreciated help from Henry Hewes, Jeff Sweet, Clara Rotter of the New York *Times,* Hobe Morrison of *Variety,* Ralph Newman of the Drama Book Shop, Alan Hewitt, scores of patient and forbearing staff members of theater production offices on, off and off off Broadway — and ever and always, Jonathan Dodd of Dodd, Mead & Co., publishers of the *Best Plays* yearbooks since Burns Mantle's first volume in the season of 1919-20, and the editor's supportive and apparently untiring wife.

We aren't a picture book, but only Best Plays carries the most penetrating and distinguished of *all* graphic art on the theater: Al Hirschfeld's incomparable drawings of major attractions of the New York season. Only *Best Plays* reproduces outstanding scenic and costume designs in their original creative form (this year thanks to Edward Gorey and Geoffrey Holder). Only *Best Plays* synopsizes *all* of one show in photographs, to record the full look and pattern of a contemporary production (this year *The Best Little Whorehouse in Texas,* thanks to the fine photos of Ilene Jones). And *all* outstanding Broadway and off-Broadway shows and performances are represented in our *Best Plays* photographs, together with representative major cross-country and off-off-Broadway productions (this year for the first time placed, not in a single photo section as in the past, but throughout the book to illustrate coverage in the text), thanks to the camera work of Bert Andrews, Mark Avery, Linda Blase, James C. Clark, Sy Friedman, Gerry Goodstein, Roger Greenawalt, Ken Howard, J.E.B., Joe B. Mann, Marinaro, Cliff Moore, Frederic Ohringer, Gary Sweetman, Martha Swope, Jay Thompson and Michael Uffer.

And only *Best Plays* looks at the season from the wide angle that reveals it *all:* the written word which is the true breadth of theater, not the expertise and/or glamor of the performer (though it helps) nor the adroitness of the production (though it can greatly enhance a script). Only *Best Plays* reserves the center ring of its multiple coverage not for the star but for the author in its selection, synopses and excerpting of the Best Plays themselves, marking out the theater's literary foundation.

So once again in this volume as in past volumes, all of us involved in the preparation of *Best Plays* have done it *all* as it was given to us to do by our far-flung, flourishing theater. Here it *all* is in these pages as it was onstage in 1977-78.

OTIS L. GUERNSEY Jr.

July 1, 1978

CONTENTS

Drawings by HIRSCHFELD

CONTENTS   xi

SUMMARIES
OF THE
SEASONS

Armelia McQueen, Ken Page, Charlaine Woodard, Andre De Shields, Nell Carter and Hank Jones in *Ain't Misbehavin'*

○
○
○
THE SEASON IN NEW YORK
○
     By Otis L. Guernsey Jr.
○
○

THE 1977-78 season in New York was a castle built on sand, an arresting demonstration of how to succeed in show business without really trying. To call it average would be kind to its whole but unkind to its parts — the average show is as hard to find as the average man, with always an exceptional emotion, laugh, idea, performance, tune or piece of business even in the shortest-lived efforts (like Stuart Ostrow's *Stages* or Gus Weill's *The November People,* which lasted only one performance on Broadway, or the musical *Angel,* which lasted only five). To call it memorable would be true in the sense that Broadway shattered all previous box-office records with a year's gross of more than $100 million but untrue in the sense that production was off, with a total of only one effective new musical in the traditional Broadway style (*On the Twentieth Century*), in a used-car-lot atmosphere of shows borrowed from other centers of stage activity and from the past. To fill the musical void, memorable scripts and scores and even performances were awakened like Sleeping Beauty to arouse the affections of a recently-metamorphosed audience which never saw live theater before the days of *Grease, Pippin* and *The Wiz* and therefore look upon *Hello Dolly, Man of La Mancha* and *The King and I* as fresh experiences, or at least as something they've seen before only in the movies.

To dwell upon the season's brightest aspect — its ten Best Plays — Broadway and off Broadway were in balance with five Bests each (last season only one appeared off and nine on). Broadway offered two indelible geriatric studies, Hugh Leonard's soft-focus *"Da"* and D.L. Coburn's sharp-focus *The Gin Game;* Ira Levin's intriguing murder game, *Deathtrap;* a new Neil Simon, *Chapter Two,* raising the emotional questions of second marriage; and a new Bernard Slade, *Tribute,* weighing contrasting values of pleasure-seeking and commitment. Off Broadway played more than a supporting role, providing the best musical comedy of the season, the cheerful and high-spirited *The Best Little Whorehouse in Texas* by Larry L. King, Peter Masterson and Carol Hall. Independent off-Broadway production took over the center ring for a change with David Mamet's parable of youth and age, *A Life in the Theater,* and Dick Goldberg's chess game of family hostility, *Family Business.* The cream of the organizationally-produced crop was Thomas Babe's police-station drama *A Prayer for My Daughter* at New York Shakespeare Festival Public Theater and Lanford Wilson's assortment of character studies in *The 5th of July* at Circle Repertory Company.

Most of these bests were not, alas, indigenous to the New York commercial

3

The 1977-78 Season on Broadway

PLAYS (13)

THE GIN GAME
Some of My Best Friends
An Almost Perfect Person
Golda
CHAPTER TWO
The November People
Cheaters
DEATHTRAP
The Water Engine (transfer) & Mr. Happiness
Stages
Patio/Porch
The Mighty Gents
TRIBUTE

MUSICALS (5)

The Act
On the Twentieth Century
Angel
Runaways (transfer)
Working

REVUES (4)

Beatlemania
Dancin'
A History of the American Film
Ain't Misbehavin'

FOREIGN PLAYS IN ENGLISH (4)

The Night of the Tribades
The Merchant
Do You Turn Somersaults?
"DA"

FOREIGN-LANGUAGE PLAYS (1)

Estrada

REVIVALS (14)

Circle in the Square 1977:
The Importance of Being Earnest
The Cherry Orchard (transfer)
Circle in the Square 1978:
Tartuffe
Saint Joan
13 Rue de l'Amour
Man of La Mancha
Hair
Dracula
Jesus Christ Superstar
A Touch of the Poet
Cold Storage (revision)
Timbuktu (Kismet)
Hello, Dolly
The Effect of Gamma Rays on Man-in-the-Moon Marigolds

SPECIALTIES (5)

Miss Margarida's Way (Transfer)
Comedy With Music
Bully
Paul Robeson
Diversions & Delights

HOLDOVERS WHICH BECAME HITS IN 1977-78 (2)

Side by Side by Sondheim
Your Arms Too Short to Box With God

Categorized above are all the new productions listed in the "Plays Produced on Broadway" section of this volume.
Plays listed in CAPITAL LETTERS have been designated Best Plays of 1977-78.
Plays listed in *italics* were still running June 1, 1978.
Plays listed in **bold face type** were classified as hits in *Variety*'s annual estimate published May 31, 1978.

stage. *"Da"* had its world premiere in Olney, Md. in 1973 (though it's an Irish play by an Irish author) and meandered to Broadway via Dublin, the Ivanhoe Theater in Chicago and the Hudson Guild Theater OOB. *The Gin Game* was done at American Theater Arts in Hollywood, at Actors' Theater, Louisville and pre-Broadway in this production at the Long Wharf, New Haven. *A Life in the Theater* was previously produced at the Goodman Theater, Chicago. *Family Business* (which, with *The Gin Game* and *A Life in the Theater* were cited by the American Theater Critics Association in our 1976-77 volume as outstanding new cross-country plays) prepped at Stockbridge, Mass. *The Best Little Whorehouse in Texas* had been tried out OOB in the Actors Studio workshop before venturing into commercial production, and *A Prayer for My Daughter* had an experimental staging at the O'Neill Playwrights Conference before being further developed in Joseph Papp's workshop.

Chapter Two went before Los Angeles audiences pre-Broadway, but — as one of our most faithful correspondents, Alan Hewitt, the actor and theater archivist, pointed out to us in the matter of *California Suite* last season — it doesn't qualify as regional-theater-originated because it was aimed in the direction of New York by its author and its New York producer from the outset. *Tribute* and *Deathtrap* were New York shows, prepared in out-of-town tryouts, the former's so successful that it paid off the production cost before the show opened on Broadway (*Tribute* opened there June 1, technically the first day of a new season, but it had started playing previews in May and can logically be classified as a 1977-78 production — which it is in this volume). *The 5th of July* was developed in and for New York by Marshall W. Mason's group, where its author is playwright-in-residence.

New growth? *The Gin Game* is its author's first play, and the circumstances of his deciding to write it are the stuff of fantasy (see D.L. Coburn's biographical sketch in the Best Plays section of this volume). *Family Business* is Dick Goldberg's New York playwriting debut. *The Best Little Whorehouse in Texas* is the first produced play of its book authors, King and Masterson, and the professional stage debut of its composer-lyricist, Carol Hall.

As in every season, the number ten shrinks as the months go by, until it's finally incapable of fitting in all the standouts of the New York theater year. 1977-78 shows that came very close to the top ten were, in the order they opened, Patrick Meyers's *Feedlot,* Per Olov Enquist's *The Night of the Tribades* (as translated by Ross Shideler), William Gibson's *Golda,* Betty Comden's, Adolph Green's and Cy Coleman's *On the Twentieth Century,* Elizabeth Swados's *Runaways,* Sam Shepard's *Curse of the Starving Class,* Istvan Orkeny's *Catsplay* and Richard Wesley's *The Mighty Gents.*

To turn from the sublime subject of esthetic accomplishment to the ridiculous economics of today's theater, these were boom times in New York both on and offstage. The city played host to an all-time-high 16,500,000 visitors during the year. They spent an estimated $1,600,000,000 and "generated" another $4,800,-000,000, a fair portion of this at theater box offices. For the third straight season, according to *Variety's* figures, the total Broadway gross was an all-time record high. In 1976-77 it was $93.4 million, 31.8 per cent above the previous year's $70.8 million, in a different world from the previous historical high of

$58.9 million in 1967-68. This season it climbed again by 11 per cent to $103,-846,494 — jumping over the $100 million moon for the first time and, in combination with the grosses of Broadway shows on the road, jumping twice as high as that to a galactic combined gross of $209,543,379.

As we fill our lungs to rejoice at this good news, we're arrested in mid-breath by other, doubt-casting numbers: Broadway production had thinned from 54 to 41 productions (not counting specialties). Playing weeks (if ten shows play ten weeks, that's 100 playing weeks) were up only slightly to 1,360 from 1,348 last season and attendance was down from 8.8 to 8.6 million, per *Variety's* figures. This leads us to the conclusion that the record gross was at least as much the result of inflation (see our report on the $25 ticket in the "Offstage" chapter of this report) as of popularity — plus a little bit of unexpected luck with massively successful revivals led by the $12 million-grossing *The King and I.* Among the 1977-78 shows, there were only four new works and three revivals established as hits as of the end of the season, according to *Variety* estimate, and only two holdovers had become hits since the end of 1976-77.

In the ebb and flow of box office activity, *A Chorus Line* was bringing in $475,000 a week from its Broadway and two touring companies. *Pippin* finally closed after 1,944 performances and a $1,659,207 profit so far on its $500,000 investment, but a long run was no guarantee of long numbers in the bank account — *Shenandoah* had recouped only about 80 per cent of its cost after 1,050 performances. Broadway producers looked enviously at their opposite numbers in the concert field, some of whom were using Broadway theaters for conspicuously lucrative rock concerts and solo shows (*Beatlemania* grossed more than $7 million in a season at the Winter Garden and was still going strong at season's end). Liza Minnelli's musical showcase, *The Act,* was in the black by about $175,000 when it closed in July.

Attempts to showcase acting stars didn't usually come off so well. Liv Ullmann's adventure in *Anna Christie* last season turned an estimated $150,000 profit, but the effort to bring Mary Martin back to Broadway with Anthony Quayle in a Russian comedy about middle-aged romance, *Do You Turn Somersaults?,* dropped all of its $400,000 cost. So did the Ted Knight vehicle *Some of My Best Friends,* a comedy in which the TV star played a disenchanted business man looking for happiness and escape from the rat race by opening up a dialogue with plants and animals. This one lost its entire $250,000. So did *The Night of the Tribades,* a dark study of Strindberg's emotional life translated from the Swedish, with Max Von Sydow, losing its comparatively modest $225,-000 stake.

The most conspicous characteristic of the Broadway year as a whole was its very great scarcity of musical inspiration. It's possible that the Broadway musical as we have known it is an endangered species suffering the environmental impact of rising production costs and dwindling esthetic nourishment. There are at least four contemporary concentrations of effort to shelter and nurture the stage musical in special circumstances outside New York until it finds its feet again: the Musical Theater Lab in Washington, D.C., the Lenox, Mass. Arts Center/Music-Theater Performing Group, the American Musical Theater Center at Duke University, Durham, N.C. and the Goodspeed Opera House,

ON THE TWENTIETH CENTU-
RY—*Above,* Keith Davis, Quitman
Fludd III, Ray Stephens and Joseph
Wise as porters, with Robin Wagner's
train design; *right,* Kevin Kline,
Imogene Coca, Judy Kaye (*foreground,* who replaced Madeline Kahn)
and John Cullum in the leading roles of
the musical

East Haddam, Conn. In the meantime, we were making do in 1977-78 with a transferred off-off-Broadway cabaret revue, *Ain't Misbehavin'*, which won the Critics and Tony best-musical citations; another cabaret turn, *The Act,* tailored for a star; a tour de force of design and atmosphere in *On the Twentieth Century;* Bob Fosse's revue-like celebration of *Dancin';* Studs Terkel's ditto of *Working;* and a bushel basket full of revivals. What more could we have wished back there in the mid-1960s than Carol Channing in *Hello, Dolly!* or Richard Kiley in *Man of La Mancha* — or a revival of what was then a venerated old 1950s musical, *The King and I,* with Yul Brynner repeating his memorable performance as the King of Siam? It wasn't wishing that made it so all over again, more than a decade later in the season of 1977-78.

Glancing over our shoulder at the off-Broadway season, we see that the Joseph Papp skyrocket reached a point in its trajectory where it exploded in a dazzling shower of productions. His season began with Central Park engagements of his own previously-acclaimed *Threepenny Opera* and *Agamemnon,* and he put on three more revivals — *The Mandrake, The Dybbuk* and a musicalized *The Misanthrope* — among his fourteen 1977-78 offerings downtown in the nooks and crannies of the Public Theater. These comprised a half dozen new plays, two "poemplays," two musicals and a specialty, the while he was also setting up a cabaret theater under his roof and sponsoring odds and ends of guest production and workshop activity. In the damp and woundy theater climate of today, part of Papp's 1977-78 fireworks display fizzled, of course, but it achieved some spectacular bursts, notably the Best Play *A Prayer for My Daughter,* the ground-breaking musical *Runaways* and the striking novelty *Miss Margarida's Way.*

Also off Broadway, Lynne Meadow's Manhattan Theater Club finally put its toe in the water of the commercial theater with a series of five-week runs of foreign plays new to New York audiences. MTC has previously confined itself to the off-off-Broadway arena, where it has achieved mightily (for example, *Ain't Misbehavin'* was developed in its cabaret). Probably MTC will now plunge in and sink or swim — at least part-time — with the rest of off-Broadway's distinguished organizational producers: Circle, Roundabout, Chelsea, Negro Ensemble, Phoenix, LOOM and the aforementioned Joseph Papp.

Among Broadway producers, The Shubert Organization — personified by Gerald Schoenfeld and Bernard B. Jacobs — had its finger in many pies such as *The Gin Game, The Act, The Merchant, Dancin', The Mighty Gents* and *Ain't Misbehavin'.* Roger L. Stevens was active with *Deathtrap* (with Alfred de Liagre Jr.) and Kennedy Center participation in many other New York shows. Emanuel Azenberg's name was on *Ain't Misbehavin'* with others and on *Chapter Two* alone. Elliot Martin distinguished himself with a benchmark production of O'Neill's *A Touch of the Poet;* but seldom these days do you find a single producer's name above the title in your Broadway program. Apparently it takes a corporal's guard to put on a show in 1978, as witness the crowd of producers who joined the single playwright, Hugh Leonard, in accepting the Tony award for *"Da"* on TV. Joseph Papp produces them on Broadway by himself, with a little help from his associate Bernard Gersten, but he doesn't originate them there. This season he brought *Miss Margarida's Way, The*

Estelle Parsons in *Miss Margarida's Way*

Water Engine and *Runaways* up north from downtown and gave shelter to *Paul Robeson* in his *For Colored Girls, etc.* theater for a few weeks.

Directors? Standouts in 1977-78 were Mike Nichols (*The Gin Game*), Dennis Rosa (*Dracula*), José Quintero (*A Touch of the Poet*), Robert Moore (*Deathtrap*), Peter Masterson and Tommy Tune (*The Best Little Whorehouse in Texas*), Richard Maltby Jr. (*Ain't Misbehavin'*), Bob Fosse (*Dancin'*), Melvin Bernhardt (*"Da"*), Stephen Porter (*The Importance of Being Earnest* and *Tartuffe*) and Harold Prince (*On the Twentieth Century* and *Some of My Best Friends*). Outstanding designs included Robin Wagner's *On the Twentieth Century,* Edward Gorey's *Dracula,* Geoffrey Holder's *Timbuktu,* Zack Brown's several settings for classics and Santo Loquasto's for new plays.

It has to be the actors, however, who leave us with those indelible snapshots of the season's highlights, developed and ready for instant replay in the mind's eye, like the quarrelsome old couple portrayed by Hume Cronyn and Jessica Tandy . . . Jason Robards's Con Melody . . . John Wood in the maze of *Deathtrap* . . . Barnard Hughes and Brian Murray as an Irish father and son . . . Jack Lemmon finding and not entirely liking himself in *Tribute* . . . Liza Minnelli, larger than life and much larger than *The Act* . . . The superb ensemble of *Ain't Misbehavin'* and the quartet of dancing, singing porters in *On the Twentieth Century* . . . Estelle Parsons as the ruthless Miss Margarida getting her way . . . Henderson Forsythe, big-mouthed small-town sheriff of *The Best Little Whorehouse in Texas* . . . Laurence Luckinbill as a pitiless and unpitiable killer in N.Y. Shakespeare's best, *A Prayer for My Daughter* . . . William Hurt, Nancy Snyder and their ensemble of walking wounded in the Circle's best, *The 5th of July* . . . Dorian Harewood and Morgan Freeman, forbidding as a dark street in *The Mighty Gents* . . . Helen Burns as a merry Budapest widow in *Catsplay* . . . Lynn Redgrave as Joan of Arc . . . Frank Langella in a love-hate relationship with the audience in *Dracula* . . . Judd Hirsch and Anita Gillette in the emotional coils of *Chapter Two* . . . Ellis Rabb as an aging actor clinging to *A Life in the Theater* . . . Douglas Turner Ward as an elder statesman of crime in *The Offering* . . . The energetic young ensemble of *Runaways* . . . Anne Bancroft as *Golda* . . . and Anthony Quayle, Mary Martin, Victor Borge, Colleen Dewhurst, Max Von Sydow, Geraldine Fitzgerald, Ted Knight, Marian Seldes, James Whitmore, Carol Channing, James Earl Jones, Shelley Winters, George Rose, Ann Reinking, Eartha Kitt, Richard Kiley, Eddie Bracken, John Cullum, Barry Nelson and other stars and strivers establishing high profiles in an assortment of good and bad circumstances.

The ultimate insignia of New York professional theater achievement (we insist) are the citations as Best Play in these volumes, designations which are 16 years older than the Critics Award and only three years younger than the Pulitzer Prize. Each Best Play selection is made with the script itself as the first consideration, for the reason (as we've stated in previous volumes) that the script is the spirit of the theater's physical body. The script is not only the quintessence of the present, it is most of what endures into the future. So the Best Plays are the best scripts, with as little weight as humanly possible given to comparative production values. The choice is made without any regard whatever to a play's type — musical, comedy or drama — or origin on or off Broadway, or popularity at the box office or lack of same.

Above, Max Von Sydow as August Strindberg in *The Night of the Tribades; right,* Colleen Dewhurst as Irene Porter in *An Almost Perfect Person; below,* James Whitmore as Teddy Roosevelt in *Bully*

If a script of above-average quality influences the very character of a season, or if by some function of consensus it wins the Critics, Pulitzer or Tony Awards, we take into account its future historical as well as present esthetic importance to the season as a whole. This is the only special consideration we give, and we don't always tilt in its direction, as the record shows.

On the other hand, we don't take scripts of other eras into consideration for Best Play citation in this one, whatever their technical status as American or New York "premieres" which don't happen to have had a previous production of record. And we draw a line between adaptations and revivals, the former eligible for Best Play selection but the latter not, under close scrutiny on a case-by-case basis.

The ten Best Plays of 1977-78 are listed here for visual convenience in the order in which they opened in New York (a plus sign + with the performance number signifies that the play was still running on June 1, 1978).

The Gin Game
   (Broadway; 271+ perfs.)

A Life in the Theater
   (Off Broadway; 244+ perfs.)

Chapter Two
   (Broadway; 205+ perfs.)

A Prayer for My Daughter
   (Off Broadway; 127 perfs.)

Deathtrap
   (Broadway; 108+ perfs.)

Family Business
   (Off Broadway; 57+ perfs.)

The Best Little Whorehouse in Texas
   (Off Broadway; 50+ perfs.)

The 5th of July
   (Off Broadway; 35+ perfs.)

"Da"
   (Broadway; 36+ perfs.)

Tribute
   (Broadway; 1+ perfs.)

Broadway

The development of the so-called musical comedy — or latterly, just the musical — has been traced by Stanley Green and other theater historians from its roots back beyond Gilbert & Sullivan through Victor Herbert and Jerome Kern, through Cole Porter and George Gershwin, through Rodgers & Hammerstein to Stephen Sondheim and . . . beyond? Aye, there's the rub, because not since *Company* has there been significant development (the music itself excepted) in the concept of what we have come to think of as the "Broadway musical." It has taken interesting tangents like *Pacific Overtures* and *I Love My Wife,* but mutation? — not really. Maybe the nearest thing to it was *A Chorus Line,* with setpieces of dancing and character monologues strung like beads along a single theme, making a kind of connection between the book musical and the revue (*Ain't Misbehavin'*) or concert (*Beatlemania*) form. *Runaways* and *Working* went along this same line this season. Theirs is an entertainment form which is neither book musical nor revue but a *theme* musical, a little less than kin but more than kind in its resemblance to the traditional Broadway show.

Elizabeth Swados's *Runaways* was an imaginative, disciplined musical-

THEME MUSICALS—*Above*, the "Dancin' Man" number in *Dancin'; below*, a scene from *Runaways*

theater image of the runaway child, the battered casualty in flight from the family battleground. There was pity and terror in its music and dance rhythms, in the tone of its frightened young voices, in the solemnity of its performances by a part-professional, part-real-runaway cast. Accusation is its theme: accusation of parents for their selfishness and insensitivity, of society for exploiting or punishing instead of comforting the runaways (though exploitation and comfort sometimes go hand in hand, as is the case with a child prostitute who feels warmly protected by her pimp). The subject was thoroughly researched by Miss Swados and developed in workshop at Joseph Papp's Public Theater before being presented first off Broadway and then on. There was no lack of emotional contact between characters and audience in *Runaways* — what was lacking was any developmental change or progress as the show began, continued and ended on its one pounding note of helpless despair, varying little even in intensity, until you longed for an exceptional insight to break the surface. For all its poetic nature, the succession of scenes and musical numbers in *Runaways* didn't build on the image created in the opening number.

Likewise, Stephen Schwartz turned a set of Studs Terkel sketches of working people into a theme musical in *Working.* There was as much continuity of style in this series of snapshots of masons, secretaries, etc. as in the anecdotes of the dancers in *A Chorus Line,* but no such common purpose to give it momentum, other than statement and re-statement of admiration for those whose devotion to small duties often demands more endurance and self-sacrifice than is expected of those with more conspicuous responsibilities.

In *Working,* as in *Runaways,* there was again no developmental progress in the course of — or as the result of — the events/influences of the material. This is the sticking point of the theme musical at the 1978 stage of its evolution, if indeed it is an advancing musical mutation. It's highly probable that our theater artists will soon come up with a book-less show that rings profound emotional changes with the variations on its theme. It hasn't happened yet, though, and until it does we'll continue to regard the full-fledged book-musical concept like *The Best Little Whorehouse in Texas* or *On the Twentieth Century* as the co-stars of the passing show together with the unalloyed and exceptional revue like *Ain't Misbehavin'.*

There's mileage in the old form yet (*Grease, Annie*) but it is footsore from repetition. With the cost of a Broadway-sized musical now in the forbidding neighborhood of $1 million, and with the expenses of an out-of-town shakedown now so high that it's getting to be impossible to take a big show out on a tryout tour, it's safest to rely on a proven classic or a proven star or a musicalized play, novel or even movie that seems to have a built-in audience appeal. Even with the bets hedged, the action this year was pitiful. Only *On the Twentieth Century* succeeded in developing a concept into a full-fledged Broadway musical with book, music, lyrics and (seemingly) cast of thousands. This Betty Comden-Adolph Green adaptation took a firm hold on the era as well as the material of its Hecht-MacArthur source, and nostalgia proved to be its best and winning bet. The train itself stole the show, dazzlingly represented onstage in Robin Wagner's chromium plated art deco designs, a vestige of the 1930s as it powered sleekly from New York to Chicago by means of turntables, miniatures, cutaways and other stage devices, and with the Cy Coleman score pounding out the rhythm of the rails.

On the Twentieth Century could run a train onstage, but it didn't — perhaps couldn't — quite evoke the overwhelming glamor that a top-ranking movie star radiated with her mere presence in those days. Consequently the activities of the passengers, in particular the Broadway impresario trying to change his bad luck by signing a movie actress to star in his next play, lost much of their comic pressure; and no amount of arm-waving by John Cullum as the producer, of posing by Madeline Kahn as the star or of acrobatics by Kevin Kline as her lover could restore it. Imogene Coca added a dash of flavoring as a religious fanatic in a manic phase. But the train was the best part. Those closest to it — namely, Keith Davis, Quitman Fludd III, Ray Stephens and Joseph Wise as four self-satisfied porters — fared best of all.

The *Shenandoah* team (Philip Rose, Gary Geld and Peter Udell) put together the only other book musical that got as far as Broadway this season: *Angel,* adapted from the Ketti Frings play and Thomas Wolfe novel *Look Homeward, Angel.* They had only slightly more success (5 performances) than the producers of *The Prince of Grand Street, Nefertiti* and *Spotlight,* which folded out of town.

Others had better luck whipping up entertainments which avoided some of the challenges of the traditional Broadway musical. For example, *Beatlemania,* a concert-style rock musical recreating and imitating the Beatles' performance of their best-liked numbers, grossed more than $7 million during the season at the Winter Garden. Liza Minnelli also won applause on Broadway in a tailor-made wrap-around called *The Act,* about how a night club singer makes it to the top (Las Vegas) — thus giving the singer, Miss Minnelli, her cue to do her thing continuously, almost concert-style, to the outer limits of her colorful stage presence and voice, with Barry Nelson coming on and off once in a while as her mentor in a barely discernable shadow of a book. Musical or concert, *The Act* was an entertainment that drew the crowds to see Miss Minnelli in what was clearly the year's standout performance by an actress in a musical.

Likewise, *Ain't Misbehavin'* celebrated the works of Thomas "Fats" Waller in a concert-style revue (almost no dialogue; song number following song number) that originated in the mind's ear of Richard Maltby Jr., was put on by him as a Manhattan Theater Club cabaret and then brought to Broadway. This toe-tapping compendium of about 30 numbers written or made famous in performance by Waller differed from the idea of *Beatlemania* in that it attempted no impersonation of its honored subject. But it certainly recreated the ebullient Waller spirit up on that stage with a minimum of fuss and a maximum of talent embodied by the singing ensemble — squeaky Nell Carter, buxom Armelia McQueen, zany Charlaine Woodard, stylish Andre De Shields and the cut-up Ken Page — with Hank Jones playing Fats Waller piano and conducting a fine jazz combo. *Ain't Misbehavin'* riffled up and down the whole keyboard of moods from the haunting "Black and Blue" in the bass to the outburst of "Your Feet's Too Big" in the high treble. It was a huge success, deservedly, and ran away with the Critics and Tony Awards for best musical. We agree — *Ain't Misbehavin'* certainly was the best "musical" of the New York year, though obviously not a "play" in any sense and thus not eligible for Best Play selection in this volume.

And then there was *Dancin'*, still another kaleidoscope with choreographer Bob Fosse demonstrating what he could do with a Broadway show if he could push such extraneous distractions as book, music and lyrics out of the way and concentrate on the dance numbers. His cast of sixteen human bodies (including that of Ann Reinking) expressed themselves eloquently in line, gesture, motion and rhythm, singly and in groups, with background music chosen from the works of about two dozen composers including such tunesmiths as George M. Cohan, John Philip Sousa, Cat Stevens and Johann Sebastian Bach. *Dancin'* was uniquely a soaring celebration of the dance, if not — again — a Broadway musical in the full sense of the term.

In a similar construction there was Christopher Durang's well-traveled *A History of the American Film,* which had four regional theater productions before arriving on Broadway as its author's New York playwriting debut. It was a kaleidoscope of Hollywood movies from the silents to the disaster epics, part satire and part sweet nostalgia. It had a great deal of musical energy in scene after scene written to be recognized as reflections of past glories of James Cagney, Henry Fonda, Gary Cooper, Bette Davis, Loretta Young and other favorites. The director, David Chambers, kept it moving along in style, but it was not finally going anywhere.

Over on the straight-play side of Broadway, the traumas of aging and impending death preoccupied some of the best work of 1978 as it did in 1977. Last year it was *The Last Meeting of the Knights of the White Magnolia* and *The Shadow Box* on Broadway and *Cold Storage* off (the latter moving around the corner to Times Square this season for revival in a version revised by its author, Ronald Ribman, with Martin Balsam repeating his role of the terminal patient *vis à vis* Len Cariou as a newcomer to the hospital). This year it was *"Da," The Gin Game* and *Tribute* leading the parade, with intimations of mortality making themselves felt in other works all the way down the line.

"Da," the Critics and Tony best-play winner, is every inch an Irish play, with an Irish author (Hugh Leonard, veteran Dublin dramatist and director of the 1978 Dublin Festival); Irish characters played by a multi-national ensemble headed by Barnard Hughes as a crusty patriarch, Brian Murray as his adopted son, Sylvia O'Brien as his wife and Lester Rawlins as a prosperous neighbor; an Irish setting in the kitchen of a humble cottage with a view of the Mountains of Mourne; and an Irish flavor of life endured and death accepted. (Irish as it may be, it had its world premiere at Olney, Md. — as David Richards reminds us in his report on Washington, D.C. in "The Season Around the United States" section of this volume — before being produced in Dublin and then bouncing back here to Chicago and New York.) "Da," as the son always called his father, has died as the play opens, after a life of hard work as an underpaid gardener on a nearby estate, with the compensation of solid family and community relationships. But Da has been such a strong influence that his son can't put him out of mind and memory, however hard he tries; and so Da is very much with us as scene follows vivid scene in the son's remembered growing-up with love, anger, pride, failure, hope, frustration and fulfillment. Directed by Melvin

Liza Minnelli in *The Act*

Bernhardt and acted with full power; lilting in its emotional rhythms as the brogue in which all its characters speak; never very far from either laughter or tears, *"Da"* was a shade the best of the year's Best Plays.

This season's Pulitzer Prize winner, *The Gin Game,* was more than a shade its best American play. Its two characters are welfare cases in a home for the aged. They begin to find a little solace in getting together over a game of gin rummy, only to have the game's aberrations expose the worst side of their natures, until they lose their last pitiful vestiges of both mutual and self respect. *The Gin Game* is full of sympathy but devoid of comfort, a first play by an author — D.L. Coburn — who has only just turned 40 but seems to have as unerring an instinct for the *terra incognita* of creeping senility as he does of playwriting. Hume Cronyn and Jessica Tandy played the couple in what will surely go down as one of the theater's memorable dual performances, the equal of their married couple in *The Fourposter.* They are strangers who meet, make connections through a ritual of card-playing which turns out to be a no-win game, and finally part as strangers returning to their no-win lives. Under the combined power of the spare but effective script and the Cronyns' performance, the play is unnerving, not depressing. When Mike Nichols, who directed it, was reminded during the out-of-town tryout that it had "only" two characters, he replied, "Who counts characters?" It's true, in *The Gin Game* these two uncommunicating old people are, finally, almost everybody.

The season's overcast of somber preoccupation darkened even Neil Simon's newest comedy, *Chapter Two,* as it posed the question: is there life for a devoted husband after the untimely death of his beloved wife? The widower (Judd Hirsch) is besieged by well-meaning but ill-advised efforts to find a new someone for him; then he discovers to his own astonishment that he's willing to try again with a young divorcee (Anita Gillette) as balky and bright as himself; and then he plunges them both into a maze of despair and recrimination, which they will escape some day only if they hold tight to each other's hands and refuse to yield to panic. The dialogue flashes with emotional gallows humor, the mood is as contemporary as tomorrow and the insights are something special and probably a bit personal. Simon, recently a widower, is now married to Marsha Mason, and some of his *Chapter Two* strains and stresses were certainly autobiographical.

What does Neil Simon now have in common with Philip Barry, Moss Hart, Eugene O'Neill, George S. Kaufman and Maxwell Anderson? Yes, that too, but in addition to possessing exceptional playwriting skill he is now a member (the only living one) of this supremely distinguished company of authors who wrote ten or more Best Plays — *Chapter Two* is Simon's tenth. He is, however, unique among these in that he has never won a Critics, Pulitzer or Tony Award.

In *Tribute,* Bernard Slade, author of the long-run comedy hit *Same Time, Next Year,* also underlined his humor with a black streak of mortality, in his study of a modern-day jester battling leukemia and forced to take a long look at himself and his past life, in particular his relationship with his only son, in a strange new twilight. A towering performance by Jack Lemmon as a pleasure-loving sort who has plenty of talent but always goes for the laugh instead of the achievement — and therefore has a great many friends but few medals —

Right, Lester Rawlins as Drumm in *"Da"; above*, Anne Bancroft as Golda Meir in *Golda*

dominated and informed this somewhat flawed script with total conviction and endless nuance.

Slade has seen fit to offer up his play with a tacky frame around it: it begins with and keeps returning to a testimonial gathering, the "tribute" of the title, while the play flashes back to key incidents in the guest of honor's recent past. But performances like Lemmon's cannot hold up, as it did, without solid members beneath them; and Slade's play is buttressed firmly with wit and feeling in the important scenes, whatever its structural flaws may be. Jack Lemmon's performance and Bernard Slade's play were a jackpot-winning entertainment combination, and we've taken the minute liberty of including them among the bests of 1977-78, even though this show, which began its New York performances in May, didn't hold its formal opening until June 1, technically the first day of the 1978-79 season.

Another Best Play, Ira Levin's *Deathtrap,* had a great deal to do with mortality but nothing whatever to do with geriatrics or sympathy for those who are about to suffer it somewhere in the coils of its sardonic murder-game involvements. This comedy thriller was like an elaborately constructed apparatus for an exceptionally gifted circus acrobat: you couldn't imagine how all the trapezes and taut wires are to be used, but you were certain they would be because they were there. A deathtrap is indeed hidden somewhere in the relationship of a middle-aged playwright envious of his student's work. Discovering the exact nature of the trap was as difficult as it should be in a first-rate mystery, and being fooled time after time was part of the fun of seeing how it came out. John Wood gave a brilliant circus performance as the playwright, timing his comedy inflections and angular movements with the play so that trapeze met hand at exactly the right instant, time after time. Much of the credit belongs to Robert Moore's concise direction, more to Levin's clever script, but even more to Wood in one of the acting gems of his sparkling career.

Among new Broadway scripts with a fairly serious thrust was William Gibson's docu-drama *Golda,* a review of events in Israel's 1973 Yom Kippur War and in the life of its great prime minister, Golda Meir. The play benefited hugely from Anne Bancroft's presence in the title role. Head thrust aggressively forward, snapping a verbal whip at the savageries of statecraft, Miss Bancroft combined imitation, admiration and insight into to the subject in a commanding performance. The author has announced that the script produced on Broadway isn't the version of his heart's desire, so that when *Golda* reappears on world stages it will be in different, but official, form. For this reason we can't consider it for Best Play selection at this time, for which, otherwise, it would have been in the running.

Richard Wesley's *The Mighty Gents* was another work of considerable power, reflecting the contemporary undersociety in characterizations of grown-up members of a one-time Newark, N.J. black youth gang who can now find or make no place for themselves, no identity in the grownup world. The performances of Dorian Harewood as a former youth gang leader, Howard E. Rollins Jr. as a gangster and Morgan Freeman as a derelict wino who refuses to be ignored as a non-person were scathing setpieces. Their rage was convincing, their fate pitiable but their play lacked a spine to make it stand up straight, even though it was tried out twice off off Broadway, at Manhattan Theater Club and Urban Arts Corps. In this form it was more polemic than play.

David Mamet's second New York playwriting year consisted of two show-biz stories: the Best Play *A Life in the Theater* off Broadway and *The Water Engine* which began off and was brought uptown. The latter is a radio-play-within-a-staged-play about a vulnerable inventor up against ruthless business interests, staged as if in a Chicago radio station in the 1930s (and consequently more memento than drama), on a bill with a curtain raiser, *Mr. Happiness,* a Mamet monologue for an offensively cheerful radio announcer. Among other on-balance-comic matters this year were the romantic vagaries of a hard-hitting female politician (Colleen Dewhurst), in *An Almost Perfect Person;* spouse-swapping with all the devious opportunities it offers to performers like Lou Jacobi and Jack Weston, in *Cheaters;* and the manners and conversational styles of Texas women in Jack Heifner's chatty one-acters, *Patio/Porch.*

On the list of the year's imports along with *"Da," The Night of the Tribades* and *Do You Turn Somersaults?* was an effort by Arnold Wesker to place the people and events of Shakespeare's *The Merchant of Venice* in a new stage perspective entitled *The Merchant* — new but not especially revealing. The only foreign-language visitor to Broadway was *Estrada,* a Russian variety show which stopped by for a week of circus and musical numbers.

The specialty productions were certainly something special this year. Hard-driving Estelle Parsons gave the season's outstanding female performance as a totally self-centered and fanatically domineering schoolteacher in *Miss Margarida's Way,* Roberto Athayde's play which drafted the audience in the role of Miss Margarida's classroom full of browbeaten pupils. Joseph Papp brought this extraordinary tour de force of acting, writing and direction (also by Athayde) uptown to Broadway after a run at the Public. Papp also sheltered Phillip Hayes Dean's biographical study *Paul Robeson,* starring James Earl Jones, by putting it into repertory with the long-running *For Colored Girls,* etc. when it otherwise would have closed after only a short Broadway run and a longer siege of controversy (see the "Offstage" section of this report).

James Whitmore brought Theodore Roosevelt into characterization in Jerome Alden's *Bully!,* as did Vincent Price with Oscar Wilde in John Gay's *Diversions & Delights.* And then there was Victor Borge, uniquely inimitable in still another welcome *Comedy With Music* sojourn on Broadway.

Here's where we list the *Best Plays* choices for the top individual achievements of the season. In the acting categories, clear distinctions among "starring," "featured" or "supporting" players can't be made on the basis of official billing, in which an actor may appear as a "star" following the title (not true star billing) or as an "also starring" star, or as any of the other career-building typographical gimmicks. Here in these volumes we divide acting into "primary" and "secondary" roles, a primary role being one which carries a major responsibility for the show; a role which might some day cause a star to inspire a revival in order to appear in that character. All others, be they vivid as Mercutio, are classed as secondary (and of course, there are shows that don't have any primary roles at all, like *Ain't Misbehavin').*

Furthermore, this year's list of individual bests is somewhat more flexible

On these pages are samples of Edward Gorey's scene and costume designs for *Dracula,* including the act curtain, a bell pull and costume designs for Count Dracula and Lucy Seward. In a scene from the melodrama, the costumes are on the floor as Dracula (Frank Langella) prepares to have his way with helpless Lucy (Ann Sachs)

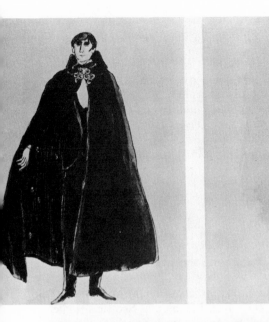

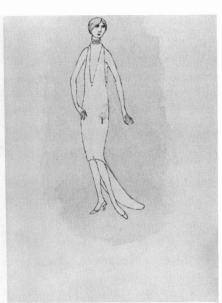

than in past volumes. This season as never before we've asked ourselves: how could we balance Jason Robards against Hume Cronyn, Jessica Tandy against Estelle Parsons, and what useful purpose could possibly be served by forcing ourselves into such arbitrary judgements? Echo replies, "We can't," and "None whatever." Consequently, when we come upon multiple examples of supreme artistry in any category of bests, henceforth we'll include them all in our list, and devil take the one-track, one-best minded.

Here, then are the *Best Plays* bests of 1977-78:

PLAYS

BEST PLAY: *"Da"* by Hugh Leonard

BEST AMERICAN PLAY: *The Gin Game* by D.L. Coburn

BEST REVIVAL: *Dracula* by Hamilton Deane and John L. Balderston, directed by Dennis Rosa

BEST ACTOR IN A PRIMARY ROLE: Hume Cronyn as Weller Martin in *The Gin Game;* Barnard Hughes as Da in *"Da";* Jack Lemmon as Scottie Templeton in *Tribute;* Jason Robards as Cornelius Melody in *A Touch of the Poet*

BEST ACTRESS IN A PRIMARY ROLE: Helen Burns as Mrs. Bela Orban in *Catsplay;* Estelle Parsons as Miss Margarida in *Miss Margarida's Way;* Jessica Tandy as Fonsia Dorsey in *The Gin Game*

BEST ACTOR IN A SECONDARY ROLE: Morgan Freeman as Zeke in *The Mighty Gents;* Lester Rawlins as Drumm in *"Da"*

BEST ACTRESS IN A SECONDARY ROLE: Marian Seldes as Myra Bruhl in *Deathtrap;* Nancy Snyder as Gwen in *The 5th of July*

BEST DIRECTOR: Robert Moore for *Deathtrap;* Mike Nichols for *The Gin Game;* José Quintero for *A Touch of the Poet*

BEST SCENERY: Edward Gorey for *Dracula*

BEST COSTUMES: Edward Gorey for *Dracula*

MUSICALS

BEST MUSICAL: *Ain't Misbehavin'*

BEST BOOK: *The Best Little Whorehouse in Texas* by Larry L. King and Peter Masterson

BEST SCORE: *Ain't Misbehavin'* by Thomas "Fats" Waller and others; *On the Twentieth Century* by Cy Coleman, Betty Comden and Adolph Green

BEST REVIVAL: *Timbuktu* by Luther Davis, Charles Lederer, Robert Wright, George Forrest and Alexander Borodin, production directed by Geoffrey Holder

BEST ACTOR IN A PRIMARY ROLE: Henderson Forsythe as Sheriff Ed Earl Dodd in *The Best Little Whorehouse in Texas*

BEST ACTRESS IN A PRIMARY ROLE: Liza Minnelli as Michelle Craig in *The Act*

BEST ACTOR IN A SECONDARY ROLE: Andre De Shields and Ken Page in *Ain't Misbehavin';* Kevin Kline as Bruce Granit in *On the Twentieth Century*

BEST ACTRESS IN A SECONDARY ROLE: Nell Carter, Armelia McQueen and Charlaine Woodard in *Ain't Misbehavin'*

BEST DIRECTOR: Richard Maltby Jr. for *Ain't Misbehavin';* Peter Masterson and Tommy Tune for *The Best Little Whorehouse in Texas*

BEST CHOREOGRAPHER: Bob Fosse for *Dancin'*

BEST SCENERY: Robin Wagner for *On the Twentieth Century*

BEST COSTUMES: Geoffrey Holder for *Timbuktu;* Florence Klotz for *On the Twentieth Century*

Off Broadway

To get a close look at the seething ferment of 1977-78 theater activity on the fringes of Broadway and beyond, you have to follow the action to the ends of narrow alleys undisturbed since Peter Stuyvesant's day; to lofts reachable only up multiple flights of stairs that would tax the stamina of a Sherpa guide; even across bridges to the *terra incognita* that Brooklyn has become since the Dodgers left. It's been many years since one "off" sufficed to identify this bubbling cauldron of theater; and now "off off" scarcely suffices to cover all the contingencies of stage production in New York.

At the tributary theater's highest professional level, where most of the bubbles are, is what we call "off Broadway" (hyphenated when used as an adjective, not so when used as a noun). By the lights of these *Best Plays* volumes, an off-Broadway production is defined as one (a) with an Equity cast (b) giving 8 performances a week (c) in an off-Broadway theater (d) after inviting public comment by critics on an opening night or nights. And according to Paul Libin, president of the League of Off-Broadway Theaters, an off-Broadway theater is a house seating 499 or fewer and situated in Manhattan *outside* the area bounded by Fifth and Ninth avenues between 34th and 56th Streets, and by Fifth Avenue and the Hudson River between 56th and 72d Streets.

Obviously there are exceptions to each of these rules. No dimension of off Broadway can be applied exactly. In each *Best Plays* volume we stretch these definitions somewhat in the direction of inclusion — never of exclusion. For example, the word "Manhattan" means what we want it to mean, *Alice in Wonderland*-wise, when we include Brooklyn's Chelsea Theater Center and Academy of Music programs. Casts are sometimes only part-Equity and schedules sometimes take in 7 and in rare cases 6 performances a week (but we don't knowingly list 5-a-weekers, which are distinctly off off Broadway).

The point is that off Broadway isn't an exact location, it's a state of the art (generally advanced), a structure of production costs (generally reduced, but climbing), a level of expertise and effort. The point we must make with increasing emphasis as the seasons pass is that the borderline between professional off-Broadway and semi-professional off off Broadway (OOB for short) has all but disappeared. OOB groups often use part-Equity casts under special showcase arrangements, while off-Broadway groups do not always meet all the off-Broadway standards in all their shows. As for the level of professional quality in the finished work, consider that this year's best-of-bests, *"Da,"* came directly into the limelight from OOB in a Hudson Guild Theater production brought to Broadway virtually intact, as did the best musical, *Ain't Misbehavin',* reaching the Broadway pinnacle with its Manhattan Theater Club cabaret OOB production.

With all measurement blurring, the New York *Times* has ceased trying to categorize off Broadway in its annual summary, and *Variety* has all but given up trying to keep a complete count. We'll continue making the distinction between off and off off here in the *Best Plays* volume, however, as long as it seems useful to do so for the record, while reminding all who read these lines that formal distinctions are no longer as clear as they were and we tend to include rather than exclude — and that elsewhere in this volume we publish the most comprehensive list of 1977-78 OOB productions anywhere.

This said, let's immediately welcome Manhattan Theater Club into the off-Broadway ranks. That 73d Street OOB group has established a commanding presence in the New York Theater under the artistic direction of Lynne Meadow. This season for the first time a part of its multiple production activity — its Downstage schedule of five scripts from abroad — was produced with off-Broadway contracts. The importation from Hungary of Istvan Orkeny's *Catsplay* in the Clara Gyorgyey translation was the standout offering of MTC's first off-Broadway year. The script is a vehicle for a wide-ranging performance by an actress (in this case the admirable Helen Burns) playing a woman in her mid-60s writing letters to her sister — and speaking them aloud in the long descriptive monologues which comprise much of the play — about her life as a widow alone in Budapest and her ongoing romance with a has-been opera singer who was once her lover and is now her hedge against loneliness. Full of laughter and sympathy in good measure, this production was moved from MTC to another off-Broadway theater for a second run into the summer under independent auspices.

MTC's 1978 Downstage schedule also took in Peter Nichols's *Chez Nous,* about a British couple experimenting with sex and lifestyles; Athol Fugard's *Statements After an Arrest Under the Immorality Act,* about regulations of sexual apartheid in South Africa on a double bill with *Scenes From Soweto;* the British *Strawberry Fields* by Stephen Poliakoff, a clash between right-wing activists and a hitchhiker they take into their van as they move along a British turnpike; and the first New York productions of Samuel Beckett's *That Time* and *Footfalls* on a one-act play program with his *Play.* It's typical of today's shifting boundaries that MTC's most prominent 1977-78 show was *not* on this off-Broadway list, but its OOB production *Ain't Misbehavin'* which went from MTC cabaret to its Critics and Tony Award-winning Broadway engagement.

In the midst of rivals like MTC and Circle Repertory, and divested of his Lincoln Center responsibilities, Joseph Papp is still the king of the off-Broadway hill with his Public Theater complex, his Delacorte schedule, his workshops, cabarets and Broadway hits — and especially his instinct for challenging theater. Tops on his schedule of new work this season was Thomas Babe's *A*

Helen Burns in *Catsplay*

Prayer for My Daughter a Best Play which — like Babe's previous Best Play about Southern women in confrontation with General Sherman in his march to the sea — traps its characters in a situation not of their choosing and rubs their skin off until flesh and nerves are exposed. In *A Prayer for My Daughter* they are two police officers who have taken into custody two suspects in a particularly callous murder and are going to extract confessions from them if it takes all night (and it happens to be the small hours of the morning of July 4). Identities become somewhat confused in the heat of the night, with overlapping streaks of brutality and sexual involvement, as one of the policemen insists on staying to do his duty and beat up the prisoners even though his daughter is in trouble and has threatened to kill herself, and as one of the criminals fingers the other for the murder. The performances by Laurence Luckinbill (killer) and George Dzundza (cop) and the direction by Robert Allan Ackerman were as strong as the play.

Another particularly striking 1978 offering at the Public was Sam Shepard's *Curse of the Starving Class,* a metaphor of the human condition and of the way *not* to go, in its study of hunger physical and hunger spiritual as both a blight and a weapon of the exploiters against the exploited. In addition, Papp's downtown 1978 kaleidoscope of innovative off-Broadway theater comprised three more new plays, an Improvisational Theater offering, three revivals, two

Mark J. Soper and Joseph Ragno in *Feedlot*

musicals, two "poemplays", a one-woman-performance specialty *Miss Margarida's Way* which made it to Broadway, plus all kinds of experimental activity. The new work in this imposing total of 14 off-Broadway productions included, besides the Babe and Shepard scripts, John Guare's widely-admired *Landscape of the Body* about a young woman under stress in the big city; Paul Sills's improvisations and Martin Buber dramatizations in *Tales of the Hasidim;* Ntozake Shangé's "poemplay" study of cruelty, *A Photograph,* and Jessica Hagedorn's of growing up in Manila, *Mango Tango;* David Mamet's 1930s radio-play-within-a-stage-play, *The Water Engine,* which also made it to Broadway; Tina Howe's *Museum* in which paintings were watching people; and the musicals *Runaways* and *I'm Getting My Act Together and Taking It on the Road,* the latter an energetic Gretchen Cryer-Nancy Ford show celebrating the status of the liberated woman on the threshold of middle age, emotional adjustments and all.

Papp never found his feet at Lincoln Center, but his stance at the Public is ever more firm on a foundation of new scripts of dramatic quality — but not *just* quality. They also tend to be innovative but not *just* innovative; sensitive but not just sensitive; courageous but not just courageous; socially concerned but not just concerned. Papp's downtown 1978 season had something of all of these, in a concept of theater unmatched in its inborn respect for striving artists and adventurous audiences.

Another invariably stimulating and highly successful producing group is Marshall W. Mason's Circle Repertory Company which, sure enough, came up with a Best Play this season: Lanford Wilson's *The 5th of July,* a group of characters in search of themselves, youngish folk who were the right age to take part in the uproar of the 1960s and who now, in the 1970s, are trying to get to the bottom of their identities. They've come together for a holiday weekend visit (the actual date has as little importance here as it does in *A Prayer for My Daughter*) at a Missouri country place owned by a Vietnam veteran who lost both his legs in the war and so must rely on his male lover for both physical and emotional support. His guests are his sister and her fatherless and obnoxious sub-teen-age daughter, two former high school chums (an heiress who'd rather be a pop singer and her ambitious husband), a Nashville-bound guitar player and a widowed aunt who is as cool as any of the younger members of the house party. *The 5th of July* is closer to its author's *The Hot l Baltimore* than to his more recent Best Play *Serenading Louie* (both produced by Circle Rep under Mason's direction), in that it is a not-very-tightly structured study of the human spirit in the aftermath of stress. In *The Hot l Baltimore* they are perhaps going to lose the hotel; here they're perhaps going to give up the old family place, and that's about it as far as plot is concerned. But with Wilson's insights, Mason's stagecraft and the coordination of a first-rate acting ensemble, this was one of the year's best entertainments.

Another standout on the Circle's schedule was Patrick Meyers's *Feedlot,* a drama of love/hate relationships among men in the long hours of the night while tending a large cattle-fattening operation, directed by Terry Schreiber of off-off-Broadway fame. Circle Rep's schedule of new scripts also took in an allegorical play by Albert Innaurato, *Ulysses in Traction,* about students rehearsing a play while a riot is going on outdoors, not exactly a laughing matter but hilarious in its overtones; and a pair of one-acters, *Brontosaurus* by Lanford Wilson and *Cabin 12* by John Bishop.

The Phoenix Theater rose again on schedule under the managing directorship of T. Edward Hambleton, offering a sampling of new scripts including Wendy Wasserstein's reflections on bright "Seven Sisters" college years, *Uncommon Women and Others;* Jack Gilhooley's *The Elusive Angel* about a childless couple trying for an adoption; a Canadian version of the pool hustler vs. gamblers conflict in David French's *One Crack Out;* and *Hot Grog,* a Jim Wann-Bland Simpson musical about the pirate Blackbeard, developed at the Musical Theater Lab in Washington, D.C.

American Place, under Wynn Handman's direction, frequently occupied itself with guest productions like the Acting Company's repertory of revivals. It also came up with four challenging new scripts: Elaine Jackson's *Cockfight,* about the macho pose when there is naught behind it; Steve Tesich's *Passing Game,* a deadly one played by two wife-abusers, one black and one white; Maria Irene Fornes's *Fefu and Her Friends,* a gathering of women staged by the author so that the action (and the audience) sometimes broke into several parts in separate

The 1977-78 Season Off Broadway

PLAYS (28)

Public Theater:
Landscape of the Body
The Water Engine
A PRAYER FOR MY DAUGHTER
Museum
Curse of the Starving Class
The Passion of Dracula
American Place:
Cockfight
Passing Game
Fefu and Her Friends
Conjuring an Event
Circle Repertory:
Feedlot
Ulysses in Traction
Two From the Late Show
THE 5TH OF JULY
Old Man Joseph and His Family
A LIFE IN THE THEATER
The Running of the Deer
Phoenix:
Uncommon Women and Others
The Elusive Angel
Esther

NEC:
The Offering
Black Body Blues
The Twilight Dinner
The Contessa of Mulberry Street
FAMILY BUSINESS
The Neon Woman
International Stud
The Ventriloquist's Wife

SPECIALTIES (13)

The 2d Greatest Entertainer in the Whole Wide World
The Square Root of Soul
Public Theater:
Miss Margarida's Way
Tales of the Hasidim
A Photograph
Mango Tango
The Grand Kabuki
I
Housewife! Superstar!
A Man and His Women
Joe Masiell Not at the Palace
My Astonishing Self
23 Skiddoo

MUSICALS (6)

Public Theater:
Runaways
I'm Getting My Act Together and Taking It on the Road
Hot Grog
Green Pond
A Bistro Car on the CNR
THE BEST LITTLE WHOREHOUSE IN TEXAS

FOREIGN PLAYS IN ENGLISH (9)

Survival
Rum an Coca Cola
Manhattan Theater Club:
Chez Nous
Play and Other Plays
Statements After an Arrest Under the Immorality Act &
Scenes From Soweto
Catsplay
Strawberry Fields
One Crack Out
The Biko Inquest

REVUES (6)

Unsung Cole
Children of Adam
The Present Tense
Nightsong
By Strouse
The Proposition

REVIVALS (45)

Delacorte:
Threepenny Opera
Agamemnon
LOOM:
H.M.S. Pinafore
The Pirates of Penzance
The Merry Widow
Naughty Marietta
The Vagabond King
Ruddigore
The Mikado
The Sorcerer & Trial by Jury
Iolanthe
Mlle. Modiste
The Grand Duchess of Gerolstein
Patience
The Gondoliers
Stage Blood
Public Theater:
The Misanthrope
The Mandrake
The Dybbuk

Counsellor-at-Law
Roundabout:
Naked
You Never Can Tell
Othello
The Promise
The Show-Off
Pins and Needles
Lulu
CSC:
A Midsummer Night's Dream
Rosmersholm
Musgrave's Dance
The Maids
The Madwoman of Chaillot
Joseph and the Amazing Technicolor Dreamcoat
The Beard
BAM:
The Devil's Disciple
The Play's the Thing
Julius Caesar
Waiting for Godot
P.S. Your Cat Is Dead
Acting Company:
Mother Courage
King Lear
Duck Variations
Life of Galileo
Ludlam Repertory:
Stage Blood
Camille

Categorized above are all the plays listed in the "Plays Produced off Broadway". Plays listed in CAPITAL LETTERS have been designated Best Plays of 1977-78. Plays listed in *italics* were still running June 1, 1978.

sections of the theater; and Richard Nelson's *Conjuring an Event,* examining the power of journalism to cause as well as report an action.

Over in Brooklyn, Robert Kalfin's Chelsea Theater Center continued to explore byways of theater and share its findings with Manhattan audiences by bringing its productions across the river to the Westside Theater following their Brooklyn runs. These included *Rum an Coca Cola,* a study of a Trinidadian Calypso artist and his young pupil, by the much-admired London playwright Mustapha Matura; *Green Pond,* the Robert Montgomery-Mel Marvin musical of 1970s attitudes, first produced by Stage South, S.C.; and Biblical Joseph's childhood presented as a folk tale in Romulus Linney's *Old Man Joseph and His Family.*

Douglas Turner Ward and Robert Hooks steered their Negro Ensemble Company into three dramatic examinations of the black experience, two of them by Gus Edwards: *The Offering,* a confrontation of the generations, and *Black Body Blues,* a clash of lifestyles, both giving off showers of sparks under Ward's direction. NEC's season concluded with Lennox Brown's *The Twilight Dinner,* a confrontation of two black friends of the 1960s from different countries, now discovering new problems in their relationship. And Charles Ludlam's Ridiculous Theatrical Company brought his *The Ventriloquist's Wife* up from OOB in a late-season Ludlam repertory, the rest of which were revivals.

The whole range of off-Broadway production, both organizational and independent, provided only one Best Play in the 1977 season — *Ashes* at the Public Theater — but it took an abrupt upturn in 1978 with five of the ten. Three of these — *A Life in the Theater, Family Business* and *The Best Little Whorehouse in Texas* — came forth in independent production to join the institutionally-sponsored *A Prayer for My Daughter* and *The 5th of July* on this year's Best Plays list. They were the first off-Broadway independents to make the list since 1974.

David Mamet's *A Life in the Theater* is an opposite of his last season's Best Play, *American Buffalo:* light with personality where the other was darkly repressed, buoyed with aspiration where the other was weighed down with ignorance and failure. The new work uses a backstage setting with two actors (Ellis Rabb and Peter Evans) as a metaphor of life and its irresistable passage of time. The elder actor is accomplished but on the downhill slant, the younger with a lot of talent and a lot to learn on the way up, communicating now and again but not as clearly as they should in this shared experience of the youth-age relationship. Little scraps of their "performances" in plays they're doing out front (burlesquing theater cliches like war melodrama or drawing-room comedy) are sometimes visible. More often, though, these two are seen in dressing-room encounters, adjusting to each other and to the changing circumstances of their lives and careers, in a comic coat-of-many-colors.

Also in independent production was Dick Goldberg's *Family Business,* a very well-made and deeply-considered play about four brothers trying to settle their lives as they settle their father's estate. The patriarch's death throws them off balance (they were already teetering), and they grab at each other trying to maintain their equilibrium: the plodding storekeeper, the profligate psychiatrist, the wild one and the mama's boy who'd like to keep them all together under the old roof, whatever compromise and/or forgiveness is necessary to do so. As played by Richard Greene, David Rosenbaum, Joel Polis and David Garfield (in the order of the characters named above) under the direction of John Stix, their emotional abrasion gave off showers of sparks with its steady, grinding pressure.

The best book musical of 1978 has at least two things in common with *Grease:* it originated off Broadway in the theater at the corner of 12th Street and Second Avenue now called Entermedia, and it has an unappetizing title. *The Best Little Whorehouse in Texas* was certainly the best little new musical play in town this this season, but it was not, as its name suggests, an exploitation of sex or a thinly-disguised burlesque show. There may be one or two bits of business or dialogue that would offend your Aunt Minnie, but probably not if she had a glass of wine with dinner before the show. The moralists are the villains, yes, in this book by Larry L. King and Peter Masterson about do-gooders using TV as a means of publicizing and closing down a beloved rural institution devoted to sexual pleasures. But this place is strictly and decorously overseen by all-seeing, all-knowing, handsome Madam Mona (Carlin Glynn) who runs the kind of place you can take the whole football team to after the homecoming game.

The character themes in both book and score had a way of suddenly going deeper than you expected; for example in the case of a shy young hayseed (Joan Ellis) who has left home to escape her father's advances, or a hamburg-joint waitress (Susan Mansur) who stopped the show with a song about her frustrated dreams, "Doatsey Mae." Carol Hall's music and lyrics aren't showy, but they are vigorous, with echoes of country rock; the book's tone ranged all the way from touching to hilarious; and Tommy Tune's musical staging was as imaginative as it was energetic. Henderson Forsythe's performance as a fire-breathing Texas sheriff provided the finishing touch, throwing the temple of femininity into full masculine perspective. *The Best Little Whorehouse in Texas* maintained its balance of taste on its tightrope of a subject and added a generous portion of entertainment to the season, both downtown where it began and uptown where it followed *Grease* to Broadway in June.

The additional conglomeration of independent production off Broadway evinced no marked trend or fad. It roamed free through revue-style commentaries on contemporary life and events in shows like *Children of Adam, The Present Tense, Nightsong, The Proposition* and, from Canada, the musical *A Bistro Car on the CNR*. It offered a delightful medley of once and future Charles Strouse numbers in the revue *By Strouse;* a collection of unjustly obscure Cole Porter numbers in *Unsung Cole;* a popular new rendition of the Dracula tale by Bob Hall and David Richmond, *The Passion of Dracula,* off Broadway's long-run contribution to this Dracula season; A Tom Eyen-style, far-out burlesque of mystery plays in *The Neon Woman*. It provided an outlet for two more cries of South African pain, *The Biko Inquest,* dramatized by Norman Fenton and Jon Blair from transcripts of the inquest into the death of Stephen Biko, and *Survival,* a set of prison episodes created by the cast and director. It viewed the life, times and emotions of a drag queen in Harvey Fierstein's *International Stud* and the legendary Queen of Persia in C.K. Mack's *Esther.* Among its variety of subjects were family life in Little Italy in Nicholas D. Bellitto's *The Contessa of Mulberry Street* (emergent from OOB's

Gene Frankel Workshop) and the last months of 1776 in America in Karen Sunde's *The Running of the Deer,* which grew out of activity at CSC, of which she is a member, and which attests to the internal vitality of that repertory company otherwise devoted to the production of revivals.

The off-Broadway specialties this season included visits from two foreign troupes: Japan's world-renowned national treasure, The Grand Kabuki, with a program of two Kabuki plays; and a Belgian multimedia group, *23 Skiddoo,* a series of extravagant audio-visual comments on the perplexing present and dark future. Performers who came on in solo showcases were Dick Shawn (*The 2nd Greatest Entertainer in the Whole Wide World*), Adolph Caesar (*The Square Root of Soul*), Anne West (*I*), Barry Humphries (*Housewife! Superstar!*), Craig Russell (*A Man and His Women*), Joe Masiell (*Joe Masiell Not at the Palace*) and Donal Donnelly (as Shaw in *My Astonishing Self*).

The time when the off-Broadway plateau was a fertile field for experimental theater has long passed (except occasionally, in the shelter of a producing institution like New York Shakespeare, Circle Repertory or American Place), what with ever more stringent contractual obligations and costs, within the continuing outside limitation of a 499-seat house (and most are nowhere near that large). But venture is still possible even though raw experiment generally is not; and off Broadway ventured widely in 1977-78. Viewed in perspective, its season also rated high in results, with five of the Best Plays; and in versatility, since three of these top-notch shows appeared in independent production. While Broadway was racing forward, widening its lead in pursuit of the $25 ticket, and off off Broadway was treading on its heels, off Broadway seemed to be settling into a steady stride for a long race.

Revivals

The attenuation in the number of Broadway revivals from 28 in 1975-76 to 17 in 1976-77 continued into 1977-78, when a mere 14 oldies were displayed in Broadway showcases — but their importance on the theater scene had attenuated not one bit. As previously noted, *Man of La Mancha* with Richard Kiley in his original role of the impossible dreamer Don Quixote, *Hello, Dolly!* with Carol Channing in her original role of Dolly Gallagher Levi dazzling the waiters with that entrance and even *Hair* and *Jesus Christ Superstar* padded the slender musical season in all the right places. Also, the colorful and romantically tuneful *Kismet,* in a rendition entitled *Timbuktu!* and transposed from Bagdad to an African setting, demonstrated some of the enduring possibilities waiting on the American musical library shelf. With an arresting Eartha Kitt performance, fanciful costumes, choreography and direction by Geoffrey Holder and the twice-familiar Borodin airs which became "Baubles, Bangles and Beads," "Stranger in Paradise," "Night of My Nights" and "This Is My Beloved" in passing through the hands of Robert Wright and George Forrest, this was a handsomely refinished antique, the most innovative musical revival of the season.

The same distinction in the straight-play category belongs to *Dracula,* the old Hamilton Deane-John L. Balderston dramatization of Bram Stoker's novel.

Here again was a triumph of style and design in Edward Gorey's bat-winged scenery and elegant costumes, in a superbly molded and modulated performance by Frank Langella in the title role. It was the show's vampirish concept under Dennis Rosa's direction that it settle down to play *Dracula* with 100 per cent conviction, letting the baroque curlicues of the ghostly story move the audience to chills or laughter when and where it pleased. The result was a show that actually chilled more than it chuckled.

Then there was the José Quintero *A Touch of the Poet,* with Jason Robards in a landmark performance of Con Melody. Robards had already played a number of major O'Neill roles with major distinction, but never this one until now, when he made it his own in one of the season's several first-rate acting achievements. In other revival production, a somewhat revised version of Ronald Ribman's *Cold Storage* gave Martin Balsam a chance to repeat on Broadway his outstanding performance of a terminal patient talking out an ending, offered last year off Broadway at American Place opposite Michael Lipton as his companion patient and this year opposite Len Cariou. John Wood's *Tartuffe* and Lynn Redgrave's *Saint Joan* at Circle in the Square also were major ornaments of the Broadway year.

Elsewhere in its schedule Circle in the Square mounted an attractive Feydeau farce, *13 Rue de l'Amour,* adapted and translated by Mawby Green and Ed Feilbert from *Monsieur Chasse;* and, in June 1977, *The Importance of Being Earnest* as last season's caboose production (this season's was a revival of *Once in a Lifetime* in June 1978).

In early 1977 summer, Joseph Papp brought Andrei Serban's production of *The Cherry Orchard* back for his swan-song offering at the Vivian Beaumont in Lincoln Center. At the other end of the season, Paul Zindel's *The Effect of Gamma Rays on Man-in-the-Moon Marigolds* spent a moment or two in the Broadway limelight.

Off Broadway, where established organizations provide whole seasons of shows from the theater library shelves, there was an imposing total of 45 revivals in 1977-78. Joseph Papp opened the season with a pair of return engagements in Central Park of his own acclaimed Lincoln Center productions — *Threepenny Opera* and *Agamemnon* — and salted his Public Theater schedule with a musical *The Misanthrope* and new looks at *The Mandrake* (Machiavelli's *Mandragola*) and *The Dybbuk.* William Mount-Burke's Light Opera of Manhattan played right around the calendar in a 13-operetta revival year, mixing golden oldies of Victor Herbert, Rudolf Friml, Franz Lehar, etc. with Gilbert & Sullivan, and adding three new productions to their repertory: Victor Herbert's Parisian hat-shop idyll *Mlle. Modiste* (with Alfred Simon consulting in the production), Jacques Offenbach's send-up of war and other human vanities, *The Grand Duchess of Gerolstein,* and G & S's *The Sorcerer* (on a bill with *Trial by Jury*).

In eclectic revival production, the senior group is Gene Feist's and Michael Fried's Roundabout Theater Company, a midtown fixture now operating out of two theaters in a season-long series of dance and other entertainments in addition to its major effort of producing a whole range of playscripts, classic to only-yesterday nostalgic, many of them long forgotten by other New York producers.

Jason Robards and Geraldine Fitzgerald in *A Touch of the Poet*

Roundabout's five-play season took in Pirandello's *Naked,* Shaw's *You Never Can Tell,* Shakespeare's *Othello* directed by Gene Feist on a bare stage, the Russian play *The Promise* of a few Broadway seasons back, directed by Michael Fried, Kelly's *The Show-Off* and, for a caboose production, Harold Rome's *Pins and Needles,* the famous garment-center revue originally produced by the ILGWU and never before revived on the New York professional stage, with Philip Campanella, an accomplished actor who has doubled for many seasons as the Roundabout's music man, serving the show as musical director and performer at one of the twin pianos which constituted its pit orchestra.

Another revival-producing organization with an eclectic policy is Classic Stage Company (CSC), only three seasons old in off-Broadway status but with a wide grasp in its repertory schedule. This year the CSC put on a new play by one of the members of its acting company (Karen Sunde, as mentioned previously in the off-Broadway section of this report) and a new English version of Ibsen's *Rosmersholm* written and directed by the group's artistic director, Christopher Martin. There was a Shakespeare in its season — *A Midsummer Night's Dream* — and there was also a John Arden (*Serjeant Musgrave's Dance*), a Jean Genet

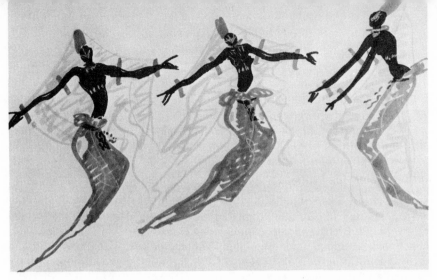

Here are examples of Geoffrey Holder's costume designs for *Timbuktu*, with Melba Moore (*at left* in photo) and Eartha Kitt in a scene from the musical reworking of *Kismet*

(*The Maids* with an all-male cast) and the Jean Giraudoux-Maurice Valency *The Madwoman of Chaillot.*

Over in Brooklyn, Frank Dunlop's BAM Theater Company went into its second season with a Shaw (*The Devil's Disciple*) a Molnar (*The Play's the Thing*) a Shakespeare (*Julius Caesar* with George Rose in the title role, Rene Auberjonois as Brutus and Austin Pendleton as Marc Anthony) and Samuel Beckett's own English version of *Waiting for Godot* (which he had staged at Berlin's Schiller Theater) with Sam Waterston and Austin Pendleton as Didi and Gogo.

John Houseman's Acting Company was a guest of American Place for a repertory of a Brecht (*Mother Courage and Her Children*), a Shakespeare (*King Lear*) and a second look at David Mamet's *Duck Variations* which was produced off Broadway last season. Charles Ludlam's Ridiculous Theatrical Company revived *Stage Blood* twice, in July and later in May in a repertory of Ludlam plays including his version of *Camille.* And a new group, the New York Actors' Theater, arose at Columbia's Havemeyer Hall, with Laurence Luckinbill as one of the artistic directors, making a wholly creditable first effort with Brecht's *Life of Galileo.*

The only revival in independent off-Broadway production was a revision by James Kirkwood of his *P.S. Your Cat Is Dead.* This play about a trapped burglar attempting the homosexual seduction of his intended victim was first produced at the Arena Stage in Buffalo, then came to Broadway in the 1975 season for only 16 performances. As of the end of the 1978 season off Broadway it had already played more than five times that long and was still running strong.

Elmer Rice and Michael McClure (*Counselor-at-Law* and *The Beard* at the Quaigh), Frank Wedekind (*Lulu* at Circle Repertory) and Tim Rice and Andrew Lloyd Webber (*Joseph and the Amazing Technicolor Dreamcoat* at BAM) were also among those present in 1977-78 New York revival production, Its breadth in time from Aeschylus to David Mamet and in character from Dracula to Dolly was enormous; and its value to a versatile, well-balanced season was the same.

Offstage

Driven by its own internal dynamism or merely following the crowd up the inflation spiral, the New York theater was subject to ever-rising costs in 1977-78 (a $1 million price tag for a full-fledged Broadway musical would be a commonplace, if full-fledged Broadway musicals were still commonplace; and some producers, notably The Shubert Organization have now decided that it's too expensive to take a big show out of town for a trial run). The box office was presenting the theatergoing public with prices to match. The double-sawbuck barrier had scarcely been leaned on by last year's revival of *Fiddler on the Roof,* when it collapsed under *The Act's* announcement of a $22.50 top on weekend evenings ($20 weeknights) to hear Liza Minnelli in a show which at that time was admittedly in pre-Broadway trouble and had only just brought in Gower Champion to help spruce it up.

That announcement proved to be an underestimate. By the time anyone could get to the box office, *The Act* was asking and getting a $25 top for Saturday night. Upward went prices at other Broadway shows until, at season's end, the price of a top ticket was $22.50 at *Dancin'* and *On the Twentieth Century,* $20 at *Ain't Misbehavin'* and $19.50 at *Annie* and *Timbuktu* — and a $17.50 top was routine at the more attractive straight plays. Successful off-Broadway productions operating outside subsidy were asking and getting $9.95 for some tickets, while *The Best Little Whorehouse in Texas* was wall-to-wall with customers at an $11.50 top ($19.50 after it moved uptown to Broadway). If there are any forces at work to prevent Broadway from becoming a $25-$30 theater and off Broadway a $10-$15 theater, they aren't visible at this time.

It was a restive year for critics. Richard Eder replaced Clive Barnes in his play-reviewing function at the New York *Times,* and then Barnes departed the *Times* to become play and dance reviewer for the New York *Post,* where Martin Gottfried's services were less and less in demand until he began doing pieces for *Cue,* where Marilyn Stasio had resigned her play-reviewing post to join the *Trib,* which suspended publication before she could get started. In January, *Variety* reported that an alert reader had noticed that a section of a T.E. Kalem review of *A Touch of the Poet* in *Time* had re-used comments by Louis Kronenberger, former *Time* drama critic and *Best Plays* editor, published in 1958 first in a *Time* review and then reprinted as part of Kronenberger's summary of the New York season in *The Best Plays of 1958-59.* Kalem characterized his action as "a kind of salute" to Kronenberger, whom he credits as being one of his mentors.

No one threw anything at John Simon, critic of *New York* magazine, as far as we know, but a number of producers voted to take his name off their first night list after he'd been heard to use a four-letter word to describe *The Shadow Box* on a TV talk show (and many were incensed by his derogatory description of Liza Minnelli's physical appearance in *The Act*). The New York Drama Critics Circle voted 13-4 at its annual meeting in October to protest this action to the League of New York Theaters and Producers as a form of censorship. Members of the League argued that it was not censorship because Simon was free to buy tickets to their shows if he chose; rather, they said, it was a fair protest against Simon's caustic style of reviewing. Not all members of the League supported this Simon-censuring action taken by a majority of those members who responded to a recommendation of the League's Media Committee. It turned out to be pretty much a token protest, with many producers sending first-night tickets to the magazine rather than its critic, and with Simon re-acquiring his freebies to most shows by season's end.

The Critics Circle dispatched the routine business of its year by electing Emory Lewis of the Bergen *Record* as its president, replacing Douglas Watt of the *Daily News,* whose term had expired, and Jack Kroll of *Newsweek* to replace Lewis as the Circle vice president. Henry Hewes, formerly of *Saturday Review* and a valued contributor to *Best Plays,* became a member emeritus of the Circle, as did Alan Rich, onetime drama critic of *New York.*

In an atmosphere of steeply rising costs and prices, Actors' Equity and the producers negotiated a new three-year contract in efficient fashion, the new actors' minimum being $355 weekly the first and second years and $400 for the third (the old minimum was $285), with the road minimums going to $547.50, $582.50 and $645 expenses included (the old road minimum was $395) and with stage managers' fees rising proportionately from a former $500 to $900 at musicals and from $420 to $805 at plays. Among other provisions: actors will not be required to wear other actors' shoes; and nude performances are forbidden except with the actors' written consent and control over the release and use of photos. A proposed change in the Equity showcase code calling for a "tiered" system of higher payments for actors at better-financed theaters — which OOBA perceived as damaging to this fragile, experimental movement — was rejected by the Equity membership at an April meeting. Instead, it was voted that Equity and OOBA get together and work out a new relationship acceptable to both sides.

The Dramatists Guild, an organization of playwrights, composers, lyricists and librettists, was in the process of exploring with the League the possibilities for changes in the Minimum Basic Agreement between them, a script-leasing arrangement of royalty percentages and provisions that has defined the author-producer relationship since the 1920s. Meanwhile, a rift developed between the Dramatists Guild and the League over the Tony Awards telecast, sponsored and overseen by League-appointed committees and a League-member producer, Alexander H. Cohen. Dramatists were all but invisible on the Tony show June 4, as though their contribution to the bests of Broadway were secondary in importance to that of the limelight-holding actors, directors — and, yes, producers. The author of the Tony-winning Best Play *"Da,"* Hugh Leonard, was all but obscured on camera by the throng of producers who came to the podium to accept the award with him, and the musical authors who won Tonys in their categories — Adolph Green, Betty Comden and Cy Coleman — were given their awards off camera like the inventors of some new gadget at the Academy Award presentation. The Dramatists Guild protested this treatment and will take a long, hard look at the whole Tony Awards process.

The Dramatists Guild also took a position in the case of Phillip Hayes Dean's *Paul Robeson,* which prior to its Broadway opening, came under attack by an *ad hoc* committee in newspaper ads and elsewhere for supposedly misinterpreting some of the facts and goals of its title character's life, in a group pre-judgment by signatories some of whom hadn't seen or read the play. In an open letter over the signatures of 33 leading dramatists including all the Guild officers (Stephen Sondheim president, Richard Lewine vice president, Dore Schary treasurer, Sheldon Harnick secretary) and Edward Albee, Lillian Hellman, Arthur Miller and Richard Rodgers among others, the Guild agreed that "a playwright must be prepared to accept criticism, no matter how bitter or even unfair," but "group censorship of a play violates the principles of the First Amendment," in this case by an action which "assailed the accuracy and integrity of the play in an attempt to pre-judge it for theatergoers . . . . . If the practise of group censorship takes root in the American theater, freedom of expression will be gravely imperiled."

The Off Off Broadway Alliance (OOBA), a loose organization of more than 60 going OOB concerns, did some self-examination at the request of its directors and decided that the strength and integrity of OOBA are essential to the health of OOB, nurturing its conditions and processes and "addressing the theaters' mutual problems of credibility and accessibility." It thereupon appointed a new

James Earl Jones (*foreground*) as Paul Robeson and Burt Wallace as Lawrence Brown in *Paul Robeson*

executive director, Ellen A. Rudolph, rolled up its sleeves and prepared to become "an organization which its member theaters will not outgrow."

The Association of Theatrical Press Agents and Managers elected Merle Debuskey to his sixth term as its president. A new theater publication, *New York Theater Review* came upon the scene under Ira J. Bilowit's editorship and is more national in its outlook than its name implies. Still another new publication which covered theater, *The Trib,* a daily New York newspaper, was as short-lived as a moderate Broadway success, opening Jan. 9 and closing in early April. For dramatists seeking outlets for their work outside the New York commercial theater, it was a year of win one, lose one. Arthur Ballet's Minneapolis-based, Rockefeller-funded Office for Advanced Drama Research (OADR) shut up shop after 15 years of operation in which it managed to get 114 new scripts produced across the country. At the same time down in Durham, N.C., Broadway producer Richard Adler formed a production unit for developing Broadway-style musicals sponsored, housed and funded by Duke University. "Call it Broadway away from Broadway," Adler commented as he set out to put on shows expected to play first at Duke and then move around the country to large and larger cities, ending up — perhaps — in New York, where astronomical costs and other circumstances have cut the production of full-scale Broadway musicals almost to the vanishing point.

For the third time in Broadway history, all the marquees went dark at the same time on purpose, in the absence of any blackout, on Aug. 5. The occasion was an observance of the death of Alfred Lunt at 84 two days previously — or rather, not so much to mark his death as to express the whole theater's deep admiration of his life, so much of which was lived with such great distinction on Broadway. The two previous marquee blackouts took place in honor of Gertrude Lawrence and Oscar Hammerstein II. An entertainment era which had long since passed away was buried in 1978 with Alfred Lunt — and, in other media, with Bing Crosby and Charles Chaplin.

All the mighty institutions of government were at the theater's service — to the usual feeble extent. The National Endowment for the Arts found $6,004,160 to aid the theater in fiscal 1977-78, a brave $102,000 more than the previous year and many millions less than any other civilized country in the Western World. The New York State Council on the Arts, considerably more aware (under the chairmanship of Kitty Carlisle Hart) of the importance and value of the theater as a regional and national arts treasure, spread $3 million over 150 theater organizations in 34 counties. Other support was on the way in the form of two bills in Congress: Congressman Fred Richmond's H.R. 1042 calling for a checkoff of $5 to $50 for the arts on Federal income tax forms (a companion bill, S. 1082, is in the Senate) and Congressman Jack F. Kemp's H.R. 9985 calling for a 50 per cent tax credit for gifts to qualified arts organizations. Much advocacy of these measures was being put forward in 1977-78, but none of those who remained silent was holding his breath.

We began this offstage report with Liza Minnelli's $25 top and we'll end it by noting the Nov. 9 *Variety* headline: "Liza's Lip-Synch in *The Act* Shocks Purists." Miss Minnelli's performance was a strenuous one — dancing, singing and dancing *while* singing — so that at certain places in the show it would be physically impossible to summon enough breath to project the notes distinctly, let alone the lyrics. The obvious measure was taken, therefore, for brief intervals, of synchronizing the star's recorded voice over the theater's loud speakers with the movement of her lips and gestures — "lip-synching" it's called, the staple of every movie musical and a number of rock shows.

The *Variety* story called those who object to using such a device in live theater "purists" and concluded: "Maybe they should be sentenced to attend a special performance of *The Act* without lip-synching. That would sink 'em."

We'd go much farther than that. We'd suggest that such purists keep their $25 in their pockets. We'd suggest that they be entirely deprived of *The Act* and all shows like it, which deserve the warm welcome of Las Vegas and/or Radio City Music Hall, where they belong, and equally deserve a cold shoulder from our demanding, puristic legitimate stage, where they do not. We aren't ignorant of the fact that all Broadway musicals are now more or less heavily electronic both onstage and in the pit (we had to hold our hands over our ears, for example, at moments in *The Best Little Whorehouse in Texas* and *Ain't Misbehavin'*) and maybe that's one reason why there are so few of them around these days. Electronic gimmickry is all too obtrusive in the present show biz environment — and where did all those fabulous dinosaurs go?

Live contact and close relationship between performer and audience are the vital signs of living theater, and *anything* interposed between them is unhealthy in the long run. The $25 Broadway ticket top is only a damned nuisance compared to the life-threatening symptom of electronic faking of live performance (no reflection on Miss Minnelli, who when she catches her breath can belt a song out into the middle of 45th Street). Let the star sing *or* dance with her own breath; we'll be satisfied, maybe even $25 worth. Let the theater's illusions be electric in the cosmic sense, not electronic. Let it use all available devices to enhance, not replace, the uniquely warm-blooded illusions of what the purists hope is to remain the eternally warm-blooded living stage.

THE 1977-78 SEASON OFF OFF BROADWAY

By Marion Fredi Towbin

Playwright and critic, author of *Three Easy Pieces, Bed & Breakfast,* etc.

AIN'T MISBEHAVIN'. "DA." THE GIN GAME. 1977-1978 was a season when the most applauded shows on Broadway originated off off Broadway.

OOB's tremendous activity culminated with this season's opening of Theater Row: eight historic buildings on 42d Street between Ninth and Tenth Avenues, buildings which were converted from massage parlors and pornography shops into New York's newest cultural complex. As Joseph Papp observed during the opening festivities, "It's nice to see that the second oldest profession in the world has managed to overcome the first oldest profession."

The concept for Theater Row was the brainchild of OOB producer Robert Moss, whose Playwrights Horizons has been situated on this block since 1975. Moss rightly believed that the block's identity (and, by extension, the identity of the entire Clinton neighborhood) would benefit from the influx of other theaters. He was helped immensely by Fred Papert, a real estate developer whose 42d Street Redevelopment Corporation swiftly incorporated the idea of a Theater Row into its own plans for the neighborhood.

There was much toe-tapping OOB this season; it seemed quite the year for musical revues. *Lyrical and Satirical,* the songs of Harold Rome, was given a jaunty production by the Joseph Jefferson Theater Company, while the Manhattan Theater Club's cabaret reverberated to the tunes of Rome, Eubie Blake and *Ain't Misbehavin's* Fats Waller. The Richard Maltby Jr. musical moved to Broadway, where it became one of this season's hottest tickets.

While *"Da,"* Hugh Leonard's beautiful memory play, moved from OOB's Hudson Guild to Broadway's Morosco, another rather similar play, Harry Granick's *The Bright and Golden Land,* was given a stunning production at Shelter West. While waiting for their new 42d Street home to be completed, the Lion Theater Company, under Gene Nye's direction, turned the old Westside Bus Terminal into the old West with Len Jenkin's *The Death and Life of Jesse James.* On a much lighter note was the Hudson Guild's *My Mother Was a Fortune Teller,* an autobiographical, one-person musical written by, and starring,

Phyllis Newman. Arthur Laurents, who'd just won numerous awards for his film *The Turning Point,* directed.

The Encompass Theater, located above an Orange Julius stand a stone's throw from Broadway, presented a vibrant series of staged readings entitled *Hear Their Voices: Women Founders of the American Theater 1910-1945.* Included were Sophie Treadwell's expressionist *Machinal,* Rachel Crothers's *Expressin' Willie* and Susan Glaspell's *Alison's House.* Guest speakers for the series included producer Jean Dalrymple. Veteran actor Alexander Scourby was featured in the cast.

Among the season's outstanding OOB revivals were Lawrence and Lee's *Inherit the Wind,* powerfully directed by John Henry Davis at Joseph Jefferson, and Elmer Rice's *Counsellor-at-Law,* at the Quaigh, which later had an off-Broadway run.

Colonnades Theater Lab (directly opposite the Public) garnered much critical acclaim with its ambitious production of *Molière in Spite of Himself,* based on Mikhail Bulgakov's *A Cabal of Hypocrites.* The *Times's* Richard Eder voted it the best play of the season in the Drama Critics Circle balloting. Colonnades founder and director Michael Lessac was also the first recipient of the New Drama Forum's Rosamond Gilder Award for Creative Achievement.

Government funding of OOB and audience development went hand in hand this season. Walter Kerr noted in the *Times* that the current Broadway theatergoer had "stopped going to plays and had begun going to theater." He attributed this healthy change in attitude to the TKTS half-price booths in Times Square and in the financial district, and to the organization behind the booths: Theater Development Fund.

"One of the more important contributions that Theater Development Fund has made to this changing universe," Executive Director Hugh Southern noted, "has been the effective restoration of price/demand elasticity in the purchasing of tickets by the public. Many producers offering tickets through these facilities have been able to adjust successfully to the changing levels of demand by offering more or fewer tickets for half price sale. The effect of this has been to prolong the life of many productions. This, in turn, generates large increments of receipts through other channels of sale and, of course, additional employment, royalties, theater rentals and revenues in restaurant, transportation, parking and other services within and around the theater district."

While OOB shows that moved to Broadway were helped by TDF, so was OOB directly — by the voucher program. Those eligible for TDF vouchers (students, professionals, union members, clergy, retired folk) could purchase a set of five vouchers for a total of $7.50, each good for one OOB admission later redeemed by TDF for $3. This season, 206 theaters received $140,498 in vouchers for 56,119 admissions.

A new Theater Row . . . new subsidized housing for the performing artist (Manhattan Plaza) . . . lots of new plays . . . outstanding revivals . . . 1977-1978 was a good season OOB.

○
○
○
THE SEASON
AROUND THE UNITED STATES

with

A DIRECTORY OF PROFESSIONAL
REGIONAL THEATER

and

OUTSTANDING NEW PLAYS
CITED BY
AMERICAN THEATER CRITICS
ASSOCIATION
○
○
○

Including casts and credits of new plays, selected Canadian programs, children's programs, dinner theater and extended coverage of the Los Angeles and Washington seasons

THE American Theater Critics Association (ATCA) is the organization of more than 125 leading drama critics of all media in all sections of the United States. One of this group's stated purposes is "To increase public awareness of the theater as a *national* resource" (italics ours). To this end, ATCA has cited a number of outstanding new plays produced this season across the country, to be listed and briefly described in this volume; and has designated one of them for us to offer as an introduction to our coverage of "The Season

Around the United States" in the form of a synopsis with excerpts, in the same manner as Best Plays of the New York season.

The critics made their citations, including their principal one of Marsha Norman's *Getting Out,* in the following manner: member critics everywhere were asked to call the attention of an ATCA committee — chaired by Dan Sullivan, drama critic of the Los Angeles *Times* — to outstanding new work in their areas. Scripts of these nominated plays were studied by committee members who made their choices, as the editor of this volume makes his New York Best Plays choice, on the basis of script rather than production. There were no eligibility requirements (such as Equity cast or formal resident-theater status) except that a nominee be the first full professional production of a new work outside New York City within this volume's time frame of June 1, 1977 to May 31, 1978. A very few promising scripts were eliminated from ATCA's consideration by their authors, who termed them works in progress not yet ready for formal recognition.

The list of the 1977-78 plays nominated by members of ATCA as outstanding presentations in their areas, with descriptions written by the critics who saw and nominated them, follows the synopsis of *Getting Out.* The synopsis itself was prepared by the *Best Plays* editor.

Time: The present

Place: A dingy one-room apartment

ACT I

SYNOPSIS: The apartment is furnished only with a bed, one chair and a suggestion of kitchen equipment with sink, etc. Three doors lead to bathroom, closet and hall, and the single window is barred behind its dirty curtains. Above the stage stretches a catwalk serving as the corridor of a prison, with cell areas connecting to it.

Five minutes before the house lights dim, droning announcements are heard over the loud speaker, similar to the following: "Kitchen workers, all kitchen workers report immediately to the kitchen. Kitchen workers to the kitchen. The library will not be open today. Those scheduled for book check-out should remain in morning work assignments. Kitchen workers to the kitchen. No library hours today. Library hours resume tomorrow as usual. All kitchen workers to the kitchen. Frances Mills, you have a visitor at the front gate . . . . ."

Neither time, place nor personality are defined in the usual way here. The action switches between past and present and sometimes contemplates them simultaneously. Furthermore, there are two protagonists, "Arlie" and "Arlene": *"Arlie is the violent kid Arlene was until her last stretch in prison. Arlie's presence is not acknowledged on the stage by any of the other characters and she does not pay any attention to them. Some of her scenes should take place in a space apart from the apartment, but she should also walk through the apartment freely at appropriate times. In a sense, she is Arlene's memory of herself. There should be hints in both physical type and gesture that Arlie and Arlene are the same person seen at different times in her life. They both speak with a country twang, but Arlene is suspicious and guarded, withdrawal is always a possibility. Arlie is unpredictable and incorrigible."*

As the house lights go to black, the prison warden's voice is heard over the loud speaker announcing Arlene Holsclaw's release on parole after serving eight years for second degree murder at Pine Ridge, an Alabama penitentiary. Though she has an extensive record of juvenile delinquency in Kentucky, her home state, the authorities now believe she's a good prospect for successful rehabilitation.

A spotlight comes up on Arlie seated downstage center. She remembers how she and her sister June once stole the neighbor boy's collection of pet frogs and threw them out in the street for cars to run over. Her manner is callous but not unaware of the horror of her tale: ". . . . . This little kid comes out in his back yard lookin for his stupid frogs an he don't see any an he gets so crazy, cryin an everthing. So me an June goes over an tells him we seen this big mess out in the street and he goes out an sees all them frog legs an bodies an shit all over everywhere an, man it was so funny. We bout killed ourselves laughin. Then his mother come out an she wouldn't let him go out an pick up all the pieces, so he jus had to stand there watchin all the cars go by an smush his little babies right into the street."

Arlene enters the apartment, followed by Bennie, a former prison guard in his late 50s and still wearing his uniform, dragging a trunk. Bennie is obviously worried about how Arlene will fare in her effort to make a new start on the outside. Arlene assures him forcefully: "Arlie girl landed herself in prison. Arlene is out, O.K.?"

Bennie has escorted Arlene from Alabama to her new home here in Kentucky, not as an official duty but in personal concern. He was afraid she might pick up a soldier on the bus or give her twenty prison dollars to the first pusher she met and wind up back in trouble. (Arlie, interpolating acid comments having nothing to do with the Bennie-Arlene conversation but merely whatever comes into her mind, would have indeed become an instant recidivist. Arlie now goes to the cell area and screams for somebody to come clean up her cell; she's apparently thrown her dinner against the wall, as she boasts, "I kin git outta here any time I want.")

Arlene notices the bars on the apartment window; Bennie guesses they're to keep out burglars. Arlene is determined to have them taken out (as Arlie pantomimes a breaking-and-entering and arrogantly confronting the policeman who arrests her). Bennie warns her that she can't alter the room without the landlord's permission. He suggests masking the bars with plants.

At Arlene's orders, Bennie hangs a cheaply-framed picture of Jesus in a spot where she can see it first thing in the morning when she wakes.

The focus of the play shifts to Arlie in her cell, lighting a fire which brings a guard running to put it out, followed by the doctor, who gives her an injection to keep her quiet. The guard looks for the matches he knows must be hidden under the toilet seat (they aren't). He looks forward to searching Arlie's body for them and is disappointed when he finds them under her mattress.

In the apartment, Bennie suggests they'd feel better if he went out and got them something to eat, but Arlene isn't hungry. He finally reveals to her that he has quit his job as a prison guard (she thought he had merely taken some time off to bring her here, partly to help her out but mostly because he'd always wanted to see Kentucky and never had). Bennie is actually considering staying here and maybe getting into the hardware business: "Nails. Always wanted to. Some little store with bins and barrels fulla nails and screws. Count em out. Put em in little sacks."

Bennie suggests that Arlene take a bath while he goes out and gets some chicken and cole slaw. Bennie exits as, in the prison, a guard brings Arlie some food.

ARLIE: Ain't you got somebody to go beat up somewhere?
GUARD: Gotta see you get fattened up.
ARLIE: Whatta you care?
Arlene goes into the bathroom.
GUARD: Oh, we care all right.
Setting the food down on the table.

Got us a two-way mirror in the shower room. (*She looks up, hostile.*) An you don't know which one it is, do you?

> *Sits her down, hard.*

Yes, ma'm. Eat. (*Pointing to the food.*) We sure do care if you go gittin too skinny. (*Walks away, folding his arms and standing, watching her, her anger building, despite her hunger.*) Yes, ma'm. We care a hog lickin lot.

ARLIE: Sons a bitches.

> *Throws the whole carton at him. Mother's knock is heard on the apartment door.*

MOTHER: Arlie? Arlie girl, you in there?

> *Arlene walks out of the bathroom and stands still, looking at the door. Arlie hears the knock at the same time and comes out of the closet, putting the pillow between her legs and holding a yellow teddy bear Arlene has unpacked.*

(*Knocking louder.*) Arlie?

ARLIE (*pulling herself up weakly on one elbow, speaking with the voice of a very young child*): Mama? Mama?

> *Arlene walks slowly toward the door.*

MOTHER (*now pulling the doorknob from the outside, angry that the door is locked*): Arlie? I know you're in there.

ARLIE: I can't git up, Mama. (*Hands between her legs.*) My legs is hurt.

MOTHER: What's takin you so long?

ARLENE (*smoothing out her dress*): Yeah, I'm comin.

> *Puts Bennie's hat out of sight under the bed.*

Hold on.

MOTHER: I brung you some stuff, but I ain't gonna stand here all night.

> *Arlene opens the door and stands back. Mother looks strong but badly worn. She is wearing her cab driver's uniform and is carrying a plastic laundry basket stuffed with cleaning fluids, towels, bug spray, etc.*

ARLENE: I didn't know if you'd come.

MOTHER: Ain't I always?

ARLENE: How are you?

> *Moves as if to hug her. Mother stands still, Arlene backs away.*

MOTHER: Bout the same.

ARLENE: I'm glad to see you.

MOTHER: You look tired.

ARLENE: It was a long drive.

MOTHER: Didn't fatten up none, I see. (*Walks around the room.*) You always was too skinny.

> *Arlene straightens her clothes again.*

Shoulda beat you like your daddy said. Make you eat.

ARLIE: Nobody done this to me, Mama. (*Protesting, in pain.*) No! No!

MOTHER: He weren't a mean man, though, your daddy.

ARLIE: Was . . . (*Quickly.*) My bike. My bike hurt me. The seat bumped me.

MOTHER: You remember that black chewing gum he got you when you was sick?

ARLENE: I member he beat up on you.

MOTHER: Yeah (*Proudly.*) an he was real sorry a coupla times. (*Looking in the cabinet.*) Filthy dirty. Hey! I brung you all kinda stuff. Just like Candy not leavin you nuthin. (*Walking back to the basket.*) Some kids I got.

ARLIE (*curling up into a ball*): No, Mama, don't touch it. It'll git well. It git well before.

This was her sister Candy's room that Arlene is taking over, and her mother has brought her a few things to brighten it up, like colored towels and a teapot sent by June. Arlene asks after her little boy Joey (while Arlie protests, "Daddy didn't do nuthin to me. Ask him. He saw me fall off my bike."). Arlene's mother saw Joey a couple of years ago but didn't speak to him. She remembers him as skinny and stringy-haired like Arlene (who resents this description, for the child as well as herself). Joey's in a foster home now because another sister of Arlene's, Shirley, didn't feel like taking care of him.

Arlene figures some day she could bring Joey here (and Arlie screams, "No Daddy! I didn't tell her nuthin. I didn't, I didn't.") Her mother helps make the bed, while Arlene informs her she's to be known by her full name now, not "Arlie" for short. (Arlie is questioned by a woman who is curious about money in the child's possession. Arlie explains that she earned it "Doin' things . . . . . for my daddy." The woman decides she can no longer permit Arlie to continue as a disturbance in the regular school. Arlie must now be sent to a special school for problem children.)

Arlene's mother has been driving the taxi herself for the past seven years. Her husband has been too sick to drive it. Arlene had some training as a beautician at the prison, though in this state ex-convicts can't get a license to practise this craft, so she'll probably have to settle for working at something else.

The mother goes out to get a broom. Arlene talks to herself, trying to reconcile herself to being skinny and having stringy hair (while Arlie anguishes with the traumas of childhood, remembering aloud that her mother "drives the cab to buy us stuff, cause we don't take no charity from nobody, cause we got money cause she earned it . . . . . She drives at night cause people needs rides at night. People goin to see their friends that are sick, or people's cars broken down an they gotta work at the . . . . . Nobody calls my momma a whore!").

The mother comes back with the broom and starts to sweep up the room, as she wonders why, since she isn't hateful, "I got so many hateful kids." Arlene hints that she'd like to come to her mother's on Sunday for some of her pot roast with all the trimmings. The mother, sweeping all the dirt into a piece of paper, tells Arlene she doesn't want her exerting a bad influence on the two younger children still at home.

Arlene hopes that if she can earn a little money she can take care of Joey. Her mother reminds her of how delinquent and unfit a child Arlene herself was.

At the same time, Arlie and a doctor are having it out. Arlie is refusing to go away to camp, though she can't come and go as she pleases without the doctor's permission.

ARLIE: I don't feel good. I'm pregnant, you know.

DOCTOR: The test was negative.

ARLIE: Well, I should know, shouldn't I?

DOCTOR: No. You want to be pregnant, is that it?

ARLIE: I wouldn't mind. Kids need somebody to bring em up right.

DOCTOR: Bringing up children is a big responsibility, you know.

ARLIE: Yeah, I know it. I ain't dumb. Everybody always thinks I'm so dumb.

DOCTOR: You could learn if you wanted to. That's what the teachers are here for . . .

ARLIE: Shit.

DOCTOR: . . . or so they say.

ARLIE: All they teach us is about geography. Why'd I need to know bout Africa? Jungles an shit.

DOCTOR: They want you to know about other parts of the world.

ARLIE: Well, I ain't goin there, so whatta I care?

DOCTOR: What's this about Cindy?

ARLIE (*hostile*): She tol Mr. Dawson some lies about me.

DOCTOR: I bet.

ARLIE: She said I fuck my daddy for money.

DOCTOR: And what did you do when she said that?

ARLIE: What do you think I did? I beat the shit out of her.

DOCTOR: And that's a good way to work out your problem?

ARLIE: She ain't done it since.

DOCTOR: She's been in traction, since.

ARLIE: So? Whadda I care? She say it again, I'll do it again. Bitch!

ARLENE (*looking down at the pile of dirt her mother has swept up*): I ain't got a can. Just leave it.

MOTHER: An have you kick it under the bed after I go?

> *She wraps the dirt up in a piece of newspaper and puts it in her laundry basket.*

Arlene's mother spies Bennie's hat and demands to know who it belongs to. Arlene explains about Bennie, how he happened to drive her here from Alabama. Her mother thinks she is giving Bennie quid pro quo, but Arlene insists, "I ain't like that no more." Her mother is angry because she feels Arlene is entertaining a man here and doesn't appreciate what she's done for her, getting the room for her and coming to see her; taking her mother for granted and expecting more; hinting about pot roast. "Same hateful brat, right?" Arlene challenges. Her mother echoes this phrase and exits angrily. Arlene calls an appealing "Mama?" after her, but her mother doesn't answer. (And Arlie repels the advances of a boy named Ronnie so forcefully that he needs the doctor's attention.)

Arlene, in her bathroom, hears a knock on her door and a voice shouting for her to open it. When Arlene doesn't answer the door, the caller, Carl, kicks it in and enters.

> *Carl is thin and cheaply dressed. Carl's walk and manner are imitative of black pimps, but he can't quite carry it off.*

CARL: Where you at, Momma?

ARLENE: Carl?

CARL: Who else? You 'spectin Leroy Brown?

ARLENE: I'm takin a bath.

CARL (*walking toward the bathroom*): I like my ladies clean.
    Puts hand on doorknob.
Matter of pro-fessional pride.

ARLENE: Don't come in here.

CARL (*mocking her tone*): Ain't nothin I ain't seen before.

ARLENE: Hold your horses.

CARL: Come out here and do it for me.

ARLENE: I'm gittin out. Sit down or something.

CARL (*talking loud enough for her to hear him through the door*): Ain't got the time.
    Searches the trunk.
Just come by to tell you it's tomorrow. We be takin our feet to the New York street. (*As though she will be pleased.*) No more fuckin around with these jiveass Southern turkeys. We're goin to the big city, baby. We get you some red shades an some red shorts an the johns'll be linin up fore we hit town . . . four tricks a night, how's that sound? No use wearin out that cute ass you got . . . Way I hear it, only way to git busted up there's be stupid, an I ain't lived this here long bein stupid.

Carl, like Arlene, is an ex-convict. At present he is an escapee. Arlene once escaped but was captured and brought back, and, emerging from the bathroom, she warns Carl that he'll be caught too. Arlene informs Carl that she isn't going away with him.

ARLENE: I ain't seen you since Birmingham. How come you think I wanna see you now?

ARLIE (*comes over to confront Carl*): I ain't goin with that dude, he's weird, Carl.

CARL: Cause we gotta go collect the john's money, that's "how come."

ARLIE: I don't need you pimpin for me.

ARLENE: I'm gonna work.

CARL: Work?

ARLENE: Yeah.
    Arlie has hands on hips, furious.

CARL: What's this "work"?

ARLIE: You always sendin me to them ol droolers . . .

CARL: You kin do two things, girl . . .

ARLIE: They slobberin all over me.

CARL: Breakin out and hookin.

ARLIE (*yelling*): They tyin me to the bed.

ARLENE: I mean real work.

ARLIE (*now screaming, as she gets further away from him*): I could git killed workin for you. Some sicko, some crazy drunk . . . No way, Carl.

CARL: You forget, we seen it all on TV in the dayroom, you bustin outta Lakewood like that. Fakin that palsy fit, beatin that guard half to death with his own key ring. Whoo-ee, then that spree you went on . . . stoppin at that fillin station for some cash, then kidnappin the old dude pumpin the gas.

ARLENE: Yeah.

CARL: Then that cab driver comes outta the bathroom an tries to mess with you an you shoots him with his own piece. (*Fires an imaginary pistol.*) That there's nice work, Momma. (*Going over to her.*)

ARLENE: That gun . . . It went off, Carl.

CARL: That's what guns do, doll. They go off.

Bennie comes in carrying the chicken dinners. Carl orders him out, but Bennie is obstinate; he doesn't want to fight Carl, but he won't back down either. Arlene explains who Bennie is, what he's doing here. Carl leaves, hostile and threatening, warning Arlene he'll return to take her away.

Arlene slips on a dress while Bennie advises her to stay away from the likes of Carl; the parole officer wouldn't approve. Arlene explains to Bennie that Carl was the man who accompanied her on the ill-fated trip to Alabama, where thanks to him she was arrested for forgery. Carl is also Joey's father, though Carl doesn't know it. (Bennie wishes he had a child, but he and his wife Dorrie, now dead, could never manage it.) The prison authorities tried to get Arlene to have an abortion, but she refused. They took the baby away from her after it was born, "An I guess I went crazy after that. Thought if I could jus git out an find him." (In the cell area, Arlie is hugging a pillow, pretending it's her baby, speculating on what it'll be when it grows up, telling it protectively, "People is mean to babies so you stay right here with me so nobody kin git you'n make you cry an they lay one finger on you . . . . . an I'll beat the screamin shit right out of em.")

Bennie and Arlene have finished dinner. Both are tired and ready for bed. Arlene wants to be let alone, but Bennie insists on fondling her, excessively forceful in his attentions. It becomes increasingly obvious that he's trying to make love to her. Arlene resists. Finally, they are struggling.

BENNIE (*overpowering her capably, prison-guard style*): Little outta practise, ain't you? (*This amuses him.*)

ARLENE (*screaming*): I'll kill you, you creep.
    The struggle continues, Bennie pinning her arms under his legs as he kneels over her on the bed. Arlene is terrified and in pain.

BENNIE: You will? You'll kill ol Bennie . . . kill ol Bennie like you done that cab driver.
    A cruel reminder he employs to stun and mock her. Arlene looks as if she has been hit. Bennie is still fired up, he unzips his pants and undoes his belt.

ARLENE (*suddenly passive and coldly bitter*): This how you got your Dorrie, rapin?

BENNIE (*unbuttoning his shirt*): That what you think this is, rape?

ARLENE (*looking at the zipper now*): I oughta know.

BENNIE: Uh-huh.
ARLENE: First they unzip their pants.
Bennie pulls his shirt off.
Sometimes they take off their shirt.
Bennie starts to pull his arms out of his shirt.
But mostly, they jus pull it out an stick it in.
Bennie stops, one hand goes to his fly, finally hearing what she has been saying. Finding it open, he straightens up, obviously shocked. He pulls his pants up and stands up.
BENNIE: Don't you call me no rapist. (*Pause, then insistent.*) No, I ain't no rapist, Arlie.
Gets up, begins to zip up his pants.
ARLENE: An I ain't Arlie.
Arlene remains on the bed.
BENNIE: No, I guess you ain't.
ARLENE (*quietly and painfully*): Arlie coulda killed you.
Curtain.

ACT II

Prison announcements are heard on the loud speaker before the house lights dim, as before Act I. After the announcements the curtain rises to reveal Arlene asleep in her bed and Arlie obviously penned in a very small cell in the prison area. She is in "segregation," and to amuse herself she goes over a dorm count of all her former roommates. Finally she starts hassling the guard, screaming and calling for the nurse.

Arlene doesn't wake up. Bennie is the guard stationed at the far end of the prison catwalk, as the warden enters to see what's going on. The guards have the situation in hand, but they are tired of Arlie's making trouble for them. After the warden leaves, a guard comments to Bennie, "I can wait . . . . . til the day she tries gettin out an I'm here by myself. I'll show that screechin slut . . . . ."

Bennie demonstrates to the other guard the way to pacify Arlie: drop some chewing gum where she can reach it — but it has to be her brand.

The sounds of a siren and a jackhammer out in the street awaken Arlene. She is disoriented at first, grabbing the bars in the window, finally realizing that she has slept in her clothes and that it is late in the morning. She explains aloud to herself, "People don't sleep in their clothes, Arlene. An people git up fore noon." Arlie too is trying to adjust to her situation, as the warden comes to her segregated cell.

ARLIE: When am I gittin outta here?
WARDEN: That's up to you.
ARLIE: The hell it is.
WARDEN: When you can show you can be with the other girls, you can get out.
ARLIE: How'm I sposed to prove that bein in here?
WARDEN: And then you can have mail again and visitors.

ARLIE: You jus fuckin with me. You ain't ever gonna let me out. I been in this ad-just-ment room four months. I think.

WARDEN: Arlie, you see the other girls in the dorm walking around, free to do whatever they want? If we felt the way you seem to think we do, everyone would be in lockup. When you get out of segregation, you can go to the records office and have your time explained to you.

ARLIE: It won't make no sense.

WARDEN: They'll go through it all very slowly . . . when you're eligible for parole, how many days of good time you have, how many industrial days you've earned, what constitutes meritorious good time . . . and how many days you're set back for your write-ups and all your time in segregation.

ARLENE: Now then . . . (*Sounds as if she has something in mind to do. Looks as if she doesn't.*)

ARLIE (*screaming*): Get outa my hall!

WARDEN: Remember, Arlie, it's up to you.

ARLIE: An I want the chaplain!

Arlene gets some of last night's slaw from the refrigerator. In the prison area, a guard brings Arlie a plate of scrambled eggs, minus a fork as usual — Arlie isn't allowed to possess anything as dangerous as a fork. She throws the plate of eggs back through the slot in her cell door.

Arlene lays some money from her purse out on the bed and starts budgeting the bills for food, cosmetics, etc. There is a banging on the door and Ruby (the woman upstairs, in her late 30s) is shouting for $5 that the previous occupant of the room, Arlene's sister Candy, owes her. Arlene puts away her money and admits Ruby, who explains that she needs the $5 for some shoes she is buying, and Candy promised it would be here. In a friendly manner, Ruby offers her phone for Arlene's use and advises Arlene that Candy probably won't be coming by, as she has been taken away by her pimp; she's now a prostitute and has been using this place to entertain clients. This information depresses already-depressed Arlene even further.

Ruby has done time herself and shares her feelings about getting out: "Hell, I heaved a whole gallon of milk right out the window my first day . . . . . It bounced! Made me feel a helluva lot better. I said, 'Ruby, if a gallon a milk can bounce back, so kin you.' " Ruby even got so she believed it after a year or so.

Arlene remains silent and moody, and this worries Ruby.

RUBY: . . . . . You don't seem like Candy said.

ARLENE: She tell you I was a killer?

RUBY: More like the meanest bitch that ever walked. I seen lots worse than you.

ARLENE: I been lots worse.

RUBY: Got to you, didn't it? (*Arlene doesn't respond, but Ruby knows she's right.*) Well, you just gotta git over it. Bein out, you gotta . . .

ARLENE: Don't you start in on me.

RUBY (*realizes her tone*): Was about to, wasn't I? Get right up'n start preachin. No booze, no men. No buyin on credit. Shit like that. Ex-cons is the worst. I'm sorry.

ARLENE: It's O.K.

RUBY: Done that about a year ago. New waitress we had. Gave my little goin straight speech'n she quit that very night. Stole my fuckin raincoat on her way out. Some speech, huh? (*Laughs, no longer resenting this theft.*)

Ruby works in a restaurant as a cook, she tells Arlene. Sensing that Arlene may be hungry, she offers her some raisin toast. Arlene, suspicious of any sudden friendliness from women after her experiences in prison, refuses coldly and proceeds to fix her stopped-up sink, while Arlie launches into a diatribe about the behavior of the "bunch of weirdos" she's cooped up with, especially one Lucille who gave her a present of some hair rollers: "I's stupid. I's thinkin maybe she were different from all them others. Then that night everbody disappears from the john and she's wantin to brush my hair. Sure, brush my hair. How'd I know she was gonna crack her head open on the sink? I jus barely even touched her . . . . . You ain't asked what she was gonna do to me. Huh? When you gonna ask that? You don't give a shit about that cause Lucille such a good girl."

Ruby tells Arlene about a dishwashing job open at the restaurant. She further suggests they might have a game of cards some time, but Arlene continues to be wary of Ruby's friendliness. Ruby again offers Arlene the use of her phone to call her parole officer, but Arlene would prefer to use the one in the A & P. Ruby offers to charge Arlene a dime if that will make her feel better. This time, to Ruby's amusement, Arlene replies "O.K."

Ruby departs. Arlene notices a smudge on the picture of Jesus, wipes it off, then goes out on her errand, as Bennie appears outside Arlie's cell on the catwalk. Bennie is friendly and talkative; Arlie is mainly concerned with the chaplain's next visit. "What's he tell you anyway, get you so starry-eyed?" Bennie wants to know. "He jus talks to me," is all Arlie will tell him.

Arlene comes back with a bag full of groceries. The bottom of the bag breaks open, spilling cans and other purchases all over the floor. Arlene stares at the mess, then picks up a package of pickle loaf and hurls it against the door.

ARLENE: Bounce? (*In disgust.*) Shit.
> *Arlene sinks to the floor. She tears open the package of pickle loaf and eats a piece of it, tearing off the bites in her mouth. She is still angry, but is completely unable to do anything about her anger.*

ARLIE: He says I'm gonna get to fly. No shit! Me flying roun singin. An you don't never have to eat or try an look nice cause you got on this dress don't ever git messed up. An nobody's tellin you you're too skinny or brush your teeth or nuthin cause everbody looks jus the same but they know who you are an all.
> *Pauses.*

The hell they will! Once you're in, creep, you're in for-ever-more. An I ain't seein your face up there, that is for sure. Cause you gonna be fryin, fatso. An maybe, jus maybe, If I git to feelin real sorry for you, I might make it rain on you a few drops. But it won't help you none cause it'll be jus like in Mama's fryin pan when she drops in some water it pops an fizzles but it goes right on fryin. (*Revenge being sweet and all.*)

ARLENE (*finally she draws her knees up to her chest, wraps her arms around them and then rests her head on her arms*): Jus gotta git a job an make some money an everything will be all right. You hear me, Arlene? You git yourself up and go find a job. (*Continues to sit.*) An you can start by cleanin up this mess you made. Cause food don't belong on the floor.

Carl appears, and Arlene orders him, "Fuck off!"; then, reconsidering in the light of her new commitment, she changes it to "Go away." But Carl hangs in there, finding a cache of knitted baby clothes, suggesting to Arlene's annoyance that they sell these things for extra money for the trip. Carl tells her she is to pay her own fare; Arlene replies she isn't going with him under any circumstances.

Arlene has noticed that Carl is on the lookout for pursuers, and that he is sniffing and scratching, sure signs of a dope habit. She tells him, "You got cops lookin for you and you ain't scored yet this morning. You better git yourself back to prison where you can git all you need."

Arlene explains that she means to stay out (which means not seeing ex-convicts like Carl) and earn money so she can take care of Joey. Carl ridicules her, "You ain't gonna get rich workin on your knees." She argues that Ruby has a real job and seems to be doing all right. Carl lays out the economics for her: work eight hours a day six days a week at dishwashing and bring home $75, which she can easily earn in two hours working for Carl. Arlene is thinking not about the money but about Joey. Carl challenges her, "If you was a kid, would you want your mom to git so dragged out washin dishes she don't have no time for you, an no money to spend on you? You come with me, you kin send him big orange bears an Sting-Ray bikes with his name wrote on the fenders."

Arlene would prefer to be with Joey, and she doesn't want to risk going back to prison. Ruby interrupts them, knocking on the door. Carl grabs Arlene's arm in a possessive gesture but turns her loose when Ruby barges in to see whether Arlene wants anything more from the store. There is immediate hostility between Ruby and Carl, who refuses to discuss his affairs further with Ruby present. He gives Arlene a dollar for a taxi, orders her to meet him at a bar later, where he'll have a car to take them north, gives her a match book with the bar's name and address, and goes.

Arlene explains to Ruby who Carl is and what he has done. Ruby understands immediately that Carl has painted a grim picture for Arlene of life on the outside. Ruby admits the hard truth about trying to go straight as an ex-con, "But," Ruby adds, "when you make your two nickels, you can keep both of em."

Arlene is in despair at the thought of a threadbare existence without luxury or even a decent job. "It's outside," Ruby reminds her, but that's not enough for Arlene. She didn't make the effort of casting out hate just to live in some slum for the rest of her life. The word "slum" annoys Ruby, who lives here too, and Arlene tries to explain further how she feels.

ARLENE: They said I's . . . he tole me if . . . I thought once Arlie . . . He said the meek . . . meek, them that's quiet and good . . . the meek . . . As soon as

Arlie . . .(*Becoming completely irrational.*)

RUBY (*really concerned, trying to snap her out of this*): What, Arlene? Who said what?

ARLENE: At Pine Ridge there was . . . I was . . . this chaplain . . .
        Not doing much better, pointing to the picture of Jesus.

RUBY (*trying to call her back from this hysteria*): Arlene . . . .

ARLENE: I was in lockup . . . I don't know . . . years . . .

RUBY: Yeah . . .

ARLENE: This chaplain said I had . . . said Arlie was my hateful self an she was hurtin me an God would find some way to take her away. An it was God's will so I could be the meek . . . the meek that's quiet and good and git whatever they want . . . I forgit that word . . . they git the earth.

RUBY: Inherit.

ARLENE: Yeah. An that's why I done it.

RUBY: Done what?

ARLENE: What I done. Cause the chaplain he said . . . I'd sit up nights waitin for him to come talk to me.

RUBY: Arlene, what did you do? What are you talkin about?

ARLENE: They tol me after . . . After I's out an it was all over . . . They said after the chaplain got transferred . . . I didn't know why he didn't come no more til after . . . They said it was three whole nights at first, me screamin to God to come git Arlie an kill her. They give me this medicine and they thought I's better . . . Then that night it happened, the officer was in the dorm doin count . . . and they didn't hear nuthin but they come back out where I was and I'm standin there tellin em to come see, real quiet I'm tellin em, but there's all this blood all over my shirt and I got this fork I'm holdin real tight in my hand . . .
        Clenches one hand now, the other hand fumbling with the buttons on her dress, as if she's going to show Ruby.
. . . this fork, they said Doris stole it from the kitchen an give it to me so I'd kill myself and shut up bothering her . . . an there's all these holes all over me where I been stabbin myself an I'm sayin Arlie is dead an it's God's will . . . I didn't scream it, I was jus sayin it over and over . . . Arlie is dead, Arlie is dead . . . they couldn't git that fork outta my hand til . . . I woke up in the infirmary an they said I almost died. They said they's glad I didn't. (*Smiling*) They said did I feel better now an they was real nice, bringin me chocolate puddin . . .

RUBY: I'm sorry, Arlene.

ARLENE: I'd be eatin or jus lookin at the ceiling an git a tear in my eye, but it'd jus dry up, you know, it didn't run out or nuthin. An then pretty soon, I's well, an officers was tellin me they's seein such a change in me and how'd I like to learn to knit sweaters an how'd I like to have a new skirt to wear an sometimes lettin me chew gum. They said things ain't never been as clean as when I's doin the housekeepin at the dorm. (*So proud.*) An then I got in the honor cottage an nobody was foolin with me no more or nuthin. An I didn't get mad like before or nuthin. I jus done my work an knit . . . An I don't think about it, what happened, 'cept . . . (*Now losing control.*) People here keep callin me Arlie an . . . (*Has trouble saying "Arlie."*) . . . I didn't mean to do it, what I done.

Susan Kingsley as Arlene and Lynn Cohen as Ruby in a scene from
Getting Out

Arlene goes over the edge into hysterics. Ruby comforts and calms her. Outside on the stair a crash is heard — it's Bennie, who has dropped a box of plants.
He comes in bearing what's left of them and is introduced to Ruby. One plant is
intact, and Bennie puts it where the others were also intended to go, on the window sill to hide the bars, telling Arlene, "I just thought, after what I done last
night . . . I jus wanted to do somethin nice."

Arlene thanks Bennie for this gesture of apology. Bennie explains to Ruby
that he's fond of Arlene and has no intention of going anywhere until he sees her
settled. Bennie gives Arlene his phone number where he's staying at a motel and
assures her as he exits, "Any ol thing now. Jus any ol thing. You even run outta
gum an you call."

Arlene picks up the match book Carl left her and holds it with Bennie's piece
of paper with the phone number; then she drops them both in the waste basket,
suggesting that Ruby get out the cards for a game of Old Maid, after Arlene
finishes a couple of chores. Arlene watches her go, then attends to the groceries
spilled over the floor.

> *Slowly, but with great determination, she picks up the items one at a*
> *time and puts them away in the cabinet above the counter.*

ARLIE (*as Arlene stops, remembering this incident*): Hey! You 'member that
time we was playin policeman an June locked me up in Mama's closet an then

took off swimmin? An I stood around with them dresses itchin my ears and crashin into that door tryin to git out a there? It was dark in there. So finally . . . (*Quite proud of herself.*) I went aroun and peed in all Mama's shoes. But then she come home an tried to git in the closet only June taken the key so she said, "Who's in there?" an I said, "It's me!" an she said, "What you doin in there?" an I started gigglin an she started pullin on the door and yellin, "Arlie, what you doin in there?" (*A big laugh.*)

ARLIE and ARLENE (*Arlene has begun to smile during the story, now they say together*): Arlie, what you doin in there?

Arlie laughs, Arlene shakes her head.

ARLENE (*now beginning to put the things away again, still smiling and remembering, stops, stage dark except for one light on her face*): Aw, shoot.

Light dims on her fond smile as Arlie laughs once more. Curtain.

Other Plays Cited
By American Theater Critics Association Members

Hello! by the Play Group Ensemble; final script by David McIntosh on the basis of improvisations by Beth Stubblefield, Chris Brown, Jon Craven and Mac Pirkle. (Knoxville, Tenn.: Play Group Theater. Nashville, Tenn.: Advent Theater) — Set in a seedy hotel, or at least a vine-overgrown suggestion of a hotel, in the present. *Hello!* is an amusing two-act comedy satirizing contemporary fantasies and mores. Described by its creators as "a slapstick concerto, a poem about time, an essay on fantasy and isolation, and a relic of cultural memory and various theatrical forms," it has four characters and an offstage voice billed as "Chickenman." The others talk about him a lot as they enact each other's fantasies or puncture them in this series of jocularly irreverent vignettes set in the context of "International Pickle Week." While the audience never meets him, Chickenman-Godot has a definite identity as the One Greatest Fantasizer of Them All. Bubbles Babylon, Captain Alexander Dumas ("Dumb-Ass"), Orange (listed as principal zany) and Tom Edison (may be blind, maybe not, but a rag-tag catch-all of inventive trivia) cast their brash, witty glances at virtually every cliche of our time, revealing all of them as the emotional junk food on which everyone has been weaned and fattened and now stands in need of the salvation of a redeeming crash diet.

The Morning Star by Henry C. Haskell (Kansas City: Missouri Repertory Theater) — The time is the 12th century, the place France, and the drama that of Heloise and Abelard, whose historic relationship is examined over a period of 26 years. Unlike most accounts of the lovers, this one concentrates more on Heloise, both as Abelard's passionate soulmate and a woman of rare intellect. A prologue introduces Heloise, now a nun, when she learns of Abelard's death in a monastery. Flashbacks then present the couple at salient moments of their relationship: their first mental and physical infatuation; their dawning love affair, realized in a playful-erotic scene in a garden; Heloise's refusal to marry Abelard and thus jeopardize his intellectual career; their flight together from Heloise's hostile guardian, Fulbert; their decision to marry after all, following the birth of a child; Fulbert's violent revenge, the emasculation of Abelard; and finally, the couple's poignant last meeting before each takes up holy orders. Lucid, moving, at times witty, with finely-drawn, vivid characters, the drama is written in elegiac iambic pentameters that read as "structured prose" (Haskell's term). Most of all, it is a work of beautifully controlled passion, its lovers brought achingly, sensuously alive.

Reunion and **Dark Pony** by David Mamet (New Haven: Yale Repertory Theater) — In *Reunion,* a long one-act, a father and daughter meet after decades of separation; and, tentatively and with gentle humor, they begin to communicate and to understand one another. They reveal their mutual need. The play is preceded by *Dark Pony,* a brief curtain-raiser, also about a father and his daughter, an idealization of the older couple at a younger age. On a long motor trip home, the father tells his child their favorite story — about a dark pony — and the girl snuggles down in contentment. The portrait is lyrical and elegiac and beautifully matched with *Reunion.*

Seduced by Sam Shepard (Providence, R.I.: Trinity Square Repertory Company) — The hero of this play has a long beard, long fingernails and a history as an aeronautical pioneer and a financial wizard. He is the richest man in the world. He is, of course, based on Howard Hughes, with that billionaire's morbid obsession with isolating himself, but he is also a marvelous figment of the playwright's perfervid imagination. Shepard's Hughes is facing death and, before he departs, he sends for two voluptuous women from his past and dreams about one last flight. Strange and mysterious, the play is a cat's cradle of laughter and intrigue.

Terminus by Thomas O. Cullen (Atlanta, Ga.: Kelly Feed & Grain Theater) — Playing on the original name of Atlanta, Terminus, this non-realistic play is an apocalyptic drama in which the destruction of Atlanta stands in for all wars. The central action is the entire cast's rejection of Lumpkin, the commonsense voice of survival. Somewhat obvious in its message, the play's best effects are long speeches — set pieces — in which the rhetoric of jingoism, of science, of sports is turned into a kind of oblique lyricism.

Wings by Arthur Kopit (New Haven: Yale Repertory Theater) — Kopit has written a poetic, romantic exploration of the mind of a stroke victim, a former aviatrix. It's a beautifully carpentered platform for a tour-de-force performance by an accomplished, charismatic actress. The play began life as a radio play, commissioned by Earplay, the drama project of National Public Radio. Its origins are evident, and it's essentially static and verbal. But on stage the 80-minute exploration of a stroke victim's plight is both dramatically viable and written with real sensitivity. Kopit has a kaleidoscopic way with words and has leavened what could be a harrowing experience with sudden flashes of light humor and romantic images of early aviation. Since most of *Wings* takes place in the mind of the stroke victim, the play is fragmentary and fleeting. The dialogue is often as fractured as the victim's thought processes as she struggles to express herself coherently. There are other characters in the play — doctors, nurses and other stroke victims — but *Wings* is essentially a one-woman theater piece. In it, Kopit has allowed us to share in what must be involved in the reestablishment of a stroke victim.

The Woods by David Mamet (Chicago: St. Nicholas Theater) — This is an end-of-summer romance between a young man and a young woman who are sharing the man's family house in the north woods. The two-character play whirls with undercurrents as the pair turns from being a loving couple into being a warring couple and finally reach a kind of mutual understanding. The woman is headstrong and convivial, the man a quiet, safe harbor.

Peter Weller and Patti LuPone in *The Woods* at the St. Nicholas Theater

A DIRECTORY OF PROFESSIONAL
REGIONAL THEATER

Compiled by Ella A. Malin

Professional 1977-78 programs and repertory productions by leading resident companies around the United States, plus selected Canadian programs and major Shakespeare festivals including that of Stratford, Ontario (Canada), are grouped in alphabetical order of their locations and listed in date order from May, 1977 to June, 1978. This list does not include Broadway, off-Broadway or touring New York shows (unless the local company took some special part), summer theaters, single productions by commercial producers or college or other non-professional productions. The Directory was compiled by Ella A. Malin for *The Best Plays of 1977-78* from information provided by the resident producing organizations at Miss Malin's request. First productions of new plays — American or world premieres — in regional theaters are listed with full cast and credits, as available. Figures in parentheses following title give number of performances and date given is opening date, included whenever a record of these facts was obtainable from the producing managements.

Augmented reports on other than regional theater production in Los Angeles by Ron Pennington and Washington, D.C. by David Richards are included under those cities' headings in this listing. A section on U.S. dinner theater by Francine L. Trevens appears at the end of this Directory.

Summary

This Directory lists 585 productions of 426 plays (including one-acters, workshops, staged readings and plays-in-progress productions) presented by 61 groups in 105 theaters in 57 cities (50 in the United States, 7 in Canada) during the 1977-78 season. Of these, 242 were American plays in 164 full productions and 86 workshop productions. 59 were world premieres, 13 were American premieres, 5 were professional premieres and 1 was an English-language premiere (Canadian production). In addition, 23 groups presented 59 children's theater productions of 56 plays, not including improvisational, story theater and participation programs at the home theaters and on tour. Many groups presented selected plays from their regular repertory at special matinees for junior and senior high school students. Guest productions were not included in this summary unless the host theater was directly involved in the production, or was the first point of origin. Community outreach programs, tours of special productions for senior citizens, hospitals and institutions for the physically handicapped, audience participation seminars, as well as theater classes, many of them conservatory training programs preparing for the professional theater, continued on the increase.

Frequency of production of individual scripts was as follows:

1 play received 10 productions (*A Christmas Carol*)
1 play received 9 productions (*Vanities*)
1 play received 6 productions (*Ashes*)
5 plays received 5 productions (*A Moon for the Misbegotten, Absurd Person Singular, Much Ado About Nothing, The Shadow Box, Travesties*)
11 plays received 4 productions (*Equus, The Glass Menagerie, Hamlet, The Imaginary Invalid, The Mousetrap, The Night of the Iguana, Private Lives, Richard III, The Sea Gull, That Championship Season, Living Together*)
19 plays received 3 productions (*As You Like It, Comedians, The Club, Henry IV, Part 1, The Importance of Being Earnest, Loot, Macbeth, The National Health, Old Times, The Runner Stumbles, The Royal Family, Round and Round the Garden, Sleuth, She Stoops to Conquer, Sizwe Banzi Is Dead, Streamers, The Two Gentlemen of Verona, Table Manners, Uncle Vanya*)
52 plays received 2 productions
335 plays received 1 production (a production sometimes consisted of 2, 3 or 4 one-acters)

Listed below are the playwrights who received the greatest number of productions. The first figure is the number of productions; the second figure (in parentheses) is the number of plays produced, including one-acters.

Shakespeare	46 (24)	Simon	5 (4)
Ayckbourn	15 (5)	Barry	4 (3)
Shaw	14 (10)	Feydeau	4 (3)
Molière	13 (11)	George Kelly	4 (3)
Williams	12 (5)	Arthur Miller	4 (3)
Chekhov	11 (6)	Christie	4 (2)
Coward	9 (6)	Wilder	3 (5)
O'Neill	8 (7)	Durang	3 (3)
Ibsen	7 (6)	O'Casey	3 (3)
Brecht	6 (5)	Shepard	3 (3)
Strindberg	6 (4)	Preston Jones	3 (2)
Peter Shaffer	6 (3)	Marsha Norman	3 (2)
Cristofer	6 (2)	Ionesco	2 (2)
Mamet	5 (5)	Lanford Wilson	2 (2)
Fugard	5 (4)	Wasserstein	2 (2)
Hailey	5 (4)	Zindel	2 (2)
Pinter	5 (3)	Horovitz	2 (1)
Kaufman	5 (2)		

ABINGDON, VA.

Barter Theater — Mainstage

(Artistic director-producer, Rex Partington; founder, Robert Porterfield)

ALL MY SONS (21). By Arthur Miller. June 8, 1977. Director, John Olon-Scrymgeour. With Rex Partington, Virginia Mattis, Con Roche, John W. Morrow Jr., Mary Shelley, Robert Rutland, Beverly Jensen.

HAY FEVER (21). By Noel Coward. June 29, 1977. Director, Dorothy Marie. With Beth McDonald, Robert Rutland, Cleo Holladay, Gwyllum Evans, Jane Ridley.

THE PLAYBOY OF THE WESTERN WORLD (21). By John Millington Synge. July 20, 1977. Director, John Beary. With Beth McDonald, Raymond McBride, Rex Partington, Mary Shelley, Con Roche, Gwyllum Evans.

MAN WITH A LOAD OF MISCHIEF (21). Book, Ben Tarver; music, John Clifton; lyrics, John Clifton and Ben Tarver; based on the play by Ashley Dukes. August 10, 1977. Director, Ada Brown Mather; musical director, Byron Grant; choreographer, William Van Keyser. With Peter More, Elizabeth Torgerson, Rosalind Harris, Mel Cobb, Gwyllum Evans, Mary Shelley.

BUBBA (21). By Sam Havens. August 31, 1977 (world premiere). Director, John Olon-Scyrmgeour; scenery, Don Coleman; lighting,

Grant Clifford Logan; costumes, Sigrid Insull.
Glenn Dorsett .... Lee Jines
Bubba Dorsett .... Beverly Jensen
Casey Hooker .... Gwyllum Evans
Bambi .... Beth McDonald
Time: The present, autumn. Place: Glen and Bubba's apartment in Chicago. Act I, Scene 1: Morning. Scene 2: Midnight. Act II, Scene 1: Morning, two days later. Scene 2: That evening.

In Repertory:
THE MOUSETRAP (24). By Agatha Christie. September 21, 1977. Director, Dorothy Marie. NEVER TOO LATE (24). By Sumner Arthur Long. September 29, 1977. Director, Owen Phillips. With Gwyllum Evans, George Clark Hosmer, Cleo Holloday, Beverly Jensen, Lee Jines, Beth McDonald, John W. Morrow Jr., Rex Partington, Robert Rutland, Mary Shelley.

TWO GENTLEMEN OF VERONA (23). By William Shakespeare. April 4, 1978. Director, Ada Brown Mather. With Sam Blackwell, John Schak, Beverly Jensen, Ellen Donkin.

THE MOUSETRAP (28). By Agatha Christie. May 2, 1978. (Same production as previously noted).

Barter Theater: Barter Playhouse

I DO! I DO! (23). Book and lyrics, Tom Jones; music, Harvey Schmidt; based on Jan de Hartog's *The Fourposter.* May 24, 1978. Director, Owen Phillips; designer, Greg Buch; musical director, Byron Grant. With Gary Daniel, Sandra Laufer.

Workshop premieres:
PRETEXTS (12). By Robert Elwell. July 1, 1977. Director, Owen Phillips.

AFTER WORDS (12). By Paula Schwartz. July 22, 1977. Director, Michael S. Montel.

BY APPOINTMENT ONLY (12). By Ronald Mielech. August 12, 1977. Director, John Morrow Jr.

Performed by the Barter Intern Ensemble: Elizabeth Allen, Carol A. Chittum, David Givens, Douglas Hopkins, Michael O'Brien, Catherine Rhea, Narii Ruesch, Dana Smith, Joan Varnum.

Designers: scenery, Parmalee Welles, Bennet Averyt, Don Coleman; lighting, Grant Clifford Logan, Tony Partington; costumes, Sigrid Insull, Carr Garnett.

Barter Theater: Barter Playhouse — Children's Theater

(Director, Deborah Jean Templin)

THE CONTEST (14) by Sally Ann Sockwell; MEMORY CAKE (14) compiled by Apprentice Ensemble; BALLOONS, BUFFOONS AND BUBBLES (16) a clown show, conceived by the Apprentice Ensemble (June, July, August 1977). Directed by Deborah Jean Templin. Designed and performed by the Barter Apprentice Ensemble: Stephanie Glick, Prentiss Hollenbeck Jr, Randy McKey, Dennis Moser, Betsey Nichols, Steven Rickert.

Note: Barter Theater also presented *Shakespeare: Love, Intrigue and Majesty* compiled by Rex Partington and *An Evening With Teyve,* a program of story and song from *Fiddler on the Roof,* as well as Old World folklore and literature, with Jerry Jarrett, August 8, 1977. *Hay Fever* and *The Nature of Comedy,* conceived by the Intern Ensemble in 1974, toured Virginia, appearing before adult and high school groups.

ANCHORAGE, ALASKA

Alaska Repertory Theater: Sydney Laurence Auditorium

(Producing director, Paul V. Brown; artistic director, Robert J. Farley)

SHERLOCK HOLMES: *And the Curse of the Sign of Four or "The Mark of the Timber Toe"* (12). By Dennis Rosa; based on Sir Arthur Conan Doyle's novel. January 25, 1978. Director, Robert J. Farley. With Philip Pleasants, Mitchell Edmonds; Mary Anne Dempsey, Lou Favreaux, Philip Piro, Frank Geraci, Joseph Botz, James Morrison, Geoffrey Hill, Steve McKean.

THE FOURPOSTER (12). By Jan de Hartog. February 15, 1978. Director, Clayton Corzatte. With Mitchell Edmonds, Tanny McDonald.

THE ECCENTRICITIES OF A NIGHTINGALE (12). By Tennessee Williams. March 8, 1978. Director, Dennis Brite. With Dana Ivey, Philip Pleasants, Deirdre Owens, Marco St. John, Margaret Hilton, Tony Vita.

DIAMOND STUDS (17). Book by Jim Wann; music and lyrics by Bland Simpson and Jim Wann. March 29, 1978. Director, Robert J. Farley. With Nicholas Cosco, Warren Elkins, Dana Hart, John Mason, Steve McKean, Gina McMather, Susan Mendel, Scott Merrick, Jim Morrison, Tim Morrissey, Ernie Norris, Dave Roth, Don Ruddy, Luan Schooler.

Alaska Repertory Theater: Fairbanks, University of Alaska Theater

DIAMOND STUDS (5). April 20, 1978. (Same as above)

THE FOURPOSTER (5). April 27, 1978. (Same as above)

Designers: scenery and costumes, James Greenleaf; lighting, James Sale.

ASHLAND, ORE.

Oregon Shakespearean Festival: Elizabethan Stagehouse (Outdoors)

(Founder, Angus L. Bowmer; producing director, Jerry Turner; general manager, William W. Patton)

THE MERCHANT OF VENICE (33). By William Shakespeare. June 17, 1977. Director, Michael Addison. With James Edmondson, Ronald Edmundson Woods, Christine Healy, Barry Mulholland, Jahnna Beecham, Kenned MacIver, Keith Grant, Michael Santo.

KING HENRY VI, PART III (33). By

William Shakespeare. June 18, 1977. Director, Pat Patton. With Larry R. Ballard, Mimi Carr, Robert Smith, Joseph DeSalvio, Jean Smart, Ronald Stanley Sopyla.

ANTONY AND CLEOPATRA (33). By

William Shakespeare. June 19, 1977. Director, Robert Loper. With Ted D'Arms, Elizabeth Huddle, Robert Smith, Catherine Butterfield, David Hudson, John Shepard.

Oregon Shakespearean Festival: Angus Bowmer Theater (Indoors)

A STREETCAR NAMED DESIRE (45). By Tennessee Williams. June 18, 1977. Director, Elizabeth Huddle. With Mary Turner, Bruce Williams, Terry Hays, John Procaccino.

MEASURE FOR MEASURE (31). By William Shakespeare. June 19, 1977. Director, Jerry Turner. With Dan Kremer, James Ed-

mondson, Brian Thompson, Judd Parkin, JoAnn Johnson Patton, Christine Healy.

THE RIVALS (30). By Richard Brinsley Sheridan. June 21, 1977. Director, William Glover. With William Moreing, Allan Nause, Catherine Butterfield, Kenned MacIver, Ronald Edmundson Woods, Mimi Carr, Joseph DeSalvio, Michael Santo.

Oregon Shakespearean Festival: Black Swan Theater

A MOON FOR THE MISBEGOTTEN (53). By Eugene O'Neill. July 17, 1977. Director, Jerry Turner. With Jean Smart, Denis Arndt,

Robert Smith, Jack Wellington Cantell, Richard Denison.

Oregon Shakespearean Festival Stage II: Angus Bowmer Theater

TARTUFFE (24). By Molière; English verse translation by Richard Wilbur. February 3, 1978. Director, Sabin Epstein. With Rex Rabold, Larry R. Ballard, JoAnn Johnson Patton, Fredi Olster, John Shepard, Kenned MacIver, Richard Farrell, Ronald Edmundson Woods.

PRIVATE LIVES (25). By Noel Coward, February 4, 1978 (matinee). Director, Dennis Bigelow. With Kenned MacIver, Michael San-

to, Richard Rossi, Fredi Olster, Clista Strother.

MOTHER COURAGE AND HER CHILDREN (19). By Bertolt Brecht. February 4, 1978 (evening). Director, Jerry Turner. With Margaret Rubin, Terry Hays, Rick Hamilton, Richard Farrell, Ronald Edmundson Woods, John Shepard, Jack Wellington Cantwell, Melody Ann Page.

Oregon Shakespearean Festival Stage II: Black Swan Theater

THE EFFECT OF GAMMA RAYS ON MAN-IN-THE-MOON MARIGOLDS (56). By Paul Zindel. February 5, 1978. Director,

William Glover. With Mimi Carr, Jahnna Beecham, Cameron Dokey, Ruth Elodie King, Kristin Patton.

Designers: Scenery, Richard L. Hays, William Bloodgood; lighting, Dirk Epperson, Robert Peterson; costumes, Jeannie Davidson, Merrily Ann Murray, Phyllis A. Corcoran.

BALTIMORE

Center Stage

(Managing director, Peter W. Culman; artistic director, Stan Wojewodski Jr.)

THE GOODBYE PEOPLE (36). By Herb Gardner. November 1, 1977. Director, Robert Allan Ackerman. With Russell Horton, John

Kellogg, Marcia Rodd, Douglas Roberts, Stanley Weiman, Sammy Smith.

THE RIVALS (36). By Richard Brinsley Sheridan. December 6, 1977. Director, Stan Wojewodski Jr. With Paddy Croft, Denise Koch, Robert Pastene, Edmond Genest, Paul Thomas.

THE RUNNER STUMBLES (36). By Milan Stitt. January 17, 1978. Director, Stan Wojewodski Jr. With Terry O'Quinn, Pat Karpen, Robert Pastene, Dan Szeleg.

THE NIGHT OF THE IGUANA (36). By Tennessee Williams. February 21, 1978. Director, Edward Berkeley. With Janet Sarno, Paul Collins, Meg Wynn Owen, Randall Duk Kim, Tana Hicken.

ASHES (36). By David Rudkin. March 28, 1978. Director, Stan Wojewodski Jr. With Terry O'Quinn, Tana Hicken, George Taylor, Ellen Parks.

BLITHE SPIRIT (36). By Noel Coward. May 2, 1978. Director, Marcia Rodd. With Paddy Croft, Munson Hicks, Pamala Lewis, Helen Cary.

Designers: scenery, Charles Cosler, Eldon Elder, Hugh Landwehr, Peter Harvey, Clark Crolius; lighting, Charles Cosler, Ian Calderon, Judy Rasmuson, Arden Fingerhut; costumes, Elizabeth P. Palmer, Bob Wojewodski, Hilary Rosenfeld, Dona Granata.

Note: Center Stage's Young People's Theater toured two productions during 1977-78 season. *The Boy Who Wanted To Be King,* adapted and directed by Jeffrey Rodman, with Fred Sanders, Rudy Roderson, Brenda Thomas, Ellen Parks, David Hodge, Preston Boyd, Allen Silver, Rocco Sisto performed for elementary schools throughout the State. *The Black, the Blue and the Gray,* a Civil War documentary by Irene Lewis and Edward Emanuel, directed by William Yaggy and Donald Hicken, with Rocco Sisto, Ellen Parks, Fred Sanders, Hubert Kelly, toured high schools.

BERKELEY, CALIF.

Berkeley Repertory Theater

(Producing director, Michael Leibert; associate director, Douglas Johnson)

PRIVATE LIVES (39). By Noel Coward. June 10, 1977. Director, George Kovach. With Linda Lee Johnson, Paul Laramore, Douglas Johnson, Anne Swift, Kendell Jackson.

OUR TOWN (39). By Thornton Wilder. July 22, 1977. Director, Douglas Johnson. With Robert Hirschfeld, Sheldon Feldner, J. C. Sealy, Alice Rovik, Steve Knox, Kendell Jackson, James Dean.

A FLEA IN HER EAR (39). By Georges Feydeau; translation by John Mortimer. September 16, 1977. Director, George Kovach. With Douglas Johnson, Dale Elliott, Linda Lee Johnson, Julie Odegard, Nicole Baptiste.

REP! (38). By Stanley Greenberg. October 28, 1977 (world premiere). Director, Michael Leibert; scenery, Jeff Whitman, Christopher M. Idoine; lighting, Matthew Cohen; costumes, Lesley Skannal; musical director and composer, Mark Mueller; choreographer, Nicole Baptiste.

Black Actor .... Alphonso McVay Jr.
Girl Apprentice .... Heidi Hutner
Character Actor .... Troy Evans
Leading Actress .... Karen Ingenthron

Leading Actor .... James Dean
Ingenue .... Kendell Jackson
Young Actor .... Dale Elliott
Character Actress .... Julia Odegard
Boy Apprentice .... Shelly Lipkin

MAJOR BARBARA (41). By George Bernard Shaw. December 9, 1977. Director, George Kovach. With Anne Swift, Troy Evans, Mark Geiger, Paul Laramore, Karen Ingenthron, Robert Hirschfeld, Shelly Lipkin.

MAD OSCAR (39). By Sheldon Feldner. January 27, 1978 (world premiere). Director, Peter Donat; scenery, Robert Blackman; lighting, Christopher M. Idoine; costumes, Marie Anne Chiment.

Oscar Wilde .... Michael Leibert
Lord Alfred Douglas .... Paul Laramore
Robert Ross .... George Kovach
Frank Harris .... Don West
"Reggie" Turner .... Dale Elliott
Harold Mellor .... Troy Evans
Leonard Smithers .... Robert Haswell
    Time: November 30, 1900. Place: A room in the Hotel D'Alsace, Paris. Two intermissions.

THE SERVANT OF TWO MASTERS (39).

By Carlo Goldoni; translated by Joan Lipman; adapted by Joe Spano, Joan Liepman, Albert Kutchins. March 8, 1978. Director, Joe Spano; masks, Marie Anne Chiment. With Scott Paulin, Nicole Baptiste, Shelly Lipkin, Will Jenkins, Alice Rovik, John Vickery, Dale Elliott, Susan Kampe, Troy Evans.

A MOON FOR THE MISBEGOTTEN (39). By Eugene O'Neill. April 19, 1978. Director, Michael Leibert. With Anne Swift, Robert Haswell, Dale Elliott, Don West, George Kovach.

Designers: scenery, George Kovach, Tom Odegard, Ron Pratt, Gene Angell, Andrew DeShong, Jeff Whitman; lighting, Matthew Cohen; costumes, Marie Anne Chiment, Lesley Skannal, Diana Smith.

BUFFALO

Studio Arena Theater

(Executive producer, Neal Du Brock)

SUNSET (38). Book by Louis LaRusso II; music by Gary William Friedman; original concept and lyrics by Will Holt. September 30, 1977 (world premiere). Director Tommy Tune; scenery, Douglas W. Schmidt; lighting, Jeffrey Schissler; costumes, Joseph G. Aulisi; multimedia creations, Sheppard Kerman; musical director, Uel Wade; arranger/orchestrator, Gary William Friedman.

Lila Halliday .... Alexis Smith
Randy Gold .... Buddy Vest
Jamie Bradbury .... Bill Starr
Crystal Newcomb .... Lisa Mordente
D. J. Rollins .... Roland Perlman
Twins ...Yolanda Ray Raven, Terry Rieser
    Session Singers: Cheryl Alexander, Christine Faith, Diva Gray.
    Time: Now. Place: Los Angeles. No intermission.
    Musical Numbers: "Sunset City," "Back With a Beat," "Nothing But," "Rock Is My Way of Life," "Destiny," "Disco Destiny," "Waltz," "Retreat," "1945," "Moments," "Montage," "Trials and Tribulation," "I Like You, If," "True Music," "Retreat," "Good Time Song," Finale.

SEMMELWEISS (29). By Howard Sackler. November 4, 1977 (world premiere). Director, Edwin Sherin; scenery, John Wulp; lighting, Marc B. Weiss; costumes, Ann Roth.
Arneth; Niedermann; Professor
Kiwisch; Student;
    Doctor .... Chet Carlin
Michaelis .... Kent Broadhurst
Semmelweiss .... Lewis J. Stadlen
Klein .... Jack Bittner
Sophie; Nurse; Lizabet
    Slovic .... Kathy Bates

Rokitansky .... Shepperd Strudwick
Rosas .... Leslie Barrett
Julia .... Kim Hunter
Kolletschka; Birly; Professor;
    Faculty .... Peter Blaxill
Braun .... Mel Cobb
Anna Hoffman; Nurse;
    Woman in Labor .... Kathleen Gray
Eva Gruen; Woman; Girl .... K. McKenna
Head Midwife ....Elizabeth Parrish
Skoda .... Dennis Patella
Hebra; Thorenson; Hoffman;
    Faculty .... Joel Stedman
Chiari; Scanzoni ..... Stephen Mark Weyte
    All Other Parts: Sally Bagot, Steven Cooper, Tyson A. J. Group, Greg Houston, Timothy J. Hunter, Pamela Kilburn, Philip Knoerzer, Deborah Kelly Kloepfer, Roderic B. MacDonald, Priscilla Manning, Michelle Maulucci, Scott R. Peal, George Scheitinger, Carl E. Schoonover, Chris Wittington, Mary Martha Zoll.
    Act I, Scene 1: The dissection room. Scene 2: Admissions Hall, Obstetrical Division. Scene 3: The morgue. Scene 4: Ward, Section One. Scene 5: Professor Rokitansky's study. Act II, Scene 1: Corridor, Section One. Scene 2: Obstetrics lecture room. Scene 3: Ward, Section One. Scene 4: Greenhouse, Botany Department. Scene 5: Meeting hall of faculty. Act III, Scene 1: Semmelweiss's consulting room. Scene 2: Meeting hall of faculty. Scene 3: Semmelweiss attic. Scene 4: Dr. Birly's Midwife School. Scene 5: Semmelweiss parlor. Scene 7: Lecture room. Scene 8: Corridor, Section One. Scene 9: Greenhouse. Scene 10: The morgue.

SAME TIME, NEXT YEAR (39). By Bernard

Slade. December 2, 1977. Director, Michael Montel. With Rosemary Prinz, Richard Greene.

THE CRUCIFER OF BLOOD (39). Written and directed by Paul Giovanni; based on characters by Arthur Conan Doyle. January 6, 1978. With Paxton Whitehead, Glenn Close, Timothy Landfield, Stephen Keep, Bill Herndon, Christopher Curry.

THE SHADOW BOX (30). By Michael Cristofer. February 10, 1978. Director, Warren Enters. With Suzanne Costallos, Joan Croydon, David Daniels, Eileen Letchworth, Pat McNamara, Gerald Richards.

COME INTO THE GARDEN, MAUD and A SONG AT TWILIGHT (30). By Noel Coward. March 10, 1978. Director, Richard Barr. With Michael Allinson, Carolyn Coates, Gwyda Donhowe, James Mastrantonio.

WHO'S AFRAID OF VIRGINIA WOOLF? (30). By Edward Albee. April 7, 1978. Director, Richard Barr. With Estelle Parsons, James Noble, Peter Burnell, Linda Kampley.

Designers: scenery, William Ritman, Robert P. Van Nutt, Larry Aumen, Michael Healy; lighting, Peter Gill, Robby Monk; costumes, Diane R. Schaller, Donna Eskew, Clifford Capone.

BURLINGTON, VT.

Champlain Shakespeare Festival: Royall Tyler Theater, University of Vermont

(Producer-director, Edward J. Feidner)

TWO GENTLEMEN OF VERONA (20). By William Shakespeare. July 6, 1977. Director, Edward J. Feidner. With Jock MacDonald, Michael Kluger, Neave Rake, Evelyne Germain, John Hutton, Dan Baumgarten.

MACBETH (16). By William Shakespeare. July 13, 1977. Director, E. Keith Gaylord. With Jennifer Cover, Ray Aranha, Deborah Gwinn, Evelyne Germain, Kent Cassella, John Hutton, Neave Rake, Kim Bent.

HENRY IV, PART 1 (10). By William Shakespeare. August 3, 1977. Director, Edward J. Feidner. With John Hutton, Jock MacDonald, Craig A. Toth, Kim Bent, Deborah Gwinn, Muriel A. Stockdale.

Designers: scenery, Lisa M. Devlin, F. Patrick Orr; lighting, Steven J. Sysko, Lisa M. Devlin, F. Patrick Orr; costumes, Polly Smith.

CHICAGO

Academy Festival Theater: Drake Theater, Lake Forest

(Producer, William Gardner)

TOO TRUE TO BE GOOD (21). By George Bernard Shaw. June 7, 1977. Director, Philip Minor. With Jean Marsh, Katharine Houghton, Charles Kimbrough, Jack Gwillim, Bruce Gray, I. M. Hobson.

THE LANDSCAPE OF THE BODY (21). By John Guare. July 5, 1977 (world premiere). Director, John Pasquin; scenery, John Wulp; lighting, Jennifer Tipton; costumes, Laura Crow.
Captain Marvin
 Holahan ....F. Murray Abraham

Betty ....Shirley Knight
Rosalie ....Peg Murray
Raulito ....Richard Bauer
Bert ....Paul McCrane
Donny ....Anthony Marciona
Joanne ....Alexa Kenin
Margie ....Bonnie Deroski
Masked Man; Dope King .....Jay Sanders
Durwood Peach ....Rex Robbins
 Place: A ferry to Nantucket and Greenwich Village. One intermission

TOBACCO ROAD (21). By Jack Kirkland; adapted from the novel by Erskine Caldwell. August 2, 1977. Director, Marshall W. Mason. With Barbara Bel Geddes, Barnard Hughes, Matthew Cowles, Anne Ives, Nancy Snyder, Helen Stenborg.

OLD TIMES (21). By Harold Pinter. August 28, 1977. Director, Marshall W. Mason. With Irene Worth, Beatrice Straight, Raul Julia.

Designers: scenery, Fred Kolouch, John Lee Beatty; lighting, Fred Kolouch, Dennis Parichy; costumes, Laura Crow.

Goodman Theater: Mainstage

(Artistic director, William Woodman; managing director, Janet Wade)

SAINT JOAN (44) By George Bernard Shaw. September 23, 1977. Director, John Clark. With Lynn Redgrave, Wyman Pendleton, Robert Moberly, Joseph Bova, James Noble, Paul Shyre, Christopher Raynolds.

THE SEAGULL (44). By Anton Chekhov; adapted by Jean-Claude van Itallie. November 11, 1977. Director, Gregory Mosher. With Ruth Ford, Deborah Baltzell, Christopher Raynolds, Jeremiah Sullivan, Robert Thompson, Linda Kimbrough.

WORKING (44). Adapter/director, Stephen Schwartz; from the book by Studs Terkel. December 30, 1977 (world premiere). Songs by Craig Carnelia, Micki Grant, Stephen Schwartz, James Taylor, Susan Birkenhead and Mary Rodgers; dance and incidental music, Michele Brourman; musical director/arranger, Stephen Reinhardt; choreographer, Graciela Daniele; scenery, David Mitchell; lighting, Pat Collins; costumes, Marjorie Slaiman.
Cast: Fred Ringley, printing salesman — Joe Ponazecki. Kate Ringley, housewife — Jo Henderson. John Ringley, newsboy — Jay Footlik. Al Calinda, parking lot attendant; Pete Keeley, ex-boss — Jay Flash Riley. Nora Watson, editor; Sharon Atkins, receptionist; Barbara Herrick, writer-producer; Cathleen Moran, hospital aide — Robin Lamont. Diane Wilson, process clerk; Mrs. Will Robinson, bus driver's wife; Heather Lamb, telephone operator; Lois Keeley, Keeley's daughter — Lynne Thigpen. John Fortune, ad copy chief; Marco Camerone, hockey player; Jerome Koslo, priest; Henry Koslo's son — Steven Boockvor. Herb Rosen, Ringley's boss; Booker Page, seaman; Joe Zutty, ex-shipping clerk; Henry Koslo, steelworker — Rex Everhart. Rose Hoffman, teacher; Babe Secoli, supermarket checker; Fran Swenson, hotel switchboard operator; Ann Bogen, executive

secretary; Mrs. Ringley, Fred Ringley's mother — Bobo Lewis. Brett Mylett, boxboy; Tim Devlin, salesman; Charlie Blossom, copy boy — David Patrick Kelly. Emilio Hernandez, migrant worker; Juan Ortega, baseball pitcher; Jack Hunter, professor of communications; Jack Currier, son of corporate executive — Joe Mantegna. Conrad Swibel, gas meter reader; Tom Patrick, fireman; Ralph Werner, department store salesman — Matt Landers. Grace Clements, felting mill worker; Delores Dante, waitress; Roberta Victor, call girl; Henrietta Koslo, Henry Koslo's wife — Anne DeSalvo. Bud Rolfing, football coach, Mike LeFevre, steel worker — Brad Sullivan. Carla Jonas, photographer; Jill Torrence, model — Terri Treas. Benny Blue, bar pianist — Stephen Reinhardt.
Musical Numbers — Act I: "All the Livelong Day" ("I Hear America Singing" by Walt Whitman; music and additional lyrics by Stephen Schwartz), "American Dreaming," "Lovin' Al," "Neat To Be a Newsboy," "Nobody Tells Me How," "Treasure Island Trio," "Un Mejor Dia Vendra," "Just a Housewife" "Millwork," "Night Skate," "Joe," "If I Could've Been," Act II; "Nobody Goes Out Anymore," "Brother Trucker," "The Working Girl's Apache," "It's an Art," "Fathers and Sons," "Something to Point To."

MUCH ADO ABOUT NOTHING (44). By William Shakespeare. February 10, 1978. Director, William Woodman. With Nicolas Surovy, Laura Esterman, Katie McDonough, Christopher Raynolds, Richard Clarke, Michael Tezla, Patrick Hines, Robert Scogin.

THE NIGHT OF THE IGUANA (44). By Tennessee Williams. March 31, 1978. Director, George Keathley. With Alan Mixon, Ruth Roman, Barbara Rush, Robert Thompson, Rebecca Taylor.

OTHERWISE ENGAGED (44). By Simon Gray. May 12, 1978. Director, William Woodman. With Philip Kerr, Benjamin Hendrickson, James Greene, Barry Boys, Marion Lines, Jack Roberts, Sarah-Jane Gwillim.

Designers: scenery, David Jenkins, Joseph Nieminski, Herbert Senn, Helen Pond; lighting, F. Mitchell Dana, Pat Collins, Stephen Ross, Robert Christen; James Edmund Brady, Virgil C. Johnson, Marsha Kowal.

Goodman Theater: Stage II: William Wrigley Theater

HAIL SCRAWDYKE! (24). By David Halliwell. January 10, 1978. Director, Michael Maggio. With Tom Mula, Timothy Jenkins, Gisli Bjorgvinsson, A. C. Weary, Claudia Bohard.

ANNULLA ALLEN: AUTOBIOGRAPHY OF A SURVIVOR (20). By Emily Mann and Annulla Allen. March 16, 1978. Director, Emily Mann. With Barbara Bryne.

BATTERING RAM (16). By David Freeman. April 9, 1978 (American premiere). Director, Gregory Mosher.

Nora .... Barbara E. Robertson
Irene .... Lynn Cohen
Virgil .... W. H. May
Six scenes over the course of ten days. One intermission after Scene 4.

THE PRAGUE SPRING (24). Book and lyrics by Lee Kalcheim; music by Joe Raposo. May 23, 1978. Director, Dennis Zacek; musical director, Carol Loverde. With Steve Fletcher, Mike Genovese, Tony Flacco, Christine Anderson, Laurence Russo, Roger Mueller.

Goodman Theater: Stage II — Mandel Hall, University of Chicago

SIZWE BANZI IS DEAD (8). By Athol Fugard, John Kani, Winston Ntshona, March 14, 1978. Director, Gregory Mosher. With Meshach Taylor, Lionel Smith.

Designers; scenery, Michael Merritt, Robert Christen, Barry Robinson, Maher Ahmad; lighting, Robert Christen, Philip Eickhoff, Robert Shook; costumes, Julie Jackson, Barry Robinson, Christa Scholtz, Michelle Demichelis.

St. Nicholas Theater Company: Mainstage

(Artistic director, Steven Schachter; managing director, Peter Schneider)

ASHES (31). By David Rudkin. September 28, 1977. Director, Steven Schachter. With Carole Lockwood, John Malkovich, Allison Giglio.

THE WOODS (31). By David Mamet. November 16, 1977 (world premiere). Director, David Mamet; scenery, Michael Merritt; lighting, Robert Christen.
Ruth .... Patti LuPone
Nick .... Peter Weller
Time: Early September. Place: The porch of a summer house. Scene 1: Dusk. Scene 2: Night. Scene 3: Morning. One intermission after Scene 2. (See review in the introduction to this section.)

YOU CAN'T TAKE IT WITH YOU (31). By George S. Kaufman and Moss Hart. January 25, 1978. Director, Gerald Gutierrez. With George Womack, Marge Kotlisky, Gerald

Walling S.J., Audrie J. Neenan, Barbara E. Robertson, Steve Fletcher.

UNCOMMON WOMEN AND OTHERS (31). By Wendy Wasserstein. March 15, 1978. Director, Mike Nussbaum. With Annabel Armour, Belinda Bremner, Cynthia Sherman, Pat Terry, Jane Voice.

BARNABY SWEET. By Glenn Allen Smith. May 3, 1978 (world premiere). Director, Steven Schachter; music, Alaric Jans; scenery, Christopher Harris; lighting, Tom Herman; costumes, Jessica Hahn.
Mike .... Jason Brett
Pat .... Lois Hall
Barnaby Sweet ...... Thomas Stechschulte
Fay .... Marge Kotlisky
Plug .... Michael Sassone
Mrs. Williams .... Sheila Keenan

Alice ....Kay Heberle
Joe ....Don Moffett
Time: 1919-1942. Place: Beaulah, Okla.;

Hong Kong; on board the U.S.S. President
Madison; Tacoma, Wash.; Panama Canal;
Hollywood; at sea. One intermission.

St. Nicholas Theater: Children's Theater

THE ADVENTURES OF CAPTAIN
MARBLES AND HIS ACTING SQUAD:
EPISODES III and IV. CLIFF NOTES (6).
By William H. Macy and David Kovacs.
February 18, 1978. WHEN YOU WISH
UPON A COOKIE (6). By William H. Macy.
March 11, 1978. Based on characters by John
Stasey; music and lyrics by Alaric Jans and
Hugh Hart. With James T. Murphy, Tom
Aulino, Susan Bugg, Marty Levy, Linda Jones,
Michael Gorman, Alaric Gans.

THE REVENGE OF THE SPACE
PANDAS, OR BINKY RUDICH AND THE
TWO SPEED CLOCK (15). By David Mamet.
November 19, 1977 (world premiere). Director,
Steven Schachter; scenery, David Emmons;
costumes, Julie A. Nagel.
Binky Rudich .... Mark K. Nutter
Vivian Mooster ..... Barbara E. Robertson
Bob the Sheep .... Kathleen Gavin
Edward Farpis ....Robert Falls
George Topax .... Jay Jens
Place: Outer space and the planet Crestview.

St. Nicholas Theater Company: New Work Ensemble Series

Showcase premieres:
THE NUCLEAR FAMILY by Mark Frost;
SPIDER by Bobby Joyce Smith; I'D
RATHER BE IT, conceived and written by the
women of the New Work Ensemble; THE
SLOW HOURS by Bruce Burgun; MARTY

by Paddy Chayefsky. Directed, designed and
performed by members of the Ensemble and
selected students from the St. Nicholas Theater
School.

Note: *Cliff Notes* and *When You Wish Upon a Cookie* toured Illinois between April and May,
1978.

CINCINNATI

Playhouse in the Park: Robert S. Marx Theater

(Producing director, Michael Murray; managing director, Robert W. Tolan)

THE THREEPENNY OPERA (32). Book
and lyrics by Bertolt Brecht; music by Kurt
Weill; English adaptation by Marc Blitzstein.
October 11, 1977. Director, Michael Murray;
musical director, Fred Goldrich. With Keith
Prentice, John Newton, Grace Keagy, Pamela
McLernon, Judith Lander, Roy K. Stevens.

THE IMAGINARY INVALID (32). By
Molière; translated by Betty Schwimmer;
adapted by R. G. Davis. November 22, 1977.
Consulting Director, R. G. Davis. With
Michael Connolly, Sidney Armus, George
Deloy, John Grassili, Caroline Kava, Andrea
Snow.

BENEFIT OF A DOUBT (32). By Edward
Clinton. January 3, 1978 (world premiere).
Director, Michael Murray; scenery and

lighting, Neil Peter Jampolis; costumes, Annie
Peacock Warner.
Laurie Cassidy .... Tania Myren
Sadie .... Elizabeth Council
John Cassidy ....William Andrews
Kay .... Etain O'Malley
Eileen Cassidy ....Nancy Donohue
Dandelion ....P. Jay Sidney
    Place: A small city in West Virginia. Act I: A
Saturday in September. Act II, Scene 1: A
Saturday in October, 10 a.m. Scene 2: 11:30
a.m. Act III, Scene 1: A Saturday in
November, morning. Scene 2: The same, eve-
ning.

OF MICE AND MEN (32). By John
Steinbeck. February 14, 1978. Director, Robert
Brewer. With Kent Broadhurst, Lanny Flaher-
ty, Peter Bosché, Susanne Marley, Eric Uhler.

THE HOUSE OF BERNARDA ALBA (32). By Federico Garcia Lorca. March 28, 1978. Director, Michael Murray. With Claudine Catania, Sylvia Gassell, Vera Visconti Lockwood, Rochelle Parker, Marian Primont, Jana Robbins, Margaret Warncke, Toni Wein.

THE ROYAL FAMILY (40). By George S. Kaufman and Edna Ferber. May 9, 1978. Director, John Going. With Barbara Caruso, Elizabeth Council, Ellen Fiske, Sam Gray, Dan Hamilton.

Playhouse in the Park: Shelterhouse Theater

VANITIES (48). By Jack Heifner. June 7, 1977. Director, John Going. With Robin Groves, Lynn Ritchie, Mercedes Ruehl.

Designers: scenery, Neil Peter Jampolis, Karl Eigsti, John Lee Beatty, Joseph A. Varga; lighting, Neil Peter Jampolis, Marc B. Weiss, Jay Depenbrock; costumes, Jill Hamilton, Annie Peacock Warner, Jennifer Von Mayrhauser, Caley Summers.

Note: The Cincinnati Playhouse brought back its guest production of *What's a Nice Country Like Us Doing in a State Like This?*, conceived and performed by the Footlighters, Inc. for an additional 8 performances in September, 1977. The Karamu Performing Arts Theater production of *Sizwe Banzi Is Dead* was presented as another Guest Production for 8 performances in November, 1977 at the Kresge Auditorium. The summer production of *Vanities* toured Texas and Ohio following its regular run. High School students in Ohio, Indiana and Kentucky saw 5 performances each of *The Threepenny Opera, The Imaginary Invalid, Of Mice and Men, The House of Bernarda Alba* and *The Royal Family.*

CLEVELAND

The Cleveland Play House: Euclid-77th Street Theater

(Director, Richard Oberlin; associate director, Larry Tarrant)

LIVING TOGETHER (23). October 5, 1977. ROUND AND ROUND THE GARDEN (24). November 6, 1977. By Alan Ayckbourn. Director, Paul Lee. With Sharon Bicknell, June Gibbons, Harper Jan McAdoo, Douglas Jones, David O. Frazier, Kenneth Albers.

In Repertory, The Norman Conquests: ROUND AND ROUND THE GARDEN (8). December 4, 1977. TABLE MANNERS (8). December 8, 1977. LIVING TOGETHER (5). December 9, 1977. By Alan Ayckbourn. Director and cast as above. The entire trilogy, with lunch and dinner breaks, was performed on December 11, 1977.

THE PRAGUE SPRING (26). By Lee

Kalcheim; music by Joe Raposo. January 6, 1978. As originally conceived and directed by J. Ranelli. With Norm Berman, Sharon Bicknell, Richard Halverson, Joe D. Lauck, Wayne S. Turney, Richard Oberlin.

KNOCK KNOCK (32). By Jules Feiffer. February 10, 1978. Director, Paul Lee. With Sharon Bicknell, Norm Berman, Richard Halverson, Wayne S. Turney, Harper Jan McAdoo, John Danielich.

THE CLUB (40). By Eve Merriam. March 24, 1978. Director, Terri White. With Sharon Bicknell, June Gibbons, Harper Jane McAdoo, Dee Hoty, Marge Adler, Gay Marshall, Terri White.

The Cleveland Play House: Drury Theater

THE LEARNED LADIES (26). By Molière; translation by Richard Wilbur. October 21, 1977. Director, Ray Walston. With Maeve McGuire, Richard Halverson, Evie McElroy, Allan Leatherman, Jo Farwell, Ray Walston.

GREAT EXPECTATIONS (41). By Paul Lee; adapted from the novel by Charles Dickens. November 25, 1977 and April 7, 1978 (world premiere). Director, Jonathan Bolt; scenery and lighting, Richard Gould; costumes, Estelle Painter.

Pip as a Boy .... David Natale/
                              Kenneth Dolin
Pip .... James Richards
Estella as a Girl .... Erica Tarrant/
                              Ellery Siegler
Estella .... Lizbeth MacKay
Mrs. Gargery .... Jo Farwell
Joe Gargery .... Allen Leatherman
Magwitch .... Paul Lee
Uncle Pumblechook .... Robert Snook
Herbert Pocket .... Wayne S. Turney
Jaggers .... Richard Halverson
Miss Havisham .... Evie McElroy
Bentley Drummle;
    Soldier 1 .... John Danielich
Waiter; Compeyson .... Joe D. Lauck
Soldier 2 .... Todd Mandel
Porter's Wife .... Carol Schultz
    Time: Early 1800's. Place: England. Two intermissions.

THE LITTLE FOXES (30). By Lillian Hellman. January 20, 1978. Director, Evie McElroy. With Maeve McGuire, David O. Frazier, June Gibbons, Allen Leatherman,
Lizbeth Mackay, Robert Snook, James Richards, Mary Bradley, Gerald Gould.

THE ROMANTICS (26). By Maxim Gorky; translated by William Stancil. March 3, 1978 (world premiere). Director, Larry Tarrant; scenery and lighting, Richard Gould; costumes, Estelle Painter.

Konstantine Lukich
    Mastakov .... Kenneth Albers
Elena Nikolaevna .... Lizbeth Mackay
Nikolai Potekhin .... Joe D. Lauck
Bukol Potekhin .... James Kisicki
Olga .... Carol Schultz
Matrena Ivanovna
    Medvedeva .... Evie McElroy
Zina .... Cheryl Kempe
Vasili .... James Richards
Alexandra .... Ann Goldman
Osip .... Robert Snook
Miron .... Allen Leatherman
    Time: Late spring, 1910. Place: Two cottages in a resort area outside Moscow. Act I, Scene 1: Evening. Scene 2: Late afternoon, several days later. Act II, Scene 1: Sundown, several days later. Scene 2: Later the same day.

Designers: scenery, Richard Gould, Barbara Leatherman, Paul Rodgers; Lighting, Richard Gould, Jack Stewart, Paul Rodgers; costumes; Harriet Cone, Estelle Painter, David Smith.

The Cleveland Play House: Chautauqua (N.Y.) — Norton Hall

A MOON FOR THE MISBEGOTTEN (2). By Eugene O'Neill. June 30, 1977. Director, Larry Tarrant. With Evie McElroy, Dan Desmond, Paul Lee, Kenneth Albers, Richard Halverson.

MAN AND SUPERMAN (2). By George Bernard Shaw. July 7, 1977. Director, Paul Lee. With Clayton Corzatte, Lizbeth Mackay, Robert Snook, Sharon Bicknell.

LADYHOUSE BLUES (2). By Kevin O'Morrison. July 14, 1977. Director, Larry Tarrant. With Christina Moore, Sharon Bicknell, Mary Gallagher, Jo Farwell, Evie McElroy.

THE YELLOW JACKET (2). By George C. Hazelton and J. H. Benrimo. July 21, 1977. Director, William Rhys. With Richard Halverson, Jonathan Farwell, Tedd Rawlins, Liz Mackay, John Buck Jr.

ARE YOU NOW OR HAVE YOU EVER BEEN ... (2). By Eric Bentley. July 28, 1977. Director, Larry Tarrant. With William Rhys, Carol Schultz, Richard Oberlin and the Cleveland Play House Company.

THE HOLLOW CROWN (2). Devised by John Barton. August 4, 1977. Director, Larry Tarrant. With Richard Halverson, James Richards, Dan Desmond, Tedd Rawlins, Liz Mackay. Sharon Bicknell.

TABLE MANNERS (2). August 11, 1977. LIVING TOGETHER (3). August 18, 1977. By Alan Ayckbourn. Director, Paul Lee. With John Buck Jr., Kenneth Albers, June Gibbons, Sharon Bicknell, Jonathan Farwell, Harper Jane McAdoo.

Note: The Cleveland Play House Youtheater presented two productions: We're Talespinners Too! based on The Talespinners by Jonathan and Jo Farwell, tongue-in-cheek adaptations of fairy tales and straight versions of Robert Browning's The Pied Piper of Hamelin, William Shakespeare's

Pyramus and Thisbe, and several Aesop fables (at the Brooks Theater, December 28-31, 1977), director, Jonathan Farwell, and *The Odyssey of Runyon Jones* by Norman Corwin (at the Drury Theater, March 22-25, 1978), directors Jonathan Farwell and Carol Schultz. Performers were Youtheater students. Two puppet productions were presented at the Drury Theater: *A Show of Hands* by George Latshaw, the evenings of January 13 and 14, 1978, for adults and children, hand and glove puppets with material from Tennessee Williams, Shakespeare and Japanese Kabuki; and, during the afternoon of January 14, 1978, Les Petites Amis, using rod puppets in two performances of their version of *Hansel and Gretel.*

COHOES, N.Y.

Cohoes Music Hall

(Executive director, Louis J. Ambrosio)

THE GLASS MENAGERIE (23). By Tennessee Williams. October 29, 1977. Director, Louis J. Ambrosio. With Robert Bacigalupi, Elaine Hausman, Maureen O'Sullivan, Peter Webster.

VANITIES (23). By Jack Heifner. November 26, 1977. Director, Bill Ludel. With Ellen Donkin, Donna Emanuel, Elaine Hausman.

A MOON FOR THE MISBEGOTTEN (23). By Eugene O'Neill. December 31, 1977. Director, Thomas Gruenewald. With Robert Bacigalupi, Jon DeVries, Richard Karmel, Kaiulani Lee, Gerald Richards.

THE UNEXPECTED GUEST (23). By Agatha Christie. January 28, 1978. Director, Louis J. Ambrosio. With Yusef Bulos, Virginia Downing, Richard Harmel, John Leighton, Ted Spian.

PRIVATE LIVES (23). By Noel Coward. February 25, 1978. Director, Harold DeFelice. With Robert Bacigalupi, Christine Baranski, Richard Harmel, Elaine Hausman, Dale Hodges.

Designers: scenery, Michael Anania; lighting, Toni Goldin; costumes, Bob Wojewodski, Dona Granata.

COSTA MESA, CALIF.

South Coast Repertory Theater

(Artistic directors, David Emmes, Martin Benson)

PRIVATE LIVES (47). By Noel Coward. September 17, 1977. Director, David Emmes. With Anni Long, Charles Lanyer, John-David Keller, Caroline Smith, Lee Shallat.

THE LAST MEETING OF THE KNIGHTS OF THE WHITE MAGNOLIA (47). By Preston Jones. November 5, 1977. Director, Martin Benson. With Bill Cobbs, Wayne Grace, Don Tuche, Art Koustik, Hal Landon Jr., Ronald Boussom, John-David Keller, Howard Shangra, Ron Michaelson.

A DOLL'S HOUSE (47). By Henrik Ibsen. January 7, 1978. Director, David Emmes. With Anni Long, Charles Lanyer, Hal Landon Jr., Lee Shallat, Don Tuche.

VOLPONE (62) By Ben Jonson. March 11, 1978. Director, Daniel Sullivan. With Michael Keenan, Charles Lanyer, Marilyn Prince, Caroline Smith, James E. DePriest, Anni Long.

COMEDIANS (47). By Trevor Griffiths. April 29, 1978. Director, Martin Benson. With Hal Landon Sr., Ron Boussom, Charles Hutchins, Richard Doyle, Michael Keenan, Howard Shangra, Hal Landon Jr., John Ellington, John-David Keller, Art Koustik.

Designers: scenery, Michael Devine, Cliff Faulkner, Susan Tuohy; lighting, Thomas Ruzika, Dawn Chiang; costumes, Charles Tomlinson, Louise Hayter, Barbara C. Cox.

Note: South Coast Repertory Theater toured the schools during 1977-78 with a production of *Tomato Surprise*, written by Robin Frederick and directed by John-David Keller. Five members from the regular company performed in this vaudeville dealing with nutrition.

DALLAS

Dallas Theater Center: Kalita Humphreys Theater

(Managing director, Paul Baker)

EQUUS (33). By Peter Shaffer. May 31, 1977. Director, Ryland Merkey. With John Figlmiller/Randy Moore, Tom Zinn/Jim Marvin, Mary Rohde, John Henson, Jacque Thomas, Deborah Allen.

ABSURB PERSON SINGULAR (33). By Alan Ayckbourn. July 12, 1977. Director, Ken Latimer. With Mary Rohde, Steven Mackenroth, Jacque Thomas, Ryland Merkey, Shannon Wilson, John Figlmiller.

THE IMAGINARY INVALID (39). By Molière; translated by Alec Stockwell. October 11, 1977. Director, Albert Millaire; musical director, Pam Nagle; choreographer, Robyn Flatt; music, Berthold Carriere. With Randolph Tallman, Shannon Wilson, Alex Winslow, Rebecca Logan, Steven Mackenroth, Randy Moore.

VANITIES (42). By Jack Heifner. November 29, 1977. Director, Ryland Merkey. With Cindy Holden, Mary Rohde, Shannon Wilson.

THE NIGHT OF THE IGUANA (39). By Tennessee Williams. January 24, 1978. Director, Judith Davis. With Mary Sue Jones, Warren Hammack, Celeste Varricchio, Randolph Tallman.

THREE MEN ON A HORSE (39). By John Cecil Holm and George Abbott. March 14, 1978. Director, Ken Latimer. With Randolph Tallman, Chelcie Ross, John Figlmiller, Allyn Winslow, Shelley McClure, Susan Sleeper, Russell Henderson, Ryland Merkey, Fitzhugh G. Houston.

FIREKEEPER (39). By Mark Medoff. May 2, 1978 (world premiere). Director, Paul Baker; designer, Virgil Beavers; lighting, Randy Moore.

Father Pascal .... John Figlmiller
Antonia Noche .... Ronni Lopez
Feliciana Noche .... Diana Gonzalez
Eulogio Noche .... Carlos Juan Gonzalez
Thomas Beavers . Tim Green/Leroy Mason
Angus Childress .... Preston Jones
    Time: 1932, the last day of Lent. Place: a small Catholic chapel on the Childress Ranch near Tenango, New Mexico.

Designers: scenery, Sallie Laurie, Yoichi Aoki, M. G. Johnston, Cheryl Denson, George Pettit; lighting, Robyn Flatt, Linda Blase, Allen Hibbard, Randy Moore, Sally Netzel; costumes, Cheryl Denson, Rodger M. Wilson, Rayanne Miller.

Dallas Theater Center: Down Center Stage

DOOR PLAY (15). By Sallie Laurie. November 1, 1977 (world premiere). Director, Mary Sue Jones; scenery, Denise Drennen; lighting, Paul R. Bassett; costumes, Rodger Wilson.
Jan .... Robyn Flatt
Jake .... Chris Hendrie
    Place: A room. One intermission.

CIGARETTE MAN (15). By David Blomquist. December 6, 1977 (world premiere). Director, Ken Latimer; scenery, Linda Blase; lighting, Bill Wheat; costumes, Denise Drennen.

June Barnett; Anita Eliot;
    Doris Pletske .... Deborah Allen
Ken Eliot .... Wayne Lambert
Carrie Markley .... Janis Myer
Julian "Boomer"
    Cassman .... Mark Brenton Henager
    Act I: Boomer's Apartment, New Year's Eve, 1960. Act II: Boomer's House, New Year's Eve, 1968. Act III: The True Gospel Convalescent Home, New Year's Eve, 1973.

THE NIGHT VISIT (15). By Roy Hudson. January 10, 1978 (world premiere). Director, John Logan; scenery, Suzanne Chiles; lighting,

Mark Momberger; costumes, M. G. Johnston.
Scott Brumloew .... Tim Haynes
L. G. Haynes .... Dick Trousdell
Myrna Hicks .... Michelle Clay
Mr. Goins .... Allyn Winslow
Little Gary .... Clay Broussard
Laura Sue .... Pamela Hurst
Carl Gillem .... Keith Dixon
    Time: June 1. Place: The Ranch Motel, Palace, Tex. Four scenes, one intermission.

LADY BUG, LADY BUG, FLY AWAY HOME (15). By Mary Rohde. February 14, 1978 (world premiere). Director, Chris Hendrie; scenery, James Eddy; lighting, Roy Hudson; costumes, Deborah Allen.
Mama Alice Kayro .... Cheryl Denson
Tish Kayro .... Synthia Rogers
Margie Lynn Kayro
    Bunton .... Eleanor Lindsay
Jack Kayro .... Michael Scudday
Jimmy Bunton .... Chris McCarty
C.C. .... Nancy Wilkins
Ginger .... Gail Homer
Shorty .... Beverly Renquist
Eula Simmons .... Alex Winslow
    Time: Mid-August of 1975. Place: Mama Alice's duplex in Polly, Tex., located southwest of San Antonio. Act I, Scene 1: The Lovely Lady Beauty Shop at Mama Alice's, mid-afternoon. Scene 2: The same, two days later at

4 a.m. Act II, Scene 1: Mama Alice's living room, a few minutes later. Scene 2: The Lovely Lady, mid-afternoon of the next day.

INSIDE THE WHITE ROOM (15). By Paul R. Bassett. April 18, 1978 (world premiere). Director, Dick Trousdell; scenery, Yoichi Aoki; lighting, Michael Scudday; costumes, Shannon Wilson.
Spencer .... Chris Hendrie
Velinda .... Cheyanne Boyd
Renquist .... Beverly Renquist
Padre .... Jeffrey Kinghorn.
    Time: The present. Place: A room. Act I: A morning in late summer. Act II: Several weeks later. Act III: Two months later.

INTERWEAVE (15). Developed by Dallas Theater Center's Mime Act from a scenario by Robyn Flatt; music by Marc Momberger and Alex Winslow. May 16, 1978 (world premiere). Directors, John R. Stevens, Robyn Flatt; scenery and costumes, Rodger M. Wilson; lighting, Suzanne Chiles; woven curtains, Sally Askins. With Robyn Flatt, Martha Goodman, Jane Farris, Janet Meier, Michael Mullen, John R. Stevens, Robert A. Smith, Beverly Renquist, Riho Mitachi, Karon Cogdill.
    Act I: "Aligning the threads." Act II: "Working the patterns." Act III: "Interweaving."

Dallas Theater Center: Magic Turtle Children's Theater

EQUEPOISE (8). Book and lyrics by Phil Penningroth; music by Howard Quilling. October 22, 1977 (world premiere). Director, Celeste Varricchio; scenery, Suzanne Chiles; lighting, Michael Scudday; costumes, Mark Momberger; musical director, Pam Nagle; choreographer, Fitz Houston.
Mary Rose Mallory ...... Eleanor Lindsay
Gene Mallory .... Jeffrey Kinghorn
Linda Mallory .... Nancy Wilkins
Alexander .... Paul Munger
Valiant Pasha .... Dennis Vincent
Hagenwood .... Tim Haynes
Chivas Regal .... Deborah Linn
Count Nero .... Philip Reeves
Magnificence .... Fitzhugh G. Houston
Marilyn Stucup .... Pamela Hurst
Announcer .... Roberta Cashwell
Ring Crew .... Lawrence Corwin,
                        John Christian Smith
Magic Turtle .... Mark Beardsley

SNOW WHITE (7). Music and lyrics by Alex

Winslow and Mark Momberger. December 17, 1977 (world premiere). Directors, Robyn Flatt and John Stevens; scenery, Steven John Yuhasz; lighting, Jim Eddy; costumes, Sandra Howell.
Snow White .... Kristine Rue
Queen .... Dallas L. McCurley
Mirror .... Janis Myer
King .... Bill Wheat
Huntsman .... Fitzhugh G. Houston
Prince .... Mark Momberger
Doc .... Andrew C. Gaupp
Happy .... Michelle Clay
Sneezie .... Janelle Haley
Sleepy .... Steven John Yuhasz/
                        Rodger Wilson
Grumpy .... Russell Henderson
Bashful .... Debra Blizzard
Dopey .... Jim Marvin/Dennis Vincent
Magic Turtle .... Alan Gordon
    One intermission.

THE TIGER IN TRACTION (8). Book and

Preston Jones, John Figlmiller and Ronni Lopez in *Firekeeper* at Dallas Theater Center

lyrics by Gifford Wingate; music by Robert R. Smith Jr. February 11, 1978. Director, Bryant J. Reynolds; scenery, Michael Krueger; lighting Wayne Lambert; costumes, Diana Gonzalez; music directors, Mark Momberger, Pam Nagle; choreographer, Deborah Linn. With Bruce Kellerhouse, Lawrence Corwin, Jo Ann Zvares, Brent Williams, Julie Dale, Alan Gordon, Sandra Howell. Magic Turtle, Lorlee Bartos.

THE ADVENTURES OF TOM SAWYER

(7). Book, lyrics and music by Sam L. Rosen; adapted from Mark Twain's novel. April 8, 1978. Directors, Hanna Cusik, Wayne Lambert; scenery, Sandra Howell; lighting, Kathy Moberly; costumes, Deborah Linn; music director, Pam Nagle; choreographer, Rodger Wilson. With Dennis Vincent, John Holloway, Gail Homer, Cynthia Waldron, Philip Reeves, Charles Hukill, Ken Monson, Michael Krueger, Sally Askins, Julie Dale, Alan Gordon, Pamela Hurst, Chris Smith. Magic Turtle, Molly Houston.

Note: Dallas Theater Center toured two productions during 1977-78: *Scapino!* (27) adapted from Molière's comedy by Frank Dunlop and Jim Dale and *The Oldest Living Graduate* (13) by Preston Jones, through 15 states. DTC continued its affiliation with Trinity University in San Antonio, staffing the theater arts program from the professional company.

EVANSTON, ILL.

North Light Repertory Company (formerly Evanston Theater Company)

(Producing director, Gregory Kandel)

THE GOODBYE PEOPLE (21). By Herb Gardner. September 27, 1977. Director, George Keathley. With Tom Alderman, William Munchow, Judith Ivey, Ronald Parady, Barry Cullison, Nathan Davis.

THE MOUND BUILDERS (21). By Lanford Wilson. November 1, 1977. Director, Gregory Kandel. With Ronald Parady, Camilla Hawk,

Helen Crowley, Barry Cullison, Timothy Oman, Judith Ivey, Mary Seibel.

OH COWARD! (21). Devised by Roderick Cook; words and music by Noel Coward. January 10, 1978. Director, Dennis Zacek; musical director, Carol Loverde; choreographer, Tracy Friedman. With John Newton-Fletcher, Judith Ivey, Greg McCaslin.

Designers: scenery, Maher Ahmad; lighting, Robert Atkins, Maher Ahmad; costumes, Christa Scholtz, Marsha Kowal.

HARTFORD, CONN.

Hartford Stage Company: John W. Huntington Theater

(Producing director, Paul Weidner; managing director, William Stewart; associate director, Irene Lewis)

ALL THE WAY HOME (44). By Tad Mosel; based on the book by James Agee. October 14, 1977. Director, Paul Weidner. With Tana Hicken, Teresa Wright, Alan Gifford, David O. Petersen, Anne Shropshire, Stephen Stout.

PAST TENSE (42). By Jack Zeman. November 25, 1977 (world premiere). Director, Paul Weidner; scenery, Hugh Landwehr; lighting, Judy Rasmuson; costumes, Claire Ferraris.
Moving Man .... Robert Underwood
Emily Michaelson .... Barbara Baxley
Moving Man .... Frank Rudnick
Ralph Michaelson .... George Grizzard.
  Time: The present. Place: A suburban home. Act I: A late summer afternoon. Act II: A half-hour later.

A FLEA IN HER EAR (43). By Georges Feydeau; translated by John Mortimer. January 6, 1978. Director, Norman Ayrton. With Stephen Stout, Jacqueline Coslow, Edwin McDonough, Sigourney Weaver, Jill Tanner, Jeffrey Jones, Ted Graeber, Theodore Sorel.

RAIN (44). By Somerset Maugham; adapted by John Colton and Clemence Randolph,

February 17, 1978. Director, Paul Weidner. With Jean DeBaer, Mark Dempsey, Ted Graeber, Richard Mathews, Julia Curry, Gertrude Blanks.

HOLIDAY (44). By Philip Barry. March 31, 1978. Director, Edward Berkeley. With Linda Atkinson, John Getz, Joyce Fideor, Robin Haynes, Ron Randell.

THEY'D COME TO SEE CHARLIE (44). By James Borrelli. May 17, 1978 (world premiere). Director, Irene Lewis; scenery, Hugh Landwehr; lighting, Arden Fingerhut; costumes, Linda Fisher.
Al Buckley .... Madison Arnold
Louie .... Tom Pedi
Charlie Campagna .... Joseph Mascolo
Tony Scalesi .... Val Bisoglio
Vince Campagna .... Michael Dinelli
Francine .... Peg Shirley
Shrimp .... Peter Carew
Booker .... George Lee Miles
Miles .... Ellis Williams
Two Men ..... Clyde Bassett, Jake Estrada
  Time: The mid-70's, an early evening in late spring. Place: The Vegas Bar on Manhattan's Lower East Side. No intermission.

Designers: scenery, John Conklin, Hugh Landwehr, Marjorie Kellogg, Edward Berkeley; lighting, Peter Hunt, Arden Fingerhut, Beverly Emmons; costumes, Claire Ferraris, James Guenther, David Murin.

THE SEASON AROUND THE UNITED STATES 83

Hartford Stage Company: The Old Place

EVE (8). By Larry Fineberg. February 2, 1978
(U. S. premiere). Director, Irene Lewis;
scenery, Hugh Landwehr; lighting, Judy
Rasmuson; costumes, Linda Fisher.

Burt .... Joseph Sullivan
Eve .... Beverly May
Neil .... John Carroll
Pat .... Daniel Snyder
Johnny .... Michael Galloway
Kim .... Alexandra Johnson
    One intermission.

MACKEREL (9). By Israel Horovitz. March
23, 1978 (world premiere). Director, Mark
Lamos; lighting, Spencer Mosse; costumes,
Bob Wojewodski; sound, Jon King.

Ed Lemon .... Gerald Hiken
Edna Lemon .... Cynthia Crumlish
Emma Lemon .... Janet Ward
Eileen Lemon .... Jani Brenn
Fortunini .... Chris Ambrose
    Time: Late fall. Place: The dining room of
the Lemon family's seaside home. One inter-
mission.

Note: The Hartford Stage Company Touring Theater is a professional troupe, under the egis of
HSC, presenting documentary dramas and children's productions to schools, civic and church
groups. *The Black, the Blue and the Gray* (50), compiled by Irene Lewis and Edward Emmanuel,
directed by Paul Weidner, designed by James Guenther, with James Kalwin, Tara Loewenstern,
David McCarver, Thurman Scott, toured between February 27 and April 15, 1978.

HOUSTON

Alley Theater: Large Stage

(Producer-Director, Nina Vance)

MARY STUART (38). By Friedrich Schiller;
adapted by John Reich and Jean Stock
Goldstone. October 20, 1977. Director, Nina
Vance with Beth Sanford. With Diana
Barrington, Pauline Flanagan, Maurice Good,
Kenneth Dight, Joyce Campion, Claude Bede.

THE IMPORTANCE OF BEING
EARNEST (42). By Oscar Wilde. December 8,
1977. Director, Leslie Yeo. With Maurice
Good, Dale Helward, Cristine Rose, Marilyn
Lightstone, Pauline Flanagan.

ECHELON (37). By Mikhail Roschin; English
translation by Michael Henry Heim. January
25, 1978 (American premiere). Director,
Galina Volchek with Beth Sanford; scenery,
Matthew Grant; lighting, Jonathan Duff;
costumes, Bobbie Hodges; musical director,
Paul Dupree.
Author .... Joel Stedman
Katya .... Cristine Rose
Galina .... Bettye Fitzpatrick
Masha .... Bella Jarrett
Lavra .... Lillian Evans
Savvishna .... Pauline Flanagan
Nina .... Angela Wood
Tamara .... Donna O'Connor
Lena .... Gale Childs
Iva .... Lenore Harris

Yesenyuk .... Dale Helward
Fydor Kadych .... Bernard Frawley
Old Woman .... Miriam Phillips
Irina .... Robin Bradley
Yurka .... Martin Rizley
Sanya .... Patti Slover
Larisa .... Chesley Santoro
Lyusya .... Judy Mueller
Volodya .... Gram Smith
Nika .... Lealan Markham
Oska .... Shawn Glanville
Gypsy Woman .... Dorothy Price
Ukranian Woman .... Che Knight
Deaf Mute .... Michael Guido
Percussionist .... George Honea
    Time: 1941. Place: Russia. One intermission

THE SHADOW BOX (38). By Michael
Cristofer. March 9, 1978. Director, Beth San-
ford. With Philip Davidson, Bettye Fitzpatrick,
Gram Smith, Robert Symonds, Michael Tylo,
Bella Jarrett, Miriam Phillips, Gale Childs,
David Wurst.

ABSURD PERSON SINGULAR (46). By
Alan Ayckbourn. April 20, 1978. Director,
Robert Symonds. With Judy Mueller, David
Wurst, Joel Parks, Cristine Rose, Robert
Symonds, Lillian Evans.

Alley Theater: Arena Stage

ROOT OF THE MANDRAKE (22). By Niccolo Machiavelli. January 19, 1978. Director, Robert Symonds. With Anthony Manionis, Eric House, Maurice Good, Dorothy Ann Haug, Philip Davidson, Dixie Taylor.

Designers: scenery, Matthew Grant, Michael Olich; lighting, Jonathan Duff, Matthew Grant; costumes, Michel J. Cesario, Bobbie Hodges, Michael Olich.

Note: Alley Theater presented Denise LeBrun in a one-woman show entitled *Denise LeBrun: Lifesize* for 34 performances in the newly-opened Penthouse Theater; director, Beth Sanford; musical direction, Paul Dupree; December 27, 1977-January 29, 1978. *The Yellow Brick Road,* a musical for children adapted by Irene Siff from the *Wizard of Oz,* was presented for 2 performances by the Merry-Go-Round, Alley Theater's training wing for young people, January, 1978.

HUNTINGTON STATION, N.Y.

PAF Playhouse

(Producer, Jay Broad; general manager, Joel Warren)

EVENTS FROM THE LIFE OF TED SNYDER (43). Written and directed by Jay Broad. October 7, 1977. With Gordon Oas-Heim, Pierre Epstein, Pirie MacDonald, Victoria Boothby, Clement Fowler, Michael Hendricks.

GIVE MY REGARDS TO BROADWAY (43). By Dennis Turner. November 18, 1977 (world premiere). Director, Anthony Stimac; scenery and lighting, Eldon Elder; costumes, Susan Hum Buck.

Louis Holtzer .... David Christmas
Artie .... Brian Brownlee
Lawrence Graham .... Jay Garner
Beverly Henderson .... Annie Kravat
Bryce Roberts .... Joseph Warren
    Time: The present. Place: The study of Lawrence Graham's house in Connecticut. Act I, Scene 1: A late evening in April. Scene 2: The next morning. Act II: A half-hour later.

DOWN AT THE OLD BULL AND BUSH (43). Devised by Dolores Sutton and Roderick Cook. December 30, 1977 (world premiere). Director, Roderick Cook; musical director, Robert Billig; choreographer, George Bunt; scenery, Herbert Senn, Helen Pond; lighting, Mitchell Dana; costumes, Laura Crow.

The Ladies:
Miss Fanny Darby .... Maria Karnilova
Miss Biddy Molloy ..... Charlotte Fairchild
Miss Annie Aardvark .... Patti Perkins
The Gentlemen:
Mr. Archie Twiggam .... George Hall
Mr. Bertie Bloggs .... Buck Hobbs

Mr. Clarence Crimmins ...... John Sloman
Chairman .... George S. Irving
    Time: The 1890's. Place: A Victorian Music Hall, with authentic English music hall song numbers.

THE KILLING OF YABLONSKI: *Scenes of Involvement in a Current Event* (43). By Richard Nelson. February 10, 1978 (world premiere). Director, Peter Mark Schifter; scenery, John Arnone; lighting, Marc B. Weiss; costumes, William Ivey Long; sound, Leslie A. Deweerdt Jr.

Reporter .... Richard Bey
Buddy; Doctor B.;
    Reporter .... Joe Regalbuto
Yablonski; Miss K.;
    Waitress .... Elizabeth Parrish
Claude Edward; Mr. A.;
    Reporter .... Jon Polito
John L. Jr.; Joe; Paul ..... Michael Miller
Jock Yablonski .... Jack Ramage
Charlotte Yablonski;
    Waitress .... Deborah Mayo
    Act I: The death of John L. Lewis. Act II: Yablonski's campaign for the union's presidency. Act III: The killings. Act IV: The interrogation of the current event. Act V: The trip into the current event. One intermission following Act III.

THE GOLD STANDARD by Kenneth Koch and HANCOCK'S LAST HALF HOUR by Heathcote Williams (American premiere) (43). March 24, 1978. Director, Jay Broad; scenery and costumes, William Ivey Long; lighting,

In *Down at the Old Bull and Bush* at PAF Playhouse: (*front row*) John Sloman, George Hall and Buck Hobbs; (*back row*) Patti Perkins, Maria Karnilova and Charlotte Fairchild

David F. Segal. *The Gold Standard* with Jon Polito, James Cahill. *Hancock's Last Half Hour* with Jon Polito as Tony Hancock. Place: A hotel room in Australia.

JUNO'S SWANS (43). By Elaine Kerr. May 5, 1978 (world premiere). Director, Michael Flanagan; scenery and lighting, Marc B. Weiss; costumes, David Toser.

Cary .... Anna Shaler
Doug .... Tom Mason
Cecil .... Elaine Kerr
Tsigounis .... Clement Fowler.
    Time: January of this year. Place: Cary's apartment on Manhattan's Upper West Side. Two intermissions.

PAF Playhouse Theater For Young People: PAF/McDonald's Theater

TO KILL A MOCKINGBIRD (61). Narrative dramatization of Harper Lee's novel. November 3, 1977. RAZZLE DAZZLE (33). Revue. January 9, 1978. THE MARVELOUS ADVENTURES OF TYL (25). By Jonathan Levy. March 29, 1978. Director, Kelly Walters. Youth Theater Acting Company; Hilary Bader, Tamara Bond, Deirdre Brennan, Jay Bond, Dan Howard, Jamie Oliviero, William Pisarra, Tom Spiller.

Designers: scenery, David Chapman, Jimmy Cuomo; lighting Richard Harden, Leslie A. DeWeerdt Jr.; costumes, Carol Oditz, Alison Ford, Virginia Johnson.

INDIANAPOLIS

Indiana Repertory Theater

(Producing director, Benjamin Mordecai; artistic director, Edward Stern)

THE PHILADELPHIA STORY (22). By Philip Barry. October 21, 1977. Director, Edward Stern. With Wanda Bimson, Bruce Gray, Munson Hicks, Bernard Kates, Christina Whitmore.

THE BIRTHDAY PARTY (22). By Harold Pinter. November 18, 1977. Director, Thomas Gruenewald. With Alfred Hinckley, Beverly May, Robert Stattel, Valery Daemke, Bernard Kates, Jon DeVries.

THE COUNTRY GIRL (22). By Clifford Odets. December 16, 1977. Director, William Guild. With Bernard Kates, Sara Woods, John Lagioia.

VANITIES (22). By Jack Heifner. January 13, 1978. Director, Charles Kerr. With Beth Collins, Gun-Marie Nilsson, Mercedes Ruehl.

THE SEAGULL (22). By Anton Chekhov; translated by Jean-Claude van Itallie. February 17, 1978. Director, Edward Stern. With Margaret Phillips, Benjamin Hendrickson, Joseph Warren, Wanda Bimson, David Gale, Allison Giglio.

HOW THE OTHER HALF LOVES (22). By Alan Ayckbourn. March 17, 1978. Director, Edward Stern. With Bernard Kates, Sara Woods, John Bergstrom, Barbara Berge, Gary Garth, Allison Giglio.

Designers: scenery, John Doepp, David Potts, Van Phillips, Ursula Belden, Eric Head, Marjorie Kellogg; lighting, John Doepp, Gregg Mariner, Jeff Davis, Paul Gallo, Geoffrey T. Cunningham, Arden Fingerhut; costumes, Elizabeth Covey, Arnold S. Levine, Susan Tsu.

Note: *Stepping Back* by Michael Warner; director, Kenneth Kaplan; with Thomas Stechschulte, Peter Thoemke and Christina Whitmore was given a staged reading on November 20, 1977 as part of IRT's Off-Night Series. Other presentations were James Beard's adaptation of *A Christmas Carol* on December 5 and December 10, 1977, and Kay Erin Thompson in *An Evening With Dorothy Parker,* on January 16, 1978. This year's IRT touring production was an adaptation of Harper Lee's *To Kill a Mockingbird* directed by Richard Harden, designed by Thomas Beall, Gersh and Arnold S. Levine. It toured schools, clubs and other community facilities in 20 cities across Indiana.

KANSAS CITY, MO.

Missouri Repertory Theater: University of Missouri at Kansas City — Danciger Auditorium of the Jewish Community Center

(Producing director, Patricia McIlrath)

THE MISANTHROPE (14). By Molière; verse translation by Richard Wilbur. July 7, 1977. Director, Cyril Ritchard. With Barry Boys, Walter Atamaniuk, Juliet Randall, Robin Humphrey.

OLD TIMES (14). By Harold Pinter. July 14, 1977. Director, James Assad. With Ellen Crawford, Mike Genovese, Jackie Burroughs.

MARY STUART (14). By Friedrich Schiller; adapted by John Reich and Jean Stock Goldstone. July 21, 1977. Director, John Reich. With Alice White, Harriet Levitt, John Mad-

dison, Juliet Randall, Barry Boys, Daniel Barnett.

THE HOSTAGE (14). By Brendan Behan. August 4, 1977. Director, Francis J. Cullinan. With Steve Meyer, Jackie Burroughs, Michael Tylo, Eden Lee Murray, Rolla Nuckles, Robin Humphrey.

THE MORNING STAR (14). By Henry C. Haskell. August 11, 1977 (world premiere). Director, Harold Scott; scenery, James Leonard Joy; lighting, Joseph Appelt;

costumes, Judy Dolan; sound design, Harold
Scott and Susan Selvey.

Gardener .... James Armstrong
1st Nun ....Harriet Levitt
Heloise ....Jackie Burroughs
2d Nun ....Jane Dick
Abbot of Cluny .... John Maddison
Margot .... Ellen Crawford
Abelard ....Barry Boys
Beadle .... James Armstrong
Flower Vendor .... David Stenstrom
Bishop of Poitiers .... Rolla Nuckles
Canon Fulbert .... Walter Atamaniuk
Martin .... John Houston
Woman .... Lorca Peress
Landlord ....Steve Meyer
Spy ....Steve Doolittle
Denyse .... Robin Humphrey
Abbess of Argenteuil .... June Finell
Young Nun .... Patton Hasegawa
  Girls: Margaret Heffernan, Sally Longan,
Val Scassellati, Judy Goldman, Mary Kay
Moran. Students: Daniel Barnett, William
Cook, George Comiskey. Servants, Carolers,
Agents of Canon Fulbert played by appren-
tices.
  Prologue: Troyes, the garden of the Paraclete
Convent, morning in April, 1142. Scene 1:
Paris, the Seine Embankment, an afternoon in
April, 1116. Scene 2: Paris, Abelard's apart-
ment, evening, a few days later. Scene 3: Paris,
a room in Canon Fulbert's house, morning, a
week later. Scene 4: Paris, the courtyard of
Canon Fulbert's, an afternoon in July of the
same year. Scene 5: Near Paris, an inn, Christmas Eve, 1116. Scene 6: Brittany, Denyse's
orchard, an early morning in May, 1118. Scene
7: Paris, a room in Canon Fulbert's house,
night, a month later. Scene 8: Argenteuil, an
anteroom in the Benedictine Convent, an afternoon in January, 1119. One intermission. (See
review in the introduction to this section.)

PURLIE VICTORIOUS (14). By Ossie Davis.
August 18, 1977. Director, Robert L. Smith.
With Von H. Washington, Alfreda Williams,
Robert Elliott, Madelyn Porter, John Cothran,
Buckner Gibbs.

In repertory, February 2-26, 1978:
THE IMAGINARY INVALID by Molière;
translated and directed by John Reich; original
music by Marc-Antoine Charpentier. With
Richard Brown, Edith Owen, Mary-Linda
Rapelye, Ellen Crawford, Mike Genovese,
Alan Zampese, Robert Elliott.
ALL MY SONS by Arthur Miller. Director,
James Assad. With Alan Zampese, Edith
Owen, Robert Elliott, Steve Keener, Marilyn
Lynch, Mike Genovese, Ellen Crawford.

Designers: scenery, James Leonard Joy, Frederick James, John Ezell, Max Beatty; Baker S.
Smith, Jack Montgomery; lighting, Joseph Appelt, Curt Ostermann, James Shehan, Michael
Scott; costumes, Vincent Scassellati, Barbara Medlicott, Judy Dolan.

Note: MRT's productions of Molière's *The Misanthrope* and Brendan Behan's *The Hostage*
toured Kansas, Missouri and Oklahoma for two weeks in October 1977. In 1978, following their
regular run, Molière's *The Imaginary Invalid* and Arthur Miller's *All My Sons* toured two dozen
communities in Kansas.

LAKEWOOD, OHIO

Great Lakes Shakespeare Festival

(Artistic director, Vincent Dowling; general manager, William H. Witte)

HAMLET (16). By William Shakespeare. June
30, 1977. Director, Vincent Dowling. With
Dennis Lipscomb, Bairbre Dowling, Edith
Owen, Robert Lanchester, Bruce Somerville,
Bernard Kates.

PEG O' MY HEART (15). By J. Hartley
Manners. July 7, 1977. Director, Vincent Dowl-
ing. With Bairbre Dowling, Edith Owen, John
Q. Bruce, George F. Maguire, Holmes
Osborne, Lucy Bredeson, Clive Rosengren.

IN A FINE FRENZY (8). Devised by
Frederik N. Smith; conceived and directed by
Roger Hendricks Simon. July 21, 1977. Direc-
tor/composer, Stuart W. Raleigh; additional
music, Bill Berset. With Gusti, Bernard Kates,
Michael LaGue, Robert Lanchester, Dennis
Lipscomb, MichaelJohn McGann, Barbara
Weikamp. Sara Woods.

THE GLASS MENAGERIE (10). By
Tennessee Williams. July 28, 1977. Director,

Vincent Dowling. With Edith Owen, Bruce Somerville, Bairbre Dowling, John Q. Bruce.

THE IMPORTANCE OF BEING OSCAR (6). By Micheal MacLiammoir; selected and arranged from the writings of Oscar Wilde. August 11, 1977. Director, Roger Hendricks Simon. With V. G. Dowling.

THE TAMING OF THE SHREW (12). By William Shakespeare. August 18, 1977. Director, Daniel Sullivan. With Dennis Lipscomb, Sara Woods, Janice Akers, Michael LaGue, Norm Berman, Bernard Kates, Clive Rosengren.

Designers: scenery, John Ezell; lighting, Richard Coumbs; costumes, Michael Olich, Algesa O'Sickey.

LOS ANGELES

Center Theater Group: Ahmanson Theater

(Managing director, Robert Freyer)

CHAPTER TWO (56). By Neil Simon. October 7, 1977 (world premiere). Director, Herbert Ross; scenery, William Ritman; lighting, Tharon Musser; costumes, Noel Taylor.
Jennie Malone .... Anita Gillette
Faye Medwick .... Ann Wedgeworth
George Schneider .... Judd Hirsch
Leo Schneider .... Cliff Gorman
    Time: The present, from late February to mid-spring. Place: Jennifer Malone's Upper East Side apartment and George Schneider's Lower Central Park West apartment. One intermission.

THE DEVIL'S DISCIPLE (56). By George Bernard Shaw. December 16, 1977. Director, Frank Dunlop; scenery and costumes, Carl Toms, lighting, F. Mitchell Dana. With Rex Harrison, Chris Sarandon, Carole Shelley, Barnard Hughes, Margaret Hamilton.

ABSURD PERSON SINGULAR (56). By Alan Ayckbourn. February 17, 1978. Director, Stephen Porter; scenery, Edward Burbridge; lighting, Robert Randolph; costumes, Noel Taylor. With Eve Arden, Stockard Channing, Laurence Guittard, Roberta Maxwell, John McMartin, Lawrence Pressman.

PAL JOEY '78 (136). Book by John O'Hara; music by Richard Rodgers; lyrics by Lorenz Hart; adapted by Jerome Chodorov and Mark Bramble. April 21, 1978. Director, Michael Kidd; scenery and lighting, Robert Randolph; costumes, Robert Fletcher; musical director, John Myles; choreographer, Claude Thompson. With Lena Horne, Josephine Premice, Clifton Davis, Louisa Flaningam, Norman Matlock, Marjorie Barnes, John La Motta.

Center Theater Group: Mark Taper Forum — Mainstage

(Artistic director, Gordon Davidson; associate director, Edward Parone)

FOR COLORED GIRLS WHO HAVE CONSIDERED SUICIDE/WHEN THE RAINBOW IS ENUF (52). By Ntozake Shangé. August 11, 1977. Arranger/director, Oz Scott; choreographer, Paula Moss. With Jonelle Allen, Barbara Alston, Beverly Anne, Trazana Beverley, Candy Brown, Marilyn Coleman, Alfre Woodard.

COMEDIANS (54). By Trevor Griffiths. November 3, 1977. Director, Edward Parone. With Jim Dale, Philip Charles MacKenzie, Gerrit Graham, Avery Schreiber, John Devlin, Henry Jones, Scott Hylands, Keene Curtis.

A CHRISTMAS CAROL (12). By Charles Dickens; adapted by Doris Baizley. December 22, 1978. Director, John Dennis; music adapter/arranger, Susan Harvey. Performed, sung, danced and juggled by The Improvisational Theater Project/Resident Ensemble.

GETTING OUT (54). By Marsha Norman. February 16, 1978. Director, Gordon Davidson. With Janette Lane Bradbury, Susan Clark, Hugh Gillin, Collin Wilcox, Sarah Cunningham, Conchata Ferrell, Bill Cobbs.

Andra Akers, Diana Scarwid, Joyce Van Patten and James Sloyan in *Gethsemane Springs,* produced at Mark Taper Forum's New Theater for Now

BLACK ANGEL (54). By Michael Cristofer. May 18, 1978 (world premiere). Director, Gordon Davidson; scenery and costumes, Sally Jacobs; lighting, Tharon Musser.

Martin Engel	Joseph Maher
Simone Engel	Tyne Daly
Claude	Neil Flanagan
Louis Puget	Richard Dysart
August Moreault	David Spielberg
1st Hooded Man	Vincent Duke Milana
2d Hooded Man	Bob Basso
3d Hooded Man; M.P.	Richard Riner
Andy Raines; M.P.; 4th Hooded Man	Art LaFleur
Bob Hawkins; M.P.	Jonathan Banks

One intermission

Center Theater Group: Mark Taper Forum — New Theater For Now

GETHSEMANE SPRINGS (22). By Harvey Perr. September 29, 1977 (world premiere). Director, John Sullivan; scenery, Sally Jacobs; lighting, Dawn Chiang; choreographer, Robert Talmage; vocal director, Arthur Samuel Joseph.

Mira	Andra Akers
David	Mathew Anden
Claude	John Anderson
Mme. Hervé	Tyne Daly
Snodgrass	Paul Hampton
Louise	Joanne Linville
Shulamith	Diana Scarwid
Victor	Charles Shull
Hopkins	James Sloyan
Elena	Gail Strickland
Marianne	Joyce Van Patten

Time: Now, and Marianne's Then. Place:

Gethsemane Springs, two adjoining sitting rooms in the Hervé home. Two intermissions.

THE WINTER DANCERS (22). By David Lan. April 6, 1978 (American premiere). Director, Kenneth Brecher; scenery, Ralph Funicello; lighting and projections, Pamela Cooper; costumes, Julie Weiss.

Carver .... John Kauffman
Betsy Hunt .... Constance Sawyer
Kettle .... Marcy Mattox
Fool .... Sab Shimona
Mountain Peak; Forest;
Life Owner .... Yuki Shimoda
One Foot; Mouse; Sky ..... Haunani Minn
Blood Lip; Whale .... Ernest Harada
Well Washed Stone;
Dancer .... Ralph Brannen
Bear .... Ken Ganado
Place: Vancouver Island and the mainland of British Columbia. Act I, Scene 1: Autumn, 1871. Scene 2: Autumn, 1873. Scene 3: Winter, 1875. Scene 4: Spring, 1876. Act II, Scene 1: Winter, 1886. Scene 2: Summer, 1891.

ZOOT SUIT (22). By Luis Valdez. April 20, 1978 (world premiere). Director, Luis Valdez; scenery, Robert J. Morales; lighting, Dawn Chiang; costumes, Peter J. Hall; dance consultant, Roberta Esparza.

El Pachuco .... Edward James Olmos
Press .... Arthur Hammer
Henry Reyna .... Daniel Valdez
Enrique Reyna .... Abel Franco
Benjamin Villareal .... Julio Medina
Dolores Reyna .... Lupe Ontiveros
Lupe Reyna .... Christine Avila
Joey Castro .... Pepe Serna
Bertha Villareal .... Rachel Levario
Tommy Roberts .... David E. Worden
Smiley Torres .... Mike Gomez
Alice Springfield .... Sheila Larken
Rudy Reyna .... Domingo Ambriz
Della Barrios .... Evelina Fernandez
George Shearer .... Noah Keen
Judge Charles; Lt. Edwards;
Prison Guard ...... Vincent Duke Milana
Ramon Gilbert; Detective
Gallindo .... Nelson D. Cuevas
Act I, Scene 1: Prologue. Scene 2: Pachuco Boogie. Scene 3: El Pachuco and the press. Scene 4: Morning, November 8, 1944. Scene 5: La Ganza de 38th Street. Scene 6, Afternoon, November 8. Scene 7: The Sleepy Lagoon. Scene 8: Dragnet, interrogation and Grand Jury. Scene 9: The mass trial. Act II, Scene 1: San Quentin. Scene 2: Evening, November 8, 1944. Scene 3: The Zoot Suit Riots. Scene 4; Midnight, November 8, 1944.

Designers: Ming Cho Lee, Peter J. Hall, Charles Berliner, Edward Burbridge, Sally Jacobs, Ralph Funicello, Robert J. Morales; lighting, Marilyn Rennagel, Peter J. Hall, Charles Berliner, John Gleason, Tharon Musser, Dawn Chiang, Pamela Cooper, Martin Aronstein; costumes, Judy Dearing, Pamela Cooper, Peter J. Hall, Sally Jacobs, Julie Weiss.

Center Theater Group: Mark Taper Forum — Forum/Laboratory

All programs workshop premieres:

TRUE ROMANCES (6). By Susan Yankowitz. September 12, 1977. Director, Judy Chaikin; music, Elmer Bernstein; lyrics, Susan Yankowitz; designers, Terence Tam Soon, Michael M. Bergfeld; musical director, David Spear; musical stager, James Mitchell. With Regina Baff, Joseph Burke, Alix Elias, Donna Fuller, Karen Hensel, John LaMotta, John Lansing, Ann McCurry, James Mitchell, Peter Riegert, Carol Schlanger, Tom Skerritt.

MGMT (4). By Jon Arlow. October 10, 1977. Director, Robert Calhoun; designers, Erik Brenmark, Joyce Aysta, Thomas Ruzika. With Barry Brown, Russell Johnson, Edwin Owens, James G. Richardson, Donegan Smith, Kent Smith, Herb Voland.

SALOME (4). By Kim Milford. December 3,

1977. Director, Gordon Hunt; designers, Scott Johnson, Mary Malin, Dawn Chiang; musical director/arranger, Ron Stockhert; choreographer, Robert Talmage. With Paul Ainsley, Marco Alpert, Doug Altman, Dennis Belfield, Beverly Bremers, Steve Bonino, Randy Books, Annette Charles, Dennis Cooley, James Dybas, Robert Fischer, Gail Heideman, Joe Kelly, Mickey McNeil, Kim Milford, Penelope Milford, Ron Stockert.

TRIPTYCH (5). By Oliver Hailey. February 3, 1978. Director, Michael Flanagan; designers, Peter Clemons, Donna Casey, Karen M. Katz. With Eileen Brennan, Jerry Hardin, Darryl Hickman, Bob Hogan, Heather MacRae.

AT THE END OF LONG ISLAND (4). By Richard Lees. March 10, 1978. Director, Asaad

Kelada; designers, Bruce Ryan, Lesley Nicholson, Roger Gorden. With Gretchen Corbett, Robert Hays, Louise Latham, Neva Patterson, John Randolph, Carol Rossen, William Schallert.

BIG APPLE MESSENGER (5). By Shannon Keith Kelley. April 7, 1978. Director, Jonathan Estrin; designers, Inge Dunn, Virginia Lisa Wells, Alan Blacher. With Sid Conrad, John Creamer, Bill Henry Douglass, Richard Erdman, Alan Feinstein, Jack Fletcher, Rick Hamilton, Ric Mancini, Rudy Ramos, Peter Riegert, Mike Robelo, Maurice Sneed, Dolph Sweet, Sal Viscuso.

OMER LOCKLEAR (5). Book and lyrics by Marc Norman; music by Tony Greco. May 12, 1978. Director, Marc Norman; designers, Erik Brenmark, Christine Ann Lewis, Karen M. Katz; choreographer, Sandra Duffy. With Jeff Altman, Susan Krebs, Darrell Larson, Laura Owens.

THE TAKING AWAY OF LITTLE WILLIE (5). By Tom Griffin. June 2, 1978. Director, Wallace Chappell; designers, Keith Hein, Cheryl Odom, Paulie Jenkins. With Harry Basch, Robin Gammell, Cooper Neal, Sara Rush, Shirley Slater, Timothy Wead, Nina Wilcox.

Note: Mark Taper Forum had an Improvisational Theater Project for young theatergoers which presented a fall season (October 5-November 23, 1977) and a spring season (January 24-May 5, 1978). The Impact Company of ITP ran a fall season (October 13-November 30, 1977) and a spring season (January 9-September 5, 1978). Both projects of ITP are under the supervision of John Dennis.

The Season Elsewhere in Los Angeles

By Ron Pennington

Theater critic of the *Hollywood Reporter*

The 1977-78 season in Los Angeles brought an increase in theatrical activity, both under Equity contracts and in the Equity waiver situations (theaters with 99 seats or less, for which the union waives all restrictions except for the subsidiary rights agreement in regard to original works).

One of the highlights of the season was James A. Doolittle's new production of Peter Shaffer's *Equus,* directed by Anthony Hopkins, who also starred with Thomas Hulce for a limited four-week run at the Huntington Hartford Theater. During the rest of the season the Hartford housed such attractions as Linda Hopkins, Lily Tomlin and her sensational array of characters in *Appearing Nitely,* and *Side by Side by Sondheim,* starring Hermione Gingold, Larry Kert, Millicent Martin and Barbara Heuman.

The Los Angeles Civic Light Opera, headed by Cy Feuer and Ernest Martin, which takes over the Music Center complex each summer, closed its 1977 season with a return engagement of *The Wiz;* Liza Minnelli on her way to New York in her Vegas-act-disguised-as-a-musical-play, *The Act;* and a sensational new reworking of Irving Berlin's *Annie Get Your Gun* by Gower Champion, starring Debbie Reynolds. The 1978 CLO season has so far included *Chicago,* with most of the original Broadway cast reunited, and the organization's first coproduction attempt with Robert Fryer's Ahmanson Theater subscription operation, *Pal Joey '78.* This was a disastrous stab at turning *Pal Joey* into a vehicle for Lena Horne (who looked good and sounded great), with a disco beat added to the Rodgers & Hart score.

Producer Norman Twain's final offering at the Westwood Playhouse before he lost the lease there was an exciting West Coast premiere of David Rabe's *Streamers*, in which director Milton Katselas and his cast played up the humor and then subtly built to the horror. John and Lynda Loesser have since taken over the theater and have booked only one production to date, Donal Donnelly in his one-man piece about George Bernard Shaw, *My Astonishing Self*.

Rudy Solari's theater in Beverly Hills tried a new "dramatic musical" about World War I titled *Dolls*, adapted by Tom Orth and Richard John Miller from the novel *Company K* by William March. It was one of those efforts that just didn't work. More successful were; *The Last of the Marx Brothers Writers*, an excellent new serious comedy by Louis Phillips that had earlier been done in San Diego, with Victor Buono starring in both productions, and Dick Shawn in his brilliant evening as *The 2nd Greatest Entertainer in the Whole Wide World*.

Los Angeles gained a new legit house in the El Rey, converted from a movie theater, which opened with Terrence Shank's imaginative and atmospheric production of Ray Bradbury's *The Martian Chronicles*. Shanks originally developed the environmental piece with his Colony waiver group at the Studio Theater Playhouse. The show only held for an eight-week run at the El Rey, but producer Paul Gregory plans an extensive college tour this fall. This was followed by the R. Scott Lucas, Robert G. Lubell and Richard Kallman production of *Merry-Go-Round*, a musical revue about middle age by Don Tucker that had enjoyed successful runs in Chicago and Las Vegas. Mel Goldberg was brought in to provide a book (flat comedy sketches) for this production, which opened to fair-to-poor reviews.

A Chorus Line finally ended its record-breaking run at the Shubert Theater on New Year's Eve after a total of 632 performances. It was immediately followed by *Beatlemania*, which was still playing in the Century City house as of May 31.

The Las Palmas was put back in operation after a fire last year with a new version of Cole Porter's *Out of This World*, rewritten and retitled *Heaven Sent* by Lawrence Kasha (who also directed) and David Landay. Starring Charlotte Rae, it proved to be an enjoyable streamlining of the original, carried along by bright style and pacing.

James Nederlander's schedule of touring musicals at the Pantages included *Grease* (playing Los Angeles for the third time), Howard Keel and Jane Powell in *South Pacific*, Carol Channing in *Hello, Dolly!*, *Shenandoah* and Richard Kiley in *Man of La Mancha*.

Close to 300 productions were mounted in waiver theaters during the season. These ranged from several excellent new plays, West Coast premieres and revivals to an abundance of showcases and tryouts of original scripts that are best left unmentioned.

The Los Angeles Actors Theater, founded by Ralph Waite, which keeps quite active with mostly new material, had especially notable entries in Jim Kennedy's *Perfume*, Richard Jordan's *The Venus of Menschen Falls* and Ted Pezzulo's *Skaters*.

Other impressive waiver-theater offerings included Arthur Miller's *After the*

Fall and Preston Jones's *The Oldest Living Graduate* at the Company of Angels (which had a success in Jones's *The Last Meeting of the Knights of the White Magnolia* last season); the West Coast premiere of Albert Innaurato's *The Transfiguration of Benno Blimpie,* starring Allen Goorwitz (aka Allen Garfield) and directed by Richmond Shepard at his theater. Don Eitner's American Theater Arts gained quite a bit of critical attention with *Devour the Snow,* a new play by Abe Polsky about the Donner Party incident in the mid-19th century, in which snowbound travelers in the Sierras were forced to feed off the corpses of fellow party members to survive.

The Odyssey Theater Ensemble scored with artistic director Ron Sossi's productions of *An Evening of Dirty Religious Plays* (Peter Barnes's *Noonday Demons* and the world premiere of Robert Coover's *A Theological Position*) and an environmental staging of *The Threepenny Opera.* The Odyssey also housed an outstanding West Coast premiere of Martin Duberman's haunting *Visions of Kerouac,* directed by Lee D. Sankowich.

The following is a selection of some of the outstanding productions mounted in Los Angeles during the 1977-78 season. The list does not include touring shows or the Center Theater Group productions at the Ahmanson and Mark Taper Forum (see the regional theater listing above).

ANNIE GET YOUR GUN (56). Music and lyrics by Irving Berlin; book by Herbert and Dorothy Fields, restructured by Gower Champion. June 21, 1977. Director-choreographer, Gower Champion; scenery and lighting, Robert Randolph; costumes, Alvin Colt; musical director, Jack Lee. With Debbie Reynolds, Harve Presnell, Art Lund, Bibi Osterwald, Gavin McLeod. Produced by Cy Feuer and Ernest Martin for the Los Angeles Civic Light Opera Association at the Dorothy Chandler Pavilion.

AN EVENING OF DIRTY RELIGIOUS PLAYS (27). *Noonday Demons* by Peter Barnes and *A Theological Position* by Robert Coover (world premiere). August 5, 1977. Director Ron Sossi. With Garret Pierson, Gary Guidinger *(Noonday Demons)*; Ron Sossi, Beth Hogan, Stephen Bassford Hunter *A Theological Position*). At the Odyssey Theater.

EQUUS (28). By Peter Shaffer. August 16, 1977. Director, Anthony Hopkins; scenery and costumes, John Napier. With Anthony Hopkins, Thomas Hulce, Dorothy French, Judith Searle, John O'Leary, Joi Staton, Sandy Sprung. Produced by James A. Doolittle's Southern California Theater Association at the Huntington Hartford Theater.

STREAMERS (183). By David Rabe. December 14, 1977 (West Coast premiere). Director, Milton Katselas; scenery, Joe

Tompkins; lighting, Thomas Ruzika; costumes, Diana Eden. With Richard Thomas, Bruce Davison, Herb Jefferson Jr., Richard Lawson, Charles Durning, Ralph Meeker. Produced by Norman Twain at the Westwood Playhouse.

THE LAST OF THE MARX BROTHERS WRITERS (42). By Louis Phillips. January 10, 1978. Director, Rudy Solari; scenery, Peggy Kellner; lighting, Steph Storer; costumes, Donna Couchman. With Victor Buono, Sandy McCallum, Carole Marget, William Halliday, Tris Solari. Produced by Niki Solari at the Solari Theater.

THE TRANSFIGURATION OF BENNO BLIMPIE (48). By Albert Innaurato. January 27, 1978 (West Coast premiere). Director, Richmond Shepard; scenery and costumes, Halima McMaster; lighting, Steve Stein. With Allen Goorwitz, Nathan Adler, Lynne Harry, Robin Maria, Norman Parker. At the Richmond Shepard Studio.

DEVOUR THE SNOW (32). By Abe Polsky. February 10, 1978 (world premiere). Director, Don Eitner; scenery, Paul Lopez; lighting, Ward Russell; costumes, Sherrie Rae Norris. At American Theater Arts.
John A. Sutter .... Hal Bokar
James Reed ....John Terry Bell
Sheriff McKinstry .... Ed Willkie
Ned Coffeemeyer ....Tony Venture

William Eddy ....Jeff Gallucci
Bill Foster .... Howard Sampson
Phillipine Keseberg .... Rolly Fanton
Margaret Reed .... Judie Carroll
Georgiz Donner ....Nora Morgan
Fallon "Le Gros" .... Joseph Ruskin
Two intermissions.

THE VENUS OF MENSCHEN FALLS (31).
By Richard Jordan. February 10, 1978 (world
premiere). Director, Richard Jordan; scenery,
David L. Snyder; lighting, Paulie Jenkins;
costumes, Roberta Weiner. Produced by
William H. Bushnell Jr. at the Los Angeles Ac-
tors' Theater.
Carl Straker .... Stanley Brock
Max Knee .... Bruce French
Dotty Simpson ....Jessica Quillen
Herman Praxelles .... Richard Sanders
Barry Tayle .... Vance Sorrells
Judge Hugh Caliber ...... Richard Venture
M. T. Head .... Arthur Hammer
Lowery Putter .... Redmond Gleeson
Clement Simpson .... Maury Cooper
Arty Fischer .... Barry Michlin
Minerva Krull ....Toni Sawyer
Frank Ogilvy .... Charles Parks
Mirabel Bothay .... Laurie Prange
Eugene Amory ....Milan Dragicevich
Two intermissions.

THE MARTIAN CHRONICLES (64). By
Ray Bradbury. February 14, 1978. Director,
Terrence Shank; scenery, J. Everett Templin;
lighting, Stuart Lancaster; Earth costumes,
Don Woodruff; Martian costumes, masks,
wigs, makeup, Patrick Duffy Whitbeck,
Conrad Wolff. With Burton Cooper, E.D.
Harris, Barbara Beckley, Carol Newell, Leon
Charles. Produced by Paul Gregory at the El
Rey Theater.

HEAVEN SENT (34). Music and lyrics by
Cole Porter; book by Lawrence Kasha and
David Landay, based on Out of This World by
Dwight Taylor and Reginald Lawrence. May 8,
1978 (world premiere). Director, Lawrence
Kasha; choreographer, Scott Salmon; musical
director, Don Sheffey; scenery and costumes,
Charles Lisanby; lighting, George Gizienski.
Produced by William Ward, Steven Lane,
Mikel Pippi and Fortunamill Inc. at the New
Las Palmas Theater.
Juno .... Charlotte Rae
Mercury .... Michael Byers
Jupiter .... Walter Farrell
Helen ....Teri Ralston
Art .... Timothy Jerome
Chloe .... Robin Taylor
Nicky ....Paul Latchaw
No intermission.

LOS GATOS, CALIF.

California Actors' Theater: Old Town Theater

(Executive producer, Sheldon Kleinman; artistic director, James Dunn.)

In repertory, October 6-November 27, 1977
HENRY IV (28) and HENRY V (28). By
William Shakespeare; adapted and directed by
Dakin Matthews. With Kurtwood Smith,
Byron Jennings, Gregory Mortenson, Tony
DeFonte, Malcolm Young, Stefan Fischer,
Michael Keys-Hall, Carolyn Reed, Brandon
Smith, Margaret Laurence, Will Huddleston,
Merle McDill, Dann Harvey Florek.

SCAPINO! (28). By Frank Dunlop and Jim
Dale; adapted from Molière's Les Fourberies
de Scapin. December 1, 1977. Director, James
Dunn. With Gregory Mortenson, Martin
Ferraro, Dann Harvey Florek, Janet Steiger,
Kurtwood Smith, Tony DeFonte, Tom
Ramirez, Anita Birchenall.

STEAMBATH (28). By Bruce Jay Friedman.
January 5, 1978. Director, Harvey Susser. With

Kurtwood Smith, John McDill, Tom Ramirez,
Stefan Fischer, Bette Besuner, Joan Pirkle.

THE PRICE (28). By Arthur Miller. February
2, 1978. Director, G. W. Bailey. With
Kurtwood Smith, Bonnie Gallup, Zachary
Berger, Dakin Matthews.

SAVE GRAND CENTRAL (28). By William
Hamilton. March 2, 1978 (world premiere).
Director, Edward Hastings; scenery, Ronald
Krempetz; lighting, Eric Chasanoff; costumes,
Elaine Saussotte; sound, Joseph Broido.
Lucy Maynard ....Leslie Harrell
Maria ....Merle McDill/Bette Besuner
Roger Maynard .... Dakin Matthews
Luis Apaka .... Martin Ferrero
Cristina Malcolm ....Carolyn Reed
Charles Malcolm .... Michael Keys-Hall

Tom McKay .... Michael X. Martin
Sally Hooker .... Bonnie Gallup
Peter Whitesides .... Joe Conti
Muffy Stockton .... Anita Birchenall
Jacques .... Malcolm Young
One intermission.

YOU CAN'T TAKE IT WITH YOU (28). By
George S. Kaufman and Moss Hart. March 30,
1978. Director, James Dunn. With Karen
Ingenthron, Bette Besuner, Stefan Fischer,
Harry Kersey, Joan Pirkle, Michael Keys-Hall,
Tom Ramirez, Bonnie Gallup.

WILD OATS or, The Strolling Gentlemen
(28). By John O'Keeffe. April 27, 1978
(American premiere). Director, Douglas Johnson; scenery and lighting, Eric Chasanoff;
costumes, Elaine Saussotte.
John Dory .... Stefan Fischer

Sir George Thunder ....David Ogden Stiers
Ephraim Smooth ....Tom Ramirez
Lady Amaranth ....Carolyn Reed
Harry Thunder .... Brandon Smith
Zachariah; Lamp;
  Coachman .... Tony DeFonte
Midge (Muz); Waiter;
  Ruffian .... Gregory L. Mortensen
Rover .... Byron Jennings
Farmer Gammon .... Kurtwood Smith
Sim .... Martin Ferrero
Jane ....Joan Pirkle
Banks .... Joe Conti
Amelia .... Bonnie Gallup
Trap; Landlord;
  Ruffian .... Malcolm Young
Twitch; Waiter .... Michael X. Martin
Time: 1791. Place: Rural England. One in-
termission.

Designers: scenery, Ronald Krempetz; Marguerite Robinson, Eric Chasanoff; lighting, Eric
Chasanoff; costumes, Barbara Affonso, Elaine Saussotte.

California Actors' Theater: Children's Theater

THE THWARTING OF BARON
BOLLIGREW (10). By Robert Bolt. January
15, 1978. Director, Frank C. Silvey; scenery,
The Company; costumes, MaryAnn Stewart.

THE MAGIC ISLE (10). By Wesley Van
Tassel; music and lyrics by Mark Ollington.
February 12, 1978. Director, Ken Barton Jr.

RUMPELSTILTSKIN (10). Written and
directed by Lee Kopp; from Grimms Fairy

Tales. April 9, 1978. Costumes, Pamela Hoyt-
Heydon.

AESOP'S FALABLES (10). Book by Ed
Graczyk; songs by Bill Smillie, J. P.
Nightingale, D. C. Johnson; additional
material by John and Pam Wood, D. C. John-
son. May 7, 1978. Director/choreographer,
Dennis Collins Johnson.

Company: Karen Lamb Barton, Richard Carlson, James Coyle, Mary Carole Frederickson,
Bruce W. De Les Dernier, Ken Embree, Janice Gartin, Will Huddleston, Michael Keys-Hall, Alan
Loebs, Brandon Smith, Janet Steiger.

LOUISVILLE, KY.

Actors' Theater of Louisville: Pamela Brown Auditorium

(Producing director, Jon Jory)

ROUND AND ROUND THE GARDEN
(13). By Alan Ayckbourn. September 21, 1977.
Director, Elizabeth Ives. With Peggy Cowles,
Ray Fry, Vinnie Holman, William McNulty,
Adale O'Brien, James Secrest.

LIVING TOGETHER (26). By Alan
Ayckbourn. October 6, 1977. Director,
Elizabeth Ives. Cast as above.

In repertory:
GETTING OUT (12). By Marsha Norman.
November 2, 1977 (world premiere). Director,
Jon Jory; scenery and lighting Paul Owen;
costumes, Kurt Wilhelm.
Arlie .... Denny Dillon
Arlene .... Susan Kingsley
Bennie ....Bob Burrus
Guard .... Brian Lynner
Doctor .... Thurman Scott

Teacher .... Nan Wray
Woman ....Jeanne Cullen
Mother .... Anne Pitoniak
Woman .... Maggie Riley
Male Teacher .... Michael Kevin
Carl .... Leo Burmester
2nd Guard .... Jim Baker
Warden .... Ray Fry
Ruby .... Lynn Cohen
    Time: Last year. Place: Louisville, Ky. One
intermission (See synopsis in the introduction
to this section).

DOES ANYBODY HERE DO THE
PEABODY? (12). By Enid Rudd. November 4,
1977. Director, Chuck Kerr. With Ann
Hodapp, Adale O'Brien, Lois Holmes,
Margaret Castleman, John H. Fields, Peter
Ekstrom.

A CHRISTMAS CAROL (28). By Charles
Dickens; adapted by Barbara Field. December
1, 1977. Director, Charles Kerr. With Bob
Burrus, Ray Fry, Louie Frederick, William
McNulty, Adale O'Brien.

ANDRONICUS (28). By William
Shakespeare. December 29, 1977. Director, Jon

Jory; music and lyrics by Jerry Blatt; musical
arranger, Joe Morton. With Michael Kevin,
Jim Baker, John H. Fields, Ray Fry, Adale
O'Brien, Jeanne Cullen.

THE FRONT PAGE (28). By Ben Hecht and
Charles MacArthur. January 26, 1978. Direc-
tor, Jon Jory. With Victor Jory, David Leary,
Adale O'Brien, Jeanne Cullen, Anne Pitoniak,
Brian Lynner.

LU ANN HAMPTON LAVERTY
OBERLANDER (28). By Preston Jones.
February 23, 1978. Director, Patrick Tovatt.
With Dawn Didawick, Michael Kevin, Ray
Fry, Barry Corbin, Bob Burrus, Jim Baker.

THE MOUSETRAP (33). By Agatha Christie.
March 23, 1978. Director, Elizabeth Ives. With
Marsha Korb, James Secrest, William
McNulty, Dee Victor, Ray Fry, Susan
Kingsley, John H. Fields, Jim Baker.

PEG O' MY HEART (28). By J. Hartley
Manners. April 27, 1978. Director, Ray Fry.
With Dawn Didawick, Bob Burrus, Anne
Pitoniak, Ray Fry, Nan Wray, James Secrest,
Jim Baker, Adale O'Brien, William McNulty.

Actors' Theater of Louisville: Victor Jory Theater

THE LOUISVILLE ZOO (13). By Various
Louisvillians at whispered meetings in the dark
of the night. November 1, 1977 (world
premiere). Director, Ray Fry; scenery and
lighting, Paul Owen; costumes, Kurt Wilhelm;
music composed, directed and performed by
Peter Ekstrom. With Jeanne Cullen, John H.
Fields, William McNulty, Adale O'Brien,
Helen Halsey, Vaughan McBride, Ronald L.
McIntyre, Anne Pitoniak.

In repertory (evenings):
DADDIES (11). By Douglas Gower.
November 1, 1977 (professional premiere).
Director, Michael Hankins.
George .... Joe Morton
Carl .... Stephen Van Benschoten
    Time: Christmas. Place: An apartment in
San Francisco. One intermission.
THE BRIDGEHEAD (8). By Frederick
Bailey. November 5, 1977 (professional
premiere). Director, Charles Maryan; scenery,
Paul Owen; lighting, Michael Hottois;
costumes, Kurt Wilhelm.
Tatum .... Thurman Scott
Carmichael .... William McNulty
Prisoner .... Dennis Sakamoto
Hagerty .... Vaughan McBride

Moxley ....Steven M. Hollow
Sawyer .... Bob Burrus
Gallo ....Jim Baker
Pike .... Leo Burmester
Highsmith .... Brian Lynner
Rubinoff .... Michael Kevin
Girl .... Sonya Harris
Molinaro .... Joe Morton
Phillips .... Stephen Van Benschoten
McGlade .... Clint Vaught
    Time: Early 1970. Place: An enemy installa-
tion in a denied area.

AN INDEPENDENT WOMAN (17). Written
and directed by Daniel Stein. November 7,
1977 (world premiere). Scenery and lighting,
Paul Owen; costumes, Kurt Wilhelm. With
Peggy Cowles as Anna Dickinson.

SIZWE BANZI IS DEAD (23). By Athol
Fugard, John Kani and Winston Ntshona.
January 25, 1978. Director, Joe Morton; assistant director, Michael Hankins. With Joe Morton, Robert Jackson.

THIRD AND OAK (26). By Marsha Norman.
March 22, 1978 (world premiere). Director, Jon
Jory; scenery and lighting, Paul Owen;
costumes, Kurt Wilhelm.

Alberta .... Anne Pitoniak
DeeDee .... Dawn Didawick
Shotter .... Joe Morton
Willie .... John Hancock

Time: The present. Place: Louisville, Ky. Act I: Laundromat. Act II: Pool hall. One intermission.

Designers: scenery, Paul Owen, David Hager, Richard Gould, Michael Hottois, Richard Kent Wilcox; lighting, Paul Owen, Ronald Wallace, James Stevens, Jeff Hill, David Hager, Michael Hottois; costumes, Kurt Wilhelm.

Note: ATL presented *Rogues And Vagabonds,* the Stratford Ontario Festival production devised by Michael Meyer, directed by Robin Phillips, with Nicholas Pennell and Marti Maraden, in the Pamela Brown Auditorium on December 5, 1977. *Getting Out* by Marsha Norman and *The Bridgehead* by Frederick Bailey were the winners of ATL's first annual Great American Play Contest. *Getting Out* was cited by the American Theater Critics Association as an outstanding new play for 1977-1978 (see the introduction to this section).

MADISON, N.J.

New Jersey Shakespeare Festival: Drew University

(Artistic director, Paul Barry)

MUCH ADO ABOUT NOTHING (22). By William Shakespeare. June 28, 1977. Director, Paul Barry. With Eric Tavaris, Margery Shaw, Robert Beseda, Robin Leary, Nesbitt Blaisdell, Geddeth Smith.

TITUS ANDRONICUS (23). By William Shakespeare. July 5, 1977. Director, Paul Barry. With Geddeth Smith, Eric Tavaris, Margery Shaw, Robin Leary, Dana Mills, Richard Graham, Roger Alan Brown.

CYRANO DE BERGERAC (22). By Edmond Rostand. July 26, 1977. Director, Paul Barry. With Paul Barry, Jody Catlin, Dana Mills, Eric Tavaris, Ronald Steelman, Geddeth Smith.

AN ENEMY OF THE PEOPLE (22). By Henrik Ibsen. August 23, 1977. Director, Paul Barry. With William Myers. Ronald Steelman, Virginia Mattis, Eric Tavaris, Tom Brennan, Jody Catlin, Richard Graham.

THE HOT L BALTIMORE (21). By Lanford Wilson. September 13, 1977. Director, Davey Marlin-Jones. With Ronald Steelman, Jody Catlin, Virginia Mattis, Sue Lawless, Richard Graham, Tom Brennan, Margery Shaw, Kale Brown.

THE GLASS MENAGERIE (30). By Tennessee Williams. October 4, 1977. With Virginia Mattis, Curt Williams, Ellen Barry, Kale Brown.

Designers: scenery, Ron A. Coleman; lighting, Gary C. Porto; costumes, Jeffrey L. Ullman, Dean H. Reiter.

Note: New Jersey Shakespeare Festival again presented 12 "Monday Night Specials" consisting of dance, music, mime and poetry, July 4-September 19, 1977 and continued its Intern Workshop in the fall.

MILWAUKEE

Milwaukee Repertory Theater Company: Todd Wehr Theater

(Artistic director, John Dillon; managing director, Sara O'Connor)

RICHARD III (44). By William Shakespeare. September 16, 1977. Director, John Dillon. With Richard Cox, Joyce Fideor, Henry

Strozier, Rose Pickering, James Pickering, Daniel Mooney.

In repertory November 4-January 22, 1978 (92):

LONG DAYS JOURNEY INTO NIGHT and AH, WILDERNESS! by Eugene O'Neill. Director, Irene Lewis. With Robert Burr, Regina David, Anthony Heald, Ronald Frazier, Jacqueline Britton, Kristie Thatcher, Rose Pickering.

FRIENDS (44). By Kobo Abe; translated by Donald Keene. January 27, 1978 (American premiere). Director, John Dillon; scenery, Grady Larkins; lighting, R. H. Graham; costumes, Carol Oditz; music; Mark Van Hecke.

Father	Henry Strozier
Mother	Ruth Schudson
Grandmother	Peggy Cowles
Daughters	Penelope Reed, Faith Catlin, Susan Monts
Sons	Tom Blair, Daniel Therriault, Larry Shue
Man	Barry Boys
Man's Fiancee	Linda Loving
Fiancee's brother	Amlin Gray
Building Superintendent	Sirin Devrim Trainer
Policeman	Hench Ellis

One intermission.

HIGH TIME (44). By Frank Cucci. March 10, 1978 (professional premiere). Director, Kenneth Frankel; scenery, Fred Kolouch; lighting, Joseph Tilford; costumes, Rosemary Ingham.

Mama	Geraldine Kay
Marie	Rosemary De Angelis
Gus	Larry Shue
Connie	Daniel Mooney

Time: The present, early November. Place: Paterson, N.J. Act I, Scene 1: Early Wednesday evening. Scene 2: Later that night. Act II, Scene 1: Friday, the following week. Scene 2: Evening, a few days later. Act III: Scene 1: Later that night. Scene 2: The following Saturday morning.

NAMESAKE (44). By Amlin Gray. April 21, 1978 (world premiere). Director, John Dillon; scenery, Stuart Wurtzel; lighting, Spencer Mosse; costumes, Susan Tsu.

Richard	Ronald Frazier
Yolanda	Kristie Thatcher
Mr. Beckersteth	Larry Shue
Leora Hoxie	Carol Morley
Cilla Hoxie	Rose Pickering
Dick Hoxie	Henry Strozier

Act I: The salon of a first-class suite on an ocean liner, afternoon. Act II: The same, immediately afterward.

Milwaukee Repertory Theater: Pabst Theater

A CHRISTMAS CAROL (29). By Charles Dickens; adapted by Nagle Jackson. December 2, 1977. Director/composer, Norman Berman; choreographer, Arthur Faria. With Henry Strozier, Larry Shue, Vicki Childers, George Fehrenback, Michael Thompson, Daniel Mooney, Barry Boys.

Milwaukee Repertory Theater: Court Street Theater

JUST A LITTLE BIT LESS THAN NORMAL (17). By Nigel Baldwin. March 9, 1978 (American premiere). Director, Barry Boys; scenery and lighting, Joseph Tilford; costumes, Marc L. Longlois.

Spud	Daniel Therriault
Lin	Susan Monts
Mum	Ruth Schudson
Dad	Henry Strozier
Jerv	Bruce Somerville
Policeman; Clergyman	Hench Ellis

Danny	Tom Blair

Time: The present. Place: London.

CUSTER (17). By Robert Ingham. March 30, 1978. Director, Sanford Robbins. With Tom Blair, James Pickering, Barry Boys, Susan Monts.

MEDAL OF HONOR RAG (35). By Tom Cole. April 20, 1978. Director, Sharon Ott. With James Pickering, Steven Williams, Daniel Mooney.

Designers: scenery, Fred Kolouch, David Chapman, Stuart Wurtzel, R. H. Graham, Grady Larkins, Valerie Kuehn, Elizabeth Mahrt, Christopher Idoine; lighting, R. H. Graham, Arden Fingerhut, Spencer Mosse, Dennis J. McHugh. Joseph Tilford; costumes, Randy Barcelo, Carol Oditz, Susan Tsu, Rosemary Ingham, Barbara Murray, Elizabeth Covey.

Henry Strozier in *Friends* at Milwaukee Repertory Theater

Note: Following the regular run in 1978, *Ah, Wilderness!* and *Long Day's Journey Into Night*, toured 15 communities in nine states in the upper midwest and west. From December 27, 1977 through January 22, 1978, MRT in association with Artreach Milwaukee, presented *The Portable Play*, a 1940s broadcast like *The Shadow*, to institutions and rehabilitation centers. It was created and directed by Amlin Gray, Sanford Robbins and Jewel Walker. Special sound effects were created by Gregory S. Murphy; music by Rod Pilloud; costumes by Rosemary Ingham; with James Pickering, Susan Monts, Jacqueline Britton, John Mansfield, Kristie Thatcher.

MINNEAPOLIS

The Cricket Theater

(Producing director, William Semans; artistic director, Lou Salerni)

THE TRIP BACK DOWN (20). By John Bishop. October 21, 1977. Director, Lou Salerni. With Richard Hilger, Joe Horvath, Gerald Quimby, Zoaunne LeRoy, William Schoppert, Gretchen Trapp.

RED ROVER, RED ROVER (20). By Oliver Hailey. November 25, 1977 (world premiere). Director, Michael Flanagan; scenery, Barry Robison; lighting, Thomas J. Hamilton; costumes, Christopher Beesley.

Nell	Zoaunne LeRoy
Eddie	Fred Thompson
Joe	James Harris
Harris	Richard Hilger
Leigh	Mari Rovang
Vic	Camille Gifford

Time: The present. Place: A comfortable home in Southern California. One intermission.

THE CLUB (20). By Eve Merriam. December 30, 1977. Director/choreographer, Nicola

Crafts-Foster; music director, Martha Van Cleef; arranger, Alexandra Ivanoff. With Martha Van Cleef; Krista Neumann, Rita Vassallo, Zoaunne LeRoy, Carole Kastigar, Jill Rogosheske, Terri Raynelle.

THE SHADOW BOX (20) By Michael Cristofer. February 3, 1978. Director, Lou Salerni. With Clive Rosengren, Zoaunne LeRoy, John Newcome, Henry J. Jordan, Joe Horvath, Carol Thibeau, Gwen Jackson, Camille Gifford, Helena Power.

INDULGENCES IN THE LOUISVILLE HAREM (20). By John Orlock. March 10, 1978. Director, Lou Salerni; music, Christopher Block; mesmerist song, John Orlock. With Zoaunne LeRoy, Carole Kastigar, Allen Hamilton, Robert Breuler.

AND IF THAT MOCKINGBIRD DON'T SING (20). By William Whitehead; music by David Huffman, Howard Platt, Tony Swartz. April 14, 1978 (world premiere). Director, Davey Marlin-Jones; scenery and lighting, Dick Leerhoff; costumes, Christopher Beesley;

music director, Christopher Bloch.

Coffeemate .... David Harris
Darlene .... Barbara Montgomery
Cassidy .... C. Michael Leopard
Belcher ....Jimmie Wright
Butcherbird ....Robert Breuler
Casey; K.C. ....Zoaunne LeRoy
Earl .... Sedgwick Howard
Hampton ....David Willis
Jenkins ....Joe Horvath
Eddie ....James Wallace
Hopper .... Richard Costigan
Waxahachie .... David Colacci
Buba ....Stephen Schmid
Patrolman .... C. Michael Leopard.
    Time: The present including 1958, 1960, 1968, and 1970. Place: Wofford's Silverdollar Cafe, a truck stop near Hobbs, N. M. One intermission.

STREAMERS (20). By David Rabe. May 19, 1978. Director, Lou Salerni. With William Schoppert, Harley Venton, David Harris, Joe Horvath. James Craven, Robert Breuler, Clive Rosengren.

Designers: scenery, Dick Leerhoff, Barry Robison, Thom Richards, Phillip Billey; lighting, Christopher Beesley, Thomas J. Hamilton, Phillip Billey.

Cricket Theater: Works-In-Progress

DEFICIENT (2). By Michael Chepiga. October 27, 1977. Director, Sean Michael Dowse. MABEL FURLOW by Monroe A. Denton Jr.; THE ASSASSINATION OF THE POPE by Jonathan Billman (2). November 10, 1977. Director, Philip Zarilli. THE MEMOIRS OF THE NEW AMERICAN HEROINE by Xavier Varner, as told to Sim Varner; director, Sean Michael Dowse; PLAY #3, OPUS 1 by Robert Breuler;

director, Gary O'Brien (2). December 8, 1977. SWEETHEARTS (2). By Ted Nameth. January 19, 1978. Directors, Kathleen Perkins, Sean Michael Dowse. THE LAST DEER IN THE FOREST (1). By William Whitehead. April 18, 1978. Director, Tom Hamilton. THE D.B. COOPER PROJECT (2). By John Orlock. May 4, 1978. Director, Sean Michael Dowse. ADAM & SON (1). By Sim Varner. June 9, 1978. Director, Sean Michael Dowse.

The Guthrie Theater Company: Guthrie Theater

(Artistic director, Michael Langham; managing director, Donald Schoenbaum)

SHE STOOPS TO CONQUER (53). By Oliver Goldsmith. June 6, 1977. Director, Michael Langham. With Helen Carey, Richard Russell Ramos, Barbara Bryne, Karen Landry, Peter Michael Goetz, Jeff Chandler, James Hurdle.

A MOON FOR THE MISBEGOTTEN (32). By Eugene O'Neill. June 8, 1977. Director, Nick Havinga. With Sharon Ernster, Peter

Michael Goetz, Peter Aylward, Richard Russell Ramos.

LA RONDE (30). By Arthur Schnitzler. June 22, 1977. Director, Ken Ruta. With Jeff Chandler, Helen Carey, James Hurdle, Cynthia Carle, Roger Kozal, Patricia Fraser, Paul Ballantyne, Maura Shaffer.

CATSPLAY (25). By Istvan Orkeny; adapted

by Clara Gyorgyey. August 3, 1977. Director, Stephen Kanee. With Helen Burns, Mary Hara, Patricia Fraser, Barbara Reid, Michael Laskin, Oliver Cliff.

THE WHITE DEVIL (32). By John Webster. August 24, 1977. Director, Michael Blakemore. With Holly Palance, Peter Michael Goetz, Jeff Chandler, James Hurdle, Roger Kozal, Ken Ruta, Barbara Bryne.

DESIGN FOR LIVING (40). By Noel Coward. October 12, 1977. Director, Michael Langham. With Ken Ruta, Jeff Chandler, Patricia Conolly, Richard Russell Ramos.

A CHRISTMAS CAROL (38). By Charles Dickens; adapted by Barbara Field. November 30, 1977. Director, Jon Cranney; music, Hiram Titus; musical director, Dick Whitbeck. With Jeff Chandler, Jim Sewell, Norah McNellis, Peter Michael Goetz, Oliver Cliff.

PANTAGLEIZE (34). By Michel de Ghelderode; translated by George Hauger; adapted by Barbara Fields. January 18, 1978. Director, Stephen Kanee. With Richard Russell Ramos, Arnold Wilkerson, Peter Michael Goetz, Sharon Ernster, Oliver Cliff.

The Guthrie Theater Company: Guthrie Two

In repertory:
ASHES (22). By David Rudkin. September 14, 1977. Director, Emily Mann. With Karen Landry, James Hurdle, Jack McLaughlin, Maura Shaffer.
NOT I, KRAPP'S LAST TAPE, PLAY (20). By Samuel Beckett. September 17, 1977. Director, Henry Pillsbury. With Guy Paul, Sharon Ernster, Mary Hara.

THE CONVERSION OF AARON WEISS (22). By Mark Medoff. October 13, 1977 (world premiere). Director, J. Ranelli; scenery, William Marshall; lighting, Richard Borgen; costumes, Jack Edwards. With Joel Brooks as Aaron Weiss, and Jack McLaughlin, Patricia Fraser, Sharon Ernster, Robert Breuler, Cynthia Carle, Barbara Reid, Don R. Fallbeck,

Don Amendolia, James Hartman, James Noah, Maura Shaffer, James Stephen Sweeney, Frank S. Scott, Peter Aylward, Karen Landry.
   A 1960s activist trying to cope with mainstream life in the 1970s.

DEAR LIAR (24). By Jerome Kilty; adapted from the correspondence of George Bernard Shaw and Mrs. Patrick Campbell. December 1, 1977. Director, Mark Lamos. With Ken Ruta, Patricia Conolly.

REUNION (12). By David Mamet. January 19, 1978. Director, Emily Mann. With Cynthia Carle, Jack McLaughlin.

Designers: Ralph Funicello, John Conklin, John Ferguson, Pat Robertson, Annena Stubbs, Jack Barkla, William Marshall, Maurice Palinski, Barry Robison; lighting, Duane Schuler, Robert Bye; costumes, Lewis Brown, Annena Stubbs, Jack Edwards.

Note: Following the end of the Guthrie season in February 1978, *A Moon for the Misbegotten* toured the midwest for five weeks.

MONTCLAIR, N.J.

The Whole Theater Company

(Managing director, Karen Ann Shafer)

MOTHER COURAGE AND HER CHILDREN (20). By Bertolt Brecht; translation by Eric Bentley; music by Paul Dessau. October 21, 1977. Directors, W. T. Martin and Arnold Mittelman. With Olympia Dukakis, Jessica Allen, Jason Bosseau, Gerald Fierst, Tom Brennan, Apollo R. Dukakis, Remi Barclay.

THE SEDUCTION, from *The Good Doctor* by Neil Simon; adapted from Anton Chekhov; A MARRIAGE PROPOSAL by Anton Chekhov, translated by Theodore Hoffman; THE BRUTE by Anton Chekhov; translated by Eric Bentley (20). December 9, 1977. Director, Arnold Mittelman; choreographer, Gila Zalon. With Apollo Dukakis, W. T. Martin,

Judith Delgado, Jim Hillgartner, Glenna Peters. Dancers: George Bohn, Kathy Kroll, Shirley Oakes.

FATHER'S DAY (20). By Oliver Hailey. January 27, 1978. Director, Bernard Hiatt. With Maggie Abeckerly, Jessica Allen, Judith L'Heureux, Gerald Fierst, James Rebhorn, Apollo Dukakis.

AND MISS REARDON DRINKS A LITTLE (20). By Paul Zindel. March 17, 1978.

Directors, Bernard Hiatt and Louis Zorich. With Maggie Abeckerly, Marjorie Fierst, Georgia Hester, Carol Rosenfeld, Daniel Pollack.

ONE FLEW OVER THE CUCKOO'S NEST (20). By Dale Wasserman; adapted from Ken Kesey's novel. May 3, 1978. Director, Olympia Dukakis. With Tom Brennan, Marjorie Fierst, Jessica Allen, Apollo Dukakis, Gerald Fierst, Jason Bosseau, W. T. Martin, Stefan Peters, Ernie Schenk.

Designers: scenery, Raul Dorphley, Raymond C. Recht, Tony Negron; lighting, Marshall Spiller; costumes, Veronica Dersler, Sigrid Insull. Mary-Margaret Bergamini-Tobias.

NEW HAVEN

Long Wharf Theater

(Artistic Director, Arvin Brown; executive director, M. Edgar Rosenblum)

HOBSON'S CHOICE (33). By Harold Brighouse. October 13, 1977. Director, Arvin Brown. With Joyce Ebert, William Swetland, Frank Converse, Laurie Kennedy, Susan Sharkey, Richard Backus.

THE LUNCH GIRLS (33). By Leigh Curran. November 17, 1977 (world premiere). Director, Arvin Brown; scenery, David Jenkins; lighting, Ronald Wallace; costumes, Bill Walker.
Clare .... Pamela Payton-Wright
Kate .... Leigh Curran
Charlene .... Suzanne Lederer
Danusha .... Carol Androsky
Vicky .... Phyllis Somerville
Rhonda .... Susan Sharkey
Edie .... Carol Williard
Chef .... Stephen D. Newman
Henri .... Philip Polito
Jesus .... Octavio Ciano
    Time: October, 1969. Place: A men's key club in New York City. Act I: The waitresses' locker-room. Act II: The kitchen. Act III: The locker room.

THE RECRUITING OFFICER (33). By George Farquhar. December 29, 1977. Director, Davey Marlin-Jones. With John Horton, John Tillinger, Katherine McGrath, Francesca James, Helena Carroll, Max Wright, Emery Battis.

SPOKESONG (33). By Stewart Parker; music by Jimmy Kennedy. February 2, 1978 (American premiere). Director, Kenneth Frankel; scenery, Marjorie Kellogg; lighting,

Ronald Wallace; costumes, Bill Walker; musical director, Thomas Fay; cycle coach, Jon Jenack.
Trick Cyclist .... Joseph Maher
Frank .... John Lithgow
Daisy .... Virginia Vestoff
Francis .... Josef Sommer
Kitty .... Maria Tucci
Julian .... John Horton.
    Time: The early 1970s and the 80 years preceeding them. Place: A bicycle shop in Belfast, Northern Ireland. One intermission.

THE MOON OF THE CARIBBEES; IN THE ZONE; BOUND EAST FOR CARDIFF: THE LONG VOYAGE HOME (33). By Eugene O'Neill. March 9, 1978. Director, Edward Payson Call. With Robert Lansing, David Clennon, Emery Battis, Peter Iacangelo, Beeson Carroll, Frederick Coffin, Owen Hollander, Lance Davis, Bob Harper, William Swetland, William Newman, Richard Jamieson, Dick Sollenberger, Edwin J. McDonough, Victor Argo, Carol Jean Lewis, C.C.H. Pounder, Shirley Martelly, Helen Chivas Hatten, le Clanche du Rand, Marlena Lustik, Nora Chester.

THE PHILADELPHIA STORY (33). By Philip Barry. April 13, 1978. Director, Arvin Brown. With Blair Brown, Frank Converse, Douglas Stender, George Hearn, Emery Battis, William Swetland, Jan Miner.

MACBETH (33). By William Shakespeare. May 18, 1978. Director, Edward Gilbert. With

Charles Cioffi, Joyce Ebert, Emery Battis, William Newman, Michael Shannon, Donna Haley, Julie Follansbee, Cynthia Mason, Myra Carter.

Long Wharf Theater: Stage II

TWO BROTHERS (19). By Conrad Bromberg. March 3, 1978 (world premiere). Director, Arvin Brown; scenery, Steven Rubin; lighting, Ronald Wallace; costumes, Mary Strieff.

Joseph Morris .... Tony Musante
Mrs. Morris .... Beverly May
David .... David Spielberg
Agnes .... Joyce Ebert
Sylvia .... Barbara Eda-Young
Lizzie .... Andrea Gurwitt
Dr. Markle .... James Noble

Penny .... Anna Levine
Dr. Horlick .... John Tillinger
Miss Cruz .... Patricia Triana
Time: 1975. Place: Los Angeles. One intermission.

STARTING HERE, STARTING NOW (16). Lyrics by Richard Maltby Jr; music by David Shire. March 28, 1978. Director, Patrick Adiarte. With Annie McGreevey, Eron Tabor, Laura Waterbury.

Designers: scenery, David Jenkins, John Conklin, John Jensen, Mark Louis Negin, Sally Cunningham; lighting Jamie Gallagher, Ronald Wallace; costumes, Bill Walker, John Conklin, Linda Fisher, Mark Louis Negin, Rebecca Carroll.

Long Wharf Theater: Monday Night New Play Readings

(Literary manager/series director, John Tillinger; workshop productions, one performance each)

FORMER THINGS by Peter John Bailey. April 3, 1978. WANT by Arthur Morey. April 24, 1978. FREE FIRE ZONE by Jascha Kessler. May 1, 1978. BUSY BEE GOOD FOOD ALL NIGHT DELICIOUS and

BORDERS by Charles Eastman. May 8, 1978. JO ANNE!!! by Ed Bullins. June 2, 1978. ALMS FOR THE MIDDLE CLASS by Stuart Hample. June 12, 1978.

Note: A special Christmas show, consisting of stories, music and poems appropriate to the season, was presented December 19-24, 1977. Performers who compiled and put together the program were Eileen Atkins, Victor Garber, Edward Herrmann, Joan Moore, John Tillinger, William Swetland. The Access Theater Company, Long Wharf Theater's community outreach program for children and adults, presented Folktales, Tales From the Brothers Grimm and an Improvisational Workshop performance, October 1977-May 1978 on the Mainstage, Stage II, on tour at schools and community facilites throughout the northeast and at training and rehabilitation facilities in the New Haven area. The Company comprised Terrence Sherman, artistic director; Kelley O'Rourke, coordinator; with Terry Griess, Barbara MacKenzie, James Neissen and Bari K. Willerford.

Yale Repertory Theater

(Director, Robert Brustein)

THE GHOST SONATA (32). By August Strindberg; translated by Evert Sprinchorn. September 30, 1977. Director, Andrei Serban. With Max Wright, Stephen Rowe, Patrizia Norcia, Mary Van Dyke, Douglas Simes, Brenda Currin.

REUNION and DARK PONY (16). By David Mamet. October 14, 1977 (world premiere). Director, Walt Jones.

Reunion
Bernie Cary .... Michael Higgins
Carol Mindler .... Lindsay Crouse
Time: Sunday afternoon in early March, 1973. Place: Bernie's apartment.
Dark Pony
Father .... Michael Higgins
Daughter .... Lindsay Crouse
Time: Night. Place: An autombile. No intermission between plays. (See review in the introduction to this section.)

TERRA NOVA (24). By Ted Nally. November 18, 1977 (world premiere). Director, Travis S. Preston; scenery and costumes, Jess Goldstein; lighting, Robert Jared; projections, William B. Warfel.

Scott .... Arthur Hill
Amundsen .... Michael Higgins
Bowers .... Jeremy Geidt
Oates .... Michael Gross
Wilson .... Max Wright
Evans .... Stephen Rose
Kathleen .... Lindsay Crouse
Time: 1912. One intermission.

THE FLYING DOCTOR; THE FORCED MARRIAGE; SGANARELLE; A DUMB SHOW, based on *The Doctor in Spite of Himself* (29). By Molière; translated by Albert Bermel. January 20, 1978. Director, Andrei Serban. With Mark Linn Baker, Norma Brustein, Peter Crombie, Joyce Fideor, David Marshall Grant, Jeremy Geidt, Michael Gross, Richard Grusin, Jonathan Marks, Patrizia Norcia, Elizabeth Norment, Marianne Owen, William Roberts, Eugene Troobnick, Jonathan Walker.

MAN IS MAN (23). By Bertolt Brecht and Elisabeth Hauptmann; translated by Steve Gooch. February 17, 1978. Director, Ron Daniels; music, William Bolcom. With Estelle Parsons, Joe Grifasi, John Shea, John Seitz, Patrizia Norcia, Timothy O'Hagan, Richard Grusin, Michael Gross, Jeremy Geidt.

WINGS (28). By Arthur Kopit. March 3, 1978 (world premiere). Director, John Madden; scenery, Andrew Jackness; lighting, Tom Schraeder; costumes, Jeanne Button; music, Herb Pilhofer.

Emily Stilson .... Constance Cummings
Amy .... Marianne Owen
Doctors .... Geoffrey Pierson, Roy Steinberg

Nurses ...... Caris Corfman, Carol Ostrow
Billy .... Richard Grusin
Mr. Brownstein .... Ira Bernstein
Mrs. Timmins .... Betty Pelzer
No intermission. (See review in the introduction to this section.)

THE WILD DUCK (24). By Henrik Ibsen; translated by Michael Meyer. April 7, 1978. Director, Robert Brustein. With Shepperd Strudwick, Christopher Walken, Jeremy Geidt, Eugene Troobnick, Bruce A. Siddons, Marianne Owen, Blanche Baker, Lee Richardson, William Roberts.

Special Production:
THE 1940'S RADIO HOUR (16). Written and directed by Walt Jones. December 28, 1977 (World premiere). Designer, Nancy Thun; lighting, Robert Heller; music arranger/director, Gary Fagin; vocals arranger/director, Paul Schierhorn; choreographers, Wesley Fata, Joe Grifasi, Rebecca Nelson, Eric Elice, Caris Corfman.

Biff Baker .... John Doolittle
Sammy Bryant .... Eric Elice
Johnny Cantone .... Stephen Rowe
Clifton Fediman .... Walt Jones
Buddy Gibson .... Richard Bey
Mimi LaRoche .... Rebecca Nelson
Connie Miller .... Caris Corfman
Natalia Navarro .... Shaine Marinson
Babs Ritchie .... Joe Grifasi
Evelyn Vaughn .... Nancy Mayans
Skip Willis .... Tom Derrah
Pop .... James Haverly
Grip .... H. Lloyd Carbaugh
Best Boy .... Richard Houpert
With the Zoot Doubleman Orchestra.
Time: December 28, 1942-January 14, 1943. Place: The Hotel Astor's Algonquin Room, New York City.

Designers: scenery, Michael H. Yeargan, Kate Edmunds, Jess Goldstein, Nancy Thun, Jeanne Button; lighting, Thomas Skelton, William Conners, Robert Jared, James H. Gage, William B. Warfel; costumes, Dunya Ramicova, Kate Edmunds, Jess Goldstein.

Note: Yale Repertory Theater and School of Drama continued to sponsor Yale Cabaret, playwrights workshops, Sunday series of new play readings, as well as a student repertory series with students, faculty and members of the professional company, all of which were open to the public. Plays given at the Cabaret, October 1977-May 1978 included: *Big Mother* by Charles Dizenzo, *Wednesday Sharp* by Robert Auletta, *Dentity Crisis* by Christopher Durang, *When Dinah Shore Ruled the Earth* by Christopher Durang and Wendy Wasserstein. The Sunday Series workshop readings presented *Trade-Offs* by Lonnie Carter, *Farmyard* by Franz Xaver Kroetz, adapted and directed by Jack Gelber, *Death Comes to Us All, Mary Agnes* by Christopher Durang, *From the Memoirs of Pontius Pilate* by Eric Bentley, *We're on the One Road* by Philomena Muinzer, October 30, 1977-May 7, 1978. The Yale School of Drama series included new plays, *Doubt and Resolution* by Paavo Hall director, Bill DeLuca; *The Complete Works* by Robert Gulack; director, Katherine Mendeloff; *Pas de Deux* by James Kuslan, director, Christopher J. Markle; *Off Season Rates* by Michael Stephens, director, Randolph Foerster; *Heinz* by Allan Havis, director, Charles Cowing; *3 Unnatural Acts* by Dick D. Zigun (all workshop productions) and Sam Shepard's *Mad Dog Blues* directed by Andrei Serban which was given 4 performances at the Fort Nathan Hale Beach.

PHILADELPHIA

Philadelphia Drama Guild: Walnut Street Theater — Mainstage

(Artistic director, Douglas Seale; managing director, James B. Freydberg)

THE SHOW-OFF (23). By George Kelly. November 2, 1977. Director, Michael Montel. With David Leary, Betty Leighton, Ellen Tovatt, Joseph Costa, Heather MacDonald.

TRAVESTIES (23). By Tom Stoppard. November 30, 1977. Director, Douglas Seale. With Paxton Whitehead, Edward Atienza, Donald Ewer, David Rounds, Domini Blythe, Valerie Von Volz, Louise Troy, Douglas Wing.

SAINT JOAN (23). By George Bernard Shaw. January 4, 1978. Director, Douglas Seale. With Domini Blythe, James Maxwell, Douglas

Wing, David Rounds, Tony van Bridge, Geddeth Smith, Douglas Seale.

HOBSON'S CHOICE (23). By Harold Brighouse. February 1, 1978. Director, Brian Murray. With Tony van Bridge, Ellen Tovatt, Louise Troy, Geddeth Smith, David Rounds.

UNCLE VANYA (23). By Anton Chekhov; translated by William Stancil. March 1, 1978 Director, Douglas Seale. With David Rounds, Robert Murch, Jack Gwillim, Louise Troy, Sherry Steiner, Donald Ewer, Tarina Lewis.

Philadelphia Drama Guild: Second Stage — Theater 5

G. K. CHESTERTON (6). Compiled and edited by Tony van Bridge from the writings of G. K. Chesterton. January 9, 1978. With Tony van Bridge.

STARTING HERE, STARTING NOW (23).

By Richard Maltby Jr. and David Shire. January 17, 1978. Director, Richard Maltby Jr.; musical direction, Manford Abrahamson. With Loni Ackerman, Margery Cohen, Harvey Evans.

Designers: scenery, John Kasarda; lighting, Spencer Mosse; costumes, Kristina Watson, David Murin.

PITTSBURGH

Pittsburgh Public Theater: Mainstage — Allegheny Theater.

(General director, Ben Shaktman)

FATHER'S DAY (43). By Oliver Hailey. September 28, 1977. Director, Michael Flanagan. With Ivar Brogger, Elaine Kerr, Sharon Laughlin, Monica Merryman, Robert Murch, David Snell.

YOU NEVER CAN TELL (34). By George Bernard Shaw. November 9, 1977. Director, John Going. With Robert Blackburn, Ivar Brogger, Richard Dix, Avril Gentles, Gun-Marie Nilsson, Erika Petersen, John Seidman.

BALYASNIKOV (43). By Aleksei Arbuzov; translated by Michael Henry Heim; adapted by Ben Shaktman. December 21, 1977 (premiere of new adaptation). Director, Ben Shaktman; scenery and costumes, Henry Heymann; lighting, Bennet Averyt.

Fyodor Balyasnikov ...... Joseph Wiseman
Khristofor Blokhin ....I. M. Hobson
Kuzma Balyasnikov .... John Abajian
Man from Gdov ....William Rhys
Viktoria Nikolaevna .... Wanda Bimson

Lev Hartwig .... John Seidman
    Time: Late 1960's. Place: Studio and apart-
ment of Fedya Balyasnikov in the
Bohemian/artist section of Moscow called the
Arbat. Act I, Scene 1: A late morning in early
fall. Scene 2: Late evening of the same day.
Scene 3: A week later. Act II, Scene 1: Late
afternoon the next day. Scene 2: Ten days later.
Scene 3: A few days later.

In repertory:
SLOW DANCE ON THE KILLING
GROUND (21). By William Hanley. February
1, 1978. MEDAL OF HONOR RAG (15). By
Tom Cole. February 3, 1978. Director, Terry
Schreiber. With Jane Galloway, Damien
Leake, Robert Nichols, Harry O'Toole.

Designers: scenery, Fred Kolouch, John Lee Beatty, Virginia Dancy, Elmon Webb, Karl Eigsti;
lighting, Fred Kolouch, Dennis Parichy, Bennet Averyt; costumes, Laura Crow, David Toser.

Pittsburgh Public Theater: New Play Development Program

(Plays in progress, two performances each)

AND FURTHERMORE by Oliver Hailey.
October 10, 1977. Director, Michael Flanagan.
With Ginger Bongle, Sharon Laughlin, David
Snell, Monica Merryman, Robert Murch.
THE SEMINARY MURDER by David Reid.
November 21, 1977. Director, Ike Schambelan.

With Robert Blackburn, Ivar Brogger, John
Seidman, Richard Dix. THE FALL. Adapted
and performed by Daniel Nagrin from the
novel by Albert Camus; translation, Justin
O'Brien. February 13, 1978.

PORTSMOUTH, N.H.

Theater By The Sea: Ceres Theater

(Producing director, Jon Kimbell; resident
director, Russell Treyz)

SLEUTH (45). By Anthony Shaffer.
September 29, 1977. Director, Miriam Fond.
With Roby Brown, John K. Carroll.

JUBALAY (45). Book and lyrics by Merve
Campone; music by Patrick Rose. November
10, 1977 (U. S. premiere). Director, Russell
Treyz; musical director, John Clifton; scenery,
John Shaffner; lighting, Ned Hallick;
costumes, Varel McComb. With Sydney
Anderson, D. Michael Heath, Michael
Maurice, Robert Molnar (as Old Zip), Donna
Pelc.
    Musical Numbers — Act I: "Share With
You," "Jubalay," "The Last Man," "Eighty-
Seven Cents," *"Bring Back Swing,"
**"Yesterday's Lover," "Oh God, I'm Thir-
ty," "The Sailor," "What Am I Bid?", "Street
Music," "Senator Bach," "Ready or Not,"
"C.N.R.," "Wailing Wall." Act II: "Peace
Will Come Again," "Opiate for the Masses,"
"The Guitarist," *"La Piece Bien Faite,"
"Dewey and Sal," "Remember Me," "Old
Jocks," "La Belle Province," "The Anarchist,"
"Lullaby," "20th Century."

*Lyrics by E. Henderson. **Lyrics by D.
Berwick. One intermission.

MY THREE ANGELS (45). By Sam and
Bella Spewack; based on Albert Husson's *La
Cuisine Des Anges*. December 22, 1977. Direc-
tor, Alfred Gingold. With James Ross Smith,
Ginny Russell, Darcy Crandall, Nancy Walton
Fenn, Tom Celli, Frederic Major, Edward
Trotta.

THE SUNSHINE BOYS (45). By Neil Simon.
February 2, 1978. Director, Thomas Lee
Sinclair. With Sy Travers, Tom Celli, Bill
Farley, Thomas Reardon.

THE SHADOW BOX (45). By Michael
Cristofer. March 16, 1978. Director, Alfred
Gingold. With Thomas Reardon, Frederic
Major, Jake Elwell, Helen Aurbach, Tom
Celli, Robert Lowry, Holly Barron, Stephanie
Voss, Nancy Walton Fenn.

THE GLASS MENAGERIE (45). By
Tennessee Williams. April 27, 1978. Director,
Russell Treyz. With Benay Venuta, Chet
Carlin, Alice Elliott, Robert Lowry.

Marilyn Chris and Herschel Bernardi in *The Confirmation* at the McCarter Theater

Designers: scenery, James E. Carroccio, Leslie E. Rollins, Larry Fulton; lighting, Daniel Raymond; costumes, Varel McComb, Kathie Iannicelli.

Note: Theater By The Sea also presents a season at the open amphitheater at Prescott Park during July and August.

PRINCETON, N.J.

McCarter Theater Company: McCarter Theater

(Producing director, Michael Kahn)

THE CONFIRMATION (17). By Howard Ashman. October 6, 1977 (world premiere). Director, Kenneth Frankel; scenery, Marjorie Kellogg; lighting, Marc B. Weiss; costumes, Jennifer Von Mayrhauser.

Sherrie Polen	Marilyn Chris
Rachel Polen	Tara King
Ed Abrams	Alan Manson
Sidney Polen	Robert Rissel
Arnold Polen	Herschel Bernardi
Flo	Rosanna Carter
Harry	Phillip Lindsay
Mrs. Priscilla Fowlkes	Minnie Gentry
Rozzi Bender	Mara Mellin

Act I, Scene 1: Shortly after 4 o'clock, one afternoon in late spring, 1962. Scene 2: That evening. Act II, Scene 1: Early the following evening. Scene 2: Shortly before midnight.

THE UTTER GLORY OF MORRISSEY HALL (17). By Clark Gesner. November 3, 1977. Director, Nagle Jackson; scenery and lighting, Howard Bay; costumes, David Graden; musical director, Jay Blackton; choreographer, Michael Maurer. With Patricia Falkenhain, Jane Rose, Margaret Hilton, Lois De Banzie, Jeffrey Jones, Robert Henderson, Daniel Arden.

THE HAPPY JOURNEY TO TRENTON AND CAMDEN; QUEENS OF FRANCE; THE LONG CHRISTMAS DINNER (17). By Thornton Wilder. December 1, 1977. Director, Michael Kahn; scenery, Raymond Recht; lighting, Richard Nelson; costumes, Jane Greenwood. With Carolyn Coates, Alice Drummond, Diane Franklin, Nicholas Kepros, Karl Light, James Noble, Ricky Paul, Jobeth Williams.

THE TORCH-BEARERS (17). By George Kelly. January 19, 1978. Director, Michael Kahn, scenery, Ed Wittstein; lighting, John

McLain; costumes, Jane Greenwood. With Peggy Cass, Tovah Feldshuh, Farley Granger, Dina Merrill, Martha Greenhouse.

TOYS IN THE ATTIC (17). By Lillian Hellman. March 12, 1978. Director, Pat Hingle; scenery, Christopher Nowak; lighting, John McLain; costumes, Bob Wojewodski. With Catherine Byers, Stanja Lowe, Deborah Offner, David Selby.

MUCH ADO ABOUT NOTHING (17). By William Shakespeare. March 30, 1978. Director, William Woodman; scenery, Herbert Senn and Helen Pond; lighting, Richard Nelson; costumes, Virgil C. Johnson (scenery, properties and costumes provided by the Goodman Theater). With Laura Esterman, Heather MacDonald, Nicholas Surovy, Kenneth Marshall, William Roerick, Norman Snow, Merwin Goldsmith.

McCarter Theater Company: Playwrights-at-McCarter — Princeton University Art Museum

(Project director, Ben Levit; literary advisor, Michael Earley; staged readings of new plays in progress, 1 performance each)

WHEN THE STARS BEGIN TO FALL by Lloyd Gold. February 6. 1978. DREAMS AND BEASTS, *an American Humoresque* by Richard Cook. February 20, 1978. THE BODY PARTS OF MARGARET FULLER by E.M. Broner. March 13, 1978. THE EXTRA-SPECIALS by J.J. Foster. March 27, 1978. PUT THEM ALL TOGETHER by Anne Commire. April 10, 1978. BRIGHT WINGS by Lloyd Gold. April 24, 1978.

PROVIDENCE, R. I.

Trinity Square Repertory Company: Lederer Theater — Upstairs

Producer-director, Adrian Hall)

ETHAN FROME (35). By Edith Wharton; dramatization by Owen and Donald Davis. October 11, 1977. Director, Adrian Hall. With Richard Jenkins, Margo Skinner, David Kennett, William Damkoehler, Barbara Orson.

ROSMERSHOLM (32). By Henrik Ibsen; new adaptation by Adrian Hall and Richard Cumming. November 25, 1977. Director, Adrian Hall. With Richard Kneeland, Margo Skinner, George Martin, Russell Gold.

A CHRISTMAS CAROL (20). By Charles Dickens; adaptation by Adrian Hall and Richard Cumming. December 20, 1977. Director, Adrian Hall; original music and lyrics by Richard Cumming; choreography, Sharon

Jenkins. With Richard Kneeland, George Martin, Daniel Von Bargen, Robert Black, Howard London, David Kennett, William Damkoehler, Barbara Orson, David Flaxman/Arthur H. Roberts.

EQUUS (47). By Peter Shaffer. February 14, 1978. Director, Larry Arrick. With Richard Kneeland, Kevin Sessums, Barbara Meek, Barbara Orson, Russell Gold, Bonnie Sacks, Daniel Von Bargen.

AS YOU LIKE IT (22). By William Shakespeare. February 27, 1978. Director, Ann McBey Brebner. With Robert Black, Margo Skinner, Nancy Nichols, Ken Bradford.

Trinity Square Repertory Company: Lederer Theater — Downstairs

THE SHOW-OFF (44). By George Kelly. October 18, 1977. Director, George Martin. With Robert Black, Anne Gerety, George Martin, Bonnie Sacks, Daniel Von Bargen.

BOESMAN AND LENA (24). By Athol Fugard. December 6, 1977. Director, Larry Arrick. With Zakes Mokae, Barbara Meek, Ricardo Pitts-Wiley.

VANITIES (44). By Jack Heifner. January 3, 1978. Director, William Radka. With Melanie Jones, Amy Van Nostrand, Cynthia Strickland.

AMERICAN BUFFALO (30). By David Mamet. February 21, 1978. Director, George

Martin. With Norman Smith, Peter Gerety, Richard Jenkins.

SEDUCED (35). By Sam Shepard. April 25, 1978 (world premiere). Director, Adrian Hall; scenery and lighting, Eugene Lee; costumes, James Berton Harris; properties, Thomas Waldon; production stage manager, William Radka.

Henry Malcolm Hackmore ..George Martin
Raul ....Richard Jenkins
The Dollies:
    Luna .... Margo Skinner
    Miami .... Cynthia Wells
    Place: a hotel room — anesthetized impersonal plastic. (See review in the introduction to this section.)

Designers: scenery, Eugene Lee, Robert D. Soule; lighting, Eugene Lee, Sean Kevin Keating, John F. Custer; costumes, Ann Morrell, Betsey Potter, James Berton Harris.

Note: Trinity Square's *Project Discovery,* a theater experience program offered to high school students, presented *Rosmersholm.*

ROCHESTER, MICHIGAN

Oakland University Professional Theater Program: Meadow Brook Theater

(General director, Terence Kilburn; assistant, Frank F. Bollinger)

SHE STOOPS TO CONQUER (29). By Oliver Goldsmith. September 29, 1977. Director, John Ulmer. With Jeanne Arnold, Larry Gates, Elizabeth Horowitz, Lynn Ann Leveridge, Richard Pilcher, Tom Spackman, Eric Tavaris.

PICNIC (29). By William Inge. October 27, 1977. Director, Terence Kilburn. With Eric Tull, Jane Badler, Bella Jarrett, Michel Cullen.

TABLE MANNERS (29). By Alan Ayckbourn. November 24, 1977. Director, John Ulmer. With Marion Brasch, Michel Cullen, Mary Gallagher, Peter McRobbie, Barbara Sohmers, Eric Tavaris.

THE CORN IS GREEN (29). By Emlyn Williams. December 29, 1977. Director, Charles Nolte. With Tom Spackman, Jeanne Arnold, Marianne Muellerleile, Patricia Reilly, Leo Leyden.

THE TEMPEST (29). By William Shakespeare. January 26, 1978. Director,

Terence Kilburn. With G. Wood, Michel Cullen, Ginni Ness, Gilbert Cole, Richard Hilger, Louis Edmonds, Michael Hendricks, Michael Rothhaar.

THE RUNNER STUMBLES (29). By Milan Stitt. February 23, 1978. Director, Charles Nolte. With Jeffrey McLaughlin, Charlotte Bova, William Le Massena, Cheryl Giannini, Michel Cullen, Peter McRobbie.

THE MALE ANIMAL (29). By James Thurber and Elliott Nugent. March 23, 1978. Director, Terence Kilburn. With Edgar Meyer, Priscilla Morrill, Harold Roe, Thom Bray, William Le Massena, Marianne Muellerleile

COLE (37). Devised by Benny Green and Alan Strachan; based on the words and music of Cole Porter. April 20, 1978. Director-choreographer, John Sharpe; musical director, Jim Hohmeyer. With Marianne Challis, Connie Coit, Nancy Grahn, Henry J. Jordan, Michele Mullen, Frank Root, Richard Walker, Kevin Wilson.

Designers: scenery, Peter Hicks, Donald Beckman, Larry A. Reed, C. Lance Brockman, Doug Wright; lighting, Nancy Thompson, Fred Fonner, Jean A. Montgomery, Larry A. Reed; costumes, Mary Lynn Bonnell.

Note: Following the regular run of *The Male Animal,* The Meadow Brook Theater gave 20 performances of the production in 16 communities in Michigan, from April 21 to May 13, 1978.

ROCHESTER, N.Y.

GeVa Theater

(Artistic director, Gideon Y. Schein; managing director, Jessica L. Andrews).

THE FRONT PAGE (20). By Ben Hecht and Charles MacArthur. October 12, 1977. Director, Gideon Y. Schein. With Ron Siebert, Ben Kapen, Lance Davis, Arva Holt, Shirley Brown Bays, Sonya Raimi.

DEATH OF A SALESMAN (20). By Arthur Miller. November 9, 1977. Director, Gideon Y. Schein. With James L. Lawless, Helen Harrelson, David Chandler, William (Chip) Brenner, Cyril Mallett, Frank Borgman.

THE FARCE OF SCAPIN (24). By Molière. December 7, 1977. Director, Nancy Rhodes. With Lance Davis, Michael John McGann, Joe Regalbuto, Michelle Giannini, Ryan Hilliard, Win Atkins, Martha Kearns, Cyril Mallett.

THE CARETAKER (18). By Harold Pinter. January 25, 1978. Director, Gideon Y. Schein. With David Chandler, Roger Forbes, Cyril Mallett.

A RAISIN IN THE SUN (19). By Lorraine Hansberry. February 22, 1978. Director, Woodie King Jr. With Constance Thomas, Minnie Gentry, Samuel L. Jackson, Jessie Saunders, David Sutton, Reuben Green, Thommi Blackwell, Cyril Mallett, David Shakes.

VANITIES (18). By Jack Heifner. March 22, 1978. Director, Gideon Y. Schein. With Linda Swenson, Lucy Holmes, Cindy Cooper.

Designers: scenery, Seth Price, Danica Eskind, C. Richard Mills, Karen Schulz, Richard H. Isackes; lighting, Seth Price; costumes, Danica Eskind, Linda Figdor, Edna Watson.

Note: GeVa On Tour, a lunchtime theater project (play plus box lunch), presented the following productions, between October 18, 1977 and June 30, 1978, Tuesdays through Thursdays at 12:15 p.m.: *The Weak Spot* by George Kelly, *The Bald Soprano* by Eugene Ionesco, *The Russian Hut* by Larry Carr (based on Slavic folk tales), *Infancy* and *The Happy Journey to Trenton and Camden* by Thornton Wilder, *A Pair of Lunatics* by W. R. Walkes, *Box and Cox* by John Madison Morton, *Star Quality* by William Morris and Mark Long. Director, Larry Carr; designers, Philipp Jung, Caroline Lentz, Marcia E. Cohen, Seth Price, Ian O'Connor, Sandy Struth, Linda Vigdor; Company: Christopher Fazel, Molly DePree, Sharon James, Frederick Nuernberg, Naomi Kay, S. Jay Rankin, Tony Pasqualini; stage manager, Marcy Gamzon.

SAN DIEGO, CALIF.

Old Globe Theater: San Diego National Shakespeare Festival

(Producing director, Craig Noel)

In repertory, May 31–September 11, 1977
HAMLET (49). By William Shakespeare. Director, Jack O'Brien. With Mark Lamos, Mary-Joan Negro, Maureen Anderman, Eric Christmas, Richard Kneeland, Norman Snow. THE TAMING OF THE SHREW (46). By William Shakespeare. Director, Laird Williamson. With Maureen Anderman, Daniel J.

Travanti, Mary-Joan Negro, John H. Napierala, Richard S. Fullerton. TIMON OF ATHENS (32). By William Shakespeare. Director, Eric Christmas. With Richard Kneeland, Daniel J. Travanti, Byron Jennings, John McMurtry, Anne Matthews, Deborah Taylor, Dale Raoul.

Old Globe Theater: Regular Season

THE LAST OF THE MARX BROTHERS WRITERS (35). By Louis Phillips. October 4, 1977 (professional premiere). Director, Craig Noel; scenery, Peggy Kellner; lighting, Stephen Storer; costumes, Donna Couchman.

Jimmy Bryce .... Victor Buono
Julius Dumont .... Sandy McCallum
Alice Upjohn MacLoy ......Carole Marget
Bellhop .... Lary Ohlson
Frank Clandenburg .... Edwin L. Kotula
Voice from the Whirlwind .... Himself
Voice on Loudspeaker ..... Deborah Taylor
Time: The present. Place: A room in a run-down hotel in Los Angeles. Act I: Afternoon. Act II, Scene 1: Immediately following. Scene 2: Immediately following.

TOO TRUE TO BE GOOD (35). By George Bernard Shaw. November 15, 1977. Director, Mark Lamos. With Deborah Taylor, Helen Wilson, George A. Noe Jr., Valerie Snyder, Kelsey Grammer, John H. Napierala, Paul Eggington.

SLEUTH (35). By Anthony Shaffer. January 3, 1978. Director, Sandy McCallum. With Mack Owen, Tom McCorry, Robert Williams.

THE SUNSHINE BOYS (29). By Neil Simon. February 14, 1978. Director, Jack Tygett. With Patrick J. Kearns, Al Sklar, Grant Goulet.

THE LION IN WINTER (35). By James Goldman. March 28, 1978. Director, Ken Ruta. With Helen Marquardt, Martin Gerrish, Nancy C. Thornes, Scott William Kinney, James Fagerle, Sean Sullivan, Mark Kincaid.

Old Globe Theater: Carter Center Stage

CHARLEY'S AUNT (88). By Brandon Thomas. June 21, 1977. Director, Wayne Bryan. With Mark Pinter, Aaron Fletcher, Michael Byers, Chris Shaffer, Edith Taylor Hunter, Lindy A. Nisbet, Hugh Monahan.

THAT CHAMPIONSHIP SEASON (35). By Jason Miller. September 20, 1977. Director, Arthur Wagner. With Mark Yavorsky, Jack Krill, J. Stanley Nesnow, Allan Singer, Sheldon Gero.

EXIT THE KING (35). By Eugene Ionesco; translated by Donald Watson. November 1, 1977. Director, Kevin Tighe. With Neil Flanagan, Bette Laws, M. Sue Hiatt, Anne Matthews, S. James Goffard, Richard Bradshaw.

THE SEA GULL (35). By Anton Chekov; translated by Stark Young. January 17, 1978. Director, Craig Noel. With Gail Baldi Mackler, Allan McKenzie, Deborah Taylor, Stephen Lynewood Brown, John H. Napierala, Kathy Logan.

OLD TIMES (35). By Harold Pinter. February 28, 1978. Director, Jack Bender. With Denis Arndt, Kandis Chappell, Julia Brandley Frampton.

LOOT (35). By Joe Orton. April 11, 1978. Director, Eric Christmas. With Mack Owen, Amelia White, Lary Ohlson, Andy Tighe, Tom McCorry, Jack Winans, Michael Cintas.

Old Globe Theater: Play Discovery Project — Carter Center Stage

(Coordinator, Diane Sinor; staged readings, 1 performance each)

TURN OF THE CENTURY by Craig Finch, January 23, 1978, director, Craig Finch. MOTHER EARTH: EMMA GOLDMAN AND FREE SPEECH IN SAN DIEGO by Sanford A. Lakoff, March 13, 1978, director, Michelle O. Serries; THE MAN WHO DECEIVED HIS WIFE by Scot Paxton, English version of Oscar, Ou Le Mari Qui Trompe Sa Femme by Eugene Scribe and M. Duveyrier, April 23, 1978, director, Helen Wilson.

Designers: scenery, Peggy Kellner, Steve Lavino, Dan Dryden, Russell Redmond, Stephen Storer, Margaret Perry; lighting, John McLain, William Greenspan, Amarante L. Lucero, Stephen Storer; costumes, Robert Morgan, Peggy Kellner, Donna Couchman, Dianne Holly.

Note: Old Globe's Shakespeare Festival performed Hamlet and The Taming of the Shrew in Scottsdale, Ariz. The Globe Educational Tour performed in schools throughout San Diego City and County from October 31, 1977-April 18, 1978, *Romeo and Juliet* (72 performances) and *The Two Gentlemen of Verona* (99 performances) directed by Sandy McCallum, designed by Steve Lavino and Donna Couchman; with Mary Barry, Richard Bradshaw, Mark Brey, Jeffrey Eiche, James Fagerle, J. C. Goebel, Edith Taylor Hunter, Mark Kincaid, Maile Klein, Patrick McMinn, Hugh Monahan, Lary Ohlson, Mary Pipes, Jonathan Perpich and Kristin Reeves.

SAN FRANCISCO

American Conservatory Theater: Geary Theater

(General director, William Ball)

JULIUS CAESAR (29). By William Shakespeare. October 14, 1977. Director, Edward Payson Call with Eugene Barcone. With Ray Reinhardt, Jay O. Sanders, Marrian Walters, Diane Salinger, William Paterson, Daniel Davis, Raye Birk.

THE MASTER BUILDER (26). By Henrik Ibsen; translator-director, Allen Fletcher. October 18, 1977. With Peter Donat, Barbara Dirickson, Anne Lawder, Joseph Bird.

A CHRISTMAS CAROL (16). By Charles Dickens; adaptation by Laird Williamson and Dennis Powers. December 6, 1977. Director, Laird Williamson; associate director, James Haire; music, Lee Hoiby; choreographer, Angene Feves. With William Paterson/Sydney Walker, Raye Birk, Deborah May, William McKereghan, Delores Y. Mitchell.

HOTEL PARADISO (28). By Georges Feydeau and Maurice Desvallieres; translated by Peter Glenville. February 14, 1978. Director, Tom Moore. With Raye Birk, Ruth Kobart, Elizabeth Huddle, Michael Winters, Sydney Walker, Diane Salinger.

ABSURD PERSON SINGULAR (32). By Alan Ayckbourn. March 14, 1978. Director, Allen Fletcher. With Daniel Davis, Susan E. Pellegrino, William Paterson, Marrian Walters, Jay O. Sanders, Barbara Dirickson.

THE NATIONAL HEALTH (30). By Peter Nichols. April 4, 1978. Director, Nagle Jackson; associate director, Eugene Barcone. With Libby Boone, Franchelle Stewart Dorn, Daniel Kern, Sydney Walker, Bruce Williams, James R. Winkler.

TRAVESTIES (9). By Tom Stoppard. May 2, 1978. Director, Nagle Jackson; associate director, Eugene Barcone; music, Larry Dellinger, choreographer, Tony Teague. With Raye Birk, Sydney Walker, Michael Winters, James R. Winker, Barbara Dirickson, Susan E. Pellegrino.

SHAKESPEARE'S PEOPLE (12; Geary Theater Special). Devised and compiled by Alan Strachan from William Shakespeare's plays and sonnets. September 12, 1977. Director, Edward Hastings. With Michael Redgrave, David Dodimead, Hope Alexander-Willis, Stephen Schnetzer, George Ceres.

Designers: scenery, Richard Segar, Ralph Funicello, Robert Blackman, John Jensen, Christopher Idoine; lighting, Richard Devin, F. Mitchell Dana, Dirk Epperson; costumes, John Conklin Robert Morgan, Cathy Edwards, Robert Blackman, Robert Fletcher, Elizabeth Covey.

American Conservatory Theater: Marines' Theater

DIVERSIONS AND DELIGHTS: OSCAR WILDE (16). By John Gay; based on the writings of Oscar Wilde. July 14, 1977 (world premiere). Director, Joseph Hardy; associate director, Trace Johnston; scenery and lighting, H. R. Poindexter; costumes, Noel Taylor. With Vincent Price.

S. MILES IS ME (12). Written and performed by Sarah Miles. February 6, 1978 (world premiere). Director, Peter Hunt; musical staging, Onna White; music, Chad Stuart, Sarah Miles.

FESTIVAL (40). Book, music and lyrics by Stephen Downs; based on the medieval chantefable *Aucassin and Nicolette*. April 26, 1968 (world premiere). Directors, Jack Rowe, Michael Shawn; scenery and lighting, Russell Pyle; costumes, Madeline Anne Graneto;

musical director/arranger, Daniel Troob; choreographer, Michael Shawn; orchestrations, Eddie Sauter.

Troubador; Narrator .... Gregory Harrison
Aucassin .... Bill Hutton
Nicolette .... Lois Young
Count de Beaucaire; King of
  Carthage .... Randal Alan Martin
Count de Valence .... Tim Bowman
Viscountess .... Roxann Parker
Lady of Beauclaire;
  Queen Torelore .... Leslie Esterbrook
  Shepherds, Shepherdesses, Soldiers, Pirates, Wierd Sisters, etc.: Pamela Cordova, Kenneth

Henley, Roger Case, Alyson Reed and all other cast members except Aucassin and Nicolette.

Time: Then. Place: There. Scenes: Prologue, Provence, The War, The Prison, The Forest, Torelore, Pirates, Carthage. No intermission.

Musical Numbers: Prelude, "Our Song," "Ribbons Song," "Beata, Biax (Beautiful, Beautiful)," "She," "The Confrontation," "Special Day," "The Time Is Come," "Fairlight Glen," "When the Lady Passes," "Gifts to You," "The Escape," "Torelore!" "Pirates Song," "I Can't Remember," "One Step Further," "Oh Dear!" "Let Him Love You," Finale, "Unfinished Song," "Our Song" (Reprise).

American Conservatory Theater: Plays In Progress

DAVID (5). By Arthur Hoppe. November 14, 1977. Director, Raye Birk.
David Carpenter .... Robert Smith
Mary Carpenter .... Penelope Court
Joe Carpenter .... Gerald Lancaster
Pete .... Bruce Williams
Maggie .... Heidi Helen Davis
Jules .... Thomas Oglesby
Delia Tugwell .... Kate Fitzmaurice
Bishop Speedwell .... Jay O. Sanders
Sen. Robert Swazey .... Daniel Davis
Herbert 43X .... Melvin Buster Flood
A television director ..... Laurence Feldman
Time: Spring in the early 1970's. Place: Washington, D. C. Act I: A tent on the mall of the Washington Monument. Act II, Scene 1: The offices of the Happiness-Through-Poverty Foundation. Scene 2: A television studio.

A VAST DIFFERENCE (6). By R. Norman Lehman and Bernard Pechter. January 9, 1978. Director, Peter Donat.
Joanne Woods .... Susan E. Pellegrino
Harry Rogers .... Michael Winters
Richard Henshaw .... Wayne Alexander
Cruising Chef .... Bruce Williams
Barbara Rogers .... Kate Fitzmaurice
Time: The present. Place: Harry Roger's apartment, San Francisco. Act I, Scene 1: An afternoon, late May. Scene 2: A morning, 28 days later. Act II: Later the same day.

FATHER DREAMS (6). By Mary Gallagher. March 13, 1978. Director, Dolores Ferraro.

Paul .... Peter Davies
Mom .... Cecil Mackinnon
Joan Hogan .... Heidi Helen Davis
Dad .... Gerald Lancaster
Time: An afternoon in summer, 1977. No intermission.

AFTERNOONS IN VEGAS (5). By Jack Gilhooley. April 27, 1978. Director, Elizabeth Huddle.
Bonnie .... Cecil Mackinnon
Candy .... Libby Boone
Bunny .... Heidi Helen Davis
Roxie .... Delores Y. Mitchell
Randy .... Randall Smith
Time: The mid-1970s. Act I: An afternoon in Las Vegas, Nevada, Rocco Moranzo's Pussycat Lounge. Act II: An afternoon a week later, the same.

SHOE PALACE MURRAY (5). Book and lyrics by William M. Hoffman and Anthony Holland; music by David H. Kent. May 18, 1978. Director, Joy Carlin.
Texas Guinan .... Patricia Sherrick
Murray Howard .... Thomas Oglesby
Benny Vogel .... Bruce Williams
Sally Kirkwood .... Diane Salinger
Lucille Doyle .... Elizabeth Huddle
Marion Rinzler .... Kerry Lee Korf
Alla Nazimova .... Marrian Walters
Time: Wednesday morning, August 26, 1926. Place: I. Miller's Theatrical Shoe Department, Broadway and 46th Street, N. Y. C.

Note: ACT's Young Conservatory toured five productions to schools and organizations between November 1977 and May 1978. They were: a story theater presentation of *A Thousand Jewels* (5) adapted by Lura Dolas from James Thurber's *13 Clocks; Behind and Below* (3) an interspace fantasy with book by Barbara Abbate and music by Susan Moss; *The Ice Wolf* (5), by Joanna Kraus; the Mime Troupe in "theater of premeditated spontaneity; *The Bremen Town Musicians* (5), book by Pat Hale; music by Al Bahret, based on *Grimms Fairy Tales*. ACT guest-sponsored a production of *Grease* by Jim Jacobs and Warren Casey; director, Tom Moore, at the Geary Theater from August 2-28, 1977. The sixth annual ACT tour performed *All The Way Home* by Tad Mosel and *Ah, Wilderness!* by Eugene O'Neill at the Pearl City campus of Leeward Community College in Honolulu, Hawaii from June 13-25, 1978, and at the new Sagetsu Kaiken Theater in Tokyo, Japan (under a partial government grant), June 30-July 9, 1978.

SARASOTA, FLA.

Asolo State Theater: Ringling Museum's Court Playhouse—Mainstage

(Artistic director, Robert Strane; managing director, Howard J. Millman; executive director/founder, Richard G. Fallon)

SATURDAY, SUNDAY, MONDAY (23). By Eduardo de Filippo; adapted by Keith Waterhouse and Willis Hall. July 1, 1977. Director, Robert Strane. With Bradford Wallace, Isa Thomas, David S. Howard, Kelly Fitzpatrick.

CROMWELL (16). By David Storey. July 29, 1977 (American premiere). Director, Richard G. Fallon; scenery, Robert C. Barnes; lighting, Martin Petlock; costumes, Catherine King.

Logan .... Milt Tarver
O'Halloran .... Kelly Fitzpatrick
Morgan .... Trent Jones
Proctor .... Walter Rhodes
Chamberlain; Boatman .. David S. Howard
Moore .... William Leach
Mathew .... Steven J. Rankin
Margaret .... Isa Thomas
Joan .... Deanna Dunagan
Kennedy .... Bill Herman
Broome .... John C. Wall
Cleet .... Ritch Brinkley
Wallace .... Howard A. Branch Jr.
Drake .... John Green
Soldiers .... Tom Case, Robert Walker
  Time: 1649-1650. Place: Ireland. Two intermissions.

CYRANO DE BERGERAC (33). By Edmond Rostand. September 3, 1977. Director, John Ulmer. With William Leach, Trent Jones, Bradford Wallace, Steven Ryan, Susan Borneman, Bette Oliver.

THE ROYAL FAMILY (23). By George S. Kaufman and Edna Ferber. February 16, 1978.

Director, Howard J. Millman. With Isa Thomas, George Brengel, Brit Erickson, Robert Strane, Elizabeth Horowitz, Bradford Wallace.

JUNO AND THE PAYCOCK (19). By Sean O'Casey. February 24, 1978. Director, George Keathley. With Bradford Wallace, David S. Howard, Isa Thomas, Elizabeth Horowitz, Hal Carter, Robert Beseda, Bette Oliver.

SHE STOOPS TO CONQUER (26). By Oliver Goldsmith. March 3, 1978. Director, Robert Strane. With George Brengel, Bette Oliver, Deanna Dunagan, William Pitts, Brit Erickson, Robert Beseda, Stephen Van Benschoten.

THE SCHOOL FOR WIVES (24). By Molière; translation by Eberle Thomas. March 31, 1978. Director, Thomas Edward West. With Eberle Thomas, Elizabeth Horowitz, Hal Carter, David S. Howard, Joseph Reed, Ritch Brinkley.

TRAVESTIES (22). By Tom Stoppard. April 7, 1978. Director, Bradford Wallace. With Stephen Van Benschoten, Robert Beseda, Max Howard, Bradford Wallace, Deanna Dunagan, Brit Erickson, Isa Thomas.

RICHARD III (26). By William Shakespeare. May 5, 1978. Director, Paul Barry. With Eberle Thomas, Deanna Dunagan, Robert Beseda, Neal Kenyon, Isa Thomas, Bette Oliver, Arthur Hanket, Stephen Van Benschoten, Joseph Reed, Brit Erickson, David S. Howard.

Asolo State Theater: Downtown Theater—Stage Two

SCAPINO! (22). By Frank Dunlop and Jim Dale; adapted from Molière's *Les Fourberies de Scapin*. November 4, 1977, Director,

Thomas Edward West. With Arthur Hanket, Joseph Reed, Kim Ivan Motter, John Green,

Walter Rhodes and Deanna Dunagan in David Storey's *Cromwell* at Asolo State Theater

Howard A. Branch Jr., Jean McDaniel, Eric Overmyer, Lou Ann Csaszar.

A CHRISTMAS CAROL (22). By Charles Dickens; adapted by David Ball and David Feldshuh. December 16, 1977. Director, Don Gaughf. With David S. Howard, Joseph Reed, Angela Lloyd, James St. Clair, Carolyn Blackinton, Miles Larsen, Evan Parry.

Designers: scenery, Rick Pike, David Emmons, John Scheffler, Jeff Dean, Robert C. Barnes, Sandro La Ferla, Holmes Easley; lighting, Martin Petlock, David Malcolm, Paul D. Romance, Jim Rynning; costumes, Rick Pike, Catherine King, Flozanne John.

Asolo State Theater: Theater For Young People

A TROUPE IN A TRUNK (16). Conceived by director/choreographer Jim Hoskins; based on the commedia dell'arte scenario, *The Betrothed;* music and lyrics by John Franceschina; book by the company. August 4, 1977 (world premiere). Scenery, Jeff Dean; lighting, Paul D. Romance; costumes, Paige Southard; masks and weapons, Bob Naismith; stage fights, Steven J. Rankin.

Musician ....John Franceschina
Cantarina .... Angela L. Lloyd
Ballerina ....Maryann Barulich

Dr. Gratiano ....Joseph Reed
Oratio ....Robert Walker
Isabella .... Lou Ann Csaszar
Pantalone .... Kim Ivan Motter
Flaminia ....Jean McDaniel
Captain Spavento ....John Green
Arlecchino ....Arthur Hanket
Franceschina .... Kathleen Archer
Pedrolino ....Howard A. Branch Jr.
Buranttino ....Tom Case
    Time: A long time ago. Place: In front of Pantalone's house on a street in Venice.

Note: The Asolo Conservatory Company acted, directed and designed Stage II productions and Stage II workshop productions of Neil Simon's *The Good Doctor* and Oscar Wilde's *The Importance of Being Earnest*; gave one-person shows; toured schools throughout the state; and during 1978 appeared in free-to-the-public understudy performances of *She Stoops to Conquer,* March 5; *The Royal Family,* March 9; *Juno and the Paycock,* March 12; *Travesties,* April 14; *The School for Wives,* May 11; *Richard III,* May 19.

SEATTLE

A Contemporary Theater

(Artistic director, Gregory A. Falls; general manager, Andrew M. Witt)

AS YOU LIKE IT (23). By William Shakespeare. May 12, 1977. Director, Gregory A. Falls. With Kurt Beattie, Clayton Corzatte, John Gilbert, Kathleen Heaney, Marion Lines, Mark Murphey, Jeffrey L. Prather.

TRAVESTIES (23). By Tom Stoppard. June 9, 1977. Director, Bill Ludel. With Clayton Corzatte, Kathleen Heaney, Nicholas Hormann, Marion Lines, Glen Mazen.

LADYHOUSE BLUES (23). By Kevin O'Morrison. July 7, 1977. Director, Kent Paul. With Patricia Cosgrove, Anne Gerety, Kathleen Heaney, Kathy Lichter, Constance Miller.

STREAMERS (23). By David Rabe. August 4, 1977. Director, M. Burke Walker. With Lee Corrigan, Justin Deas, Teotha Dennard, Jay Fernandez, James W. Monitor, Merritt Olsen, James W. Pearl, Les Roberts, Marcus Smythe, Ben Tone, Steve Tomkins.

THE CLUB (27). By Eve Merriam. September 1, 1977. Director, Judith Haskell; musical arrangements by Alexandra Ivanoff. With Katherine Benfer, Jean Bonard, Mary Fain, Karen McLaughlin, Judith Moore, Carolyn Val-Schmidt, Suzanne Walker.

ABSURD PERSON SINGULAR (29). By Alan Ayckbourn. September 29, 1977. Director, Raymond Clarke. With Barbara Berge, Robert Cornthwaite, Saylor Creswell, Donald Ewer, Barbara Lester, Marion Lines.

A CHRISTMAS CAROL (39). By Charles Dickens; adapted by Gregory A. Falls; music by Robert MacDougall. December 2, 1977. Director, Gregory A. Falls. With John Gilbert, John Michael Hosking, Marie Mathay, Jim Royce, Mark Sather, Robert John Zenk.

HENRY IV, PART 1 (23). By William Shakespeare. May 11, 1978. Director, Gregory A. Falls. With Denis Arndt, Shaun Austin-Olsen, Jack Bittner, Ted D'Arms, Marie Mathay, Barry Mulholland, Elaine Nalee.

Designers: scenery, Karen Gjelsteen, William Forrester, Shelley Henze Schermer, Jerry Williams; lighting, Phil Schermer, Al Nelson, Paul W. Brayan, Jody Briggs; costumes, Sally Richardson.

Note: ACT-Seattle toured *The Odyssey* by Homer, adapted by Gregory A. Falls and Kurt Beattie, through six western states and the state of Washington, between October, 1977 through April, 1978, playing 105 performances. The company included Richard Hawkins, John Hosking, Richard Lee, Marie Mathay, Marcy Mattox, James W. Monitor, Merritt Olsen, Robert John Zenk, David Colacci, Brenda Hubbard.

Seattle Repertory Theater: Seattle Center Playhouse—Mainstage

(Artistic director, Duncan Ross; producing director, Peter Donnelly)

THE ROYAL FAMILY (28). By George S. Kaufman and Edna Ferber. October 26, 1977. Director, Daniel Sullivan. With Augusta French, Denis Arndt, Eve Roberts, Janet Zarish, Jeffrey L. Prather, Herman O. Arbeit, Donald Barton.

THE DREAM WATCHER (26). By Barbara Wersba; adapted from her novel. November 30, 1977 (world premiere). Director, Brian Murray; scenery, Ed Wittstein; lighting, Patricia Collins; costumes, Lewis D. Rampino.

Albert Scully	Tim Wilson
Helen Scully	Geraldine Court
John Scully	J. T. Walsh
Mr. Finley; Pusher	Peter Bartlett
Sheila Morris; Neighbor	Susan Kay Logan
Rick Hollander	Mark Bendo
Bob Trautman	Adam Dales
Mrs. Orpha Woodfin	Eva Le Gallienne
Chuck Forbes	Gregory Abels
Nurse	Elsa Raven
Mrs. Turner	Shirley Bryan

Mrs. Stein .... Minerva Pious
Place: A New Jersey suburb in the spring.
One intermission.

THE NATIONAL HEALTH (30). By Peter
Nichols. January 4, 1978. Director, Duncan
Ross. With Denis Arndt, Herman O. Arbeit,
Andy Backer, Molly Dodd, Gardner Hayes, Lil
Henderson, Jean Marie Kinney, Lori Larsen,
Michael McKee, Marguerite Morrisey, Jeffrey
L. Prather, Rick R. Ray.

UNCLE VANYA (30). By Anton Chekhov.
February 8, 1978. Director, Duncan Ross. With
James Cahill, Philip Kerr, Megan Cole,
Suzanne Collins, Richard E. Arnold, Andy
Backer, Dorothy Chace.

MUCH ADO ABOUT NOTHING (41). By
William Shakespeare. March 15, 1978. Direc-
tor, Duncan Ross. With Harry Groener,
Megan Cole, Peter Webster, Gun-Marie
Nilsson, Jon Peter Benson, John Abajian,
Richard Dix, David O. Petersen.

13 RUE DE L'AMOUR (33). By Georges
Feydeau; adaptation by Mawby Green and Ed
Feilbert. April 26, 1978. Director, Daniel
Sullivan. With Sharon Spelman, Clayton Cor-
zatte, Robert Loper, Jean Smart, Liz Otto,
Stuart Warmflash, Deems Urquhart, J. V.
Bradley.

Seattle Repertory Theater: Second Stage—Play in Progress

EMINENT DOMAIN (4). By Percy Granger.
April 17, 1978. Director, Jack Bender.
Holmes Bradford .... Biff McGuire
Victor Salt .... Warren Buck
Katie Bradford .... Jeannie Carson
Stoddard Oates .... David Mong
John Ramsey .... Brian Thompson
Roberta Sharron .... Cheri Becvar
Time: February, two years ago. Place: A uni-
versity town in the southwest.

Note: Seattle Repertory Theater presented William Windom in his one-man show, *By-Line: Ernie
Pyle* on October 15, 1977. In January and February, 1978, The MOB (Mobile Outreach Bunch)
made a six-week swing around the state in *Metric Show*, a song-dance-mime explanation of the in-
tricacies of the metric system. *Much Ado About Nothing* gave 8 free performances for area school
children, and following its regular run, toured eight northwest cities from April 17-May 13, 1978.
Rep 'n' Rap, Seattle Rep's summer project, toured *Discovering Tutankhamun* to 16 cities, June 5-
17, 1978, written by Phil Shallat; directed by Lori Larsen; with Norman Bernard, Dana Cox, Dean
Erickson, Marcella Hayden, Allenda Yvonne Jackson. This production preceded the
Tutankhamun exhibition at the Seattle Art Museum from July 15 to November 15, 1978.

STAMFORD, CONN.

Hartman Theater Company

(Producing directors, Del and Margot Tenney; managing director, Roger L. Meeker)

THE MOUSETRAP (22). By Agatha Christie.
October 26, 1977. Director, Del Tenney. With
Joanne Gibson, Stephen Temperley, Frederick
Sperberg, Sally Chamberlin, John Wardwell,
Margot Tenney. George Morfogen, Tom
Mason.

THE MIRACLE WORKER (22). By William
Gibson. November 30, 1977. Director, Tony
Giordano. With Karen Ludwig, Emily Hacker,
Patricia O'Connell, George Morfogen.

THE MIDDLE AGES (23). By A. R. Gurney
Jr. January 4, 1978 (world premiere). Director,
Melvin Bernhardt; scenery, John Lee Beatty;

lighting, Dennis Parichy; costumes, June
Stearns.
Barney .... Peter Coffield
Eleanor .... Swoosie Kurtz
Charles .... Douglass Watson
Myra .... Patricia O'Connell
Place: The trophy room of a men's club in a
midwestern city. One intermission.

OTHELLO (22). By William Shakespeare.
February 1, 1978. Director, Robert W. Smith.
With Ron O'Neal, Kate Mulgrew, David
Canary, John Blazo Jr., Margot Tenney.

THE ANIMAL KINGDOM (22). By Phillip

Barry. March 1, 1978. Director, John Going. With David Snell, Giulia Pagano, Laurie Kennedy.

JEROME KERN AT THE HARTMAN (22). Conceived by William E. Hunt. April 5, 1978. Director, William E. Hunt; musical direc- tor/arranger, Gil Martin; choreographer, Rudy Tronto. With David-James Carroll, Mercedes Ellington, Jeanne Lehman, James J. Mellon, Joyce Nolen, Michael Radigan, Jonathan Lehman, Jonathan Sprague, Sally Ann Swarm. Selection of Jerome Kern's songs for the stage and the movies.

Designers: scenery, Roger Meeker, J. D. Ferrara, Zack Brown, Hugh Landwehr, Ruth A. Wells; lighting, Richard Butler, Roger Meeker, Jeff Schissler; costumes, June Stearns, Gerda Proctor, Annette Beck, Linda Fisher, Ruth A. Wells.

Hartman Theater Company: Company Store

(Director, Larry Arrick; associate director, David F. Eliet)

THE SERVANT OF TWO MASTERS (18). By Carlo Goldoni; adaptation by Kenneth Cavander; music and lyrics by Barbara Damashek. November 16, 1977. Director, Larry Arrick; musical director, Barbara Damashek.

YERMA (18). By Federico Garcia Lorca; translated by James Graham-Lujan and Richard L. O'Connell. December 14, 1977. Director, Robert S. Eichler; musical director, Stephen Roylance.

RIBBONS by David F. Eliet. (world premiere), directed by Wendy Chapin; and THE MAIDS by Jean Genet, directed by Larry Arrick (18).

January 18, 1978.
Ribbons
Wena .... Molly Thompson
Deirdre .... Anne W. Scurria
  Scenery, Leslie Taylor; lighting, Peggy Peterson; costumes, Toni Spadafora.
The Maids
  With Barbara Sieck, Rosalyn R. Farinella, Shami Jones.

LA RONDE (18). By Arthur Schnitzler. February 15, 1978. Director, David F. Eliet.

THREE SISTERS (18). By Anton Chekhov. March 15, 1978. Director, Wendy Chapin.

Conservatory Company: Priscilla Cohen, Mercy Cook, Robert Eichler, Karen Fisher, Joan M. Friedman, Lee Holder, Shami Jones, Elizabeth J. Moyer, John Olesen, David Pilat, Tina Rose Rosselli, Stephen Raylance, Anne W. Scurria, Barbara Sieck, Joy Smith, Philip Soltanoff, Susan Strickler, Molly Thompson, Sterling Taylor, Timothy Warren, Steve White, James Zachar.

Designers: scenery, Kathleen Egan, Toni A. Spadafora, Leslie Taylor, Stephen Studnicka; lighting, Peggy Peterson, Wendy Chapin; costumes, Karen D. Miller, Toni A. Spadafora.

Hartman Theater Company: The Candy Store — Theater for Young People

THE ADVENTURES OF MRILE (13). Adapted by Elizabeth J. Moyer from an African folk tale. November 3, 1977. Director, William C. Sandwick; musical director, Anne W. Scurria; designer, Elizabeth J. Moyer; lighting, Steven Hirschberg. With Ben Strout, John Olesen, Joy Smith, Susan Strickler, Mallory Kubicek.

JUMPING MOUSE (14). Adapted by Larry Arrick; music, lyrics and direction by Barbara Damashek. January 13, 1978. Assistant direc- tor, Stephen Berwind; designer, Elizabeth J. Moyer; lighting, Peggy Peterson. With Stephen Roylance, Joan M. Friedman, Joy Smith, Elizabeth J. Moyer, Susan Strickler, Robert S. Eichler and members of the Conservatory Company.

ST. LOUIS

Loretto-Hilton Repertory Theater: Mainstage

(Producing director, David Frank)

MACBETH (32). By William Shakespeare. October 14, 1977. Director, David Frank. With Robert Darnell, Joan Matthiessen, Joneal Joplin, Patricia Ball, Keith Jochim, Robert Spencer, Clyde Burton.

LU ANN HAMPTON LAVERTY OBERLANDER (32). By Preston Jones. November 18, 1977. Director, Davey Marlin-Jones. With Mickey Hartnett, Dana Mills, Joneal Joplin, Wil Love, Robert Darnell, Patricia Kilgarriff, Robert Spencer.

THE DEVIL'S DISCIPLE (32). By George Bernard Shaw. December 30, 1977. Director, David Frank. With Dana Mills, Joneal Joplin,

Cara Duff-MacCormick, Brendan Burke, Patricia Kilgarriff, Rita Sand.

THE RUNNER STUMBLES (32). By Milan Stitt. February 3, 1978. Director, Norman Gevanthor. With David Faulkner, Cara Duff-MacCormick, Robert Darnell, Keith Jochim, Joneal Joplin, Mary Fogarty.

CANTERBURY TALES (32). By Martin Starkie and Nevil Coghill; based on Chaucer's Tales; music by Richard Hall and John Hankins. March 10, 1978. Director, Carl Schurr; musical director, Terrence Sherman. With Brendan Burke, Joneal Joplin, Wil Love, Patricia Kilgarriff, Karen Looze, Helen Hedman, Alan Clarey.

Loretto-Hilton Repertory Theater: Studio Theater

ASHES (23). By David Rudkin. April 2, 1978. Director, Geoffrey Sherman. With Steven

Gilborn, Marilyn Redfield, Michael Thompson, Stephanie Lewis.

Designers: scenery, Grady Larkins, Heidi Landesman, John Conant, John Kavelin; lighting, Glenn Dunn, Peter E. Sargent, David Hitzert; costumes, John Carver Sullivan, Carr Garnett, Catherine Reich.

Note: Loretto-Hilton's Imaginary Theater Company toured three states, performed in and around St. Louis and at the theater itself. *Holiday Tales* (November 29 to December 23, 1977) was given for senior citizens at homes, hospital and centers. *Tales of Fantasy* and *People and Choices* (January 21 to April 23, 1978) was presented to elementary and junior high school audiences. Directed by Michael P. Pitel III, stage-managed by Jim R. Sprague, the company consisted of Jonathan Daly, J. Patrick Martin, Eric Singerman, Susan Maloy Wall and Addie Walsh.

SYRACUSE

Syracuse Stage

(Producing director, Arthur Storch; managing director, James A. Clark)

LOVE LETTERS ON BLUE PAPER by Arnold Wesker (world premiere) and THE END OF THE BEGINNING by Sean O'Casey (30). October 14, 1977. Director, Arthur Storch; scenery, Eldon Elder; lighting, Judy Rasmuson; costumes, Lowell Detweiler.
Love Letters on Blue Paper
Victor Marsden .... John Carpenter
Sonia Marsden .... Myra Carter
Professor Maurice Stapelton Richard Clarke
Trade Union Official .... Jay Devlin

Time: The present — summer, covering a period of about three months. Place: Yorkshire, England.
The End of the Beginning
Darry Berrill .... John Carpenter
Lizzie Berrill .... Myra Carter
Barry Derrill .... Jay Devlin
Time: Some time ago. Place: A farmhouse somewhere in Ireland.

THE PLOUGH AND THE STARS (39). By

Sean O'Casey. November 18, 1977. Director, Peter Maloney. With Dan Diggles, Ellen Fiske, Moultrie Patten, Robert Shrewsbury, Dee Victor, Nancy Reardon.

TARTUFFE (39). By Molière; verse translation by Richard Wilbur. December 23, 1978. Director, John Going. With Munson Hicks, Moultrie Patten, Nancy Reardon, Dee Victor, Dan Diggles, Ellen Fiske, Gene O'Neill, Thomas Ruisinger.

THAT CHAMPIONSHIP SEASON (39). By Jason Miller. January 27, 1978. Director, Bill Putch. With Stephen C. Bradbury, David J. Forsyth, Thomas Connolly, Robert Fields, Edmund Lyndeck.

CANDIDA (39). By George Bernard Shaw. March 3, 1978. Director, Bill Ludel. With Penelope Allen, Robert Stattel, Daniel Zippi, Beth Dixon, Michael Parish, Donald C. Moore.

VANITIES (39). By Jack Heifner. April 7, 1978. Director, John Going. With Roxanne Hart, Susanne Peters, Rebecca Hollen.

Designers: scenery, Elmon Webb, Virginia Dancy, William Trotman, William Schroder, Neil Peter Jampolis; lighting, Lee Watson, Judy Rasmuson, James E. Stephens, Neil Peter Jampolis; costumes, Linda Fisher, James Berton Harris, Liz Bass, Nanzi Adzima.

Syracuse Stage: Sunday New Playreading Series

THE LESSON by John O'Toole; A BETTER PLACE by Robert Hogan; DROPHAMMER and THE DODO BIRD by Emanuel Fried. Directors, David Semonin and George Johnston. With Carlton Colyer, Munson Hicks, Jonathan Putnam, Stephen C. Bradbury, Thomas Connolly, Aloma Noble, David J. Forsyth, Gerardine Clark, Nancy Reardon, Sam Winters, Ellen Fiske, Gene O'Neill, Ruth Fenster, Thomas Ruisinger, Darcy Pulliam. (1 performance each, December 1977, January and February, 1978).

Note: Following its run at the theater, *Candida* toured Rochester, Fredonia, Seneca Falls, Keuka Park, Batavia, Geneva, Morrisville and Binghamton in New York State, a total of 11 performances between April 6-22, 1978. Syracuse Stage also toured *Musical Mirage Express* and *Journeys End in Lover's Meeting,* two musicals written and compiled by Gerardine Clark, to Syracuse elementary and high schools, in February and March, 1978.

TUCSON

Arizona Civic Theater: Tucson

(Artistic director, Sandy Rosenthal; managing director, David Hawkanson)

PYGMALION (22). By George Bernard Shaw. November 10, 1977. Director, Sandy Rosenthal. With John McMurtry, Molly McKasson, Ivor Barry, Stephen Barker, Robert Ellenstein.

SLOW DANCE ON THE KILLING GROUND (14). By William Hanley. December 8, 1977. Director, David Gardiner. With Robert Ellenstein, Carlos Carrasco, Penny Metropulos.

EQUUS (22). By Peter Shaffer. January 5, 1978. Director, Mark Lamos. With John McMurtry, Daniel Tamm, Dee Maaske, Mark Pinter, David Byrd, Harriet Medin.

ON THE HARMFULNESS OF TOBACCO by Anton Chekhov; based on a concept by Patrick Tovatt; acting version by Philip Baker Hall, Dianna Lewis Hall, Patrick Tovatt; directors, Susan Bay and Philip Baker Hall.
BLACK COMEDY by Peter Shaffer; director, Susan Bay. (22). February 2, 1978. With Mark Pinter, Molly McKasson, Dee Maaske, Philip Baker Hall, John McMurtry, Howard Allen, Penny Metropulos, Henry M. Kendrick.

THE SHADOW BOX (14). By Michael Cristofer. March 2, 1978. Director, Sandy Rosenthal. With Robert Ellenstein, Tad Feldman, Sandy Christopher, John McMurtry, Mark Pinter, Susan Bay, Dee Maaske, Roberta Streicher.

RODGERS AND HART: *A Musical Celebration* (22). Concept by Richard Lewine and John Fearnley; music by Richard Rodgers; lyrics by

Lorenz Hart. March 30, 1978. Director/ choreographer, Judith Haskell; musical director, Charles Ross Perlee. With Dale Christo-

pher, Christian Grey, Lowell Harris, Penny Metropulos, Thom Rogers, Suzanne Walker, Evellyn Ward, Polly Wood.

Arizona Civic Theater: Scottsdale Center for the Arts

VANITIES (6). By Jack Heifner. March 11, 1978. Director, Sandy Rosenthal. With Penny Metropulos, Barbara Sammeth, Ellen Tobie.

EQUUS (10). By Peter Shaffer. March 17, 1978. Same production as in Tucson season.

Designers: scenery, Reagan Cook, Jack Schwanke, J. Michael Gillete; lighting, Dan T. Willoughby; costumes, Peggy Kellner, Sandra Mourey.

WALTHAM, MASS.

Brandeis University: Spingold Theater

(Chairman, Theater Arts Department, Charles Werner Moore; general manager, John-Edward Hill)

PAL JOEY (10). Book by John O'Hara; music by Richard Rodgers; lyrics by Lorenz Hart. October 19, 1977. Director/designer, Howard Bay; musical director, Fred Frabotta; choreographer, Cheryl G. McFadden. With James Sherman, Carol Bruce, Marshall Hambro, Susan Rarus.

UNCLE VANYA (9). By Anton Chekhov; translated by David Magershack. December 7, 1977. Director, Vivian Matalon. With Michael Angelo Castellana, David Lewis, Sheila Rose Bland, Lawrence Reese, Jennifer McLogan.

ARTAUD AT RODEZ (9). Written and directed by Charles Marowitz. March 8, 1978. With Clive Merrison, Jan Alan Ginsberg, Lawrence Reese, Sandra Guberman, Michael Angelo Castellana.

THE IMAGINARY INVALID (9). By Molière; translated by Arthur P. Chiasson. May 3, 1978. Director, Daniel Gidron. With Scott Richards, Sandra Guberman/Sarah Pearson, Lawrence Reese, James Luse.

Brandeis University: Laurie Theater

MISS IN HER TEENS, *or The Medley of Lovers* and BON TON, *or High Life Above Stairs* (6). By David Garrick. October 11, 1977. Director, James Luse. With John Cook, David Lewis, Stephen McConnell, Deborah Quayle, Pamela Pascoe, Scott Richards, Daniel Scott, Lawrence Reese.

HEARTBREAK HOUSE (5). By George Bernard Shaw. November 22, 1977. Director, Charles Werner Moore. With Patricia Riggin, Michael Kluger, Joe Hukills, Hershell Norwood, Dan Scott, Sandra Guberman, Diane Dowling.

NOAH (6). By Andre Obey; translated by Earle D. Clowney and Judith D. Suther. November 29, 1977. Director, Annie Thompson. With Brock Putnam, Edith Agnew, Scott Richards, James Silverman, William H. Dean, Sarah Pearson, Deborah Quayle, Sioux Saloka.

LYSISTRATA (6). By Aristophanes. February 28, 1978. Director, Brock Putnam. With Lin Parker, Christal Miller, Stephanie D. Clayman, John C. Cook, Bob Stachel, Lis Adams.

A THIN THREAD (6). By D. Matry Scott. April 4, 1978 (world premiere). Director, Charles Werner Moore; scenery, Mary Therese D'Avignon; lighting, Richard S. Osann; costumes, Susan Smith White.

Jane Sorrentino	Lori Cymrot
Patient	Ellen Robbins
Samantha Vallachia	Ellen D. Levine
Jennie Andrews	Katherine Ravenhall
Brunette	Lori Oshansky
Frank	William H. Dean
Tara	Gail A. Collins
Mrs. Tucker	Lori Lee
Henry	Hershell Norwood

Alice O'Brien .... Edith Agnew
Freddie .... Wendy Colman
Dr. Raymond .....Stephan M. Markusfeld

Mrs. Strong .... Lin Parker
Time: The present. Place: A hospital and
nurses' school. One intermission.

Brandeis University: Merrick Theater — Playwrights Festival

BOX by David Crane, directed by Jim Luse;
THE BIG SELL by Paul Mroczka, directed by
Bill Miller; OUR GENERATION WEARS
SANDALS LIKE THE VIETNAMESE by

Dan Gurskis, directed by Fred Zollo (5). April
12, 1978. Three one-act plays in progress. With
members of the acting company.

Designers: scenery, Melinda Leeson, Michael Lincoln, Robert Little, Kati Slaton, Steve Saklad,
Robert Alpers, Marc C. Anderson; lighting, Dennis J. Cohen, Michael Lincoln, Jim Maran, Paul
W. Gorfine, Amanda J. Klein, David Sumner, John Lam; costumes, Gail Brassard, Charlene
Tuch, Chris Kaseta, Karen Gerson, Kati Slaton, David Sumner.

WASHINGTON, D.C.

Arene Stage: Kreeger Theater

(Producing director, Zelda Fichandler; associate producing director, David Chambers)

COMEDIANS (55). By Trevor Griffiths.
January 18, 1978. Director, David Chambers.
With Robert Prosky, Andrew Davis, Joel
Colodner, Mark Hammer, Timothy Meyers,
John Madden Towey, Joe Palmieri, Terrence
Currier.

GEMINI (47). By Albert Innaurato. April 19,
1978. Director, Douglas C. Wager. With Mel
Shrawder, Leslie Cass, Bill Randolph, Deborah
Baltzell, Joshua Mostel, Dick Boccelli, Doris
Belack.

Arena Stage: Arena Theater

THE NATIONAL HEALTH (39). By Peter
Nichols. October 19, 1977. Director, David
Chambers. With Stanley Anderson, Leslie
Cass, Terrence Currier, Mark Hammer,
Robert Prosky, Halo Wines, Veronica
Castang, Leonardo Cimino.

THE CAUCASIAN CHALK CIRCLE (39).
By Bertolt Brecht; translated by John
Holmstrom. December 7, 1977. Director, Mar-
tin Fried. With Christine Estabrook, Robert
Prosky, Stanley Anderson, Leslie Cass,
Veronica Castang, Leonardo Cimino, Paula
Desmond, Faizul Khan.

A STREETCAR NAMED DESIRE (39). By
Tennessee Williams. February 8, 1978, Direc-
tor, Marshall W. Mason. With Diane Kagan,
Edward J. Moore, Lindsay Crouse, Stanley
Anderson.

HAMLET (47). By William Shakespeare.
March 29, 1978. Director, Liviu Ciulei. With
Kristoffer Tabori, Christine Estabrook,

Richard Bauer, Elizabeth Franz, Joel
Colodner, James David Cromar, Leonardo
Cimino.

DUCK HUNTING (39). By Alexander Vam-
pilov; translated by Alma H. Law. May 10,
1978 (American premiere). Director, Zelda
Fichandler; scenery, Karl Eigsti; lighting, Hugh
Lester; costumes, Marjorie Slaiman; music,
Robert Dennis.
Zilov .... Stanley Anderson
Galina .... Halo Wines
Sayapin .... John Madden Towey
Kuzakov .... George Clark Hosmer
Kushak .... Mark Hammer
Irina ....JoAnne Hrkach
Vera .... Gale Garnett
Valeriya ....Linda Selman
Dima ....Clarence Felder
Young boy .... Andrew Prosky
Time: The present, the beginning of the duck
hunting season in Soviet Russia. Place: Zilov's
room. Two intermissions.

Arena Stage: Old Vat Room — In the Process

(Plays-in-progress premieres; coordinators, Douglas C. Wager, George Spalding)

SEPARATIONS (9). By Janet Neipris. April 21, 1978. Director, Susan Einhorn. With Robin Groves, Peter Alzado, Ben Hammer, Rebecca Schull, Estelle Omens, Joyce Pinson.

THE DESERT DWELLERS (9). By Sidney Renthal. May 12, 1978. Director, Steven Rob-

man. With Richard Bauer, Robyn Goodman, John Gilliss, John Wylie, Robert Prosky, Christopher McHale, Frank Muller, Terrence Currier.

TRAPPERS (9). By Anthony Giardina. June 2, 1978. Director, Douglas C. Wager.

Designers: scenery, Tony Straiges, Christopher Nowak, Karl Eigsti, Santo Loquasto, Ming Cho Lee; lighting, William Mintzer, Hugh Lester; costumes, Marjorie Slaiman, Rebecca Carroll, Santo Loquasto.

Arena Stage: Special Productions

NIGHTCLUB CANTATA (47). Written and directed by Elizabeth Swados. October 12, 1977 (Kreeger Theater). With Jossie deGuzman, Karen Evans, Rocky Greenberg, Paul Kandel, JoAnna Peled, David Schechter, Mark Zageski; Robert Fisher, pianist; David Sawyer, percussionist.

STARTING HERE, STARTING NOW (127+) by Richard Maltby Jr. and David Shire. November 23, 1977 (Old Vat Room). Director,

Richard Maltby Jr. With Loni Ackerman/Catherine Cox, Walter Bobbie/Eron Tabor, Margery Cohen/Laura Waterbury.

ANGEL CITY (3). By Sam Shepard. January 13, 1978 (Arena Theater). Director, Douglas C. Wager. With John Gilliss, JoAnne Hrkach, Christopher McHale, Frank Muller, David Toney. Free workshop performances by the Arena's acting apprentices.

Note: *Living Stage,* headed by Robert Alexander, Arena Stage's professional improvisational outreach company, presented *Faces of Fascism,* dramatization dealing with the mistreatment of children in public institutions based on Kenneth Wooden's *Weeping in the Playtime of Others: Americas's Incarcerated Children,* at the 1977 experimental New Theater Festival, June 11-19, at the University of Maryland in Baltimore, and at Villa Julle College in Steyenson, Md.

Folger Theater Group

(Producer, Louis W. Scheeder)

TEETH 'N' SMILES (39). By David Hare; music and lyrics by Nick and Tony Bicat. October 17, 1977 (American premiere). Directors, Jonathan Alper and Louis W. Scheeder; scenery, David Chapman; lighting, Hugh Lester; costumes, Bob Wojewodski; musical direction, Paul Schierhorn.

Arthur	Peter Phillips
Inch	James Dean
Laura	Pamela Brook
Nash	Hubert Kelly
Wilson	Paul Schierhorn
Peyote	M. Jonathan Steele
Snead	Earle Edgerton
Smegs	Larry Dilg
Anson	Nicholas Woodeson
Maggie	Gale Garnett
Saraffian	George Taylor

Randolph	Allan Carlsen

Time: June 9, 1969. A college campus in Cambridge, England. The members of an itinerant rock band, playing an engagement on a college campus, discover that they've all been living on borrowed time and fraudulent dreams. One intermission.

THE TWO GENTLEMEN OF VERONA (55). By William Shakespeare. December 5, 1977. Director, Louis W. Scheeder. With Michael Tolaydo, Allan Carlsen, Mikel Lambert, Franchelle Stewart Dorn, Terry Hinz, Peter Vogt.

HAMLET (56). By William Shakespeare. February 6, 1978. Director, Jonathan Alper. With Michael Tolaydo, Albert Corbin, Mikel

Lambert, Margaret Whitton, Peter Vogt, Allan Carlsen, David Butler.

MACKEREL (31). By Israel Horowitz. April 20, 1978 (premiere of revised version). Director, Louis W. Scheeder; scenery, David Chapman; lighting, Elizabeth Toth; costumes, Sheila McLamb; sound score, William Penn.

Emma Lemon ....Jo Henderson
Ed Lemon .... Brian Hartigan
Edna Lemon ....Pat Karpen
Eileen Lemon ....Elizabeth Kemp
Time: Late fall. Place: The dining room of

the Lemon family's seaside home in Gloucester, Mass. The shiftless Lemon family finds itself caught up in a series of back-firing get-rich-quick schemes, after a hurricane washes a 300,-000 pound mackerel into the dining room. One intermission.

RICHARD III (3). By William Shakespeare. May 29, 1978. Director, Louis W. Scheeder. With Paul Collins, Peter Vogt, Mikel Lambert, Elaine Bromka, John Neville-Andrews, David Cromwell.

Designers: scenery, David Lloyd Gropman, Hugh Lester; lighting, Elizabeth Toth, Paul Gallo, Hugh Lester; costumes, Dona Granata, Bob Wojewodski, Susan Tsu.

Note: Folger Theater Group toured *Black Elk Speaks* (67 performances) by Christopher Sergel; based on the book by John G. Neihardt; music by Philip J. Lang; in 18 states from January through May, 1978. Director, Louis W. Scheeder; scenery and lighting, Hugh Lester; costumes, Karen M. Hummel; choreographer, Jane Lind. With Carl Alexander, Henry "Kaimu" Bal, Richard Camargo, Clayton Corbin, Michael Lamond, Jane Lind, Maria Antoinette Rogers.

The Season Elsewhere in Washington

By David Richards

Drama Critic of the Washington *Star*

Zelda Fichandler, the vital producing director of Arena Stage, was not being overly pessimistic when she remarked that "it is in the theater's basic nature to fail. The artistic success is the miraculous exception." After all, Arena manages the miraculous event more often than any other theater in town, and the observation came during the run of *Duck Hunting,* easily the most provocative play Washington saw all year.

Yet, her comment bore a distressing pertinence to the season in general. Despite a slew of big names, big-name shows and the kind of box-office grosses that put envy in producers' eyes, it was a lackluster year. Of course, the crowds turned out with a vengeance for such shows as *Annie,* which tried out here the year before and was back for a four-month stay, *A Chorus Line* and Lily Tomlin's one-woman outing. Henry Fonda and Jane Alexander, as Supreme Court Judges, were a huge draw in *First Monday in October,* a battle of wits by Jerome Lawrence and Robert E. Lee. Eartha Kitt and acres of costumes were enough to send the receipts soaring for *Timbuktu!,* and even *Grease,* returning for the umpteenth time, cleaned up, although one is beginning to wonder where the customers are coming from.

Beyond the pre- or post-Broadway fare that has once again become the exclusive property of the Kennedy Center empire (the Eisenhower, the Opera House and the National), what was there? Not a great deal.

The Folger Theater Group made some significant strides with its productions of Shakespeare, achieving a clarity and an ease not always evident in the past.

Left, Brian Hartigan in Folger Theater Group's *Mackerel; below*, Clarence Felder and Stanley Anderson in Arena Stage's production of *Duck Hunting*

The two original plays it staged this season were busts, though. David Hare's *Teeth 'n' Smiles* was a cool phantasmagoria about a British rock band coming apart along with the times, which happened to be the late 1960s. But it was indulgently acted and directed, and Hare's stoned musicians, too hip to call out for the help they needed, proved a tedious lot. Israel Horovitz had a splendid premise for *Mackerel*: What if a hurricane (or God) washed a 300,000 pound mackerel into the dining room of a shiftless Gloucester fisherman and his family? For every inventive detail, there were, alas, three facile ones, and the production was so concerned with the serious implications of the fable that its true zaniness was left to flounder on the stage, rather like the big fish itself.

Olney Theater had solid revivals of *The Tenth Man* and *Philadelphia Here I Come!*, but its long-standing, immensely fruitful relationship with Irish playwright Hugh Leonard was apparently over, after seven plays. When *"Da"* swept the Tony awards this year, no mention was made that the play got its first hearing at Olney in 1973 or that James D. Waring subsequently staged the work for Chicago and Dublin. Like children, the theater can be thankless.

Ford's Theater was back dipping into its dependable one-man show repertory again — Vincent Price's Oscar Wilde, James Whitmore's Will Rogers and Max Morath's ragtime music. The American Dance Machine gave the historic theater its one big hit, although that group's ambition to preserve memorable Broadway dance numbers was more laudable than its actual execution of them.

For the non-Equity experimental theaters, the landscape was also looking bleak. Both ASTA and the New Playwrights' Theater of Washington spruced up their quarters, then had trouble finding anything worthwhile to put in them. While old art is assiduously preserved in this city, new art is not encouraged with equal zeal. This season, yet another alternative theater group, the Washington Theater Lab, bit the pavement after five tiring years of trying to find a permanent home and a loyal audience.

What excitement there was could mostly be found at Arena Stage, and even it had some low points with *Nightclub Cantata, A Streetcar Named Desire* and *Gemini*. Rumanian director Liviu Ciulei, however, came up with a visually arresting production of *Hamlet*, which he viewed as "a play about rooms, closets and whispers." To an American, it looked suspiciously like a Watergate *Hamlet*. David Chambers, who will take over the artistic direction of Arena for the next two seasons, while Mrs. Fichandler goes on sabbatical, contributed an incisive staging of *Comedians*. And in the Old Vat Room, Richard Maltby Jr.'s and David Shire's revue of show tunes, *Starting Here, Starting Now,* found four months' worth of fast friends.

The real note of distinction, however, was provided by *Duck Hunting*, a sharp, ironic Soviet play by Alexander Vampilov about a Russian bureaucrat who is ill at ease with himself, his life and his society. The alienated man is not officially recognized in Soviet art, so it was astounding to discover a play not only written about the specimen, but written with such compassion and understanding. Stanley Anderson's performance as Zilov, the misfit, rivaled any on Washington's stages all season.

Otherwise, Mrs. Fichandler's doleful observation seemed all too accurate. For a long time, Washington has been over-inflated with cultural hubris. This season, at least, there was just cause for dispassionate theatergoers to wonder why.

Ford's Theater

HOLD ME! (30). By Jules Feiffer. November 16, 1977. Director, Gene Borio; scenery, Kert Lundell; lighting, Tom Grond; costumes, Ruth Morley. With Maria Cellario, Rhoda Gemignani, William Lodge, Ray Stewart, Britt Swanson.

THE AMERICAN DANCE MACHINE (67). Revue composed of dance numbers from celebrated Broadway shows. February 5, 1978 (world premiere). Director, Lee Theodore; lighting, Jeremy Johnson; costumes, Rolande Guizart; musical direction, David Baker, Danny Hurd. With Swen Swenson, Janet Eilber, Harold Cromer, Barry Preston and members of the American Dance Machine Company.

Musical Numbers — Act I: "Popularity" (*George M,* choreography, Joe Layton); "June Is Bustin' Out All Over" (*Carousel,* choreography, Agnes DeMille); "Whip Dance" (*Destry Rides Again,* choreography, Michael Kidd); "All abroad for Broadway" (*George M,* choreography, Joe Layton); "Monte Carlo Crossover" and "Up Where the People Are" (*The Unsinkable Molly Brown,* choreography,

Peter Gennaro); "Harlem Makes You Feel" (*Bubbling Brown Sugar,* choreography, Billy Wilson); "The Telephone Dance" (*Cabaret,* choreography, Ron Rield); "You Can dance With Any Girl at All" (*No, No, Nanette,* choreography, Donald Saddler). Act II: "Satin Doll" (choreography, Carol Haney); "Come to Me, Bend to Me" and "Funeral Dance" (*Brigadoon,* choreography, Agnes DeMille); "Quadrille" (*Can-Can,* choreography, Michael Kidd); "I've Got Your Number" (*Little Me,* choreography, Bob Fosse); "Clog Dance" (*Walking Happy,* choreography, Danny Daniels).

THE ROBBER BRIDEGROOM (21). Musical by Alfred Uhry; music by Robert Waldman; lyrics by Alfred Uhry. May 14, 1978. Director, Mary Porter Hall; scenery, Douglas W. Schmidt; lighting, David Segal; costumes, Jeanne Button; choreography, Norman Snow. With Tom Wopat, Rhonda Coullet, Glynis Bell, Suzanne Costallos, John Goodman, Rosalind Harris, Trip Plymale, Ernie Sabella, David Sinkler.

Note: The Ford's Theater season also included touring productions of *Will Rogers' U.S.A., Max Morath at the Turn of the Century* and The Acting Company's *Mother Courage and Her Children,* and the pre-Broadway production of *Diversions and Delights.*

Hartke Theater (Catholic University)

BIRDS, BEASTS AND FLOWERS (2). Program of poetry and prose devised by John Carroll. March 3, 1978. With Princess Grace of Monaco, Richard Pasco. Produced by Arthur Cantor.

Note: The Hartke's professional productions also included *My Astonishing Self* and Emlyn Williams's one-man show, *The Playboy of the Weekend World.*

John F. Kennedy Center: Eisenhower Theater

THE MASTER BUILDER (41). By Henrik Ibsen; translated by Sam Engelstad and Jane Alexander. June 4, 1977. Director, Edwin Sherin; scenery, John Wulp; lighting, Roger Morgan; costumes, Ann Roth. With Richard Kiley, Jane Alexander, Teresa Wright, Thomas Toner, Shepperd Strudwick, Joel Stedman. Mary Catherine Wright.

FIRST MONDAY IN OCTOBER (70). By Robert E. Lee and Jerome Lawrence.

December 28, 1977 (world premiere). Director, Edwin Sherin; scenery, Oliver Smith; lighting, Roger Morgan; costumes, Ann Roth.
Custodians ....John Stewart, Ellsworth Wright
Chief Justice Crawford .... Larry Gates
Justice Josiah Clewes .... Earl Sydnor
Associate Justice
    Thompson ....Maurice Copeland
Justice Daniel Snow .... Henry Fonda
Justice Harold Webb ....John Wardwell

Justice Ruth Loomis ...... Jane Alexander
The Marshall .... John Newton
Mason Woods .... Tom Stechschulte
Associate Justice
  Quincy .... Alexander Reed
Associate Justice
  Carey .... Eugene Stuckman
Associate Justice
  Halloran .... Patrick McCullough
Miss Birnbaum .... Carol Mayo Jenkins
Photographer .... John Stewart
Blake .... Ron Faber
  Time: The present. Place: Backstage at the
U.S. Supreme Court. The first woman ap-
pointee to the Supreme Court, an arch-
conservative from Orange County, Calif.,
causes consternation in the ranks of her fellow
judges. One intermission.

THE AMERICAN COLLEGE THEATER
FESTIVAL. Tenth annual two-week festival of
representative college productions, selected
from across the country. April 10-23, 1978.
Produced by Kennedy Center in conjunction
with the Alliance for Arts Education, the
American Theater Association and the Amoco
Oil Company. Named best production was
SIDESHOW (3). Musical by Rick Smith.
April 10, 1978. Director, Raymond Carver;
scenery, Raymond Carver; costumes, Juanita
Norris, Jim Weisman; musical direction, Larry
Brown; choreography, Peggy Brillo, Raymond
Carver; musical arrangements, Jerry Taylor.
Produced by Angelo State University, San
Angelo, Texas.
John Nance Garner .... Brent Scott
Siamese Twins .... Richard Nance,
                              Don Pearson
Tallest Man in the World .... Jim Weisman
World's Littlest Woman .... Karen Pearson
Mechanical Man .... Craig Torrence
World's Strongest Man ...... Don Hale II
Oldest Living Supreme
  Court Justice .... Carlton Smith
Sideshowgirls .... Peggy Brillo,
                            Dixie Pederson
  Time: The 1930s. Place: A sideshow tent.

The life and career of Vice-President John
Nance Garner, presented as a circus sideshow.
One intermission.
  Musical Numbers—Act I: "Sideshow," "I'm
a Barker," "We Can Get Along," "A Little
Woman," "One of These Days," "It's Lonely
Up Here," "Strike a Blow for Liberty," "I Got
Ettie," "An Idea Whose Time Has Come." Act
II: Entr'acte and "Follow the Crowd," "It's
Magic Time," "It's Only Money," "Rags to
Riches," "Put Your Foot Down," "It's Time to
Save the U.S.A.," "A Barker's Wife,"
"Strong! I'm Strong!," "Old," "We Can Get
Along," "I've Got a New Perspective,"
"Sideshow."
  The festival also included: WHEN YOU
COMIN' BACK, RED RYDER? (3) by Mark
Medoff, University of Montana, Missoula;
THE ROBBER BRIDEGROOM (3) by Alfred
Uhry and Robert Waldman, Rhode Island
College; THE AMOROUS FLEA (3) by Jerry
Devine and Bruce Montgomery, Wayne State
University; THE BRIG (3) by Kenneth H.
Brown, University of Detroit; THE
LEARNED LADIES (3) by Molière, trans-
lated by Richard Wilbur, Smith College;
EQUUS (2) by Peter Shaffer, Portland State
University.

GRACIOUS LIVING (30). By Samuel
Taylor. May 7, 1978 (world premiere). Direc-
tor, Edwin Sherin; scenery, Oliver Smith;
lighting, Roger Morgan; costumes, Jane
Greenwood.
Donald Renshaw .... Paul Hecht
Steve Miller .... Gerald Hiken
Victoria Blunt .... Tammy Grimes
Daisy Bowhistle
Tuttle .... Patricia Routledge
Donald (Sonny) Tuttle .... Jamie Ross
  Time: Spring of a year in the 1970s. Place:
Beverly Hills and London. An aging movie star
is confronted with the full-grown evidence of his
youthful indiscretions when he returns to Lon-
don to star in a revival of Hamlet. One inter-
mission.

Note: The Eisenhower season also included pre-Broadway productions of Do You Turn Somersaults?, The Merchant, A Touch of the Poet and The Mighty Gents, and a touring production of
Absent Friends.

Note: The John F. Kennedy Opera House season included the D'Oyly Carte, The Grand Kabuki,
Marcel Marceau, touring productions of Porgy and Bess, Pippin and A Chorus Line, Victor Borge
and the pre-Broadway production of Timbuktu!

John F. Kennedy Center: Chautauqua Tent

WALT (16). One-man show based on the writings of Walt Whitman. November 29, 1978 (world premiere). Director, Anne Occhiogrosso; costumes, Tim Evans. With Randall Duk Kim. Produced by the American Players Theater. No intermission.

National Theater

FDR (24). One-man show by Dore Schary. November 8, 1977. Director, Jeff Bleckner; scenery and lighting, H. R. Poindexter; costumes, Noel Taylor. Produced by Don Gregory, Bill Loeb and James Davis. With Robert Vaughn.

SPOTLIGHT (6). Musical by Richard Seff; music by Jerry Bressler; lyrics by Lyn Duddy. January 11, 1978 (world premiere). Director, David Black; scenery, Robert Randolph; lighting, Roger Morgan; costumes, Robert Mackintosh; choreography, Tony Stevens; musical direction, Jack Lee; orchestrations, Will Schaeffer; dance arrangements, Wally Harper.

Jack Beaumont .... Gene Barry
Siggy Zimmer .... Marc Jordan
Holly Beaumont .... D'Jamin Bartlett
Chip Beaumont ...... David-James Carroll
Mr. Kleinsinger .... William McClary
Carey .... John Leslie Wolfe
Cosmo .... Garon Douglass
Charlie; Waiter .... James Braet
Myrna .... Clare Culhane
Marie .... Lenora Nemetz
Louisa May .... Debbie Shapiro
Brawn .... Gary Daniel
Mona .... Cynthia Stewart
1st Contender .... Freda Soiffer
2d Contender;
  Young Woman .... Michelle Stubbs
3d Contender .... Eileen Casey
Lu Ellen .... Terry Calloway
Janet; Night Woman ..... Michon Peacock
Passerby .... Loyd Sannes
Leaflet Man .... Wayne Mattson
Young Man .... Jeffrey Spielman
Louise Pembley .... Polly Rowles
  Time: 1955 to the present. Place: Jack Beaumont's home in Beverly Hills; a Hollywood studio: New York City. A faded Hollywood song and dance man looks back over his life and career. One intermission.
  Musical Numbers — Act I: "No Regrets," "What Am I Bio," "Spotlight," "You Need Someone," "Round and Round," "Tricks of the Trade," "Notice Me," "Everything." Act II: "Didn't You Used to Be Him?," "Such a Business," "The Stranger in the Glass," "You Are You," "Where is Everybody?," "Spotlight."

Note: The National season also included touring productions of *Lily Tomlin in Appearing Nitely, Bubbling Brown Sugar, For Colored Girls Who Have Considered Suicide/When the Rainbow is Enuf, Paul Robeson, Grease, Annie,* and the pre-Broadway production of *Man of La Mancha.*

Olney, Md. Theater

THAT CHAMPIONSHIP SEASON (21). By Jason Miller. May 31, 1977. Director, James D. Waring; scenery and lighting, James D. Waring; costumes, Kaye A. Byars. With Herb Voland, Ben Slack, John C. Capodice, Robert Murch, David Snell.

TOWARDS ZERO (21). By Agatha Christie. June 21, 1977. Director, Leo Brady; scenery, Rolf Beyer; lighting, James D. Waring; costumes, Meryl Schaffer. With Judith McGilligan, Roger Baron, J. Robert Dietz, Alan Share, Mimi Salamanca, Linda Patchell.

ABSURD PERSON SINGULAR (21). By Alan Ayckbourn. July 12, 1977. Director, James D. Waring; scenery and lighting, James D. Waring; costumes, Meryl Schaffer. With Anita Dangler, Michael Rothhaar, George Taylor, Judith McGilligan, Pat Karpen, Rudolph Willrich.

THE TENTH MAN (21). By Paddy Chayefsky. August 2, 1977. Director, Leo Brady; scenery, Rolf Beyer; lighting, James D. Waring; costumes, Meryl Schaffer. With Albert M. Ottenheimer, Roger De Koven, Pat Karpen, Rudolph Willrich, Carl Don, J. Robert Dietz, Bernie Passeltiner, David Little.

PHILADELPHIA HERE I COME! (21). By Brian Friel. August 23, 1977. Director, James

D. Waring; scenery, Rolf Beyer; lighting, James D. Waring; costumes, Lillian Mikiver; special music, The Celtic Folk. With Pauline

Flanagan, Tom-Patrick Dineen, Jarlath Conroy, Roger De Koven, Helena Carroll, Judith McGilligan.

Shakespeare Summer Festival

ROMEO AND JULIET (30). By William Shakespeare. July 5, 1977. Director, Roger Meersman; scenery and lighting, C. H. Vaughan III; costumes, Marjorie Slaiman.

With Lanny Thomas, Helena Light, Shepard Sobel, John Elko, Leah Kremer, Carter Reardon. Produced by Ellie Chamberlain in cooperation with the National Park Service.

Wolf Trap Farm Park

SOUTH PACIFIC (7). Musical by Oscar Hammerstein II and Joshua Logan; music by Richard Rodgers; lyrics by Oscar Hammerstein II. August 22, 1977. Director, Donald Driver; scenery, Peter Wolf; costumes, Brooks

Van-Horn; choreography, Arthur Faria: musical direction, Herbert Hecht. With Jane Powell, Howard Keel, Brandon Maggart, Queen Yahna, Joanna Pang, James Ferrier.

WATERFORD, CONN.

Eugene O'Neill Theater Center: National Playwrights Conference

(President, George C. White; artistic director, Lloyd Richards; assistant to artistic director, Nancy Quinn; designers, Fred Voelpel, Bil Mikulewicz, Arden Fingerhut, Ian Calderon. All programs new works in progress)

Barn Theater (indoors)

TERRA NOVA (2). By Ted Tally, July 15, 1977. Director, John Dillon; dramaturg, Edith Oliver.
Scott .... Ron Randell
Amundsen .... Robert Burr
Bowers .... Richard Backus
Wilson .... John Heard
Oates .... Paul Collins
Evans .... Michael Sacks
Kathleen .... Cara Duff-MacCormick
    Time: The winter of 1911-1912. One intermission.

THE LAST AMERICAN DIXIELAND BAND (2). July 20, 1977. Director, Dennis Scott; dramaturg, Edith Oliver.
Bessie .... Ethel Ayler
Reggie .... Reuben Green
Joy Boy .... George Lee Miles
Catman Davis .... Richard Ward
Sporty Ody .... Joe Seneca
Alice Lemures .....Cara Duff-MacCormick
Peter King .... Ron Randell
    Time: The recent past. Place: Chicago. One intermission.

GAZELLE BOY (2). By Ronald Tavel, July 23, 1977. Director, John Dillon; dramaturg, Arthur Ballet.
Dorcas (Timothy Ingsley) ...John Pielmeier
Delarai Edelston .... Grayson Hall
Fiona Grovner ....Rosemary De Angelis
Michael Northshield ....William Metzo
Margaret Malaroy .... Jane Cronin
Archdeacon .... Richard Backus
    Attendants at the Agamemnon Home, Members of the Congregation of the Mission of St. George, Royal Canadian Mounted Police: John Heard, Jeanne Ruskin, Michael Sacks John Seitz, Tom Waites. Stage directions read by Paul Collins.
    Time: 1946 and early the following summer. Place: Province of British Columbia, Canada. Act I, Prologue: The compound of the Agamemnon Mental Home at Earls Cove, spring 1946. Scene 1: Anglican Mission of St. George outside a small coastal town in the wilderness north of Vancouver, September 1946. Act II, Scene 1: The Archdeacon's residence on Vancouver Island, October. Scene

2: The loft of the Mission, October. Scene 3: The Mission, third Sunday in November. Act I staged in Barn Theater, Act II staged in Amphitheater (outdoors).

UNCOMMON WOMEN AND OTHERS (2). By Wendy Wasserstein. July 26, 1977. Director, Steven Robman; dramaturg, Marilyn Stasio.
Man's Voice .... Bryan Clark
Kate .... Kate Mulgrew
Samantha .... K. McKenna
Holly .... Kathryn Grody
Muffet .... Judith Light
Rita .... Swoosie Kurtz
Mrs. Plum .... Jo Nichols
Leilah .... Jeanne Ruskin
Susie Friend .... Stacey Nelkin
Carter ....Anna Levine
One intermission.

EMINENT DOMAIN (2). By Percy Granger. July 29, 1977. Director, Lynne Meadow; dramaturg, Arthur Ballet.
Holmes Bradford ....Ron Randell

Amphitheater (Outdoors)

CUSTER (2). By Robert E. Ingham. August 5, 1977. Director, Robert Ackerman; dramaturg, Arthur Ballet.
Custer .... Frank Converse
Reno .... Jeffrey DeMunn
Benteen ....John Seitz

Instant Theater (Outdoors)

SCOOTER THOMAS MAKES IT TO THE TOP OF THE WORLD (2). By Peter Parnell. July 13, 1977. Director, Dennis Scott; dramaturg, Marilyn Stasio.
Dennis ....John Pielmeir
Scooter ....Tom Waites
No intermission.

WINDFALL APPLES (2). By Roma Greth. July 18, 1977. Director, John Desmond; dramaturg, Arthur Ballet.
June Eisenhart ....Anna Levine
Wally Eisenhart .... Bryan Clark
Lorraine Eisenhart .... Jane Cronin
Danielle .... Stacey Nelkin
Tony ....Tom Waites
Martin ....Alan Rosenberg
Time: Early November of 1943. Place: A small American town. Two intermissions.

TWO SMALL BODIES (2). By Neal Bell.

Katie Bradford .... Jane Cronin
Victor Salt .... John Heard
Stoddard Oates ....Richard Backus
John Ramsey .... Edmund Lyndeck
Robert Sharron .... Gilbert Lewis
Time: The present. Place: A university town in the Midwest. One intermission.

AT THE END OF LONG ISLAND: AN ENDSUMMER DAYDREAM (2). By Richard Lees. August 1, 1977. Director, Sheldon Larry; dramaturg, Marilyn Stasio.
Jonathan ....Nicholas Saunders
Vera .... Joan Croydon
Barbara .... Kim Hunter
Jamie ....Anna Levine
Josh ....Alan Rosenberg
Mr. Burdin ....Alfred Hinckley
Mrs. Burdin .... Jo Nichols
Jason .... Jeffrey DeMunn
Time: August 10, 1974, a Saturday, the day after Richard Nixon has left Washington for good: Place: A summer home at the end of Long Island. One intermission.

Libbie Custer .... Judith Light
Company: Richard Backus, John Heard, Alan Rosenberg Jeanne Ruskin, Tom Waites.
Time and place: The here and now. One intermission.

July 22, 1977. Director, Lynne Meadow; dramaturg, Marilyn Stasio.
Lt. Brann .... Frank Converse
Eileen Maloney .... Swoosie Kurtz
One intermission.

PRAYER FOR MY DAUGHTER (2). By Thomas Babe. July 28, 1977. Director, Robert Ackerman; dramaturg, Edith Oliver.
Jack .... Jeffrey DeMunn
Jimmy ....Alan Rosenberg
Sean .... Michael Sacks
Kelly ....John Seitz
One intermission. Title later changed to A Prayer for My Daughter.

THE ELUSIVE ANGEL (2). By Jack Gilhooley. August 3, 1977. Director, Steven Robman; dramaturg, Edith Oliver.
Carlton Pine .... Michael Sacks
Mary Pine .... Swoosie Kurtz

Slick Jessup .... Graham Beckel
Bo Peep Braxton .... K. McKenna
Lucy ....Anna Levine

Ken Harrison ....Bryan Clark
One intermission.

WEST SPRINGFIELD, MASS.

Stage West

(Managing director, Stephen E. Hays; artistic director, Rae Allen)

THE LITTLE FOXES (23). By Lillian Hellman. November 5, 1977. Director, Rae Allen. With Carrie Nye/Jan Ferrand, Nancy Sellin, Richard Lupino, Alley Mills, Robert Nichols, Jack R. Marks, Douglas Stender.

A CHRISTMAS CAROL (36). By Charles Dickens; adapted by Rae Allen and Timothy Near. December 4, 1977. Director, Timothy Near. With Ronald Bishop, Jan Farrand, Richard Lupino, Kathleen Bernard.

In Repertory

LOOT (13). By Joe Orton. January 6, 1978. Director, Peter Mark Schifter. With Gwyllum Evans, Nancy Sellin, Douglas Stender, Chris Romilly, Ronald Bishop, John Wallace Spencer.

RIB CAGE (17). By Larry Ketron. January 8, 1978 (world premiere). Director, Rae Allen;

scenery, Thomas Cariello; lighting, Barley Harris; costumes, Christina Weppner.
Vernie ....Alley Mills
Hodge .... David Selby
Sheryl ....Janet Ward
Richard ....John Strasberg
Carolyn .... Ellen Endicott
Posten .... James Hilbrandt
Time: The mid-1970's. Place: A house in South Carolina. Act I: Late afternoon. Act II: An hour or so later.

THREE SISTERS (22). By Anton Chekhov. February 11, 1978. Director, Rae Allen. With Zina Jasper, Nancy Sellin, Judy Jurgaitis, George Touliatos, Jeffrey Horowitz.

VANITIES (38). By Jack Heifner. March 11, 1978. Director, Larry Carpenter. With Timothy Near, Anne Cohen, Nancy Sellin.

Designers: scenery, Lawrence King, Jerry Rojo, Thomas Cariello; lighting, Barley Harris, John Gisondi, Barbara Ling; costumes, Christina Weppner.

Note: *A Bag Full of Stories* by Peter Elbling and Timothy Near, dealing with the frustrations and discoveries of elementary school age children, was toured by Stage West during January and February, 1978 to schools in the area. Timothy Near directed; with Bev Lubin, Anne Cohen, Kit Randall, Phillip C. Curry, Judy Jurgaitis, Thomas Dillon (all members of the regular company).

CANADA

CALGARY, ALBERTA

Theater Calgary: Mainstage

(Artistic director, Harold G. Baldridge; associate director, Rick McNair)

THAT CHAMPIONSHIP SEASON (23). By Jason Miller. October 17, 1977. Director, Brian Rintoul. With Doug McGrath, Sean McCann, James B. Douglas, Ken James, John Bentley.

SLEUTH (28). By Anthony Shaffer. November 17, 1977. Director, Barry Morse. With Christopher Gaze, Barry Morse.

THE CONDEMNED OF ALTONA (23). By Jean-Paul Sartre. January 5, 1978. Director, Harold G. Baldridge. With Douglas Campbell, Terry Tweed, Sheila Junor-Moore, Michael Ball, Alex Diakun.

THE PLAYBOY OF THE WESTERN WORLD (26). By John Millington Synge.

February 9, 1978. Director, Frances Hyland. With Mary Haney, Brian MacGabhann, Michael Hall, David Ferry, Patricia Phillips, Des Smiley.

STREAMERS (23). By David Rabe. March 23, 1978. Director, Harold G. Baldridge. With L'yn Ivall, John Hamelin, Dino Shorte, Brian

Paul, Elliot McIver, Michael Ball, Robert Koons.

THE IMPORTANCE OF BEING EARNEST (26). By Oscar Wilde. April 27, 1978. Director, Harold G. Baldridge. With Michael Ball, Stephen Hair, Sheila Haney, Brigid Johnston, Robert Koons.

Theater Calgary: Second Stage

HOSANNA (7). By Michel Tremblay; translated by John Van Burek and Bill Glassco. December 14, 1977. Director, Alex Dmitriev. With Nicholas Campbell, Jack Ackroyd.

BOILER ROOM SUITE (7). By Rex Deverell. March 8, 1978. Director Rick McNair. With

Sheila Junor-Moore, Des Smiley, David Yorston.

TRAVESTIES (7). By Tom Stoppard. May 24, 1978. Director, Harold G. Baldridge. With Stephen Walsh, Stephen Hair, John Hamelin, Brigid Johnston, Maureen Thomas, David Yorston.

Designers: scenery, Judith Lee; scenery and costumes, Pat Flood, Terry Gunvardahl, Richard Roberts, Ted Roberts, William Layton, David Lovett, Douglas MacLean; lighting, Gavin Semple, Pat Flood, Jeffrey Dallas.

Note: The Stage Coach Players, Theater Calgary's touring company, was established in 1977 to tour schools and communities in Calgary and Southern Alberta. From November 17, 1977 to March 28, 1978, they presented an adaptation of *Beowulf* (123); two new plays, *Dr. Bernardo's Pioneers* (43) and *Dollars and Dreams* (8) written and directed by Rick McNair; scenery and costumes, Pat Flood, Ron Fedoruk, Paul Joyal; with Milton Branton, Vicki Hargreaves, Duval Lang, Grant Lowe, Sandy Mayzell, Bill Woodward.

HALIFAX, NOVA SCOTIA

Neptune Theater

(Artistic director, David Renton)

ARMS AND THE MAN (24). By George Bernard Shaw. November 14, 1977. With Nicola Lipman, Florence Paterson, Melody Ryane, Dan MacDonald, John Dunsworth, Joseph Rutten, Douglas Chamberlain.

THE SNOW QUEEN (28). By Ray Whitley and Mark DeWolf; adapted from Hans Christian Andersen. December 10, 1977. Director, David Renton; composer/music director, John Roby; dance coordinator, Douglas Chamberlain. With Melody Rayne, Florence Paterson, Deni Allaire, Bruce Armstrong, Barrie Baldaro, Greg Wanless.

THE GINGERBREAD LADY (24). By Neil Simon. January 8, 1978. Director, William Davis. With Mary McMurray, Toby Tarnow, George Merner, Melody Ryane, Don Allison, Deni Allaire.

A DOLL'S HOUSE (24). By Henrik Ibsen; translated by Michael Meyer. February 6, 1978. Director, Bernard Hopkins. With Diana Leblanc, Chuck Shamata, Daniel Buccos, Pam Rogers, David Renton.

SAME TIME, NEXT YEAR (34). By Bernard Slade. March 6, 1978. Director, David Renton. With Joan Gregson, David Brown.

Designers: scenery and costumes; Robert Doyle, Art Penson; lighting, Trevor Parson, R. A. Elliot.

Note: *Same Time, Next Year* toured the Provinces of Nova Scotia, New Brunswick and Prince Edward Island from March 29-April 9, 1978.

MONTREAL, QUEBEC

Centaur Theater Company

(Artistic director, Maurice Podbrey)

EVE (50). By Larry Fineberg; based on *The Book of Eve* by Constance Beresford-Howe. November 10, 1977. Director, Maurice Podbrey. With Helen Hughes, Gillie Fenwick, Lawrence Benedict, Ian De Voy, Steptimiu Sever, Susan Gibson.

THE SEA (32). By Edward Bond. January 5, 1978. Director, Elsa Bolam. With Griffith Brewer, Peter Froehlich, Raymond Clarke, Moya Fenwick, Wendy Dawson.

TORONTO (33). By David Fennario. February 2, 1978 (world premiere). Director, Eric Steiner; designer, Shawn Kerwin; lighting, Steven Hawkins.

Jerry	Brian Smegal
Linda	Marie Romain Aloma
Randall	Tom Butler
Harry Brown	Mitchell Jason
Brian	Geoffrey Bowes
Joan	Diane Polley
Newton	Myron Natwick
Rae	Wayne Robson

No intermission.

BACK TO BEULAH (32). By W. O. Mitchell. March 16, 1978. Director, Maurice Podbrey. With Helen Hughes, Griffith Brewer, Janet Barkhouse, Clare Coulter, Diane Dewey, Victor Knight, Philippe Robert.

THE DREAM PLAY (50). By August Strindberg; English translation by Anthony Ibbotson and Bill Glassco; adaptation by Jean Herbiet. April 13, 1978. Directors, Jean Herbiet, Felix Mirbt; director of voices, Maurice Podbrey; scenery and costumes, Michael Eagan; lighting, Pierre-René Goupil; puppets created by Felix Mirbt; assisted by Carolyne Davis. With voices: Joy Coghill, Ian de Voy, Jill Frappier, Vlasta Vrana; puppeteers: Louis Di Bianco, Felix Mirbt, Robert More, Robert Pot, Michael Rudden.

THE ISLAND (32). By Athol Fugard, John Kani and Winston Nishona. May 25, 1978. Director, Maurice Podbrey. With Alton Kumalo, Errol Slue.

Designers: scenery and costumes, Alison Green, Michael Eagan, Barbra Matis, Shawn Kerwin, Wendell Dennis; lighting, Marsha Sibthorpe, Harry Fehner, Vladimer Svetlovsky, Steven Hawkins, Pierre-René Goupil.

Special Productions:

CRUEL TEARS (33). By Ken Mitchell and Humphrey and the Dumptrucks. October 13, 1977. An Arts Club Theater production. Director, Brian Richmond; musical director, the Dumptrucks; choreographer, Gisa Cole. With Winston Rekert, Anne Wright, Alex Diakun, Janet Wright, Norman Browning, Bruce Greenwood, Harry Kalensky, Beth Kaplan and other members of Arts Club Theater Company.

SIZWE BANZI IS DEAD (9). By Athol Fugard. March 28, 1978. Director, Maurice Podbrey. With Alton Kumalo and Errol Slue. A Centaur Theater Company production, following national tour.

LE SONGE (THE DREAM PLAY). French-language production of the National Arts Center, Ottawa. May 24, 1978.

Note: Centaur Theater Company sent two productions on tour during 1977-1978 to Ontario and Quebec: *Sizwe Banzi Is Dead,* which played at the Centaur Mainstage following the tour (as noted in foregoing listing) and the 1976-77 Centaur production of *Nothing to Lose* by David Fennario. Centaur Theater Company operates two theaters, Centaur I and Centaur II but prefers not to designate which productions are scheduled for each.

Jo-Ann Quérel and Michel Coté in *Floralie* at National Arts Center Theater Company

OTTAWA, ONT.

National Arts Center Theater Company: Mainstage — English

(Director general, Donald MacSween)

FLORALIE (18). By Roch Carrier; translated by Sheila Fischman. November 28, 1977 (English language premiere). Director, Jean Gascon; scenery, Michel Catudal; lighting, Francois Bedard; costumes, Solange Legendre, Francois Barbeau; music, Michel Hinton; choreographer, Brian MacDonald.

Floralie .... Jo-Ann Querel
Anthyme .... Michel Cote
Father; Nombrillet .... Guy L'Ecuyer
Mother; Envy .... Claire Faubert
Cure; Avarice .... Gilles Provost
Candidate; Jos Violon;
   Neron .... Pierre Theriault
Idiot; Dwarf .... Yves Jacques

Germaine; Pride .... Veronique Le Flaguais
Robaudi; Lust .... Jacques Zouvi
Eugenie; Gluttony .... Claudia Theriault
1st Worker; Juste;
   Wrath .... Pierre Collin
Anatole; Sloth .... Denis Lacroix
2d Worker; Julien .... Gerard Anderson
   Villagers: Renejean Dufour, Denise Robert, Claire Saint-Denis, Jeffrey Prentice.

Time: 1910. Place: Rural La Beauce, Quebec, One intermission.

TROILUS AND CRESSIDA (18). By William Shakespeare. January 9, 1978. Director, John Wood. With John Graham-Davies,

Benedict Campbell, Jennifer Dale, Denise Fergusson, Eric Donkin, Claude Bede, Lee J. Campbell.

CAMINO REAL (18). By Tennessee Williams. February 20, 1978. Director, John Wood. With Page Fletcher, Edward Atienza, Donald Davis, Lee J. Campbell, Ray Jewers, Joyce Campion, Nicola Lipman, Denise Fergusson.

WILLIAM SCHWENCK AND ARTHUR WHO? OR SHADES OF G. AND S. (18).

Conceived and directed by Alan Laing and John Wood; words and music by W. S. Gilbert and Arthur Sullivan. May 29, 1978. With members of the National Arts Center English-speaking Company.

Studio Theater — English:
THE FATHER (18). By August Strindberg. May 8, 1978. Director, Donald Davis. With Jean Gascon, Monique Mercure, Nicky Guadagni, Jack Medley, Edward Atienza, Joan Orenstein.

Designers: scenery, Michel Catudal, John Fergusson; lighting, Francois Bedard, Nick Cernovitch, Richard C. Reinholdt, Robert Thomson; costumes, Solange Legendre, John Fergusson, Susan Benson.

National Arts Center Theater: Special Productions — English

SAME TIME, NEXT YEAR (18). By Bernard Slade. October 10, 1977. Director, Warren Crane. With Barbara Rush, Tom Troupe.

BACK TO BEULAH (18). By W. O. Mitchell. October 31, 1977. Director, John Wood. Neptune Theater Company production.

SIZWE BANZI IS DEAD (18). By Athol Fugard, John Kani and Winston Ntshona. February 13, 1978. Director, Maurice Podbrey. Centaur Theater Company production.

National Arts Center Theater Company: French

BREAK OF NOON *(Partage de Midi)* (21). By Paul Claudel. October 3, 1977. Director, Olivier Reichenbach. With Sophie Clement, Jean-Marie Lemieux, Guy Nodon, Rene Gagnon.

THE DREAM PLAY *(Le Songe)* (14). By August Strindberg. Adapted by Jean Herbiet. December 5, 1977. Directors, Jean Herbiet, Felix Mirbt; puppets by Felix Mirbt with Carolyn Davis. The voices, Monique Brasseur,

Hubert Gagnon, Rene Gagnon, Hedwige Herbiet; puppeteers, Louis Di Bianco, Felix Mirbt, Robert More, Robert Pot, Michael Rudder.

THE SEA GULL (*La Mouette*) (28). By Anton Chekhov; translated by Arthur Adamov. April 3, 1978. Director, Olivier Reichenbach. With Kim Yaroshevskaya, Paul Savoie, Christiane Raymond, Jean-Marie Lemieux, Jean Dalmain, Michele Magny.

Designers: scenery, Guy Neveu, Michael Eagan; lighting, Michel Beaulieu, Pierre-Rene Goupil, Nick Cernovitch; costumes, Francois Barbeau, Michael Eagan.

National Arts Center Theater: Special Productions — French

THE FLYING DOCTOR *(Le Médecin Volant)* and THE DOCTOR IN SPITE OF HIMSELF *(Le Médecin Malgre Lui)* by Molière (8). November 8, 1977. Director, Jean Gascon. Le Théâtre Populair du Quebec production.

THE ENRAGED WIDOW *(La Veuve Enragée)* (8). By Antonine Maillet. February 3, 1978. Director, Yvette Brind'Amour. Mercedes Palomino production.

THE HEIRLOOM VASE *(La Cruche Cassee).* (8). By Henri Kleist; translated by Alfred de Lostalot; adapted by Jean-Louis Roux. March 17, 1978. Director/designer, Robert Prevost. Le Théâtre du Nouveau Monde production.

THE HOSTAGE *(Un Otage).* By Brendan Behan; French adaptation, Jean Paris. (8). May 5, 1978. Director, Daniele J. Suissa. Theater du Rideau Vert.

STRATFORD, ONT.

Stratford Festival: Festival Stage

(Artistic director, Robin Phillips; director of Festival Stage, William Hutt; founder, Tom Patterson).

A MIDSUMMER NIGHT'S DREAM (24). By William Shakespeare. June 6, 1977. Director, Robin Phillips. With Maggie Smith, Lewis Gordon, Alan Scarfe, Domini Blythe.

ALL'S WELL THAT ENDS WELL (36). By William Shakespeare. June 7, 1977. Director, David Jones. With Martha Henry, Margaret Tyzack, William Hutt, Tom Wood, Richard Monette, Nicholas Pennell.

RICHARD III (37). By William Shakespeare. June 8, 1977. Director, Robin Phillips. With Brian Bedford, Eric Donkin, Max Helpmann, Martha Henry, Mary Savidge, Alan Scarfe, Maggie Smith, Margaret Tyzack.

MUCH ADO ABOUT NOTHING (13). By William Shakespeare. August 16, 1977. Director, Marigold Charlesworth. With Martha Henry, William Needles, Alan Scarfe.

AS YOU LIKE IT (14). By William Shakespeare. August 18, 1977. Director, Robin Phillips. With Brian Bedford, Domini Blythe, Bernard Hopkins, Maggie Smith.

Designers: scenery, Susan Benson, Tanya Moiseiwitsch, Daphne Dare, Brian Jackson; lighting, Gil Wechsler.

Stratford Festival: Avon Theater

ROMEO AND JULIET (39). By William Shakespeare. June 6, 1977. Director, David William. With Leo Leyden, Marti Maraden, Richard Monette, Florence Paterson, Nicholas Pennell, Leslie Yeo.

GHOSTS (35). By Henrik Ibsen; translated by John Lingard. June 7, 1977. Director, John Wood. With Eric Donkin, William Hutt, Marti Maraden, Nicholas Pennell, Margaret Tyzack.

MISS JULIE (20). By August Strindberg. June 8, 1977. Director, Eric Steiner. With Domini Blythe, Pamela Hyatt, Douglas Rain.

THE GUARDSMAN (28). By Ferenc Molnar. June 9, 1977. Director, Robin Phillips. With Brian Bedford, Eric Donkin, Mary Savidge, Maggie Smith.

HAY FEVER (14). By Noel Coward. September 27, 1977. Director, Robin Phillips. With Domini Blythe, Richard Curnock, William Hutt, Pamela Hyatt, Marti Maraden, Richard Monette, Florence Paterson, Maggie Smith, Tom Wood.

Designers: John Ferguson, John Pennoyer, Daphne Dare, Lawrence Schafer; lighting, Gil Wechsler, Michael Whitfield; costumes, Janice Lindsay, Daphne Dare, John Pennoyer, Berthold Carriere.

VANCOUVER, B.C.

The Vancouver Playhouse: Queen Elizabeth Playhouse — Mainstage

(Artistic director, Christopher Newton)

PYGMALION (23). By George Bernard Shaw. October 7, 1977. Director, Derek Goldby. With Christopher Newton, Nicola Cavendish, Terence Kelly, Robert Clothier, Andrew Gillies.

ARSENIC AND OLD LACE (26). By Joseph Kesselring. December 2, 1977. Director, Christopher Newton. With Joy Coghill, Heather Brechin, Jim Mezon, Robert Clothier, John Innes, Laura Press.

OEDIPUS (29). By Seneca; adapted by Ted Hughes. January 6, 1978. Director, Yurek

Bogajewicz. With Terence Kelly, Margaret Robertson, Robert Clothier, Jim Mezon, Laura Press, Al Kozlik.

THE CONTRACTOR (29). By David Storey. February 17, 1978. Director, Roger Hodgman. With Robert Clothier, Jim Mezon, Laura Press, Shirley Broderick, Nicola Cavendish, John Innes.

TWELFTH NIGHT (30). By William Shakespeare. March 31, 1978. Director, Derek Goldby; special music, Roger Perkins; choreographer, Judith Marcuse. With Nicola Cavendish, Patricia Gage, Jim Mezon, Glenn MacDonald, Heather Brechin, Terence Kelly, Andrew Gillies, Christopher Newton, Herbert Foster.

The Vancouver Playhouse: David Y.H. Lui Theater — New Series

ASHES (23). By David Rudkin. September 9, 1977. Director, Susan Ferley. With Terence Kelly, Heather Brechin, Nicola Cavendish, John Innes.

A RESPECTABLE WEDDING (23). By Bertolt Brecht. November 4, 1977. Director, Derek Goldby. With Heather Brechin, Andrew Gillies, Shirley Broderick, Terence Kelly, Nicola Cavendish.

JACK SPRAT (23). By Joe Wiesenfeld. January 27, 1978 (world premiere). Director, Pamela Hawthorn; designer, Judith Lee; lighting, Jeffrey Dallas.
Jack Sprat .... Tom McBeath

Woman; Waitress, etc. ....Hilary Strang
Dorrie Sprat ....Diana Belshaw
Dunsmuir; Fox; Alfred;
   Doberman .... Reg Tupper
Abbot; Plover; Jake;
   Jackson .... Guy Bannerman
Eddie Foyer .... Brian Tope
Marlie .... Sherry Bie
   Time: The present. Place: Vancouver. One intermission.

LOOT (23). By Joe Orton. March 10, 1978. Director, Paul Reynolds. With Collin Miller, Susan Chapple, Ian Deakin, Ron Halder, Richard Gishler, Gary Chalk.

Designers: scenery and costumes, Cameron Porteous, Judith Lee; lighting, Jeffrey Dallas.

Note: The Vancouver Playhouse production of *Loot* played 28 performances in 24 communities in British Columbia and Alberta, April 3-20, 1978.

WINNEPEG, MANITOBA

Manitoba Theater Center: Mainstage

(Artistic director, Arif Hasnain)

THE LAST CHALICE (24). By Joanna Glass. October 7, 1977 (world premiere). Director, Arif Hasnain; scenery and costumes, James Bakkom; lighting, Neil McLeod.
Cam Mackenzie .... Roland Hewgill
Ruth ....Irene Hogan
Jean ....Philippa King
Duncan ....Frank Aldous
Ken Hamilton .... Robert S. Buck
Roy Cross .... Tom Celli
Billy Bradley ....David Clement
Mr. Johnson .... John Gardiner
Miss Halverson .... Patricia Hamilton
Ernie Staychuk .... Adam Henderson
Tommy ....Tim Whelan
Mike Melzewski ....George Sperdakos
   Time: 1950's. Place: Saskatoon, Saskatchewan.

KNOCK KNOCK (24). By Jules Feiffer. November 18, 1977. Director, George Keathley. With Hy Anzell, Bernie Passeltiner, Harriet Hall, Richard Blair.

THE CONTRACTOR (24). By David Storey. January 6, 1978. Director, Edward Gilbert. With Ian D. Clark, Tom-Patrick Dineen, Terence Durrant, Alan Gifford, Dorothy D'Arcy Goldrick, Robert Haley, Louisa Martin, Margaret Martin, Antony Parr, Patrick Sinclair, Cedric Smith, Gordon Stokoe.

THE NIGHT OF THE IGUANA (27). By Tennessee Williams. February 10, 1978. Director, Kurt Reis. With John McEnery, Patricia Hamilton, Araby Lockhart, Carol Teitel, Alan Gifford.

MEASURE FOR MEASURE (24). By William Shakespeare. March 17, 1978. Director, Arif Hasnain. With James Blendick, Brenda Curtis, Alan Gifford, Neil Vipond, Peter Dvorsky.

THE ROYAL HUNT OF THE SUN (24). By Peter Shaffer. April 21, 1978. Director, Timothy Bond; music, John Mills-Cockell; choreographer, Salvatore Aiello. With James Blendick, Peter Jobin, Alan Gifford, Dan Macdonald, Adam Henderson.

Manitoba Theater Center: Warehouse Theater

HELLO AND GOODBYE (15). By Athol Fugard. October 13, 1977. Director, Timothy Bond. With Peter Jobin, Toby Tarnow.

OH COWARD! (15). Devised by Roderick Cook; words and music by Noel Coward. November 24, 1977. Director, Irene Hogan; musical direction, Roger Perkins. With Pat Galloway, David Brown, Paul Craig.

THE SEA HORSE (15). By Edward J. Moore. February 23, 1978. Director, Irene Hogan. With Kathleen Perkins, Robert Haley.

ASHES (15). By David Rudkin. April 6, 1978. Director, Stephen Katz. With Leslie Carlson, Dixie Seatle, Dorothy-Ann Haug, Wayne Robson.

Designers: scenery and costumes, Peter Wingate, James Bakkom, Mark Negin, Michael Eagan, Debra Hanson, Charles Dunlop; lighting, Donald Acaster, Gilbert V. Hemsely Jr, Neil McLeod, Joan Arhelger, Monty Schneider, Bill Williams, Edsel Hilchie.

Manitoba Theater Center: Warehouse Theater — Plays in Progress

LOVE IS MEANT TO MAKE US GLAD (6). A musical revue devised and performed by Pat Galloway and David Brown. December 19, 1977. Director, Irene Hogan; musical direction, Roger Perkins; choreographer, Stephanie Ballard.

FOR LOVE AND CHICKEN SOUP (6). By Brad Leiman. May 1, 1978. Director, Alex Dmitriev.

Sammy Fleischman ...... E. M. Margolese
Howard .... Carey Castle
Ada Goldstein .... Pat Van Der Tol
Time: The present. Place: Winnipeg's North End.

Note: Prior to its Mainstage opening, Knock Knock played 7 performances (November 9-16, 1977) for students from 25 rural centers in the province of Manitoba. Snow White and the Seven Dwarfs, a new adaptation by Clive Endersby, gave 9 performances (December 23-28, 1977) at MTC; director, Gregory Tuch; scenery and costumes, Debra Hanson; lighting, Bill Williams; with members of the company. Two mime programs were presented at the Warehouse Theater: The Potato People (40), devised by the company for elementary school students (January 9-February 3, 1978); and short plays and vignettes, plus The Potato People (8), given for adults in the evenings (January 13-February 4, 1978) — created, directed and performed by the Theater Beyond Words Mime Company: Harro Maskow, artistic director, and Paulette Hallich, Terry Judd, Larry Le Febvre, Robin Patterson.

DINNER THEATER

Year of Breakthroughs

By Francine L. Trevens

Playwright, producer and co-founder of Readers and Playwrights Theater, Springfield, Mass.

This was the year that dinner theaters broke through in significant directions:

Angel, the first Broadway production which was an outgrowth of a dinner-theater premiere, came from Northstage in Glen Cove, L.I., where it premiered under the title *Look Homeward, Angel.*

General Entertainment Associates organized to find new scripts for the ever-hungry dinner-theater market.

Equity President Theodore Bikel, a frequent dinner theater star, flew to Roanoke, Va. to launch the new Equity Barn Dinner Theater with press conferences and radio and TV appearances.

Many dinner theaters were following the lead of summer and regional theaters opening cabaret spots on their premises to keep the entertainment going longer and later.

Shakeup story of the year was the dissolution of the five-and-a-half-year association of the Belkins of Coachlight Dinner Theater and their producing director, Cash Baxter. Baxter, who staged over 40 shows for the theater in that period, departed in the midst of his most successful *Pippin* in its dinner-theater debut. From there the show was to have a tour of the summer circuit.

Baxter came to Coachlight after three successful years with the Windmill Dinner Theaters in Texas. The Belkins came from the fields of engineering and merchandising. They built one of the most attractive dinner theaters in the country six years back and have had phenomenal success in maintaining high standards and strong audience support, even when a rival theater opened directly across the road within that first year. Coachlight in Warehouse Point, Conn. has long been known for its concern for audiences. Seldom can you arrive at the theater without one of the Belkins themselves — Sam, Ruth or daughter Janis — greeting you at the door and being available at the end of the evening for your expressed reactions to their play.

Theater managers who tackle new material are not always as optimistic as Northstage, which finds that pre-Broadway material draws well during their off-peak season. They feel it is worth doing such new material and note that "we create the Broadway production at a lesser cost and a greater convenience for our open audience." Since Northstage is on Long Island and competes directly with Broadway, it is natural that they would be conscious of themselves in relation to the Broadway scene.

Ed Veranth of the Country Dinner Playhouse in Dallas feels dinner theaters expose countless audiences to "theaters and plays which, without dinner theater, they would never see." One such new play was *The Latest Mrs. Adams,* which premiered starting in April, 1977 and played well into this season, traveling to the Country Dinner Playhouse in Columbus, Ohio, through June 26, 1977, then to the Beef 'n' Boards Dinner Theater through July 31, then on August 2-21 to the Harlequin Dinner Theater, Atlanta, Ga. This is one example of how a dinner-theater chain can give a new play and a fine cast (Kathryn Crosby, Mary Frances Crosby, Carter Mullally Jr., Richard Maggi, etc.) a long run and lots of audience feedback.

The Golden Apple Dinner Theater in Sarasota is another which inaugurates shows for long-term dinner-theater tours. Its plays travel under the Coastal Theater Productions, Inc. banner, their packaging subsidiary. Thus Henry Denker's *Second Time Around* played at Miami Beach Performing Arts Center, Ft. Lauderdale's Parker Playhouse, Golden Apple's Deauville Hotel branch in Miami, the Music Hall for the Performing Arts in Detroit and the Country Dinner Playhouse in St. Petersburg.

The Alhambra Dinner Theater in Jacksonville, Fla., which has a strong preference for new shows (four in one calendar year) notes that "inflation is our biggest problem." Although they do new material, dinner theaters are not subsidized, as are many regional theaters and off-off Broadway companies which launch new works. Mike Clark, general manager of the Firehouse Dinner Theater, which has done new plays in the past, noted that they'd do a new show "anytime we have a good property. Our audiences hope to see a big hit in its beginnings." He feels his Omaha theater has been "educating the audience to the vast appeal of theater and that it is now easier" to experiment more. Their all-time greatest success was their premiere production of *Red Dawg*.

There is a relaxed, family feeling at many dinner theaters, where repeat business over the years has made audience members feel they are part of the show. Seldom, however, do they get into the act as actively as an 81-year-old customer at a Sunday brunch performance of *Last of the Red Hot Lovers* at the Firehouse. During intermission she whipped out her harmonica and played three tunes which brought the house down, making it difficult for Barney Cushman and Bobbi Michelle to follow with their scripted act.

The Alhambra finds it can provide both old and new fare despite being in a situation where the Jacksonville Electric Authority keeps blowing substations, which causes city-wide blackouts not unlike those that have plagued New York's audiences. "I have learned to live with them and work around them, having my patrons eat by emergency lights and actors make up by candle light," says producer W. C. Hartigan. His theater's philosophy is that since many audiences become acquainted with theater through exposure to dinner theater, it is therefore essential that the material being produced be good, whether it is new or old. To that we can all add "Amen."

These shows premiered in dinner theaters during the 1977-78 season:

HOT SHOT (5 weeks) by Don Appell. May 31, 1977. Directed by Don Appell; scenery, Ham Waddell; lighting, Rob Chase; costumes, Sherry Stewart. With Gene Barry, Joy McConnochie, Maida Severn, Michael Graves, David Coxwell, Mark Leiberman, Elmore Vincent, Michael Piontek, Betty Claire Barry. Alhambra Dinner Theater, Jacksonville, Fla.

LOOK HOMEWARD, ANGEL (8 weeks) based on the novel by Thomas Wolfe; book by Ketti Frings and Peter Udell; music by Gary Geld, lyrics by Peter Udell. January 6, 1978. Directed by Philip Rose; scenery, Ming Cho Lee; lighting, David Kissel; costumes, Pearl Somner; musical direction, William Cox; choreography, Robert Tucker. With Frances

Sternhagen, Fred Gwynne, Don Scardino, Joel Higgins, Leslie Ann Ray, Peg Lamprey, Patti Allison, Justine Johnston. Northstage Dinner Theater, Glen Cove, L.I.

SECOND TIME AROUND (4 weeks) by Henry Denker. January 17, 1978. Directed by Robert Ennis Turoff; scenery, Ray Perry; lighting, David Ferguson; costumes, James Delaney Collum. With Molly Picon, Frank Bara, Philip LeStrange, Lydia Franklin, Kathleen Klein, J. Robert Dietz, Peter Ivanov. Golden Apple Dinner Theater, Sarasota, Fla.

WHO WANTS FAT HAIR? (7 weeks) by George Tibbles. February 28, 1978. Directed by Jack Hallett; scenery, Ham Waddell; lighting, Rob Chance; costumes, Sherry Stewart. With Morey Amsterdam, Donald McGrath, Donna Drewes, Melva Williams, Robbie Fian, Lee H. Doyle. Alhambra Dinner Theater.

KINDLING (3 weeks) by Don Appell, April 11, 1978. Directed by Don Appell; scenery, Ham Waddell; lighting, Ron Chance; costumes, Sherry Stewart. With Cyd Charisse, John Brandon, Angus Duncan, Sandy Freeman. Alhambra Dinner Theater.

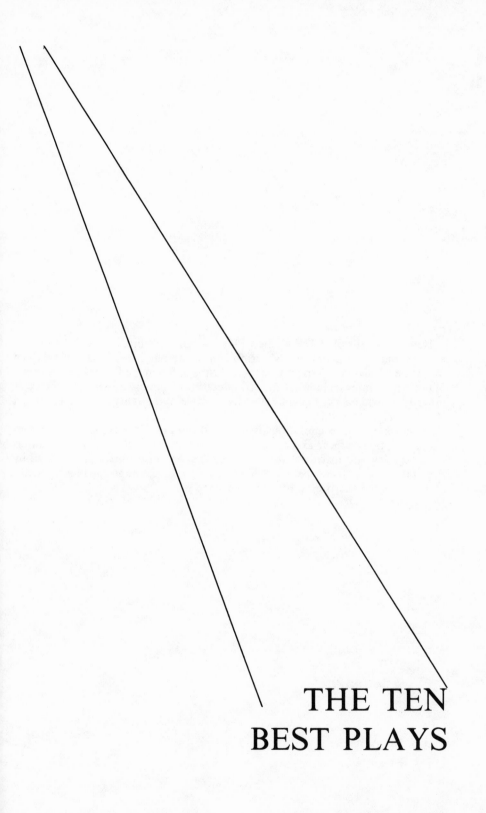

THE TEN
BEST PLAYS

Here are details of 1977–78's Best Plays — synopses, biographical sketches of authors and other material. By permission of the publishing companies which own the exclusive rights to publish these scripts in full in the United States, some of our continuities include substantial quotations from crucial/pivotal scenes in order to provide a permanent reference to style and quality as well as theme, structure and story line.

In the case of such quotations, scenes and lines of dialogue, stage directions and descriptions appear *exactly* as in the stage version or published script unless (in a very few instances, for technical reasons) an abridgement is indicated by five dots (. . . . .). The appearance of three dots (. . .) is the script's own punctuation to denote the timing of a spoken line.

THE GIN GAME

A Play in Two Acts

BY D. L. COBURN

Cast and credits appear on pages 354-355

D. L. COBURN was born in Baltimore Aug. 4, 1938 and was educated at the public high school. He served as an enlisted man in the Navy aboard a destroyer from 1958 to 1960. Sensing as yet no particular motivation toward a writing career, he moved to Dallas in 1968, working as a creative consultant in market- ing and other types of special problems for clients in Mexico City, Houston, Dallas and New York.

A couple of years ago, Coburn happened to attend a performance by Tom Troupe in a stage version of Diary of a Madman. *The show aroused some in- stinct deep within him and he began to think of himself as a serious writer. After returning to several more performances of the play, he went backstage to talk to Troupe, introducing himself as a playwright. Soon afterward Coburn translated the name into action and wrote a play, his first,* The Gin Game, *which had its first performance September 24, 1976 at American Theater Arts, Hollywood, and was subsequently staged by the Actors Theater in Louisville and the Long Wharf Theater in New Haven before opening on Broadway October 6, 1977 with the Cronyns and receiving a Best Play citation and the Pulitzer Prize.*

Coburn still lives in Dallas where he plays baseball with a sandlot hardball team, the Dallas Retreads (so named by him because some of its members are in the full prime of life), soars aloft in gliders whenever he can and pursues a more sedentary interest as a self-described novice Civil War buff. He is married for the second time, with two children by his first wife.

"The Gin Game": by D. L. Coburn. Copyright © 1977, 1978 by D. L. Coburn. Reprinted by per- mission of Flora Roberts, Inc. See CAUTION notice on copyright page. The complete play is pub- lished by Drama Book Specialists, 150 West 52nd Street, New York, N.Y. 10019. Inquiries con- cerning stock and amateur acting rights should be addressed to: Samuel French, Inc., 25 West 45th Street, New York, N.Y. 10036. All other inquiries should be addressed to the author's represen- tative: Flora Roberts, Inc., 65 East 55th Street, New York, N.Y. 10022.

We represent The Gin Game *in these pages with an illustrated synopsis in order to record moments from the outstanding performances of Jessica Tandy and Hume Cronyn in the play's two roles under Mike Nichols's direction, in addition to the structure of the script. The photographs of* The Gin Game *accompanying the text on the following pages depict scenes as presented by The Shubert Organization and produced by Hume Cronyn and Mike Nichols October 6, 1977 at the John Golden Theater, with scenery by David Mitchell, costumes by Bill Walker and lighting by Ronald Wallace.*

Our special thanks are tendered to the producers and their press representatives, David Powers and Barbara Carroll, for making available these selections from Zoe Dominic's excellent photographs of the show.

Time: The early 1970s

Place: The sun porch of the Bentley Nursing and Convalescent Home for the Aged

ACT I

Scene 1: Sunday afternoon, visitors day

SYNOPSIS: The Bentley Home's large sun porch has a look of disuse, loneliness and musty decay — and so does the man, Weller Martin, aged 70-75, seated at a card table playing solitaire and wearing an old bathrobe as though there were nothing to get dressed for any more, even though today is visitors day. The noisy, happy reunions with relatives and friends, whose greetings and chatter can be heard from the living room offstage, are not for him.

Through the french doors upstage comes Fonsia Dorsey, aged 65-70, also a lonely refugee from visitors day, also not quite fully dressed and groomed, with her hair severely confined in a hairnet. She is embarrassed at invading Weller's privacy and tries to ignore him, elaborately studying the greenery which decorates the porch. But Weller insists on striking up a conversation, finding that Fonsia is new here and suffers from chronic diabetes. Weller is in good health except for old age, that incurable disease from which all Bentley residents suffer. Weller and Fonsia agree that Bentley is better than one of those homes which ask you to give them all your money before they'll take you in.

Weller rises and paces with his cane (he has a slight limp). Finally he suggests a game of gin. Fonsia protests that she's not a card player; she was raised Old Time Methodist, but she used to play an occasional game of rummy. Weller promises to teach her the gin version of rummy, Hollywood scoring and all.

They sit, Weller deals and explains the game to her (as in photo above), with Jessica Tandy as Fonsia and Hume Cronyn as Weller.

While the game progresses, Fonsia tells Weller that she was once married for four years and has a son, Larry, 45, who doesn't come to see her on visitors day because he lives far away, in Denver, and hasn't been home in more than a year.

Fonsia notices that she has gin and lays down her cards. Weller is amused at her beginner's luck.

Weller deals the cards again and under Fonsia's questioning replies that he has three children, all grown, who moved away in the custody of their mother after a divorce. While they talk, Fonsia suddenly goes gin again.

During the next game, Weller tells her of his business, a marketing research firm — and this time he curses when Fonsia again goes gin.

As the next game begins, Weller hints that his business partners treated him unfairly. The sound of singing from the living room leads Weller to complain that they are over-entertained in this home by a succession of choirs, magicians, etc.

All at once, Weller senses that his next discard will be the card Fonsia is waiting for. He's right — Fonsia picks it up and goes gin. Exasperated by this steady string of defeats, Weller bangs his cane on the floor. *Curtain.*

Scene 2: Sunday afternoon, one week later

On the following Sunday, a sunny visitors day, Fonsia seeks out Weller on the porch and finds that the cards are ready on the table. Both look more presentable than on the previous Sunday. They have had little contact all week, but now Weller invites Fonsia to a re-match, which Fonsia happily accepts. For a few moments, though, they are content simply to enjoy each other's company, looking down their noses at the patronizing ways in which other people's visitors treat their elderly relatives.

Weller seldom talks to any of the other residents, who seem to be either catatonic or complaining. At last the two settle down to their game, and soon Fonsia is beating him again, knocking with three. The second hand has scarcely begun when Fonsia goes gin.

Fonsia has a moment of dizziness — probably caused by pills she is taking. Weller confesses that he too has spells, attacks of nerves, moments of inexplicable panic. Fonsia remembers those also; she had them for a while after her divorce, but they disappeared in time.

Suddenly Fonsia goes gin again, and Weller is doubly peeved to learn that she had been saving queens, so that he could have knocked earlier and beaten her. Weller tells her that saving queens is a dumb tactic, but the proof of the pudding is, she won the game.

Weller admits that he is frustrated by Fonsia's incredible run of luck. As he deals again, he is muttering about thievery at the Bentley Home and the inferior quality of the underpaid help. Again they play, and again (as in series of photos above), Fonsia goes gin.

This time Weller loses control, shouting "Jesus Christ! Do you have to win all the Goddam time??? I mean it. Can't you lose just once???"

Fonsia would rather stop playing if it makes Weller act like this. Weller promises to curb his temper and insists that they keep on with the game. He deals. They both have good hands, Weller soon needing only one of several cards to go gin. But Fonsia goes gin first, and Weller's anger becomes rage. He rises, shouts an obscenity, sweeps the cards from the table and finally overturns the table itself, frightening Fonsia as the curtain falls.

ACT II

Scene 1: The following evening, shortly after dinner

Weller comes onto the porch looking for Fonsia, who is out in the garden (the audience area) but comes back when Weller calls her name. He's embarrassed, ingratiating (photo next page), calling her Fonsie, apologetic about his behavior the previous afternoon. Fonsia admits she enjoys his company, except for his emotional reaction to losing at gin. Weller takes this as a teasing challenge; he goes to fetch the cards. When she won't play with him, he deals a game of solitaire.

Cynically, Weller characterizes the other residents as having ceased to think or feel, now merely stored here in this home waiting for their bodies to die. He also points out that he and Fonsia don't seem to have taken on much popularity in the outside world, judging from the fact that no one comes to see them on visitors day. He scoffs at the do-good attempts to cheer them all up here at the home. He convinces Fonsia that since there is really nothing much else to do here, they might as well play a few hands of gin.

As they play, Fonsia tells Weller that she had to take a job after her divorce and had an unnatural fear that she would misspell a word and allow her employers to find out that she had no education. She never even graduated from high school. While she is talking she finds that he has gin.

Weller's temper is under control, with sarcasm showing only a little around the edges as he deals the cards again. This time Fonsia discards a jack which she should have known Weller wanted because he picked up a jack a moment ago. It gives him gin, but he is angry now because he believes that Fonsia threw the game, deliberately letting him win one (photo on opposite page).

Weller now permits himself to be consumed by a kind of mad compulsion to prove that Fonsia is winning through some sort of divine intervention or other supernatural guidance. She goes gin again, and Weller demands she admit God Himself gave her the card she needed. When she does, Weller takes it as patronizing sarcasm and calls her a bitch. Instinctively, she slaps him.

Weller pulls himself together and apologizes. But he deals again, feverishly, promising that after just one more short hand they'll go in. As he plays, Weller's every other word is a curse. Fonsia makes gin and merely lays down her hand

face up, not daring to say the word aloud. Weller, again furious, goads her until she shouts it: "GIN — GODDAMIT!!! GIN!!!"

Weller rises and, limping more heavily than ever, exits, leaving Fonsia alone and shocked into stillness; angry and frightened. *Curtain.*

Scene 2: The following Sunday afternoon

Weller is alone on the sun porch, fidgeting, while a thunderstorm slowly gathers in the afternoon sky. Fonsia enters, tentatively; Weller has told one of the attendants to tell Fonsia that her sister from Ottawa is waiting on the porch to see her. Fonsia has easily seen through the transparent ruse.

Fonsia warns him that she will not play another hand of the game that seems to drive Weller crazy. Fonsia has complained to the office about Weller's violent behavior, putting him in peril of a visit from the psychiatrist, which sometimes leads to commitment to the State Mental Hospital. Weller resents her interference, though she pleads that she was only trying to get him the help he might need, even if it costs him some money.

Weller has given Fonsia the impression that as the ex-owner of his own business he must have some kind of a nest egg. Weller now admits that his money vanished into his partners' pockets, plus medical expenses after he had a heart attack, so that he is a penniless Welfare case here at the home.

Angry at Fonsia because she has wrung this confession from him, Weller characterizes her as a rigid perfectionist who finds fault with everything and probably alienated her son so that he can't stand the sight of her — that's why he never visits her, not because he lives far away in Denver. Under this goad, Fonsia in her turn becomes so angry and defensive that in spite of herself she admits that what Weller has surmised is true. Her son lives right here in town but never visits her, perhaps even hates her.

Reduced to tears, Fonsia confesses that she too is penniless and on Welfare — she once owned a little house but gave it to the church to spite her son. The thunderstorm breaks as she recalls her son expressing a wish to look up his father — it was the last straw for her in their deteriorating relationship.

Weller comforts Fonsia, calming her down even as a bolt of lightning strikes nearby. He suggests a soothing game of gin. Fonsia enjoys Weller's company, but she refuses even to discuss playing that game again. Weller taunts her: secretly she takes pleasure in beating him time after time and watching him get angry. He tries to force her to the card table but she resists, warning him that his violent behavior will bring action from the authorities. Weller accuses her of vindictiveness, infuriating her with another reference to her treatment of her son. Fonsia in turn accuses him of vindictive obsession with cards at the expense of all else, but she is now angry enough to sit at the table and confront Weller by means of the game.

Weller deals the cards. Now there is nothing between them except open hostility. Weller is sure he's going to win this time, that his luck will be different. With deliberate cruelty, Fonsia taunts him with using luck as an excuse — maybe Weller is just a rotten gin player, and maybe in earlier life he was also just a rotten business man, so that luck and/or his partners had nothing to do with his failure.

Weller shouts an obscenity at her. Fonsia calls him "a filthy foulmouth," like her husband, upon whom she had her revenge when he came home one night intoxicated and found all his possessions and himself thrown out into the street.

Fonsia makes the mistake of mentioning her bad luck with men, and Weller picks her up on it — she also is leaning on luck as an alibi for her failures. He has made his point, as she made hers before. In their anger they have torn away each other's pretensions and left themselves exposed, defenseless.

They play the game, cursing at each other. Suddenly Fonsia goes gin. For Weller this is the end of the line. He rises, out of control now, and strikes the table with his cane (as above on opposite page), punctuating each blow with his cry, "GIN! GIN! GIN! GIN! GIN! GIN! GIN!"

Suddenly, Weller stops, stares at Fonsia for a moment and then, limping, slowly exits looking very much like an empty, sleepwalking old man (below). Fonsia is alone, whimpering. *Curtain.*

Ellis Rabb as Robert and Peter Evans as John in a scene from *A Life in the Theater*

A LIFE IN THE THEATER

A Play in One Act and 26 Scenes

BY DAVID MAMET

Cast and credits appear on pages 411-412

DAVID MAMET was born Nov. 30, 1947 in Flossmoor, Ill. He graduated from Goddard College in Vermont with a B.A. in English literature in 1969, after having observed creative theater at close quarters as a busboy at Second City in Chicago and having studied it for a year or two at a professional school in New York. From 1971 to 1973 he was artist-in-residence at Goddard. In 1974 he became a member of the Illinois Arts Council faculty and in 1975 he helped found and served for a time as artistic director of St. Nicholas Theater Company in Chicago, which mounted the first productions of some of Mamet's scripts including Reunion, Squirrels, Duck Variations *and* Sexual Perversity in Chicago. *He continues to serve St. Nicholas as playwright-in-residence.*

Mamet's first New York production was Duck Variations *off off Broadway at St. Clements in May, 1975, followed by* Sexual Perversity *at the same group in September, 1975. His* American Buffalo *moved from its world premiere at Chicago's Goodman Theater Stage Two in October, 1975 to St. Clements in January, 1976, and Mamet received the 1975-76 Obie as best new playwright for these latter two works.*

Mamet's career on the professional New York stage began with the off-Broadway program of Duck Variations *and* Sexual Perversity *which opened at the Cherry Lane in June, 1976 and ran for 273 performances. His* American Buffalo *was produced on Broadway in February, 1977 and was named a Best Play of its season and won the Critics Award for best American play. His second Best Play,* A Life in the Theater, *opened off Broadway on Oct. 20 and was still running as this season ended. Another Mamet script,* The Water Engine, *was produced this season Dec. 20 at the New York Shakespeare Festival Public*

"A Life in the Theater": by David Mamet. Copyright © 1975, 1977 by David Mamet. Reprinted by permission of Grove Press, Inc. See CAUTION notice on copyright page. All inquiries should be addressed to the publisher: Grove Press, Inc., 196 West Houston Street, New York, N.Y. 10014.

155

Theater for 63 performances and then brought uptown to Broadway on a bill with a curtain-raiser Mamet wrote especially for this occasion, Mr. Happiness, *March 6 for 16 more performances.*

Mamet's long list of playwriting awards and grants includes Joseph Jefferson Awards for distinguished Chicago shows to Sexual Perversity *in 1975 and* American Buffalo *in 1976; a New York State Council on the Arts Plays for Young Audiences grant in 1976 for* The Revenge of the Space Panda, or Binky Rudich and the Two-Speed Clock; *a Rockefeller playwriting-in-residence grant in 1976, and a CBS Fellowship at Yale in 1977.*

The following synopsis of A Life in the Theater *was prepared by Jeff Sweet. Parentheses around lines of dialogue are the playwright's punctuation intended, in his own words, "to mark a slight change of outlook on the part of the speaker — perhaps a momentary change to a more introspective regard."*

Time: The present

Place: Various spots around a theater

Scene 1

SYNOPSIS: Backstage, Robert and John discuss that evening's performance — the opening night of the newest offering of the regional theater with which they are associated. They congratulate each other and comment on the intelligence of the audience. "I feel perhaps they saw a better show than the one we rehearsed," Robert says. Robert, *"an older actor,"* is given to making pronouncements on the Art of the Theater. John, younger, and apparently new to the company, listens dutifully, intent on winning the other's approval.

Robert asks about John's immediate plans. John says he's going out to eat. Now that the show is open, he has his appetite back.

John says again that he liked Robert's work that night. Robert thinks one of his own scenes, a courtroom scene, was off. John insists that it was fine, though he thought that another of Robert's scenes, a doctor scene, may have been a bit "brittle." Though he doesn't say so, Robert is a bit taken aback, and John, sensing this, begins to hedge and qualify his comment. Robert, regaining his composure, insists he values the younger actor's opinion. John hedges a little more, saying that the fault lay with the actress with whom Robert was playing the scene, that "it's a marvel you can work with her at all."

That's what being a pro is about, Robert indicates, graciously accepting the compliment: "You have a job to do. You do it by your lights, you bring your expertise to bear, your sense of rightness . . . fellow feelings . . . etiquette . . . professional procedure . . . there are tools one brings to bear . . . procedure."

John finds Robert's statement "inspiring." They criticize the actress severely for mugging, mincing and stilted diction.

ROBERT: She would make *anyone* look brittle.
JOHN: Mmm.
ROBERT: You bring me the man capable of looking flexible the moment that she (or those of her ilk) walk on stage.
JOHN: I can't.
ROBERT: No formal training.
JOHN: No.
ROBERT: No sense of right and wrong.
JOHN: She exploits the theater.
ROBERT: She does.

She even lacks beauty, they decide. John repeats that he finds it a marvel Robert can work with her at all. "I tune her out," Robert explains, "When we're on stage she isn't there for me."

They chat about another scene, one Robert found particularly satisfying. John makes appropriate comments.

Robert again asks John where he is going now, John repeats his intention of getting a bite. Robert says he doesn't eat at night for fear of gaining weight. John volunteers that Robert looks fit. "Then that makes it worthwhile," says Robert. Robert plans to walk or maybe read. John asks if Robert would care to join him, if not for a snack then for coffee? Robert is agreeable.

John notices Robert has greasepaint still on his face, runs off to get a tissue, returns and takes off the older actor's overlooked makeup. Robert suggests they go. *"John casually tosses the crumpled tissue toward the trash receptacle stage right. It misses the container and falls on the floor."* Pointedly, Robert picks up the tissue and deposits it where it belongs. All right, now they may go. "I'm famished," says Robert, as they exit.

Scene 2

In the wardrobe area, the two actors dress for a performance. "Am I in your way?" John asks. No, Robert replies.

Scene 3

Onstage in front of an audience, John and Robert play a scene from a cliche-ridden World War I trench melodrama. They are *"smoking the last fag."*

JOHN: They left him up there on the wire.
ROBERT: Calm down
JOHN: Those bastards.
ROBERT: Yeah.
JOHN: My God. They stuck him on the wire and left him there for target practise.
ROBERT (*of cigarette*): Gimme that.
JOHN: Those dirty, dirty bastards.
ROBERT: Yeah.
JOHN: My God.

ROBERT: Calm down.

JOHN: *He* had a home. *He* had a family. *(Pause.)* Just like them. *He* thought he was going home . . .

ROBERT: Relax, we'll all be going home.

JOHN: On the last day, Johnnie, on the *last day* . . .

ROBERT: That's the breaks, kid.

JOHN: Oh, my God, they're signin' it at noon. *(Pause.)* Poor Mahoney. Goes to raise the lousy flag, the Jerries cut him down like wheat. . . . .

John's character rushes offstage to avenge Mahoney. *"A single shot is heard, then silence."* "Well, looks like that's the end of it," says Robert's character philosophically. End of play.

Scene 4

"Robert and John have just completed a curtain call for an Elizabethan piece." Robert tells John he's doing their duel wrong and coaches him in what he insists is the proper way. "We don't want any blood upon the stage," says Robert, knocking wood. There is a pause. "Please knock on wood," says Robert. John does. Robert thanks him.

Scene 5

They are working out in a dance room. Robert lectures on the importance of good tone in speech.

ROBERT: Do you know when I was young my voice was very raspy.

JOHN: No.

ROBERT: But I was vain, I was untaught. I felt my vocal quality — a defect, in effect — was a positive attribute, a contributory portion of my style.

JOHN: Mmm.

ROBERT: What is style?

JOHN: What?

ROBERT: Style is *nothing*.

JOHN: No?

ROBERT: Style is a paper bag. Its only shape comes from its contents. *(Pause.)* However, I was young. I made a fetish of my imperfections.

JOHN: It's a common fault.

ROBERT: It makes me blush today to think about it.
        Pause.

JOHN: Don't think about it.
        Pause.

ROBERT: You're right. You start from the beginning and go through the middle and wind up at the end.

JOHN: Yes.
        Pause.

ROBERT: A little like a play. Keep your back straight.

Ellis Rabb and Peter Evans in *A Life in the Theater* duel scene

JOHN: Mmm.
ROBERT: We must not be afraid of process.
JOHN: No.
ROBERT: We must not lie about our antecedents.
JOHN: No.
ROBERT: We must not be second-class citizens. *(Pause.)* We must not be clowns whose sole desire is to please. We have a right to learn.
       Pause.
JOHN: Is my back straight?
ROBERT: No. *(Pause.)* Do you *follow* me?
JOHN: I think I do.
ROBERT: We must not be afraid to *grow.* We must support each other, John. This is the wondrous thing *about* the theater, this potential.

JOHN: Mmm.

ROBERT: Our history goes back as far as Man's. Our aspirations in the Theater are much the *same* as man's. *(Pause.)* (Don't you think?)

JOHN: Yes.

Pause.

ROBERT: We *are* society. Keep your back straight, John. The mirror is your friend. *(Pause.)* For a few more years. *(Pause.)* What have we to fear, John, from *phenomena? (Pause.)* We are explorers of the *soul.*

Pause.

JOHN: Is my back straight?

ROBERT: No.

Scene 6

> *The end of a day. John is on the backstage telephone.*

JOHN: Oh, no. I can't. I'm going out with someone in the show. *(Pause.)* No, in fact, an *Actor. (Pause.)* I don't know . . . Midnight. *(Pause.)* I'd like that very much. *(Pause.)* Me, too. *(Pause.)* How have you been?

> *Robert enters.*

ROBERT: You ready?

JOHN *(covering phone)*: Yes. *(Into phone.)* I'll see you then. *(Pause.)* 'Bye.

> *He hangs up telephone.*

ROBERT: We all must have an outside life, John. This is an essential.

JOHN: Yes.

ROBERT: Who was it?

Pause.

JOHN: A friend.

Scene 7

John and Robert greet each other coming in for a morning rehearsal.

Scene 8

"Before a performance at the makeup table." After some chitchat, Robert makes a request. He asks that the younger actor "do less" in their scene together. John is not overjoyed.

JOHN: Do you mean I'm walking on your scene? *(Pause.)* What do you mean?

ROBERT: Nothing. It's a thought I had. An esthetic consideration.

JOHN: Mmm.

ROBERT: I thought maybe if you *did* less . . .

JOHN: Yes?

ROBERT: *You* know.

JOHN: If I *did* less.

ROBERT: Yes.

JOHN: Well, thank you for the thought.

ROBERT: I don't think you have to be like that.

JOHN: I'm sorry.

ROBERT: Are you?
JOHN: I accept the comment in the spirit in which it was, I am sure, intended.
    Pause.
    ROBERT: It *was* intended in that spirit, John.
    JOHN: I know it was.
    ROBERT: How could it be intended otherwise?
    JOHN: It couldn't.
    ROBERT: Well, you *know* it couldn't.
    JOHN: Yes, I know.
    ROBERT: It hurts me when you take it personally.

Robert discovers the zipper of his costume is broken. John helps him improvise an unsatisfactory solution.

Scene 9

Robert plays a scene onstage trying to hide the defective fly. It is a dreadfully civilized scene in which John's character accuses Robert's of getting his wife pregnant. Robert misses a line. John helps him cover.

Scene 10

Backstage, Robert is ranting about something. John doesn't understand what and doesn't make much of an effort to find out.

Scene 11

They're onstage again, doing another play, this one Chekhovian in style, which gives them the opportunity to stripmine for subtext and pause a lot.

Scene 12

Backstage, Robert and John exchange small talk as they change clothes.

Scene 13

At Robert's request, John lights the older actor's cigarette.
They are backstage, reading through a scene in a new script. Robert takes the opportunity to comment extensively on the author's symbolism. John would just as soon read through the scene and be done with it, but he restrains his impatience, responding to Robert's insights monosyllabically.

Scene 14

"Robert and John are eating Chinese food at the makeup table between shows." Robert questions John on an audition John had that afternoon. John believes it went well but is not eager to elaborate. Robert says there are some things one can control and others one cannot. One can control one's intentions. One cannot control what others think of one's work. "If they hadn't liked you,

that would not have signified that you weren't a good actor," says Robert. "No. I think I know that," John says, closing a conversational door.

Scene 15

In the dressing room, Robert expresses his opinion that they should do the current show in blue jeans and T-shirts. John responds monosyllabically.

Scene 16

Robert is onstage, tearing into a monologue about bread and revolution. "To the barricades!" he cries.

Scene 17

"At the makeup table," Robert rhapsodizes about the wonders of greasepaint. John, irritated, asks him to shut up. A moment's silence.

ROBERT: Am I disturbing you?
JOHN: You are.
     Pause.
ROBERT: Enough to justify this breach of etiquette?
JOHN: What breach? What etiquette?
ROBERT: John . . .
JOHN: Yes?
ROBERT: When one's been in the theater as long as I . . .
JOHN: Can we do this later?
ROBERT: I feel that there is something here of worth to you.
JOHN: You do?
ROBERT: Yes.
JOHN *(sighs):* Let us hear it then.
ROBERT: All right. You know your attitude, John, is not of the best. It isn't. It just isn't.
JOHN *(pause):* It isn't?
ROBERT: Forms. The theater's a closed society. Constantly abutting thoughts, the feelings, the emotions of our colleagues. Sensibilities *(pause)* bodies . . . *forms* evolve. An etiquette, eh? In our personal relations with each other. Eh, John? In our personal relationships.
     Pause.
JOHN: Mmm.
ROBERT: One generation sows the seeds. It instructs the preceding . . . that is to say, the *following* generation . . . from the quality of its actions. Not from its discourse, John, no, but organically. *(Pause.)* You can learn a lot from keeping your mouth shut.
JOHN: You can.
ROBERT: Yes. And perhaps this is not the place to speak of attitudes.
JOHN: Before we go on.
ROBERT: Yes, but what is "life on stage" but attitudes?
JOHN *(pause):* What?

ROBERT: Damn little.
    Pause.
JOHN: May I use your brush?
ROBERT: Yes. *(Hands John brush.)* One must speak of these things, John, or we will go the way of all society.
JOHN: Which is what?
ROBERT: Take too much for granted, fall away and die. *(Pause.)* On the boards, or in society at large. There must be law, there must be a reason, there must be tradition.
    Pause.
JOHN: I'm sorry that I told you to shut up.
ROBERT: No, you can't buy me off that cheaply.
JOHN: No?
ROBERT: No.
    Pause.
JOHN: Would you pass me the cream, please?
ROBERT: Certainly. *(Passes the cream.)* Here is the cream.
JOHN: Thank you.

Scene 18

Robert and John are onstage performing the play they were rehearsing in Scene 13. It's about two men adrift in a lifeboat, dying from lack of drink. John's character breaks into a fevered, despairing monologue and then breaks down. The scene ends with Robert's character spotting a ship.

Scene 19

"John and Robert are standing in the wings. John is about to go on." John has gone blank. He can't remember a line in the scene he is about to play. Robert tries to help. He volunteers to get the script. John tells him to keep quiet as he's trying to hear his cue to enter. Moments pass. John thinks he's missed his cue. He's not certain. He watches, listens. Still not certain, but he thinks he missed it. Should he go on now? *Robert shrugs.* John decides he will but doesn't move. "Get *out* there . . . "says Robert. John makes his entrance with, "Missus Wilcox?? Missus Wilcox, ma'am? The men all got together . . ."

Scene 20

John is dressing backstage as Robert enters, brooding about something. Robert compliments John on his sweater. John pays little attention.

Scene 21

Robert engages John in a rhetorical conversation on the actor's life as John waits on hold on the backstage phone. Robert suggests they get a drink and urges John to hang up. But John is waiting to make a date with someone called Bonnie. While John is talking to Bonnie Robert goes off stiffly, alone.

Scene 22

Robert and John are taking off their makeup. Robert is complaining about critics. John has gotten wonderful reviews, and Robert is telling him that he deserves praise, but not for what the critics have applauded. Robert's diatribe is getting on John's nerves.

JOHN: I thought they were rather to the point.
ROBERT: You did.
JOHN: Yes.
ROBERT: Your reviews.
JOHN: Yes.
ROBERT: All false modesty aside.
JOHN: Yes.
ROBERT: Oh, the Young, the Young, the Young, the Young.
JOHN: The Farmer in the Dell.
ROBERT: Oh, I see.
JOHN: Would you hand me my scarf, please?
         Pause.
ROBERT: You fucking TWIT.
JOHN: I beg your pardon?
ROBERT: I think that you heard me.
         Takes towel from John's area and begins to use it. Pause.
JOHN: Robert.
ROBERT: What?
JOHN: Use your own towels from now on.
ROBERT: They're at the laundry.
JOHN: Get them back.

Scene 23

John is rehearsing on a dark stage. He is working on a soliloquy. He is alone. Rather, he *thinks* he is alone. He has hardly started when Robert's voice from offstage dispels that illusion. "Ah, sweet poison of the actor, rehearsing in an empty theater upon an empty stage . . ." John is irritated by the interruption but holds the irritation in check as Robert, still offstage, compliments the younger actor.

ROBERT: . . . . You're very good, John. Have I told you that lately? You are becoming a very fine actor. The flaws of youth are the perquisite of the young. It is the perquisite of the young to possess the flaws of youth.
JOHN: It's fitting, yes . . .
ROBERT: Ah, don't mock me, John. You shouldn't mock me. It's too easy. It's not good for you, no. And that is a lesson which we have to learn. *(Pause.)* Which you have to learn.
JOHN: And what is that?
ROBERT: That it is a hurtful fault, John, to confuse sincerity with weakness. *(Pause.)* And I must tell you something.

JOHN: Yes.

ROBERT: About the Theater — and this is a wondrous thing about the Theater — and John, one of the ways in which it's most like life . . .

JOHN: And what is that?

Pause.

ROBERT: Simply this. That in the Theater (as in life — and the Theater is, of course, a *part* of life . . . No?) . . . Do you see what I'm saying? I'm saying, as in a grocery store, that you cannot separate the *time* one spends . . . that is, it's all part of one's *life. (Pause.)* In addition to the fact that what's happening on *stage* is life . . . of a sort . . . I mean, it's part of your *life. (Pause.)* Which is one reason I'm so *gratified* (if I may presume, and I recognize that it may be a presumption) to see you . . . to see the *young* of the *Theater* . . . (And it's *not* unlike one's children) . . . following in the footpaths of . . . following in the footsteps of . . . those who have gone before. *(Pause.)* Do you see what I am saying? I would like to think you *did.* Do you? John? *(Pause.)* Well . . . well. Goodnight, John.

Pause.

JOHN: Goodnight.

ROBERT: *Good*night. I'll see you.

Robert leaves. At least, he makes a show of leaving. John starts his soliloquy again, then stops. He has a sense the older actor is still watching him from the wings.

JOHN: . . . . I *see* you in there. I see you there, Robert.

ROBERT (offstage voice): I'm just leaving.

JOHN: You were not just leaving, you were . . . *looking* at me.

ROBERT: On my way *out,* John. On my way *out.* Christ, but you make me feel small. You make me feel *small,* John. I don't feel good.

Pause.

JOHN: Are you crying? Are you crying, Robert, for chrissakes? *(Pause.)* Christ. Are you crying?

ROBERT: Yes.

Pause.

JOHN: Well, stop *crying.*

ROBERT: Yes, I will.

JOHN: No, stop it *now.* Stop it. Please.

Pause. Robert stops crying.

ROBERT: Better?

Pause.

JOHN: Yes. *(Pause.)* Are you all right?

ROBERT: Oh, yes. I'm all right. I'm fine. Thank you, John. *(Pause.)* Well, I suppose I'll . . . (You're going to work summore, eh?)

JOHN: Yes.

ROBERT: Then I suppose I'll . . . (Well, I was leaving *anyway.) (Pause.)* Goodnight. Goodnight, John.

Pause.

JOHN: Are you all right now? *(Raising his voice.)* Robert! Are you all right now?

ROBERT *(far offstage)*: Yes. Thank you. Yes. I'm all right now.

John is about to begin his declamatory rehearsal again, when Robert calls to him for assurance that he's not angry. John assures Robert he's not, takes the stage and starts speaking, but then stops.

JOHN: Robert . . . . . are you out there?

ROBERT: Yes, John.

JOHN *(sotto voce)*: Shit.

Scene 24

Robert and John are playing doctors in the middle of an operation. Robert gets lost in the scene. John tries to correct him, but Robert won't pick up the hints about "a curious growth near his spleen." Improvising in hospitalese, Robert and John wage a battle over what the lines in the script should be, trying to make it sound like part of the scene so the audience won't notice. But their improvising soon becomes a shambles of cross-purposes and, finally, mercifully, the curtain comes down.

Scene 25

"Backstage. Robert appears, holding his left wrist with his right hand." He has cut himself. John is concerned. Robert insists it was an accident. John suggests going to the hospital. Robert resists. He insists he'll be fine. He's just tired. Needs a rest. No, he doesn't want a doctor. He just wants to go home and rest. No, thanks, he doesn't want John to take him home. He just wants a moment alone, and then he'll go home. He'll be his old self tomorrow. *"John looks to Robert for a moment, then exits. Robert remains onstage alone for a moment, then slowly exits."*

Scene 26

After a performance, John and Robert compliment each other's work. Robert wistfully remarks that his father always wanted him to be an actor. John asks Robert for a cigarette. Robert gives him one. John is going to a party. Robert has no plans in particular. He mentions that he is not eating well lately. "Not hungry," he says. John accepts Robert's offer to light his cigarette.

ROBERT: A life spent in the theater.

JOHN: Mmm.

ROBERT: Backstage.

JOHN: Yes.

ROBERT: The bars, the house, the drafty halls. The penciled scripts . . .

JOHN: Yes.

ROBERT: Stories. Ah, the stories that you hear.

JOHN: I know.
ROBERT: It all goes so fast. It goes so quickly.
       Long pause.
JOHN: You think that I might borrow twenty 'til tomorrow?
ROBERT: What, you're short on cash.
JOHN: Yes.
ROBERT: Oh. Oh. *(Pause.)* Of course.
       He digs in his pocket. Finds money and hands it to John.)
JOHN: You're sure you won't need it?
ROBERT: No. No, not at all. No. If I don't know how it is, who does?
       Pause.
JOHN: Thank you.
ROBERT: Mmm. Goodnight.
JOHN: Goodnight.
ROBERT: You have a nice night.
JOHN: I will.
ROBERT: Goodnight.
       John exits. Pause.
Ephemeris, ephemeris. *(Pause.)* "An actor's life for me."
       *Robert composes himself and addresses the empty house. He raises
       his hand to stop imaginary applause.*
You've been so kind . . . Thank you, you've really been so kind. You know, and
I speak, I am sure, not for myself alone, but on behalf of all of us . . . *(Composes
himself.)* . . . All of us here, when I say that these . . . *these* moments make it all
. . . they make it all worthwhile.
       Pause. John quietly reappears.
You know . . .
       Robert sees John.
JOHN: They're locking up. They'd like us all to leave.
ROBERT: I was just leaving.
JOHN: Yes, I know. *(Pause.)* I'll tell them.
ROBERT: Would you?
JOHN: Yes.
       Pause.
ROBERT: Thank you.
JOHN: Goodnight.
ROBERT: Goodnight.
       Pause. John exits.
ROBERT *(to himself*: The lights dim. Each to his own home. Goodnight. Good-
night. Goodnight.
       Curtain.

The author (Neil Simon, *center*) of *Chapter Two* joins his characters Jennie Malone (Anita Gillette) and George Schneider (Judd Hirsch) on the stage in this photograph.

CHAPTER TWO

A Comedy in Two Acts

BY NEIL SIMON

Cast and credits appear on page 359

NEIL SIMON was born in the Bronx, N.Y. on July 4, 1927. After graduating from DeWitt Clinton High School he managed to find time for writing while serving in the army. Writing soon became his profession without the formalities of college (except for a few courses at New York University and the University of Denver). His first theater work consisted of sketches for camp shows at Tamiment, Pa. in collaboration with his brother Danny. He became a TV writer, supplying a good deal of material for Sid Caesar (Caesar's Hour) *and Phil Silvers* (Sergeant Bilko).

On Broadway, Simon contributed sketches to Catch a Star *(1955) and* New Faces of 1956. *His first Broadway play was* Come Blow Your Horn *(1961), followed by the book of the musical* Little Me *(1962). His next play, the comedy* Barefoot in the Park *(1963), was named a Best Play of its season, as was* The Odd Couple *(1965). Neither of these had closed when the musical* Sweet Charity, *for which Simon wrote the book, came along early in 1966; and none of the three had closed when Simon's* The Star-Spangled Girl *opened the following season in December 1966 — so that Simon had the phenomenal total of four shows running simultaneously on Broadway during the season of 1966-67. When the last of the four closed the following summer, they had played a total of 3,367 performances over four theater seasons.*

Simon immediately began stacking another pile of blue-chip shows. His Plaza Suite *(1968) was named a Best Play of its year. His book of the musical* Promises, Promises *(1969) was another smash and his* Last of the Red Hot Lovers *(1969) became his fourth Best Play and third Simon show in grand simultaneous display on Broadway.* Plaza Suite *closed before* The Gingerbread

"Chapter Two": by Neil Simon. Copyright © 1978 by Neil Simon. Reprinted by permission of Random House, Inc. See CAUTION notice on copyright page. All inquiries should be addressed to Random House, Inc. 201 East 50th Street, New York, N.Y. 10022.

Lady *(1970, also a Best Play) opened, so that Simon's second stack was "only" three plays and 3,084 performances high.*

There followed The Prisoner of Second Avenue *(1971, a Best Play),* The Sunshine Boys *(1972, a Best Play),* The Good Doctor *(1973, a Best Play) and* God's Favorite *(1974). There was no new Neil Simon play on Broadway the following year because he was moving himself and his family from New York to California, partly for personal reasons and partly to write for the screen. Movies or no movies, by April 1976 he had* California Suite *ready for production at Center Theater Group in Los Angeles and brought it to the Eugene O'Neill Theater — which he owns — in June 1976 as his 15th Broadway show and ninth Best Play.*

To continue: this season's Neil Simon Best Play (his tenth and his 16th Broadway production), presented in synopsis hereinunder, is Chapter Two, *a semi-autobiographical script also produced at Center Theater Group before coming on to New York in December 1977. And certainly there will be more.*

In addition to the recent Academy Award nominee The Goodbye Girl, *Simon's movie scripts have included* The Cheap Detective, Murder by Death, The Out-of-Towners, The Heartbreak Kid *and the screen versions of his own* Barefoot in the Park, The Odd Couple, Plaza Suite, The Prisoner of Second Avenue *and* The Sunshine Boys. *Simon's second wife is Marsha Mason, who starred in* The Goodbye Girl. *He has two daughters by his first marriage.*

Time: **The present, a late February afternoon continuing through to mid-spring**

Place: **Jennifer Malone's upper East Side apartment and George Schneider's lower Central Park West apartment**

ACT I

Scene 1

SYNOPSIS: The setting represents two separate apartments in different parts of New York and of entirely different styles. At left, George Schneider's is in an old, high-ceiling, West Seventies building; at right, Jennifer Malone's is more compact and simple, as though in one of today's new buildings. The two living rooms are appropriately furnished with sofas, etc., and the entrance doors to the apartments are visible upstage.

It is 10:30 p.m. At left, George Schneider opens the door to his apartment and enters carring a suitcase and an attache case. ("*George is 42 years old, an attrac-*

tive, intelligent man who at this moment seems tired and drawn.") He is obviously returning home after a trip; his mail is piled up on a table. His brother Leo ("*about 40 . . . . . wearing a suede sheepskin coat, scarf and gloves*") enters carrying George's other suitcase. The apartment is cold and the gas is leaking. George is too preoccupied with his own thoughts even to notice such trivial matters, which Leo soon puts to rights. Most of the mail consists of letters of condolence. One of them, most sensitively expressed, sets George to thinking out loud about his recently dead wife, Barbara.

GEORGE: Barbara knew a whole world of people I never knew . . . She knew that Ricco, the mailman, was a birdwatcher in Central Park and that Vince, the butcher in Gristede's, painted miniature portraits of cats every weekend in his basement on Staten Island . . . She talked to people all year long that I said hello to on Christmas.

LEO *(looks at him)*: I think you could have used another month in Europe.

GEORGE: You mean I was supposed to come home and forget I had a wife for twelve years? . . . It doesn't work that way, Leo . . . It was, perhaps, the dumbest trip I ever took in my whole life. London was bankrupt, Italy was on strike. France hated me . . . Spain was still in mourning for Franco . . . why do Americans go to grief-stricken Europe when they're trying to get over being stricken with grief?

LEO: Beats me. I always thought you could have just as rotten a time here in America.

GEORGE: . . . What am I going to do about this apartment, Leo?

LEO: My advice? . . . Move . . . Find a new place for yourself.

GEORGE: It was very spooky in London . . . I kept walking around the streets looking for Barbara . . . Harrod's, King's Road, Portobello . . . Sales clerks would say, "See what you want, sir?" and I'd say, "No, she's not here" . . . I know it's crazy, Leo, but I really thought to myself, "It's a joke. She's not dead. She's in London waiting for me. She's just playing out this romantic fantasy . . . The whole world thinks she's gone, but we meet clandestinely in London, move into a flat, disappear from everyone and live out our lives in secret!" . . . She could have thought of something like that, you know.

LEO: But she didn't. *You* did.

GEORGE: In Rome I got sore at her . . . I mean *really* mad . . . How dare she do a thing like this to me? . . . I would *never* do a thing like that to her . . . Never! . . . Like a nut, walking up the Via Veneto one night, cursing my dead wife.

LEO: In Italy, they probably didn't pay attention.

GEORGE: In Italy, they agree with you . . . (*He shrugs.*) Okay, Leo, my sweet baby brother, I'm back . . . Chapter Two in the life of George Schneider . . . Where the hell do I begin?

Leo suggests poker, a Knicks game, a dinner at his house with his wife Marilyn. He sees that George's distress is so acute that he can't think of making plans. Leo embraces George and goes. George picks up his attache case and heads for the bedroom, reminding himself, "Okay, let's take it one night at a time, folks." The lights slowly go to black.

Scene 2

Jennie Malone enters her apartment at stage right, carrying a suitcase. She flicks on the light. It is 4:30 on a cold February afternoon. She is *"an attractive woman, about 32 . . . . . wears a camel's hair coat, leather boots and a woollen hat,"* and she is followed by her friend, Faye Medwick, *"about 35 . . . . . dresses a bit more suburban, not chic but right for the weather,"* carrying Jennie's makeup case.

Faye admires Jennie's organization — she has prearranged to have the heat turned up and an order of groceries delivered. Jennie has been out West divorcing her husband of six years, and she too is suffering the pangs of getting used to being by herself. Faye complains about her own husband, Sidney. Jennie believes that Faye should tell Sidney how she feels about their marriage.

FAYE: . . . . . I can't get an appointment with his secretary.
        Putting on coat.
JENNIE: I don't understand you. I know more about what's wrong with your married life than Sidney does . . . Why don't you speak up? What are you afraid of? What do you think would happen to you if you told him what you tell *me* in the privacy of this room?
FAYE: . . . That next time you'd be picking *me* up at the airport.
JENNIE: Oh, God, that infuriates me. Why are we so intimidated? I wasted five lousy years living with Gus trying to justify the one good year I had with him . . . Because I wouldn't take responsibility for my own life . . . Dumb! You're dumb, Jennie Malone! . . . *All* of us . . . We shouldn't get alimony, we should get the *years* back . . . Wouldn't it be great if just once the judge said, "I award you six years., three months, two days and custody of your former youthful body and fresh glowing skin!"
FAYE: I would be in such terrific shape if you were my mother.
JENNIE: Don't give me too much credit. I *talk* a terrific life . . . Now go on home. I want to crawl into bed and try to remember what my maiden name was.
FAYE: Are you sure you'll be all right? All alone?
JENNIE: No. But I want to be.
        They embrace.
FAYE: You can call me in the middle of the night. Sidney and I aren't doing anything.
        Faye exits. Jennie gets suitcase, takes it off into the bedroom.

Scene 3

About 5 p.m. the next night, George is on the telephone with a divorcee who has called trying to date him, when Leo enters. George gets rid of the woman as gently as he can and complains to Leo that he is besieged with offers like this, when all he wants is to be let alone. Leo advises him, "Listen, George, next to Christmas, loneliness is the biggest business in America."

Leo is trying to find George some female companionship, but George complains that the last one he arranged for him to meet showed up in an electric dress. This time, Leo assures George, he has found the right one, a girl he happened to meet in "21." George wants none of her — he'll return to circulation some day, all right, but in his own good time. Leo leaves him the girl's phone number just in case and departs.

Scene 4

In Jennie's apartment, Jennie is packing a suitcase when the phone rings. It's her ex-husband, Gus, calling to say hello. Jennie tries to keep the conversation bright and casual, telling Gus her plan to perhaps do a year of repertory at Arena Stage in Washington after she finishes in her current soap opera — but she is near tears when she finally hangs up the phone.

Faye comes in with the glad news that she has a part in *As the World Turns*; and that a friend of hers, Leo Schneider, has a brother George, a novelist, who has just lost his wife and may be looking for a little companionship. Jennie will have none of him — the last date Faye arranged for her was six feet eight inches tall. She informs Faye: "I have dated and I have gone to parties and I have had it. If one more man greets me at the door with his silk shirt unbuttoned to his tanned navel, his chest hair neatly combed and wearing more jewelry around his neck than me, I am turning celibate."

Anyhow, Jennie is on her way to Cleveland to visit her family. The phone rings and Faye pleads with her to answer it, but Jennie picks up her suitcase and exits.

Scene 5

About two weeks later at 9 p.m., George is on the phone to Leo's wife Marilyn. Leo was going to put George in touch with a veteran lady researcher who once worked for the Harvard library, for some information, and George has mislaid the phone number.

While he is talking, George finds Leo's slip of paper with a phone number on it hidden under the telephone. He ends his conversation with Marilyn and dials the number. The phone rings in Jennie's apartment just as Jennie comes in the door. She turns on the lights and answers the ringing phone. George identifies himself.

JENNIE: Oh . . . God! . . . Yes . . . George Schneider . . . It seemed so long ago . . . I'm sorry, you caught me at a bad time. I just got off a plane and walked in the door.

GEORGE: Oh, I didn't know. I'm sorry. Can I call you back?

JENNIE: Well . . . Yes, I suppose so, but, er . . . I'll be very honest with you, Mr. Schneider . . . I'm going through sort of a transition period right now and I'm not planning to date for awhile.

GEORGE: *Date?* . . . Did Leo say I was going to call you for a date?

JENNIE: Well, he said you were going to call, so I assumed —

GEORGE: No, no. This wasn't a date call. I'm very surprised at Leo. Miss, er . . . is it Jenkins or Jurgens?

JENNIE: Is what?

GEORGE: Your name.

JENNIE: It's Malone. Jennifer Malone.

GEORGE (*confused, looks at paper*): Jennifer Malone? No, that's wrong.

JENNIE: I could show you my driver's license.

GEORGE: That's not the name he gave me . . . (*He looks on back of the paper.*) Oh, geez, it's on the other side. I couldn't read his writing. Serene Jurgens was the one I wanted. She's an elderly woman, about 85 years old.

JENNIE: Well, you know what you want better than I do.

GEORGE: Look, I am so embarrassed. I really was going to call you socially. At another time. I mean, really I was.

JENNIE: Well — let's see how it goes with Serene first. OK? Goodbye.
        She hangs up.

George immediately dials Jennie back and explains that he now realizes she's the girl Leo met in "21" and suggested he call — he mixed up the telephone numbers. Each explains to the other that he/she is going through a period of adjustment right now and not seeking involvement. Jennie accepts George's explanation and hangs up.

George calls again — this, he explains, is the charming call which follows the explaining call about the dumb call. "This is now the end of the charming call," George tells her and takes her by surprise by himself hanging up; but he calls her right back and this time she's willing to take part in one of those exploratory conversations in which each is open to receiving information about who they are, what they do and why they happen to be single. Apparently they speak much the same language.

JENNIE: . . . . . You're a very interesting telephone person, Mr. Schneider . . . However, I have literally just walked in the door and I haven't eaten since breakfast . . . It was really nice talking to you — Goodbye.
        She hangs up. Stays while he hurriedly dials. Her phone rings, she picks it up.
. . . As you were saying . . .?

GEORGE: Listen, uh, can I be practical for a second?

JENNIE: For a second . . . yes.

GEORGE: They're not going to let up, you know.

JENNIE: Who?

GEORGE: The pushers. Leo and Faye. They will persist and push and prod and leave telephone numbers under books until eventually we have that inevitable date.

JENNIE: Nothing is inevitable. Dates are man-made.

GEORGE: Whatever . . . The point is, I assume you have an active career . . . I'm a very busy man who needs quiet and a few distractions . . . So let me propose, in the interest of moving on with our lives, that we get this meeting over with just as soon as possible.

JENNIE: . . . Surely you jest.

GEORGE: I'm not asking for a date. Blind dates are the nation's third leading cause of skin rash.

JENNIE: Then what are you suggesting?

GEORGE: Just hear me out. What if we were to meet for just five minutes. We could say hello, look each other over, part company, and tell Leo and Faye that they have fulfilled their noble mission in life.

George persists, and Jennie is intrigued in spite of herself. George suggests that right now would be a good time and Jennie's apartment a good place. They agree not to build their hopes of each other too high in case they're disappointed, and both hang up.

Scene 6

Twenty minutes later in Jennie's apartment the phone rings. It's Faye, and Jennie admits she's asked George over and he's arriving any minute. The doorbell rings.

> *She hangs up. She tucks her blouse into her skirt, looks in the mirror, does a last-minute brush job, then crosses to the door. She takes in a deep breath, then opens it. George stands there, arm extended, leaning against the door frame. They look at each other . . . Finally he smiles and nods his head.*

GEORGE: Yeah! . . . Okayyyyyy!
JENNIE: Is that a review?
GEORGE: No. Just a response . . . Hello.
JENNIE (*smiles*): Hello.
> *They are both suddenly very embarrassed and don't quite know what to say or how to handle this situation.*
GEORGE (*good-naturedly*): . . . This was a dumb idea, wasn't it?
JENNIE: Extremely.
GEORGE: (*nods in agreement*): I think I've put undue pressure on these next five minutes.
JENNIE: You could cut it with a knife.
GEORGE: I think if I came in, it would lessen the tension.
JENNIE: Oh, I'm sorry. Please, yes.

George steps in and Jennie closes the door. They decide to have a glass of white wine. As Jennie goes to the kitchen to get it, George notices a photograph of a football player in action — Gus, Jennie's former husband, who was a wide receiver for the Giants.

Jennie pours the wine, and, somewhat awkwardly, George tries to turn on the charm. He explains that Leo's other suggestions turned out to be so disastrous that he was unduly wary and flippant when he first talked to Jennie on the phone. In contrast, he finds Jennie "an attractive, intelligent and what appears to be, a very nice girl." Jennie in her turn admits she enjoyed her phone conversations with George and found him "very bright." She asks about George's work. He explains that he writes popular spy novels under a pseudonym, which she recognizes, and unpopular serious novels under his own name. George insists on telling her his age — 42 — and she replies with hers — 32. For the first time they look directly at each other and hold their gaze; they decide they like what they see. But five minutes are up, and it's time for George to go.

George proposes a full-fledged date for the next evening. Jennie accepts. He exits, leaving her smiling.

Scene 7

A week later about 6:30 p.m. in Jennie's apartment, Jennie is trying on a new backless dress to see whether Faye thinks it suits her (she does), because Jennie has been going out with George for several nights in a row and wants to keep his attention. "After six days I think I'm nuts about him," she tells Faye, as they exit talking about George.

Scene 8.

Later that night, George and Jennie come into George's apartment. George is feeling dizzy and unwell, probably from something he's just eaten. Solicitously, Jennie sits him down, loosens his tie and helps him with his shoelaces. George apologizes for passing out and ruining their date. Jenny soothes him, kissing his hand, and George gently kisses her on the mouth. Jennie and George agree that they feel as though they've known each other a long, long time and are picking up where they left off. They kiss again, but this time, to Jennie's dismay, tears come into George's eyes. He fights his emotions as Jennie comforts him.

JENNIE: It's all right . . . Whatever you're feeling, it's all right.

GEORGE: I keep trying to push Barbara out of my mind . . . I can't do it, I've tried, Jennie.

JENNIE: I know.

GEORGE: I don't really want to. I'm so afraid of losing her forever.

JENNIE: I understand and it's all right.

GEORGE: I know I'll never stop loving Barbara but I feel so good about you . . . and I can't get the two things together in my mind.

JENNIE: It all happened so fast, George. You expect so much of yourself so soon.

GEORGE: On the way over in the cab tonight, I'm yelling at the cab driver, "Can't you get there faster?" . . . And then some nights I wake up saying, "I'm never going to see Barbara again and I hope to God it's just a dream."

JENNIE: I love you, George . . . I want you to know that.

GEORGE: Give me a little time, Jennie. Stay next to me. Be with me. Just give me the time to tell you how happy you make me feel.

JENNIE: I'm not going anywhere, George . . . You can't lose me . . . I know a good thing when I see it.

GEORGE (*managing a smile*): Jeez! I thought I had food poisoning and it's just a mild case of ecstasy.

Jennie promises to share George's feelings, no matter what. George now feels strong enough to get up and show Jennie the apartment — the bedroom first.

Judd Hirsch and Anita Gillette in a scene from *Chapter Two*

Scene 9

Three days later in George's apartment, Leo has come over to consult George about his own problem: his wife Marilyn wants to leave him. She has a long list of complaints, the first being that Leo never comes home until the wee small hours — he is a theater press agent and must work at night. Leo, too, feels he is stagnating in marriage and wishes he could get away from it now and again.

In turn, George confides to Leo that he is crazy in love with Jennie, the girl Leo found for him, and means to marry her — on this coming Monday, in fact. It's all arranged. Leo can't believe George means to marry someone he's known for only two weeks. George tells him that he knew after the third date with Barbara, his late wife, that she was the girl for him, and it's the same with Jennie. He wants Leo and Marilyn to come to the wedding. Leo begs George to wait a month, offering to stay with Marilyn for a month if George will put off his wedding, but it's no deal.

Leo begs George at least to let him go to see Jennie and talk to her, alone. Reluctantly George agrees, commenting, "A half hour with her and you'll come back wondering why I'm waiting so long." Leo leaves, and George goes to the phone and dials. The phone rings in Jennie's apartment.

JENNIE: Hello?

GEORGE: I love you. Do you love me?

JENNIE: Of course I do . . . Who is this?

GEORGE: You're going to get a call from my brother. He thinks we're crazy.

JENNIE: Of course we are. What else is new?

GEORGE: Jennie, I've been thinking . . . Let's call it off. Let's wait a month. Maybe a couple of months.

JENNIE: All right . . . Whatever you say.

GEORGE: And I'd like you to move in here with me . . . Until we decide what to do.

JENNIE: I'll move in whenever you want.

GEORGE: I'm crazy about you.

JENNIE: I feel the same way.

GEORGE: Then forget what I said . . . It's still on for Monday morning.

JENNIE: I'll be there with my little bouquet!

> *They hang up. Jennie looks thoughtful. George's gaze is drawn to a framed photo of Barbara. Curtain.*

ACT II

Scene 1

The next afternoon, in George's apartment, George is on the phone telling his doubting mother what a wonderful woman he is going to marry.

The doorbell rings, and George puts down the phone to answer it. It's Jennie, come with a present: the two books which George considers his serious work, bound in leather. Jennie gets on the phone to Mrs. Schneider and tells her what a wonderful son she has.

George has a present for Jennie too, which he now gives her: an engagement ring for the two days left before their marriage. Jennie is as touched by the ring as George is by the books. Overcome with emotion, she runs out while George continues his phone conversation with his mother, who is now obviously resigned to her son's new marriage.

Scene 2

In Jennie's apartment the doorbell rings — it's Faye come to ask Jennie a favor. Jennie's lease on the apartment runs for another two months, and Faye would like to borrow a key.

At this moment George, having finished his long phone conversation with his mother, dials Jennie. They exchange a few reassuring jokes and then hang up, leaving Jennie to cope with Faye, who wants to borrow the key so that she can use the apartment to consummate a love affair. Wise or unwise, this is what Faye wants to do, for the same reason Jennie's marrying a man she's known only two and a half weeks: "Because yesterday was lousy and it seems right today. I'll worry about tomorrow the day after."

Faye leaves with the key, planning to use it in a few days. After another call from George, Jennie answers the doorbell and finds that George's brother Leo has come to call. Leo and Marilyn and George and Jennie apparently got along very well together over the dinner table recently, but still Leo thinks Jennie and George are moving too quickly into marriage. He's concerned about his brother's happiness — and he's concerned about Jennie's too. He feels they need more time.

Jennie asks to hear about Barbara and George's reaction to her death. No matter how painful, the truth might help Jennie to understand George better.

LEO (*thinks, takes his time*): All right . . . They were very close. I mean, as close as any couple I've ever seen. After ten years, they still held hands in a restaurant. I'm married eleven years and I don't pass the salt to my wife . . . When George first found out how ill Barbara was, he just refused to accept it. He knew it was serious, but there was no way she was not going to beat it. He just couldn't conceive of it . . . And Barbara never let on to a soul that anything was ever wrong . . . Her best friend, at the funeral, said to George, "I just didn't know" . . . She was beautiful, Jennie, in every way. And then in the last few months you could see she was beginning to slip . . . George would go out to dinner or a party and leave early, trying not to let on that anything was wrong . . . and especially not letting on to themselves . . . And then one morning George called me from the hospital . . . and he said very quietly and simply, "She's gone, Leo" . . . and it surprised me because I thought when it was finally over George would go to pieces. I mean, I expected a full crackup, and it worried me that he was so held together . . . I saw him as often as I could, called him all the time and then suddenly I didn't hear from him for about five days. He didn't answer the phone, I called the building, they said they didn't see him go in or out and I got plenty scared . . . I went up there, they let me in with the pass key, and I found him in the bedroom sitting in front of the television set, with the picture on and no sound. He was in filthy pajamas, drenched in perspiration. There was a container of milk on the floor next to him that had gone sour . . . He must have dropped eight or nine pounds . . . And I said to him, "Hey, George, why don't you answer your phone? Are you okay?" . . . And he said, "Fine . . . I'm fine, Leo" . . . Then he reached over and touched my hand and for the first time in a year and a half the real tears started to flow . . . He cried for hours, through that whole night . . . I still couldn't get him to eat, so the next morning I got our doctor to come over and he checked him into Mount Sinai . . . He was there for ten days. And he was in terrible shape. His greatest fear was that I was going to commit him someplace . . . When he came out, he stayed with me about a week. I couldn't even get him to take a walk. He had this panic, this fear, he'd never make it back into the house. I finally got him to walk down to the corner and he never let go of my arm for a second. We started across the street and he stopped and said, "No, it's too far. Take me back, Leo" . . . A few weeks later he went into therapy. A really good doctor. He was there about a month and then suddenly he decided he wasn't going back. He wouldn't explain why. I called the doctor and he explained to me that George was making a very determined effort not to get better . . . Because getting better meant he was ready to let go of Barbara and there was no way he was going to let that happen . . . .

Then one day, just as suddenly, George took off for Europe to revisit all the places he'd been with Barbara. Leo admits he tried to supply George with the wrong kind of female companionship until he met Jennie, who, he is sure, is right for George — if she will just give him a little more time to make the final adjustment to the loss of Barbara.

What Leo has told her frightens Jennie. She's willing to wait as long as necessary, but it's George who wants the wedding right away. Jennie has her own emotional problems which she hopes the relationship with George will put right. She means to go ahead with it, and she promises Leo, "Even if what we're doing is not right, I'll *make* it right." Leo leaves, reassured.

Scene 3

On Monday morning at 9 a.m. in George's apartment, George is dressed in a blue suit and has cut himself shaving. He is very nervous, and as though seeking support he dials his doctor. The doctor is busy with a patient. George leaves a message on the answering machine, telling the doctor he's getting married today as though he expected the doctor to intervene with some objection. He leaves the doctor the number of the judge's chambers where he is to be married, just in case.

Leo comes in, also in a blue suit, wearing a white carnation. He tries to hurry George; they can't keep the judge waiting.

GEORGE (*looks at Leo*): . . . Who is she, Leo? . . . I'm marrying a girl, I don't know who she is.

LEO: Don't start with me! . . . Don't give me trouble, George! . . . drove me and all your friends half crazy and now suddenly you want information?

GEORGE: I can't breathe . . . What a day I pick not to be able to breathe. What should I do, Leo?

LEO: I'll buy you a balloon, you can suck on it! . . . George, I've got to know. Are you calling this off? . . . Because if you are, I can still catch a workout at the gym.

GEORGE (*yells, annoyed*): Will you have a little God damn compassion!!! . . . I can't even get my ex-analyst on the phone. A lot *they* care. Fifty dollars an hour and all they do is protect you from doing neurotic things in *their* office.

George gets his carnation from the frigidaire. Leo helps him with it and hustles him out of the apartment.

Scene 4

In Jennie's apartment later that same day, Faye is wearing a sexy black negligee and is clearly awaiting adventure. Leo rushes into George's apartment, grabs the phone and dials. It rings in Jennie's apartment. Faye answers it somewhat reluctantly. Leo explains that George has forgotten his airplane tickets, and George and Jennie are waiting at the airport to begin their honeymoon. Leo can't meet Faye this afternoon as planned. He postpones their meeting before rushing out.

Scene 5

A week later about 8 p.m., in George's apartment, George and Jennie enter laden with luggage, tired, *"and there is some degree of tension between them."* Their moods are unmatched: Jennie is making an effort to be cheerful while George, unbending and solemn, reminds her of the eight glasses of wine she had on the plane to ease her fear of flying. When Jennie remarks "It's a little glum in here" she isn't talking only about the lighting of the room. She's beginning to resent George's solemnity, and she shows it.

JENNIE: I've tried everything, including my funniest faces, to get a smile out of you since eight o'clock this morning.
GEORGE: Why don't you try an hour of quiet?
> *Pops Tylenol.*
JENNIE: I tried it in Barbados and it turned into twenty-four hours of gloom.
GEORGE: . . . Listen, I'm walking a very fine line tonight . . . There are a lot of things I would like to say that would just get us both in trouble . . . I don't want to deal with it now. Let's just go to bed and hope that two extra-strength Tylenol can do all they claim to do — okay?
JENNIE: . . . I'd just as soon hear what you had to say.
GEORGE: I don't think you do.
JENNIE: Why don't you be in charge of saying it and I'll be responsible for not wanting to hear it.
> *He looks at her, nods, then looks around and decides to sit opposite her. She looks at him. He stares at the floor.*
GEORGE: . . . As honeymoons go, I don't think you got much of a break.
JENNIE: Really? I'm sorry if you felt that way. *I* had an intermittently wonderful time.
GEORGE: Well, I don't know what you experienced in the past. I'm not a honeymoon expert but personally, I found me unbearably moody.
JENNIE: Two days in seven isn't much of a complaint, which I never did . . . And I think we ought to limit this conversation to present honeymoons.
GEORGE: Why?
JENNIE: Because that's where we're living.
GEORGE: You can't get to the present without going through the past.

Jennie is willing to hear anything George wants to say, but she's sorry they have to face these frightening emotional problems their first night together in

Judd Hirsch and Anita Gillette in *Chapter Two*

Mr. and Mrs. Neil Simon (Marsha Mason)

this apartment. George demands that she think back and make some sort of comparison with her honeymoon with her ex-husband Gus, who, George imagines, was a bit of a buffoon. For all the good it will do him, Jennie tells him that "What happened to you and me in Barbados was something I never dreamed was possible."

Jennie hates confrontations, but she is determined to see this one through and counter-demands that George look back and rate his own honeymoon with Barbara in Europe. But the pain of the memory saps all of George's strength, leaving him unresponsive, apologetic. Jennie tries to reassure him.

JENNIE: I'm in no hurry. What you're giving now is enough for me. I know the rest will come.

GEORGE: *How* do you know? How the hell did you become so wise and smart? . . . Stop being so goddamn understanding, will you? It bores the crap out of me.

JENNIE: Then what *do* you want? Bitterness? Anger? Fury? You want me to stand toe to toe with you like Barbara did? Well, I'm not Barbara. And I'll be damned if I'm going to recreate *her* life, just to make *my* life work with you . . . This is *our* life now, George, and the sooner we start accepting that, the sooner we can get on with this marriage.

GEORGE: No, you're not Barbara. That's clear enough.

JENNIE (*devasted*): Oh, Jesus, George. If you want to hurt me, you don't have to work that hard.

GEORGE: Sorry, but you give me so much room to be cruel, I don't know when to stop.

JENNIE: I never realized that was a *fault* until now.

GEORGE: I guess it's one of the minor little adjustments you have to make. But I have no worry, you'll make them.

JENNIE: And you resent me for that?

GEORGE: I resent you for *everything*.

JENNIE (*perplexed*): *Why*, George? . . . Why?

GEORGE: Because I don't feel like making you happy tonight! . . . I don't feel like having a wonderful time . . . I don't think I *wanted* a "terrifically wonderful" honeymoon! . . . You want happiness, Jennie, find yourself another football player, will ya? . . . I resent everything you want out of marriage that I've already had . . . And for making me reach so deep inside to give it to you again . . . I resent being at L or M and having to go back to A! . . . And most of all, I resent not being able to say in front of you — that I miss Barbara so much . . .

> *He covers his eyes, crying silently. Jennie has been cut so deeply, she can hardly react . . . She just sits there, fighting back her tears.*

Oh, Christ, Jennie, I'm sorry . . . I think I need a little outside assistance.

JENNIE (*nods*): . . . What do you want to do?

GEORGE (*shrugs*): I don't know . . . I don't want to make any promises I can't keep.

JENNIE: Whatever you want.

GEORGE: We got, as they say in the trade, problems, kid.

> *Goes to her, embraces her head, then goes into bedroom, leaving her stunned and alone. Dimout.*

Scene 6

In Jennie's apartment at 3 o'clock on a sunny afternoon two days later, Faye enters from the bedroom wrapped in a sheet, followed by Leo, who has just put on his pants and is bare from the waist up. Their assignation has been a disaster, partly because Leo interrupted it to take an incoming phone call worth $30,000 to him — thus increasing Faye's fear of being found out because Leo revealed this phone number to someone.

Faye admits that she is "nervous and clumsy" in this unaccustomed role. Leo reassures her, insists that she dance a few steps with him and is trying to soften her mood, when she freezes him with questions about how many times before this he's had affairs. Leo tries other ways to please her, but to no avail; she's upset, confused, wanting and not wanting to make love, reminding Leo that they've known each other since childhood, were attracted to each other and might — Faye speculates — have made a go of marriage.

Realizing that the game is up for the time being, at least, Leo starts putting on the rest of his clothes while telling Faye that he could never have been monogamous: "I can't be faithful to my wife and I hate the guilt that comes with playing around. So I compromise. I have lots of unpleasurable affairs . . . And what makes it worse, I really do care for Marilyn."

Leo isn't looking for romance, all he wants is "a little dispassionate passion." Faye realizes she has picked the wrong partner to sublimate her romantic fantasies; nevertheless, she likes Leo and he likes her. They come together for a friendly kiss before parting, a kiss which becomes passionate just as Jennie comes into the apartment to pick up some summer clothes. Embarrassment reigns supreme and puts a period to this episode as Leo exits, slamming the door.

Scene 7

In George's apartment about an hour later, George — in hat and coat and carrying a suitcase — is in the process of departing and leaving a note for Jennie, when Jennie enters. George tells her he's on his way to Los Angeles, where someone is interested in one of his books for a movie.

JENNIE: When did all this come up?
GEORGE: Two weeks ago.
JENNIE: Why didn't you tell me?
GEORGE: I had no reason to go two weeks ago.
JENNIE: Leave it to you to make a point clear. How long will you be gone?
GEORGE: I don't know.
JENNIE: Where will you stay?
GEORGE: I don't know.
JENNIE: . . . Just going to circle the airport for a few days?
GEORGE: You never lose your equilibrium, do you?
JENNIE: You think not? I'd hate to see an X-ray of my stomach right now.
GEORGE: I don't think being apart for a while is going to do us any damage.
JENNIE: Probably no worse than being together the past few days.

GEORGE: But if it's really important to get in touch with me, Leo will know where I am.

JENNIE: And I'll know where Leo is.

Their bitterness increases until Jennie, angry, starts swinging at George, who throws her to the floor. She comes up defiant, talking, telling George she will not give up no matter how hard he tries to push her away. In spite of their problems she feels good about herself: "I'm nuts about me! . . . And if you're stupid enough to throw someone sensational like me aside, then you don't deserve as good as you've got! . . . I am sick and tired of running from places and people and relationships . . . And don't tell me what I want because *I'll* tell you what I want . . . I want a home and I want a family . . . and I want a career, too . . . And I want a dog and I want a cat and I want three goldfish . . . I want *everything!* . . . ."

George admits he is crazy about Jennie and would like to take her in his arms, but he is stuck, inhibited in some way: "I'm fighting to hold on to self-pity and just my luck I run into the most understanding girl in the world." He wants to go to Los Angeles for a while, alone, to try to get himself unstuck. Jennie is resigned to his leaving but doesn't want to stay in this apartment by herself. She will go back to her own apartment till George returns.

Scene 8

In Jennie's apartment the next day, Faye is in the living room when the doorbell rings. It's Leo, come to fetch his wallet which he dropped there the day before. Leo and Faye are going their separate ways, Faye to Jennie's psychiatrist and Leo home to his wife.

Jennie comes in, dressed in a bathrobe and drying her hair. Leo exits and Faye confesses to Jennie that the man she's really wanted to have an affair with all these years is Jennie's ex-husband Gus. Instead, Faye and Sidney have decided to spend the weekend at a motel in New Jersey. Faye departs leaving Jennie feeling she's lived through all this before.

Scene 9

George, travel-weary, comes into his apartment and turns on the lights, calling for Jennie. She's in her own apartment, still in her bathrobe. She has decided to phone George at the Los Angeles hotel, so her line is busy when George tries to phone her from his apartment. Before Jennie finishes dialing she hangs up, having decided she should be patient a little longer.

George is still trying to reach her, so that when Jennie hangs up her phone rings at once. Jennie can't hide her delight at hearing George's voice. She learns that George got no farther than the Los Angeles airport when he turned around and came home.

GEORGE: I never even checked into the Chateau Marmont. I got unstuck in the TWA lounge . . .

JENNIE: Oh, George . . .

GEORGE: I sat there drinking my complimentary Fresca, and I suddenly remembered a question Dr. Ornstein told me to ask myself whenever I felt trouble coming on. The question is: "What is it you're most afraid would happen *if?*"

JENNIE: I'm listening.

GEORGE: So I said to myself, "George . . . What is it you're most afraid would happen — *if* you went back to New York . . . to Jennie . . . and started your life all over again?" . . . And the answer was so simple . . . I would be happy! . . . I have stared happiness in the face, Jennie — and I embrace it.

JENNIE (*tearfully*): Oh, George . . . you got any left to embrace me?

GEORGE: From here? No. You need one of those long-armed fellas for that.

JENNIE: Well, what are we waiting for? Your place or mine?

GEORGE: Neither . . . I think we have to find a new one called "Ours."

JENNIE: Thank you, George. I was hoping we would.

GEORGE: Thus, feeling every bit as good about me as you do about you, I finished the last chapter of the new book on the plane.

He takes up manuscript. The last few pages are handwritten.
I've got it with me. You want to hear it?

JENNIE: The last chapter?

GEORGE: No. The whole book.

JENNIE: Of course. I'll be right over.

GEORGE: No, I'll read it to you. I don't want to lose my momentum.

He opens book, settles back, so does she. He reads.
You ready? . . . *Falling Into Place,* by George Schneider . . . Dedication . . . To Jennie . . . A nice girl to spend the rest of your life with . . .

He turns page.
Chapter One . . . "Walter Maslanski looked in the mirror and saw what he feared most . . . Walter Maslanski . . .

Curtain starts.
" . . . Not that Walter's features were awesome by any means . . . He had the sort of powder-puff eyes that could be stared down in an abbreviated battle by a one-eyed senior citizen canary . . ."

Curtain.

Jeffrey De Munn as Jack, Laurence Luckinbill as Simon, George
Dzundza as Kelly and Alan Rosenberg as Jimmy in a scene from
A Prayer for My Daughter

A PRAYER FOR MY DAUGHTER

A Play in Two Acts

BY THOMAS BABE

Cast and credits appear on pages 393, 396

THOMAS BABE was born March 13, 1941 in Buffalo, N.Y. and went to high school in Rochester prior to Harvard, where he received his B.A. in 1963. He went on to Yale Law School, graduating in 1972, but he'd already been bitten by the playwriting bug, having won the first Phyllis Anderson Award at Harvard in 1963 for his script The Pageant of Awkward Shadows. *His second play was* Kid Champion *with which Babe made his professional playwriting debut in January, 1975 in a 48-performance production by Joseph Papp at the Public Theater, who also produced his first Best Play,* Rebel Women, *in May, 1976 for 40 performances, and this season his second Best Play,* A Prayer for My Daughter, *for 127 performances.*

Among other Babe scripts are Mojo Candy, *produced by Yale Summer Cabaret in 1975;* Billy Irish, *produced at Manhattan Theater Club in January, 1977;* Great Solo Town *and* Fathers and Sons. *He recently directed another author's work at Playwrights Horizons, and he has written poems published in English magazines. With Timothy S. Mayer he founded and ran the Summer Players at Agassiz Theater, Cambridge, Mass. from 1966 to 1978. He lives in New Haven, was married and is now divorced, with one daughter.*

"A Prayer for My Daughter": by Thomas Babe. Copyright © 1977 by Thomas Babe. Reprinted by permission of The Lantz Office Incorporated. See CAUTION notice on copyright page. All inquiries concerning stock and amateur acting rights should be addressed to: Samuel French, Inc., 25 West 45th Street, New York, N.Y. 10036. All other inquiries should be addressed to the author's representative: The Lantz Office Incorporated, 114 East 55th Street, New York, N.Y. 10022.

Time: The present, 1 a.m. on July 4

Place: The squadroom of a downtown precinct

ACT I

SYNOPSIS: In the early morning hours of the holiday, the empty police station *"has all its affinities to a toilet bowl,"* with a litter of paper and paper cups left by the day shift, battered desks and chairs, dirty windows, typewriters and other equipment. On top of this mess, the place has been decorated to celebrate the Fourth with red, white and blue streamers and balloons.

Two policemen enter through the door up left, escorting two manacled suspects. The policemen are Francis Xavier Kelly *("heading for a fat 40s, beer-gut and all")* and Jack Delasante (in his 30s, *"lean, more than a little cruel look-ing, more than a little dangerous"*). Their captives are Jimmy Rosario (a.k.a. Jimmy Rosehips, in his 20s, *"pure punk with the aspect of a choir boy"*) and Sean (Simon Cohen, a.k.a. Sean de Kahn, in his 40s, *"bearded and lean, has a little of the professor about him, the air that he is the cleanest thing that's been in this room in a decade or two"*).

Kelly begins removing the party decorations while Jack orders the others to sit, pushing Jimmy into a chair. Jack remarks to Kelly that it's not only the Fourth of July but also the full of the moon, so anything can happen. Kelly remembers that "Fourth of July last year, they booked that transvestite whoor for stabbing somebody with a flag."

Jimmy asks for a glass of water (Sean explains that the boy is a former drug addict whose mouth sometimes gets dry). Jack gets a cup of water from the cooler and teases Jimmy with it, then throws it in his face.

Meanwhile, Kelly has found an important message left on his desk. Jack sits down at a typewriter to make out a report, Kelly dials and is on the phone talk-ing to his daughter Margie.

JACK *(with many papers and files, reading)*: What's the woman's name again?
SEAN: The who?
JACK: You killed, the one of you.
JIMMY: Got no idea of the drift of *this* conversation.
JACK: Yeah? Maybe. *(Pause. Looking at papers. Sings.)*
    You are my sunshine,
    My only sunshine,
    You make me happy —
KELLY *(Hand over receiver, to Jack)*: Hey, could you?
JACK *(continuing to sing, softly)*:
    When skies are gray,
    You'll never know, dear,
.   How much I miss you —
SEAN *(correcting)*: Love you!

JACK: Yeah, *love* you . . . *(Sings.)*
  Please don't take my sunshine away.
(Spoken.) Yep.
  KELLY *(to phone)*: I told you I didn't think you ought to, sweetie, I mean, I don't like him, you don't like him. No, I don't think you did. *(Pause.)* You did.
  Long pause.
Goddamit! *(Pause.)* I said, goddamit. You whoor. *(Pause.)* No, I didn't say that. I didn't mean that. I meant you should've — *(Pause.)* Aw, for the Christ's sake, don't cry. *(Pause.)* No, look, I'll bring you some ice cream later, you can't sleep. Tell him to walk. *(Pause.)* You got the .38, lock the door. We got a little garbage to clean up here . . . . .

Kelly tells his daughter he loves her, hangs up and curses, informing Jack that his daughter married "that number one asshole . . . . . a faggot" in secret last week. Jack advises Kelly to go kick the guy's head in, but Kelly has work to do here.
  Out of earshot of their captives, Kelly suggests that they skip the usual "I'm-a-good-cop and you're-a-bad-cop" psychological ploy and knock them around to get a quick confession and wrap up the case so that Kelly can go pay some attention to his emotionally disturbed daughter. Jack opts for applying mental pressure, but Kelly is too tired for such tactics, it's too late at night.

  KELLY: . . . . . I say they're nothin', hit them a lot. I don't trust your instinct to impress the bright ones.
  JACK: That's what you're afraid of?
  KELLY: I told you.
  JACK: You really think that, don't you?
  KELLY: I told you. I'm tired. I wanna straighten my kid. Okay?
  JACK: Maybe you're right. Maybe you'd get a little close to the vest with that kid, anyway. He's pretty.
  KELLY: Don't bait me. You're wasting a z-hour here.
  JACK: Maybe you're right, yeah, you son of a bitch. *(Pause.)* You don't trust me?
  KELLY: Aw, come on.
  JACK: You don't really fuckin trust me?
  KELLY: Jackie, I'm shit out flat and my brain feels like it's fading and I just wanna operate when I still have the last little edge. I wanna straighten Margie. You're a good cop.
  JACK: You bet your fuckin fat ass.
  KELLY: I said it.

Kelly trusts Jack, but he believes that Sean, whom he calls "the beard," is a clever one, and Jack tends "to get entranced with the wilies," while Kelly treats them all alike.
  The phone rings. It's Kelly's wife, worried about what their daughter Margie has threatened to do. Kelly tries to reassure her and promises to see Margie as soon as he can. He hangs up the phone, and he and Jack split the assignment:

Jack will try to befriend the young one in the other room while Kelly interrogates the older one here in the squadroom. "I figure the bearded homo pulled the trigger," Kelly remarks. Jack disagrees, and they make a bet before Jack disappears upstage into another room with Jimmy.

Sean (whose real name, Kelly knows, is Simon Cohen) gives his name as "Sean de Kahn" and asks to phone his attorney. Kelly remembers that Sean's parents live in Brooklyn and looks up their number in the phone book. When he threatens to call them instead of an attorney, Sean agrees to talk, telling him that the youth with him is "deeply disturbing," giving Kelly the idea (which Sean denies) that Sean will place the blame for the killing on him.

KELLY: I figure either of you two could've actually blown Mrs. Linowitz away. Old cons like you got ice water for blood, but young guys like Jimmy, they can be very impetuous.

SEAN: I know.

KELLY: I know you know.

SEAN: You're silly. We'll beat it.

KELLY: I know. That's why we did this.

SEAN: What's "this?"

KELLY: We try and sneak in a little punishment before the court has a chance to decide you don't deserve it on a technicality, like you were born incurable homo, or I didn't read you your rights Shakespeare-perfect.

SEAN: No one's read me my rights.

KELLY: I don't read 'em to homos.

SEAN: Then what you're doing here is a dreadful farce.

KELLY: You wanna talk Miranda and Escobedo with me, Sean, okay. You're entitled to a lawyer, except you're not really entitled to a lawyer, because you got blood on your hands and it stinks. Now this is my house, Sean, I make the rules. That's your warning, you have the right to be very careful around me, O.K.?

SEAN: You're worse than silly — you're insane.

KELLY: I'm tired, Sean. Got this daughter who's got her head wedged up in trouble, you know, family stuff, I stake a dry cleaning establishment all day, my ass is sore, you and your friend treat me to an old woman, her head half off — I'm just not as used to shit like that, like you imagine I am: I get tired, edgy.

Sean still insists he's entitled to call a lawyer, but Kelly ignores his request. Sean assures Kelly that though they can easily frighten Jimmy into signing anything up to and including a confession, he, Sean, will let hell freeze over before he talks.

From Sean's rap sheet, Kelly observes that Sean is jobless in an apparently aimless existence. Sean claims he's a teacher — Jimmy's teacher, for example, teaching him a way of life, "eclectic spritualism," looking upon him as he'd look upon a son — or more accurately, a daughter. As for his sex life, Sean claims he's celibate.

Kelly decides to smooth things out a little by taking a drink. This alarms Sean, and rightly so, Kelly admits: Kelly intends to get a bit drunk and beat

Sean up, whether or not he confesses to murder. "I may be . . . *(Pause.)* . . . insane," Kelly tells Sean, who worries about protecting his face while Kelly prepares to beat him up: "I never hit faces. I'm not sadistic."

Jack enters, interrupting with the information that Jimmy needs a fix. Jack feels that Jimmy is on the point of confessing and will do so if he gets some junk, but Kelly orders Jack not to give him any.

As Jimmy comes to the door of the other room, the phone rings. Kelly answers it; it's his despondent daughter again, this time telling her father she's got the barrel of the .38 in her mouth, so that Kelly can't understand what she's saying (he puts Jack on another phone to trace the call).

Kelly tries to soothe Margie, telling her he loves her. She hangs up, but Jack has been able to trace the call to some Bronx rooming house. Kelly orders Jack to alert the "loonie squad" immediately. Jack is surprised that Kelly doesn't plan to go to his daughter himself. Kelly explains with the cryptic observation, "Suicides are a disgrace. They don't even get buried in church ground."

JACK: Go see her.
KELLY: What, dead?
JACK: You ain't sure what's happening.
KELLY: I got a feelin'. *(Walks up to Jimmy.)* If you don't go back in there and sit down, I'm gonna break you over my knee like a pencil. Now park your fuckin toosh.
    Jimmy backs off.
JACK *(on the phone)*: That was the trace, Morris. baby. She says she has a gun, Kelly says he thinks she took somethin as well . . . Naw, he don't want to . . . I don't know why . . . Kelly?
KELLY: I got nothin to say. Morris knows his job.
JACK *(to phone)*: He's got nothin to say. He says you know your job. Yeah. *(Hangs up.)* He says he'll try, but fuck you.
KELLY *(sudden energy)*: Okay, I'm taking Sean de Kahn in the other room, you drag Narcissus out here. I want somethin quick from him, from you, all of you. The kid's his daughter, if you follow that.
JACK *(one last try):* Kelly, if you wanna go see about Margie . . .?
KELLY *(ignoring)*: And no junk!

Sean signals Jimmy to keep his mouth shut as he's forced into the other room by Kelly. Jimmy tries to act tough but is obviously nervous (this is his first arrest). Jack takes a bag of powdered dilaudid, a potent drug, out of one of the desk drawers — it's another policeman's evidence in another case — and prepares a fix with it in front of Jimmy.

JIMMY: How come he didn't go?
JACK: Who?
JIMMY: The other officer.
JACK: Go where, Jimmy?
JIMMY: Ain't he got a suicide working there?

JACK: He didn't want to go. He's seen one dead person today. The old lady you did.

JIMMY: He must be a fun man, he must be a real fun sugar daddy he can't move his ass for . . . whoever it was.

JACK: Who was it?

JIMMY: His daughter, man, I heard that. I wasn't supposed to, but I heard.

JACK: I mean who was it, which one of you killed Mrs. Linowitz?

JIMMY: From nothin I know nothin from. *(Pause.)* You wanna know about my daughter?

JACK: Nope.

JIMMY: I wanna tell you.

JACK: I don't want to hear. I want to know how it was Mrs. Linowitz had to get killed for twenty-six dollars and fifteen cents.

JIMMY: You don't give a shit. My daughter —

JACK: I'm bored. When I get bored, I get shitty.

   Holds up the loaded fix.
There she is.

JACK: You're a bastard. How do I know what that is? How do I know that ain't sodium pentathol? That's sodium pentathol or it's milk sugar.

JACK: You're milk sugar. This is for me.

   Rolls up his sleeve; fixes during the following.
How I got it figured is that Sean says, Jimmy, just this once, Jimmy, honey, a little money and you and me, we'll settle out a bit, and Jimmy says, Look man, I don't do nothing with an armory in it, I'm clean, I take teevees, class-C felonies only, and Sean de Kahn says, Jimmy, this Mrs. Linowitz keeps a pile in a tin box under the presser, she don't trust banks, and we take this, we make ten thousand minimum and no old lady is gonna offer any resistance, she reads the papers, she'll think we're garbage, she'll remember the grandchildren and get scared like all ladies of any type, she'll cave right in, and Jimmy says, I don't know, and Sean de Kahn gets Jimmy a little hit and the next thing you know, there's Jimmy and Sean, and Sean has a gun in his hand and Jimmy is scraping up the money and suddenly Jimmy hears this terrible roaring explosion and fire by his ear and sees this poor dumb old woman get blasted backwards and he says, Shit, Sean, why'd you do that, man? and old Sean just smiles and smiles and says it was necessary, philosophically necessary. Right?

   Pause. Jack relaxes into a sort of euphoria, but alert.
Hey, Jimmy, it's pins and needles for about eight seconds, then it's whoosh. This dilaudid, what can I say about it, hunh? Nectar for the gods.

Jimmy wants a fix badly, and Jack promises to give him one if he talks. Jimmy promises to talk, and Jack hands him a loaded hypodermic. Jimmy pumps the dilaudid into his vein, while expressing his philosophy (as euphoria creeps up him): darkness is a permanent condition into which a little light comes briefly once in a while. "The darkness is the evil, the black everywhere, all the time; it's permanent, the dark, unloseable, and you and me and everybody are the only real source of illumination we got . . . people . . . . ."

Laurence Luckinbill and George Dzundza in a scene from *A Prayer for My Daughter*

Jimmy also remarks that if Sean were watching now he'd call the stuff in the hypodermic dark, not light. Jack had a good Catholic education (his father was a cop, while Jimmy's was a crook) which taught him the light, not the dark, would inevitably conquer.

Jimmy, on cloud nine, offers to answer any question. Instead of questioning him about the murder, Jack questions him about his philosophy. Jimmy thinks the dark is a contrast necessary to perceive light. Jack, as taught by the fathers, believes the dark to be unnecessary. He'd like to serve as a teacher to Jimmy, as Sean does.

Jack can't understand how, if Jimmy has a daughter, he can also be a "daughter" to Sean. Jimmy tries to explain that "There are guys flattered if they think somebody looks at them the way somebody — that person — might look at a real pretty chick." Jimmy is one of those guys, and he craves affection:

"I mean, no guy but an upfront deviate is gonna make it with his own daughter, but there's affection there, a lot of just affection. The kind most guys don't hand out to sons. Who's gonna kiss his own son a lot or pat him on the ass, like that, without the bullshit, hunh?"

Jimmy sometimes feels ashamed of his relationship with Sean — he admits — and at such times he goes home. Jack doesn't believe that Jimmy really has a daughter, because Jimmy is a punk, and no woman would let him make love to her. Jack darkens the atmosphere by telling Jimmy, "You're shit." The policeman expects increased hostility from the suspect, but instead his remark brings tears to Jimmy's eyes.

Disconcerted, Jack is now prepared to believe Jimmy's story about a daughter, aged five, with "hair like the top of a candle." Suddenly Jack returns to the subject of the murdered woman, and Jimmy finally admits that he was confused, he doesn't know for sure who fired the gun, but he thinks it was probably Sean: "I think he did. He did. He did it. I hate guns. He did it. I don't know."

Jack pushes Jimmy into the chair as Kelly come back into the room, rubbing his knuckles, with Sean, who is doubled over in pain. Kelly is contemptuous of his victim's softness. Sean, a onetime medical technician, fears he has a ruptured spleen. Sean warns Kelly that if he dies Kelly will be in trouble; the autopsy will show he was beaten, for sure.

At Kelly's command, Sean sits. He tries to persuade the officers to end this interview and book them promptly, so that he can receive medical attention and the policemen can go home at last. Jack reminds Kelly that his daughter Margie needs him, but Kelly is prepared to stay here until the night's work is done.

Sean again questions Kelly's sanity, and Jimmy, who is now "hummin' like a filament," sugests maybe Kelly hates his daughter and wonders, "Don't it hurt you someplace that you got a daughter who's gonna kill herself cause you're her total-darkness daddy on the phone? No pain, nothin'?"

Angrily, Kelly replies that he hurts, yes, but he is proud of his ability to take the blows. Kelly can't help remembering that his father was a hero (Jack recalls that *his* father was a bum to his family, though to some he was "a good cop"). Jimmy now admits that he lied when he said his father was a crook — he never knew a father. Sean tells them his father is a saint, but Kelly remembers that Sean's father is "a commie traitor."

Kelly is glad to learn that Sean is feeling no worse, so his spleen probably isn't injured after all.

KELLY: . . . . . I mean, I just wanted to punish you, not kill you.
    Takes a drink.
Shit, you don't have to tell me, Delasante, the kid blamed the beard.
    JACK: You got it.
    SEAN: I would've thought it was disturbing . . .
    KELLY: What?
    SEAN: To have a daughter. That would be a very deeply disturbing thing.
    KELLY: Who can say?
    Pause. Kelly takes a drink. Jimmy starts to giggle; he can't help himself.

And you gave him a pop, Delasante?

JACK: Yeah, I gave him a pop.

KELLY: Jesus, what a bunch of hyperventilated creeps. I don't know.

Kelly drinks again. Jimmy stifles his giggles.

What it is there is that Margie's the only person in the world I'm on a sure foot with. I don't want anything from her, except I'm her father and she's my daughter and that will never get removed. It goes back to the times she was little and all the stuff along the way, and the smiles, and she'd shout at me and get pissed off sometimes . . . but that there is permanent; even when she sticks it to me, it's permanent. It's more like a thing I read about Alfred Einstein, who invented the big bomb, who said when he was a kid he read a lot of dead scientists and authors and said he didn't feel alone, he didn't think he ever would feel alone, because those dead guys were his unloseable friends. That's how I think of her, my daughter, my unloseable friend. And I don't want a goddam thing from her but she knows it, she's unloseable, and she prospers. That's the limit of it.

Pause. Jimmy giggles again.

SEAN: "Feeling does not influence even in the smallest degree the subject's thought processes," the Army concluded after they gave me a psychological test. "Very highly unusual," they concluded.

Jimmy starts to laugh. Kelly pins him with a glance.

KELLY: You and me, sonny, we talk next, make book on it.

JACK *(sings)*:

You are my sunshine,
My only sunshine,
You make me happy
When skies are grey —

The phone rings.

KELLY: Jesus Christ, with the music . . .!

JACK *(sings)*:

You'll never know, dear —

Jack answers the phone.

What?

Pause.

KELLY: So? Who is it?

JACK: Disconnect.

He starts to hang up phone. Blackout. Curtain.

ACT II

Sometime later, Jimmy is asleep on a desk, Sean is sitting and Jack is reading a book, while Kelly is trying to get in touch with his other daughter, who lives in Vermont and has no telephone in her home. Through the state police Kelly passes along an urgent message to have his daughter phone him from a neighbor's house.

After giving Sean a cup of coffee, Jack suggests to Kelly that they decide both of their prisoners are equally guilty and call it a night. "No, I gotta do something," Kelly decides, and he adds: "I have reserves of energy. It comes from bein even with everybody. I still live with my woman, Delesante, I have a sense of obligation."

Jack is certain that Kelly would really rather be out looking after Margie, and again Kelly contradicts him: "You don't know shit. If you care so much, why don't you go out and tell her all that intolerable grief she says she has is really tolerable . . . . ."

Kelly decides he's going to take Jimmy on, while Jack works on Sean: "I want the beard to sing." Kelly pushes Jimmy into the other room and follows him after cautioning Jack to listen for the phone and let him know if there are developments.

Jack is still brooding over Kelly's earlier remark that he doesn't trust him: "You think you work with a man and suddenly it appears on the horizon he doesn't trust you, on the horizon where the sun rises, the light you know, you being into the light and all, he doesn't trust you, and that's the futile black; right, Sean, I mean, in other words, Simon? Right?"

Sean doesn't reply. Jack, curious about Sean's sex life, questions him about it. The subject seems irrelevant to Sean, who claims to have been intimate with several women, speaking in a way which makes Jack feel Sean is condescending to him. Again, Jack asks Sean to make a statement about the murder.

SEAN: Tell me what to say.

JACK: You know, whichever way, in your own words, twist the idiom a little, so it don't sound like we wrote it and some bullshit lawyer makes some bullshit judge laugh at Kelly and me for bein a little old fashioned and goin to the source of the felony. Like that. Whatever. The truth.

SEAN: I don't want to condescend to you, officer.

JACK: Delasante. Jack.

SEAN: I'd rather we were square.

JACK: Me, too. I want the kid for this one. I get no pleasure from burning you.

SEAN: You can have him.

JACK: All the way. I want him stapled in a shroud.

SEAN: Take him. What should I say?

JACK: Hey, let's resist a little. I thought you had some love for him, he was your daughter.

SEAN: You can have him.

Jack can't understand Sean's willingness to put the blame for the killing on Jimmy. He knows quite a lot about Sean's sexual and other habits from the police package on him begun ten years before, after an extortion arrest. It disturbs Sean that they know so much about him (once, while Sean was in a state of delerium at Bellevue, the police sat beside him and wrote down everything he said, because "we just knew, we were gonna see you again"). Sean beat that extortion rap and therefore, he tells Jack, all that information should have been removed from his file.

There is something Sean wants to say, and Jack is here to listen. Once in Vietnam where he was a medical technician (Sean tells Jack) he noticed a shirtless man, covered with blood and dirt, leaning against a tree smoking a marijuana cigarette. The man noticed Sean, waved and said something Sean couldn't hear.

When the man stood up to shout he was hit in the neck by a sniper's bullet. Sean cradled the dead man's head in his lap and hung on to it for 12 hours, giving himself shots of morphine to keep from weeping.

Sean knows he should have taken Kelly's beating better than he did, and it disturbs him greatly to think that remembered Vietnam emotion may be creeping up on him again.

SEAN: . . . . . You know how many times I didn't say a thing and didn't do a thing, not one goddam thing, and I know you'll find that hard to believe, considering my package, but I was good a long time, a very long time, until I was overwhelmed with it. *(Pause; a different tone; sad.)* There's a woman inside me, officer, and she aches for the men she has known. She flirts with them and cries for them when they have to go in the morning; she likes to please them but she likes to have her cigarette lit, at least when I used to smoke . . . and I hate her so much that most often I want to kill her, because she loves her men so completely that it terrifies me . . . and she says to me, whenever I think there is no woman in me, that I am a liar and a fool, and she is the one who makes me cry and she's the one who makes me sing goddam songs to men . . . live men, dead men, it doesn't matter. *(Pause.)* And he was her first, my woman, her first man. Nothing came of it but that I ran my fingers through his hair for, they tell me, twelve hours, and I sang: "You are my so forth, My only so forth, You make me so forth . . ." *(Pause. Sean's tone changes slightly back to its old crispness.)* Does a word of this make the least little sense to you?

JACK: Oh, I'm gettin' it all, but it's a little vague . . . . .

Jack suggests that maybe a psychiatrist could help Sean. Jack is curious about people like Sean, because he's known only one way — heterosexuality — married three times, with two daughters, a compelling need for regular female companionship and four shots of hard drugs a day.

Jack has decided: "If you need them, you can't live *with* them, you think about murder all the time." The only woman Jack really loved was his first wife, Debby, until he caught her one night staring at him when she thought he was asleep: "She's thinking I want to sneak off, and I'm thinking, she wants to slip it to me." She was just watching her man for no reason, Sean thinks, an action he perfectly understands.

Jack cites the sex book in which he's been reading about the weakness of the male and strength of the female spermatozoa, from which he draws the conclusion: "Women always kill the men, given half a chance. And I don't give 'em half a chance."

The phone rings. It turns out to be Kelly's Vermont daughter, whose name is Sasha. Kelly can't come to the phone right away, so Jack puts Sasha on hold and returns to Sean.

JACK: And we agree, Jimmy pulled the chain on the old lady?
SEAN: Right on.
JACK: And he *did,* right?
SEAN: What do you think?
JACK: I think he did.

SEAN: Then he did.
JACK: And you really think so, I mean . . .?
SEAN: I'm pretty committed to thinking he did, yeah.
JACK: Yeah.

Jack declares "There's no woman in me," and he advises Sean not to talk too much about the woman inside him to others, or it's possible a smart lawyer will rip Sean and his sworn statement (when he makes it) apart in front of a jury.

Jack goes back to the phone, reassures Sasha her father will be with her directly, then goes back to Sean: "We dispose of Jimmy . . . . . and it doesn't matter a lot whether he pulled the trigger or not, *he's* the one I want tonight." Jack is set on pinning the crime on Jimmy because Jimmy is such an obvious deviate.

Kelly enters pushing Jimmy ahead of him, ordering him to sit and then taking Sasha's call. Kelly fills Sasha in on what's happening to Margie — hasty marriage, suicidal depression. Kelly wants Sasha to get on the phone with Margie, if it can be arranged, to try to talk her sister out of doing further harm to herself. Sasha's immediate reaction, judging from Kelly's end of the conversation, is that her father isn't making a maximum effort himself in this emergency, that he is unfeeling, made of stone. Kelly slams the phone down in anger.

Jack takes Sean into the next room to write out the statement that he is obediently willing to provide, leaving Kelly alone in the room with Jimmy. Kelly feels a need to explain himself, gruffly: "I'm here because I don't want to be there in the Bronx with Margie, and I couldn't stand to be anywhere else. And since I wanna be here, you gotta be here, and Sergeant Delasante, and Sean de Kahn gotta be here. And since I never figured out how to ask for anything I really wanted, I don't ask, I tell. And if I want, or wanted, anything from you, you wouldn't know unless I told you, which I don't intend to. *(Pause.)* I wanted all that clear."

Jimmy asks no one in particular, "Who said to be a man was easy?" and insists to Kelly he didn't kill anybody (Kelly never thought he did). Kelly can guess how Jimmy got his high on dilaudid. Kelly orders Jimmy to strip so that he can be searched for more narcotics. Jimmy takes his clothes off, while telling Kelly that Jack gave him the drug (Kelly warns him nobody would believe that a policeman gave him a fix in a station house while he was under arrest as a murder suspect). When Jimmy is naked Kelly can see he's not concealing anything.

KELLY: Shit-Jesus, I'm ashamed, you know. *(Pause.)* Put the clothes on.
JIMMY: I don't want to.
KELLY: I said, put your clothes on.
JIMMY: I don't know.
KELLY: What don't you know? Who done it?
JIMMY: That's not it, that's not what I don't know.
KELLY: I get so pissed off at people saying they don't know, I do.
JIMMY: Does she say "I don't know" a whole lot?
KELLY: Who?

JIMMY: Your daughter.
KELLY: Don't touch my daughter, Jimmy.
JIMMY: Okay, yeah, I'm sorry, I thought you might wanna say.
KELLY: Get dressed, would you?
JIMMY *(after a pause)*: It's okay.
KELLY: I know that, I know it's okay.
KELLY: You want me to fight you still, is that it?
KELLY: Just a little.
JIMMY: I'm way out of my depth here.
KELLY: Are you? I wonder.
JIMMY: It's just not easy, man.
KELLY: Sergeant.
JIMMY: No, man, it's "man," Sergeant.
KELLY: Who said easy? I can't figure the taking of a human life, your own, somebody else's, and that's the only last fuckin thing on God's green earth I can't figure. Every other sin is bullshit.
    Pause.
JIMMY: I know, and it's okay, it really is.
KELLY: Christ I'm tired.
JIMMY: If you're tired, I'm just dead.
KELLY: Yeah, I know.
    As he takes Jimmy in his arms; a moment.
There was a time for months, years even, after she was born, I couldn't say her name. I had to say something else but her real name — I'd call her Margarine, she liked that, Magpie, Mag-poos, from the mess she used to leave in her diapers, Mugs, Mike, even Mikey, and then some day there, she dawned on me like Margaret, which is her real name, and Margie, which is her real nickname, and I had possession of the belief that my daughter was the most extraordinary human being who ever moved shoes over the earth. I couldn't for the life of me tell you what happened there later, how she got moody, how she smart-assed me around and sneaked around with those pin-dicks she was always callin "My man" — maybe all that started when she started to get her monthlies, but nobody's ever got from me what she got with her sayin crap, her sayin "Hi, daddy . . ." her sayin "I love you, daddy . . ."
    Kisses Jimmy on the head.

Kelly has noticed that Jimmy feels no arousal in Kelly's embrace, though Kelly himself does, somewhat. Kelly takes Jimmy's gestures as a sign of affection, but what Jimmy is really doing is stealing Kelly's gun. Kelly is almost indifferent as to whether Jimmy shoots him or not; Jimmy, now in possession of the gun and holding it behind his back, assures Kelly he has no intention of doing so.

KELLY: I'd like the gun back.
JIMMY: I know.
KELLY: Tell you, let's make a deal.
JIMMY: What deal?

KELLY: Let's just stand like we were, before, just relaxed, close our eyes, feel nothin . . . nothin at all.
Kelly makes to be affectionate.
JIMMY: Stop doin that, it's not that hand.
KELLY: I figured that. Let's just relax.
JIMMY: It's —
Gunshot.
Aw, shit, you're such bad luck.
KELLY: I know. Get me a chair.
JIMMY: How bad is it, hunh?
KELLY: I don't know, but it hurts like a son of a bitch. Get dressed, hunh, get dressed fast, I mean, this is a constabulary.
JIMMY *(doing so)*: O.K., I'm gettin dressed.

Jimmy talks of getting a doctor, though Kelly feels strangely comfortable "for the first time in a long time." Jack comes in to check the commotion. Jimmy points the gun at him. Jack's first reaction is to suggest that Jimmy put the gun down, as Kelly advises: "Jackie, don't get big about this."

Jack inspects Kelly's wound and finds that the bullet hit Kelly's back pocket where he was carrying his wallet and did no damage that can't be handled with the application of a towel to stop the superficial bleeding. Kelly agrees "My time's comin' five, ten years from now — myocardial infarction."

The phone rings. Jimmy, still holding the gun on Jack, lets him answer it. Jack listens, then hangs up and tells the others a prayer is in order — the police found Margie too late to prevent her death. She was still alive when they got there ("her voice was proud") but she had shot herself in the head and died, inevitably, a half hour later.

Kelly comments "Bingo" and then, apparently unmoved by this terrible news, returns to business: did Jack get a signed statement from Sean? Yes. Okay, Jack has won the bet on which one was the killer — "So," Kelly continues, "would you disarm the felon so we can go someplace . . . home, to sleep, whatever?"

Jack moves to obey, but Jimmy warns them he'll blow somebody's brains out if they don't let him talk — he wants to tell them about the day his girl, Lisa, went to the hospital. Lisa, the nurses and the doctor persuaded Jimmy to stay and watch the birth, though he didn't want to. Things went well at first, but then the baby got stuck; and everyone helped the mother push until suddenly the infant, a girl, popped out into the world. "All the light I ever had ran to her," Jimmy tells them, wondering whether Kelly, apparently unmoved by his own daughter's death, ever felt the same.

KELLY: I'll tell you, since you wanna know all that crap. When Jack just told me bingo and brains on the wall, I'll tell you how I felt. I felt okay. I felt like the stone is off my chest. She's safe now. Now I'm gonna love her a lot and think about her, I'm gonna be closer to her than I ever been in my life, because all that stuff is past now and it was so complicated. Now she's set kind of perfect, bein' dead, and bingo! . . . I find myself relieved.
Jimmy points the gun at Kelly's temple for a long moment, then tosses the gun on the desk in defeat.

JIMMY: All right, Sergeant, man, you win.

KELLY: Okay, Jackie, he ain't got the gun any more. So you beat him up a little now, right?

JACK: Yeah, I can, but I'm not going to, Kelly, you know, in other words, not now. Jimmy, he ain't got a prayer of surviving his next birthday, look at him.

KELLY: You're all bullshit, Jackie.

JACK: Yeah?

KELLY: Yeah?

JACK: Yeah, maybe, Frannie, and I'm not gonna tell you what I finally conclude about you, not now. This is Margie's wake. I'm gonna write my reports up, and yours, like a very good police officer, which is what I happen to be. And here's how it comes out, just so everybody knows, including the Sergeant there — that Sean has given me a statement that makes Jimmy take the whole big total fall, which Jimmy knows, and Jimmy's got nothin to say in his own defense, really, because he knows, after all, he's the rabbit here, everybody's darlin little girl, which Sean knows likewise, and I know, and the Sergeant there knows. Just like we all know, in reality, that Sean, in reality, killed the old lady and Jimmy was so hopped up at the time he's practically innocent. I don't know why things turn out like this, but they do, they always do. And I'm gonna wait five seconds for anybody here to tell me I'm out of line, in other words, wrong.

Pause.

Okay, Jimmy.

JIMMY: Say what you want, but I know why you all gotta be rid of me and I don't kiss off so easy.

JACK: Yeah? Whatever gets you through the night, but just so you know, honey, just so the record's straight, that's all. In other words, happy Fourth of July, friends.

Day is dawning, and it looks like it's going to be a hot one. Kelly ignores a comment by Sean that he could have stopped his daughter from killing herself if he'd wanted to; he orders the handcuffs put on the prisoners so they can be moved to jail. Jack cuffs them, as Kelly suggests they all say a prayer for his daughter, "Because you pray, or you pretend to pray, because that's what people do to balm the griefs all, and you know that."

Kelly prays silently, but Sean decides to sing "You Are My Sunshine" from beginning to end. By the time he gets to the last line of the song, Kelly has finished his prayer and Jack is watching while Jimmy beats out a derisive rhythm.

SEAN *(sings)*:
. . . . . Please don't take my sunshine away.

Sean laughs. They are frozen for a moment after the song. Noise outside intrudes; Kelly busts it by moving; he and Jack are then suddenly businesslike.

KELLY: Move, garbage. The bus for the Tombs leaves in five minutes. You boys'll just make it.

They go, perfectly cop and crook. Blackout. Curtain.

John Wood in *Deathtrap*

DEATHTRAP

A Play in Two Acts

BY IRA LEVIN

Cast and credits appear on page 363

IRA LEVIN was born in New York City in 1929 and was educated at Horace Mann, Drake University in Des Moines and New York University. His first novel, written at 22, was the thriller A Kiss Before Dying *which won the Mystery Writers of America designation as the best first novel of the year. After military service, at 25, he adapted Mac Hyman's* No Time for Sergeants *into a TV script and then, two years later, into his first play, a Broadway comedy that opened Oct. 20, 1955, ran for 796 performances, launched Andy Griffith into stardom and was named a Best Play of its season.*

Levin's playwriting career has continued through the Broadway productions Interlock *(1958),* Critic's Choice *(1960),* General Seeger *(1962),* Drat! The Cat! *(1965, a musical for which he wrote the book and lyrics),* Dr. Cook's Garden *(1967),* Veronica's Room *(1975) and now his second Best Play* Deathtrap. *Offstage his best-known work is* Rosemary's Baby.

Levin's more recent work includes the novels The Stepford Wives *and* The Boys From Brazil, *recently transposed to film. Levin has three sons by a marriage which terminated in divorce.*

EDITOR'S NOTE: Ira Levin's *Deathtrap* is a suspense thriller which depends heavily — and most adroitly — on the element of surprise. Here's what some of the reviewers wrote about it after its Broadway opening.

Clive Barnes in the New York *Post:* "For critics, thrillers are notoriously dif-

"Deathtrap": by Ira Levin. Copyright © 1978 by Ira Levin. Reprinted by permission of Howard Rosenstone & Company, Inc. See CAUTION notice on copyright page. All inquiries concerning amateur acting rights should be addressed to: Dramatists Play Service, Inc., 440 Park Avenue South, New York, N.Y. 10016. All other inquiries should be addressed to the author's representative: Howard Rosenstone & Company, Inc., 850 Seventh Avenue, New York, N.Y. 10019.

ficult to write about — simply because you can only hint at the story . . . . .
Deathtrap is about death and about two hours. I shouldn't say more."

Douglas Watt in the *Daily News:* "Ethical considerations prevent my going
any further (than the first scene) with the plot."

Richard Eder in the New York *Times:* "It is a rule in writing about this kind
of play that the ending should not be revealed."

Edwin Wilson in the *Wall Street Journal:* "It is an unwritten law that
reviewers do not give away surprises in a mystery."

Jack Kroll in *Newsweek:* "Then there's the . . . . . unexpected developments,
a brilliant description of which I just threw in my waste basket."

In effect, *Deathtrap* is a play of surprises, and so successful a one that it's
likely to be running and/or touring long after this Best Plays volume is off the
presses. We wouldn't want to give away its author's treasure any more than the
reviewers quoted above, so we cannot offer in these pages a full synopsis of the
script, as we do in the case of most other Best Plays.

Ours is a theater yearbook which pays close attention to the literary underpin-
nings of the performing art — the script. Instead of a full, plot-revealing synopsis of *Deathtrap,* however, we've arranged to present one scene — Act I, Scene 2
— in its entirety, so that our record of the theater year's Best Plays will include a
detailed example of the style, characterizations and construction of Ira Levin's
script without giving away its later secrets, as follows:

Time: The present

*Place: Sidney Bruhl's study in the Bruhl home in West-
port, Conn.*

ACT I

Scene 1: An afternoon in October

SYNOPSIS: Sidney Bruhl's study is a converted stable with a stairway to the
second floor, entrances to kitchen, front door and living room upstage and
french doors leading to a patio at right. Prominent features of the room are a
desk and large collection of weapons displayed on the wall.

Sidney Bruhl (*"about 50, an impressive and well-tended man, wearing a car-
digan sweater over a turtleneck shirt"*) is sitting at his desk. His wife Myra (*"in
her 40s, slim and self-effacing, in a sweater and skirt"*) comes in just as Sidney
finishes reading the script of a murder play which he feels will be "highly commercial." Unfortunately for him, it's not his work (though he is a well known
and successful playwright) but a script entitled *Deathtrap* which came in the
mail from a former student, Clifford Anderson, who wants Sidney's opinion of
it. Sidney tries to remember which of his students was Anderson — perhaps the
enormously fat one.

Thrillers are Sidney's specialty, but his last four plays have been flops. He's envious of his student for having written so promising a script. Myra comforts him with a kiss and suggests that Sidney collaborate with the student on revisions — and of course take top billing when the script is finally produced. Sidney decides this might be a good idea and playfully declares that he'd commit murder if necessary to have another hit.

Sidney phones Anderson at his home in nearby Milford. From Sidney's end of the conversation Myra can deduce that Anderson is unmarried, wrote *Deathtrap* in total isolation and has shown it to no one else. He typed the original and only one carbon which he mailed to Sidney.

Myra hears Sidney drag in the subject of collaboration and pretend that one of his scripts was once doctored and rescued by the late, great George S. Kaufman. Sidney informs his former student that he's working on a play now himself, about a Dutch clairvoyant named Helga ten Dorp who happens to be living nearby in Westport. It's title is *The Frowning Wife,* Sidney says, noting Myra's disapproving look. But Sidney will drop what he is doing if Anderson will come by train this very evening to discuss revisions of *Deathtrap,* bringing the original typescript with him so they can use it in consultation. Anderson agrees to come, and the phone conversation ends.

Myra remarks, "He probably has another carbon copy filed away somewhere." Sidney agrees: "More than likely. And all his notes and outlines, early drafts . . . Opening night of my dazzling triumph his gray-haired mother comes down the aisle accompanied by the Milford and Westport Police Departments."

Sidney persuades Myra to go to the movies with a friend, while he goes to meet the train. Sidney has aroused his wife's curiosity, if not suspicion — would he really do murder to steal a hit play? Sidney smiles and reassures her — certainly not. He suggests, however, that there might be a future play idea in this situation of a student who sends a promising script to a former teacher who is suffering a dry period. Sidney taps the manuscript and comments, "Pity he's got the title *Deathtrap,"* as Myra goes off to the movies and the lights fade to black.

Scene 2: That evening

> *As the lights come up, Sidney has unlocked the front door from the outside and is showing Clifford Anderson into the foyer, while Myra, who has been fretting in the study, hurries to greet them. The draperies are drawn over the french doors, and all the room's lamps are lighted. Sidney has replaced his sweater with a jacket; Myra has freshened up and perhaps changed into a simple dress. Clifford is in his mid-20s and free of obvious defects; an attractive young man in jeans, boots and a heavy sweater. He carries a bulging manila envelope.*

SIDNEY: Actually it was built in seventeen *ninety*-four but they were out of nines at the hardware store so I backdated it ten years.

CLIFFORD: It's a beautiful house . . .

SIDNEY: (*closing the door*): Historical society had kittens.

MYRA: Hello!
> *She offers her hand. Clifford shakes it warmly.*
SIDNEY: This is Clifford Anderson, dear. My wife Myra.
CLIFFORD: Hello. It's a pleasure to meet you.
MYRA: Come in. I was beginning to worry . . .
SIDNEY (*simultaneously*): Watch out for the beam.
> *Ducking, Clifford comes into the study. Sidney follows.*
You can always tell an authentic Colonial by the visitors' bruised foreheads.
> *Myra smiles nervously. Clifford looks about, a bit awed.*
CLIFFORD: The room you work in?
SIDNEY: How did you guess.
CLIFFORD: The typewriter, and all these posters . . .
> *He moves about, studying the window cards. Sidney watches him;*
> *Myra glances at Sidney. Clifford touches the Master's covered*
> *typewriter, then points at the wall.*
Is that the mace that was used in *Murderer's Child?*
SIDNEY: Yes. And the dagger is from *The Murder Game.*
> *Clifford goes closer, touches the dagger blade.*
Careful, it's sharp. The trick one was substituted in Act Two.
CLIFFORD (*moves his hand to an ax handle*): *In for the Kill?*
SIDNEY: Yes.
CLIFFORD: I can't understand why that play didn't run . . .
SIDNEY: Critics peeing on it might be the answer.
> *Clifford goes on with his inspection.*
MYRA: The train must have been late.
> *Sidney pays no notice.*
Was it?
CLIFFORD (*turning*): No, Mr. Bruhl was. The train was on time.
SIDNEY: I had to get gas, and Frank insisted on fondling the spark plugs.
CLIFFORD (*points at a window card*): Do you know that *Gunpoint* was the first play I ever saw? I had an aunt in New York, and I came in on the train one Saturday — by myself, another first — from Hartford. She took me to the matinee. I was twelve years old.
SIDNEY: If you're trying to depress me, you've made it.
CLIFFORD: How? Oh. I'm sorry. But that's how I got hooked on thrillers.
SIDNEY: *Angel Street* did it to me. "Bella, where is that grocery bill? Eh? What have you done with it, you poor wretched creature?" I was fifteen.
MYRA: It sounds like a disease, being passed from generation to generation.
SIDNEY: It is a disease: *thrilleritis malignis,* the fevered pursuit of the one-set five-character moneymaker.
CLIFFORD: I'm not pursuing money. Not that I wouldn't like to have some, so I could have a place like this to work in; but that isn't the reason I wrote *Deathtrap.*
SIDNEY: You're still an early case.
CLIFFORD: It's *not* a disease, it's a tradition: a superbly challenging theatrical framework in which every possible variation seems to have been played. Can I conjure up a few new ones? Can I startle an audience that's *been* on Angel

Street, that's dialed "M" for murder, that's witnessed the prosecution, that's played the murder game . . .

SIDNEY: Lovely speech! And thanks for saving me for the last.

CLIFFORD: I was coming to *Sleuth*.

SIDNEY: I'm glad I stopped you.

CLIFFORD: So am I. I'm a little — euphoric about all that's happening.

SIDNEY: As well you should be.

MYRA: Would you like something to drink?

CLIFFORD: Yes, please. Do you have some ginger ale?

MYRA: Yes. Sidney? Scotch?

SIDNEY: No, dear, I believe I'll have ginger ale too.
> *Which gives Myra a moment's pause, after which she goes to the liquor table.*

CLIFFORD: These aren't *all* from your plays, are they?

SIDNEY: God no, I haven't written *that* many. Friends give me things now, and I prowl the antique shops.

MYRA: *There's* a disease.

SIDNEY: (*taking his keys out*): Yes, and a super excuse for not working.
> *Indicating a pistol while en route to the desk.*
I found this in Ridgefield just the other day; eighteenth-century German.

CLIFFORD: It's beautiful . . .

SIDNEY: (*unlocking the desk's center drawer*): As you can see, I'm taking very good care of my "spiritual child." Lock and key . . .

CLIFFORD: (*unfastening his envelope*): I've got the original . . .

SIDNEY: (*taking the manuscript from the drawer*): Thank God. I should really be wearing glasses but my doctor told me the longer I can do without them, the better off I am.
> *Offering the manuscript in the wrong direction.*
Here you are. Oh, there you are.
> *Clifford smiles; Myra turns to look and turns back to her ice and glasses. Clifford takes a rubber-banded manuscript from the envelope.*

CLIFFORD: It's not in a binder. For the Xeroxing . . .

SIDNEY: Makes no never-mind.
> *They exchange manuscripts.*

CLIFFORD: I've got the first draft here too. (*Sits at right of desk.*) There's a scene between Diane and Carlo in Act One that I may have been wrong to cut, and the Diane-and-Richard scene starts earlier, before they know Carlo is back.

SIDNEY: (*sitting behind the desk*): Did you do several drafts?

CLIFFORD: Just the one. It's a mess, but I think you'll be able to decipher it, if you'd like to see those two scenes.

SIDNEY: I would. By all means.
> *Clifford extracts a less tidy manuscript from the envelope.*
I had a feeling there was a Diane-and-Carlo scene I wasn't seeing . . . Before the murder?

CLIFFORD: Yes. I was afraid the act would run too long.
> *Hands the second manuscript over.*

SIDNEY: Thanks. What else do you have in there?

CLIFFORD: Oh, the outline, which I departed from considerably. I made it the way you suggested, a page per scene, loose leaf. And some lines I jotted down and never got to use.

SIDNEY: Threw away the ones you did use as you used them?

CLIFFORD: Yes.

SIDNEY: Same way I work . . .

Myra crosses with glasses of ginger ale.

CLIFFORD: Everything was in the one envelope, so I just grabbed it. Thank you.

MYRA: You're welcome.

She gives Sidney his glass, along with an intent look.

SIDNEY: Thanks . . .

CLIFFORD: It's a two-hour walk to the station, so I had to leave right after we talked.

Myra withdraws.

SIDNEY: *Two hours?*

CLIFFORD: I walk longer than that; I'm one writer who's not going to get flabby. I work out with weights every morning. I came *this close* to making the Olympic decathlon team.

SIDNEY: Really?

CLIFFORD (*hands apart*): Well, *this* close.

SIDNEY: I'll be careful not to argue with you. I'm on the Olympic sloth team. Gold medal. Fall asleep in any position.

Raises his glass, falls asleep, wakes up.

Deathtrap.

CLIFFORD: *Deathtrap.*

MYRA: *Deathtrap.*

Sidney turns. Myra is seated glass in hand, needlework in her lap. It'll be toasted with more than ginger ale some day, if Sidney is right about it, and I'm sure he is.

CLIFFORD: I hope so. I toasted it with beer the other night.

MYRA: We have some. Would you rather?

CLIFFORD: No, no, this is fine, thanks.

SIDNEY: Are you planning to stay in here?

MYRA: Yes.

CLIFFORD (*manuscript open on his lap*): Do you think I overdid the set description? All the exact locations for each piece of furniture?

SIDNEY: The set description? (*Looking in the original manuscript.*) I don't remember anything wrong with it . . . No, this is perfect, couldn't be better.

Turns pages.

You certainly type beautifully . . . Electric?

CLIFFORD: No. I can't see electric typewriters; if there's a power failure you can't work.

SIDNEY: That's the whole point in owning one.

Turning another page.

No, the real trouble with them, I find — with Zenobia here, at any rate — is that

John Wood as Sidney Bruhl, Marian Seldes as Myra Bruhl and Victor Garber as Clifford Anderson in a scene from *Deathtrap*

you can make only one decent carbon. The second carbon is so muddy as to be almost illegible.

> *Clifford turns a page. Myra leans forward nervously.*

You don't have that problem with . . .

MYRA: (*interrupting the question*): Sidney has some wonderful ideas for improving the play, Mr. Anderson!

CLIFFORD: I'm — sure he does. I'm looking forward to hearing them.

SIDNEY: Couldn't you do that in the living room, dear?

MYRA: There's no good work light in there.

SIDNEY: I seem to recall a paisley chair with a light beside it bright enough for the engraving of Bibles on pinheads.

MYRA: It's *too* bright, and the chair is too low. I'll be quiet.

SIDNEY: Darling, this is Clifford's first play and I'm the first person to read it. I'm sure he'd prefer our discussion to be private. (*To Clifford.*) Wouldn't you? Don't be embarrassed to say so.

CLIFFORD: No, I don't mind Mrs. Bruhl being here. In fact I like it. It makes me feel a little less as if I've been summoned to the principal's office.

SIDNEY: Oh.

> *Myra settles in.*

I'm sorry if I awe you.

CLIFFORD: You do. All those plays, and the things you say . . . I never thought of calling my typewriter anything but Smith-Corona.

SIDNEY: As long as it answers . . .

CLIFFORD: *You're* welcome to read the play too, Mrs. Bruhl, if you'd like to.

MYRA: I would.

CLIFFORD (*to Sidney*): I'm curious to know how women are going to react to Diane's decision. About the gun.

MYRA: Sidney told me a little about it at dinner, but he stopped at the surprises. I don't even know who kills whom.

CLIFFORD: Good, you shouldn't. (*To Sidney.*) I think that was the trouble with *Murderer's Child,* if you'll forgive me for saying so. From the opening curtain it was so obvious that Dr. Mannheim was going to bash poor Teddy. You didn't leave any room for doubt. I mean, the audience should suspect, yes, but they shouldn't be absolutely certain, should they? Doesn't that tend to diminish the suspense?

SIDNEY: Hmm . . . You may have a point there . . . I wish you had mentioned on the phone that you wanted Myra to read it. I'd have told you to bring another carbon, and she could be reading right now while we have our talk.

CLIFFORD: I didn't know she'd be interested, and anyway I don't have one.
Myra is sitting forward again.

SIDNEY: You don't have another carbon?

CLIFFORD: I only made the one. I thought I'd be Xeroxing the original as soon as I was through.

SIDNEY: Of course. There's no need for two or three any more in the age of Xerox . . .
His eyes meet Myra's and glance away. Clifford gestures with his manuscript toward Myra.

CLIFFORD: She could read this one, and we could pass the pages back and forth. Or I could sit next to you.

SIDNEY: Wait, let me think. I want to think for a moment.
Sidney thinks — hard. Myra tries to contain her growing anxiety but can't.

MYRA: Mr. Anderson, Sidney is bursting with creative ideas about your play! I've never seen him so enthusiastic! He gets plays in the mail very often, finished plays that are ready for production supposedly; from his agent, from producers, from aspiring playwrights; and usually he just laughs and sneers and says the most disparaging things you could possibly imagine! I know he could improve your play tremendously! He could turn it into a hit that would run for years and years and make more than enough money for everyone concerned!
She stops. Clifford stares. Sidney studies her.

SIDNEY: Is that what you meant by "I'll be quiet?"

MYRA (*putting her needlework aside*): I *won't* be quiet. I'm going to say something that's been on my mind ever since your phone conversation. (*Rising, advancing on Clifford.*) It's very wrong of you to expect Sidney to give you the fruit of his years of experience, his hard-won knowledge, without any quid pro quo, as if the seminar were still in session!

CLIFFORD: He *offered* to give me . . .

MYRA (*turning on Sidney*): And it's very wrong of *you* to have offered to give it to him! *I* am the one in this household whose feet are on the ground, and whose eye is on the checkbook! Now, I'm going to make a suggestion to you, Sidney. It's going to come as a shock to you, but I want you to give it your grave and thoughtful and earnest consideration. Will you do that? Will you promise to do that for me?
Sidney, staring, nods.
Put aside the play you're working on. Yes, put aside the play about Helga ten

Dorp and how she *finds murderers,* and keys under clothes dryers; put it aside, Sidney, and help Mr. Anderson with *his* play. Collaborate with him. *That's* what I'm suggesting. *That's* what I think is the fair and sensible and *rational* thing to do in this situation. *Deathtrap,* by Clifford Anderson and Sidney Bruhl. Unless Mr. Anderson feels that, in deference to your age and reputation, it should be the other way around.

SIDNEY: Hm. That *is* a shocker . . . Put aside — *The Drowning Wife?*

CLIFFORD: I thought it was "frowning."

SIDNEY: *Frowning?* No. What kind of title would that be? *The Drowning Wife* is what I'm calling it, at the moment. It has these Women's Lib overtones, plus the ESP . . . (*Looking doubtfully at Myra.*) It's such a *timely* play . . .

MYRA: *It will keep,* Sidney. People are always interested in psychics who can point at someone (*Points to him.*) and say — (*Swings her finger to Clifford.*) "This man — murdered that man." (*Pointing at Sidney again. She lowers her hand.*) Put it aside. Please. Do for Mr. Anderson — what George S. Kaufman did for you.

SIDNEY (*gives her a look, then thinks*): That's awfully persuasive, Myra . . . (*To Clifford.*) How does it grab *you?*

CLIFFORD: Oh wow. I suddenly feel as if I'm on the spot.

SIDNEY: You are, really. Myra's put you there, put us both there.

MYRA: I felt it should be brought up now, before — anything was done.

SIDNEY: Yes, yes, you were quite right. Quite right.
     Clifford is thinking.
What's your reaction, Clifford?

CLIFFORD (*rises*): Well, first of all, I'm overwhelmed, really honored and — staggered, that Sidney Bruhl would ever *consider* the idea of putting aside one of his own plays to work with me on mine. I mean, there I was, sitting in that theater when I was twelve years old, and who would think that some day I'd be standing *here,* weighing the chance to . . .

SIDNEY (*interrupting him*): We get the gist of this passage.

CLIFFORD: It's a golden opportunity that I'm sure I ought to seize with both hands.

MYRA: You should. Yes.

CLIFFORD: But . . . the thing is . . . it's as if I went to a doctor, one of the world's leading specialists, and he recommended surgery. Well, even with my respect for his eminence and his experience — I would still want to get a second opinion, wouldn't I? I'm sure your ideas are terrific, but you're right, Mrs. Bruhl, it wouldn't be — fair for me to hear them now, without some sort of an understanding or arrangement. And to be perfectly honest, right now, *without* having heard them, I feel that *Deathtrap* is very good as it is. Not perfect certainly; I guess it could still use a little fine-tuning. But — I'm not sure it needs surgery. What I ought to do, I think, is Xerox a few copies tomorrow morning and send them off to some of those agents you recommended to us. If they say too that it needs major rewriting, then I'll be coming back here begging you to do what Mrs. Bruhl suggested, and I'll be willing to make whatever arrangement you think is right. The same one you had with Mr. Kaufman, I guess. I hope I haven't offended you.

SIDNEY: Not at all.

MYRA: Mr. Anderson, please. Agents know about contracts; they don't know . . .

SIDNEY (*interrupting her, gathering the two manuscripts together*): Don't, Myra. Don't beg him. He'll think he has the wealth of the Indies here, and we're Mr. and Mrs. Jean Lafitte.

CLIFFORD: I'd never think anything like that, Mr. Bruhl. I'm grateful that you're willing to go out of your way to help me.

SIDNEY: But I'm not, really. Now that I've had a moment to consider the matter, I would never put aside a play as timely and inventive as *The Drowning Wife* to do wet-nurse work on one as speculative as *Deathtrap*.
       Hands the manuscripts over.
Sit down, Myra. You're making me nervous, standing there hyperventilating.
       Myra withdraws a bit, warily.
Do as you said; show it to a few agents. And if you decide that major rewrites *are* in order, get in touch. Who knows, I might hit a snag; it's happened once or twice.

CLIFFORD (*fitting the two manuscripts into the envelope*): Thank you, I will.
       Myra withdraws farther.

SIDNEY: Though I doubt I shall; I have it completely outlined and I'm more than halfway done. And I have another play ready to go next, based on the life of Harry Houdini.

CLIFFORD: Oh?

SIDNEY (*rising*): Yes, magic is very in now. Look at the success of *The Magic Show*. Houdini's always been an idol of mine.
       Taking them from the wall.
These are a pair of his handcuffs . . .

MYRA (*on edge again*): Sidney . . .

SIDNEY: Relax, darling; Clifford isn't the type of person who would steal someone else's idea. (*To Clifford.*) You wouldn't do that, would you?

CLIFFORD: Of course not.

SIDNEY: See ? No cause for alarm. "His heart is as far from fraud as heaven from earth." A remarkable man, Houdini. Made all his own magical apparatus, did you know that?

CLIFFORD: No, I didn't.

SYDNEY: Magnificent craftsmanship. Have a look.
       Tosses the open handcuffs to Clifford.

MYRA: Sidney, *please!*

SIDNEY: *Sit down, Myra.*

MYRA: Don't! I beg you! For God's sake, *think!*

SIDNEY: He's an *honest young man!* Now will you sit down and stop being so all-fired suspicious of everyone who comes through that door? (*To Clifford.*) We had a very nasty experience a few years back involving a plagiaristic playwright whose name I won't mention, since he's gone to his maker, recalled for repairs. Ever since, Myra has gotten alarmed if I so much as tell a fellow writer the language I'm working in. Don't take it personally. Have a good look at those; they're quite remarkable.

Myra has turned away in fearful anxiety. Sidney glances uneasily at her while Clifford, who has rested his envelope and bound manuscript against the leg of his chair, examines the antique handcuffs. Myra sits.

CLIFFORD: They look so old . . .

SIDNEY: They were made to. And apparently solid and escape-proof.

CLIFFORD: They certainly seem that way.

SIDNEY: Be my guest.

CLIFFORD: You mean put them on?

SIDNEY: Yes. That's what I mean when you're holding my prize pair of twelve-hundred-dollar Houdini handcuffs and I say "Be my guest": "Put them on."

CLIFFORD: Twelve hundred dollars . . . Whew!

Impressed, he locks the handcuffs onto his wrists. Myra sits wincing.

SIDNEY: Now turn your wrists like this, press, and pull.

Clifford follows the directions — and is still handcuffed.

You didn't do it right; it's got to be a single quick motion. Try again.

Clifford does; no dice.

Turn, press, pull; all in one.

Clifford makes several more tries.

CLIFFORD: No, they're not opening.

SIDNEY: Hm. They did for me yesterday morning; it's not a question of their not being oiled.

CLIFFORD: (*still trying*): I guess I'm just not Houdini . . .

SIDNEY: It's all right, I've got the key here. Somewhere.

Begins rummaging nervously about the desktop.

Don't go on fussing with them; you're liable to ruin them.

CLIFFORD: Sorry.

He sits still. Myra turns around, slowly, fearfully. Clifford smiles sheepishly at her; she tries to smile back. Sidney goes on searching.

SIDNEY: Key, key, key, key. Where are you, little brass key?

He begins looking in drawers. Clifford looks at his handcuffed wrists, and at Myra, and at Sidney, and gets an idea.

CLIFFORD: Do you know, this could be a good thriller!

Sidney looks at him.

It could! I mean it!

SIDNEY: How so?

CLIFFORD: Well . . . a young playwright sends his first play to an older playwright who conducted a seminar that the young playwright attended. Nobody else has read it, and then he comes to *visit* the older playwright, *to get some ideas for rewrites,* and he brings along the original and all his notes and everything. Of course you'd have to have the Xerox breaking down, to explain why there are only the two copies, and the play would have to be a very good one — the one the young playwright wrote, I mean — and the older playwright would have to have nothing much going for him at the time . . .

SIDNEY: An enormous concatenation of unlikely circumstances, don't you think?

CLIFFORD: Yes, maybe . . . But we've almost got it here, haven't we? The only difference is that you've got *The Drowning Wife* and the Houdini play, and *Deathtrap* probably isn't worth killing for. I'll bet nobody even saw me getting into your car . . .

SIDNEY: Well there you are: you've licked the second-play problem.
Resumes searching.

CLIFFORD: I think it could be turned into something fairly interesting . . . What do you think, Mrs. Bruhl?

MYRA: I — don't like it. It frightens me.

SIDNEY (*turning to the weapons on the wall*): I wonder if I could have put it up here somewhere . . .

Clifford looks curiously at Myra, and at Sidney nervously touching the various weapons, and at his handcuffed wrists. He thinks a bit. And a bit more. And a lot more. He thinks very hard.

CLIFFORD: Oh, I forgot to mention, I should be getting a phone call any minute now.
Sidney turns and looks at him.
There's a girl who's coming to see me at eight-thirty — that's around what it is now, isn't it? — and I couldn't reach her before I left, so I left a note on the hall mirror telling her where I am and giving the number (*Rising.*) so she can call and find out what train I'll be taking back. So she can pick me up at the station. One two-hour walk per day is just about enough for me. (*Turns and smiles.*) So I hope you find the key soon or else you're going to have to hold the phone for me.

SIDNEY (*stands looking at him for a moment*): How is she going to get in to *read* the note?

CLIFFORD: She has a key.

SIDNEY: You're not a very conscientious house-sitter.

CLIFFORD: She's honest.

SIDNEY: You said in the car that you don't know anyone in Milford except a few tradespeople.

CLIFFORD: She's from Hartford. Her name is Marietta Klenofski and she teaches at Quirk Middle School. Phys Ed.

SIDNEY: Where did you get the number? It's not listed.

CLIFFORD: They gave it to me at the university, along with your address. I'm friendly with Mrs. Beecham there.

SIDNEY: Beecham?

CLIFFORD: The short red-haired lady. With the eyeshade.

SIDNEY: I hope she gave you the right number. I had it changed a few weeks ago — an obscene caller was boring us — and I didn't notify old U. of Conn. What number did you leave with Ms. Klenofski?

CLIFFORD: I don't remember it.

SIDNEY: Two-two-six, three-oh-four-nine? Or two-two-six, five-four-five-seven?

CLIFFORD: The first one. Three-oh-four-nine.

SIDNEY: The new number. Hm. I must have notified the university and clean forgot about it. How strange, and how untypical of me.

CLIFFORD: Would you go on looking for the key, please?

SIDNEY: Certainly. (*Turns, considers, reaches to the wall.*)

MYRA: *My heart won't take it!*

SIDNEY (*plucking something from a ledge*): Won't take what, dear? *Turning, showing it.*
My finding the key? (*Looks at Myra, and at Clifford.*) I do believe the two of you thought I was going to grab the mace and do a Dr. Mannheim . . . Clifford? Is that why you've withdrawn so far upstage?

CLIFFORD (*shrugs uncomfortably, points toward his chair*): You can't write a play like that and not have a mind that — envisions possibilities . . .

SIDNEY: True, very true. I'm slightly paranoid myself. (*Coming around the desk.*) What's *your* excuse, oh loyal and trusting wife?

> *Myra looks at him — as he puts the key on a table by Clifford's chair — and turns away.*

Eleven years of marriage and she thinks I'm capable of a flesh-and-blood murder. There's a lesson for you in that, Clifford. Come uncuff yourself. *Deathtrap* is promising, but it's not *that* promising. (*Moves back around the desk.*)

CLIFFORD (*going toward the chair*): I'm glad it isn't.

SIDNEY: No, I think your best invention so far is the name "Marietta Klenofski." That's lovely. I congratulate you.

CLIFFORD: Thanks.

> *Sitting in the chair, he picks up the key and leans his hands into the lamplight.*

SIDNEY: I can see the sweat on her forearms after the basketball game . . . Mrs. Beecham's eyeshade, I thought, was a bit much.

CLIFFORD: I thought it was the kind of convincing detail you told us to try for. Are you sure this is the right key?

SIDNEY (*coming around to him*): Ye gods, Houdini opened them inside a milk can under ten feet of water; do you mean to say you can't do it in . . .

> *He whips a garrotte around Clifford's throat, and pulling at its two handles, hauls him upward from the chair. Clifford, choking, tries to get his fingers under the wire but can't. Myra whirls, screaming.*

MYRA: *My God, Sidney! Stop! Stop it!*

SIDNEY: *Stay back! Stay away!*

MYRA: *Oh my God! My God!*

> *Clifford has thrust his manacled hands back over his head, trying to find Sidney's head, while Sidney, grimly determined, strains at the garrotte handles. The chair tumbles. Myra turns away, her hands over her face, moaning and crying. Sidney hauls Clifford about by the garrotte, evading his groping hands, his kicking legs. A lamp falls. Clifford catches one of Sidney's hands and wrenches at it. Blood trickles down Clifford's wire-bound throat. Myra turns and looks and turns away again, never stopping her moaning and lamentation. Clifford, pop-eyed and hawking, falls forward before the fireplace, his shackled arms outflung; Sidney goes down with him and kneels astride him, keeping his fierce hold on the handles. When Clifford is finally and surely dead, Sidney relaxes his grip, lets go, sits for a moment on Clifford's back, then reaches forward and feels*

at a wrist within its handcuff. Myra sits weeping, moaning.
> *Sidney gets up, breathing hard, trembling a little. He gets out his handkerchief, wipes his hands and his face, looks at Myra. He rights the chair, picks up the lamp, puts it in its place and straightens its shade — not very successfully because his hands are shaking badly now. He holds them a moment, then turns to the desk, picks up a key, and crouching beside Clifford, unlocks and removes the handcuffs. He rises, wiping the cuffs with the handkerchief, and goes and replaces them on the wall, then returns to Clifford's body. Myra is staring at him.*

SIDNEY: Right on the rug. One point for neatness.
> *He crouches again and unwinds the garrotte from Clifford's throat, then turns the ends of the hearth-rug over Clifford's body. Rising, he wipes the garrotte with the handkerchief and meets Myra's wondering stare.*

Your heart seems to have taken it.

MYRA (*keeps staring at him awhile*): Barely.

SIDNEY (*looks away, wipes at the garrotte*): We'll give it a rest on the Riviera, after the opening. And we'll have a housekeeper again, so you can take things easy. Another car too, a goddamn Rolls.
> *Looks at the blood-streaked handkerchief, wipes the garrotte more.*

MYRA: We're going to be in prison!

SIDNEY (*throws the handkerchief into the fireplace*): A young would-be playwright walks away from his house-sitting job. The police won't even bother to yawn.
> *Puts the garrotte in its place.*

MYRA: Leaving his clothes? And his typewriter?

SIDNEY: Why not? Who can figure these young people nowadays? Especially the would-be writers. Maybe he realized he *wouldn't* be —
> *Picking up the envelope and the bound manuscript.*
— and went off to preach ecology. (*going back behind the desk.*) Or to join the Reverend Sun Myung Moon.
> *Puts the envelope and manuscript down, opens the manuscript.*
Who knows, the place might be broken into, and poor little Smith-Corona stolen.
> *Tears out the first page and puts it aside; unfastens the envelope and takes out the two unbound manuscripts; removes their first pages.*

MYRA: What are you — going to do with him?

SIDNEY: (*examining other papers that were in the envelope*): Bury him. Behind the garage. No, in the vegetable patch; easier digging.
> *He examines the last scraps of paper and puts them down; opens the desk's center drawer and puts the three manuscripts into it; closes and locks it. Myra puts her face into her hands, overcome by grief and shock again. Sidney gathers the papers and loose pages, the envelope, the letter that came with the play.*

Take a brandy or something . . .
> *He goes to the fireplace and, crouching by Clifford's body, tosses*

everything in; takes a match from a holder, strikes it, and sets the papers afire. He tosses the match in, rises, watches, then moves away and faces Myra, who is studying him.

I'm going to be a winner again! All our dear friends are going to see *you* living on *my* money! Picture their confusion.

Myra looks into her lap. Sidney goes and throws open the draperies, unbolts and opens the french doors. He looks toward the treetops.

Full moon all right . . .

He comes back to the hearth and, crouching, rearranges Clifford's body for carrying.

I hope this isn't going to become a monthly practise . . .

He straightens up, takes his jacket off and puts it on a chair, rubs his hands and readies himself; meets Myra's gaze.

Would you mind helping me carry him?

Myra looks at him for a moment, and looks away.

It's been *done*, Myra. I don't see the point in my getting a hernia.

Myra looks at him and, after a moment, rises and comes over. The lights begin dimming as Sidney lifts Clifford's rug-wrapped shoulders. Myra lifts his feet. They heft him up between them and carry him toward the french doors, Sidney going backwards.

Thank God he wasn't the fat one.

The lights fade to darkness. Curtain.

EDITOR'S NOTE: As for what ensues in Act I, Scene 3 (*"Two hours later"*) and in Act II, Scene 1 (*"Two weeks later, morning"*), Scene 2 (*"A week later, night"*) and Scene 3 (*"A week later, afternoon"*) we direct your attention to the nearest box office of the New York and touring *Deathtrap*, and to the play's program note over the signatures of its producers, Alfred de Liagre Jr. and Roger L. Stevens: "We hope *Deathtrap* holds a few surprises for you, and, if it does, that you'll help us keep them as surprises for future audiences." We will of course comply, as did all the New York reviewers, who nevertheless offered a few hints as to the tone and quality of subsequent events in Ira Levin's play, as follows:

Clive Barnes: "Its Byzantine complexities, the surrealistic weavings of its dramatic grammar, its deathshead jokes, its murderous wit and graveyard humor, all need to be taken in the special, cheerfully artificial context of its genre."

Richard Eder: *"Deathtrap* . . . . . is a series of endings that keep taking over from each other."

Edwin Wilson: *"Deathtrap* has more twists and turns than a slalom race."

John Beaufort, *Christian Science Monitor:* "Mr. Levin has a fiendishly clever way of mixing chills and laughter, clues and climaxes . . He can twist a plot until it almost cries out for mercy."

Jack Kroll: *"Deathtrap* is like a ride on a good roller coaster, when screams and laughs mingle to form an enjoyable hysteria . . . . . Ira Levin has performed the engaging feat of writing a real thriller that is also a satire on thrillers."

Harold Gary as Isaiah Stein, David Rosenbaum as his son Phil and
Richard Greene as his son Bobby in *Family Business*

FAMILY BUSINESS

A Play in Three Acts

BY DICK GOLDBERG

Cast and credits appear on page 423

DICK GOLDBERG was born in Winston-Salem, N.C. in 1947 and by the age of 12 he was writing material for performance (and since then has done no other kind of professional writing). He was educated at Brandeis University, getting his B.A. in 1969, his M.F.A. in 1971 and serving as a visiting lecturer at Brandeis's Graduate School of Theater in 1973. His first produced play was Apostle of the Idiot, *done at Brandeis in 1969. His next was* Black Zion *in 1971 in Cambridge, Mass. by the National Jewish Theater, which he served for a time as producer.*

Goldberg's first professional and first New York production and first Best Play is Family Business, *which was also staged last season at the Stockbridge, Mass. Festival and was then cited as one of the outstanding new cross-country plays by the American Theater Critics Association in* The Best Plays *of 1976-77. Goldberg now lives in Columbia, S.C. where until recently he was the producer of Stage South, the state theater of South Carolina. He is married to his childhood sweetheart and they have one child, a boy.*

The following synopsis of Family Business *was prepared by Jeff Sweet.*

"Family Business": by Dick Goldberg. Copyright © 1976, 1978 by Dick Goldberg. Reprinted by permission of Brett Adams Limited. See CAUTION notice on copyright page. All inquiries should be addressed to the author's representative: Brett Adams Limited, 36 East 61st Street, New York, N.Y. 10021.

Time: Late autumn, 1974

Place: The main room of Isaiah Stein's home in Beverly, Mass.

ACT I

SYNOPSIS: At rise, Isaiah Stein sits asleep in his wheelchair. It is late afternoon and the room is dark, but we can see something of its dimensions. Upstage center, a staircase leads to the second floor. To the right of this is a foyer leading to the front door. To the left is the door to Isaiah's room. In the right wall is an arch leading to the kitchen. The left side of the room is a formal dining area.

In his sleep, Isaiah calls out for "Miriam." A second later, Jerry, his youngest son — around 20 — enters through the front, turning on the lights and greeting his father. Isaiah, awakening, tells Jerry he was dreaming of his wife, Jerry's mother.

Jerry is in a hurry to change, but Isaiah prevails upon him to stay and talk. Isaiah asks Jerry about how his interview for admission to Harvard went. Will Jerry be able to stay for the family meeting he's called? Jerry begs off, saying he's meeting friends in Boston.

Isaiah is instantly certain that, in reality, Jerry is going to take a girl into Boston. The old man is clearly delighted, but he tells his son to be sure to be back early enough to say goodnight to him.

Norman, the second youngest son, enters through the front, as Jerry heads upstairs to change. Norman makes his presence known to his father. Isaiah is brusque with him. He tells Norman that he will not be needed at the family conference. As Norman arranges with Margaret, the housekeeper, for dinner (Margaret is offstage, in the kitchen), the phone rings.

Norman returns, answers the phone. It is the second-oldest of Isaiah's four sons, Phil. Norman is about to chat when Isaiah demands the phone. From the conversation, we gather Phil is nearby and will soon arrive; also that Phil is a doctor, is married to a woman named Ruth and has children. Isaiah talks warmly with Phil, in contrast to the curt tone he uses with Norman. The conversation over, he has Norman hang up for him.

Jerry comes downstairs for a bit, telling Isaiah more about his date, supposedly with a well-endowed homecoming queen. We gradually realize what Norman knows and what Isaiah doesn't grasp — that the date is a fiction. Jerry is not meeting a girl.

Jerry hints that he hasn't enough money for the evening. Isaiah compels Norman to give his brother five dollars. Jerry suggests that Norman could write a check for even more. Isaiah thinks that's a fine idea, and Jerry goes upstairs to fetch Norman's checkbook.

Norman suggests that it might not be a good thing for Jerry to go through money as quickly as he does. He also tells his father that he doesn't think Jerry is going on a date. Isaiah will hear nothing against Jerry, however, telling Norman to stick to his own business.

ISAIAH: You worry about getting through college — a boy twenty-eight who's just in his second year!

NORMAN: When's Jerry starting school?

ISAIAH: He went for an interview today — at Harvard!

NORMAN: When?

ISAIAH: I already told you. Today.

NORMAN: What time?

ISAIAH: This afternoon.

NORMAN: I saw him in town this afternoon.

ISAIAH: This morning! He went this morning! How long was it before you decided to go to college — Salem State College?

NORMAN: I wanted to go, but you wanted me to work for you.

ISAIAH: Your mother didn't die right when you were all set to take on the world. An "A" student who could go anywhere, who *will* go anywhere. You want to rush that boy and that will kill him.

NORMAN: Maybe he should get a job, like I did.

ISAIAH: Maybe you should mind your own business.

NORMAN: Dad, it's not good —

ISAIAH: I know what's good for my sons.

NORMAN: Dad, you don't see what's happening to Jerry.

ISAIAH: What's happening to Jerry? You tell me.

NORMAN (*thrown off by this sudden direct question*): He's a wonderful kid, Dad, don't get me wrong, but he's — he doesn't know what he's doing.

ISAIAH: Are you finished?
            Norman doesn't respond.
I'll think about what you have had to say.

NORMAN: Pop —

ISAIAH: I'm tired. Take me to my room. I want to lie down before dinner.
            *Norman begins to take his father into his room. Jerry comes
            downstairs again. Isaiah doesn't see him, but Jerry and Norman ex-
            change looks.*

Bobby, the oldest of the four brothers, enters. He and Jerry begin to roughhouse, miming a basketball game. Norman returns. Bobby suggests the three of them go to a Lakers game on Friday. Jerry begs off with the excuse of a supposed previous engagement. Maybe another night, says Bobby agreeably as he heads upstairs.

Alone with Norman, Jerry produces the checkbook and applies pressure to get Norman to sign the check. Norman refuses. He tells Jerry that, in a conversation with Dr. Cohen, he has discovered that their father's recent tests turned out badly. His heart is in very bad shape. Jerry doesn't seem to care very much, returning to the subject of the check.

NORMAN: You unfeeling bastard —

JERRY: That's me. Write your name, Norman.
They start talking in whispers.
NORMAN: My gay little brother — I wonder what father would do if I told him you were gay?
JERRY: He'd throw you out of the house.
NORMAN: If I told him — maybe; but if I told Bobby or Phil and then they said something.
JERRY: Can it, Norman. Bobby would knock the little shitsies out of you if you said anything like that about his baby brother. And you may not have noticed, but I don't like to hang around Phil, the shrink, too much whenever he deigns to visit. Pretty clever of me, don't you think?
NORMAN: There are ways — other ways.

Norman offers Jerry a deal. If Jerry will stick around until Phil arrives, he'll sign the check. Jerry wants to know why it's so important that he stay. Norman tries to explain: "Mama would have wanted this — for him to see us all together — brothers . . . . . You know how much our being a family meant to her. I mean's that's . . . that's what she lived for — Friday nights and holidays and the family all together. It's something we ought to do for her. Before he . . ."

Norman thinks that somehow it would make a difference if, before their father dies, Isaiah would be surrounded by all his four sons. Jerry mocks Norman's sentimental nature, but he agrees to the plan on the condition that Norman make the check out for $35. He will cash the check and then return for ten minutes of family togetherness.

To satisfy Norman, Jerry goes to the door of Isaiah's room and tells his father he'll be back in a few minutes. Then he takes Norman's check. He is about to step out when Bobby comes downstairs. "You got a date again tonight?" Bobby asks him. Jerry tells him yes and Bobby, smiling and in full view of Norman, gives him $10. Jerry exits out the front door.

Bobby makes drinks for Norman and himself. He hopes the family meeting won't last long, as he has business to attend to at one of the toy stores the family owns. Norman volunteers to help, but Bobby insists Norman can help best by studying. They haven't seen their brother Phil for some time, despite the fact he and his family don't live very far away.

Bobby asks how Isaiah is feeling today. Norman tells him the bad news from Dr. Cohen and asks Bobby if he thinks they should get a second opinion. Bobby doesn't think they'd be told anything different.

Bobby complains about the housekeeper. He would like to get rid of Margaret. Norman thinks they should hold off on that. After all, Isaiah likes her, even though she can't cook worth a damn.

Bobby thinks Jerry is leading pretty close to the ideal life — sleeping late, getting laid a lot. Norman expresses his doubts about the latter. Bobby continues, saying that he shares Isaiah's pleasure in Jerry's high spirits, "like he was my kid or something." "I bet if you and Alice had had kids, they would have been . . ." Norman begins. Bobby cuts Norman off. Apparently Alice is a subject he'd rather not discuss. Changing his tack, Norman tells Bobby he thinks they have spoiled Jerry. Bobby doesn't take the comment very seriously.

The phone rings, and Bobby answers. It's Ruth, Phil's wife. She's wondering where Phil is. Norman tells Bobby that Phil is nearby and on his way, but Bobby doesn't relay this to Ruth. He promises her he'll have Phil call as soon as he turns up. The phone call over, Bobby tells Norman that he thinks if anyone has been spoiled it is their psychiatrist brother Phil.

BOBBY: Livin' in that fancy house, always psychin' people out, starting that foundation. Boy, if that isn't the most profit-making non-profit business I ever heard of. He wouldn't be worth two bits if it wasn't for all the money Pop gave him — money that I earned down at the store.

NORMAN: Pop asked you before he lent Phil the money, didn't he?

BOBBY: Asked? The last time your father asked my opinion of something was when the store in Salem was losing money, and he asked me when he should close it. I told him give it another six months. He said to me, "What do you know? All you know about toys is that you play with them." Then, two weeks later he got his first attack and he couldn't do a thing. And I made a go of that toy store in less than 90 days. And you know when we'll see all that money? The same money he turned around and lent Philip? When Philip is good and dead. And you know how he'll croak? Death by drowning! You see, one day he'll be down in Cohasset pissing away money, and all of a sudden, he won't be able to stop — nickels and dimes and dollar bills just flowing out of him like the Mystic River. Ruth'll come home, open the door, and — woosh! it'll all pour out — all that money — and the remains of Dr. Philip M. Stein with his hands still holding his pecker.

Bobby roars with laughter.

NORMAN *(genuinely):* You're pretty funny, Bobby.

BOBBY: Yeah — I laugh at myself all the time.

NORMAN: You like Phil and you know it.

BOBBY: Who said anything about not liking the bastard? I just think the boy should remember where he got all that grade A butter he spreads on his bread.

The doorbell rings. Norman answers it — it's Phil. He asks after their father, as Bobby exits upstairs. Norman tells him Dr. Cohen's news. As he exits into the kitchen to heat up dinner, he reminds Phil to call Ruth. Phil makes the call, and from it we gather he is very badly in debt and needs to raise a substantial amount of money in 30 days. Ruth apparently asks where they're going to get the money. Phil testily replies that they'll discuss it later, when he gets home, and slams down the phone.

Norman returns from the kitchen, and Bobby comes back downstairs. Phil and Bobby exchange a little banter, Bobby making disparaging comments about psychologists, Phil taking them good-naturedly. Phil wonders what Isaiah has planned for the family meeting. Bobby assures him their father wouldn't make demands on his precious time if it weren't for something he considered important.

Norman tells Phil that Jerry will be returning soon and is looking forward to seeing him again. He intimates Jerry has a problem that he'd like Phil to give attention, but he doesn't specify the nature of the problem.

Norman goes and wheels out Isaiah, who makes a great show of affection for Phil. Isaiah orders Norman to serve the food (Margaret having left by now) and also rather forcefully suggests that Norman eat in the kitchen while he and the two oldest brothers talk. Reluctantly, Norman serves them and disappears.

Isaiah gets to the point of the meeting. He knows he will die soon and, following his usual practise of taking Phil and Bobby into his confidence when making important decisions, he tells them he has changed his will. Before, the will divided the approximately $1 million estate among the four boys, with some going to charity. But Isaiah's been thinking of the old days when he worked in a shoe factory and was involved in organizing his fellow workers. "A lot of us were socialists in those days, probably a few out-and-out reds then too, and we all did a lot of talking about from each according to his ability, to each according to his need. And that seemed a lot fairer in this situation."

Also, he's been thinking of what he'd imagine their mother would have liked. The upshot is that Bobby and Norman would get joint title to the house and his share of the stores. All of his stocks would be put in trust for Phil's foundation. And the savings and the insurance would go to Jerry. "If you don't like it, tell me," says Isaiah. "You're the ones who are going to have to live with it, not me."

Phil doubts the wisdom of letting Jerry have a quarter of a million dollars in cash. Isaiah explains that he won't; he'll get the interest — about $15,000 a year. If Jerry wants any more, he'll have to come to Bobby and Phil, who are to be trustees for the rest.

Phil still isn't happy. He'd prefer to go back to the old will, with the liquid assets evenly divided. Isaiah says he hasn't heard any convincing reasons to change what he has done. Phil, getting more agitated, doesn't think the arrangement is fair to Norman. When is Isaiah going to stop punishing Norman for having been the driver when Miriam, Isaiah's wife, died in an automobile accident?

Tempers flare. Isaiah says he'll stick to this version of the will. Phil responds with the accusation that Isaiah called this meeting without any intention of considering anyone else's perspective on the matter. The matter is settled, Isaiah says.

PHIL: It was settled before you opened your mouth.

ISAIAH: Philip, I won't take much more of this.

PHIL: I know, Pop, you're dying.

ISAIAH: You want me to die, don't you?

PHIL: I don't know.

ISAIAH: What kind of an answer is that?

PHIL: An honest one. And I guess I really shouldn't expect you to be able to deal with it.

ISAIAH: A son tells his father he wants him to die.

PHIL: That's not what I said. Why don't you ever listen to what I say? To what anybody says? You only hear and see what you want.

ISAIAH: I'll tell you what I hear and see now. That it should have been me in that car instead of your mother.

BOBBY: Don't talk like that, Pop. Come on, Pop.

ISAIAH: Because living to this ripe old age only to find stupidity and greed and hatred all around me, I didn't need.

PHIL: I'm sorry that's what you see.

ISAIAH: I don't want your sympathy. I don't want anything from you. All I want is for you to leave my house and to know that in the morning, I'm calling Mr. Gross and making other arrangements.

PHIL: Dad, I said I was sorry.

ISAIAH: Thank you. We're finished with dinner. You can go back to your home now. Bobby, go to the store. *(To Bobby.)* Take me to my room.

Bobby wheels Isaiah off and returns. He tells Phil Isaiah will relent and not cut him out of the will. Phil has doubts. Bobby says he'll talk to Mr. Gross, the lawyer, and see what he can do to cool Isaiah down.

Suddenly, Isaiah is screaming for Jerry, his voice filled with pain. Bobby runs into Isaiah's room. Norman emerges from the kitchen and follows him. Phil is alone onstage. Bobby appears at the door and tells Phil that Isaiah is having a bad attack and asks Phil to call the doctor. Bobby disappears into Isaiah's room again. Phil goes to the phone and dials.

PHIL: . . . . . Hello . . . may I speak with Dr. Cohen, please . . . Hello, Dr. Cohen, this is Dr. Stein . . . Philip Stein, Isaiah Stein's son.
         As if a knife were being thrust into his spine.
No . . . no . . . Dad seems fine — he looks great in fact. That's why I was calling . . . I was wondering . . . I was wondering . . . whether you had the results of my father's last tests . . .

ACT II

Seven days later, in early evening, it is the last day of the house being open for mourners of Isaiah's death. The guests have all gone, including the rabbi. At rise, Norman is onstage alone as Bobby comes downstairs. Bobby is on his way out to an appointment with Chip Schwartz, a realtor. Bobby wants to sell the house. Norman is dead set against the idea and tries to discourage Bobby's visit. Bobby leaves anyway.

Phil comes downstairs looking for Bobby, having something he wants to discuss with him, but Bobby has already left. Jerry, who has entered from the kitchen, announces his intention to change out of "creepy" mourning clothes and get out of the house for the night. Norman asks where he plans to go. Jerry lies, saying he hasn't decided. Norman prevails on Phil and Jerry to help clear the table of the plates and remnants of food that had been served to the mourners.

As soon as his brothers are out of the room, Norman calls the realtor's office to say that Bobby will not be able to keep the appointment because of snow on the roads. Call finished, Norman exits into the kitchen as Phil and Jerry return.

Phil wants to talk to Jerry. Jerry seems eager to get downtown. In response to

Phil's questions, he says he's thinking of investing some of his money in a club, and his date in town relates to the deal. Phil says he'll be happy to give Jerry a lift after they've talked. Caving in under the pressure, Jerry calls to tell his friend David, with whom he had made the date, that he'll be a little late. It is obvious to the audience that David is something more than Jerry's prospective business partner.

Phil starts hitting Jerry with his pitch. Instead of investing his money in a club, Phil says, Jerry should invest in something more reliable. The bottom line is that he wants Jerry to "invest" in his clinic to the tune of $35,000. Jerry reminds Phil that he doesn't have access to the principal of his inheritance, that he receives only the interest, which makes it impossible for him to lend that much money. Phil says that all that is necessary to get to the principal is the agreement of the two trustees, of whom he is one and Bobby is the other. So all it comes down to is getting Bobby to agree. Jerry hesitatingly agrees to let Phil approach Bobby on the matter. Phil releases Jerry to go upstairs and change.

Norman enters shortly after Jerry's exit. Norman confides in Phil his concern about Jerry's having been left so much money.

NORMAN: He's just not ready to handle that kind of responsibility.
PHIL: I couldn't agree with you more.
NORMAN: And I think he'd be better off staying home, don't you agree?
PHIL: I don't know.
NORMAN: He's been talking about moving out.
PHIL: And you'd like him to stay here?
NORMAN: Not for me. I just think he needs someone to look after him.
PHIL: You know Norman, Jerry's a pretty hard-headed kid.
NORMAN: You could get to him.
PHIL: Well, I don't know what I would say. What would you like me to say?
NORMAN: Just tell him you think he'd be better off staying right where he is for a few years.
PHIL: I've got to have some reasons. I admit, he may respect me, but it's not going to sway him for me to dart up to his room and say, "Stay, kid."
NORMAN: He's setting patterns — isn't that what people do?
PHIL: Yes.
NORMAN: I know Pop and all of us kind of spoiled him after Mama died. He was kind of special, being born so late in their lives. Well, I guess it really wasn't good for him — us letting him get away with so much, I mean.
PHIL: You're probably right.
NORMAN: I want to make it clear. I don't have anything against him. I want him to stay here. He's my brother, and maybe he does need to fool around a little more before he goes off to school.

Phil begins to get the idea there's more to the matter than Norman is saying. He presses Norman for the full story. After making Phil promise not to tell Bobby, Norman reveals that Jerry is gay and asks Phil if there's anything he can do to treat Jerry's condition. Phil says he'll be glad to talk to Jerry and see what he can do. And yes, Phil tells Norman, he thinks in light of this perhaps it would be better if Jerry were to stay in the house. Since Bobby seems intent on moving out, that would mean Jerry would be largely Norman's responsibility. Norman thinks he could handle it and would be pleased to try. And it is Phil's turn to ask Norman a favor — to put in a word with Bobby in support of the idea of Phil handling some of Jerry's money. Norman can see nothing wrong with this, and he agrees.

Phil goes upstairs to "reason" with Jerry. "I can't promise you complete results tonight," he tells Norman as he exits, "but I'll loosen him up."

Bobby returns, mad as hell. When he arrived at the realtor's office, Schwartz was not there. Instead, There was a "For Sale" sign and a note to Bobby saying, "Sorry you couldn't make it this evening; why don't you go ahead and stick this in the ground." He intends to give Schwartz a piece of his mind tomorrow.

Norman tells Bobby that Phil is upstairs talking to Jerry about letting him handle some of his trust money. Bobby knows what that means — Phil wants Jerry's money for his own purposes. Norman asks Bobby why he can't be more charitable towards Phil. After all, they're brothers. As far as Bobby is concerned, that is only an accident of biology. And no, he's not going to let Phil get his hands on Jerry's money. "I don't like my brother," says Bobby, "I don't like him in a big way. And I really don't like the way he goes through money — money that I worked my ass off for." What's more, Phil is a bad risk. He doesn't pay his debts.

Norman tells Bobby that he won't allow him to sell the house unless Bobby agrees with whatever Phil and Jerry decide about the money.

BOBBY: You're saying if I agree to whatever the hell it is, you'll sell the house.

NORMAN: You know I don't want to sell the house, Bobby — that I think you'd be better off here.

BOBBY: If we sell or if we don't, Norman, I'm getting out.

NORMAN: So go. I hope you'll be very happy coming to visit Jerry and me.

BOBBY: Jerry is leaving, too, Norman. I think you've been cooped up in this house too long.

NORMAN: Shut up, Bobby. I am perfectly all right. I'm the one who doesn't want to run out, who wants to stay where he belongs.

BOBBY: I'll tell you where you belong all right — I'll tell you where —

NORMAN: Not another word!

He pushes Bobby into sofa.

BOBBY *(after a moment)*: Norman, are you all right?

NORMAN: Yes. I just don't like people saying I'm — I'm different. First Dad, and now you.

BOBBY: I didn't mean anything by it.

NORMAN: I know you didn't. Bobby, don't go.

BOBBY *(gently)*: Norman, we don't need this house. It's too big. It was too big when Pop was alive.

NORMAN: I need it.

BOBBY: You'll be happy some place else — I'm sure you will.

NORMAN: No, I won't. You don't understand. It wouldn't have to be for very long. Just a few years until . . .

BOBBY: Until what, Norman?

NORMAN: I don't know. Jerry got married, you got married. You could find someone again — someone like Alice. You could raise a family — here!

BOBBY: That's never going to happen, Norman.

NORMAN: Yes, it is.

BOBBY: She's dead. That's all there is to it. Alice got sick and died.

NORMAN: If you had gone ahead and gotten married . . .

BOBBY: Okay, Norman.

NORMAN: People die . . . but you can find other people, people to take their place.

BOBBY: Okay.

NORMAN *(crosses to shiva stool and sits)*: Mama loved me more than she loved Pop . . . did you know that, Bobby? She loved me more than she loved Pop. Every day, for as long as I can remember, she would leave him at the store to come home and be with me. She was here before I got home from school almost always. We would watch TV upstairs . . . we'd sit together on the couch with only the desk lamp on in the room . . . and I'd make patterns with the cookies she had given me. From three o'clock to five o'clock. Every day. A little after five, she'd wake Jerry from his nap, and you and Phil'd get home from practise. And then I'd be the one to come down and wait for Pop. I'd be the one. I'd stand by the window and say to myself, "The sixth car to come by going up the street will be Pop's." Different days I'd guess different numbers. I was right a lot, too. But I didn't tell him when I guessed it. Because Pop would laugh. He'd always laugh. At me . . . and at Mama.

> *Pause.*

I did not kill her. I was home, and Pop wanted someone to take her to the store to pick up some things for dinner. *He* wanted something special for dinner.

> *Pause.*

She loved me. She loved me more than she did Pop.

> *Long pause. Bobby is moved but unable to reach out to him.*

I'll find something for us in the kitchen, okay? Some cake or something.

BOBBY: Sure.

> *Norman exits into the kitchen.*

Phil and Jerry come downstairs, Jerry looking not at all well. Norman returns with coffee for the four of them. Phil cues Jerry, and Jerry begins. He wants to lend Phil $35,000 from his principal, ostensibly for construction on Phil's house. "What about collateral?" Bobby asks. Phil says that, considering it's in the family, doesn't Bobby think that the formalities of regular business practise could be relaxed. Bobby isn't buying this. He tells Jerry that Phil's record for repaying loans is not the best. Jerry says he isn't worried.

Phil asks Bobby what he has against the idea. Is it something personal? Bobby denies any personal prejudice, but, if they're taking about a deal with money involved, he believes it's best to approach it in a sensible, businesslike manner. Phil accuses Bobby of putting up barriers out of jealousy. "You don't want me to have anything you don't have. Like a nice house . . . or a wife . . . or anything." Bobby replies that if Phil chooses to look at it in that light, then there's nothing more to talk about.

Joel Polis as Jerry and David Garfield as Norman in a scene from
Family Business

Phil calls Norman and Jerry to his defense. Jerry, now very afraid, tries to make a plausible case for lending the money, but it is obvious that the merits of the proposed loan have little to do with Jerry's arguments. Bobby is now suspicious. Something is going on under all of this, and he'll know what before he signs over any money. Jerry makes another plea, but Bobby turns it aside.

"I can't do it, Phil," Jerry says. "All right, Jerry . . ." says Phil, a hint of threat in his tone.

Hysterically, Jerry begins to rail at Bobby, "I hate you! Why do you have to try to be like Pop? You're not Pop! You're Bobby — dumb, old Bobby. Who never was good for anything . . . and never will be . . ." Instantly, Jerry apologizes. He didn't mean to say these things. They aren't true. Only Phil made him. Bobby asks how. What hold does Phil have over him?

JERRY: I was afraid that he'd . . . he said he'd tell you . . .
BOBBY: Tell me what?!
JERRY: I'm gay. *(A beat.)* Bobby, don't.
BOBBY: You didn't say that.
    Jerry starts crying.
Tell me you didn't say that.
    JERRY: It's true. I'm gay.
        Bobby hits Jerry in the stomach. Jerry falls behind sofa, Bobby still punching. Norman runs to pull Bobby off. Bobby's strength wanes and Norman is able to restrain him. Norman then goes to stairs to Jerry and cradles him in his arms . . . . .

NORMAN: It'll be all right, Jerry! it'll be all right.

JERRY *(crying)*: I knew he'd hate me for it.

NORMAN: He doesn't hate you. He just doesn't understand. He will, though, give him time.

BOBBY: Never — never in a thousand years, Norman. Don't tell him lies.

NORMAN: Keep quiet, Bobby. Just keep quiet for a few goddamn minutes.

JERRY *(to Norman)*: You — you had to tell the goddamn supershrink. He couldn't figure it out for himself — so you told him.

BOBBY *(to Phil)*: Are you happy now? *(Laughing.)* You didn't exactly get what you want.

PHIL: You're a bastard. That's what you are. He was coming to you so that you would understand, and you beat him up.

BOBBY: What did you think was going to happen? That's why you threatened him, wasn't it?

PHIL *(taking chair to defend himself)*: I thought he was stronger.

BOBBY: Don't make excuses, Phil. You're to blame. You and your goddamn passion to be the best, to have the most. Well, you got it this time, you won; you can have your money. Take the faggot's money.

JERRY: Bobby!

BOBBY: Take any goddamn thing you want.

NORMAN: I'll take care of you, Jerry.

JERRY: Get your dumb-ass paws off me. I don't want you.

NORMAN: Jerry, calm down. Everything'll be all right.

JERRY: When are you going to wake up, you big stupid jerk? Everything is not going to be all right. Everything is never all right. Not that I've ever seen. Soon as the hell I can, I'm getting out of here and moving in with my friend, my friend David. You know what he is, Bobby?

BOBBY: I don't want to know.

JERRY: Just like me.

BOBBY: Shut up!

JERRY: Oh, no — you're going to hear it, and you're going to live with it. Cause that's what little Jerry is and he likes it.

NORMAN: Jerry, let me help you. Let me do something for you.

JERRY: You want to do something for me, Norman?

NORMAN: Sure.

JERRY: Go get me Pop's bags from the basement. Anybody mind if I take the fucking bags?

NORMAN *(taking Jerry's shoulders)*: Where are you going?

JERRY *(fights him off)*: Somebody shut this mother-fucker up! Shut him up!
    Norman crosses to the sofa and sits.

PHIL: Norman — Norman, you're tired. It's late. I have to be going.
    Into hall, puts on his coat.

BOBBY *(viciously, but quiet)*: Come back real soon, won't you?

PHIL: I'm sorry.
    No response.
I said I'm sorry. I am.

BOBBY: Goodbye, Phil. *(Sits in chair.)* Say hello to . . . Ruth for us.

PHIL: I'll make it up to you, I will.

JERRY: Don't bother, Philip, don't even bother trying.

PHIL: I didn't know what I was doing. I didn't mean what I was doing.

BOBBY *(sarcastically)*: We believe you, Philip.

JERRY: It just doesn't make any difference this time.

PHIL: Don't —

JERRY: Would you get out of here?

PHIL *(stunned, sits on hall stool; long pause)*: Oh, Papa —

ACT III

One morning three weeks later, Norman is alone onstage, busying himself with small tasks when the phone rings. Startled for a second, he regains his composure and answers. It's Phil. He's nearby and wants to stop by the house to talk. Norman maintains an even tone as best he can as he replies to Phil, telling him that Bobby is in the house at the moment, but that if Phil wants to come by in about 20 minutes, by which time Bobby will be gone, then he's welcome. The conversation over, Norman hangs up.

Bobby comes downstairs with two boxes of his stuff. He's moving out of the house and into an apartment. He suggests that Norman come visit, take a look at the building, maybe go to a party a friend is throwing, maybe consider moving into a one-bedroom place Bobby knows is available in the same building. Norman declines. He knows where he wants to stay.

"Norm, what do you need this place for?" Bobby asks. Jerry is moving out, too, so Norman will be all alone. And what is he going to do with his time here? Clean the house so that it's always the way it was when Mama was still alive? "Margaret does most of that," says Norman. Margaret does nothing, Bobby replies. There's no reason to keep her on. Norman makes it clear that he doesn't want to continue the conversation along this line.

Bobby asks Norman for help in bringing a dresser downstairs. Norman asks if they can do it another time; he doesn't feel so well. Bobby says O.K. and starts to haul the boxes out through the kitchen to his car. The doorbell rings. Norman looks outside, tells Bobby it's someone with religious literature. Bobby exits into the kitchen with the boxes.

Bobby gone, Norman answers the door. In comes a young man named David. He and Norman have met before. David asks if Jerry is in. Norman says no, then goes offstage and returns with a cup of coffee for David. Norman starts chatting a bit about the family, stretching the truth a bit when he says that Bobby is out of town on a vacation.

DAVID: Toys — you're in the toy business, right?

NORMAN: I'm not, but the family is, that is. I go to school and take care of this place — well, help Margaret take care of things. It's big place, but a nice place, a comfortable place, a big place.

DAVID: Yes, it is.

NORMAN: I forget, now where do you live?

DAVID: On Beacon Hill.

NORMAN: Ah, I bet it's small. Oh, I don't mean anything by that. But I've always heard the places on the Hill were small.

DAVID: It's not so bad.

NORMAN: You live there by yourself — right?

DAVID: Yes.

NORMAN: Have you ever thought of moving, David?

DAVID: No; I like it.

NORMAN: It's convenient to town, right? And if you live there by yourself, you must do your own cleaning, and that's easier if it's small.

DAVID: Yes.

NORMAN: Jerry has it easy — Margaret and I do everything. And did you know that the B and M takes only thirty-six minutes to get to North Station?

DAVID: No, I didn't know that.

NORMAN: You and Jerry have a lot of business together — I mean with the club and everything.

DAVID: Yes!

NORMAN: I guess that means the two of you need to be in touch a lot.

DAVID: It hasn't been much of a problem, really.

NORMAN: But isn't the deal coming through soon?

DAVID: Maybe we should discuss this with Jerry.

NORMAN *(continuing his thought)*: Then you would need to be together.

DAVID: I don't want to keep you from your books or anything.

NORMAN: He's awfully young. He doesn't know anything about cooking and cleaning. There are still lots of things to do with our father's estate. Could I get you another cup of coffee?

DAVID: I'm not quite finished —

> *Norman grabs the cup from David's hand, goes toward the kitchen, but then quickly turns toward David.*

NORMAN: Would you like to live here — you and Jerry, I mean. Bobby's room will be . . .

DAVID: Norman, that's very nice of you.

NORMAN: There would be a lot of advantages.

DAVID: Yes, I'm sure there would be.

NORMAN: You'd both save on rent.

DAVID *(trying to make light of the situation)*: What are your rates?

NORMAN: Well, since you both need your money for the club, I don't think we'd really need to charge.

DAVID: Well, if I were interested, that would be a tempting offer.

NORMAN: What do you mean — *if* you were interested?

DAVID: Norman, do you really want me to move in here?

NORMAN: Of course! It looks like it would be a good idea for any number of reasons.

DAVID: And maybe not such a good idea, too.

NORMAN: No.

DAVID: Norman, I'm your brother's lover.

NORMAN: I know that.

DAVID: I like you, Norman, and I don't think I want to be a part of hurting you. Jerry phoned after you called.

NORMAN: What?

DAVID: He *is* meeting me here. We thought we knew why you had called me. And he's coming to talk with you, to explain why we can't do it.

NORMAN: No!

DAVID: I'm sorry. I didn't want to hurt you. But I couldn't just call you back and tell you over the phone.

NORMAN *(embarrassed, almost to the point of tears)*: Excuse me — excuse me, please.

He quickly goes up the stairs.

David is alone onstage. Bobby enters, calling to Norman that he's decided to take the dresser after all. He stops short when he sees David. They identify each other awkwardly. David tells him that Jerry is on his way over. Bobby says that he wants to speak to him. Jerry comes in through the front door. Bobby asks David to leave them alone to talk, and David does.

"What do you want to talk with me about?" Jerry asks. Bobby tries to explain. He doesn't understand Jerry's lifestyle, but he wants to try. He just needs some time. Jerry coolly tells Bobby to take all the time he wants. Bobby asks that Jerry try to understand him a little in return. After all, they were close once. Jerry doesn't know that he really wants to get back to that with Bobby. Bobby continues to try for a reconciliation.

BOBBY: It takes more than a few weeks to unlearn thirty-five years of something.

JERRY: And I really don't think that you can. So why waste your energy. You better keep that for fucking your pillow . . . you know, the one you call Alice.

BOBBY: Shut up!

JERRY: Why? Is mine the only perversion open to discussion? At least what I do I do with people . . . not with a fucking ghost.

BOBBY: You know what I feel like doing right now? Slapping you around again . . . to try to knock some sense into you.

JERRY: Go ahead, Bobby, that's what you're good at. Norman's not here to stop you this time. You could get in a lot of good belts.

BOBBY: Jerry . . . Jerry, please.

JERRY: Or are you afraid you'll kill me this time?

BOBBY: Goddamn you!

JERRY: For what? For what I am? We are all blessed and equal in His sight. It's just the likes of you that rank some of us a little lower on the scale.

BOBBY: I don't, Jerry, please believe me . . . I don't.

JERRY: Two minutes ago you were begging forgiveness . . . Ten seconds ago you wanted to beat up the fairy. I don't trust you, Bobby, it's as simple as that.

BOBBY: Up yours!

JERRY: That's just the way I like it.

BOBBY: That's right . . . prance and describe it to me and talk about Alice, and do everything else you know how to do . . . and you know how to do a hell of a lot . . . to keep me away.

JERRY: I didn't go after you: I didn't strike you.

BOBBY *(backing Jerry against wall)*: Well, go ahead if it will make you happy.

JERRY: Sorry . . . I'm not into that.

BOBBY: Go ahead . . . then we can start from ground zero.

JERRY: I don't think I want to touch you.

BOBBY: Why not?

JERRY: Forget it, Bobby.

BOBBY: I want you to hurt me.

JERRY: Go get that some place else.

BOBBY: I want it from you.

JERRY: Go see Phil! You need Phil!

BOBBY: I probably do . . . but I need you more.

JERRY: Get away from me! Get out of my life! No "Bobby's" wanted here.

BOBBY: I love you.

JERRY: Up yours, you bastard.

BOBBY: I love you.

JERRY: Keep it to yourself.

BOBBY: I love you.

JERRY: Say it enough and maybe you'll believe it.

BOBBY: What do I have to do to make you believe it?

JERRY: Ain't no way.

BOBBY: Why? Answer me that and I'll leave you alone for good.

JERRY: I don't have to . . .

BOBBY: Well, then you'll just have me hanging around.

JERRY: I'll try not to go the same places as you.

BOBBY: Come here, Jerry.

JERRY *(loudly calling off as Bobby moves in on him)*: Norman! *(To Bobby)* Where's Norman?

BOBBY: I don't know.

JERRY: Don't come near me, Bobby.

BOBBY: Then you come to me.

JERRY: No!

> Slowly, Bobby moves towards Jerry and embraces him. Jerry simply allows this to happen. After a long moment, Bobby lets him go. Without saying anything, Bobby turns and exits through the kitchen. Jerry is standing alone as Norman enters from upstairs.

NORMAN: Did you call me?

JERRY: I gotta go, Norman. I just wanted to say —

> Jerry bolts from the room and out the front door, passing Phil as he does so.

Phil tries to call Jerry back, but it's no use. Norman asks Phil what he wants. Phil explains that he is selling his house to pay debts. He wants to move himself, his wife and children into this house. Norman says no. He doesn't want Phil around. "I like my life a lot better when you're not a part of it."

Phil tries to appeal to Norman's fraternal instincts. Norman is unmoved.

"Look," he says, "I may not be very bright, but I know who comes first with you, who comes first in a big way." "You need a family," says Phil. No, Norman replies, he doesn't need anybody to take care of him. He's been taking care of himself — not to mention his father — for years. He'll do all right.

Phil tells Norman that, after the confrontation between the four of them three weeks ago, he nearly gave in to the impulse of letting the car swerve off the road and being done with it. The impulse passed, and he fought to keep in control, to stay alive. But Phil realizes that, though he can be good in a pinch, "for the long haul . . . for what I really want . . . I haven't got the goods."

PHIL: . . . . . I let Pop die.
NORMAN: Pop died of a heart attack.
PHIL: But when I called Doc Cohen . . . I told him . . .
NORMAN: . . . That everything was all right.
PHIL: Yes.
NORMAN: And he told me even if he had gotten here the minute it happened, it wouldn't have done any good.
PHIL *(sitting in chair)*: I didn't need that money for an addition to the house. I needed it because I was $35,000 in debt . . . and still am. I was behind on everything . . . payments on the house, the cars, things for the foundation, you name it. When Pop said he was changing his will and cutting me out, I thought I had to . . . I thought I had to stop him.
NORMAN *(pause)*: He loved us, Phil. I know he did. He didn't always know how to show it, but he loved us. He loved us as much as he could.
        Pause.
And we loved him . . . as much as we could.
PHIL *(pause)*: I want to love you, Norman. I mean that!
        Pause. He rises.
If that didn't happen . . . if it didn't work out, we'd go. Whenever you'd tell us to.
NORMAN *(pause)*: Do you want your old room back? For you and Ruth, I mean.
PHIL: Yes.
NORMAN: What about the kids?
PHIL: That would be up to you.
NORMAN: Bobby's room?
PHIL: Bobby's room it is.
NORMAN: Would you like to have something?
PHIL: How about some coffee?
NORMAN: Okay.
PHIL: Let me get it.
NORMAN: There's some on the stove.
PHIL *(crosses to kitchen door and turns to Norman)*: Norman . . .
NORMAN: Uh-huh.
PHIL: Would it be okay for us to eat in the kitchen?
        Norman looks at Phil for a long moment as the curtain falls.

The company of *The 5th of July: front row,* Danton Stone as Wes, Jeff Daniels as Jed; *second row,* Helen Stenborg as Aunt Sally, William Hurt as Ken; *back row,* Nancy Snyder as Gwen, Jonathan Hogan as John, Amy Wright as Shirley, Joyce Reehling as June

THE 5TH OF JULY

A Play in Two Acts

BY LANFORD WILSON

Cast and credits appear on pages 408, 410

LANFORD WILSON was born in Lebanon, Mo., April 13, 1937 and was raised in Ozark, Mo. He was educated at San Diego State College and the University of Chicago, where he started writing plays. Arriving in New York in 1963, he gravitated to the Caffe Cino, one of the first of the off-off-Broadway situations, and made his New York playwriting debut with the one-acter So Long at the Fair, *followed by* Home Free *and* The Madness of Lady Bright, *which latter work claims an OOB long-run record of 250 performances. In 1965 his first full-length play,* Balm in Gilead, *was produced at the Cafe La Mama and directed by Marshall W. Mason, who has figured importantly in Wilson's later career. That same year the prolific author's* Ludlow Fair *and* This Is the Rill Speaking *were presented at Caffe Cino.*

During the mid-1960s, Wilson's plays began to receive productions in the professional segment, both in New York and abroad. His off-Broadway debut took place with the appearance of Home Free *on a New Playwrights Series program for 23 performances at the Cherry Lane Theater in February, 1965.* Ludlow Fair *and* The Madness of Lady Bright *appeared off Broadway and in London in 1966. The* Rimers of Eldritch *(a development of* This Is the Rill Speaking*) won its author a Vernon Rice Award off Broadway in 1967. In 1968 his* Wandering *was part of the off-Broadway program* Collision Course, *and he tried out an untitled new work with Al Carmines at Judson Poets' Theater. His*

"The 5th of July": by Lanford Wilson. Copyright © 1978 by Lanford Wilson. Reprinted by permission of International Creative Management. See CAUTION notice on copyright page. The complete play is published by Hill and Wang, a division of Farrar, Straus and Giroux, Inc. Inquiries concerning amateur acting rights should be addressed to: Dramatists Play Service, Inc., 440 Park Avenue South, New York, N.Y. 10016. All other inquiries should be addressed to the author's agent: Bridget Aschenberg, International Creative Management, 40 West 57th Street, New York, N.Y. 10019.

239

other playscripts have included No Trespassing *(1964) and* Wandering Days Ahead *(1967).*

In 1969, Wilson moved uptown to Broadway with the short-lived but favorably remembered The Gingham Dog, *following its production a year earlier at the Washington, D.C. Theater Club. His only other Broadway production to date was the almost equally short-lived but even more favorably received (in subsequent productions)* Lemon Sky *in 1970. The following year he wrote the libretto for composer Lee Hoiby's opera version of Tennessee Williams's* Summer and Smoke, *which premiered in St. Paul, Minn. and was presented by New York City Opera in 1972. He also collaborated with Williams on the film script* The Migrants *which was produced by CBS and won an Emmy nomination and a Christopher Award.*

In 1970, Wilson joined Marshall W. Mason's off-off-Broadway Circle Theater (now Circle Repertory Company) as its playwright-in-residence. His plays produced by this group have included Sextet (Yes) *in 1971; and* The Great Nebula in Orion *(named by Stanley Richards as one of the best short plays of the year),* Ikke, Ikke, Nye, Nye Nye *and* The Family Continues *during the 1972 season. They were directed by Mason, as was* The Hot 1 Baltimore *in its OOB premiere at the Circle January 27, 1973. It moved to an off-Broadway theater March 22, 1973, set a new off-Broadway long-run record for an American play of 1,166 performances, was named a Best Play of its season, won the Critics (best American play), Obie and Outer Circle awards and was adapted into a TV series.*

In 1975 Wilson's The Mound Builders *was produced at the Circle under Mason's direction, won an Obie and was filmed for the Theater in America series on WNET-TV. In 1975-76, the well-established group crossed the ill-defined boundary between OOB and the professional "off-Broadway" area. That same season Wilson's* Serenading Louie, *produced by the Circle for 33 performances, became its author's second Best Play (it had been written between* Lemon Sky *and* The Hot 1 Baltimore *and was rewritten for this production). This season the Circle produced Wilson's one-acter* Brontosaurus *and his third Best Play, the full-length* The 5th of July.

Wilson has been the recipient of Rockefeller, Guggenheim and Yale Fellowships. He is a bachelor and lives in Sag Harbor, N.Y.

The following synopsis of The 5th of July *was prepared by Jeff Sweet.*

Time: *Early evening, Independence Day, 1977, and the following morning*

Place: *The Talley place, a farm near Lebanon, Mo.*

ACT I

SYNOPSIS: It is twilight in this living room. Upstage near an exposed flight of stairs, a door leads to a downstairs guest room. A second door at right leads to the back of the house and the third at left to the front porch, part of which is visible.

Ken Talley, the owner of the house, in his 30s, with two artificial legs replacing those he lost in Vietnam (a fact of life to which everyone around him by now is entirely accustomed), is listening to a cassette recording of what can barely be perceived as vocal sounds. John, about the same age as Ken, enters from the porch. Ken tells John that an Arthur Schwartzkoff has phoned and left a message to call back. John tries, but Schwartzkoff is not there.

Gwen, John's wife — slim, nervy, attuned to all the vibes around her — enters and tells Ken she's in love with his house. It seems that she and John are thinking of buying it. She and Ken talk about the elaborate English garden that Jed, Ken's lover, is planting on the property. Apparently the garden is going to be a long-term job. "In only five years you'll be able to see the plants," as Ken comments. Such is Jed's devotion to the garden that during the winter, while Ken was living in St. Louis, Jed stayed in Lebanon to nurse it.

Jed — a handsome, stocky, essentially introverted young man — appears from the direction of the garden. The others greet him, but he remains on the fringe of the group, choosing to stay on the front porch rather than join them.

John tells his wife Gwen that if they're going to the event planned for that evening, they'll have to change their clothes. The event has something to do with a Matt Friedman whom Gwen fondly remembers as having helped straighten her out in difficult times. "Like he wouldn't let me sell my house or anything, and he wouldn't let me take flying lessons. I mean he was like a leveling influence."

John and Gwen go to the guest room to change. As soon as they've gone, Shirley, a girl in early teens dressed up in a gown that belonged to her great-grandmother, zips through the room and off, *"grandly ignoring Ken."*

The living room is quiet for the moment, Jed enters. He and Ken express relief that in less than a day John and Gwen will be out of the house and their hair. Ken marvels that, some years back, he and his sister June had the energy to live with them. (Apparently June's energy gave out, though, for she moved out sometime before Ken did.)

Ken's sister June — attractive, efficient, the mother of the girl Shirley — is also a house guest here. She enters and asks impatiently, "Are we doing this?" as though she thought they shouldn't. Ken tells her that John and Gwen are changing and that Aunt Sally's appearance is imminent. June goes out by way of the front porch to look for her daughter Shirley. No sooner has she disappeared than Shirley scampers through the room again, this time dashing out the door to the back.

Jed and Ken are alone again. They comment on Gwen and John's drug-taking. Ken observes that cocaine is an expensive habit.

JED: What does that matter to her? She probably owns Peru, or wherever it comes from.

KEN: She doesn't own Peru. She owns Montana and Colorado. Colorado owns Peru. Oh, God, all the old Berkeley days came back to wreck us last night. We called each other "man" and "cat," you would have vomited. I'll bet I said "dig it" five hundred times. It's a damned wonder we weren't down in the garden singing "We Shall Overcome." We wake you?

JED: Not me.

KEN: Even you. Even the dead. The little people in the wood. I didn't get to bed till five-thirty. All the birds were having fits: "Get the fuck off that God-damned nest, get down in the garden and get me a bug!" Got up at ten . . . that's six-thirty, seven-thirty . . .

JED: Four and a half. Did you eat?

KEN: I had coffee. I didn't even recognize it.

JED: You take your pills?

KEN: After last night my system would go into shock if I sent down one more chemical or another . . . . . Yes, yes, I took my vitamins, I took my minerals, and my protein and my birth control pill. Now, if I only had something to start it all moving. I've been up almost twelve hours, my heart hasn't beaten more than five times.

Ken and June's Aunt Sally enters carrying a dried rose. She's looking for a misplaced roll of copper wire, in the meantime expressing disappointment that the rose didn't retain its color when it dried, as a magazine article promised.

Weston Hurley, a young songwriter friend of Gwen and John's whose guitar almost seems to be a part of his body, comes in by way of the porch. He is also a guest in this house. June returns and asks Wes if Gwen and John are changing. What does she mean by "changing," Wes wants to know. "Clothes," Ken amplifies. "Oh wow," says Wes, "I had this whole metamorphosis thing going. I was reading this book about Kafka . . ." It is concluded that, though they are ostensibly changing for that night's event, Gwen and John are probably "going at it."

Aunt Sally tells Ken she doesn't think Gwen and John are seriously interested in buying the house (Gwen has enough money to buy any house in the country) and that he should accept the idea of holding onto it, staying in Lebanon and teaching at the high school. Ken replies firmly that he will not teach and that Gwen and John are indeed serious about buying — they plan to turn the place into a recording studio where they could work without involving themselves in Nashville.

SALLY: The place would be up for sale again in a year.

KEN: You know that, and I know that, but we're getting a little desperate. If Gwen hadn't shown up, I was ready to give it to the Catholics.

SALLY: Wouldn't that be a scandal. You'd be tarred.

KEN: And feathered. I love it. But don't get your hopes up, we have to get a hundred-seventy-five for it.

JED: What did you pay for the house in Sun City?

SALLY: Oh, I can't think about it.

JUNE: Ninety-five.

SALLY: I don't know why I let your father talk me into moving to California. Matt and I always hated the idea of retirement communities. Imagine choosing to live in the only place in the country that has a full one hundred percent unemployment.

JUNE: Mom and Dad love it.

SALLY: Well, I'm sorry. Retirement shouldn't be squandered on old people. It's morbid . . . . . . And I don't like the house.

KEN: You've hardly seen the house.

SALLY: No, it's too . . . big.

JUNE: Why are you buying it?

SALLY: Well, Buddy swears that I'm lonely now that Matt's gone. Really, he's only afraid of who might move in next to him. But I don't love St. Louis any more. No one does.

JUNE: There's nothing wrong with St. Louis.

JED: There's nothing right about it.

SALLY: The mayor on TV looks like he'd rather be the mayor of any other place on earth. And you aren't going to get anywhere with Shirley while I'm around.

JUNE (overlap): Don't let that worry you . . . . . .

SALLY: It's gonna rain on Harley Campbell's funeral tomorrow. It must have rained every vacation we came down here. I don't know why Matt loved it. Everyone hated him. If it rained, he went fishing. Never caught a fish. I don't think he baited his hook. Loved every minute of it. Hated catching fish. Didn't want the responsibility. Sat in the rain and laughed like a moron. They all must have thought he was mad.

KEN: Don't be absurd; he was as sane as you.

SALLY: Where have they got to now? They came back from town.

KEN: They went into their room, shut the door and are, we presume, going at it.

SALLY: Again? He certainly does try very hard to keep her occupied, doesn't he?

KEN: John has always known what side he was buttered on.

SALLY: You get the feeling the moment they're alone if she opens her mouth and doesn't sing, he sticks something in it. (To June). Was he like that when you lived with them?

JUNE: I didn't live with them. Kenny lived with them.

KEN: June moved out; if you can't stand the heat, get out of the kitchen.

JUNE: The heat didn't bother me; it was the smell of all those burning cookies.

Ken listens to more of the tape. He explains that it's a recording of a boy named Johnny Young, a junior high school student with a very high I.Q. but very little control over his vocal apparatus. On the tape is a story Johnny has recorded when he was alone with the recorder. Ken is listening to it to try to "translate" it so that he can then tell Johnny what he thinks of the story. "He communicates by scribbled messages," says Ken. "Half his problem is just tension. Fear of being anticipated. Everyone has cut him off as soon as they get the gist of what he's trying to say for so long that . . ." "Okay, okay . . ." says June, cutting him off. June makes a few catty remarks and disappears upstairs.

Sally wonders why June is in such a mood. Ken speculates that John's presence may have something to do with it. Sally wonders why June came down from St. Louis with her to visit Lebanon this Fourth of July weekend. Ken speculates that John's presence may have something to do with that, too. It seems that June and John were once an item. But isn't that firmly in the past tense? Sally asks. "Nevertheless," Ken replies. "Well, it gives her focus," says his Aunt Sally philosophically.

As Sally continues to search for misplaced objects, Jed looks through a book for a solution to a gardening problem. Ken tells Sally that Jed has a masters degree in botany.

Suddenly John runs on looking for Shirley. Apparently she was peering through the window as he and Gwen were making love. Shirley enters the room from the back, initially acting innocent, but then, to the accompaniment of John's mock threats to kill her, she goes into an exhaustively detailed description of what she saw. Gwen enters, wrapped in a sheet, raving about the orgasm she had when she realized Shirley was watching. "Shirley," she cries, "you gotta always be there!" Shirley's reaction is that she thinks what she saw was gross. "I have never seen anything so unnatural and warped and unnatural in my young life!" she exclaims.

In the midst of this, June interrupts to remind all present that this evening is to be a sober occasion, and she admonishes Shirley to put away the dress and act respectfully to Aunt Sally and to the memory of Uncle Matt. Shirley replies she has a lot of respect for Aunt Sally, "whom I consider my mother, and Uncle Matt, who was the only father I ever had . . ." What's more, she doesn't want to have anything to do with dumping Matt's ashes into the river (the solemn event for which they're all preparing).

John asks Shirley how old she is. Shirley tries to pass herself off as 19, but June reveals that she's 13. "You better watch that one," says an amused John. He follows Gwen into the guest room to change for the scattering of the ashes. Shirley shouts after John that she's going to be an artist, that artists have no age, and, as an incipient artist, she must force herself to see everything, "no matter how disgusting and how low!"

Wes is just beginning to understand what's going on: namely, that Matt has been dead over a year and that Sally has been holding his ashes all this time with the intention of scattering them. "He said don't keep my ashes in a God damned urn," says Sally. And she hasn't. She transferred them from the fancy urn from the funeral home to a candy box. She's given him a little air every day and even dried the rose in him. Ken remarks that the ashes might be put to best use as fertilizer for Jed's rose bushes. Shirley protests that if anyone says the word "ashes" again she will scream. She can't stand all this talk of death and cremation.

"I suppose the river is as good a place for him as any," Sally continues. "He used to fish there. And we made love there the first time." Sally tells how, on their second date with Matt, they saw a U.F.O. Wes, who is interested in the subject, questions her about the shape of what she saw. She remembers it didn't have a tail. She and Matt ran to get a closer look, but, arriving at the river bank, they found the U.F.O. was gone, though much of the foliage in the vicinity had been burned away. She and Matt then examined the river bank area. This happened during the war, and they thought it might be a Japanese invasion. After running around for a while, they stopped to rest and talk and look look at the moon. And one thing led to another. Every year since, they had come down from St. Louis to visit the spot.

June tells Shirley that if she's going to join them she will have to change out of the gown.

SHIRLEY: . . . . . The sooner we get back to St. Louis and you stop acting like a mother the happier I'll be.

JUNE: Just a simple decision, we don't need the production number.

SHIRLEY: Unlike either of you, I do not have a single memory of the boy friends I dated during the war in this one-horse burg.

JUNE: Where do you get the way you talk? I did not have "boy friends," we did not go on "dates." Haven't you learned anything? She spends twenty-four hours a day in the queer movie house watching Betty Grable re-runs.

SHIRLEY: Betty Grable is the greatest star Missouri ever produced.

KEN: Oh, God, I'll bet that's true.

SHIRLEY: I would think one would know better than to proclaim her chastity to her illegitimate daughter.

JUNE: There is a world of difference between making love and teasing some basketball player after the junior prom.

KEN: June certainly never teased anyone.

SHIRLEY: That from a woman who has written: "The truly liberated person is free in mind, not in body" on the wall of the apartment.

JUNE: I am going to cut your filthy tongue right out of your filthy face if you can't learn to respect people's aspirations!

Gwen and John enter, dressed with a flamboyance that is a bit out of keeping with an informal ashes-scattering ceremony. Jed heads upstairs to change. Sally goes back to looking for things she has misplaced, one of which is Uncle Matt.

SALLY: . . . . . I can't seem to remember what I've done with his box of ashes.
Ken and June at the same time overlapping.
KEN: Don't say it!
JUNE: Please don't!
Shirley screams. A beat.

WESTON: Far out.

GWEN: Oh, God, that's so great. I'd be a new person if I could do that. Ever since my shrink told me I should scream, I haven't been able to.

JUNE: Don't pay any attention to her. She's only trying to be the center of . . . Oh, God, I sound exactly like Dad, don't I?

KEN: His voice was higher.

JUNE: Men and women aren't strong enough to have children. Trees should have children.

Sally worries some more about where she left Matt. Jed shouts down from upstairs that Matt is in the refrigerator.

Apropos of nothing, Wes mentions he's been reading about the Bermuda Triangle lately. Gwen says it's a fraud. She and John spent two months down there trying to disappear without success. "Like we did everything you could think of to make ourselves conspicuous, you know. Not a fuckin' thing happened to us."

Shirley asks how long Gwen and John will be staying in Nashville. "Just a couple of days. You want to come?" says Gwen. "Yes!" says Shirley.

Addressing Ken, June says, "You can shrug it off, right?" Ken tells her not to force the issue. June dryly replies that he is the only person she knows who can express non-involvement in 45 languages. "Seven or eight," Ken corrects.

Shirley is envious of Gwen for having travelled so much. Gwen replies that the hill overlooking the river is the best place she's ever been, and she reiterates to Ken her desire to buy the property. Sally tries to discourage her over Ken's protests. Gwen, however, isn't about to be discouraged. Gwen aspires to be a singing star, and she talks with enthusiasm about building a recording studio in this house. She thinks here she might be able to get over her recording block. She can sing perfectly well, except when tape is rolling; then she freezes. It took two weeks to get her to unclench to record a demonstration tape. But it was worth it, John chimes in. He tells them that the tape impressed a top manager named Jimmy King. "Only thing he said I really should concentrate on this one thing, and like what happens to the copper business?" says Gwen (a copper factory is one of the properties she owns).

JOHN: One thing at a time, one thing at a time.

GWEN: Only I'm never sure which time to take what thing.

JOHN: You gotta learn to think about yourself.

GWEN: But wouldn't that be far out to have this really major career after you're already thirty-three years old and burned out?

JOHN: Nobody says you're burned . . .

GWEN: Everybody says I'm burned out. How can you take as many drugs and go through what I've gone through and not have your brains fried?

SHIRLEY: You are *thirty-three years old?*

GWEN: Isn't that gross? I mean like really scary-time. Like the crucifixion bit and all that.

SHIRLEY: I couldn't possibly live to be thirty.

GWEN: You always think that, but then you do.

Shirley disappears upstairs. John and Gwen ask Ken about his plans. Is it true that he's going to teach at the high school that Ken, June and John attended when they were in their teens and living in Lebanon?

KEN: Oh, hardly, no. The profession has done very nicely without me for six years. I think it will survive a while longer.

GWEN: I thought that's what you were down here for. You were going back to your old high school.

KEN: I was never that interested in teaching.

SALLY: Oh, you were so.

GWEN *(overlapping Sally)*: You used to scream about it all the time.

JOHN: Hell you weren't. That was your mission, I thought.

KEN: Well, once again, Super Fag's plans fail to materialize.

JOHN: That guy said you were the best teacher Oakland ever had.

KEN: Would you get off my back? That's all I hear from Jed and Sally and June. I don't need it from you. Yes, I was quite happy leaving our cozy abode in Oakland each morning, and walking briskly into the Theodore Roosevelt High School. Very "Good Morning, Miss Dove," very "Goodbye, Mr. Chips." And — by prancing and dancing and sleight of hand, I actually managed to get their attention off sex for one hour a day. They became quite fascinated by trochees. But I'm afraid anymore my prancing would be quite embarrassing to them.

JOHN: So you're afraid, so you'll get over it.

KEN: So everyone tells me.

JUNE: Running like a rabbit would be closer —

KEN: Fear has nothing to do with it. As I slowly realized that no accredited English department was interested in my stunningly over-qualified application, except the notoriously parochial hometown . . .

JUNE: Fine, that's where you belong.

KEN: . . . I became aware that what everyone was trying to tell me was — that teaching impressionable teenagers in my present state, I could only expect to leave quite the wrong impression. You have no idea how much noise I make falling down.

JOHN: Oh, bull. A big-deal War Hero. They'd love you.

KEN: I don't think so. And though it seems incredible to us, they don't even know where Vietnam is.

JUNE: Why don't you just admit you're vain and terrified and face it instead of —

KEN: I have simply developed an overpowering distaste for chalk.

The conversation branches off briefly into a discussion of the fact that Ken has had to go back into physical therapy because he has been walking wrong, placing the emphasis on the muscles in his arms rather than his stomach muscles to move about on the false legs and crutches. He's having to build up his stomach muscles again.

John brings the conversation back to the question of what Ken is going to do if he isn't going to teach. Ken abruptly short-circuits the conversation, calling up to Jed that it's time to get a move on. John tells Wes it's time to head out — first to the scattering of Matt, and then to the Fourth of July fireworks. Wes decides to take a pass on both.

Gwen also begins to have second thoughts about going. She's beginning to "freak out" at the thought of scattering Matt's ashes. "Tell me it isn't ashes, tell me it isn't him. Tell me it's something else," she says. Ken tells her that what they're really going to throw out is uneaten lousy candy that people sent him while he was in the hospital. Gwen is not persuaded by this fiction. She tells the others to go on without her. John says he's going to stay with her, whether she goes or stays. Impatiently, June goes onto the porch where Aunt Sally has drifted, saying, "Aunt Sally, can we do this?" "I'll go, June," says Sally. "Kenny said don't push me. You always push." She exits, presumably to fetch Matt's ashes, June following her off.

The matter of whether Gwen and John are going or staying has not been settled. While the discussion continues, Shirley enters in a different dress. John suggests to Gwen that they stay in the house with Wes and Shirley.

The phone rings. Jed answers. It's person-to-person for John. As John talks on the phone, June returns. Aunt Sally is talking to the ashes, and June is less than certain the scattering is going to happen. Gwen, still agitated, pulls out a pillbox, saying, "Does anybody want a quaalude? I'm really freaking out."

Shirley somehow gets her hands on the pillbox during the general confusion. Gwen sees this and warns Shirley not to take one. Shirley says she's just looking. Gwen says you can start off by looking and end up being burned out. She offers herself as a case in point. She's had so many operations, she jokes, there's nothing much left inside to take out.

Gwen and Wes talk about her family's ill fortune. Gwen's father has been paralyzed for four years, and her mother and brother were killed in a plane crash. And to top it all off, whenever Gwen is in the hospital, Schwartzkoff, who votes her father's stock, calls a board meeting to vote through something she is against. She asks if John is talking to Schwartzkoff on the phone. No, John replies, it's their engineer in Nashville calling about their schedule. Gwen continues to talk about her carved-up condition with an intensity that almost conveys the impression that she revels in it. John returns from the phone. Ken comments wryly that in comparison to Gwen, Cassandra had it easy.

Mention of Cassandra switches Gwen onto another subject — myths and her feeling that, properly understood, they contain all the answers. Wes chimes in that he's been reading about Eskimo folk myths. Gwen asks for an example. Wes obliges with a story about an Eskimo family whose winter food supply, a pile of caribou meat, was frozen solid and thus impossible to eat, leaving them on the brink of starvation. Then a young Eskimo warrior had the idea of thawing the meat by letting off "this tremendous, powerful fart." Sure enough, the meat thawed, but the smell was so repulsive that the meat was inedible, so everyone starved to death anyway.

The story does not go over very well. The general consensus is that it's gross. In addition, Ken and John doubt its authenticity. How can it be a folk tale when there's no heroic action? The warrior's fart doesn't qualify because, as John says, "Heroic actions must have saving results," and the warrior's action didn't save anyone. Weston gets defensive.

Wes (Danton Stone) telling his Eskimo story to Gwen (Nancy
Snyder) and Ken (William Hurt) in *The 5th of July*

WESTON: . . . . . You obviously don't have the sensitivity to understand —
SHIRLEY: I have nothing but sensitivity and I don't even understand it . . . . . .
WESTON: I only thought it was interesting because it is a completely different
culture.
JOHN: Wes, that isn't culture. That's hardship.
WESTON: No, no, it is. It's an alien culture. Like they call themselves "*The*
People" and everybody else is "The *Other* People."
KEN: Wes, every people call themselves "The People," and everyone else is the
other people.
WESTON: They have fifty different words for snow . . .
          Pause.
You don't think that shows a subtle mind?
KEN *(beat)*: Wes, of course they have fifty different words for snow.
JOHN *(beat)*: Their winters are six months long.
KEN *(beat)*: They have nothing else to talk about.
JOHN *(beat)*: Snow is all there is.
KEN *(beat)*: They have to find some way to make it interesting.
JOHN *(beat)*: The Bedouins probably have fifty different words for sand.
WESTON: They probably do. They're a very interesting people.
KEN: They call themselves "The People" and . . .
JOHN: Wes, you know why you're not going to make a successful songwriter?
Because you have too many interests.
GWEN: There's a song about syphilis, though. Songs can be about anything.
SHIRLEY: You are so depressing.

Wes retreats to the front porch with his guitar. Jed comes downstairs, having
changed for the scattering. He gives Ken some water to help him down his pills.
Gwen identifies one of them as a "horse-size pain killer." Ken flipply refers to it
as his birth control pill. Gwen expresses relief that she doesn't have to worry
about that. "Can't you have children?" Shirley asks. "That was like the first
thing to go," says Gwen. But that didn't bother her very much and, actually, the
operation had a happy side-effect: by accident the surgeons cut a nerve the result

of which is that she feels sex "like five times as intense as the normal person."

Shirley, somewhat put off by Gwen's revelations, insists she will never indulge in sex. Gwen tells her she mustn't say that because she doesn't know what she's missing. When she heard Ken was injured, Gwen continues, she didn't rest until she was assured that his sexual performance would not be impaired. Gwen suddenly spots fireflies in the back yard and runs off to get a closer look.

JUNE: Could we go now, Aunt Sally?

JOHN: Gwen can stay with Wes and Shirley.

KEN: You don't have to stay now?

JED: No, the phone call was from Schwartzkoff. He doesn't have to hang around waiting for it any more.

KEN: You running the copper business now?

JUNE: What's this country-western singer crap? That's just to keep her mind off the copper business, right?

KEN: Diversionary tactics.

JOHN: Hey, hold on, come on.

JED: "Smoke gets in your eyes."

GWEN (re-entering): Oh, God, "Smoke Gets in Your Eyes." I love that song. We gotta do that song.

SHIRLEY: I thought it was the engineer checking schedules.

JOHN: Come on, let's go. Before the kid starts up again.

SHIRLEY: I am not starting up. I said I was going to be a great artist, which I have said repeatedly for the past solid year.

JUNE: With the emphasis on repeatedly.

SHIRLEY: And you can't stop me!

JUNE: If I had it to do over again, I wouldn't give her to Aunt Sally. You live with a bat, you fly like a bat.

SHIRLEY: I don't think you were militant at all. I think you were just cross and angry.

GWEN: Are you kidding me? She was sensational.

JUNE: You have no idea of the life we led.

GWEN: Really.

JUNE: You've no idea of the country we almost made for you. The fact that I think it's all a crock now does not take away from what we almost achieved.

She grabs Shirley, who starts thrashing wildly.

KEN: June! June! O.K., O.K. Aunt Sally? I see you've got Uncle Matt in your lap. I don't think we should put this off.

SALLY (long pause): They all hated him because he was a Jew. Your mother, your father, my folks, the whole damn town hated him.

JUNE: He kept coming back down here.

SALLY: Oh, nothing bothered him except when it bothered me. And if it didn't bother him it didn't bother me. He liked young people. Shirley was a joy to him. He was very concerned about Gwen. And he was very angry when Kenny lost his legs. People said he didn't like this country, because he wasn't afraid to speak his mind.

JUNE: They say a lot.

SALLY: I think they were right. I don't think he liked this country a bit. No, I'm sorry, but if Gwen and John are going to buy the Talley place then Matt doesn't belong here.

GWEN: No, don't feel that way about it.

SALLY: He'll just have to like California.

GWEN: Listen, feel free to come anytime —

JED: Gwen and John are buying the place?

SALLY *(to Jed)*: I want to talk to you about that.

Sally has made up her mind, and she goes upstairs with the ashes. She has to get up early next morning for Harley Campbell's funeral. June is angry. "I told Dad I'd get her to dump the damn ashes before she came out there, if I had to dump them myself." She exits upstairs.

Jed asks Gwen if she's really going to buy the place. She says yes, but that they'll be glad to follow whatever instructions he leaves about the garden. Jed says that it doesn't matter. After all, it takes 20 years for a garden to come into its own, and they only started it three years ago. He looks off past the porch without expression.

Gwen tries to make Shirley appreciate the idealism that motivated June as an activist in the 1960s. As Gwen describes it, June and all the other activists were hopelessly naïve. "How straight do you have to be to see that nothing is going to come from it? But don't knock your mother, 'cause she really believed that 'Power to the People' song, and that hurts."

Shirley responds by telling them, in very intense tones, that she intends to be a great artist. The greatest artist the Midwest has ever produced. She doesn't know what she's going to do, but she's going to be astonishing. Her fantasies of grandeur build in a crescendo of self-praise, climaxed by a dramatic "fainting" spell.

June comes back downstairs at this point. John explains to her: "She recognized herself on the street and fainted." With great dignity, Shirley rises, and in a coda says that one day her name will be said in the same breath with those of Shakespeare, Michelangelo, Beethoven, Frank Lloyd Wright and Marie Curie. "And when I first achieved my first achievements," she tells John, "I was still eleven years younger than you are now," after which *"She sweeps from the room"* and exits off the front porch into the garden, stopping only to tell a bewildered Weston that she would never seriously consider marrying him. He continues to play his guitar on the front porch.

June comes downstairs, reporting that Sally has gone to bed. Jed figures it's time to change out of the clothes he was going to wear for the scattering, and he heads up to his room.

Ken, June, John and Gwen are together in the living room.

JUNE: Son-of-a-bitch; together again.

GWEN: Oh, Jesus, I loved the four of us. No shit, that was like the greatest period of my life.

JUNE: Let's don't re-run that again, I couldn't take it.

GWEN: You should have stayed with us; we had like our own little commune.

KEN: No. Four is too large for a menage, too small for a commune. Eventually, John would have cracked under the strain of all three of us chasing his tail.

JUNE: No, it was all a little too steamy for me.

JOHN: Don't sit down, baby; we're all on our way out.

GWEN: All the time we were on that fuckin' world cruise it was just like — not what we'd planned at all. I'll never forgive you for chickening out of that.

KEN: I didn't chicken out.

John goes on porch.

GWEN: No shit, it was like what the hell are John and me doing in fuckin' Europe, you know? The whole idea was going off to escape from your draft thing — it didn't make any sense.

KEN: Wait a minute, did I leave you in the lurch?

GWEN: You sure as hell did. John came back, said you weren't going; we cried like babies!

KEN: What did he tell you I said? Duty calls? My country right or wrong?

GWEN: June's really got your number; you never commit to anything . . . . .

JOHN *(enters)*: Let's go celebrate. Come on.

JUNE: You three go on.

KEN: Not tonight. I've got to turn in. I've got to work tomorrow. Afternoon. I haven't exercised today. Not tonight.

GWEN: This is the last night we're here.

JOHN: I bet that really rips them up.

KEN: No, I'm just beat.

Gwen and John head for town and the fireworks and the dance. June and Ken stay behind. Sally sneaks downstairs and joins Wes on the porch. June says goodnight to Ken and heads up to her room.

As Sally and Wes enjoy the moonlit night, Ken begins to do situps in the living room to strengthen his stomach muscles. Sally says goodnight to Ken and Wes and heads into the garden. Jed comes downstairs. Ken tells him, "I cannot teach those kids, Jed . . . We can't stay here . . . I can't walk into a classroom again . . ."

Jed picks Ken up in his arms. "I really have knocked myself out," says Ken, leaning against him. "Hang in there," says Jed, and he carries him upstairs. Wes is playing his guitar on the porch. *Curtain.*

ACT II

The front porch occupies the bulk of the stage. Behind it we can see something of the living room. It is the morning of July 5. Jed is alone at rise, writing a letter. Shirley, who obviously enjoys his company, joins him. Jed tells her that Aunt Sally has gone to the funeral. The others have been up for a while, too.

Shirley tells Jed she dreamed about being chased by a deer. Jed says he can't interpret that one for her. Shirley tells him that if she were going to compare herself to something, it would be to a flower. A little white flower that blossoms for one day only, then fades from unfulfillment. Jed suggests that perhaps she is an anemone. Shirley likes the sound of that. Jed promises to look it up in a book and show her. She thanks him; it's important to her. Jed says it's important to them all. "I know," says Shirley. Jed says, "We don't dwell on it because we try to spare you the pressure of all our expectations. We multitudes." "I know," says Shirley. "But don't. Don't spare me. It makes me strong."

Ken enters with his tape recorder and papers, reporting that Gwen has been on the phone most of the morning and June is making buns. Sally enters, having returned early from Harley Campbell's service.

Shirley mentions that she was up late the previous night, packing. She has taken Gwen's offer to go to Nashville with her and John seriously. As Sally tells them the latest news in town, June sails through, depositing the first load of her home-made buns. Ken asks Sally why she didn't call to have someone pick her up. The walk from town is a long one, particularly for someone her age. Sally waves aside his comment.

It is revealed that Jed has received a letter from Sissinghurst Castle, the site of a famous English garden. The letter is to confirm that Jed has indeed rediscovered in America a rare English rose. The letter goes on to state that, other plants having been grown from the plant he sent them, an affiliated nursery will soon — with his permission — offer the rose through its catalog that others might have the pleasure of growing it. Gwen, who has entered during this, tells Jed that in his letter he should tell them he wants a royalty.

Shirley asks Gwen how the fireworks display was. Gwen says it wasn't impressive. What she did find interesting was the gang of young farm boys at the display, "these really randy, country Republican high school juniors drinking beer out of a paper sack." Seeing them, Gwen continues, made her suddenly understand Ken and John completely. Ken protests that though he and John grew up in Lebanon, they share nothing in common with the boys of which she speaks. "John and I moved in quite a different circle from your . . . . . we were quite a different social strata from the horny river trash you're trying to associate with us." Ken may disclaim all he wants, says Gwen, but to her mind the resemblances are obvious.

During the course of the conversation, it is revealed that Ken and June's father, Buddy, made a small fortune selling mobile homes and that, when he and their mother left for the retirement village in California, Buddy gave June the house in town and Ken this house for them to do with as they please. June sold the house in town.

Wes has joined the others on the porch, and now John makes his appearance. Gwen tells John that she has called Schwartzkoff and is very upset with the latest news of what he is up to with her copper company. John says he'll handle everything and Gwen should just focus on her singing.

Changing the subject, John tells Ken that last night they ran into MacConnell, principal of the high school, and that MacConnell is still under the impression that Ken is going to teach at his school. Ken says he will disabuse him of that idea very soon.

GWEN: He was very excited about one of his students returning to the fold.

KEN: Well, the prospect excites me not at all.

GWEN: Well, listen, who can know anything. Last year when we saw you in St. Louis . . .

JED: Two years ago.

GWEN: Was that two years ago? That was all you were talking about. Jed was going to build this garden, you were going to teach . . . . . .

JUNE: Actually Kenny came down to the school this May and let his little self get frightened away. He visited the classrooms and . . .

KEN: . . . Oh, please. Yes, Jed and I visited that lovely new building this May, before school let out. Dear old Mac was a little edgy about Jed. He couldn't quite put that together . . .

JED: I think he was coming pretty close.

KEN: Probably be thrilled. An opportunity to exhibit his liberal tolerance. But other than that I found him quite pleasantly condescending, didn't you?

JED: No complaints. Said he liked gardens.

KEN: And I had the pleasure of being introduced to the four classes I would be teaching this fall.

JED: Well, actually only three . . .

KEN: Well, O.K., three. I begged off the fourth and went back to the car.

JED: Went in full of piss and vinegar, came out white as a sheet . . . . .

GWEN: What did they do?

JUNE: No one had prepared them for him . . . Mac has always been about as tactful . . .

KEN: No, I think it was more a question of a sincere lack of rapport.

GWEN: A lot of messy questions, right?

KEN: No, actually I was quite prepared for the messy questions. Dry urbanity; humorous self-deprecations.

JED: The kids wouldn't look at him.

KEN: Which God knows I should have been prepared for, but for some reason I was not.

JOHN: They were grossed out, for God's sake.

KEN: Well, if I had some deep-seated need to teach, trying to get at Johnny Young's speech problems will fulfill that quite nicely for a few more weeks.

GWEN: That's all too fuckin' humanitarian; I never trust that gig — it's creepy.

KEN: Not at all, the gimp leading the gimp; we form a very cozy symposium.

JOHN: So, do both.

JUNE: Came running back to St. Louis hot to sell the house and hit the road.

GWEN: Well, listen, more luck to me.

The conversation shifts to Ken's making wry jokes about his fiberglass legs and from that to the various relations, sexual and otherwise, John, Ken, Gwen and June shared with each other. Shirley is repelled by the idea that her mother slept with John. John comments that at that time June was sleeping with everyone. "Your mother was a bigger pop-tart than I was," Gwen tells Shirley.

Ken, coming to his sister's defense, says that June's sleeping-around days only really began when Gwen supplanted June in John's affections. Ken then recalls that, when children, he, June and John used to "diddle with each other." Ken recalls that, by the time they had headed for college at Berkeley, he had been in love with John for years. In fact, one night, when John was very drunk, Ken had fulfilled his fantasy. But, in the end, John had met and married "the Copper Queen."

GWEN: That would be me.

JUNE: Nobody said John didn't know a good thing when he saw it.

GWEN: Damn straight.

KEN: And they all lived happily ever after.

GWEN: Oh, I loved us then. I remember once we bought twenty dollars worth of daffodils and June and I ran up and down, giving them to all the stalled drivers on the San Jose Freeway.

WESTON: Why?

GWEN: June had decided they were wonderful.

JUNE: They hated us. The traffic started moving; we nearly got run down.

KEN: You were decidedly before your time.

GWEN: That fuckin' war! Damn, it fucked us. It broke my heart when we weren't together. If you'd come with us to Europe, everything would have been so different. You would never have been in Nam, you wouldn't have been injured; June wouldn't have gotten militant and estranged from us.

John would prefer that this topic not be pursued. He interrupts with a compliment for June's cooking. The next minute, Weston is talking about a book he read about the American army in Nam. This leads Ken to speak ironically about his experience there. He no longer has nightmares about his friends being blown up. Now he is more likely to dream of some general moving through the hospital, "handing out medals like aspirin." The brass were looking for heroes to decorate, and they did in fact uncover "a few heroic actions in the face of fire." Weston, remembering their conversation from the night before about how a heroic action by definition has to have a saving grace, asks Ken what the saving grace was in Nam. Ken replies by returning to Weston's Eskimo fable, saying that he would have accepted it as a myth had the family overcome its revulsion for the fart-thawed meat and eaten it. *That* he might have accepted as a heroic action. And the saving grace?

KEN: Would have been surviving. Don't choke on it, don't turn up your nose, swallow it and live, baby.

WESTON: Even if it stinks, man.

KEN: Dig it.

WESTON: Right on.

KEN: They could have forever after been known as the family who bravely ate the fart-thawed meat and went on to become . . .

SALLY: Vegetarians.

John suggests to Gwen it's time they pack if they're going to make their plane.

Shirley indicates she's ready to leave with them. June clamps down on that — no Nashville trip for Shirley. Gwen tries to get June to relent, but there's no changing June's mind. Shirley storms off, angry and disappointed.

Wes wants to know if they have enough time before leaving for him to help Jed some more in the garden. In the middle of Wes explaining, or rather trying to explain (not really understanding much about gardening), what he still has to do with Jed, the phone rings. Gwen assumes it's Schwartzkoff calling back because she hung up on him in mid-conversation. John goes off to answer the phone as Gwen complains how Schwartzkoff is thwarting her intentions for the copper company. Gwen had visited the plant and, in an impassioned speech owing something to the theories of Karl Marx, had promised the employees that she would give them a bonus at the end of the year of all of the company's profits, minus 1 per cent for her. "But they had to divide it evenly, file clerks get as much as managers," she explains. It seems Schwartzkoff is trying to get around this promise by taking the profits from the copper company to pay for capital improvements at other branches and so claim there are no profits to divide.

John returns to say that the call is for either Ken or June. June decides to get it. On her way to the phone, John indicates to her that he would like to talk to her privately. June seems none too interested, and she exits to deal with the phone.

In a prankish mood, Ken grabs Weston's hand and tells him that, having gypsy blood, he has the power to read the future in Weston's palms. At the beginning, Ken "sees" good things for Weston, but, as he builds momentum, the visions become filled with mysterious enemies. Thoroughly spooked, Weston rushes offstage, gaining his release by paying Ken ten dollars to "light a candle" for him. Ken tells Jed they'll use the money for seed for the garden.

June enters. The call was from Dr. Anderson. Apparently Aunt Sally passed out at Harley Campbell's funeral and was carried for examination to the doctor's house. No sooner had the doctor turned his back than Sally had sneaked out and walked the five miles back to the house. The doctor is on his way over now. June and Ken are upset and worried, both by her fainting spell and by her behavior. Sally will not be bullied by them, however. She feels fine now, and she doesn't want to be inconvenienced with their fussing over her. As near as she can figure (having had nurse's training at one time), she had a slight stroke and there's no real cause for worry.

She begins to muse on what the town must think of her — not just because of her fainting, but because she committed the great social sin of marrying a Jew. She goes on to discuss the appearance of Harley's corpse. She tells June to stop looking at her "as if it were only a matter of time. It's always only a matter of time." She doesn't want to talk about dying. Besides, nobody really knows anything about it. "Start talking about death, you end up talking about life, and a good thing, too," says Aunt Sally.

June mentions that Dr. Anderson said Sally left a candy box in his office. Ken asks Sally if she left Uncle Matt there. Sally's answer is that it's just as well if the candy box stays where it is.

Sally continues: Matt didn't believe in death. Nor does she. "It goes on and then it stops. You can't worry about the stopping, you have to worry about the going on." What about heaven? asks Weston, who has rejoined them on the porch. Sally doesn't buy the idea of heaven either. Gwen says that heaven for her is this house and asks what figure Ken has in mind to sell for. Whatever it is, she'll be glad to pay it. But she wants to do it quickly so she can move in soon.

John enters, having gone offstage a minute before to answer the phone, and tells Gwen that her manager wants to talk to her about business. Gwen tells John to get a price on the house from Ken and a commitment on when they could take possession. She exits into the house.

John asks Ken how much he wants. $175,000 Ken says. John's counter-offer is $125,000. Ken finds bargaining with friends disagreeable. Also, he's feeling a bit reluctant to turn the place over to people he thinks don't really have a genuine feeling for it. "I love it," John protests, "I always have."

KEN: Yeah, but what do you care where you are, as long as there's a telephone.

JOHN: As it happens, Gwen is the one who decides. Whatever she says is fine by me. Whatever makes her happy.

JED: I'm hip.

KEN: But, Jesus, John, the money you spend doing it .... I mean I know you're trying to gain the whole world, but what are you losing doing it?

JOHN: Everything gets written off. We wouldn't own it. The company would own it. We don't own anything. The company has it all.

JUNE: So she said.

KEN: Come on, we're not blind. How can you buy — what are you buying, the whole record company now? How can you buy a ...

JOHN: Oh, for Godssake. Who's doing that? She wants a chance to see if she's any good.

KEN: But how can a person buy something like that just to keep her out of the board meetings of ...

JOHN: ... Oh, fuck, Talley. Stop being such a faggot. Look around you, wake up, for Godssake. You can buy anything!

SALLY: Not for a hundred and a quarter you can't.

JOHN: OK, that was the wrong thing to say. Listen, I'm just trying to make her happy.

JUNE: Sure, but for whom? For the board of directors of —

KEN: The surrogate —

JED: Schwartzkoff.

JOHN: Yeah, see, that's not your business.
    Pause.

KEN: John, I can't sell for that price. It —

JOHN: You can't sell to me for that price or you can't sell to anybody for that price? I'm not deaf to these insinuations and innuendoes that have been floating around.
    Pause.

KEN *(level)*: I was very angry when you took off for Europe without telling me, but that's long passed.

JOHN: Don't dump that on me.

KEN: We plan for six months to go together, suddenly you leave a week ahead of schedule, what the hell would you call it?

JOHN: No, I won't take that. You can't lay your goddam fecklessness on me — I'm not responsible for anything that happened to you in . . .

KEN: O.K., forget it. Everyone loves you, everyone forgets everything. Nobody's dumping anything on you.

JOHN: What would you call it? No. I did not want you to come. I wanted me and Gwen to get out of the whole steamy situation with both of you.

KEN: Until last night when Gwen said I left you in the lurch, I thought it had been her idea. So you told her I changed my mind. O.K.

John admits that's the way it was, but he won't take responsibility for Ken's having been drafted. Ken didn't need to leave the country to escape the draft. He could have told the authorities he was gay and that would have done it. Come to think of it, John never understood why Ken allowed himself to be taken. "Did it have anything to do with Gwen and me?" he asks. "No," says Ken. "Now I hope everyone heard that," says John. Ken says he still doesn't know why he went. June says she thinks because he didn't want to make any kind of commitment, so he let the army make the commitment for him by drafting him.

John steers the conversation back to the proposed sale of the house. $130,000 is as high as he's willing to go. "A hundred thirty-five," says Sally. She's decided to bid against John for it. Ken asks for an explanation. Sally tells him that she and Jed scattered Matt's ashes in the rose garden the night before on Jed's promise that the house would not be sold. Sally is willing to go as high as $225,-000 to make sure the house doesn't leave the family.

John is irritated. He came for two reasons. One was to buy the house, and now that's off. The other was to talk to June. June wants to know why. John suggests they talk alone. June refuses. All right then, he'll talk about it here and now. He and Gwen would like to take Shirley with them, have her live with them a few months each year. The conversation becomes heated, people talking over each other in a jumble.

JUNE: You're out of your mind. You have the *balls*. You have the *balls* . . .

JOHN: Come on, I don't want Gwen to hear this, and I don't think you want Shirley to . . .

SALLY: I knew goddamned well he didn't want the house. No, young man.

JUNE: I don't give a shit who hears it. Out. You better leave now, and you better never — never mention Shirley again.

KEN *(standing on one crutch)*: You better watch what you say, buddy; you're leaving yourself open for one hell of a nonsupport suit . . .

JOHN: I have said nothing. I claim no responsibility.

JUNE: Some things you can not buy, baby! Now leave.

JOHN: All right, forget it; can it. You just by God remember you had the chance.

SHIRLEY *(arms around June's knees)*: I will live in St. Louis with my mother.

JOHN: Fine, baby, it serves you right. *(Yelling.)* Baby, we're leaving here.

Pushes Ken out of the way. Ken falls.
(To Ken.) Oh, Jesus, God. I forgot. I'm sorry, baby, I'm sorry, I forgot completely.
          Jed crosses to Ken.
JED *(to John)*: Go on. Don't touch him. Leave. Move.
KEN: I'm not hurt! I'm not hurt! It's O.K., Jed.
JOHN: I swear to God, I barely touched you!
JED: You go in to Gwen; I'll get him up.
KEN *(still on floor)*: I'm O.K.

Totally unaware of what has just occurred on the porch, Gwen and Weston come running on, filled with the fantastic and wonderful news that Columbia Records has decided to sign them, offer them big money, give them the whole star treatment. "Two weeks! Two weeks! He's going to have the fucking record on the air. On the motherfuckin' airwaves," crows Gwen. She runs off to pack for the flight to Nashville.

Quietly John addresses Ken, "Listen, I'm your friend, whether you know it or not." Ken does not reply. John exits.

Weston tells the gang on the porch that what John doesn't know is that the offer to Gwen is a *genuine* offer. It's not the one that John has been surreptitiously laying out money to set up. Columbia really thinks Gwen is hot stuff. "She's really good," says Wes. "John don't know." Weston disappears inside the house.

Jed picks Ken up. Ken allows as how he's going to have to start working on his teaching plan for next year. June asks Ken if he's figured out yet what Johnny Young is saying on the tape.

KEN: Oh, sure, just takes listening to a couple of times. He's into the future.
JUNE: Well, why not.
KEN: You'd think he'd tell me something about his past. Johnny's into science, only in a very esoteric way. Sally and Wes wouldn't like it at all, he's very positive and negative and decidedly eccentric. Space travel, transportation — and it all ends up . . .
          Turns on cassette player and reads from his yellow pad at the same time.
"After they had explored all the suns in the universe, and all the planets of all the suns, they realized that there was no other life in the universe, and that they were alone. And they were very happy, because then they knew it was up to them to become all the things they had imagined they would find."
          Turns off the cassette player. June picks up tray with the breakfast dishes and goes inside.

Sally says that perhaps she should sell the house in Sun City and use the profits to fix up this place. Ken nods, saying that it's obvious Sally shouldn't be moved. "I'm much too ill to travel . . ." says Sally. Jed agrees.

Inside, Weston calls out for them to come in and listen to the new song he and Gwen have worked up. Ken calls out to Weston that they can hear them fine from where they are. The song begins. It's a gentle ballad. Sally rises.

JED: Are you O.K.?

SALLY: Well, I can walk.

KEN: You're beatin' me.

> *Sally exits into the house. Shirley and Ken and Jed sit on the porch. Shirley begins to cry quietly.*

KEN: What's wrong, doll?

SHIRLEY *(stopping)*: I don't care. The important thing is to find your vocation and work like hell at it. I don't think heredity has anything to do with anything.

KEN: Certainly not.

SHIRLEY: You do realize, though, the terrible burden.

KEN: How's that?

SHIRLEY: I'm the last of the Talleys. And the whole family has just come to nothing at all so far. Fortunately it's on my shoulders.

> *She gets up, with the weight of the burden on her shoulders.*

I won't fail us.

> *She goes into the house. Ken and Jed sit a moment.*

KEN: We had to put in all those damn lilies. If they don't bloom it's your ass. And you and Weston have got to get cinders this afternoon for the penstemon.

JED: Oh, God. And you have to light a candle for him.

KEN: Maybe he'll write us a song.

> *He gets up. Sighs. Picks up the portable recorder.*

I've got to go talk to Johnny Young about the future.

> *Jed leans back. They look at each other a moment. The singers continue. Jed looks out over the garden, still seated. Ken begins to work his way toward the door. The song continues. Curtain.*

THE BEST LITTLE
WHOREHOUSE IN TEXAS

A Musical in Two Acts

BOOK BY LARRY L. KING AND PETER MASTERSON

MUSIC AND LYRICS BY CAROL HALL

Cast and credits appear on pages 424-425

LARRY L. KING (co-author, book) was born in Putnam, Tex. Jan. 1, 1929 and grew up working in the oil fields. He graduated from Texas Tech in 1949 and, after serving in the Army, worked for newspapers in Texas and New Mexico. His free-lance articles have appeared in many publications including Atlantic Monthly, Harper's *and* Esquire, *and it was his* Playboy *article about a beloved Texas small-town institution called "The Chicken Ranch" that inspired the book of* The Best Little Whorehouse in Texas, *its co-authors' first produced work for the stage.*

King has written five books including Confessions of a White Rapist, *nominated for a National Book Award in 1971, and the novel* Emmerich Descending. *In 1972 he won the Stanley Walker Journalism Award of the Texas Institute of Letters. He has been a Nieman Fellow at Harvard, Ferris Visiting Professor of Journalism at Princeton and a Duke University Fellow of Communications. He now lives in Manhattan and is married for the second time. He has three children, two daughters and a son, Bradley Clayton King, who was a member of the original cast of his father's musical.*

"The Best Little Whorehouse in Texas": book by Larry L. King and Peter Masterson; music and lyrics by Carol Hall. Produced by Universal Pictures. Copyright © 1978 by Larry L. King, Peter Masterson and Susannah Productions, Ltd. Lyrics copyright © 1977, 1978 by Daniel Music, Ltd., Shukat Music, a Division of The Shukat Company, Ltd. and MCA Music, a Division of MCA Inc. All rights reserved, including public performance for profit. Any copying, arranging or adapting of the lyrics contained herein without the written consent of the owners is an infringement of copyright. See CAUTION notice on copyright page. All inquiries concerning the use of the lyrics should be addressed to MCA Music, 445 Park Avenue, New York, N.Y. 10022. All other inquiries should be addressed to: The Sterling Lord Agency Inc., 660 Madison Avenue, New York, N.Y. 10021; Writers & Artists Agency, 162 West 56th Street, New York, N.Y. 10019; or The Shukat Company, Ltd., 25 Central Park West, New York, N.Y. 10023.

261

PETER MASTERSON (co-author, book) is an accomplished actor making his playwriting debut with this work, which he also co-directed with Tommy Tune. He has appeared on the New York stage in That Championship Season, *as Officer DiSantis in* The Poison Tree, *as Smitty in* The Great White Hope, *in the title role of* The Trial of Lee Harvey Oswald, *in* Marathon 33 *and in the Actors Studio production of* Blues for Mr. Charlie *which he also played in London. His major screen credits include the male lead in* The Stepford Wives *and a featured role in* The Exorcist.

Masterson is a native Texan born in Houston June 1, 1934 and a graduate of Rice with a B.A. in history in 1957. He decided to turn the story of Texas's Chicken Ranch into the musical The Best Little Whorehouse in Texas *after reading Larry L. King's article about it in* Playboy *four years ago. He is a member of the Actors Studio (where his musical was first put on in workshop) and directed many of their productions as well as others in stock, off and off off Broadway. His wife, the actress Carlin Glynn, is the leading lady of his musical. They have three children.*

CAROL HALL (music and lyrics), a native of Abilene, Kansas, grew up in Texas and became so musically accomplished so early in life that she began her public career as a piano soloist with the Dallas Symphony Orchestra at the age of 12. She was educated at Sweet Briar and Sarah Lawrence, graduating in 1960. Her musical Wonderful Beast *was produced last season at Cafe La Mama, and she also wrote a score for Lion Theater Company's* Love's Labour's Lost OOB. *Like the co-authors of the book of* The Best Little Whorehouse in Texas, *she is making her professional stage debut with this off-Broadway and Broadway production.*

The composer's other work has included the Emmy Award-winning TV special Free To Be You and Me, *and the title numbers for the movies* Death of a Gunfighter *and* Rivals, *while artists like Barbra Streisand, Mabel Mercer, Harry Belafonte, Neil Diamond and Barbara Cook have recorded her songs. She is the author of two books,* I Been There *and* Super-Vroomer. *She lives In New York City and is married, with two children.*

Our method of representing The Best Little Whorehouse in Texas *in these pages differs from that of the other Best Plays. The musical appears here in a series of photographs with synopsis and quotes from the script and lyrics, recording the overall "look" of a 1978 show, with its visually expressive concept and characters as well as its story structure and style.*

The photographs of The Best Little Whorehouse in Texas *depict scenes as produced by Universal Pictures and as directed by Peter Masterson and Tommy Tune, with the musical numbers staged by Tommy Tune, as of the opening April 17, 1978 Off Broadway at the Entermedia Theater, with scenery by Marjorie Kellogg and costumes by Ann Roth.*

Our special thanks are tendered to the producers and their press representatives, Jeffrey Richards Associates, Maurice Turet and Bruce Lynn, for making available these selections from Ilene Jones's excellent photographs of the show.

ACT I

1. The bandleader (Craig Chambers, *above*) tells of "the nicest little whorehouse you ever saw," in business since 1890, called "The Chicken Ranch" because its clients could pay in produce (as *at left*). He sings of "20 Fans" after sundown, when "The little house lay/In the stillness of night":

Twenty fans were turnin
They were turnin
Twenty fans were turnin
In every room
Fevers were a burnin
They were burnin
And they had to have
A way to cool down.

2. The present owner, Miss Mona Stangley (Carlin Glynn, *left*) runs a taut ship. She interviews a pair of waifs nicknamed Shy and Amber (Joan Ellis and Pamela Blair, *right*) looking for jobs. Amber has had some experience, Shy none. Miss Mona decides to take them on and explains the rules: customers are called "guests," not "johns" or "tricks;" no criminal records, no dope habits; no whips, no orgies, no kissing on the mouth; and come running when Miss Mona rings the bell. "Mostly we get a nice quiet group and I'd like to keep it that way," Miss Mona declares, adding comments in the song "A Lil' Ole Bitty Pissant Country Place" (opposite page).

3. MISS MONA (*sings*):
It's just a little bitty
                    pissant country place
Nothin much to see
No drinkin allowed
We get a nice quiet crowd
Plain as it can be

It's just a piddly squattin
                    ole time country place
Nothin too high toned
Jes lots of good will
And maybe one small thrill
But there's nothin dirty going on!

4. Miss Mona mentions other advantages of her stern leadership: never any trouble with the law, and "There's a group rate on Blue Cross." She pays special attention to Shy, who hangs her head when Miss Mona, trying to find out what Shy is doing here, asks her "Did your Daddy get sweet on you, honey?" Miss Mona comforts Shy in song, "Girl, You're a Woman".

As Miss Mona sings, the other girls enter and prepare Shy for action with new dress, hairdo and makeup — so successfully that the first arrival chooses Shy out of the group (as in photo *at left*), and she leads him upstairs.

5. On a local TV show, Melvin P. "Watchdog" Thorpe (Clint Allmon, *above left, "wearing a preposterous silver wig and a broad holier-than-thou smile"*) and his choir are viewing with moral alarm the existence of the Chicken Ranch.

MELVIN (*sings*):
  Texas has a whorehouse in it!
CHOIR (*sings*):
  Lord have mercy on our souls.
MELVIN (*sings*):
  I'll expose the facts
  Although it fills me
                      with disgust . . .

Please excuse the filthy,
                      dark details
And carnal lust. . . .
I'll uproot and I'll crusade
I can smell corruption and I'll
                      fight it to the top!
Loveless copulation goin on
And it must stop!

6. Meanwhile, back at the Chicken Ranch the girls are decorating the place for the annual Thanksgiving visit of seniors on the winning team of the big Texas U-Texas Aggies game. Jewel (Delores Hall, *right*), Miss Mona's helper, sings to the girls about her day off which, like the title of her song, is "Twenty-four Hours of Lovin' ".

7. Sheriff Ed Earl Dodd (Henderson Forsythe, *right*) comes to talk to Miss Mona about "Watchdog" Thorpe: "If that television idiot goes on stirrin folks up it's liable to mess up your playhouse. Mine too, for that matter" if people get to believing that the Sheriff is taking protection money from his old friends, which he isn't. Miss Mona thinks it will blow over, but the Sheriff isn't so sure. Politics and law enforcement aren't what they used to be.

The Mayor notifies Sheriff Dodd that Thorpe and his crew have set up by the courthouse and are staging a public demonstration against the Chicken Ranch. The Sheriff goes to order them off the street, but Thorpe defies him: "We're perfectly within the law here, Sheriff Dodd. As a newsman I've got First Amendment protection. The public has a right to know what's going on out here, and what kind of payoff you're acceptin to protect a notorious house of ill repute."

Sheriff Dodd informs Thorpe: "First thang. First thang is you're standin in Lanville County which by my figgerin is about a hunnert miles west of that sinkhole you call Houston, and I can't see it's a whole lot of business of yours what goes on here. Now, number two. Number two is, you ain't an officer of the law and I am, and this is my pea patch you're in. So don't go tryin to tell me what my Goddam job is. . . ."

The Sheriff's language causes one of the town's church ladies to make a hasty departure, but he has barely warmed to his task: "Three! No sawed off little shit is gonna accuse me of takin a bribe and live to tell it, 'cause I wear the badge in this Goddam county and if I get any madder I'm gonna blow your ass all the way back to Harris County and you can go see the Goddam Civil Liberties Union in tiny little pieces. If I ever see any one of you sorry shitheads in this town again, I'm gonna lock up your ass until your baby's grown. If I even dream that any one of you bastards even thought about driving through here I'm gonna hunt you down like a hound dawg would a coon. (*He fires his pistol into the air and before the echo dies the street is empty.*) Goddam wig-wearin citified son-of-a-bitch!"

8. At the Texas Twinkle Cafe, leading citizens including the newspaper editor (Don Crabtree, *right* in photo *above*) are worrying about the attention the town seems to be getting. They're particularly concerned lest Thorpe get wind of the annual visit of the football players. Sheriff Dodd stands up for the Chicken Ranch and Miss Mona. On his way out, he remarks, "Well, I gotta get myself on back to my office so's that everybody can call me up and tell me we've got a whorehouse operatin here for about a hunnerd and fifty years."

As the others talk, the waitress, Doatsey Mae (Susan Mansur, *left* and *above*), thinks her own thoughts and sings them aloud:

> Some girls have crazy
> Secret thoughts
> That can really make 'em fly
> Some girls can even
> Do the things
> They maybe think they'd like to try
> I wanted to . . . I wanted to
> But I never could
> Doatsey Mae . . . Plain as grey
> Respectable . . . Doatsey Mae
> Day by day
> Respectable . . . Doatsey Mae
> The one nobody thinks of havin
> > dreams
> Ain't as simple as she seems
> Doatsey's not as simple as she *seems*.

9. At the big game, the Angelettes (*above:* "53 per cent of these girls are enrolled in the School of Religion") cheer as the Aggies win. The Aggie seniors celebrate in their locker room and anticipate (*below*) the rewards of victory at the Chicken Ranch, singing:

We been deprived so long
But now we're gettin some . . .
I bet the girls are countin up
The minutes till we come. . . . .
We gonna whomp . . . And stomp
And whoop it up tonight

Those little gals won't never
                  ever be the same
We gonna whomp . . . And stomp
And whoop it up all right
It's even better than
             a Aggie football game

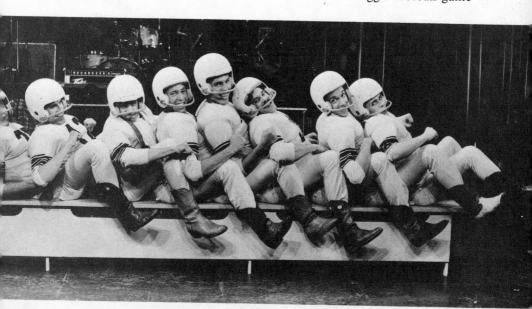

10. Aggies and a Senator escorting them are securely tucked in for the night. The Sheriff comes by to see that all is quiet. He and Miss Mona remember 20 years ago when he was a hell-raiser and she had just stepped off the bus from Amarillo. She had been meaning to go all the way to San Antone — but then something happened, as she recollects in song:

Caught a bus from Amarillo
It was goin to San Antone
Had a brand new cardboard suitcase
And a window seat alone.
And I thought that I was somethin
And I dreamed I'd travel far
Maybe be a restaurant hostess
Maybe be a movie star. . . . .

And the bus from Amarillo
Raced a train along the track
But I never looked behind me
'Cause I wasn't comin back . . . . .

Well it's hard now to determine
How a plan just disappears
How the days can turn to weeks
And how the weeks can turn to years
It's funny how you wait for things
And want that lucky day
And it's funny, when the bus stopped
I got off and walked away.

And the bus from Amarillo
I can hear it still go by
Guess I missed my only chance
And now I swear I don't know why.

11. While Miss Mona is singing, the Sheriff falls asleep. Suddenly . . . RAID! Thorpe and his cohorts have arrived. Sleepers and non-sleepers (*left*) are interrupted, and pandemonium reigns at the Chicken Ranch. *Curtain*.

ACT II

12. Following the raid, "Watchdog" cavorts with his Melvin P. Thorpe singers (*above*), and the girls are downcast at the disruption of their activities (*below*). The Senator quickly explains to the press that he has no recollection of coming to the Chicken Ranch and must have been doped by "Commonists". The Governor arrives and is questioned about the future of the Chicken Ranch (*next page*).

13. The Governor (Jay Garner, *right*) makes himself perfectly unclear. He's for virtue and knows Miss Mona only by name. He backs Thorpe but leaves it up to the local authorities to close the Ranch. He sings:

OOOOOOOOO! I love to dance
           the little sidestep
Now they see me, now they don't
I've come and gone . . .
OOOOOOOOO! I love to sweep
           around a widestep
Cut a little swath and
Lead the people on.

14. A crowd has gathered, chanting "We're gonna close Miss Mona." Miss Mona disperses them by firing shotgun into the air, then sends the girl to their rooms to keep out of sight.

Alone with Jewel (*left*), Miss Mona admits that Sheriff Dodd can't handl this problem, though there was a tim . . . she remembers a weekend i Galveston with the Sheriff, watchin Kennedy's inauguration on TV: "Tha was high cotton for me, fresh out of th Panhandle. I wasn't no older than Sh and he must have been past forty then I'd never seen salt water, I remembe the sun was shinin and the water out i the Gulf was so blue it ached my eyes."

When they got home, the Sheriff gav her a gown, and she "never felt mor like Cinderella."

Jewel sympathizes with Miss Mona then sings "No Lies":

Who said life was a roller coaster?
Who said life was a sweet surprise?
Who said life was a circus poster?
Not me! . . . Not me!
So, ask me no questions
Give me no answers
And I'll tell you no lies.

15. On the street, the town is divided pro and con the Chicken Ranch. But the town fathers deplore the publicity, and the Governor phones — he's under pressure. Sheriff Dodd knows he must close Miss Mona's place, even though (as he sings, alone in his office, *right*), she's a "Good Old Girl":

Well, she's a good old girl
We've been some long, long miles together
And thank the Lord
         she never was the clingin kind . . .

Never talked no foolish talk
Had no ties and held no rules
Hell, that good old girl and me
We ain't, we ain't damn fools you know.

We never talked too much
We didn't hold to conversation
There's lots of things I could have
            told her . . . I suppose
But what I would want to tell that good old girl
She knows.

16. At the Chicken Ranch, some of the girls (*left*) sing about what they plan to do next — sleep late, dye their hair, lose some weight, travel far away, bounce back, etc. But for all of them, their song agrees, it looks like a "Hard Candy Christmas" coming up.

17. *Above,* Thorpe receives his reward for vigilant citizenship from the Governor and the Senator (J. Frank Lucas, *right*). Miss Mona and her girls are leaving the Ranch as ordered by Sheriff Dodd, who comes to say goodbye (*below*). She is resigned, but he deplores this result of political expediency: "It just got outa hand. It ate me up before I knowed it was hungry!"

18. Miss Mona is headed for a farm, where she hopes Sheriff Dodd will visit her sometimes. The Sheriff starts to leave, but she stops him, asking him if he remembers where he was when Kennedy was inaugurated. He remembers the speech, but . . . he remembers much better where he was when Kennedy was shot: "Yeah, I'd just picked up three Meskin kids — they'd stole theirselves a goat from old man W.B. Starr and was throwin theirselves a barbecue. . . . . It's funny, there's just certain thangs you just can't hardly forget."

"A-men to that, Ed Earl," Miss Mona declares, and the Sheriff makes a rapid exit. Alone, Miss Mona ruminates while the band sings:

Oh the little house lay
In a green Texas glade
Where the trees were as coolin
As fresh lemonade
The soft summer wind
Had a trace of perfume
And a fan was turnin
In every room.

Twenty fans were turnin
They were turnin
Twenty fans were turnin
In every room
Fevers were a burnin
They were burnin
And they had to have
A way to cool down.

MISS MONA (sings:)
   It was just a little ole bitty pissant *country* place.

Miss Mona rings the bell wistfully (*left*), but this time no one is going to answer. *Curtain.*

Jack Lemmon in *Tribute*

TRIBUTE

A Play in Two Acts

BY BERNARD SLADE

Cast and credits appear on page 378

BERNARD SLADE was born May 2, 1930 in St. Catherines, Ontario, the son of an aircraft mechanic. He left Canada at age 5 for England, where he went to school until he was 18, after which he returned to Canada as an actor. He worked in stock and TV for a decade. He also became a producer when, in 1954, he opened and maintained a theater in Canada between Vineland and Niagara Falls.

In 1957 Slade branched out into writing. His first produced work was the one-hour TV play The Long, Long, Laugh, *the first of more than 100 Slade scripts which have been televised by the Canadian Broadcasting Corporation, the B.B.C. and all three American networks. It was six more years before his debut as a playwright with* Simon Says Get Married *at the Crest Theater in Toronto, followed by* A Very Close Family *at the Manitoba Theater (also produced as a two-hour TV play).*

Slade made his New York debut with the comedy hit Same Time, Next Year, *which opened March 13, 1975, was 1,344 performances old and still running at the end of the present season and was named a Best Play of its year. He made it two in a row with this season's* Tribute, *starring Jack Lemmon, which arrived in New York in May (and held its formal opening June 1) thus placing its author in a position almost unheard-of for anybody but Neil Simon, that of having more than one show running on Broadway.*

Slade recently returned to acting with his wife Jill for a brief stint in an Edmonton production of his own Same Time, Next Year *(which has already had 33 foreign productions). His writing credits also list the screen plays* Stand Up and Be Counted *and* Same Time, Next Year. *He and his wife now live in Los Angeles, and they have two children.*

"Tribute": by Bernard Slade. Copyright © 1978 by Bernard Slade. Reprinted by permission of the author's agent. See CAUTION notice on copyright page. Inquiries concerning stock and amateur acting rights should be addressed to: Samuel French, Inc., 25 West 45th Street, New York, N.Y. 10036. All other inquiries should be addressed to the author's representative: Jack Hutto.

Time: The present

Place: The living room of a New York townhouse and on the stage of a New York Theater

ACT I

Scene 1: Tonight and a morning three months ago

SYNOPSIS: The theater itself is the setting for the play's beginning. The stage is masked by a scrim with a huge Al Hirschfeld line drawing of Scottie Templeton. Lou Daniels *("a chunky, affable New Yorker in his early 50s who looks older than his years")* comes out in front of the curtain at right and commands the houselights to dim (they do). Lou explains what he is doing and what the audience is doing in this theater at this time: we are gathered here as a tribute to our old friend Scottie Templeton who has given us "the gift of friendship and the gift of laughter . . . . . he has so many friends the only place we could fit them all was in a theater."

Lou has some notes for a speech, but he crumples them into his pocket and ad libs about his own friendship with Scottie, which began in their early teens. They met in an elevator. "It was jammed with people all facing front, not saying a word as we went from the first to the fifteenth floor. Scottie was the first one off. A few feet from the elevator, he suddenly stopped, turned, held up his hands and said, 'Hold it a minute, everybody! I've got this great idea! Let's all meet a year from today.' I was the only one who laughed and we've been friends ever since."

Another particular friend of Scottie's, Dr. Gladys Petrelli *("50s, shrewd, maternal and approachable"),* appears in front of the curtain at left. She tells us how Scottie used to be something of a hypochondriac. As she does so, the stage behind the scrim is gradually illuminated while the proscenium bulbs start to dim, so that the theater setting slowly disappears (and the scrim rises) and Scottie Templeton *("51 but looks ten years younger. An elegant, charming, pixieish man. A mixture of Noel Coward, the Marx Brothers and Peter Pan")* becomes visible in a town house living room setting. Scottie is wearing a dressing gown and playing a composition of his own he calls "Scottie's Unfinished" on the piano. The living room is split-level, furnished in a comfortable modern style, with kitchen door at left, front door at center and stairs leading to a landing and the bedrooms up right.

While Scottie is playing, Sally Haines, *"a beautiful girl in her early 20s"* who works occasionally as a model, comes out of one of the bedrooms upstairs and stands on the landing. She is trying to explore Scottie's personality by throwing conversational curves at him. They've just met in the hospital, where Scottie went for tests and Sally was getting over an appendectomy, Scottie made Sally's acquaintance by putting on a doctor's robe and pretending to examine her. Sally came home with Scottie, but they have not yet been to bed together. Sally comes downstairs and goes to the kitchen, fixing breakfast and answering questions through the open door, while Scottie continues to favor her with his "Unfinished" on the piano.

Sally finally emerges from the kitchen with a tray of coffee. Scottie shows her how to push a button to make a revolving bar appear, fully equipped with all other libations.

SALLY: Hey, that's terrific. You sure have a neat place. You a writer?
SCOTTIE *(handing her coffee)*: In another life — well, a screen writer, really.
SALLY: Any I might have seen?
SCOTTIE: Not if you're lucky.
SALLY: You didn't like being a writer?
SCOTTIE: I loved being a writer. I just hated writing.
SALLY: How come?
SCOTTIE: Because you have to be in a room all alone. I like to mix. What I *really* should have been is a headwaiter.
SALLY: What do you do now?
SCOTTIE: I'm in public relations.
SALLY: What does that involve?
SCOTTIE *(he thinks for a second)*: Actually, it's a lot like being a headwaiter.
SALLY *(grins, checks watch)*: Ooops, I have to get to the unemployment office.
She moves to telephone, writes on pad.
I'll leave you my full name and telephone number. I'm available for parties, afternoon teas, conversation or almost anything.
SCOTTIE: There's no need for you to rush off, you know. You're welcome to stay and play with me.
SALLY: Thanks, but I'm sure you want to be alone with your son.
SCOTTIE: No, as a matter of fact, the first few hours are usually a bit awkward.
She picks up a small, framed photo.
This him?
SCOTTIE: Took it himself. He's always been good with a camera.
She puts photo down, picks up suitcase, looks at him.
SALLY: I want to thank you. I laughed so hard my stitches hurt.
SCOTTIE: Come here and give me a kiss. Right here.
He indicates his cheek. She moves to him and goes to kiss the spot he's pointing to on his cheek. At the last second, he turns his face so that she kisses him flush on the lips. He grins at her surprise.
I didn't think a big-city girl like you would fall for an old gag like that.
SALLY *(grins)*: I didn't. *(Exits.)*

Sally has just left when the doorbell rings. Scottie believes it's his son Jud, whom he expects momentarily, and calls out for him to come in, the door's unlocked. But his caller is Maggie Stratton, Jud's mother *("Scottie's first wife, mid-40s, feminine, intelligent, sympathetic")*, carrying one of Jud's suitcases while Jud unloads the rest of his stuff from the taxi. Scottie and Maggie embrace warmly and he catches up on his ex-wife's news: Maggie, married to a professor and the mother of two children by him, has come to New York to visit her father in a nursing home (Scottie has visited him recently, too, which amazes Maggie).

Jud enters, banging his luggage against the doorway. He is *"shy, intelligent, awkward and intense"* and embarrassed when Scottie suggests that his son give him a bear hug. Maggie announces that Jud has landed a part-time teaching job at Berkeley which will help with his tuition. Jud has decided he wants to be a teacher.

SCOTTIE: I thought you wanted to be a playwright.

JUD *(surprised)*: How'd you know that?

SCOTTIE *(easily)*: Oh, I try and keep up. *(Jud looks at him.)* I read that play you wrote a couple of years ago.

JUD: Oh?

SCOTTIE: It was wonderful.

JUD: Thanks, but Mom said you once told Sonja Henie she was a great actress.

SCOTTIE: Well, I thought you both needed encouragement. Anyway, didn't it win some sort of workshop production?

JUD: Yes — but it just confirmed my suspicions that the stage is no longer a valid platform for a serious writer.

SCOTTIE *(gently)*: Play was that much of a disaster, huh?

JUD *(dryly)*: Well, nobody said anything I could use in the ads.

SCOTTIE: Jud, at the risk of sounding like an elder statesman, don't you think you should go around the track a couple more times before settling for a seat in the grandstand?

Jud answers him, gravely describing the options a teaching career would offer if he gets his Ph.D. His job at Berkeley is suppose to start right now, but he has put it off a week so that he can visit his father.

SCOTTIE: A week? You're only going to be here a week?

JUD: If it's O.K. with you.

SCOTTIE: Well, I wish you'd consulted me.

JUD: I would have, but — *(A slight shrug.)* — I knew it wouldn't make much difference to you one way or the other.

>   *Scottie watches Jud as he moves up the stairs and exits with his bags.*
>   *He then turns to Maggie.*

SCOTTIE: Look, I know we kid around a lot, but I'd like to ask you a serious question. Who's his father? The Japanese gardener? I mean, there's not one single thing about the kid that's like me. Level with me — was it the pool man with the tight jeans and the tattoo? *(Maggie does not speak.)* How is he?

MAGGIE: He put himself through college with extra jobs, he graduated summa cum laude, he looks out for the other two kids, he's never touched drugs or alcohol and he keeps his room clean.

SCOTTIE: Yeah, he worries me. *(She grins.)* Well, doesn't he worry you? I mean, the kid's twenty years old and he dresses like he's out of a Chekhov play.

Scottie remembers that Jud wasn't always so serious — he used to fall down laughing when Scottie put on his chicken costume (Jud was eight years old at the time). Scottie feels it's very important for father and son to get to know each other. Maggie senses that Scottie has something to tell her, and Scottie confesses that he has just been to the hospital for a checkup and has been told the worst: a blood disease, fatal "no mistake and no cure . . . . . it was right out of *Dark Victory."*

Scottie is trying to joke about it and to comfort himself with the knowledge that he's lived exactly the life he chose. He's told no one else about his illness and only brought it up now because of Jud — he wishes the boy would stay longer. Scottie feels he has something of value to transfer to his son: "My first idea was to leave him a list of the two hundred best maitre d's in the country and what to tip them for a good table. After I got that nonsense out of my system, I figured out that the one thing I know how to do well is have fun. If I could teach him that, it's something."

Scottie asks Maggie to talk Jud into staying longer than a week (he's afraid if he tells Jud about being sick it will upset him). She goes upstairs to try, as Lou Daniels comes in with a handful of phone messages that have been piling up because Scottie has taken his phone off the hook. Two of them are from Scottie's doctor. Lou is curious about them, but Scottie puts him off.

Maggie comes back and sends Lou out to get her a cab while she tells Scottie it's all set — Jud considers his father's request for a longer visit after two years' absence a reasonable one. Maggie exits after promising to come back this evening for a drink.

Jud enters, and Scottie thanks him for agreeing to stick around awhile. He promises Jud a date with an exceptional girl, but Jud (who is loading and testing his camera equipment) is not much interested. He'd rather make his own friends.

SCOTTIE: Hey, whatever happened to that girl friend you had in Pennsylvania?
JUD *(puzzled)*: What girl?
SCOTTIE: No, that's not it! You're supposed to say "Erie?" and then I say, "Well, I always thought she was a little *weird."*
    Jud is still looking at him in a puzzled fashion.
It's an old vaudeville routine we used to do. Don't you remember?
JUD: I had to be six years old then.
SCOTTIE: But we used to do it practically every day. My God, how could you forget it?
JUD *(dryly)*: Maybe it's because I always had to play straight man.
SCOTTIE: Kid, you're no trouper.

Lou comes back and wants to talk business, but Scottie prefers to show Jud an old family album, with a picture of Jud's grandfather as he looked in World War I. Lou insists, and Scottie gives advice on a couple of public relations problems: a TV talk-show host wants to come out of the closet, a producer wants to talk to Scottie at a midtown hotel. Lou finally leaves, but not before advising Scottie that he doesn't look too well and ought to be taking it a bit easy.

Jud is studying a photo of Scottie's mother — an English woman — whom Jud never knew. Scottie doesn't approve of Jud's clothing and wants to take him to a tailor at once, but Jud wants to visit an exhibition at the Museum of Modern Art this morning. Scottie suggests, then, that they spend the afternoon at the track or at a 42d street divertissement. Jud fails to get the point of all this effort and attention from his father.

SCOTTIE: There is no point. It's called "having a good time."
JUD: Well, I'd prefer to have a good time my own way, okay?
        He checks watch.
I'll see you later, huh?
        Scottie nods and turns away. Jud moves to the front door.
SCOTTIE *(suddenly — abruptly)*: I want to spend time with you, Jud!
        Jud turns and looks at Scottie, too surprised at his tone to say anything.
I mean I'd like to catch up with what you've been doing with your funny little life.
JUD *(slightly puzzled)*: Sure. I'll be around. *(Exits.)*

Scottie phones Sally Haines and suggests that she go to the Museum of Modern Art this morning and pretend to have a chance meeting with his excessively shy son, as the lights fade on the living room.

Scene 2: That night

The lights come up on Hilary *("a blonde, crisp, well-groomed, attractive woman in her 30s")* on the stage of the theater, telling the gathering how she used to be in the "entertainment business" and Scottie first availed himself of her services and then became her friend. It was Hilary's ambition to save enough money to open a travel agency, but she was short of her goal when she was brought low by two arrests and an illness. She was contemplating doing away with herself. But Scottie breezed in and invited her to the Hilton Hotel where, it turned out, he'd organized a banquet in her honor, attended by a hundred of her former clients at $250 a plate. Three days later she was in the Bahamas, starting her travel agency.

The light on Hilary dims. When it comes up in the living room Jud and Sally — who, it seems, managed to make his acquaintance at the museum as suggested by Scottie — are sitting on the floor with a blanket and a bag of food, having a picnic. Sally pretends that she's never been here before and is impressed with the apartment. Jud tells her he has a hard time meeting girls, and Sally agrees: "I practically had to tackle you around the knees to stop you leaving the museum."

Jud explains that he began stuttering as a child and when the stuttering stopped, the awkwardness remained. Jud describes his father as "very — you know — glib. No — socially adept" and remembers how he used to jot down funny things in a notebook during the winter to tell his father when he saw him in the summer. But this device failed to make the contact easier for Jud. He decided to visit his father this summer because "I realized my father and I were both getting older and that this was probably the last chance we'd have to — reach some understanding."

Sally teases Jud, and, on impulse, he kisses her just as Scottie comes in the front door. Jud proudly presents Sally to his father, who declines their invitation to join the picnic until after he's fixed himself a drink. Sally offers to do it for him and, without thinking, presses the hidden button that makes the bar appear — a dead giveaway to Jud that's she's been in this apartment before. Instantly, Jud comprehends that Scottie arranged for him and Sally to meet.

SCOTTIE *(turns to Jud who is hurt and angry but is trying to cover it)*: Listen, son, I think I can explain —

JUD: Oh, come on, Dad — I knew it was a setup all along.

SALLY *(surprised)*: You did? How?

JUD: I checked in the mirror this morning and I'm not Robert Redford.
      They are both looking at him. He attempts a laugh.
Hey, who do you think you're dealing with here? I happen to be a college graduate.

SALLY: But if you knew from the start, why did you go along with it?

JUD: Listen, I never said my father didn't have *taste*. I mean I'm no dope. *(Jud turns away to the picnic.)*

SALLY: I'm really sorry, Jud.

JUD: There's nothing to be sorry about. Listen, are we going to eat or what?

SALLY *(turns to Scottie, shrugs)*: I guess I overplayed my role, Scottie.

SCOTTIE: There's no harm done, my love. It seems you got the part anyway.
      He checks wrist watch.
You know, maybe I should take a small rain check on dinner. I do have a late date and I have to perfume my body and slip into something stunning. *(Moving up stairs. He stops halfway up stairs, turns.)* Sally, don't be put off by the kid's impression of the Reverend Davidson. Underneath that grim exterior, there beats the heart of a sex maniac. At least I hope so — for his sake.

JUD *(with a slight edge)*: Yes — well, if I ever need a reference I'll certainly know where to go.

SCOTTIE *(evenly)*: Sorry, son. There'll be no more cheering from the cheap seats. *(He exits.)*

Sally and Jud agree that Scottie is a charmer. Sally knows perfectly well that Jud never saw through their deception and wonders why it should make him angry when his father was only trying to arrange a good time for him. Jud replies: "My father's made a living from being a court jester and a glorified pimp. Well, I don't like him pimping for me, O.K.?"

Sally resents Jud's implication on her own behalf. She accuses Jud of being "tight-assed" and jealous of his father, leaving him angry and confused as she exits.

Jud starts to clean up the picnic, when the doorbell rings. Jud opens the door and in comes a huge, ridiculous-looking chicken (Scottie in the chicken costume that used to amuse Jud when he was a little child). *"Jud jumps out of the way as the chicken rushes by, settles between the table and couch and lays a large football-sized white egg. Proudly the chicken bows and then collapses on its back on the floor, exhausted. When the egg is laid Jud breaks down into hysterical laughter."*

Jud picks up the egg as Scottie takes off the chicken head — he's glad to see that his son still has a laugh left in him. Scottie apologizes for the Sally incident. Jud admits he over-reacted; he all but called Sally a prostitute. Jud had wanted to impress his father with Sally, with his apparently new-found ability to meet and cope with an attractive female.

The chicken costume (which Scottie doffs) reminds Jud of the past, and of the fact that one day his father split with his mother and just disappeared out of Jud's life without any explanation, then or since. Scottie apologizes — he didn't realize how much his leaving would lastingly affect his son.

Jud indicates that he'd like very much to see Sally again. Scottie advises begging and pleading if it will get her back — even groveling if necessary.

Scottie sits and plays his "Unfinished" on the piano.

JUD: You know, a couple of years ago I came across some of the short stories you wrote before you went to the Coast.
Scottie stops playing.

SCOTTIE: You never told me that.

JUD: They were very good.

SCOTTIE: Not really.

JUD: I thought so.

SCOTTIE: Well, they fooled a lot of people. Story of my life. All the form and none of the ability.

JUD: Why did you stop writing? Didn't you feel you had anything to say?

SCOTTIE: And I didn't even say it very well.

JUD: It was that simple?

SCOTTIE: You really want the long answer? *(Jud sits on the steps. Scottie leans against the railing.)* Okay, when I was about seven — now aren't you sorry you asked? — my father took me to see a Christmas pantomime show. He knew the stage manager, and afterwards we went backstage. Well, if the show was magic — this was heaven. I mean, you'd have to be crazy to choose reality over this. I suppose I used my writing as a ticket to the show. Are we nodding off yet?

JUD: No. I was just thinking it doesn't explain the quality of the work I read.

SCOTTIE: Oh, I'm not saying I was totally without talent. I was a pretty good literary mimic. Good enough to get me to the West Coast, anyway.

JUD: And you stopped writing.

SCOTTIE: Not immediately. When I went to Hollywood, I discovered it was phony, tacky, superficial and vulgar — everything I'd ever wanted. With all these distractions, my concentration — never my strong suit anyway — dwindled to that of a monkey. The obvious solution was to become a producer. The rest, as they say, is show-biz history.

JUD: It doesn't bother you that you have nothing you can point to with any pride?

SCOTTIE: Well, I'd always rather hoped it would be you.
Jud reddens, gets up, stands awkwardly for a moment.

JUD (*formally*): Yes — well, I've enjoyed having this talk.

SCOTTIE: So have I, Mr. Carstairs, and I'll certainly talk to the little woman about that insurance policy.

JUD: I'm sorry. Sometimes — when something effects me emotionally I make inappropriate responses.

SCOTTIE: So do I, son. So do I.

The moment is broken by the front doorbell. Jud opens it to reveal a very angry Dr. Gladys Petrelli.

Scottie's doctor, Gladys, can barely spare Jud a nod. This is not a social visit, but an urgent medical mission (Jud appropriately exits). Gladys is angry because Scottie simply up and left the hospital without notice and has returned none of her calls. It's urgent that treatments begin immediately, Gladys tells him, as he knows very well because they went over it all together. But Scottie objects: "I did some reading and there are some charming little side effects you didn't mention like your hair falling out."

Gladys tries to call the hospital to get Scottie a room, but he absolutely refuses to go. Gladys still insists that it's imperative. Scottie tries, unsuccessfully, to laugh the problem off. Gladys promises him "It won't be all velvet," but with any luck Scottie can lead a fairly normal life after the treatments. She insists that she's coming to get him first thing in the morning. Scottie confesses to her that he's terrified. Gladys professes her friendship for Scottie and promises to knock herself out trying to help him. Finally she exits.

Scottie gets his mind off his troubles by playing a practical joke on his friend Lou Daniels with a fake telephone message. The doorbell rings — it's his ex-wife Maggie coming back to see him as promised. She sits while Scottie fixes her a drink. She notices that he is in a manic mood, which is a sign that he's deeply distressed — not about Jud, whom he feels he'll be able to approach, in time. It's his illness that is depressing him, of course, and Maggie offers herself as a listener if Scottie feels like talking about it. He does, as he fixes himself a drink.

SCOTTIE: Well, it's funny, you don't think about it all the time. At least I don't. I suppose the body has some built-in mechanism. The night they hit me with the news I went through the inevitable "Why me?" stage. I mean, I know some guys who wouldn't be too upset about cashing it all in, but I like it here. Always have. The weird part is that I didn't resent dying. What really bothered me was knowing when. I don't know — somehow it robs the whole event of spontaneity.

By now he has his drink and is standing on the platform above the couch where Maggie is still sitting.

I wished that I could drink more or get religion, but too much liquor makes me sick and somehow God never caught my attention. Eventually, "Why not me?" I accepted it. At this point I somehow expected some incredible revelation — but — (*He shrugs, gives a little laugh.*) It reminds me of the time I went to see a Pinter play. Halfway through, I turned to a silver-haired old lady who was sitting next to me and said, "Do you understand any of this?" She patted my hand and said, "Don't worry, my dear — all will be revealed in the last act." At the

Robert Picardo and Jack Lemmon in *Tribute*

final curtain, I looked at her and she slowly shook her head and said, "Well, I'm none the wiser."

Maggie has to go home the next day but offers to come back to New York soon if Scottie needs her. Her kindness brings sudden, unexpected tears to Scottie's eyes. Maggie comes over to comfort Scottie, cradling his head in her arms, kissing him lightly. Scottie pulls her toward him and kisses her more meaningfully, bringing her into a passionate embrace while commenting, "Times have changed. I used to laugh you into bed" The lights fade on the living room.

Scene 3: Later that night

The lights come up on Lou on the stage at the tribute, telling a story about how Scottie, as a network TV producer, was in the middle of a loud policy argument and didn't say a word for a long time. Finally, he took charge, firmly, and told the meeting: "I'm the producer of the show, I'm the one who's ultimately responsible, and I want you to know one thing — I'll go either way."

Scottie got his laugh but lost his job, Lou tells the gathering, as the lights fade on the stage and come up in the living room where Scottie and Maggie, who is dressed in Scottie's bathrobe, are amusing themselves playing a post-coitus Noel Coward scene. Scottie reviews their past through rose-colored memory: "I don't remember you ever yelling at me." Maggie can remember more accurately: "I could never *find* you. You should have been around when your child support checks bounced."

Nevertheless she holds no grudges, she has been generous enough to help Scottie feel somewhat alive again, but she knows perfectly well that their marriage failed because they were ill-matched, and it could never be revived.

As Maggie goes in to the other room to get her clothes, Jud comes back unexpectedly early, having been sent home by Sally because she thinks he ought be spending more time with his father, and anyway she hasn't quite recovered from her operation. Maggie comes in not knowing Jud is there, dressed in blouse and slip, looking for her skirt. Jud grasps the situation immediately and is infuriated, ignoring his mother's efforts to explain, accusing his father (who is perfectly willing to assume any blame): "I have a-a totally amoral — irresponsible, selfish child for a father who doesn't c-c-care who he hurts as long as he gets his own way! . . . . . How does it feel to-to — *(Close to angry tears.)* — cheapen everything you touch."

Jud pushes past his mother and goes upstairs to get his things. Scottie stamps off in the other direction, out the front door. When Jud comes down and heads for the door, Maggie stops him.

MAGGIE: Jud, you can't leave him.
JUD *(as he grabs coat)*: Why not?
MAGGIE: Because he's dying.
JUD: What?
MAGGIE: He found out a couple of days ago. That's why you can't leave him now.

Jud stands for a long moment, his face expressionless, then he drops his stuff and sits facing out front on the steps.

JUD *(finally)*: Well, I wish I could feel something. But it doesn't really change anything, does it? He's still the same man he's always been.

MAGGIE: He's still your father.

After a long moment he gets up, picks up his bags.

Jud, you'll stay?

JUD: I owe it to myself. I'm going to stick around to see if there's anything about the son of a bitch I can admire.

He moves slowly up the stairs, as the curtain falls.

ACT II

Scene 1: Tonight and the next morning three months ago

On the stage of the theater at the tribute Lou is describing some of the other adventures of Scottie's life: blackjack dealer in Reno, husband of a lady jock, tour guide, etc., etc., "but his real talent was for friendship."

Lou introduces one of Scottie's newest friends, Sally, who tells a story about Scottie trying to get her little dog onto a New York bus. The lights fade on the stage and come up in the living room the morning after the previous scene. Maggie is still there, alone, asleep on the couch. Scottie wakes her with his arrival home after a night of soul-searching, contemplation and rejection of the possibility of suicide, and finally an all-night gin game.

Maggie tells Scottie Jud finally calmed down and didn't leave after all (she pretends she didn't tell Jud about Scottie's condition). Maggie goes to ger her coat. As she is leaving, Scottie gives her his cheek to kiss — and to her surprise, at the last moment he does *not* turn his head to receive her kiss on the lips.

Scottie phones his doctor and finds that she is not in. He leaves no message. Jud appears on the balcony upstairs with a book in his hands. He comes downstairs to speak to his father.

JUD: Look — about last night. I guess I flew off the handle and said some —

SCOTTIE: Everything you said was true, Jud.

JUD: Then why did you let it happen?

SCOTTIE: A couple of years ago I was in England and stopped in a wayside inn. On the menu they had a cheese sandwich and a ham sandwich. I asked the waitress if I could have a ham and cheese sandwich. She said, *(Using Cockney accent.)* "Oh, I don't know if I can do that, do I?" I suggested they simply combine the two sandwiches and I'd pay for both. "Well, I'm going to 'ave to ask 'im, won't I?" She went off and had a lengthy discussion with the owner and then came back and said, "No, he can't do it." I asked why on earth not. "He said if we do that who knows where it would all end."

JUD *(puzzled)*: I don't understand why you told me that story.

SCOTTIE: All my life I've never given any thought to where any situation would all end. Last night I'm afraid I overdid it.

JUD *(edgily)*: Why is it that with you everything has to have a punch line?

SCOTTIE *(irritably)*: Because anybody can write the straight lines! Look, I'm very tired right now. We can talk about it later.

JUD: Let's just forget it.

   The doorbell rings. Jud moves towards front door, stops and turns.
Look, is it okay if I stick around for the summer?

SCOTTIE: That's up to you, Jud.

Jud opens the door — it's Sally with a bag of bagels and lox, coming in to brighten up their morning. Jud brings up the subject of the talentless friends, actors and directors, whom Scottie kept hiring for his pictures for friendship's sake, even though, as Jud puts it, "they always screwed up."

The doorbell rings again, ending discussion of this ticklish subject. Scottie sends Jud and Sally into the kitchen to fix breakfast while he admits Gladys, his doctor.

Scottie is still balking at going to the hospital. He remembers a friend who had treatments and was never himself again — not really alive. That was a different matter, Gladys argues — he had a brain tumor. Scottie has a real chance to gain time, she tells him.

SCOTTIE: Give me a break, will ya? Look, I don't want to hang around and *bore* everyone to death. I mean, who wants to leave with the audience wanting less? Don't you understand, Gladys? I've lost all the prelims, maybe I'll be able to win the main event.

   He stops.
Jesus, that line looked better in my head than it sounded.

GLADYS *(getting angry)*: What the hell are you talking about? You think this is one of those dumb movies you wrote?

SCOTTIE: Now wait a minute — do I criticize *your* work?

GLADYS: What about your son?

SCOTTIE *(finally)*: Sometimes you have to cut your losses and run.

GLADYS *(looks at him for a moment, sits)*: How you feeling now?

SCOTTIE: Fine, just fine.

GLADYS: That won't last long.

SCOTTIE: You know, you used to be more fun.

GLADYS: Scottie, exactly what do you plan to do?

SCOTTIE: Try not to think about it.

GLADYS: Then what?

SCOTTIE: Make a nice, clean exit.

GLADYS: How?

SCOTTIE: Well, I was rather hoping you'd provide me with a handy little escape kit.

   She looks at him for a moment.

GLADYS: Scottie, I think it's about time someone told you there's a fine line between being a living legend and a horse's ass.

Gladys wants to explain to him exactly what's wrong with his bone marrow, but Scottie doesn't want to hear the details; he prefers to keep the truth at bay with jokes as long as possible. Scottie is determined not to go to the hospital with Gladys, and he exits upstairs. She sits on the couch, equally determined to take him with her.

Jud enters. Gladys, attacking the problem head-on, tells him, "Your father has a form of leukemia. It's very serious but it's treatable. If he starts treatment right now we may have a good chance of prolonging his life — certainly months, possibly years."

Scottie refuses to go to the hospital (Gladys tells Jud) because he doesn't think he has much to live for. Jud refuses to accept any guilt for this, and he rejects Gladys's request for him to try to talk Scottie into taking the treatments; he feels that it is up to his father to decide for himself. Gladys exits, but not before annoying Jud by telling him, "I just know you can't be the selfish little prig you appear to be."

Sally comes in on the tail end of this conversation and she in turn is annoyed because Jud won't tell her what it was about. Jud apologizes — he admits he's upset because he found his father and mother together the night before. Jud tries to explain why he's so sensitive to this situation: as a child he adored his father, who then disappeared. It took Jud years to adjust.

JUD: . . . . . If you think I don't communicate now you should have seen me ten years ago. I was *not* easy to love. Then my mother met Don, my stepfather. He wanted to be my friend. At this point I wouldn't have accepted the friendship of *God*. But Don wouldn't give up — he just kept chipping away until he got to me. He's a good man. It took a while — but after my mother married him I finally believed it was going to be permanent. It was the one thing in my life I could count on. Last night my father took care of that too.

SALLY: I don't get it. How's anyone going to find out about it?

JUD *(looks at her for a moment; flatly)*: Jesus, you're just like him.

SALLY: Oh, come on, Jud, we'd all like to live neat, ordered, happy-ever-after lives, but it just doesn't work out that way. Sometimes human impulses screw us up.

JUD: I don't understand that sort of morality.

There is a pause.

SALLY: You know, I have a feeling we're never ever going to finish a meal together.

JUD: I can't be dishonest just because I want to go to bed with you.

SALLY *(wryly)*: Just my luck to get mixed up with an idealist.

She gets her purse, moves toward the front door.

You know our problem, Jud? You're too old for me. *(Turns at the door, ruefully regards the food, looks at him.)* I doubt if we'll be seeing each other again but if we do, let's make a pact, huh? Eat first — talk later. *(She exits.)*

Jud in his anger bangs at the piano, as Lou enters. Lou is glad of the chance to talk to Jud, he feels that Jud should make an effort to persuade his father to save himself for all their sakes: "Let me tell you about your father. He's a man who's misused his talent, he's avoided responsibility all his life, he's never been a fan of hard work, he's loused up every chance he ever had, he's squandered his money foolishly — and there's never been a time I didn't look forward to seeing him and I've never spent a moment with him that I wasn't amazed, amused or didn't thoroughly enjoy. And there are hundreds of people who feel just like me."

Jud can't help feeling that his father has never accomplished anything worthwhile. Lou asserts that Jud should appreciate his father's "enormous gift for taking a hamburger and making everyone around him believe they were at a banquet."

The conversation ends abruptly as a loud report is heard from upstairs. The two freeze for an instant, then move to see what has happened. They stop when Scottie appears on the landing in a fresh change of clothes, carrying a just-opened magnum of champagne and calling for orange juice to go with it. Lou goes into the kitchen to get it.

Scottie sits on the sofa and prepares to call some friends to share the champagne. He tries to avoid any serious talk with Jud, but Jud persists, telling Scottie he knows about his condition, not from the doctor, but because his mother told him before she left.

JUD: Naturally, I was sorry to hear the news.

SCOTTIE *(quietly)*: Jesus, you sound like a Hallmark card.

JUD: I'm sorry about that, too.

SCOTTIE: Is that why you decided to stay?

JUD: It's one of the reasons.

SCOTTIE: You don't have to, you know.

JUD: You're going to need all the help you can get.

SCOTTIE: There's really nothing you can do.

JUD: For one thing, I can get you to the hospital.

SCOTTIE *(rises to face Jud)*: Okay, you've made your token attempt. Now I'll say it once and then we'll forget it. I can't think of one good reason for me to change my mind.

JUD: I can. You owe it to me to stick around for as long as you can.

SCOTTIE *(coldly)*: I wasn't aware you held any of my unpaid markers. *(As Jud goes to speak.)* Look, maybe you were justified in your opinion of me last night but it didn't exactly fill me with paternal affection, so just get off my back huh?

JUD: No. You've walked away from every responsibility you've ever had. Well, I'm not going to let you walk away from this one.

Scottie looks at him for a moment.

SCOTTIE: I see. And now you expect me to be suffused with guilt and atone by making some stupid, meaningless gesture.

JUD: It's for your benefit too, you know.

SCOTTIE: My benefit?

JUD: It might just give you some self-respect!

SCOTTIE: This may come as a great surprise to you but I am loaded with self-respect.

JUD: All right, then. Do it for me.

SCOTTIE: Why the hell should I?

JUD: Because I need you. When I needed you before you weren't there. Well, dammit, I need you *now*!

SCOTTIE: Where the hell were you when I needed *you*? It's a two-way street, you know. I mean, where were you when I came back to New York and was beating my brains out trying to get a job? Even the past few years I haven't noticed you rushing down here to keep me company.

JUD: You never insisted I come.

SCOTTIE: That was your choice.

JUD: You shouldn't have given me a choice!

SCOTTIE: Okay, let's just say I'm not the father you always wanted. Has it ever occurred to you that you're not the son I always wanted? Have you ever done one crazy, funny, spontaneous thing in your entire life? Have you ever even tried?

> *There is a muffled banging on the door to the kitchen and Lou's voice.*

LOU *(offstage)*: Can someone get this door?

SCOTTIE: I'm going to tell you one thing, Jud — if that's not comedy relief we're both in a lot of trouble.

JUD *(angrily)*: Why don't you go fuck yourself!

> *He turns, runs up the stairs and exits. Scottie looks after him.*

SCOTTIE: That's spontaneous — not very funny but it's spontaneous.

Lou comes in carrying the tray of orange juice and glasses, hoping that Jud and Scottie have had a nice talk. Scottie explains that he and Jud don't talk, they have interviews, as though Jud were evaluating Scottie's life.

Jud comes downstairs carrying a suitcase. Scottie stares at it. It's Scottie's suitcase, not Jud's; Jud has packed it and is going to take Scottie to the hospital. Jud tells his father, "We need some time . . . . . I'm not ready to cry over you yet," as the lights dim in the living room with Jud and Scottie staring at each other.

Scene 2: Earlier today

The lights come up on the stage at the tribute, where Maggie is telling the gathering how Scottie loved to have people around, as on this occasion. On the other side of the stage, Jud tells the audience he's taken 2,000 photos of his father during the last three months, while his father was undergoing the treatment for his illness. Jud shows a number of the slides — Scottie in the hospital, Scottie clowning, Scottie feeling terrible, Scottie feeling better, etc. As the slide show ends, the lights gradually come up in the living room. It's the day of Scottie's tribute, and Jud is projecting slides on the wall with his own projector, wearing earphones and selecting music to go with the slide show he's going to present in the theater that evening.

Jud doesn't hear Sally come in (she's carrying a shopping bag and is all dressed for the evening). He finally sees her. They greet each other somewhat awkwardly — they've been avoiding each other for months. Jud wants to apologize to Sally for his earlier behavior — "I had no right to judge your life."

Today is Scottie's birthday. Jud has arranged the gathering at the theater with help from Lou. Everyone is pretending that they have forgotten Scottie's birthday, so that when the celebration starts it'll be a big surprise to him.

> *Scottie appears on the landing. He is wearing a bright blond Harpo Marx wig and carrying his jacket and tie.*

SCOTTIE: Listen, I need your honest opinion. Do you think this tie goes with the suit?

SALLY: Perfect. But only if you carry a horn.

SCOTTIE: Do you happen to know the date, Sally?

SALLY: Uh. *(Gives today's date.)* Why?

SCOTTIE: No reason. *(He exits into bedroom.)*

SALLY: He's exactly the same, isn't he? Only more so.

JUD: Yes. It's amazing.

SALLY: Do you talk much about it?

JUD: Well, you know this place — we're not alone that much. *(He looks up, sees her studying him.)* I tried a couple of times but he didn't seem to want to and — *(He gives a little shrug.)* I admire him too much to invade his privacy.

SALLY: Oh?

JUD *(finally)*: Yes. I have great admiration for the way he's dealt with this whole thing. It must have been very rough for him but he never once complained — at least not to me.

SALLY: You two tied up your "loose ends," huh? *(She sits beside Jud.)*

JUD: Well, I don't know — *(An attempt at lightness.)* — but I've used up a lot of film trying.

SALLY: Are you kidding?

JUD: No. I had this idea that by objectively studying the film I'd — well, I'd be able to bring him into focus. But you know my father — a "master of disguise."

Jud doesn't quite know what he wants from his father and admits "I'm a very peculiar chap." He certainly wishes he'd spent at least some of the time getting to know Sally better.

Lou comes in, preoccupied with details of the surprise: he has people including Maggie stashed in hotels all over town. He notifies Jud and Sally that they are to leave here within 15 minutes.

Scottie enters, wondering why he suddenly isn't getting any phone messages: "For three months the phone rings like I'm Truman Capote and then suddenly it stops." Sally leaves, pretending she has a modeling date, that's why she's all dressed up. Lou goes into the kitchen to make a few calls. Jud is packing up his projector, pretending he's getting ready to go home on a late plane.

Scottie asks Jud why the divorce affected him so deeply, when many children manage to come through similar situations almost unscathed. Jud has finally figured out why: when he was about 8 years old and put to bed in one of the bunks at the pool house because his parents were having a big party in the main house, he was awakened by the sound of laughter in the unlighted room and realized that Scottie was making love to a woman, unaware of the child's presence. Jud recalls that "Six months later you and Mom split up and somehow

Robert Picardo as Jud, Jack Lemmon as Scottie and A. Larry
Haines as Lou in a scene from *Tribute*

in my addled little mind I tied in the whole incident with why you had to go
away. It wasn't of course. At least not that particular woman. *(Scottie, very
shaken, takes out a cigarette, searches for a match. Jud moves to him, lights his
cigarette.)* Look, as I said it was no great tragedy. Today, I could probably handle it but when you're eight years old you're saddled with a very old-fashioned
sense of morality."

Lou comes back and "reminds" Jud that he has to go pick up his airplane
ticket. Jud exits, leaving Scottie perplexed, half-heartedly and unsuccessfully
trying to improve the mood by kidding with Lou. But then even Lou departs,
leaving Scottie alone and restless on this day of all days — his birthday. Scottie
calls the operator to make sure his silent phone isn't malfunctioning.

The doorbell rings. Scottie opens it *"to reveal a woman of indeterminate age
holding a suitcase in one hand and a small card in the other. She is wearing
glasses and a white nurse's uniform, white hose and white orthopedic shoes."*
She identifies herself as a nurse sent by Dr. Gladys Petrelli to take care of Scottie. When Scottie tells her he has no need for any nurse to "push me around in a

wheelchair like Joseph Cotten," she begins to weep because she needs this job —
her husband is out of work. Scottie takes pity on her and fixes her a drink. He
tells her it's his birthday, and she in her turn pities him, feeling sorry that she
didn't bring him some sort of small present, like cookies.

NURSE: . . . . . Well, we'll just to have to make do.
     She starts to unbutton the front of her dress.
SCOTTIE: I beg your pardon?
NURSE *(continues to undress)*: I warn you — it won't be much.
SCOTTIE: What — what are you doing?
NURSE: Look, don't think I do this for everyone — not even on their birthday.
SCOTTIE *(desperately)*: No — listen, it's okay — I'll wait for the cookies!
     She is now in a half slip and a bra and is about to take off the bra.
Seriously — Look, you have a job — you don't have to —
     He stops as he sees the two magnificent breasts in front of him.
     Slowly, recognition comes to his eyes.
Hilary! That's Hilary!
     She takes off glasses and wig.
NURSE (HILARY): Well, I'm glad there are a couple of things about me you
remember. Happy birthday, Scottie!
SCOTTIE *(looking at her breasts)*: Oh Hil — you shouldn't have.
     They embrace happily. Lou, Jud and Sally, holding a tape recorder,
     burst onto the landing.
LOU *(coming downstairs)*: Put that girl down — you don't know where she's
been.
SALLY: We got it all! We got it all on tape!
SCOTTIE: You remembered!
SALLY: Well, we thought you'd like her better than the ship with the clock in
the middle.
LOU: And it's only the beginning.
     Hilary moves to her suitcase, gets dressed in the clothes we saw her
     wearing at the tribute. Scottie looks up at Jud, who has remained on
     the landing.
SCOTTIE: Don't tell me you were in on this thing, too?
JUD *(dryly)*: Yeah, but first they made me promise I wouldn't phone the Vice
Squad.

Lou promises Scottie that there's much more to come and tells Hilary she has
only five minutes to change. He goes off after Sally to the waiting limousine.
Scottie and Hilary reminisce about the old days (she doesn't miss the action but
she misses the applause). Scottie does his trick of extending his cheek and then
turning his head to receive the kiss on the lips. Jud comes onto the landing as
Hilary, having slipped into her dress, is telling Scottie what she particularly likes
about him: he treats everybody the same, movie star and hooker.

HILARY: . . . . . Don't be embarrassed — I wouldn't say it if it weren't true.
Scottie, you're a rare creature — a man with absolutely no order of priorities.

She poses for him.
So what do you think? Do I look respectable enough to escort you to the ball?
SCOTTIE: You look divine. Go ahead love, I'll be right there.
Hilary exits. Jud crosses for Scottie's coat.
Jud, do you concur with Hilary's charming observation that I'm a man with no order of priorities?

JUD: She meant it as a compliment.
SCOTTIE: But you don't think it is.
JUD: Well, I guess I always wanted to be a priority.
SCOTTIE: Is that why you never really wanted to spend much time with me?
JUD *(holding Scottie's coat for him)*: Dad, they're waiting.
SCOTTIE: Don't patronize me! Was that your reason?
JUD: Partly. Mostly I was jealous.
SCOTTIE *(puzzled)*: Of what?
JUD: Of you. I always felt like a clod around you. You said that I wasn't the son you wanted. Well, I always knew that.
SCOTTIE: Jud —
JUD: Oh, I wanted to be. Fantasy time. Anyway, a couple of years ago, I realized that I could never be like you.
SCOTTIE: That's where you're wrong. You're exactly like me. You never made an emotional commitment in your life, either. Don't look so stricken, son. You're still young.
We hear a car horn being honked outside.
What's the matter? Does being a "chip off the old block" scare you that much.
JUD: I don't know. I'm not sure who you are.
The front door flies open to reveal an agitated Hilary.
HILARY: Scottie, if you don't get out of here soon, this damn thing's going to turn back into a pumpkin!
Jud quickly exits. Scottie stands a moment and as he turns to exit the lights dim.

Scene 3: Tonight

The lights come up on the stage at the tribute, where Lou tells the audience that in the last months he's come to realize, with admiration, that Scottie is not only a great guy, he has "the guts of a lion." A spotlight picks up Scottie sitting in a box near the stage, as Lou calls on him to speak.

Scottie steps onto the stage. He's gratified, touched at this demonstration by his friends, so much so that he's at a loss for any coherent, articulate description of his feelings. He throws out a few one-liners, tells about an aunt of his who thought she was a poached egg, addresses a remark to Jud somewhere in the audience about the one thing he'd like most to pass on to him: "If I could wish one thing for you, Jud, it's a passion — for anything — anybody — that will go the distance. *(A beat.)* You see, I never had the guts to risk failure — with you — with anyone — even myself."

Scottie has said all he can think of to say, and he is at a loss for an exit line.

He stands there, more and more embarrassed, until a voice at the back of the theater comes to his rescue.

JUD *(stuttering slightly)*: What about that girl you had in Pennsylvania?
SCOTTIE *(vaguely)*: What?
JUD: What about that girl you had in Pennsylvania?
>*Scottie peers out and we see Jud coming down the aisle, his eyes fixed on his father. He stops halfway down the aisle.*
SCOTTIE *(weakly)*: Erie?
JUD: Well, I had to admit she was a little weird. And what about your brother in Alaska?
>*The two are staring at one another, unsmiling.*
SCOTTIE: Nome?
JUD *(moving down to front of stage)*: Of course, I know'm. He's my uncle.
SCOTTIE *(just staring at him; finally)*: Would you believe that at this late stage of my career — I've forgotten my — lines.
JUD: The cat?
SCOTTIE *(looks at him, puzzled)*: I'm sorry — I'm not used to playing straight man. Did you put out the cat?
JUD: Why? Was he on fire?
>*Scottie doesn't say anything for a long moment.*
SCOTTIE *(finally)*: Come up here and give me a kiss — *(He points to his cheek.)* — here.
>*After a moment, Jud moves up on the stage and crosses to Scottie to kiss him on the cheek where he has indicated. At the last moment Scottie turns his face and kisses him on the mouth. The two embrace and cling tightly to one another. They break and look at one another. They stand for a long moment before Scottie reaches out to tousle Jud's hair in a fatherly gesture, puts his arms around his shoulder and the two move slowly offstage. As they do, Scottie's trousers slowly slip down to around his ankles and he waddles off as the lights slowly dim until the stage is in darkness. Curtain.*

Brian Murray and Barnard Hughes in "*Da*"

"DA"

A Play in Two Acts

BY HUGH LEONARD

Cast and credits appear on page 372

HUGH LEONARD was born in Dublin in 1926. Thirty years later his first long play, The Big Birthday, *was produced at the Abbey Theater. In subsequent decades he won a place among the leading dramatists of the English-speaking stage with a list of more than 20 works including* Mick and Mick, The Patrick Pearse Motel, Madigan's Lock, Some of My Best Friends Are Husbands, Thieves, Summer *and* A Suburb of Babylon.

The first two Leonard scripts produced in New York both appeared the same month, September 1967, off Broadway: The Poker Session *for 16 performances and* Stephen D *(an adaptation of James Joyce's* A Portrait of the Artist as a Young Man *and* Stephen Hero) *for 56 performances. His first and only Broadway production previous to "Da" was* The Au Pair Man, *a two-character allegory of British-Irish relations performed by Julie Harris and Charles Durning and presented by Joseph Papp's New York Shakespeare Festival at Lincoln Center in December 1973 for 37 performances.*

"Da" had its world premiere in the U.S.A. Aug. 7, 1973 at the Olney, Md., Theater. Other pre-New York productions included one at the Ivanhoe Theater in Chicago. The present production was mounted off of Broadway at the Hudson Guild Theater prior to its May 1 appearance on Broadway, where it won the Critics and Tony Awards for the season's best play.

Leonard lives near Dublin with his wife Paule and his daughter Danielle. Among his movie credits are Interlude, Great Catherine *and* Rake's Progress, *and his innumerable TV credits include adaptations of Dickens, Emily Bronte, Flaubert, Maugham, Wilkie Collins, Conan Doyle, de Maupassant and Sean O'Faolain. He was recently named director of the 1978 Dublin Theater Festival, and he writes a column for* Hibernia.

"Da": by Hugh Leonard. Copyright © 1975 by Hugh Leonard. Reprinted by permission of Curtis Brown, Ltd. See CAUTION notice on copyright page. The complete play is published by Atheneum Publishers. All inquiries should be addressed to the author's representative: Gilbert Parker, Curtis Brown, Ltd., 575 Madison Avenue, New York, N.Y. 10022.

Time: May 1968 and, later, times remembered

Place: A kitchen and, later, places remembered

ACT I

SYNOPSIS: In the center at the focal point is a small Irish kitchen-living room surrounded and surmounted by platforms which represent other places: the seaside, a hilltop, etc.

Charlie, in his early 40s, wearing suit, tie and overcoat with mourning band, is sorting papers and burning them in an old-fashioned kitchen range. At the front door, Oliver knocks and enters; he is about Charlie's age, a boyhood friend Charlie hasn't seen for 15 years (Charlie has been living and working abroad, Oliver has stayed home), come to offer his condolences on the death of Charlie's father.

Charlie pours each of them a drink of stout, reminiscing about how he pretended to his mother until the day of her death (when Charlie was 39) that he never took a drink. Oliver is now married, with four children, and his news is that he has finally acquired the theme music from *King's Row*. As Oliver remembers it, "I got billy-ho for going with you to that fillum. My mother wouldn't let me play with you over that fillum."

They remember the girls of their youth, and their ambitions — Oliver is pain-fully conscious of his failure to broaden himself, even though he took the Dale Carnegie course and joined the Rosicrucians. As Oliver is talking, Charlie's dead father — "Da" — comes in from the scullery, makes a caustic remark about Oliver and then goes out again (as though Charlie, listening to Oliver, had suddenly imagined what his father might have thought of this conversation, his thought embodied by his father's actual presence).

Before leaving, Oliver hints that he and his wife would like to get their hands on this house, if Charlie has any influence with the Corporation that owns it. Charlie has no such influence, and Oliver departs, somewhat disappointed.

Charlie faces the empty room. He sits and begins to sort the papers. He whistles loudly to himself. Da comes in. He wears working-man's clothes: Sunday best, polished boots.

CHARLIE *(refusing to look at him)*: Hoosh. Scat. Out.
DA: That wasn't too bad a day.
CHARLIE: Piss off.
    Da sits in his chair. Charlie looks at him.
Sit there, then! No one is minding you.
    He goes on with his sorting, slamming papers down right and left.
DA: I knew it would hold up for you. You were lucky with the weather when you came over at Christmas, too. *(Charlie ignores him.)* Mind, I wouldn't give much for tomorrow. When you can see the Mountains of Mourne, that's a sure sign it'll rain. Yis, the angels'll be having a pee.

CHARLIE *(whirling on him)*: Now that will do!

DA: That's a good expression. Did you ever hear that expression?

CHARLIE: Did I? Thanks to you, until I was twelve years of age every time the rain came down I had a mental picture of a group of winged figures standing around a hole in the clouds relieving themselves. Go away; I'm working, I'm clearing up. *(Working, half to himself.)* Oh, yes, that was him. A gardener all his life, intimately associated with rainfall: i.e., the atmospheric condition of warm air which, when large enough to fall perceptibly to the ground, constitutes precipitation. Hot air rises, the rain falls; but as far as he was concerned the kind of elementary phenomenon was . . .

DA: Codology.

CHARLIE: Codology. No, it was easier and funnier and more theologically oriented to say that the angels were having a pee.

He goes to the range and drops a large pile of papers in.

DA: You ought to put that down in one of your plays.

CHARLIE: I'd die first.

Da sees that Charlie's teacup is empty. Continuing in Charlie's memory to behave as he always did, Da rises and goes to get the teapot but can scarcely handle it, it's so hot. Midway between the stove and Charlie's chair Da has to set the teapot on the floor, worrying, "If herself walks in on us and sees that on the floor there'll be desolation. The gee-gees let her down today, and if the picture in the Picture House was a washout as well she'll come home ready to eat us."

Charlie picks up the pot and puts it back on the range, telling Da, "You're dead. You're in Dean's Grange, in a box, six feet under . . . with her. I carried you . . . it's over, you're gone, so get out of my head."

But as Charlie sorts out his father's belongings, he can't put Da out of his memory. Indeed, very soon his mother, in her late 50s, comes in from the scullery to join them in Charlie's thoughts. They are awaiting the arrival of an important man in the town, Mr. Drumm, who may be able to arrange Young Charlie's future by giving him a reference and who, Da recalls with great pride, once remarked to him, "Tynan, 'clare to God I never seen the beating of you for roses."

Now Young Charlie comes down the stairs, carrying a book, as grown-up Charlie winces at this apparition, this memory of himself as a lad of 17. Young Charlie's mother insists on giving him a fresh shirt for the interview with Drumm, though the boy has been wearing the one he has on for less than a week. The clean shirt is so obviously patched that the boy resists wearing it, but the mother slaps his face and puts the clean shirt on over his head, remarking, "The day you bring money in, you can start being particular. Time enough then for you to act the gentleman. You can do the big fellow in here then, as well as on the sea front."

Drumm arrives and is called "sir" by Da (to Charlie's chagrin) and given a precious cup of rationed tea. Drumm is neatly dressed and tight-lipped and formal in manner as he questions Young Charlie about his education (on scholarship to the Presentation Brothers), his favorite author (Young Charlie answers "Shakespeare") and his future.

DRUMM: And where do your talents lie?

YOUNG CHARLIE: Dunno.

DRUMM: An authority on Shakespeare shouldn't mumble. I asked, what kind of post do you want?

MOTHER: He'll take what he's offered. He's six months idle since he left school. He won't pick and choose.

DA: And if there's nothing for him, sure he can wait. There'll be any amount of jobs once the war's over.

DRUMM: Past history says otherwise. There's usually a depression.

DA: Not at all.

DRUMM: You're an expert, are you?

DA *(a stock phrase)*: What are you talking about, or do you know what you're talking about? The Germans know the Irish are their friends, and sign's on it, when the good jobs are handed out in England they'll give us the first preference.

DRUMM: Who will?

DA: The Jerries, amn't I telling you . . . when they win.

DRUMM: You support the Germans, do you?

CHARLIE *(to Da)*: Shut up. *(To Young Charlie)* Don't go red. Smile.
        Young Charlie summons up an unnatural grin. At once Drumm
        looks at him bad-temperedly.

DRUMM: Is something amusing you?

YOUNG CHARLIE: No.

DA: Hitler's the man that's well able for them. He'll give them lackery, the same as *we* done. Sure isn't he the greatest man under the sun, himself and De Valera?

MOTHER *(not looking at him)*: Now that will do . . .

DA: What the hell luck could the English have? Didn't they come into the town here and shoot decent people in their beds? But they won't see the day when they can crow it over Heil Hitler. He druv them back into the sea in 1940, and he'll do it again now. Sure what's Churchill anyway, bad scran to him, only a yahoo, with the cigar stuck in his fat gob and the face on him like a boiled shite.

Drumm does not react, but suggests that the boy come outside and walk along with him a ways so that Drumm can sound him out. Getting a job in England (where there is work available) at this time is out, because his parents don't want to part with him. Da comments, "There's good jobs going here if you keep an eye out. I'm gardening above in Jacob's these forty-six years, since I was a young lad . . . would you credit that?"

To Young Charlie's aching embarrassment, his mother tells Drumm how they adopted him when he was a ten-day-old foundling in the hospital. They began rearing him on 30 shillings a week (two pounds ten now): "He's more to us than our own." Drumm leaves with Young Charlie, promising to do what he can for the lad, informing Da, who gives him the Nazi salute, "You're an ignorant man."

Grown-up Charlie reproaches his father for not having stopped his mother from telling Drumm about the adoption, haranguing him: "You worked for fifty-eight years, nine hours a day, in a garden so steep a horse couldn't climb it, and when they got rid of you with a pension of ten shillings a week you did hand-springs for joy because it came from the Quality. You spent your life sitting on brambles, and wouldn't move in case someone took your seat."

Mother in her turn declares she's ashamed of Da for talking so about Hitler in front of Drumm and can't blame Young Charlie for feeling ashamed of his father too.

Meanwhile, Drumm and Young Charlie are strolling to the seawall, as Drumm tells the boy never to lie to him again: "Shakespeare is nobody's favorite author." They talk of girls, and of poetry, and of a job as clerk soon to be available in Drumm's office. Young Charlie is elated at the prospect of a secure job, but Drumm warns him that he may be throwing his life away for 45 shillings a week: "You'll amount to nothing until you learn to say no. No to jobs, no to girls, no to money. Otherwise, by the time you've learned to say no to life you'll find you've swallowed half of it."

It's settled, then; Young Charlie is to have the clerking job, and Drumm will need his birth certificate and his real name, not his adopted one of Tynan. The mention of his adoption again embarrasses Young Charlie to the point of tears, and Drumm reproaches him: "Don't give me that woebegone look. It's a fact, you're going to have to live with it and you may as well make a start."

Drumm advises the lad that his mother is a fine woman (even though she *will* tell everyone about the adoption, and Young Charlie can never seem to do enough to please her) but his father is in a sense "the enemy" because Young Charlie is so fond of him.

DRUMM: . . . . Once at a whist drive I heard him say that the world would end in 1940. It was a superstition that had a fashionable currency at one time among the credulous. Well, 1940 came and went, as you may have noticed, and finding myself and the county of Dublin unscathed, I tackled him on the subject. He was unruffled. He informed me that the world hadn't ended because the German bombs had upset the weather.
  Young Charlie laughs boisterously. He bangs his fists on his knees.
  Da enters and rings a doorbell. A doorbell is heard ringing.
Yes, the dangerous ones are those who amuse us.
  The bell is rung again. Da puts his pipe in his pocket and waits.
There are millions like him: inoffensive, stupid and not a damn bit of good. They've never said no in their lives or to their lives, and they'd cheerfully see the rest of us buried. If you have any sense, you'll learn to be frightened of him.
  A light is flashed on Da's face as if a door had been opened.
DA (*saluting*): That's a hash oul' day, ma'am. Certainly you know me . . . Tynan of Begnet's Villas, sure I'm as well known as a begging ass. And do you know what I'm going to tell you? . . . that back field of yours, the meadow: if you was to clear that field of the rocks that's in it and the stumps of trees and had it dug up with a good spreading of manure on the top of it, begod, you wouldn't know yourself. There's bugger-all you couldn't grow in it.
DRUMM: From people too ignorant to feel pain, may the good God deliver us!
DA: The young lad, do you see, he's starting work. Oh, a toppin' job: running an office, sure he's made for life. And the way it is, I'd think bad of him starting

off without a decent suit on his back or the couple of good shirts. Sure you couldn't let him mix with high-up people and the arse out of his trousers? Have you me?

DRUMM: I'm advising you to live in your own world, not with one foot in his.

DA: I'll come to you so on Sundays and do the field . . . sure it won't take a feather out of me. *(Embarrassed by mention of money.)* Very good, yis . . . I'll leave that to yourself: sure whatever you think. *(Saluting.)* Thanks very much, more power . . . . .

Da moves back to the kitchen and Drumm and Young Charlie wander off to listen to music being played down on the pier. Da tells Charlie he remembers that Drumm came around to see how he was getting along after Mother died, bringing him a package of cigarettes which Da still has, somewhere in the house. Charlie tells Da: "You destroyed me, you know that? Long after I'd quit the job and seen the last of Drumm, I was dining out in London: black dickie-bow, oak paneling, picture of Sarah Bernhardt at nine o'clock: the sort of place where you have to remember not to say thanks to the waiters. I had just propelled an erudite remark across the table and was about to shoot my cuffs, lose my head and chance another one, when I felt a sudden tug as if I was on a dog-lead. I looked, and there were you at the other end of it. Paring your corns, informing me that bejasus the weather would hold up if it didn't rain, and sprinkling sugar on my bread when Ma's back was turned . . . . . So how could I belong there if I belonged here?"

Charlie had asked Da to come and live with his family in London when Da was 81, but Da had refused, preferring to stay here watching over his late wife's belongings and fending for himself.

Charlie remembers an early sexual adventure with a girl named Mary Tate whom they dubbed the "Yellow Peril." To be seen with her would in itself be a loss of reputation, but Young Charlie and Oliver were drawn to her: "We always kept our sexual sights impossibly high. It preserved us from the stigma of attempt and failure on the one hand, and success and mortal sin on the other." On a certain evening, watching the Yellow Peril sitting on a bench, reading, Young Charlie sends Oliver off to the billiard hall alone (much to Oliver's angry resentment) and dares to approach her, speak to her and sit down beside her. The girl tells him, "Nothing doing for you here . . . . . Ought to have gone off with that friend of yours," but Young Charlie persists in his awkward advances, which the girl doesn't either encourage or discourage. But she advises him to wait until an approaching passerby is out of the way. The intruder turns out to be Da himself, who is astonished at finding Young Charlie in this situation. Da sits down beside them and demands to know the girl's name.

MARY *(a little cowed)*: Mary Tate.
YOUNG CHARLIE: Leave her alone.
DA: You hold your interference. From where?
MARY: Glasthule . . . the Dwellin's.
    Da makes a violent gesture, gets up, walks away, turns and points at her dramatically.

Richard Seer, Brian Murray and Barnard Hughes in *"Da"*

DA: Your mother was one of the Hannigans of Sallynoggin. Did you know that?

MARY: Yes.

DA: And your Uncle Dinny and me was comrades the time of the Troubles. And you had a sister that died of consumption above in Loughinstown.

MARY: Me sister Peg.

DA: And another one in England.

MARY: Josie.

DA: Don't I know the whole seed and breed of yous! *(To Young Charlie.)* Sure this is a grand girl. *(He nudges Young Charlie off the bench and sits down next to Mary.)* Tell me, child, is there news of your father itself?

MARY *(her face clouding):* No.

DA: That's hard lines.

MARY *(bitterly):* We don't *want* news of him. Let him stay wherever he is — we can manage without him. He didn't give a curse about us then, and we don't give a curse about him now.

DA: There's some queer people walking the ways of the world.

MARY: Blast him.

Da talks to her. She listens, nods, wipes her eyes.

CHARLIE: And before my eyes you turned the Yellow Peril into Mary Tate of Glasthule, with a father who had sailed off to look for work in Scotland five years before, and had there decided that one could live more cheaply than seven. The last thing I'd wanted that evening was a person.

DA *(rises, about to go; to Young Charlie):* You mind your manners and treat her right, do you hear me. *(To Mary.)* Don't take any impudence from him. Home by eleven, Charlie.

Da departs, leaving Young Charlie now entirely incapable of losing his virginity this evening, much to Mary's disgust. She departs, weeping, as Young Charlie prepares to join Oliver at the billiard hall.

Immediately afterward, Charlie remembers Da in his prime in 1912, taking little Charlie and their dog for a walk up to view the mountains and the sea beyond. Little Charlie is obedient, hanging on Da's every word, as Da tells him how it will be some day when they win the Sweepstake: "We won't do a shaggin' hand's turn."

It begins to get dark, and little Charlie confesses his fear of the dark, and his special fear: his Aunt Bridgie has told him that his real mother comes from Dublin at night, dressed all in black, and looks in at him through the window. Da tells the boy his real mother is out there on the Kish lightship they can see winking in the distance, cooking for the men, so she can't be spying on Young Charlie in the dark.

CHARLIE *(as a boy):* Da . . . what if she got off the Kish? What if she's at home now before us and looking through the window?

DA: Well, if she is, I'll tell you what we'll do. I'll come up behind her and I'll give her the biggest root up in the arse a woman ever got.

CHARLIE *(pleased):* Will you, Da?

DA: I will. And bejasus it'll be nothing compared to the root I'll give your Aunt Bridgie.

> *Rising, brushing his trousers-seat.*

Now where the hell is that whelp of a dog?

CHARLIE: Da, I love you.

DA *(staring at him in puzzlement):* Certainly you do. Why wouldn't you?

Grown-up Charlie fights off this wave of remembered affection. He then remembers what his mother told him about how she came to marry Da. At the time, she was attracted to a sailor named Ernie Moore.

MOTHER: . . . . . I was very great with him for a while. Then himself came to the house one day and said how he had the job above in Jacob's and he wanted to marry me. So that was that.

YOUNG CHARLIE: How?

MOTHER: It was fixed.

YOUNG CHARLIE: How fixed?

MOTHER: My father told him I would, so it was fixed. Things was arranged in them days.

YOUNG CHARLIE: Did you want to?

MOTHER: I had no say in it.

YOUNG CHARLIE: How well did you know him?

MOTHER: Well enough to bid the time of day to.

YOUNG CHARLIE: That was handy.

MOTHER: A body's not put into this world to pick and choose and be particular. I was seventeen. I done what I was told to.

YOUNG CHARLIE What about Popeye the Sailor?

MOTHER: Who?

YOUNG CHARLIE: The other one.

MOTHER: Mr. Moore in your mouth. When your time comes and you have to answer to God in the next world it makes no differ who you married and who you didn't marry. That's when everything will be made up to us.

Mother doesn't appreciate Young Charlie's jokes about sailors, and she finally declares: "When you do get married, to whatever rip will have you, I only hope you'll be half the provider for her as himself has been for me."

Young Charlie is writing a letter at his mother's direction to tell Da's employers, the Jacobs, the news that he has landed a job. Young Charlie makes a joking reference to Mr. Micawber in his letter, but his mother and Da can't identify this literary reference and deeply mistrust it. They order Young Charlie in no uncertain terms to do the letter over. Young Charlie obeys, angrily, and storms out to the billiard hall, vengefully whistling "Popeye the Sailor."

Charlie's memory returns to the hilltop with Da and the boy Charlie.

> *We hear the far-off barking of a dog.*

DA: There's the whoorin' dog gone down ahead of us in the finish. And the lights is on in the town. (*Pointing*.) That's the Ulverton Road, son, where we frightened the shite out of the Black-and Tans. And the lamp is lit in your Uncle Paddy's window.

CHARLIE: If it is, he didn't light it: he's dead these donkey's years. Uncle Paddy, Kruger Doyle, Gunjer Hammond, Oats Nolan — all your cronies — and old Bonk-a-bonk with his banjo and Mammy Reilly in her madhouse of a shop, with her money, so they said, all in sovereigns, wrapped up inside her wig. All dead. Like yourself . . . and, trust you, last as usual.

DA: That's a hash old wind starting up. We'll need a couple of extra coats on the bed tonight, son.

CHARLIE: We will.

DA: Mind your step now. If you slip and cut yourself she'll ate the pair of us. Give me your hand. Let the light from the Kish show you where the steps are.

CHARLIE: That's it, mother: light us home. Least you can do.

> *Curtain.*

ACT II

Charlie has had a few drinks at the pub and is coming home closely accompanied by his memory of himself as Young Charlie, with Da lurking near them in the shadows. Charlie tries to keep Da out of his memory by concentrating on Young Charlie, but he cannot. Da is seated comfortably in his usual armchair while Charlie resumes sorting through his effects. Young Charlie studies Charlie and decides that he's a bit of a disappointment.

CHARLIE: Oh, Yes?

YOUNG CHARLIE: I mean, I'd hoped to do better for meself.

CHARLIE: What had you in mind?

YOUNG CHARLIE: Don't get huffy. It's not that I amn't glad to see you: at least it means I'll live till I'm forty: that's something.

CHARLIE: Thanks.

YOUNG CHARLIE (*looking at Charlie's wrist*): And I like the watch.

CHARLIE: Oh, good.

YOUNG CHARLIE: I suppose I could have done worse: but you can't deny you're a bit ordinary. It gives a fellow the creeps, seeing himself at your age: everything behind him and nothing to look forward to.

CHARLIE: I get the old-age pension next year: there's that.

YOUNG CHARLIE: Yesterday I was thinking: I'm only eighteen, anything can happen to me . . . anything. I mean, maybe a smashing girl will go mad for me. Now I dunno.

> *Charlie puts on his glasses to read a receipt. Young Charlie looks at him.*

Ah, God.

CHARLIE: What?

YOUNG CHARLIE: Glasses. I'm blind as well.

Brian Murray as Charlie, Richard Seer as Young Charlie, Barnard Hughes as Da and Sylvia O'Brien as Mother in a scene from *"Da"*

CHARLIE: I'm sorry about that. The time I was castrated in a car crash, it affected my eyesight.
YOUNG CHARLIE *(horrified)*: You weren't. *(Then.)* You're so damned smart.

Young Charlie criticizes Charlie for turning everything into a joke, showing a lack of enthusiasm. Charlie in his turn reminds Young Charlie that he gave Da the inadequate gift of a package of razor blades one Christmas because he'd spent all his money on nylons for a girl. Da of course cherished the razor blades so dearly that he still has one left.

Young Charlie had intended the job with Drumm as a stopgap measure, but he stayed there 13 years. At 30, with a wife and family, Young Charlie was still subject to the clerical indignity of Drumm's reproach for mis-filing a letter. Drumm treated Young Charlie as the son he never had until, as Charlie remembers it: "One evening, I was in a hurry somewhere — to meet a girl, go to a film: I don't know. I saw him coming towards me. I didn't want to stop and talk, so I crossed over. He'd seen me avoid him. It was that simple. Except at work, he never spoke to me again."

Da finds the old razor blade and gives it to Charlie, then reproaches Charlie for putting him in a home this past January (it was a private hotel), then putting him in the poorhouse (it was a private room in an expensive psychiatric hospital, where Da, becoming senile at 83, could be well attended). At one point, Da tried to fight his way out of confinement. He tells Charlie, "You never seen me when I was riz," but Charlie remembers a time when Da was "riz" when his mother came home late for tea and Da could not imagine why. Questioning her, Da finds out that she met an old friend, the woman who finally married the sailor she fancied before she married Da, and she was treated to a glass of port at the Royal Marine Hotel. Da pretends that Ernie is long dead, but Mother knows different — she's been invited to take tea with them at their house next Thursday. Da is not invited, and he works himself into a jealous rage at the thought of his wife seeing Ernie Moore again. Da threatens her, striking his fist on the table, but she is determined: she is going.

DA: You set one foot in the Tivoli, you look crossways at a whoormaster the like of him, and be Jesus, I'll get jail for you, do you hear me? I won't leave a stick or stone standing in the kip.

MOTHER *(still a little afraid)*: Look at you . . . look at the yellow old face of you.

DA *(savagely, almost skipping with rage)*: With your . . . your port wine, and your sweet cake, and your Royal Marine Hotel.

MOTHER The whole town knows you for a madman . . . aye, and all belonging to you.

DA: Ernie . . . Ernie! You'll stay clear of him, Thursday and every other day.

MOTHER: Because you know I preferred him over you, and that's what you can't stand. Because I never went with you. Because you know if it wasn't for me father, God forgive him, telling me to —
Da makes a violent rush at her, his fist raised.

CHARLIE: Hey . . .
Da's fist comes down and stops almost touching her face, where it stays, trembling, threatening.

MOTHER *(quietly)*: Go on. Go on, do it. And that'll be the first time and the last. I'll leave here if I was to sleep on the footpath.
Pause. Da starts past her towards the scullery.
(Half to herself.) You went behind my back to him because you knew I wouldn't have you.
Da runs to the table and raises a cup, as if to dash it to pieces. Instead, he takes his pipe from the table and throws it on the ground. It breaks. He goes into the scullery. Charlie stoops to pick up the pieces of the pipe as Mother faces away from him to wipe her eyes.

CHARLIE *(still stooping)*: Will you go? On Thursday?
She faces him. Although tears are coming, there is a wry, almost mocking attempt at a smile.

MOTHER: The jealous old bags.

Charlie's memory moves forward in time to a year later when Da is 68 and his employer, Jacob, has just died. Da is summoned by Jacob's daughter, Mrs. Prynne, who's selling the house and dismissing the help (Da has heard that Cook received a parting gift of 100 pounds and he has high hopes). Young Charlie is picking loganberries so they won't go to waste, as Da joins Mrs. Prynne and gives her last-minute instructions about the care of the rose cuttings she's taking with her. He has been working here since he was 14 — 54 years — and, Mrs. Prynne tells him, he is to have a pension of 26 pounds a year and "Now, the lump sum. Poor Cook is getting on and will have to find a home of her own, so we've treated her as a special case. But I'm sure you and Mrs. Tynan won't say no to twenty-five pounds, with our best wishes and compliments."

Da conceals his disappointment, while Mrs. Prynne hints that Young Charlie should begin to think about helping out his elderly parents. She is persuaded to part with five more pounds as a wedding present for the young man. She also gives Da a family memento, a souvenir found in the ruins of the San Francisco earthquake: 30 pairs of eyeglass frames fused together into a single wiry tangle.

Mrs. Prynne departs, taking the cuttings and even Young Charlie's loganberries with her. Young Charlie belittles both the memento and the "lump sum" which works out to a gift of nine shillings and threepence a year for a lifetime of service.

Charlie remembers that his mother was disappointed, too, and tried to pawn the spectacle frames but could get nothing for them. Charlie figures they're probably still around somewhere, and if he can find them he'll throw them out, like the pieces of Da's broken pipe, Da's IRA certificate and the old photos that were gathering dust.

Charlie remembers the commotion the day he, Young Charlie, went off in an airplane to get married in Belgium (too far and too foreign for his parents to accompany him) — Mother calling him, Da afraid he'll miss the plane, Oliver bringing a present and hanging around to see him safely onto the bus. Young Charlie managed to get away without tears or loving embraces, just a wave of the hand, leaving his parents a bit regretful that they hadn't planned to go with him.

Charlie then remembers the last time he saw his father. Charlie had been advised not to bring the increasingly senile old man over to a London nursing home to die among strangers, so Charlie left him at home in Ireland and came over to see how he was getting along.

Da is in his 80s, stooped and deaf. Charlie's attitude is paternal.
DA: Hoh?
CHARLIE: I said are you eating regularly?
DA: Sure I'm getting fat. I go to Rosie for me tea and Mrs. Dunne next door cooks me me dinner. Are *you* eating regular?
CHARLIE: She's a widow. I'd watch her.
DA: Hoh?
CHARLIE: I say I'd watch her.
DA: I do.
CHARLIE: You reprobate. Do you need extra cash, for whist drives?
DA: I gave up going. Me hands is too stiff to sort the cards into suits. The last time I went, oul' Drumm was there. Do you remember oul' Drumm?
CHARLIE: Yes.

DA: He accused me of renagin'. "Why don't you," says he, "join the Old People's club and play there?" Says I to him back: "I would," says I, "only I'm too shaggin' old for them!" *(He laughs.)*

CHARLIE: That was good.

DA: Sure I have the garden to do . . . fine heads of cabbage that a dog from Dublin never pissed on. I'm kept going. I say I blacked the range yesterday.

CHARLIE: You're a marvel.

DA: I am. How's all the care.

CHARLIE: They're great. Send their love.

DA *(rising)*: I was meaning to ask you . . .

CHARLIE: What?

DA *(saluting him)*: I do often see your young one in the town.

CHARLIE: What young one?

DA: Her . . . Maggie. Your eldest. 'Clare to God, Mr. Doyle, I never seen such shiny black hair on a girl. *(Charlie stares at him. This is not a flashback to Da as a young man; it is Da in his 80s, his mind wandering.)* Sure she's like a young one out of the story books. The way it is, Mr. Doyle, I'm above at Jacob's these six years, since I was fourteen. I have a pound a week and the promise of one of the new dwellin's in the square. I'd think well of marrying her, so I would.

Charlie can't get through to Da, so he pacificies him by saying he'll speak to his "daughter" Maggie about the matter. Soon Da straightens up (in Charlie's memory) and protests, "I never carried on the like of that . . . . . Astray in the head. Thinking it was old God's time and you were herself's da."

A knock on the door signals the arrival of old Drumm, come to pay Charlie his respects following Da's funeral. Drumm offers to shake hands and forget their falling-out, which Charlie is quick to do.

DRUMM: There, that's done . . . I'm obliged. Mind, I won't say it's generous of you. *I* was the wounded party.

CHARLIE: It was a long time ago.

DRUMM *(good-humored)*: Don't play word-games with me, my friend. Time doesn't mitigate an injury; it only helps one to overlook it. *(Indicating a chair.)* May I?

CHARLIE: Please.

DRUMM *(sitting)*: Years ago I made a choice. I could have indiscriminate friendships or I could have standards. I chose standards. It's my own misfortune that so few people have come up to them.

CHARLIE: Including me.

DRUMM: You tried. You had your work cut out.

CHARLIE: I had.

DRUMM *(being fair)*: I daresay I was difficult.

CHARLIE: Impossible.

DRUMM *(bridling)*: And you've become impudent.

CHARLIE *(unruffled)*: Yes.

DRUMM: A beggar on horseback.

CHARLIE: It's better than walking.

Charlie asks after Drumm's health and learns that he's well, except for a bit of stomach trouble. Drumm started a rumor that he has cancer (which he doesn't) so that people will be more solicitous of him (they are) even if they don't like him.

Drumm tells Charlie that Da asked Drumm to come see him in the hospital and wrote out a duly witnessed will leaving everything to Charlie, the will being necessary because Charlie is not a blood relative. Charlie is certain his father had nothing to leave, but Drumm knows different. He has brought Charlie an "heirloom" — the fused spectacles which Drumm had put in a bank vault for safe keeping — and 135 pounds, more than Charlie imagined his father could possibly possess. Then it dawns on Charlie that the money is from his own checks Charlie sent Da over the years, and which Da saved instead of spending.

Drumm comments on the unfathomability of human behavior: "In seventy years the one surviving fragment of my knowledge, the only indisputable poor particle of certainty in my entire life, is that in a public house lavatory incoming traffic has the right of way. *(Acidly.)* It isn't much to take with one, is it?"

Drumm asks Charlie whether Da ever had any children of is own (several, all stillborn, Charlie has heard). Charlie wonders why Da never used the only important thing Charlie was ever able to give him, the checks, and Drumm offers the parting observation, "No manners."

Drumm goes, and Charlie shouts for Da, who comes in. Charlie calls him an "old shite" for not using the money.

CHARLIE: Since I was born, "Here's sixpence for the chairoplanes, a shilling for the pictures, a new suit for the job. Here's a life." When did I ever get a chance to pay it back, to get out from under, to be quit of you? You wouldn't come to us in London: you'd rather be the brave old warrior, soldiering on.

DA: And wasn't I?

CHARLIE: While I was the ingrate. The only currency you'd take, you knew I wouldn't pay. Well, I've news for you, mate. You had your chance. The debt is cancelled, welched on. *(Tapping his head.)* I'm turfing you out. Of here. See that?

> *He tears the black armband from his overcoat and drops it in the range.*

And this?

> *He holds up the parcel containing the spectacle frames.*

DA: You wouldn't. Not at all.

CHARLIE: Wouldn't I? You think not?

> *He bends and crushes the frames through the paper with increasing violence.*

DA: Ah, son . . .

CHARLIE: San Francisco earthquake!

DA: You'd want to mind your hand with them —

CHARLIE *(cutting his finger)*: Shit.

DA: I told you you'd cut yourself.

> *Charlie gives him a malevolent look and very deliberately shoves the parcel into the range. He sucks his hand.*

CHARLIE: Now wouldn't I?

DA: Is it deep? That's the kind of cut 'ud give you lock-jaw. I'd mind that.

CHARLIE: Gone . . . and you with it.

DA: Yis.

Taking out a dirty handkerchief.

Here, tie this around it.

CHARLIE: Get away from me. Ignorant man, ignorant life!

DA: What are you talking about, or do you know what you're talking about? Sure I enjoyed meself. And in the windup I didn't die with the arse out of me trousers like the rest of them — I left money!

CHARLIE: *My* money.

DA: Jasus, didn't you get it back? And looka . . . if I wouldn't go to England with you before, sure I'll make it up to you. I will now.

CHARLIE: You what? Like hell you will.

DA: Sure you can't get rid of a bad thing.

CHARLIE: Can't I? You watch me. You watch!

He picks up his case, walks out of the house and closes the front door. He locks the door and hurls the key from him. A sigh of relief.

He turns to go, to find Da has walked out through the fourth wall.

DA: Are we off, so? It's starting to rain. The angels must be peein' again.

CHARLIE: Don't you dare follow me. You're dead . . . get off.

DA: Sure Noah's flood was only a shower. *(Following him.)* Left . . . left . . . I had a good job and I left, right left!

CHARLIE: Hump off. Get away. Shoo. I don't want you.

He goes to the upper level. Da follows, lagging behind.

DA: Go on, go on. I'll keep up with you.

Charlie stops at the top level.

CHARLIE: Leave me alone.

Charlie slowly walks down as Da follows.

DA *(singing)*:

"Oh, says your oul' one to my oul' one:
'Will you come to the Waxy Dargle?'
And says my oul' one to your oul' one:
'Sure I haven't got a farthin'.'"

Curtain.

A GRAPHIC GLANCE

Ira Hawkins, Gilbert Price, Eartha Kitt and Melba Moore in *Timbuktu!*

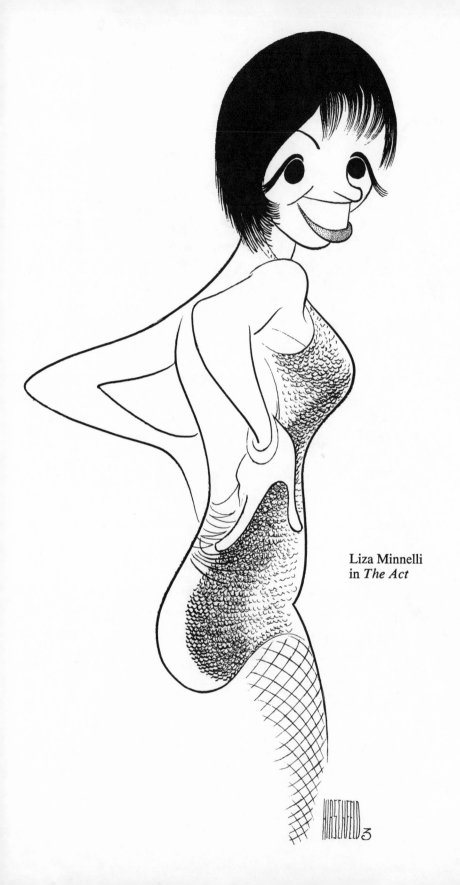

Liza Minnelli
in *The Act*

Frank Langella in *Dracula*

Kevin Kline, Dean Dittman, George Coe, John Cullum, Madeline Kahn and Imogene Coca in *On the Twentieth Century*

Mary Martin and Anthony Quayle in *Do You Turn Somersaults?*

James Earl Jones in *Paul Robeson*

British playwrights at work: Simon Gray, David Rudkin, Harold Pinter,
Alan Ayckbourn, Trevor Griffiths, Peter Shaffer and Tom Stoppard

Richard Gant, Dorian Harewood (center), Starletta DuPois and Morgan Freeman in *The Mighty Gents*

Golda Meir and Anne Bancroft
(in the title role in *Golda*)

Della Reese in *The Last Minstrel Show* (which closed out of town),
Frances Sternhagen and Fred Gwynne in *Angel*, Ken Page in *Ain't
Misbehavin'*, and some of the runaways in *Runaways*

Patricia Elliott and Louis Jourdan in *13 Rue de l'Amour*

(*Opposite*)
Richard Kiley in the revival of *Man of La Mancha*

Some of the dances in *Dancin'*

Tammy Grimes, John Wood, Patricia Elliott and Mildred Dunnock in *Tartuffe*

Carol Channing in a revival of *Hello, Dolly!*

Some of the world's greatest playwrights: Anton Chekhov, Henrik Ibsen, August Strindberg, William Shakespeare, George Bernard Shaw and Luigi Pirandello

Teri Garr and William Atherton
in the revival of *Broadway*

The cast of *Working*

Kathryn Walker, Jason Robards and Geraldine Fitzgerald in the revival of *A Touch of the Poet*

Jack Warden in *Stages*

Lynn Redgrave in *Saint Joan*

Jack Lemmon in *Tribute*

PLAYS PRODUCED
IN NEW YORK

PLAYS PRODUCED ON BROADWAY

Figures in parentheses following a play's title give number of performances. These figures are acquired directly from the production offices and do not include previews or extra non-profit performances. In the case of a transfer, the Off-Broadway run is noted but not added to the figure in parentheses.

Plays marked with an asterisk (*) were still running on June 1, 1978. Their number of performances is figured through May 31, 1978.

In a listing of a show's numbers — dances, sketches, musical scenes, etc. — the titles of songs are identified wherever possible by their appearance in quotation marks (").

HOLDOVERS FROM PREVIOUS SEASONS

Plays which were running on June 1, 1977 are listed below. More detailed information about them appears in previous *Best Plays* volumes of appropriate years. Important cast changes since opening night are recorded in the "Cast Replacements" section of this volume.

*Grease (2,600). Musical with book, music and lyrics by Jim Jacobs and Warren Casey. Opened February 14, 1972.

Pippin (1,944). Musical with book by Roger O. Hirson; music and lyrics by Stephen Schwartz. Opened October 23, 1972. (Closed June 12, 1977)

*The Magic Show (1,643). Musical with book by Bob Randall; music and lyrics by Stephen Schwartz; magic by Doug Henning. Opened May 28, 1974.

Equus (1,209). By Peter Shaffer. Opened October 24, 1974. Closed temporarily 9/11/76 after 781 performances but reopened in the same production 10/6/76 and continued. (Closed October 1, 1977)

*The Wiz (1,380). Musical based on L. Frank Baum's *The Wonderful Wizard of Oz;* book by William F. Brown; music and lyrics by Charlie Smalls. Opened January 5, 1975.

Shenandoah (1,050). Musical based on the original screen play by James Lee Barrett; book by James Lee Barrett, Peter Udell and Philip Rose; music by Gary Geld; lyrics by Peter Udell. Opened January 7, 1975. (Closed August 7, 1977)

*Same Time, Next Year (1,344). By Bernard Slade. Opened March 13, 1975.

Chicago (898). Musical based on the play by Maurine Dallas Watkins; book by Fred Ebb and Bob Fosse; music by John Kander; lyrics by Fred Ebb. Opened June 3, 1975. (Closed August 27, 1977)

*A Chorus Line (1,157). Musical conceived by Michael Bennett; book by James Kirkwood and Nicholas Dante; music by Marvin Hamlisch; lyrics by Edward Kleban. Opened April 15, 1975 off Broadway where it played 101 performances through July 13, 1975; transferred to Broadway July 25, 1975.

Bubbling Brown Sugar (766). Musical revue based on a concept by Rosetta LeNoire; book by Loften Mitchell; original music by Danny Holgate, Emme Kemp and Lillian Lopez; other music by various authors. Opened March 2, 1976. (Closed December 31, 1977)

California Suite (445). Program of four playlets by Neil Simon. Opened June 10, 1976. (Closed July 2, 1977)

Godspell (527). Musical based on the Gospel according to St. Matthew; conceived by John-Michael Tebelak; music and new lyrics by Stephen Schwartz. Opened May 17, 1971 off Broadway where it played 2,124 performances through June 13, 1976; transferred to Broadway June 22, 1976. (Closed September 4, 1978)

*For Colored Girls Who Have Considered Suicide/When the Rainbow Is Enuf (688). By Ntozake Shangé. Opened May 17, 1976 off Broadway where it played 120 performances through August 29, 1976; transferred to Broadway September 15, 1976.

*Oh! Calcutta! (710). Revival of the musical devised by Kenneth Tynan; with contributions (in this version) by Jules Feiffer, Dan Greenberg, Lenore Kandel, John Lennon, Jacques Levy, Leonard Melfi, David Newman and Robert Benton, Sam Shepard, Clovis Trouille, Kenneth Tynan and Sherman Yellen; music and lyrics (in this version) by Robert Dennis, Peter Schickele and Stanley Walden; additional music by Stanley Walden and Jacques Levy. Opened September 24, 1976 in alternating performances with *Me and Bessie* through December 7, 1976, continuing alone thereafter.

Sly Fox (495). By Larry Gelbart; based on *Volpone* by Ben Jonson. Opened December 14, 1976. (Closed February 19, 1978)

Your Arms Too Short to Box With God (429). Conceived from the Book of Matthew by Vinnette Carroll; music and lyrics by Alex Bradford; additional music and lyrics by Micki Grant. Opened December 22, 1976. (Closed January 1, 1978)

Otherwise Engaged (309). By Simon Gray. Opened February 2, 1977. (Closed October 30, 1977)

American Buffalo (135). By David Mamet. Opened February 16, 1977. (Closed June 11, 1977)

Lily Tomlin in "Appearing Nitely" (84). One-woman show written by Jane Wagner and Lily Tomlin. Opened March 24, 1977. (Closed June 12, 1977)

*Mummenschanz (491). Program of Swiss pantomime. Opened March 30, 1977.

The Shadow Box (315). By Michael Cristofer. Opened March 31, 1977. (Closed December 31, 1977)

Anna Christie (124). Revival of the play by Eugene O'Neill. Opened April 14, 1977. (Closed July 30, 1977)

*I Love My Wife (469). Musical based on a play by Luis Rego; book and lyrics by Michael Stewart; music by Cy Coleman. Opened April 17, 1977.

Side by Side by Sondheim (384). Revue with lyrics by Stephen Sondheim; music by Stephen Sondheim, Leonard Bernstein, Mary Rodgers, Richard Rodgers and Jule Styne. Opened April 18, 1977. (Closed March 19, 1978)

*Annie (464). Musical based on the Harold Gray comic strip *Little Orphan Annie;* book by Thomas Meehan; music by Charles Strouse; lyrics by Martin Charnin. Opened April 21, 1977.

The Basic Training of Pavlo Hummel (107). Revival of the play by David Rabe. Opened April 24, 1977. (Closed September 3, 1977)

*The King and I (451). Revival of the musical based on the novel *Anna and the King of Siam* by Margaret Landon; book and lyrics by Oscar Hammerstein II; music by Richard Rodgers. Opened May 2, 1977.

Happy End (75). Musical revival based on a German play by "Dorothy Lane" (Elisabeth Hauptmann); music by Kurt Weill; lyrics by Bertolt Brecht; book and lyrics adapted by Michael Feingold; production newly conceived by Robert Kalfin. Opened March 8, 1977 off Broadway where it played 56 performances through April 30, 1977; transferred to Broadway May 7, 1977 matinee. (Closed July 10, 1977)

New York Shakespeare Festival Lincoln Center. Agamemnon (38). Revival of the play by Aeschylus; conceived by Andrei Serban and Elizabeth Swados using fragments of the original Greek and Edith Hamilton's translation. Opened May 18, 1977. (Closed June 19, 1977)

Toller Cranston's The Ice Show (61). Opened May 19, 1977. (Closed July 10, 1977)

*Gemini (430). By Albert Innaurato. Opened March 13, 1977 off Broadway where it played 63 performances through May 1, 1977; transferred to Broadway May 21, 1977.

PLAYS PRODUCED JUNE 1, 1977–MAY 31, 1978

*Beatlemania (447). Musical revue with songs written by John Lennon, Paul McCartney and George Harrison; editorial content by Robert Rabinowitz, Bob Gill and Lynda Obst; original concept by Steven Leber, David Krebs and Jules Fisher. Produced by David Krebs and Steven Leber at the Winter Garden. Opened May 31, 1977; see note.

The Group: Randy Clark rhythm guitar, Reed Kailing bass guitar, P.M. Howard lead guitar, Bobby Taylor drums.

Offstage Musicians: Andrew Dorfman keyboards, Larry Davidson trumpet, Sally Rosoff cello, Mort Silver woodwinds, Peter Van Dewater violin.

Production supervised by Jules Fisher; visuals director, Charles E. Hoefler; multimedia images, Robert Rabinowitz, Bob Gill, Shep Kerman, Kathleen Rabinowitz; scenery, Robert D. Mitchell; lighting, Jules Fisher; sound, Abe Jacob; musical supervision, Sandy Yaguda; arrangements, Andrew Dorfman; special consultant, Murray the K; production stage manager, Robert V. Straus; stage manager, John Actman; press, Elizabeth A. Rodman.

Concert-style revue evoking the Beatles, their music and moods of the 1960s.

Note: *Beatlemania* opened in "previews" at the Winter Garden 5/26/77 after an out-of-town tryout. It never scheduled a formal opening night but was reviewed later at various performances by most critics including that of the New York *Times* (6/17/77). By agreement with the League of New York Theaters and Producers the opening date has been set at May 31 for the record.

MUSICAL NUMBERS — Act I, Scene 1 (Camelot: Pre-Beatles): "Let's Twist Again" (by Kal Mann and Dave Appell), "Roll Over Beethoven" (by Chuck Berry), "Bye Bye Love," "Hound Dog" (by Jerry Leiber and Mike Stoller), "Roll Over Beethoven" (Reprise). Scene 2 (The Coming): "I Want to Hold Your Hand," "She Loves You." Scene 3 (Making It): "Help!," "If I Fell," "Can't Buy Me Love," "Day Tripper." Scene 4 (Listening): "Yesterday," "Eleanor Rigby," "We Can Work It Out," "Nowhere Man." Scene V (Tripping): "A Day in the Life," "Strawberry Fields Forever," "Penny Lane," "Magical Mystery Tour," "Lucy in the Sky With Diamonds."

Act II, Scene 6 (Dropping Out): "Lady Madonna," "The Fool on the Hill," "Got to Get You Into My Life," "Michelle," "Get Back." Scene 7 (Flower Power): "Come Together," "With a Little Help From My Friends," "All You Need Is Love." Scene 8 (Bottoming Out): "Revolution," "Helter Skelter," "Hey Jude." Scene 9 (Moving On): "I Am the Walrus," "The Long and Winding Road," "Let It Be."

Circle in the Square. 1976-77 schedule of programs ended with **The Importance of Being Earnest** (108). Revival of the play by Oscar Wilde. Produced by Circle in the Square, Theodore Mann artistic director, Paul Libin managing director, at Circle in the Square Theater. Opened June 16, 1977. (Closed August 28, 1977)

Algernon Moncrieff	John Glover	Cecily Cardew	Kathleen Widdoes
Lane	Munson Hicks	Miss Prism	Mary Louise Wilson
John Worthing	James Valentine	Rev. Canon Chasuble	G. Wood
Lady Bracknell	Elizabeth Wilson	Merriman	Thomas Ruisinger
Gwendolen Fairfax	Patricia Conolly		

Directed by Stephen Porter; scenery, Zack Brown; costumes, Ann Roth; lighting, John McLain; production stage manager, Randall Brooks; press, Merle Debuskey, David Roggensack.

This Wilde comedy was excerpted by Royal Shakespeare Company in its *Pleasure and Repentance* program off Broadway 4/21/74 for 5 performances. Its last full professional New York production took place off Broadway 2/25/63 for 111 performances. Its last Broadway production was 3/3/47 for 81 performances.

The Cherry Orchard (48). Return engagement of a revival of the play by Anton Chekhov; new English version by Jean-Claude van Itallie. Produced by Joseph Papp in the New York Shakespeare Festival production at the Vivian Beaumont Theater. Opened June 29, 1977. (Closed August 7, 1977)

Lopakhin	Raul Julia	Charlotta	Elizabeth Franz
Dunyasha	Christine Estabrook	Simeonov-Pishchik	C.K. Alexander
Yepikhodov	Max Wright	Yasha	Ben Masters
Anya	Marybeth Hurt	Firs	Dwight Marfield
Ranevskaya	Irene Worth	Trofimov	David Clennon
Varya	Suzanne Collins	Vagrant	C.S. Hayward
Gayev	George Voskovec	Stationmaster	William Duff-Griffin

Guests, Peasants, Servants: John Ahlberg, Bernard Duffy, Roxanne Hart, Diane Lane, Bruce McGill, Peter Philips.

Standbys: Miss Worth — Jacqueline Brooks; Messrs. Julia, Wright — Gerry Bamman. Understudies: Mr. Alexander — William Duff-Griffin; Mr. Duff-Griffin — Bernard Duffy; Misses Hurt, Estabrook — Roxanne Hart; Miss Franz — Ruby Holbrook; Miss Collins — Gloria Maddox; Mr. Masters — Bruce McGill; Mr. Clennon — Peter Philips; Messrs. Marfield, Voskovec — William Robertson.

Directed by Andrei Serban; scenery and costumes, Santo Loquasto; lighting, Jennifer Tipton; incidental music, Elizabeth Swados; dance arrangement, Kathryn Posin; associate producer, Bernard Gersten; production manager, Andrew Mihok; press, Merle Debuskey, Faith Geer.

Time: The cherry trees are in bloom but it is still cold. There is a frost. Place: Madame Ranveskaya's estate. Act I: The children's room, May, daybreak. Act II: An open field, late June, the sun will soon set. Act III: The drawing room separated from the ballroom, Aug. 22, evening. Act IV: Same as Act I, October. Most of the furniture has been removed. The play was presented in three parts with intermissions following Acts I and II.

Return engagement of the prize winning revival which played the Vivian Beaumont for 62 performances beginning 2/17/77 (see its entry in *The Best Plays of 1976-77*). This return engagement was Joseph Papp's final New York Shakespeare Festival production at Lincoln Center.

Circle in the Square. Schedule of four revivals. **Tartuffe** (88). By Molière; English verse translation by Richard Wilbur. Opened September 6, 1977; see note. (Closed November 20, 1977). **Saint Joan** (96). By George Bernard Shaw. Opened November 29, 1977; see note. (Closed February 19, 1978). **13 Rue de l'Amour** (98). By Georges Feydeau; adapted and translated by Mawby Green and Ed Feilbert. Opened March 8, 1978; see note. (Closed May 21, 1978) And *Once in a Lifetime* by Moss Hart and George S. Kaufman to

Joan of Arc (Lynn Redgrave, *center, wearing sword*) identifies the
Dauphin (Robert LuPone, *right*) in Circle in the Square's *Saint Joan*

open 6/15/78. Produced by Circle in the Square, Theodore Mann artistic director, Paul
Libin managing director, at Circle in the Square Theater.

TARTUFFE

Flipote	Ruth Livingston	Orgon	Stefan Gierasch
Dorine	Patricia Elliott	Valere	Victor Garber
Mme. Pernelle	Mildred Dunnock	Tartuffe	John Wood
Elmire	Tammy Grimes	Loyal	Roy Brocksmith
Mariane	Swoosie Kurtz	Police Officer	Jim Broaddus
Damis	Ray Wise	Deputies	Timothy Landfield,
Cleante	Peter Coffield		Steven Gilborn

Understudies: Mr. Wood — Roy Brocksmith; Mr. Coffield — Jim Broaddus; Misses Dunnock,
Elliott — Ruth Livingston; Misses Grimes, Kurtz, Livingston — Johanna Leister; Messrs. Garber,
Wise — Timothy Landfield; Messrs. Gierasch, Brocksmith, Broaddus — Steven Gilborn.

Directed by Stephen Porter; scenery and costumes, Zack Brown; lighting, John McLain; production stage manager, Randall Brooks; stage manager, James Bernardi; press, Merle Debuskey,
David Roggensack.

Time: The 17th century. Place: Orgon's home in Paris. The play was presented in two parts.

The last professional New York production of *Tartuffe* took place off Broadway in CSC repertory 10/22/76 for 19 performances. The last Broadway production was by the Compagnie de
Théâtre de Villeurbanne 7/2/68 for 6 performances in French-language repertory.

SAINT JOAN

Robert de Baudricourt; English Soldier	Roy Cooper	Steward; Warwick's Page	Armin Shimerman

Joan .... Lynn Redgrave
Bertrand de Poulengey;
   Stranger .... Peter Van Norden
Court Page .... Pendleton Brown
Archbishop of Rheims ...... Tom Aldredge
Tremouille .... Tom Klunis
Gilles de Rais .... Kenneth Gray
Capt. La Hire .... Ed Setrakian
Dauphin .... Robert LuPone
Duchess de la Tremouille Gwendolyn Brown

Dunois .... Joseph Bova
Dunois's Page;
   Canon de Courcelles .... Stephen Lang
Warwick .... Philip Bosco
Chaplain de Stogumber ... Robert Gerringer
Bishop of Beauvais .... Paul Shyre
Inquisitor .... Paul Sparer
Canon d'Estivet .... John Rose
Brother Ladvenu .... Nicholas Hormann
Executioner .... Jim Broaddus

Court Ladies, Courtiers, Soldiers, Monks: Jim Broaddus, Pendleton Brown, Kenneth Gray, Sarah-Jane Gwillim, Nicholas Hormann, Stephen Lang, John Rose, Armin Shimerman, Peter Van Norden.

Understudies: Misses Redgrave, Brown — Sarah-Jane Gwillim; Messrs. Van Norden, Setrakian, Klunis — Jim Broaddus; Mr. Rose — Kenneth Gray; Messrs. Bosco, Shyre — Tom Klunis; Messrs. LuPone, Shimerman — Stephen Lang; Messrs. Aldredge, Gerringer, Sparer — John Rose; Mr. Bova — Ed Setrakian; Messrs. Lang, Cooper — Armin Shimerman; Mr. Broaddus — Peter Van Norden; Mr. Hormann — Pendleton Brown.

Directed by John Clark; scenery, David Jenkins; costumes, Zack Brown; lighting, John McLain; production stage manager, Randall Brooks; stage manager, James Bernardi.

Scene 1: A tower of Vaucouleurs Castle, between Lorraine and Champage, Feb. 13, 1429. Scene 2: Antechamber and throne room of the Dauphin's castle at Chinon, Feb. 24. Scene 3: The north bank of the River Loire, April 29. Scene 4: The Earl of Warwick's tent in the English camp, June 23. Scene 5: Rheims Cathedral, July 17. Scene 6: The Bishop's Court, Rouen Castle, May 30, 1431. Epilogue: A bedchamber in the royal chateau 25 years later. The play was presented in two parts.

Saint Joan was last produced on Broadway by the Repertory Theater of Lincoln Center 1/4/68 for 44 performances.

13 RUE DE L'AMOUR

Marie .... Jill P. Rose
Tailor; 1st Policeman .... Jim Broaddus
Duchotel .... Bernard Fox
Moricet .... Louis Jourdan
Leontine .... Patricia Elliott

Jean-Pierre .... Richard Pilcher
Birabeau .... Laurie Main
Madame Spritzer .... Kathleen Freeman
Inspector of Police .... Ian Trigger
2d Policeman .... John Shuman

Understudies: Misses Elliott, Freeman — Jill P. Rose; Messrs. Fox, Jourdan, Main — Jim Broaddus; Messrs. Broaddus, Pilcher, Trigger — John Shuman.

Directed by Basil Langton; scenery and costumes, Zack Brown; lighting, John McLain; production stage manager, James Bernardi; stage manager, John Shuman.

Time: 1890. Place: Paris. Act I: The home of Monsieur and Madame Duchotel on an autumn afternoon. Act II: Moricet's bachelor apartment that same night. Act III: The morning room the following day.

An 1892 Feydeau bedroom farce entitled *Monsieur Chasse*, never professionally produced in New York under that title. A considerably altered adaptation by William Lestocq, *The Sportsman*, with even the character names changed, was presented by Charles Frohman 2/14/93. The play has been produced in this Green-Feilbert translation in London during the 1975-76 season; in a Jon Jory translation, *Rendezvous*, at Actors' Theater of Louisville, Ky. in 1973-74; and in a Barnett Shaw version, *The Happy Hunter*, in Dallas in 1972-73.

Note: Press date for *Tartuffe* was 9/25/77, for *Saint Joan* was 12/15/77, for *13 Rue de l'Amour* was 3/16/78.

Man of La Mancha (124). Musical revival with book by Dale Wasserman suggested by the life and works of Miguel de Cervantes y Saavedra; music by Mitch Leigh; lyrics by Joe Darion. Produced by Eugene V. Wolsk at the Palace Theater. Opened September 15, 1977. (Closed December 31, 1977)

Don Quixote (Cervantes) ......Richard Kiley	Fermina; Moorish Dancer ... Joan Susswein
Sancho ....Tony Martinez	Guitarist .... Robin Polseno
Horse; Tenorio ....Ben Vargas	Jorge .... Edmond Varrato
Mule; Jose .... Hector Mercado	Fernando; Guard .... David Wasson
Innkeeper .... Bob Wright	Antonia ....Harriett Conrad
Maria .... Marceline Decker	Housekeeper .... Margret Coleman
Pedro .... Chev Rodgers	Padre ....Taylor Reed
Anselmo; Barber ....Ted Forlow	Dr. Carrasco .... Ian Sullivan
Juan ....Mark Holliday	Captain .... Renato Cibelli
Paco .... Antony DeVecchi	Guard .... Michael St. Paul
Aldonza .... Emily Yancy	

Standby: Mr. Martinez — Edmond Varrato. Understudies: Misses Yancy, Conrad — Joan Susswein; Mr. Forlow — Edmond Varrato, Mark Holliday; Mr. Wright — Renato Cibelli; Mr. Reed — Mark Holliday, David Wasson; Mr. Sullivan — Marshall Borden, David Wasson; Miss Coleman — Marceline Decker; Miss Susswein — Kay Vance; Messrs. Rodgers, Vargas, Mercado — Antony DeVecchi; Mr. Cibelli — Michael St. Paul.

Production and musical staging by Albert Marre; musical direction, Robert Brandzel; scenery and lighting, Howard Bay; costumes, Howard Bay, Patton Campbell; arrangements, Music Makers, Inc.; assistant to the director, Gregory Allen Hirsch; production stage manager, Patrick Horrigan; stage manager, Gregory Allen Hirsch; press, John A. Prescott.

Man of La Mancha was first produced 11/22/65 for 2,328 performances and was named a Best Play of its season and won the Critics Award for best musical. It was revived on Broadway 6/22/72 for 140 performances.

The list of musical numbers in *Man of La Mancha* appears on page 387 of *The Best Plays of 1965-66.*

Estrada (7). Musical revue in the Russian language. Produced by United Euram at the Majestic Theater. Opened September 20, 1977. (Closed September 26, 1977)

Nani Bregvadze	Yefim Levinson
Grigori Davidenko	Orera
Vladimir Konovich	Pesnyary
Natalia Kriushkin	Vladimir Serov
Oleg Kriushkin	Souvenir Ensemble
Larisa Kudeyarova	

Artistic director, Nikolai Lationov; choreography, Tamara Golovanova; press, Daniel Langan, Patt Dale.

Subtitled *The Moscow Music Hall* (its title means "Variety" in Russian), a collection of musical variety and circus acts from the Soviet Union.

Miss Margarida's Way (98). By Roberto Athayde. Produced by Joseph Papp in the New York Shakespeare Festival production, Bernard Gersten associate producer, at the Ambassador Theater. Opened September 27, 1977; see note. (Closed January 1, 1978)

Miss Margarida ....Estelle Parsons	
One of Her Students .... Colin Garrey	
Rest of Her Students ....The Audience	

Directed by Roberto Athayde; scenery and costumes, Santo Loquasto; lighting, Martin Tudor; production manager, Andrew Mihok; stage managers, Penny Gebhard, Colin Garrey; press, Merle Debuskey, Sol Jacobson.

Note: This production of *Miss Margarida's Way* was presented off Broadway 7/31/77-9/4/77 for 30 performances, after which it transferred to Broadway; see its entry in the "Plays Produced Off Broadway" section of this volume.

Comedy With Music (66). Musical entertainment by Victor Borge. Produced by The

354   THE BEST PLAYS OF 1977-1978

Edgewood Organization, Inc., Lewis Friedman and John W. Ballard executive directors, at the Imperial Theater. Opened October 3, 1977. (Closed November 27, 1977)

Cast: Victor Borge, Marylyn Mulvey.
Design, Neil Peter Jampolis; associate producers, Dean Lenz, Allison McLeod; production stage manager, Don Judge; press, Gurtman & Murtha Associates.
Program of anecdotes and piano numbers, presented in two parts, devised by and with the noted Danish comedian, who appeared on Broadway in similar shows with slightly different titles 10/2/53 for 849 performances and 11/9/64 for 192 performances.

Hair (43). Musical revival with book and lyrics by Gerome Ragni and James Rado; music by Galt MacDermot. Produced by Michael Butler in association with K. H. Nezhad at the Biltmore Theater. Opened October 5, 1977 (Closed November 6, 1977)

Claude	Randall Easterbrook	Crissy	Kristen Vigard
Berger	Michael Hoit	Shopping Cart Lady	Michael Leslie
Woof	Scott Thornton	Tourist	Perry Arthur
Hud	Cleavant Derricks	Tourist; Gen. Grant	Carl Woerner
Sheila	Ellen Foley	Abraham Lincoln	Linda Myers
Jeanie	Iris Rosenkrantz	Sergeant	Byron Utley
Dionne	Alaina Reed	Parents	Lori Wagner, James Rich

Mothers: Annie Golden, Louis Mattioli, Perry Arthur. Fathers: James Rich, Eva Charney, Martha Wingate. Principals: Carl Woerner, Michael Leslie, Linda Myers.
Tribe: Perry Arthur, Emily Bindiger, Paul Binotto, Eva Charney, Loretta Devine, Doug Katsaros, Michael Leslie, Louis Mattioli, Linda Myers, Raymond Patterson, James Rich, James Sbano, Deborah Van Valkenburgh, Lori Wagner, Doug Wall, Martha Wingate, Carl Woerner, Charlaine Woodard.
Musicians: Denzil A. Miller Jr. electric keyboard; Jerry Jemmott bass, assistant conductor; Chris Alpert trumpet; Richard Hurwitz trumpet; Danny Bank baritone sax, reeds; Brian Koonin electric guitar; Billy Butler rhythm, electric guitars; Rick Cutler drums; Muhammad Abdullah percussion, hand drums.
Understudies: Mr. Easterbrook — Scott Thornton; Mr. Hoit — Doug Katsaros; Miss Foley — Deborah Van Valkenburgh; Mr. Derricks — Byron Utley; Miss Reed — Charlaine Woodard; Mr. Thornton — James Rich; Miss Vigard — Soni Moreno.

Directed by Tom O'Horgan; choreography, Julie Arenal; musical direction and vocal arrangements, Denzil A. Miller Jr.; scenery, Robin Wagner; costumes, Nancy Potts; lighting, Jules Fisher; sound, Abe Jacob; vocal direction, Patrick Flynn; associate producer, George Milman; assistant choreography, Wesley Fata; production stage manager, J. Galen McKinley; stage manager, Seth M. M. Sternberg; press, Gifford/Wallace, Inc., Eileen MacMahon.
Time: The 1960s. Place: The East Village. The play was presented in two parts.
Hair was first produced off Broadway by New York Shakespeare Festival 10/29/67 for 94 performances, after which it transferred to Broadway newly-directed by Tom O'Horgan 4/29/68 for 1,750 additional performances.
The list of musical numbers in *Hair* appears on page 375 of *The Best Plays of 1967-68*.

*The Gin Game (271). By D. L. Coburn. Produced by The Shubert Organization, Gerald Schoenfeld chairman, Bernard B. Jacobs president, at the John Golden Theater. Opened October 6, 1977.

Fonsia Dorsey	Jessica Tandy	Weller Martin	Hume Cronyn

Directed by Mike Nichols; scenery, David Mitchell; costumes, Bill Walker; lighting, Ronald Wallace; produced by Hume Cronyn and Mike Nichols (co-produced by Icarus Productions, Inc. and the Cronyn Company); production supervisor, Nina Seely; press, David A. Powers.
Act I, Scene 1: Sunday afternoon, Visitors Day. Scene 2: Sunday afternoon, one week later. Act II, Scene 1: The following evening, shortly after dinner. Scene 2: The following Sunday afternoon.

In a series of gin rummy games, two lonely people in an old folks' home peel away their defenses and reveal the inner structure of their personalities and past lives. Previously produced at American Theater Arts, Hollywood, Calif., the Actors Theater, Louisville, Ky. and the Long Wharf Theater, New Haven, Conn.

A Best Play; see page 145.

The Night of the Tribades (12). By Per Olov Enquist; translated by Ross Shideler. Produced by Burry Fredrik, Irwin Meyer, Stephen R. Friedman in association with William Donnell at the Helen Hayes Theater. Opened October 13, 1977. (Closed October 22, 1977)

Siri von-Essen-Strindberg . . . . Bibi Andersson	Marie Caroline David . . . . Eileen Atkins
August Strindberg . . . . Max Von Sydow	Photographer . . . . Bill Moor
Viggo Schiwe . . . . Werner Klemperer	

Understudies: Misses Andersson, Atkins — Katherine McGrath; Messrs. Von Sydow, Klemperer — Bill Moor; Mr. Moor — Richard Humphrey.

Directed by Michael Kahn; scenery, Lawrence King; costumes, Jane Greenwood; lighting, John McLain; associate producers, Sally Sears, Marilyn Strauss; production stage manager, Suzanne Egan; stage manager, Richard Humphrey; press, Shirley Herz, Louise Weiner Ment.

Time: March, 1889. Place: The stage of the Dagmar Theater in Copenhagen. The play was presented in two parts.

Emotional upheavals in the life of the noted playwright. A foreign (Swedish) play previously produced in many countries and at the McCarter Theater, Princeton, N.J.

*Dracula (257). Revival of the dramatization by Hamilton Deane and John L. Balderston of the novel by Bram Stoker. Produced by Jujamcyn Theaters, Elizabeth Ireland McCann, John Wulp, Victor Lurie, Nelle Nugent and Max Weitzenhoffer at the Martin Beck Theater. Opened October 20, 1977.

Lucy Seward . . . . Ann Sachs	Abraham Van Helsing . . . . Jerome Dempsey
Miss Wells . . . . Gretchen Oehler	R. M. Renfield . . . . Richard Kavanaugh
Jonathan Harker . . . . Alan Coates	Butterworth . . . . Baxter Harris
Dr. Seward . . . . Dillon Evans	Count Dracula . . . . Frank Langella

Understudies: Mr. Langella — Baxter Harris; Messrs. Dempsey, Evans, Kavanaugh, Harris — Louis Beachner; Mr. Coates — Malcolm Stewart; 2d male understudy — Charles Kindl.

Directed by Dennis Rosa; scenery and costumes, Edward Gorey; scenery supervision, Lynn Pecktal; costume supervision, John David Ridge; lighting, Roger Morgan; production supervisor, Ben Janney; production stage manager, Charles Kindl; stage manager, Bill Dodds; press, Solters & Roskin, Inc., Joshua Ellis, Milly Schoenbaum.

Time: The 1920s. Place: Dr. Seward's Sanatorium, Purley, England. Act I: The library, evening. Act II: Lucy's boudoir, evening of the following day. Act III, Scene 1: The library 32 hours later, shortly before sunrise. Scene 2: A vault just after sunrise.

Dracula was first produced on Broadway 10/5/27 for 291 performances. It was revived on Broadway 4/13/31 for 8 performances and off Broadway in the 1943-44 season. This production was previously produced by the Nantucket, Mass. Stage Company.

Some of My Best Friends (7). By Stanley Hart. Produced by Arthur Whitelaw, Jack Schlissel and Leonard Soloway at the Longacre Theater. Opened October 25, 1977. (Closed October 29, 1977)

Andrew Mumford . . . . Ted Knight	Dorothy Mumford . . . . Alice Drummond
Albert . . . . Gavin Reed	Sari . . . . Trish Hawkins
Irving Buxbaum . . . . Lee Wallace	Baby . . . . Ralph Williams
Lawrence Mumford . . . . Bob Balaban	Delivery Boy; Urchins . . . . Joseph Scalzo

Standbys: Messrs. Knight, Wallace — Lee Goodman; Miss Drummond — Lynne Stuart; Messrs. Reed, Balaban — Rudolph Willrich. Understudies: Miss Hawkins — Laure Mattos; Mr. Williams — Joseph Scalzo.

Directed by Harold Prince; scenery, Eugene Lee; costumes, Franne Lee; lighting, Ken Billington; associate producers, Donald Tick, Martin Markinson; stage manager, Joseph Scalzo; press, Max Eisen, Judy Jacksina, Barbara Glenn.

Time: The present. Place: Living room studio of Andrew Mumford in Manhattan. Act I, Scene 1: Morning. Scene 2: The following day. Act II, Scene 1: Late the same night. Scene 2: Several days later.

Middle-aged business executive can talk to his dog, his house plant, etc. (and they talk back) but finally he can't get out of his rut even with their help.

An Almost Perfect Person (108). By Judith Ross. Produced by Burry Fredrik and Joel Key Rice at the Belasco Theater. Opened October 27, 1977. (Closed January 28, 1978)

Irene Porter	Colleen Dewhurst	Announcer's
Dan Michael Connally	George Hearn	Voice ....Gary Alexander Azerier
Jerry Leeds	Rex Robbins	

Understudies: Messrs. Robbins, Hearn — Jess Osuna.

Directed by Zoe Caldwell; scenery and lighting, Ben Edwards; costumes, Jane Greenwood; associate producers, Sally Sears, Nadine Koval, William Livingston; production stage manager, Peter Lawrence; stage manager, Robert Bruyr; press, Shirley Herz, Louise Weiner Ment.

Place: Irene Porter's apartment on New York City's Upper West Side. Act I, Scene 1: The night of a Congressional election, 3 a.m. Scene 2: Noon, the following day. Act II: Later that evening.

Comedy about amorous adventures of a female Congressional candidate. Previously produced in Chicago and in summer theater.

*The Act (207). Musical with book by George Furth; music by John Kander; lyrics by Fred Ebb. Produced by The Shubert Organization, Gerald Schoenfeld chairman, Bernard B. Jacobs president, in a Feuer & Martin (Cy Feuer and Ernest H. Martin) production at the Majestic Theater. Opened October 29, 1977.

Lenny Kanter	Christopher Barrett		
Michelle Craig	Liza Minnelli	Arthur	Roger Minami
Nat Schreiber	Arnold Soboloff	Charley Price	Mark Goddard
Dan Connors	Barry Nelson	Molly Connors	Gayle Crofoot

The Boys: Wayne Cilento, Michael Leeds, Roger Minami, Albert Stephenson. The Girls: Carol Estey, Laurie Dawn Skinner. Dance Alternates: Claudia Asbury, Brad Witsger.

Understudies: Messrs. Nelson, Soboloff, Goddard — Christopher Barrett; Miss Crofoot — Laurie Dawn Skinner; Miss Minnelli (dance standby) — Claudia Asbury.

Directed by Martin Scorsese; choreography, Ron Lewis; musical direction, Stanley Lebowsky; scenery, Tony Walton; costumes, Halston; lighting, Tharon Musser; sound, Abe Jacob; orchestrations, Ralph Burns; dance music arrangements, Ronald Melrose; vocal and choral arrangements, Earl Brown; production stage manager, Phil Friedman; stage manager, Robert Corpora; press, Merle Debuskey, Leo Stern.

Time: The present. Place: The Hotel Las Vegas and in the memories of Michelle Craig. The play was presented in two parts.

While doing her Las Vegas nightclub act, a singing star remembers some of the tribulations of making her way into the limelight. Gower Champion worked on the show in its later production stages, without program credit.

Gower Champion replaced Barry Nelson 4/25/78.

MUSICAL NUMBERS — Act I: "Shine It On," "It's the Strangest Thing," "Bobo's," "Turning" (Shaker hymn), "Little Do They Know," Arthur in the Afternoon," "Hollywood, California," "The Money Tree." Act II: "City Lights," "There When I Need Him," "Hot Enough for You?", "Little Do They Know (Reprise), Finale, "My Own Space."

Gavin Reed and Ted Knight in *Some of My Best Friends*

Bully (7). One-man performance by James Whitmore in a play by Jerome Alden. Produced by Don Saxon and Kevin Krown in association with Kathy Raitt in the George Spota/Four Star International Production at the Forty-Sixth Street Theater. Opened November 1, 1977. (Closed November 5, 1977)

Directed by Peter H. Hunt; scenery and costumes, John Conklin; lighting, Peter H. Hunt; associate producer, Dan Lieberman; ragtime piano, Sam Anderson; production stage manager, Martha Knight; press, Faith Geer.

Act I: The adventures of Theodore Roosevelt. Act II: The further adventures of Theodore Roosevelt.

One-character play expressing the personality and career of the 26th President in the actor's impersonation and the playwright's dramatization of real and imaginary Roosevelt writings and "conversations" with such contemporaries as Elihu Root, Jules Jusserand, H. L. Mencken, Edith Carow Roosevelt (his second wife), William Allen White, Gifford Pinchot, Theodore Roosevelt Sr. and Martha Bullock Roosevelt (his father and mother), Joe Murray, Alice Hathaway Lee Roosevelt (his first wife), Henry Cabot Lodge, Quentin, Kermit, Theodore III and Archie Roosevelt (his sons), Bill Loeb, Baron Jutaro Komura, Minister Kogoro Takahira, Count Serge Witte and Woodrow Wilson.

Golda (108). By William Gibson. Produced by the Theater Guild, Philip Langner, Armina Marshall, Marilyn Langner producers, at the Morosco Theater. Opened November 14, 1977. (Closed February 16, 1978)

Allon; Menachem ....James Tolkan
Lior; Father; American;
   Cabinet Member .... Richard Kuss
Dayan .... Ben Hammer
Elazar .... Nicholas La Padula
Cabinet Member; TV Interviewer;
   British Commandant ....San Schacht
Golda Meir ....Anne Bancroft
Lou .... Vivian Nathan
Dinitz; Cabinet Member .... Zack Matalon
Mother; Sarile ....Frances Chaney
Golda as Child; Sarile as Child;
   Ruthie ....Justine Litchman
Sister; Arab Woman; Adolescent
   Grandchild; American Girl

                 Alice Golembo
Bodyguard; Arab; Adolescent Grandson;
   TV Crew, Cabinet Member .. Eric Booth
Morris ....Gerald Hiken
"Arab" Escort; Bar-Lev .... Ernest Graves
Arab Woman; Clara as
   Young Girl .... Corinne Neuchateau
Abdullah; Ben-Gurion;
   Religious Minister ....Sam Gray
Gideon; Modke ....Josh Freund
Grandson .... Michael Brown
Menachem as Boy; Nahum . Glenn Scarpelli
Clara .... Rebecca Schull
Israeli Citizens ....David C. Jones,
                 Robert Levine

D.P.s: Ilana Rapp and all of the above cast members except the Messrs. Schacht, Freund and Scarpelli and the Misses Bancroft and Litchman.

Standby: Miss Bancroft — Tresa Hughes. Understudies: Messrs. Kuss, Graves — David C. Jones; Misses Nathan, Chaney — Rebecca Schull; Messrs. Hiken, Gray, Matalon — Robert Levine; Miss Golembo — Corinne Neuchateau; Messrs. Scarpelli, Freund — Michael Brown; Miss Litchman — Ilana Rapp; Mr. Booth — Peter Dowling.

Directed by Arthur Penn; scenery and costumes, Santo Loquasto; lighting and projections, Jules Fisher; visuals, Lucie D. Grosvenor; production supervisor, Porter Van Zandt; stage manager, Wayne Carson; press, Joe Wolhandler, Peter Wolhandler, Silvia Perchuk.

Act I: Golda's office, Oct. 6, 1973; Kiev, Russia, 1903; War Room, Oct. 6, 1973; Amman, Trans-Jordan, 1948; Golda's office, Oct. 7, 1973; Golda's garden, Tel Aviv, 1968; Golda's house, Tel Aviv, 1931; Golda's house, Milwaukee, 1915; Golda's office, Oct. 7, 1973; Cabinet Room, October 9, 1973; Chicago, 1948; Golda's office, Oct. 9, 1973.

Act II: Golda's office, Oct. 10, 1973; Israel television station, Oct. 10, 1973; the Myerson home, Jerusalem, 1928; Golda's office, Oct. 12, 1973; D. P. camp, Cyprus, 1947; Golda's office, Oct. 12, 1973; grave site, Jerusalem, 1951; Golda's office, Oct. 13, 1973; Cabinet Room, Oct. 15, 1973.

Subtitled "a partial portrait," a documentary-style drama of the Israeli command at the climax of the Yom Kippur War, with flashbacks to earlier life of Golda Meir.

The Merchant (5). By Arnold Wesker. Produced by The Shubert Organization, John F. Kennedy Center, Roger Berlind and Eddie Kulukundis in association with SRO Productions Limited at the Plymouth Theater. Opened November 16, 1977. (Closed November 19, 1977)

Shylock Kolner ....Joseph Leon
Antonio Querini ....John Clements
Portia Contarini ....Roberta Maxwell
Nerissa .... Gloria Gifford
Jessica Kolner ....Julie Garfield
Rivka Kolner .... Marian Seldes
Abtalion da Modena .... Boris Tumarin
Tubal di Ponti ....John Seitz

Solomon Usque .... Jeffrey Horowitz
Rebecca da Mendes ....Angela Wood
Bassanio Visconti .... Nicolas Surovy
Graziano Sanudo .... Riggs O'Hara
Lorenzo Pisani ....Everett McGill
Moses of Castelazzo .... Leib Lensky
Girolamo Priuli .... William Roerick
Servant .... Rebecca Malka

Venetians: Russ Banham, Mark Blum, Philip Carroll, James David Cromar, Brian Meister, John Tyrrell.

Understudies: Mr. Leon — John Seitz; Misses Garfield, Maxwell, Gifford, Wood — Rebecca Malka; Mr. Clements — William Roerick; Miss Seldes — Angela Wood; Messrs. Seitz, Tumarin — Leib Lensky; Messrs. Horowitz, Lensky, Roerick — Philip Carroll; Mr. Surovy — James David Cromar; Mr. O'Hara — John Tyrrell; Mr. McGill — Russ Banham.

Directed by John Dexter; scenery and costumes, Jocelyn Herbert; lighting, Andy Phillips; lighting supervision, Andrea Wilson; production stage manager, Brent Peek; stage manager, Pat De Rousie; press, Merle Debuskey, Susan L. Schulman.

Time: 1563. Place: Venice and Belmont. The play was presented in two parts.
A view of Shakespeare's *The Merchant of Venice* characters, setting and events from a new angle. A foreign (British) play having its world premiere in this production.

Jesus Christ Superstar (96). Musical revival based on the last seven days in the life of Jesus of Nazareth; music by Andrew Lloyd Webber; lyrics by Tim Rice. Produced by Hal Zeiger at the Longacre Theater. Opened November 23, 1977. (Closed February 12, 1978)

Judas Iscariot ....Patrick Jude	Simon Zealotes ....Bobby London
Jesus of Nazareth .... William Daniel Grey	Peter .... Randy Martin
Mary Magdalene ....Barbara Niles	Pontius Pilate .... Randy Wilson
1st Priest .... Doug Lucas	Soldier; Tormentor ....D. Bradley Jones
2d Priest .... Richard Tolin	George Bernhard
Caiaphas ....Christopher Cable	Maid by the Fire ....Celeste Hogan
Annas ....Steve Schochet	King Herod .... Mark Syers

Apostles: Doug Lucas, Richard Tolin, David Cahn, Ken Samuels, Lennie del Duca. Soul Girls: Freida Ann Williams, Claudette Washington, Pauletta Pearson.

Understudies: Mr. Grey — Randy Wilson; Messrs. Jude, Wilson — Steve Schochet; Miss Niles — Freida Ann Williams; Mr. Cable — Doug Lucas; Chorus Understudies — Alan Blair, Kelly Carrol.

Directed by William Daniel Grey; choreography and movement, Kelly Carrol; musical direction, Peter Phillips; production stage manager, Chuck Linker; stage manager, Rick Ralston; press, Hal Zeiger.

This rock musical version of the New Testament, originally conceived for the stage by Tom O'Horgan, was previously produced on Broadway 10/12/71 for 720 performances.

The list of scenes and musical numbers in *Jesus Christ Superstar* appears on pages 315-6 of *The Best Plays of 1971-72.*

*Chapter Two (205). By Neil Simon. Produced by Emanuel Azenberg at the Imperial Theater. Opened December 4, 1977.

George Schneider .... Judd Hirsch	Jennie Malone ....Anita Gillette
Leo Schneider ....Cliff Gorman	Faye Medwick .... Ann Wedgeworth

Standbys: Messrs. Hirsch, Gorman — Dick Latessa; Miss Gillette — Andrea Adler; Miss Wedgeworth — Jean DeBaer.

Directed by Herbert Ross; scenery, William Ritman; costumes, Noel Taylor; lighting, Tharon Musser; production stage manager, Charles Blackwell; stage manager, Lani Sundsten; press, Bill Evans, Mark Hunter.

Time: The present, a late February afternoon through to mid-spring. Place: Jennifer Malone's Upper East Side apartment and George Schneider's lower Central Park West apartment. The play was presented in two parts.

The emotional upsets of a widower's second marriage. Previously produced by Center Theater Group in Los Angeles.

A Best Play; see page 169.

A Touch of the Poet (141). Revival of the play by Eugene O'Neill. Produced by Elliot Martin at the Helen Hayes Theater. Opened December 28, 1977. (Closed April 30, 1978)

Mickey Maloy .... Barry Snider	Dan Roche .... Walter Flanagan
Jamie Cregan .... Milo O'Shea	Paddy O'Dowd .... Dermot McNamara
Sara Melody .... Kathryn Walker	Patch Riley ....Richard Hamilton
Nora Melody ....Geraldine Fitzgerald	Deborah .... Betty Miller
Cornelius Melody ....Jason Robards	Nicholas Gadsby .... George Ede

Standbys: Mr. Robards — Milo O'Shea; Misses Miller, Fitzgerald — Louisa Horton; Mr. O'Shea — Walter Flanagan; Miss Walker — Linda Martin; Messrs. Ede, Hamilton, Flanagan —

Wally Peterson; Mr. Snider — Dermot McNamara; Mr. McNamara — John Handy.

Directed by José Quintero; scenery and lighting, Ben Edwards; costumes, Jane Greenwood; production stage manager, Mitchell Erickson; stage manager, John Handy; press, Seymour Krawitz, Louise Weiner Ment, Patricia McLean Krawitz.

Time: July 27, 1828. Place: The dining room of Melody's Tavern, in a village a few miles from Boston. The play was presented in two parts.

This is the second Broadway revival of this O'Neill play which premiered 10/2/58 for 284 performances. Its first was by National Repertory Theater 5/2/67 for 5 performances.

*Cold Storage (175). Revised version of the play by Ronald Ribman. Produced by Claire Nichtern and Ashton Springer in association with Irene Miller at the Lyceum Theater. Opened December 29, 1977.

Richard Landau .... Len Cariou   Joseph Parmigian .... Martin Balsam
Miss Madurga .... Ruth Rivera

Standby: Mr. Cariou — George Guidall. Understudy: Miss Madurga — Ginny Freedman.

Directed by Frank Corsaro; scenery and costumes, Karl Eigsti; lighting, William Mintzer; production stage manager, Clint Jakeman; press, Max Eisen, Judy Jacksina, Barbara Glenn.

Time: The present. Place: New York City. Act I: A hospital roof garden. Act II: Early evening, the same day.

Cold Storage was previously produced off Broadway by American Place Theater 3/27/77 for 48

Mary Martin and Anthony Quayle in *Do You Turn Somersaults?*

performances. Its script, a conversation about life and death between two hospital patients, has been revised for this production.

George Guidall replaced Len Cariou 5/29/78.

Do You Turn Somersaults? (16). By Aleksei Arbuzov; translated by Ariadne Nicolaeff. Produced by John F. Kennedy Center in association with Cheryl Crawford at the Forty-Sixth Street Theater. Opened January 9, 1978. (Closed January 21, 1978)

Lidya Vasilyevna .... Mary Martin   Rodion Nikolayevich ..... Anthony Quayle

Directed by Edwin Sherin; scenery, Oliver Smith; costumes, Ann Roth; lighting, Ken Billington; incidental music, Charles Gross; presented by arrangement with the Royal Shakespeare Theater, Stratford-on-Avon; production stage manager, Paul A. Foley; stage managers, Stephen Nasuta, Marc Schlackman; press, Fred H. Nathan, Randi Cone.

Time: August 1968. Place: On the Riga coast. Part I, Scene 1: Her sixth day, a sanatorium in Riga. Scene 2: Her eighth day, a small cafe on the seashore. Scene 3: Her 11th day, outside Domsky Cathedral, Riga. Scene 4: Her 15th day, a hospital on the outskirts of Riga. Scene 5: Her 18th day, a lounge in the sanatorium. Part II, Scene 6: Her 21st day, by the entrance to a restaurant. Scene 7: Her 23d day, a cemetery. Scene 8: Her 26th day, outside the sanatorium. Scene 9: Her 31st day, Rodion's country house.

A doctor-patient relationship blooms into a romance. A foreign play previously produced in Poland, Russia, Rumania, London (as *Old World*) and elsewhere.

The November People (1). By Gus Weill. Produced by Shelly Beychok and Jim D'Spain at the Billy Rose Theater. Opened and closed at the evening performance January 14, 1978.

Mitch .... Cameron Mitchell   Brian .... James Sutorius
Mary .... Jan Sterling   Kathleen .... Pamela Reed
Donny ....John Uecker

Standby: Mr. Mitchell — Ben Kapen. Understudies: Messrs. Sutorius, Uecker — Justin Deas; Miss Reed — Lisabeth Shean.

Directed by Arthur Sherman; scenery, Kert Lundell; costumes, Joseph G. Aulisi; lighting, Thomas Skelton; production stage manager — Alan Hall; stage manager, Richard Elkow; press, Shirley Herz, William Schelble.

Act I: Sunday morning. Act II: Sunday evening.

Homecoming of a Watergate criminal after his prison term.

Paul Robeson (77). By Phillip Hayes Dean. Produced by Don Gregory at the Lunt-Fontanne Theater. Opened January 19, 1978. Closed February 26, 1978 after 45 performances and reopened in repertory with *For Colored Girls Who Have Considered Suicide/When the Rainbow Is Enuf* March 9, 1978 at the Booth Theater. (Closed April 30, 1978)

Paul Robeson .... James Earl Jones   Lawrence Brown .... Burt Wallace

Directed by Lloyd Richards; original staging, Charles Nelson Reilly; scenery, H. R. Poindexter; costumes, Noel Taylor; lighting, Ian Calderon; produced by arrangement with Carmen F. Zollo; production stage manager, Phil Stein; stage manager, Louis Mascolo; press, Seymour Krawitz, Patricia McLean Krawitz, Louise Weiner Ment.

One-man portrayal of Paul Robeson through the many conflicts of his life and career, with Burt Wallace accompanying the singing interludes on the piano.

SCENES AND CHARACTERS — Act I: Carnegie Hall (Paul, Audience); Philadelphia (Marian); Somerville (Pop); Trolley Car (Mr. Pillgard, Ladies); Rutgers — Waiting Room (Paul), Cafeteria (German Lady), Winants Hall (Glee Club), Audition (Hans Mueller, Dr. Hoffman); New York Hospital (Reeves, Ben, William); Somerville (Pop); Rutgers (Coach Sanford, Big Red Flanagan, Team); Pop's Church (Paul at coffin); New York — Harlem (Paul, Larry), Van Vechten's mansion (Van Vechten, Essie), Wall Street (Essie, Mr. Hayden, Miss Minnie), Paul's apartment (Paul, Essie), A friend's party (Paul, Essie), YMCA Theater (Dora Williams), Provincetown Playhouse (Mr. and Mrs. Jerome Kern, Gilpin).

Act II: Russian border (Customs Officer, Civil Guard); The Kremlin (Soviet Artists, The Impassioned One, Spanish Artist); Madrid (Republican Commander); Lorca's Grave (Paul); Battlefield hospital (Abraham Lincoln Brigade); London (Lord and Lady Barclay, British Intelligence); Africa (Tribesmen, Ebo Women); Voyage to America (Paul); Statue of Liberty (Paul); Broadway (Paul); Washington, D.C. (Pres. Truman); Kansas City (Concert Audience); Peekskill, N.Y. (Audience, Police, F.B.I., Mob); Interlude (Paul, Larry Brown); Washington, D.C. (Mr. Walters, House Un-American Activities Committee); Mother Zion (Ben's Congregation); Philadelphia (Paul, Audience).

Cheaters (32). By Michael Jacobs. Produced by Ken Marsolais, Philip M. Getter and Leonard Soloway at the Biltmore Theater. Opened January 15, 1978. (Closed February 11, 1978)

Monica	Rosemary Murphy	Grace	Doris Roberts
Howard	Lou Jacobi	Michelle	Roxanne Hart
Sam	Jack Weston	Allen	Jim Staskel

Standbys: Misses Murphy, Roberts — Doris Belack; Messrs. Weston, Jacobi — Kurt Knudson; Miss Hart — Arlene Grayson; Mr. Staskel — Steve Scott.

Directed by Robert Drivas; scenery, Lawrence King; costumes, Jane Greenwood; lighting, Ian Calderon; production supervisor, Larry Forde; associate producers, Donald Tick, Martin Markinson; stage managers, Arlene Grayson, Steve Scott; press, Betty Lee Hunt, Maria Cristina Pucci.

Act I: A — A hotel in New York City, a motel in Union, N.J., an apartment in New York City. B — A home in Larchmont, N.Y., a home in Englewood, N.J. Act II: A home in Englewood, N.J. Comedy about wife and husband swapping.

*On the Twentieth Century (117). Musical based on plays by Ben Hecht, Charles MacArthur and Bruce Millholland; book and lyrics by Betty Comden and Adolph Green; music by Cy Coleman. Produced by The Producers Circle 2, Inc. (Robert Fryer, Mary Lea Johnson, James Cresson, Martin Richards) in association with Joseph Harris and Ira Bernstein at the St. James Theater. Opened February 19, 1978.

Priest	Ken Hilliard	Letitia Primrose	Imogene Coca
Bishop	Charles Rule	Redcap	Mel Johnson Jr.
Stage Manager	Ray Gill	Anita	Carol Lugenbeal
Joan	Maris Clement	Oscar Jaffee	John Cullum
Wardrobe Mistress;		Max Jacobs	George Lee Andrews
Hospital Attendant	Carol Lurie	Imelda; Dr. Johnson	Willi Burke
Actor	Hal Norman	Maxwell Finch	David Horwitz
Owen O'Malley	George Coe	Mildred Plotka/	
Oliver Webb	Dean Dittman	Lily Garland	Madeline Kahn
Congressman Lockwood	Rufus Smith	Otto Von Bismark;	
Conductor Flanagan	Tom Batten	Hospital Attendant	Sal Mistretta
Train Secretary		Bruce Granit	Kevin Kline
Rogers	Stanley Simmonds	Agnes	Judy Kaye

Porters: Keith Davis, Quitman Fludd III, Ray Stephens, Joseph Wise.

Female Singers: Susan Cella, Maris Clement, Peggy Cooper, Karen Gibson, Carol Lugenbeal, Carol Lurie, Melanie Vaughan. Male Singers: Ray Gill, Ken Hilliard, David Horwitz, Craig Lucas, Sal Mistretta, Hal Norman, Charles Rule, David Vogel.

Standby: Mr. Cullum — George Lee Andrews. Understudies: Miss Kahn — Judy Kaye; Miss Coca — Peggy Cooper; Miss Burke — Karen Gibson; Mr. Kline — Ray Gill; Mr. Andrews — Craig Lucas; Messrs. Dittman, Smith — Hal Norman; Mr. Batten — Stanley Simmonds; Mr. Coe

— David Vogel; Miss Kaye — Melanie Vaughan; Messrs. Davis, Fludd, Stephens, Wise — Mel Johnson Jr.; Swing Singers — Linda Poser, Gerald Teijelo.

Directed by Harold Prince; musical numbers staged by Larry Fuller; musical direction, Paul Gemignani; scenery, Robin Wagner; costumes, Florence Klotz; lighting, Ken Billington; orchestrations, Hershy Kay; associate producers, Sam Crothers, Andre Pastoria; assistant to Mr. Prince, Ruth Mitchell; production associates, Nina Goodwin, Edward Merrow, Rich Mandel; production stage manager, George Martin; stage manager, E. Bronson Platt; press, Bill Evans, Mary Bryant.

Time: The early 1930s. Place: Mainly on the Twentieth Century Limited from Chicago to New York.

Musicalization of the 1933 play *Twentieth* (or *20th) Century* about a colorful Broadway theater impresario and his cohorts aboard the famed New York-Chicago flyer, by Hecht & MacArthur, which was in turn based on a play by Charles Millholland.

Judy Kaye replaced Madeline Kahn 4/24/78.

ACT I

Overture

"Stranded Again" .... Bishop, Actor, Singers
"On the Twentieth Century" .... Porters, Letitia, Flanagan, Rogers, Passengers
"I Rise Again" .... Oscar, Owen, Oliver
"Indian Maiden's Lament" .... Imelda, Mildred Plotka
"Veronique" .... Lily, Male Singers
"I Have Written a Play" .... Flanagan
"Together" .... Porters, Passengers, Oscar
"Never" .... Lily, Owen, Oliver
"Our Private World" .... Lily Oscar
"Repent" .... Letitia
"Mine" .... Oscar, Bruce
"I've Got It All" .... Lily, Oscar
"On the Twentieth Century" (Reprise .... Company

ACT II

Entr'acte .... Porters
"Five Zeros" .... Owen, Oliver, Letitia, Oscar
"Sextet" .... Owen, Oliver, Oscar, Letitia, Lily, Bruce
"She's a Nut" .... Company
"Max Jacobs" .... Max
"Babbette" .... Lily
"The Legacy" .... Oscar
"Lily, Oscar" .... Lily, Oscar

---

*Deathtrap (108). By Ira Levin. Produced by Alfred de Liagre Jr. and Roger L. Stevens at the Music Box. Opened February 26, 1978.

Sidney Bruhl	.... John Wood	Helga ten Dorp	.... Marian Winters
Myra Bruhl	.... Marian Seldes	Porter Milgrim	.... Richard Woods
Clifford Anderson	.... Victor Garber		

Standbys: Misses Winters, Seldes — Jan Farrand; Mr. Garber — Ernie Townsend.

Directed by Robert Moore; scenery, William Ritman; costumes, Ruth Morley; lighting, Marc B. Weiss; production stage manager, Philip Cusack; stage manager, Lani Sundsten; press, Jeffrey Richards Associates, Bruce Lynn.

Time: The present. Place: Sidney Bruhl's study in the Bruhl home in Westport, Conn. Act I, Scene 1: An afternoon in October. Scene 2: That evening. Scene 3: Two hours later. Act II, Scene 1: Two weeks later, morning. Scene 2: A week later, night. Scene 3: A week later, afternoon.

Murder plots and counterplots, as a playwright's greed and professional jealousy are matched by his ingenuity in concocting schemes to make his dreams come true.

A Best Play; see page 205.

*Timbuktu! (105). Musical based on *Kismet;* book by Luther Davis based on the musical by Charles Lederer and Luther Davis from the play by Edward Knoblock; music and lyrics by Robert Wright and George Forrest from themes of Alexander Borodin and African folk music. Produced by Luther Davis at the Mark Hellinger Theater. Opened March 1, 1978.

Chakaba; Orange Merchant;

Antelope	Obba Babatunde	Najua; Bird in Paradise	Eleanor McCoy
Beggar; Witchdoctor	Harold Pierson	Wazir	George Bell
Beggar; Woman in Garden	Shezwae Powell	Chief Policeman	Bruce A. Hubbard
Beggar	Louis Tucker	Sahleem-La-Lume	Eartha Kitt
Hadji	Ira Hawkins	Munshi; Bird in Paradise	Miguel Godreau
Marsinah	Melba Moore	Mansa of Mali	Gilbert Price
Child	Deborah Waller	Antelope	Luther Fontaine
M'Ballah	Daniel Barton	Zubbediya	Vanessa Shaw

Three Princesses of Baguezane: Deborah K. Brown, Sharon Cuff, Patricia Lumpkin.

Citizens of Timbuktu: Obba Babatunde, Gregg Baker, Daniel Barton, Joella Breedlove, Deborah K. Brown, Tony Carroll, Sharon Cuff, Cheryl Cummings, Luther Fontaine, Michael F. Harrison, Dyane Harvey, Marzetta Jones, Jimmy Justice, Eugene Little, Patricia Lumpkin, Joe Lynn, Tony Ndogo, Harold Pierson, Ray Pollard, Shezwae Powell, Ronald Richardson, Vanessa Shaw, Louis Tucker, Deborah Waller, Renee Warren.

Understudies: Mr. Hawkins — Gregg Baker; Miss Kitt — Shezwae Powell; Miss Moore — Vanessa Shaw; Mr. Price — Bruce A. Hubbard; Mr. Bell — Louis Tucker; Mr. Godreau — Eugene Little; Mr. Hubbard — Ronald Richardson; Miss McCoy — Dyane Harvey; Mr. Barton — Jimmy Justice; Messrs. Babatunde, Fontaine — Tony Ndogo; Misses Cuff, Brown, Lumpkin — Joella Breedlove; Swing Dancers — Rodney Green, Jan Hazell.

Directed, choreographed and costumed by Geoffrey Holder; musical direction, supervision of arrangements and incidental music, Charles H. Coleman; scenery, Tony Straiges; lighting, Ian Calderon; sound, Abe Jacob; additional orchestrations, Bill Brohn; produced in association with Sarnoff International Enterprises, William D. Cunningham and John F. Kennedy Center for the Performing Arts; production stage manager, Donald Christy; stage managers, Jeanna Beldin, Pat Trott; press, Solters & Roskin, Inc., Joshua Ellis, Milly Schoenbaum, Sophronia McBride-Pope, Mark Goldstaub.

Time: In the year 1361 (of Islam 752). Place: Timbuktu in the ancient empire of Mali, West Africa. Act I: From dawn to dusk. Act II — From dusk to dawn.

The 1953 musical *Kismet* with setting and characters transposed from Baghdad to Timbuktu in Africa.

ACT I

Scene 1: The city square of Timbuktu, dawn
"Rhymes Have I" .... Hadji, Marsinah, Beggars
"Fate" .... Hadji
Scene 2: The gates of the city
"In the Beginning, Woman" .... Sahleem-La-Lume
Scene 3: The city square at market time
"Baubles, Bangles and Beads" .... Marsinah, Merchants
Scene 4: A garden of a house near the palace
Dance: Birds in Paradise Garden
"Stranger in Paradise" .... Mansa, Marsinah
Scene 5: A courtyard of the palace
"Gesticulate" .... Hadji, Council
Scene 6: An attiring pavilion in the palace
"Night of My Nights" .... Mansa, Courtiers

ACT II

Scene 1: En route to the garden
Dance: Nuptial Celebration .... People of Mali

Scene 2: The garden
"My Magic Lamp," "Stranger in Paradise" (Reprise) .... Marsinah
Scene 3: A corridor in the palace
Scene 4: The Wazir's harem
"Rahadlakum" .... Sahleem-La-Lume, Ladies of the Harem
Scene 5: Another part of the palace
"And This Is My Beloved" .... Hadji, Marsinah, Mansa, Wazir
Scene 6: Palace court
"Golden Land, Golden Life" .... Chief Policeman, Nobles of the Court
"Zubbediya" and Dances .... Zubbediya, Princess, Marriage Candidates, Acrobat
"Night of My Nights" (Reprise) .... Mansa, Marsinah, Hadji, Nobles of the Court
"Sands of Time" .... Hadji, Sahleem-La-Lume

*Hello, Dolly! (100). Revival of the musical with book by Michael Stewart; music and lyrics by Jerry Herman; based on Thornton Wilder's play *The Matchmaker*. Produced by James M. Nederlander and The Houston Grand Opera at the Lunt-Fontanne Theater. Opened March 5, 1978.

Mrs. Dolly Gallagher
Levi .... Carol Channing
Ernestina .... P. J. Nelson
Ambrose Kemper ...... Michael C. Booker
Horse .... Carole Banninger,
                        Debra Pigliavento
Horace Vandergelder .... Eddie Bracken
Ermengarde .... K. T. Baumann

Cornelius Hackl .... Lee Roy Reams
Barnaby Tucker .... Robert Lydiard
Minnie Fay .... Alexandra Korey
Irene Molloy .... Florence Lacey
Mrs. Rose .... Marilyn Hudgins
Rudolph .... John Anania
Judge .... Bill Bateman
Court Clerk .... Randolph Riscol

Townspeople, Waiters, etc.: Diane Abrams, Carole Banninger, JoEla Flood, Marilyn Hudgins, Deborah Moldow, Janyce Nyman, Jacqueline Payne, Debra Pigliavento, Theresa Rakov, Barbara Ann Thompson, Richard Ammon, Bill Bateman, Kyle Cittadin, Ron Crofoot, Don Edward Detrick, Richard Dodd, Rob Draper, David Evans, Tom Garrett, Charlie Goeddertz, James Homan, Alex MacKay, Richard Maxon, Randy Morgan, Randolph Riscol, Mark Waldrop.

Swing Dancers: Coby Grossbart, Bubba Rambo.

Understudies: Mr. Reams — Michael C. Booker; Miss Lacey — Deborah Moldow; Miss Korey — K. T. Baumann; Mr. Bracken — John Anania; Mr. Lydiard — Kyle Cittadin; Mr. Anania — Randy Morgan; Miss Baumann — Jacqueline Payne; Miss Nelson — Theresa Rakov; Mr. Booker — Rob Draper; Miss Hudgins — Barbara Ann Thompson.

Directed by Lucia Victor; choreographed by Jack Craig; musical direction, John L. DeMain; original production directed and choreographed by Gower Champion; scenery, Oliver Smith; costumes, Freddy Wittop; lighting, Martin Aronstein; production supervised by Jerry Herman; conductor, John Everly; associate producer, Robert A. Buckley; dance and incidental music arrangements, Peter Howard; production stage manager, Pat Tolson; stage manager, T. L. Boston; press, Solters & Roskin, Inc., Milly Schoenbaum, Fred Nathan.

Hello, Dolly! was first produced on Broadway 1/16/64 for 2,844 performances (fourth longest run in Broadway history) and was named a Best Play of its season. It was revived on Broadway with Pearl Bailey 11/6/75 for 51 performances.

The list of scenes and musical numbers in *Hello, Dolly!* appears on page 320 of *The Best Plays of 1963-64* and page 322 of The Best Plays of 1975-76.

The Water Engine and **Mr. Happiness** (16). By David Mamet. Produced by Joseph Papp in the New York Shakespeare Festival Production, Bernard Gerstein associate producer, at the Plymouth Theater. Opened March 6, 1978; see note. (Closed March 19, 1978)

MR. HAPPINESS
Mr. Happiness .... Charles Kimbrough

THE WATER ENGINE

Charles Lang	Dwight Schultz	Bernie	Michael J. Miller
Rita; Lily La Pon	Patti LuPone	Dave Murray	Colin Stinton
Morton Gross	David Sabin	Sound Effects Man	Eric Loeb
Lawrence Oberman	Bill Moor	Announcer	Paul Milikin
Mrs. Varec	Barbara Tarbuck	Musician	Alaric Jans
Mr. Wallace	Dominic Chianese		

Other characters: Soapbox Speaker, Chainletter, Barker, Guide at the World's Fair, Two Men Who May Be Policemen, Radio Announcer, Two Women on an Elevator, Inventor, Secretary, Worker.

Understudies: Messrs. Schultz, Stinton — Eric Loeb; Messrs. Chianese, Moor, Sabin — Paul Milikin; Mr. Miller — Dominic Chianese Jr.; Misses LuPone, Tarbuck — JoAnne Belanger.

Directed by Steven Schachter; scenery, John Lee Beatty; costumes, Laura Crow; lighting, Dennis Parichy; music, Alaric Jans; associate producer, Bernard Gersten; production supervisor, Jason Steven Cohen; production stage manager, Jason La Padura; stage manager, Harold Apter; press, Merle Debuskey, William Schelble.

Time: 1934, the second year of "The Century of Progress Exposition." Place: The studios of WCMJ Radio, New York City. The play was performed without intermission.

A radio-play-within-a-play (*The Water Engine*) about an inventor violently suppressed by industrial interests when he invents an engine that will run on water, preceded by a curtain-raising monologue. (*Mr. Happiness*) by one of those cheery radio personalities answering listeners' questions.

Note: *The Water Engine* was previously produced off Broadway at New York Shakespeare Festival Theater Cabaret 12/20/77–2/11/78 for 63 performances, after which this production transferred to Broadway; see its entry in the "Plays Produced Off Broadway" section of this volume.

The Effect of Gamma Rays on Man-in-the Moon Marigolds (16). Revival of the play by Paul Zindel. Produced by Courtney Burr and Nancy Rosenthal at the Biltmore Theater. Opened March 14, 1978. (Closed March 26, 1978)

Tillie	Carol Kane	Nanny	Isabella Hoopes
Beatrice	Shelley Winters	Janice Vickery	Lolly Boroff
Ruth	Lori Shelle		

Understudies: Misses Kane, Shelle — Lolly Boroff; Miss Boroff — Jill Karyn.

Directed by A. J. Antoon; scenery and costumes, Peter Harvey; lighting, Ian Calderon; original music, Richard Peaslee; associate producers, William King, Charles Blum; production associate, Blossom Horowitz; production stage manager, Murry Gitlin; press, Max Eisen, Barbara Glenn.

Time: The present. Place: The home of Beatrice. The play was presented in two acts.

The Effect of Gamma Rays, etc. was first produced off Broadway 4/7/70 for 819 performances, was named a Best Play of its season and won the Critics Award (Best American Play) and the Pulitzer Prize.

Stages (1). By Stuart Ostrow. Produced by Edgar Bronfman and Stuart Ostrow at the Belasco Theater. Opened and closed at the evening performance, March 19, 1978.

Stage I — Denial		Colin Dickinson	William Duell
Pianist	Roy Brocksmith	Josie	Brenda Currin
Frank Faye	Philip Bosco	Mr. Harris	Ralph Drischell
Chic Lady	Diana Davila	Theater Owner	Howland Chamberlin
Silvia	Lois Smith	*Stage II — Anger*	
Bill Blue	Tom Aldredge	Chairman	Tom Aldredge
Arnold Glickman	Max Wright	The Witness (The Actor)	Jack Warden
Jason Kahn (The Actor)	Jack Warden	Attorney for the Witness	William Duell
Jill Kahn	Caroline Kava	Counsel	Ralph Drischell
Dundeen Dickinson	Gretel Cummings	New Member	Philip Bosco

2d Member ...... Howland Chamberlin	(The Actor) .... Jack Warden
3d Member .... Roy Brocksmith	Justine; Nurse .... Lois Smith
Stage III — Bargaining	Garage Command .... Philip Bosco
Butterfly .... Diana Davila	Doctor .... Roy Brocksmith
Redheaded Sister ...... Greta Cummings	*Final Stage — Acceptance*
Blonde Sister .... Lois Smith	Abe Thibault (The Actor) .. Jack Warden
Blonde Husband .... Ralph Drischell	Gonzalo Bolivar .... Manuel Martinez
Redheaded Husband ...... Tom Aldredge	Jesse Thibault .... Philip Bosco
Father .... Max Wright	Fat Customer .... Roy Brocksmith
Constantine (The Actor) ... Jack Warden	Trench Coat
Stage IV — Depression	Customer .... Howland Chamberlin
Jack .... Max Wright	Mr. Stevens .... Tom Aldredge
Stanley .... William Duell	Lady Customer .... Lois Smith
Harold .... Tom Aldredge	Trooper .... Max Wright
Linda .... Caroline Kava	The Banker .... William Duell
Danny Steinman	

Directed by Richard Foreman; scenery, Douglas W. Schmidt; costumes, Patricia Zipprodt; lighting, Pat Collins; music, Stanley Silverman; sound, Roger Jay; production stage manager, D. W. Koehler; stage manager, Frank DiFilia; press, Betty Lee Hunt/Maria Cristina Pucci, Fred Hoot.

The play was presented in two parts with the intermission following Stage III.

Five playlets, or "Stages," unrelated except that they all center on a late middle-aged man confronted with frustration and failure. Stage II is based on testimony given before the House Un-American Activities Committee on March 21, 1951 in Washington and on May 6, 1953 in New York.

*Dancin' (75). Musical with music and lyrics by Johann Sebastian Bach, Ralph Burns, George M. Cohan, Neil Diamond, Bob Haggart, Ray Bauduc, Gil Rodin and Bob Crosby, Jerry Leiber and Mike Stoller, Johnny Mercer and Harry Warren, Louis Prima, John Philip Sousa, Carol Bayer Sager and Melissa Manchester, Barry Mann and Cynthia Weil, Felix Powell and George Asaf, Cat Stevens, Edgard Varèse and Jerry Jeff Walker. Produced by Jules Fisher, The Shubert Organization and Columbia Pictures at the Broadhurst Theater. Opened March 27, 1978.

Gail Benedict	Vicki Frederick
Sandahl Bergman	Linda Haberman
Karen G. Burke	Richard Korthaze
Rene Ceballos	Edward Love
Christopher Chadman	John Mineo
Wayne Cilento	Ann Reinking
Jill Cook	Blane Savage
Gregory B. Drotar	Charles Ward

Dance alternates: Christine Colby, William Whitener, Valerie Miller.

Directed and choreographed by Bob Fosse; music arranged and conducted by Gordon Lowry Harrell; scenery, Peter Larkin; costumes, Willa Kim; lighting, Jules Fisher; sound, Abe Jacob; orchestrations, Ralph Burns; produced by Jules Fisher; associate producer, Patty Grubman; production stage manager, Phil Friedman; stage manager, Perry Cline; press, Merle Debuskey, Susan L. Schulman, William Schelble.

A loose collection of production numbers about and expressed in dancing, with Bob Fosse's choreography and direction the primary creative inspiration.

Ross Miles replaced Gregory B. Drotar 5/30/78.

ACT I

Opening: "Prologue (Hot August Night)" and "Crunchy Granola Suite" (words and music by Neil Diamond) — Wayne Cilento, John Mineo, Company.

Recollections of an Old Dancer: "Mr. Bojangles" (by Jerry Jeff Walker). Mr. Bojangles — Christopher Chadman; Mr. Bojangles's Spirit — Gregory B. Drotar; Singer — Wayne Cilento. Alternates: Mr. Chadman — Richard Korthaze; Mr. Drotar — William Whitener; Mr. Cilento — Edward Love.

The Dream Barre: "Chaconne" (transcription from Bach's *Sonata for Violin Solo No. 4*). Boy — Charles Ward; Girl — Ann Reinking; Ballet Master — Richard Korthaze. Alternates: Mr. Ward — William Whitener; Miss Reinking — Vicki Frederick; Mr. Korthaze — Gregory B. Drotar.

Percussion: Part I — Rene Ceballos, Vicki Frederick, Linda Haberman; Part II — Christopher Chadman, Wayne Cilento, John Mineo; Part III — Sandahl Bergman, Gail Benedict, Karen G. Burke, Jill Cook, Gregory B. Drotar, Edward Love, Ann Reinking, Blane Savage; Part IV — "Ionisation" (by Edgard Varèse) — Charles Ward. Alternates: Part I — Christine Colby; Part II — Blane Savage; Part III — Christine Colby, William Whitener; Part IV — William Whitener.

ACT II

Dancin' Man: "I Wanna Be a Dancin' Man" (by Johnny Mercer and Harry Warren) — Company.

Three in One: "Big Noise from Winnetka" (by Bob Haggart, Ray Bauduc, Gil Robin and Bob Crosby) — Karen G. Burke, Wayne Cilento, Jill Cook. Alternate — Gail Benedict.

Joint Endeavor: "If It Feels Good, Let It Ride" (by Carol Bayer Sager and Melissa Manchester) and "Easy" (by Melissa Manchester). Pas de Deux — Vicki Frederick, Rene Ceballos, Sandahl Bergman, Charles Ward, Gregory B. Drotar, Blane Savage; "Easy" — Ann Reinking; Singers — Christopher Chadman, Wayne Cilento, Edward Love, John Mineo. Alternates: Pas de Deux — Christine Colby, Linda Haberman, Karen G. Burke, Gregory B. Drotar; Singer — Gail Benedict.

A Manic Depressive's Lament: "I've Got Them Feelin' Too Good Today Blues" (by Jerry Leiber and Mike Stoller) — Edward Love. Alternate — Jill Cook.

Fourteen Feet: "Was Dog a Doughnut" (by Cat Stevens) — Sandahl Bergman, Christopher Chadman, Wayne Cilento, Gregory B. Drotar, Vicki Frederick, Ann Reinking, Blane Savage. Alternates — Christine Colby, William Whitener.

ACT III

Benny's Number: "Sing, Sing, Sing" (by Louis Prima), Part I — Company; Part II, Trombone Solo — Vicki Frederick, Blane Savage, Charles Ward; Trumpet Solo — Ann Reinking; Clarinet Solo — Company; Piano Solo — Wayne Cilento, John Mineo. Alternates: Trombone Solo — Linda Haberman, Gregory B. Drotar; Trumpet Solo — Sandahl Bergman; Piano Solo — Jill Cook.

The Female Star Spot: "Here You Come Again" (by Barry Mann and Cynthia Weil) — Sandahl Bergman, Karen G. Burke, Rene Ceballos, Vicki Frederick. Alternate — Gail Benedict.

AMERICA: "Yankee Doodle Dandy" (by George M. Cohan) — Company; "Gary Owen" — Gail Benedict, Linda Haberman, Gregory B. Drotar; "American Women" — Sandahl Bergman, Vicki Frederick, Ann Reinking; "Under the Double Eagle" — Wayne Cilento, John Mineo, Blane Savage; "Dixie" — Karen G. Burke, Edward Love; "When Johnny Comes Marching Home" — Ann Reinking; "Rally Round the Flag" — Rene Ceballos; "Pack Up Your Troubles in Your Old Kit Bag and Smile, Smile, Smile" (words by George Asaf, music by Felix Powell) — Vicki Frederick, Gail Benedict, John Mineo; "The Stars and Stripes Forever" (by John Philip Sousa) — Charles Ward; "Yankee Doodle Disco" — Company (choreographed by Christopher Chadman). Alternates: "Gary Owen" — Christine Colby, William Whitener; "American Women" — Linda Haberman; "Under the Double Eagle" — William Whitener; "When Johnny Comes Marching Home" — Vicki Frederick; "Rally Round the Flag" — Sandahl Bergman; "Pack Up Your Troubles" — Gail Benedict; "The Stars and Stripes Forever" — William Whitener.

Improvisation: Dancin' (by Ralph Burns) — Company.

A History of the American Film (21). Musical revue by Christopher Durang; music by Mel Marvin. Produced by Judith Gordon and Richard S. Bright at the ANTA Theater. Opened March 30, 1978. (Closed April 16, 1978)

Cast: Maureen Anderman — Contract Player #8 (whose roles are Blessed Virgin Mother, Speakeasy Patron, Nurse, Voice of Anna Karenina, Ma Joad, Cucumber Girl, Voice of Sonja

Ben Halley Jr., Gary Bayer, April Shawhan and Bryan Clark in "Casablanca" scene from *A History of the American Film*

Henie); Gary Bayer — Jimmy; Walter Bobbie — Contract Player #1 (whose roles are Michael, Salad Chef); Jeff Brooks — Contract Player #5 (whose roles are Ticket Man, Newsboy, Young Speakeasy Patron, Young Reporter, Grandma Joad, Mickey); Bryan Clark — Contract Player #7 (whose roles are 1920s Cop, Bartender, Judge, Edward Mortimer, Voice of Vronsky, Von Leffing, Navy Officer, Victor Henreid, Voice of John, Voice of Academy Award Announcer, Voice of FBI Narrator, Voice of God, Theater Manager).

Also David Cromwell — Contract Player #4 (whose roles are Jesus, Ferruchi, Ernie the Reporter, Abdhul, Pa Joad, Makeup Man, Harkness, Uncle Sam, Marine Officer, Robot); David Garrison — Contract Player #10 (whose roles are Minstrel, Clarinet Man, "Big" Hit Man, David, Fife); Ben Halley Jr. — Contract Player #3 (whose roles are Piano Man, Viola, Indian, Ito, Sailor, Stuart); Swoosie Kurtz — Bette; Kate McGregor-Stewart — Contract Player #6 (whose roles are Orphanage Lady, Ma O'Reilly, Allison Mortimer, Prison Warden, Lettuce Girl, Gold Star Mother, a WAC); Joan Pape — Eve; April Shawhan — Loretta; Brent Spiner — Hank; Eric Weitz — Contract Player #9 (whose roles are God, "Little" Hit Man, Eric, Santa, Snare, Voice of Robot); Mary Catherine Wright — Contract Player #2 (whose roles are "Silent" Mother, Bartender's Girl, Clara Mortimer, Carrot Girl); Onstage Pianist — Robert Fisher.

Understudies: Messrs. Spiner, Bobbie — Stephen James; Misses Shawhan, Wright, Anderman — Carolyn Mignini; Messrs. Brooks, Weitz, Garrison — Robert Polenz.

Directed by David Chambers; musical staging, Graciela Daniele; musical direction, Clay Fullum; scenery, Tony Straiges; costumes, Marjorie Slaiman; lighting, William Mintzer; sound, Lou Shapiro; orchestrations, Robert M. Freedman; associate producers, Marc Howard, Sheila-Barbara-Dinah Productions; production stage manager, Ron Abbott; stage manager, Gully Stanford; press, David A. Powers, Barbara Carroll.

Cavalcade of Hollywood movies from the silents to the disaster epics, in a series of comic parodies, with music. Previously produced at the Eugene O'Neill Memorial Theater Center, Waterford, Conn.; Hartford, Conn. Stage Company; Mark Taper Forum, Los Angeles and Arena Stage, Washington, D.C.

ACT I

The Silent Years
"Minstrel Song" .... Minstrel
"Shanty Town Romance" .... Jimmy, Loretta
"They Can't Prohibit Love" .... Bette
"We're in a Salad .... Hank, Salad Girls
"Euphemism" .... Loretta
"Ostende Nobis Tosca" .... Bette, Hank, David, Eric
"The Red, the White and the Blue" .... Eve, Company

ACT II

"Pretty Pin-Up" .... Eve, Loretta, Bette, Clara
"Apple Blossom Victory" .... Bette, Eve, Singing WAC
"Isn't It Fun To Be in the Movies" .... David, Eric
"Search for Wisdom" .... Jimmy, Loretta, Company

Diversions & Delights (13). One-character play by John Gay; with Vincent Price as Oscar Wilde. Produced by Roger Berlind, Franklin R. Levy and Mike Wise at the Eugene O'Neill Theater. Opened April 12, 1978. (Closed April 22, 1978)

Directed by Joseph Hardy; scenery and lighting, H. R. Poindexter; lighting, Barry Arnold; costumes, Noel Taylor; production stage manager, David Clive; press, Seymour Krawitz, Patricia McLean Krawitz.

Time: 1899. Place: A concert hall on the Rue de la Pepiniere, Paris. The play was presented in two parts.

Subtitled "an evening spent with Sebastian Melmouth (a Wilde pseudonym) on the 28th day of November, 1899," an exiled, broken and ailing Wilde is giving a public performance shortly before his death.

Patio/Porch (21). Program of two one-act plays by Jack Heifner. Produced by Milton Justice in association with Ken Cohen at the Century Theater. Opened April 13, 1978. (Closed April 30, 1978)

Patio		*Porch*	
Jewel	Ronnie Claire Edwards	Dot	Fannie Flagg
Pearl	Fannie Flagg	Lucille	Ronnie Claire Edwards

Standby: Misses Flagg, Edwards — Tanny McDonald.

Directed by Garland Wright; scenery, John Arnone; costumes, David James; lighting, Marc B. Weiss; production stage manager, Lani Ball; press, The Merlin Group, Ltd., Patt Dale, Beatrice Da Silva, Glen Gary.

Place: A small Texas town.

Conversations between women — *Patio* between two middle-aged sisters whose lives are virtually empty, *Porch* between an overbearing mother and her longsuffering daughter.

The Mighty Gents (9). By Richard Wesley. Produced by James Lipton Productions with The Shubert Organization and Ron Dante at the Ambassador Theater. Opened April 16, 1978. (Closed April 23, 1978)

Rita	Starletta DuPois	Lucky	Mansoor Najee-Ullah
Frankie	Dorian Harewood	Eldridge	Richard Gant
Tiny	Brent Jennings	Zeke	Morgan Freeman

The cast of *The Mighty Gents* including (*at top*) Morgan Freeman and Howard E. Rollins Jr. and (*at bottom*) Dorian Harewood

Braxton .... Howard E. Rollins Jr.   Father .... Frank Adu

Standbys: Messrs. Harewood, Rollins, Adu — Charles Brown; Miss DuPois — Loretta Greene; Messrs. Najee-Ullah, Jennings, Gant — J. Herbert Kerr Jr. Understudy: Mr. Freeman — Frank Adu.

Directed by Harold Scott; music, Peter Link; scenery, Santo Loquasto; costumes, Judy Dearing; lighting, Gilbert V. Hemsley Jr.; production stage manager, David Taylor; stage manager, Joseph DePauw; press, Howard Atlee.

Time: Now. Place: On the streets of Newark, N.J. and in the apartment of Frankie and Rita. The play was presented without intermission.

Members of a former black youth gang are struggling desperately to survive as adults. Previously produced off off Broadway as *The Last Street Play.*

*"Da" (36). By Hugh Leonard. Produced by Lester Osterman, Marilyn Strauss and Marc Howard in the Hudson Guild Theater production, Craig Anderson producer, at the Morosco Theater. Opened May 1, 1978.

Charlie Now .... Brian Murray	Young Charlie .... Richard Seer
Oliver .... Ralph Williams	Drumm .... Lester Rawlins
Da .... Barnard Hughes	Mary Tate .... Mia Dillon
Mother .... Sylvia O'Brien	Mrs. Prynne .... Lois de Banzie

Standbys: Misses O'Brien, de Banzie — Ruby Holbrook; Miss Dillon — Faith Catlin. Understudy: Mr. Seer — David Naughton.

Directed by Melvin Bernhardt; scenery, Marjorie Kellogg; costumes, Jennifer Von Mayrhauser; lighting, Arden Fingerhut; production stage manager, Edward R. Fitzgerald; press, Howard Atlee, Becky Flora.

Time: May 1968 and, later, times remembered. Place: A kitchen and, later, places remembered. The play was presented in two parts.

A son is haunted by bittersweet memories of the father who has just died, and of his youth in Ireland. A foreign play produced first in Olney, Md. and then in Dublin and elsewhere including the Ivanhoe Theater in Chicago and the Hudson Guild Theater off off Broadway.

A Best Play; see page 299.

*Ain't Misbehavin' (27). Musical revue with music by Fats Waller; based on an idea by Murray Horwitz and Richard Maltby Jr. Produced by Emanuel Azenberg, Dasha Epstein, The Shubert Organization, Jane Gaynor and Ron Dante at the Longacre Theater. Opened May 9, 1978.

Nell Carter   Ken Page

Andre De Shields   Charlaine Woodard

Armelia McQueen

Standbys: Misses Carter, McQueen — Judy Gibson; Miss Woodard — Yolanda Graves; Messrs. De Shields, Page — Irving Lee.

Conceived and directed by Richard Maltby Jr.; musical numbers staged by Arthur Faria; music supervision, Luther Henderson; conductor and pianist, Hank Jones; scenery, John Lee Beatty; costumes, Randy Barcelo; lighting, Pat Collins; associate director, Murray Horwitz; orchestrations and arrangements, Luther Henderson; vocal arrangements, William Elliott, Jeffrey Gutcheon; production stage manager, Richard Evans; stage manager, D. W. Koehler; press, Bill Evans, Mark Hunter.

Recreation of the work and style (but not the impersonation) of Thomas "Fats" Waller, first produced off off Broadway at Manhattan Theater Club. In the list of numbers below, all the music was written by "Fats" Waller except where indicated; songs not written by Waller were recorded by him.

ACT I: "Ain't Misbehavin'" (music with Harry Brooks, lyric by Andy Razaf) — Company; "Lookin' Good But Feelin' Bad" (lyric by Lester A. Santly, vocal arrangement by Jeffrey

Gutcheon) — Company; "'T Ain't Nobody's Biz-ness If I Do" (music and lyric by Porter Grainger and Everett Robbins, additional lyric by Richard Maltby Jr. and Murray Horwitz) — Andre De Shields, Company; "Honeysuckle Rose" (lyric by Andy Razaf) — Ken Page, Nell Carter; "Squeeze Me" (lyric by Clarence Williams) — Armelia McQueen; "Handful of Keys" (lyric by Richard Malty Jr. and Murray Horwitz, based on an idea by Marty Grosz, vocal arrangement by William Elliott) — Company.

Also "I've Got a Feeling I'm Falling" (music with Harry Link, lyric by Billy Rose) — Carter, Company; "How Ya Baby" (lyric by J. C. Johnson) — Charlaine Woodard, De Shields, Company; "The Jitterbug Waltz" (lyric by Richard Maltby Jr., vocal arrangement by William Elliott) — Company; "The Ladies Who Sing With the Band" (lyric by George Marion Jr.) — De Shields, Page; "Yacht Club Swing" (music with Herman Autry, lyric by J. C. Johnson) — Woodard; "When the Nylons Bloom Again" (lyric by George Marion Jr.) — McQueen, Woodard, Carter; "Cash for Your Trash" (lyric by Ed Kirkeby) — Carter; "Off-Time" (music with Harry Brooks, lyric by Andy Razaf, vocal arrangement by Jeffrey Gutcheon) — Company; "The Joint Is Jumpin' " (lyric by Andy Razaf and J. C. Johnson) — Company.

Entr'acte — Ensemble.

Act II: "Spreadin' Rhythm Around" (music by Jimmy McHugh, lyric by Ted Koehler, additional lyric by Richard Maltby Jr.) — Company; "Lounging at the Waldorf" (lyric by Richard Maltby Jr., vocal arrangement by William Elliott) — McQueen, Woodard, Page, Carter; "The Viper's Drag" ("The Reefer Song," traditional) — De Shields, Company; "Mean to Me" (music and lyric by Roy Turk and Fred E. Ahlert) — Carter; "Your Feet's Too Big" (music and lyric by Ada Benson and Fred Fisher) — Page; "That Ain't Right" (music and lyric by Nat King Cole, additional lyric by Richard Maltby Jr. and Murray Horwitz) — De Shields, McQueen, Company; "Keepin' Out of Mischief Now" (lyric by Andy Razaf) — Woodard; "Find Out What They Like" (lyric by Andy Razaf) — McQueen, Carter.

Also "Fat and Greasy" (music and lyric by Porter Grainger and Charlie Johnson) — De Shields, Page; "Black and Blue" (music with Harry Brooks, lyric by Andy Razaf, vocal arrangement by William Elliott) — Company; Finale (songs by others which Fats Waller made hits) includes "I'm Gonna Sit Right Down and Write Myself a Letter" (music by Fred E. Ahlert, lyric by Joe Young) — Page; "Two Sleepy People" (music by Hoagy Carmichael, lyric by Frank Loesser) — McQueen, Page; "I've Got My Fingers Crossed" (music by Jimmy McHugh, lyric by Ted Koehler) — McQueen, Woodard, Page; "I Can't Give You Anything But Love" (music by Jimmy McHugh, lyric by Dorothy Fields) — De Shields, Woodard; "It's a Sin to Tell a Lie" (music and lyric by Billy Mayhew) — Carter, Company; "Honeysuckle Rose" (Reprise) — Company.

Angel (5). Musical from the Ketti Frings play *Look Homeward, Angel,* based on the novel by Thomas Wolfe; book by Ketti Frings and Peter Udell; music by Gary Geld; lyrics by Peter Udell. Produced by Philip Rose and Ellen Madison at the Minskoff Theater. Opened May 10, 1978. (Closed May 13, 1978)

Helen Gant	Donna Davis	Mr. Farrell	Billy Beckham
Ben Gant	Joel Higgins	Miss Brown	Jayne Barnett
Mrs. Fatty Pert	Patti Allison	Laura James	Leslie Ann Ray
Mrs. Snowden	Grace Carney	W. O. Gant	Fred Gwynne
Eugene Gant	Don Scardino	Dr. Maguire	Daniel Keyes
Eliza Gant	Frances Sternhagen	Joe Tarkington	Rex David Hays
Will Pentland	Elek Hartman	Reed McKinney	Carl Nicholas
Florry Mangle	Rebecca Seay	Tim Laughran	Norman Stotz
Mrs. Clatt	Justine Johnson	Madame Victoria	Patricia Englund
Jake Clatt	Gene Masoner		

Standbys: Mr. Gwynne — Peter Walker; Miss Sternhagen — Ann Gardner. Understudies: Miss Englund — Ann Gardner; Messrs. Scardino, Beckham — Dennis Cooley; Messrs. Higgins, Masoner — Paul Myrvold; Misses Ray, Davis, Seay — Leoni Norton; Misses Allison, Barnett — Laura Waterbury.

Directed by Philip Rose; choreography, Robert Tucker; musical direction and dance arrangements, William Cox; scenery, Ming Cho Lee; costumes, Pearl Somner; lighting, John

Joel Higgins, Don Scardino, Frances Sternhagen and Fred Gwynne
in *Angel*

Gleason; orchestrations, Don Walker; associate producers, Karen Wald, Norman Main; production stage manager, Steve Zweigbaum; stage manager, Arturo E. Porazzi; press, Merle Debuskey, Leo Stern.

Time: Autumn 1916. Place: Altamount, N.C. Act I: The Dixieland Boarding House. Act II, Scene 1: Gant's marble yard and shop, one week later. Scene 2: Dixieland Boarding House, that evening. Scene 3: Dixieland, two weeks later, just before dawn.

Look Homeward, Angel is the novelist's account of life in his family's boarding house in the South. The straight-play version on which the musical was based was produced on Broadway 11/28/57 for 564 performances and was named a Best Play of its season and won the Critics Award and the Pulitzer Prize.

ACT I

"Railbird" .... Eugene Gant
"If I Ever Loved Him" .... Laura
"A Dime Ain't Worth a Nickel" .... Ben Gant, Fatty Pert
"I Got a Dream to Sleep On" .... Eugene Gant
"Drifting" .... Eliza Gant

ACT II

"I Can't Believe It's You" .... W. O. Gant, Madam Victoria
"Feelin' Loved" ....Eugene Gant, Laura
"A Medley" ....Ben Gant, Fatty Pert, Eliza Gant, Laura
"Tomorrow I'm Gonna Be Old" .... W. O. Gant
"Feelin' Loved" (Reprise) ....Eugene Gant, Laura
"How Do You Say Goodbye" .... Laura
"Gant's Waltz" .... W. O. Gant, Eliza Gant
"Like the Eagles Fly" (Reprise) .... Eugene Gant

Runaways (21). Musical written and composed by Elizabeth Swados. Produced by Joseph Papp in the New York Shakespeare Festival Production, Bernard Gersten associate producer, at the Plymouth Theater. Opened May 13, 1978; see note.

Hubbell	Bruce Hlibok	Roby	Venustra K. Robinson
Interpreter for Hubbell	Lorie Robinson	Lazar	David Schechter
A. J.	Carlo Imperato	Eric	Evan H. Miranda
Jackie	Rachael Kelly	Iggy	Jonathan Feig
Luis	Ray Contreras	Jane	Kate Schellenbach
Nikki Kay Kane	Nan-Lynn Nelson	EZ	Leonard Brown
Lidia	Jossie De Guzman	Mex-Mongo	Mark Anthony Butler
Manny	Randy Ruiz	Melinda	Trini Alvarado
Eddie	Jon Matthews	Deidre	Karen Evans
Sundar	Bernie Allison	Mocha	Sheila Gibbs

Chorus: Paula Anderson, Kenya Brome, Jerome Dekie, Karin Dekie, Lisa Dekie, John Gallogly, Timmy Michaels, Toby Parker.

Musicians: Judith Fleisher piano, toy piano; John Schimmel string bass; Leopoldo F. Fleming congas, timbales, bongos, bells, siren, others; David Sawyer trap set, triangle, glass, ratchet; Patience Higgins saxophones, flutes; Elizabeth Swados guitar; Jeffrey Hest sax; Mark Green, Austin Hall trumpets.

Understudies: Carey Bond, Michele Dagavarian, Jerome Dekie, Katherine Diamond, Sheila Gibbs, C. S. Hayward, Michael Laylor, Timmy Michaels, Toby Parker.

Directed by Elizabeth Swados; scenery, Douglas W. Schmidt, Woods Mackintosh; costumes, Hilary Rosenfield; sound, Bill Dreisbach; lighting, Jennifer Tipton; associate producer, Bernard Gersten; horn arrangement, Larry Morton; arrangements improvised by the musicians; English-Spanish translations, Jossie De Guzman; production supervisor, Jason Steven Cohen; production stage manager, Gregory Meeh; stage managers, Peter Glazer, Patricia Morinelli; press, Merle Debuskey, Richard Kornberg.

In the words of Elizabeth Swados, "a collage around the profound effects of deteriorating families" extensively researched and partially improvised, with several actual runaways in the cast.

Note: This production of *Runaways* was presented off Broadway by the New York Shakespeare Festival at the Public Theater 2/21/78-4/30/78 for 80 performances before transferring to Broadway.

ACT I SONGS AND SPEECHES

You Don't Understand ....Hubbell
(with improvisation by Bruce Hlibok)
I Had to Go .... A.J., Schimmel
Parent/Kid Dance .... Company
"Appendectomy" .... Jackie
"Where Do People Go" .... Company

Footsteps .... Nikki, Schimmel, Lidia, Manny
    (Spanish argument by Jossie De Guzman and Randy Ruiz)
"Once Upon a Time" .... Lidia, Company
Current Events ....Eddie
"Every Now and Then" ...................................A.J., Sundar, Company
Out on the Street ....Hubbell, Lorie
    (with improvisation by Bruce Hlibok)
Minnesota Strip ....Roby
"Song of a Child Prostitute" .... Jackie, Lidia, Manny, Luis
Christmas Puppies ....Nikki
Lazar's Heroes ....Lazar
    (with improvisation by David Schechter)
"Find Me a Hero" .... Lazar, Company
Scrynatchkielooaw ....Nikki
"The Undiscovered Son" .... Eric, Fleisher, Schimmel
I Went Back Home ....Iggy, Jane
This Is What I Do When I'm Angry ...........................A.J., Nikki
"The Basketball Song" .... EZ, Company
    (dance — Luis, Mex-Mongo)
Spoons .... Manny
"Lullaby for Luis" .... Lidia, Luis, Higgins, Company
"We Are Not Strangers" .... Eric, Company

                    ACT II SONGS AND SPEECHES

In the Sleeping Line .... Company
    (A.J.'s Dream — Carlo Imperato; Roby's Dream — Venustra K. Robinson; Jackie's Dream —
    Diane Lane; Lazar's Dream — David Schechter; Eddie's Dream — Vincent Stewart; Night-
    mares in Spanish — Jossie De Guzman, Randy Ruiz, Ray Contreras)
"Lullaby From Baby to Baby" .... Melinda, Hubbell, Deidre
Tra Gog Vo in Dein Whole (I Will Not
    Tell a Soul) .... Lazar, Hubbell
"Revenge Song" .... Company
Enterprise ....Deidre, Nikki, Mex-Mongo, Company
"Sometimes" .... Roby, Lazar, Company
Clothes ....Iggy
"We Are Not Strangers" (Reprise) ....Mocha, EZ, Company
Mr. Graffiti ....Mex-Mongo
"The Untrue Pigeon" ....Nikki
"Senoras de la Noche" .... Lidia, Manny, Nikki
We Have to Die? ....Deidre
"Where Are Those People Who Did *Hair?*" ....Lazar, Deidre, Company
Appendectomy II ....Jackie, Melinda
"Let Me Be a Kid" .... Company
To the Dead of Family Wars ....Deidre
Problem After Problem ....Hubbell, Lorie
"Lonesome of the Road" ....Luis, Sundar, Company

*Working (30). Musical adapted by Stephen Schwartz from the book by Studs Terkel;
songs by Craig Carnelia, Micki Grant, Mary Rodgers and Susan Birkenhead, Stephen
Schwartz and James Taylor. Produced by Stephen R. Friedman and Irwin Meyer in
association with Joseph Harris at the Forty-sixth Street Theater. Opened May 14, 1978.

Principal Roles, Act I: Mike LeFevre, steelworker — Brad Sullivan; Al Calinda, parking lot
attendant — David Langston Smyrl; Nora Watson, editor, Roberta Victor, call girl — Patti
LuPone; John Fortune, advertising copy chief, Marco Camerone, hockey player — Steven
Boockvor; Diane Wilson, secretary — Lynne Thigpen; Herb Rosen, corporation executive — Rex
Everhart; Anthony Palazzo, stonemason, Joe Zutty, retired shipping clerk — Arny Freeman; John

The company in a scene from *Working*

Rushton, newsboy — Matthew McGrath; Rose Hoffman, teacher, Grace Clements, millworker — Bobo Lewis; Babe Secoli, supermarket checker, Terry Mason, stewardess — Lenora Nemetz; Brett Meyer, boxboy — David Patrick Kelly; Emilio Hernandez, migrant worker — Joe Mantegna; Conrad Swibel, gas meter reader, Tom Patrick; Fireman — Matt Landers; Kate Rushton, housewife — Susan Bigelow; Barbara Herrick, agency vice president — Robin Lamont; Bud Jonas, football coach — Bob Gunton.

Principal Roles, Act II: Benny Blue, bar pianist, Charlie Blossom, copy boy — David Patrick Kelly; Delores Dante, waitress — Lenora Nemetz; Heather Lamb, telephone operator, JoAnne Robinson, bus driver's wife, Maggie Holmes, cleaning woman — Lynne Thigpen; Fran Swenson, hotel switchboard operator, Lucille Page, seaman's wife — Bobo Lewis; Sharon Atkins, receptionist, Cathleen Moran, hospital aide — Robin Lamont; Frank Decker, interstate trucker — Bob Gunton; Dave McCormick, interstate trucker — Joe Mantegna; Booker Page, seaman — Rex Everhart; Will Robinson, bus driver — David Langston Smyrl; Tim Devlin, salesman, Ralph Werner, tie salesman — Matt Landers; Carla Devlin, salesman's wife — Terri Treas; Mike LeFevre, steelworker — Brad Sullivan.

Standbys: Hank Brunjes, James Congdon, Marilyn Cooper.

Directed by Stephen Schwartz; dances and musical staging, Onna White; musical direction and vocal arrangements, Stephen Reinhardt; scenery, David Mitchell; costumes, Marjorie Slaiman; lighting, Ken Billington; orchestrations, Kirk Nurock; dance and incidental music, Michele Brourman; associate to Miss White, Martin Allen; associate director, Nina Faso; production stage manager, Alan Hall; stage managers, Ruth E. Rinklin, Richard Elkow; press, Hunt/Pucci Associates, Betty Lee Hunt, Maria Cristina Pucci.

Series of character portraits of the working people listed above, in songs and sketches.

MUSICAL NUMBERS — Act I: "All the Livelong Day" ("I Hear America Singing" by Walt Whitman, music and additional lyrics by Stephen Schwartz) — Company; "Lovin' Al" (music and lyrics by Micki Grant) — David Langston Smyrl as Al Calinda, Ensemble; "The Mason" (music and lyrics by Craig Carnelia) — David Patrick Kelly; "Neat To Be a Newsboy" (music and lyrics by Stephen Schwartz) — Matthew McGrath as John Rushton, Newsboys; "Nobody Tells Me How" (music by Mary Rodgers, lyrics by Susan Birkenhead) — Bobo Lewis as Rose Hoffman; Treasure Island Trio (music by Michele Brourman) — danced by Terri Treas, Lenora Nemetz, Lynne Thigpen.

Also "Un Mejor Dia Vendra" (music by James Taylor, Spanish lyrics by Graciela Daniele and Matt Landers) — Joe Mantegna as Emilio Hernandez, Matt Landers, Migrants; "Just a

Housewife" (music and lyrics by Craig Carnelia) — Susan Bigelow as Kate Rushton, Housewives; "Millwork" (music by Michele Brourman and Stephen Schwartz) — Robin Lamont, David Patrick Kelly, Matt Landers, danced by Terri Treas; Nightskate (music by Michele Brourman and Stephen Schwartz) — danced by Stephen Boockvor as Marco Camerone; "Joe" (music and lyrics by Craig Carnelia) — Arny Freeman as Joe Zutty; "If I Could've Been" (music and lyrics by Micki Grant) — Company.

Act II: "It's an Art" (music and lyrics by Stephen Schwartz) — Lenora Nemetz as Delores Dante, Customers; "Brother Trucker" (music and lyrics by James Taylor) — Joe Mantegna as Dave McCormick, Bob Gunton as Frank Decker, David Patrick Kelly, Matt Landers; Husbands and Wives (music by Michele Brourman) — danced by Rex Everhart and Bobo Lewis as Mr. & Mrs. Booker Page, David Langston Smyrl and Lynne Thigpen as Mr. & Mrs. Will Robinson, Matt Landers and Terri Treas as Mr. & Mrs. Tim Devlin, Couples; "Fathers and Sons" (music and lyrics by Stephen Schwartz) — Bob Gunton; "Cleanin' Women" (music and lyrics by Micki Grant) — Lynne Thigpen as Maggie Holmes; "Something to Point To" (music and lyrics by Craig Carnelia) — Company.

*Tribute. By Bernard Slade. Produced by Morton Gottlieb at the Brooks Atkinson Theater. Opened June 1, 1978; see note.

Lou Daniels . . . . .A. Larry Haines	Maggie Stratton . . . . .Rosemary Prinz
Dr. Gladys Petrelli . . . . .Tresa Hughes	Jud Templeton . . . . Robert Picardo
Scottie Templeton . . . . Jack Lemmon	Hilary . . . . Joan Welles
Sally Haines . . . . .Catherine Hicks	Mrs. Everhardt . . . . .Anne Dodge

Standbys: Messrs. Lemmon, Haines — John Carpenter; Mr. Picardo — Tom Capps; Misses Hughes, Prinz, Welles, Dodge — Anita Keal; Miss Hicks — Laura Beattie.

Directed by Arthur Storch; scenery, William Ritman; costumes, Lowell Detweiler; lighting, Tharon Musser; associate producers, Ben Rosenberg, Warren Crane; production stage manager, Warren Crane; press, Solters & Roskin, Inc., Milly Schoenbaum, Fred Nathan.

Time: The present. Place: The living room of a New York townhouse and on the stage of a New York theater. Act I, Scene 1: Tonight. Scene 2: A morning three months ago. Scene 3: That night. Scene 4: Later that night. Act II, Scene 1: The next morning — three months ago. Scene 2: Earlier today. Scene 3: Tonight.

A jester maintains his sense of humor in the face of mortal illness, while coming to emotional terms with the son to whom he's never before paid much attention.

Note: *Tribute* played its previews and was "frozen" in late May, so that we identify it with the 1977-78 season despite the technicality of its opening June 1, the first day of the new season.

A Best Play; see page 277.

PLAYS WHICH CLOSED PRIOR TO BROADWAY OPENING

Productions which were organized by New York producers for Broadway presentation but which closed during their tryout performances are listed below.

The London Music Hall. Musical revue devised by John Gratton. Produced by David Stones for Rewtone, Ltd. on a pre-Broadway tour of Halifax, Nova Scotia and Boston. Opened May 18, 1977. (Closed in Boston May 28, 1977).

Jimmy Edwards	Los Ranqueles
The New Faces	Tony Wells
Tessie O'Shea	

The London Music Hall Dancersa; nikki Billyeald, Roger Finch, Carole Forbes, Richard Gough, Angela Harewood, Christine Ling, Jerry Manley, Gayna Martine, Di Palmer, Michael Scobie, John Thornton, Ken Warwick.

Directed by John Gratton; choreography, Irving Davies; musical direction, Burt Harden; scenery, John Campbell; lighting, Martin K. Hazelwood; stage manager, Ian David Tootle; press, Susan Bloch.

English vaudeville in the traditional music hall style.

ACT I: "Welcome to London" — The London Music Hall Dancers; Meet the Stars of Our Show — Tessie O'Shea, Professor Jimmy Edwards, Tony Wells, The New Faces; The Beefeaters of London Town; A Recital of Wind Instruments — Edwards.

ACT II: The London Music Hall Dancers; Tony Wells Will Entertain You; The Exciting Los Ranqueles; Tessie O'Shea; Finale.

Absent Friends. By Alan Ayckbourn. Produced by Claire Nichtern and Ashton Springer on a pre-Broadway tour of Westport, Conn., Washington, D.C. and Toronto. Opened July 4, 1977. (Closed in Toronto October 15, 1977).

Diana	Anne Jackson	Paul	Lee Richardson
Evelyn	Dale Hodges	John	Jacob Brooke
Marge	Meg Wynn Owen	Colin	Eli Wallach

Directed by Eric Thompson; scenery, Edward Burbridge; costumes, Michele Suzanne Reisch; lighting, Martin Aronstein; stage manager, Nina Seely; press, Max Eisen, Judy Jacksina.

Two-act comedy about friends who reveal their own problems in trying to console one of their number. A foreign play previously produced in London and the Long Wharf Theater, New Haven, Conn.

Nefertiti. Musical with book and lyrics by Christopher Gore; music by David Spangler. Produced by Sherwin M. Goldman in a pre-Broadway tryout at the Blackstone Theater, Chicago. Opened September 20, 1977. (Closed October 22, 1977)

Messenger	Patrick Kinser-Lau	Ipy	Michael V. Smartt
Penmut	Marilyn Cooper	Tiy	Jane White
Tushratta;		Akhnaton	Robert LuPone
Gen. Ramose	Benjamin Rayson	Scribe	G. Eugene Moose
Tadukhipa; Nefertiti	Andrea Marcovicci	Tutmose	Francisco La Gueruela
Hap	Michael Nouri		

Citizens of Mitanni, Thebes, etc.: Georgia Connor, Ann Crumb, Florie Freshman, Sylvia Miranda, Anthony Balcena, Ramon Colon, Michael Corbett, Simeon Den, Patrick Kinser-Lau, Francisco La Gueruela, G. Eugene Moose, Ernesto Pagnano.

Understudies: Miss Cooper — Florie Freshman; Mr. Rayson — G. Eugene Moose; Miss Marcovicci — Ann Crumb; Mr. Nouri — Francisco La Gueruela; Mr. Smartt — Michael Corbett; Miss White — Sylvia Miranda; Mr. LuPone — Patrick Kinser-Lau; Swings — Sal Provenza, Lynda Karen Smith.

Directed by Jack O'Brien; choreography, Daniel Lewis; musical direction, John DeMain; scenery, costumes, visuals, Sam Kirkpatrick; lighting, Gilbert V. Hemsley Jr.; orchestrations, Robert Freedman; dance music arrangements, Wally Harper; conductor, Robert Billig; production stage manager, Alan Hall; stage manager, Susie Cordon; press, Ellen Levene, Linda Cioffoletti.

Love and politics in 14th-century B.C. Egypt.

ACT I

"The Diary of a Dying Princess" ... Tadukhipa, Penmut, Tushratta, Citizens of Mitanni
"Lama Su Apapi" ... Penmut
"Penmut's Apology" ... Penmut
"Everything Is Possible" ... Tadukhipa

"The Diary of a Dying Princess" (Reprise) .... Tadukhipa, Hap, Penmut
"Breakfast at Thebes" .... Tiy, Household Staff
"Father" .... Akhnaton
"Pardon Me a Minute" .... Nefertiti
"Beautiful Has Come" .... Akhnaton, Attendants
"Whatever Happened to Me?" .... Hap
"Whatever Happened to Me?" (Reprise) .... Hap
"It Happens Very Softly" .... Nefertiti, Handmaidens
"Legions of the Night" .... Ipy, Priests
"Light Will Shine" .... Akhnaton, Citizens of Thebes
"Everything Is Possible" (Reprise) .... Nefertiti, Akhnaton

ACT II

"Under the Sun" .... Akhnaton, Nefertiti, Followers
"The New World" .... Akhnaton
"A Free Translation" .... Hap, Tushratta, Mitannites
"Someone Was Here" .... Nefertiti, Artists
"Another Free Translation" .... Hap, Tushratta
"Dinner at Thebes" .... Tiy, Ipy, Hap
"Take Off the Sandal" .... Nefertiti

The Confirmation. By Howard Ashman. Produced by Steven Wells. Gerry Lou Silverman and Michael Young in pre-Broadway tryouts at the McCarter Theater, Princeton, N.J. and the Annenberg Theater in Philadelphia. Opened October 4, 1977. (Closed in Philadelphia November 6, 1977)

Sherrie Polen	Marilyn Chris	Flo	Rosanna Carter
Rachel Polen	Tara King	Harry	Phillip Lindsay
Ed Abrams	Alan Manson	Mrs. Priscilla Fowlkes	Minnie Gentry
Sidney Polen	Robert Riesel	Rozzi Bender	Mara Mellin
Arnold Polen	Herschel Bernardi		

Directed by Kenneth Frankel; scenery, Marjorie Kellogg; costumes, Jennifer Von Mayrhauser; lighting, Marc B. Weiss; stage manager, Arthur Karp; press, Howard Atlee, Richard Seader.

Time: Late spring, 1962. Act I, Scene 1: Shortly after 4 o'clock one afternoon. Scene 2: That evening. Act II, Scene 1: Early the following evening. Scene 2: Shortly before midnight.

A suburban Jewish family tries to return to basics.

The Dream Watcher. By Barbara Wershba. Produced by Burry Fredrik in a pre-Broadway tryout at Seattle Repertory Theater. Opened November 30, 1977. (Closed December 24, 1977 matinee).

Albert Scully	Tim Wilson	Rick Hollander	Mark Bendo
Helen Scully	Geraldine Court	Bob Trautman	Adam Dales
John Scully	J.T. Walsh	Mrs. Orpha Woodfin	Eva Le Gallienne
Mr. Finley; Pusher;		Nurse	Elsa Raven
Chuck Forbes	Peter Bartlett	Mrs. Turner	Shirley Ryan
Sheila Morris;		Mrs. Stein	Minerva Pious
Neighbor	Susan Kay Logan		

Directed by Brian Murray; scenery, Ed Wittstein; costumes, Lewis D. Rampino; lighting, Patricia Collins; press, Shirley Herz.

A 14-year-old misfit finds an encouraging friend in his 80-year-old teacher.

Spotlight. Musical with book by Richard Seff; music by Jerry Bressler; lyrics by Lyn Duddy; based on a story by Leonard Starr. Produced by Sheldon R. Lubliner in a pre-

Broadway tryout at the National Theater, Washington, D.C. Opened January 11, 1978. (Closed January 14, 1978)

Jack Beaumont	Gene Barry	Louisa May	Debbie Shapiro
Siggy Zimmer	Marc Jordan	Brawn	Gary Daniel
Holly Beaumont	D'Jamin Bartlett	Mona	Cynthia Stewart
Mr. Kleinsinger	David-James Carroll	LuEllen	Terry Calloway
Carey	John Leslie Wolfe	Janet	Michon Peacock
Cosmo	Garon Douglass	Passerby	Loyd Sannes
Charlie	James Braet	Leaflet Man	Wayne Mattson
Myrna	Clare Culhane	Young Man	Jeffrey Spielman
Marie	Lenora Nemetz	Louise Pembley	Polly Rowles

Contenders: Freda Soiffer, Michelle Stubbs, Eileen Casey.

Ensémble: Steve Anthony, James Braet, Terry Calloway, Eileen Casey, Clare Culhane, Gary Daniel, Garon Douglass, David Warren-Gibson, Barbara Hanks, Clay James, Wayne Mattson, Tim Millett, Marcia O'Brien, Michon Peacock, Loyd Sannes, Rochelle Seldin, Debbie Shapiro, Freda Soiffer, Jeffrey Spielman, Cynthia Stewart, Michelle Stubbs, John Leslie Wolfe.

Directed by David Black; choreography, Tony Stevens; musical direction and vocal arrangements, Jack Lee; scenery, Robert Randolph; costumes, Robert Mackintosh; lighting, Roger Morgan; orchestrations, Will Schaeffer; dance music arrangements, Wally Harper; press, Seymour Krawitz, Louise Weiner Ment.

A star neglects his children — also performers — in favor of his own career.

MUSICAL NUMBERS: "No Regrets," "What Am I Bid," "Spotlight," "You Need Someone," "Round and Round," "Tricks of the Trade," "Notice Me," "Everything," "Didn't You Used To Be Him?", "Such a Business," "The Stranger in the Glass," "You Are You," "Where Is Everybody," "Spotlight" (Reprise).

The Prince of Grand Street. Musical with book, music and lyrics by Bob Merrill. Produced by Robert Whitehead, Roger L. Stevens and The Shubert Organization in a pre-Broadway tryout. Opened at the Forrest Theater, Philadelphia, March 8, 1978. (Closed at the Shubert Theater, Boston, April 15, 1978)

Itzak Goldfarb	Sam Levene	Mr. Gittleson; Stagehand	Bob Carroll
Nathan Rushumsky	Robert Preston	Henry Metzger	David Margulies
Jenny Abromowitz	Darlene Anders	Goldman	Alan Manson
Moishe Zweigman	Steven Gelfer	Krantz	Sammy Smith
Yetta Feinstein	Bernice Massi	Leah	Neva Small
Martin Malovsky	Derek Wolshonak	Julius Pritkin	Werner Klemperer
Sam Teitelbaum; Sexton	Duane Bodin	Maid	Susan Edwards
Mrs. Schumacher	Annette C. Winter	Stagehand; Jim	Clyde Laurents
Mrs. Schwartz	Molly Stark	Stage Manager	Walter Charles
Mr. Ginsburg; Foreman;		Mark Twain	Addison Powell
Stephen Douglas	Alexander Orfaly	Maurice Markov	Richard Muenz

Mourners: Dean Badolato, Duane Bodin, Bob Carroll, Walter Charles, Steven Gelfer, Clyde Laurents, Richard Muenz, Alexander Orfaly, Derek Wolshonak. Criers: Shellie Chancellor, Susan Edwards, Patricia Gaddonnieux, Molly Stark, Annette C. Winter. Workers: Darlene Anders, Shellie Chancellor, Susan Edwards, Patricia Gadonnieux, Patti Mariano, Nana, Molly Stark, Annette C. Winter.

Standby: Mr. Preston — Bob Carroll. Understudies: Miss Small — Darlene Anders; Mr. Klemperer — Alexander Orfaly; Mr. Levene — Duane Bodin; Miss Massi — Susan Edwards; Mr. Manson — Walter Charles; Mr. Margulies — Richard Muenz; Mr. Smith — Clyde Laurents; Mr. Powell — Walter Charles; Swing Dancers/Singers — Eleanor Treiber, Vito Durante.

Directed by Gene Saks; choreography, Lee Theodore; musical direction and vocal arrangements, Colin Romoff; scenery, David Mitchell, costumes, Jane Greenwood; lighting, Tom Skelton; orchestrations, Michael Gibson; dance arrangements, David Baker; production stage manager, William Dodds; stage manager, Wayne Carson; press, Warren Knowlton.

Time: 1908. Place: In and around the Lower East Side of Manhattan.

ACT I

Scene 1: An East Side street
Scene 2: The Grand Street Tivoli Theater
"A Grand Street Tivoli Presentation" .... Ensemble
Scene 3: Outside a local synagogue
"Fifty Cents" .... Mourners
Scene 4: Inside the synagogue
Scene 5: An East Side street
Scene 6: Kitchen of Rashumsky's residence
"I Know What It Is To Be Alone" .... Leah, Rashumsky
Scene 7: Kitchen; next morning
"I'm a Star" ....Rashumsky
Scene 8: Atlantic City, the Boardwalk
"Do I Make You Happy" .... Leah, Rashumsky
Scene 9: An Atlantic City hotel
"Stay With Me" ....Rashumsky
Scene 10: An East Side street
Scene 11: Apex Shirts and Blouses
"Sew a Button" .... Leah, Faactory Workers
Scene 12: An East Side street
Scene 13: A local cafe
"The Prince of Grand Street" .... Rashumsky, Ensemble

ACT II

Scene 1: An East Side street
Scene 2: The Grand Street Tivoli Theater
"A Grand Street Tivoli Presentation" .... Ensemble
"A Place in the World" .... Leah
Scene 3: A local cafe
Scene 4: The Grand Street Tivoli Theater
Scene 5: Mark Twain's residence, Gramercy Park
Scene 6: The Grand Street Tivoli Theater
"The Youngest Person I Know" .... Leah, Rashumsky, Ensemble
"A Grand Street Presentation" .... Ensemble
Scene 7: An East Side street
Scene 8: The Grand Street Tivoli Theater
"What Do I Do Now?" .... Leah
Scene 9: An old age home
Scene 10: A hotel room
Scene 11: The Grand Street Tivoli Theater
"What Do I Do Now?" (reprise) .... Leah

The Last Minstrel Show. Musical by John Taylor Ford. Produced by Ken Marsolais in association with Martin Markinson and Donald Tick in a pre-Broadway tryout. Opened at the Wilmington, Del., Playhouse March 30, 1978. (Closed at the New Locust Theater in Philadelphia April 30, 1978)

Forbes ....Roger Alan Brown
Black Sally .... Della Reese
J.J. Jones (Mr. Shine) ......Gregory Hines
George Cole (Mr. Tambo) .... Ned Wright
Uncle Tom Taylor
  (Mr. Salt) .... Eugene Jackson
Brother Bo Taylor
  (Mr. Pepper) ....Dick Vance
Sam Parks Jr.

(Mr. Pompey) .... Jeffrrey V. Thompson
Preacher Simmons
  (Mr. Moses) .... Howard Roberts
Jimmie White
  (Mr. Rastus) .... Tucker Smallwood
Al Perletter
  (Mr. Interlocutor) ....Ralston Hill
Bert Pine (Mr. Bones) .... Clebert Ford
Patton Bridges ....Rene Levant

Darlene Anders and Robert Preston in *The Prince of Grand Street*

Standbys: Black Sally — Sandra Phillips; Messrs. Jackson, Ford — Robert Gossett; Messrs. Vance, Roberts — John T. Grimes; Mr. Thompson — Arvell Shaw; Mr. Wright — Clyde Williams; Mr. Hines — Robert Melvin; Messrs. Hill, Smallwood — Roger Alan Brown; Mr. Brown — Frank Echols; Mr. Levant — Tucker Smallwood.

Directed by Donald McKayle; musical direction, Howard Roberts; scenery, Edward Burbridge; costumes, Robert Mackintosh; lighting, Ian Calderon, orchestrations, Howard Roberts; production stage manager, Nate Barnett; stage managers, Peter Lawrence, Frank Echols; press, Betty Lee Hunt, Maria Cristina Pucci.

Based on a 1926 incident of black picketing when the last touring minstrel show played the Variety Theater in Cincinnati.

ACT I

Scene 1: Backstage at the Variety Theater, Cincinnati, the night of March 15, 1926
Scene 2: Act I of the Minstrel Show
  Overture
  "A High Old Time in Dixie" ....Minstrels
  Wait Til the Sun Shines, Nelly ....Instrumental
  "Down Where the Watermelon Grows" ....Bones, Tambo, Minstrels
  "Shine, Shine, Shine" .... Pepper, Minstrels

"At the Garbage Gentlemen's Ball" .... Shine, Rastus, Pompey
"T'Aint No Sin" .... Salt, Pepper, Moses
Turkey in the Straw ....Instrumental
Dance: Shine, Salt, Pompey
"I'll Lend You Anything" .... Tambo, Bones, Moses
"When the Bell in the Lighthouse
Rings Ding, Dong" .... Interlocutor
"Darktown is Out Tonight" .... Interlocutor, Minstrels
"Waitin' for the Robert E. Lee" ....Minstrels
Scene 3: Backstage immediately following Minstrel Show Act 1

ACT II

Scene 1: A few seconds later
Scene 2: Act II of the Minstrel Show
"Oh, Dem Golden Slippers" .... Bones, Tambo
"Good News" .... Black Sally, Minstrels
"Happy Days in Dixieland" .... Black Sally, Minstrels
"She's Getting More Like the White Folk Every Day" ....Black Sally, Salt, Pepper
"I Don't Mind Walkin' in the Rain" .... Black Sally, Bones, Moses
"Pickaninny's Paradise" .... Black Sally, Salt, Minstrels
"Strut Miss Lizzie" .... Black Sally, Minstrels
"What He's Done for Me/Do Lord" .... Black Sally, Minstrels
"Gee, I'm Glad I'm From Dixie/Dixie" ....Black Sally
Scene 3: Backstage immediately following the Minstrel Show
"Can't You Hear Me Callin' Caroline" ....Minstrels
"Always Left Them Laughing" ....Black Sally

Broadway. Revival of the play by Philip Dunning and George Abbott. Produced by Roger Berlind, Steven Beckler and Thomas C. Smith in a pre-Broadway tryout at the Wilbur Theater in Boston. Opened April 15, 1978. (Closed May 6, 1978)

Nick Verdis	Joseph Leon	Steve Crandall	Chris Sarandon
Pearl	Jill O'Hara	Dolph	Armin Shimerman
Roy Lane	William Atherton	Porky	James Harder
Lil	Nancy Andrews	Scar Edwards	Timothy Meyers
Mazie	Marion McCorry	Joe	David J. Forsyth
Ruby	Jean De Baer	Dan McCorn	Roy Poole
Grace-Ann	Lesley Rogers	Benny	Robert D'Avi
Katie	Laura Copland	Larry	Robert Sevra
"Billie" Moore	Teri Garr		

Understudies: Misses Rogers, De Baer, O'Hara, McCorry — Laura Copland; Misses Andrews, Copland — Lynn Charnay; Messrs. Forsyth, Shimerman, Sevra, D'Avi — Jack Gianino; Messrs. Harder, Leon, Poole — David J. Forsyth; Miss Garr — Lesley Rogers; Messrs. Atherton, Sarandon, Meyers — Robert Sevra.

Directed by Robert Allan Ackerman; scenery, Karen Schulz; costumes, Carrie F. Robbins; lighting, Arden Fingerhut; musical supervisor, Jack Lee; assistant to the director, Dennis Grimaldi; production stage manager, Joe Lorden; stage manager, Jack Gianino; press, Hunt/Pucci Associates, Betty Lee Hunt, Maria Cristina Pucci, Jan W. Greenburg.

Time: 1927. Place: Private party room of the Paradise Nightclub. Act I: An evening in spring. Act II: Half hour later. Act III: The following evening.

Broadway was originally produced 9/16/26 for 332 performances and was named a Best Play of its season. It's only previous New York revival of record was off Broadway by the Laughing Stock Company in October 1950.

PLAYS PRODUCED
OFF BROADWAY

Some distinctions between off-Broadway and Broadway productions at one end of the scale and off-off-Broadway productions at the other were blurred in the New York theater of the 1970s. For the purposes of this *Best Plays* listing the term "off Broadway" is used to distinguish a professional from a showcase (off-off-Broadway) production and signifies a show which opened for general audiences in a mid-Manhattan theater seating 499 or fewer and 1) employed an Equity cast, 2) planned a regular schedule of 7 or 8 performances a week and 3) offered itself to public comment by critics at a designated opening performance.

Occasional exceptions of inclusion (never of exclusion) are made to take in selected Brooklyn productions, visiting troupes, borderline cases and a few non-qualifying productions which readers might expect to find in this list because they appear under an off-Broadway heading in other major sources of record.

Figures in parentheses following a play's title give number of performances. These figures do not include previews or extra non-profit performances.

Plays marked with an asterisk (*) were still running on June 1, 1978. Their number of performances is figured from opening night through May 31, 1978.

Certain programs of off-Broadway companies are exceptions to our rule of counting the number of performances from the date of the press coverage. When the official opening takes place late in the run of a play's regularly-priced public or subscription performances (after previews) we count the first performance of record, not the press date, as opening night — and in each such case in the listing we note the variance and give the press date.

In a listing of a show's numbers — dances, sketches, musical scenes, etc. — the titles of songs are identified wherever possible by their appearance in quotation marks (").

Most entries of off-Broadway productions which ran fewer than 20 performances are somewhat abbreviated.

HOLDOVERS FROM PREVIOUS SEASONS

Plays which were running on June 1, 1977 are listed below. More detailed information about them appears in previous *Best Plays* volumes of appropriate date. Important cast changes since opening night are recorded in a section of this volume.

*The Fantasticks (7,514); longest continuous run of record in the American theater. Musical suggested by the play *Les Romantiques* by Edmond Rostand; book and lyrics by Tom Jones; music by Harvey Schmidt. Opened May 3, 1960.

*Vanities (959). By Jack Heifner. Opened March 22, 1976.

Streamers (478). By David Rabe. Opened April 21, 1976. (Closed June 5, 1977)

The Club (674). Musical by Eve Merriam. Opened October 14, 1976. (Closed May 21, 1978)

Ashes (167). By David Rudkin. Opened January 25, 1977. (Closed July 3, 1977)

Starting Here, Starting Now (120). Musical revue with music by David Shire; lyrics by Richard Maltby Jr. Opened March 7, 1977. (Closed June 19, 1977)

New York Shakespeare Festival Public Theater. On the Lock-In (62). Musical with book, music and lyrics by David Langston Smyrl; conceived by Robert Macbeth. Opened April 14, 1977. (Closed June 5, 1977) **Creditors** and **The Stronger** (56). Program of revivals of one-act plays by August Strindberg; new translations by Palaemona Morner and R. Spacek. Opened April 15, 1977. (Closed June 5, 1977)

Der Ring Gott Farblonjet (78). Musical based on the Volsung saga; book by Charles Ludlam; music by Jack McElwaine. Opened April 27, 1977; was joined in repertory by *Stage Blood* July 1, 1977. (Closed August 14, 1977)

Roundabout Theater Center. Dear Liar (55). Revival of the play by Jerome Kilty. Opened April 28, 1977. (Closed June 12, 1977)

Circle Repertory Company. Exiles (36). Revival of the play by James Joyce. Opened May 19, 1977. (Closed June 12, 1977)

The Sunday Promenade (14). By Lars Forssell; translated by Harry G. Carlson. Opened May 24, 1977. (Closed June 5, 1977)

The Phoenix Theater. Scribes (12). By Barrie Keeffe. Opened May 26, 1977. (Closed June 5, 1977)

PLAYS PRODUCED JUNE 1, 1977-MAY 31, 1978

The 2nd Greatest Entertainer in the Whole Wide World (78). One-man show by and with Dick Shawn. Produced by Kenneth D. Laub at the Promenade Theater. Opened June 2, 1977. (Closed August 7, 1977)

Musicians: Steve Weiss piano, Lou Silverblank flute, Joseph Dick percussion.
Scenery, Akira Yoshimura; lighting, Marilyn Rennagel; stage manager, Robin Brecker; press, Gifford/Wallace, Inc.
Stand-up comedy program with music, presented in two parts.

The Square Root of Soul (28). One-man show conceived and performed by Adolph Caesar. Produced by The Negro Ensemble Company at Theater de Lys. Opened June 14, 1977. (Closed July 10, 1977)

Directed by Perry Schwartz; projections and musical score, Jothan Callins; lighting, Perry Schwartz; stage manager, Michael Nunley; press, Howard Atlee, Clarence Allsopp, Becky Flora.
An evening of 40 selections from poetry by black authors including Gwendolyn Brooks, Oscar Brown Jr., Shirley Burden, Countee Cullen, Paul Lawrence Dunbar, Zack Gilbert, Frances E.W. Harper, Langston Hughes, Frank S. Jenkins, James Weldon Johnson, Don L. Lee, Joseph A. Walker, Joseph White, Richard Wright. Previously produced in Washington, D.C.

Circle Repertory Company. 1976-77 schedule of programs ended with **Unsung Cole** (75). Musical revue with music and lyrics by Cole Porter; conceived by Norman L. Berman. Produced by Circle Repertory Company, Marshall W. Mason artistic director, Jerry Arrow executive director, at the Circle Theater. Opened June 23, 1977. (Closed September 4, 1977)

Dick Shawn in *The 2nd Greatest Entertainer in the Whole Wide World*

Gene Lindsey
Mary Louise
Maureen Moore

Anita Morris
John Sloman

Directed by Norman L. Berman; musical direction, Leon Odenz; choreography, Dennis Grimaldi; scenery, Peter Harvey; costumes, Carol Oditz; lighting, Arden Fingerhut; music and vocal arrangements, Norman L. Berman; additional music and vocal arrangements, Leon Odenz; production stage manager, Amy Schecter; press, Rima Corben.

Collection of 32 obscure Cole Porter songs, some of them dropped from shows and never before presented on the professional stage. The play was presented in two parts.

Margery Cohen replaced Anita Morris 7/3/77.

ACT I: "Pick Me Up and Lay Me Down" — Company; "Farming" — Company; "Thank You So Much, Mrs. Lowsborough-Goodby" — Mary Louise, Gene Lindsey; "The Great Indoors" — Anita Morris; "The Tale of an Oyster" — Maureen Moore; "Poor Young Millionaire" — John Sloman; "A Lady Needs a Rest" — Louise, Morris, Moore; "Ours" — Sloman, Moore; "Lost Liberty Blues" — Morris; "Olga" — Lindsey, Company; "The Queen of Terra Haute" — Louise; "Almiro" (original lyrics by Rene Pujol, adaptation by Brian Ross) — Company; "Dancin' to a Jungle Drum" — Moore; "Take Me Back to Manhattan/I Happen to Like New York" — Lindsey; "Why Don't We Try Staying Home" — Sloman, Moore; "Give Me the Land" — Company.

ACT II: "Abracadabra" — Louise, Company; "When the Hen Stops Laying" — Louise, Lindsey; "That's Why I Love You" — Morris, Sloman; "Nobody's Chasing Me" — Moore; "I'm Getting Myself Ready for You" — Louise, Sloman, Company; "Just Another Page in Your Diary" — Morris and Lindsey, Louise and Sloman; "Goodbye Little Dream Goodbye" — Lindsey, "After You Who" — Louise; "Down in the Depths" — Morris; "Love for Sale" — Sloman; "I've got Some Unfinished Business With You" — Louise; "Kate the Great" — Morris;

"If Ever Married I'm" — Moore; "Red Hot and Blue" — Louise, Morris; "Swingin" the Jinx Away" — Sloman, Lindsey, Women; "Friendship" — Company.

New York Shakespeare Festival. Summer schedule of two outdoor revivals. **Threepenny Opera** (27). Musical with book and lyrics by Bertolt Brecht; music by Kurt Weill; translation by Ralph Manheim and John Willett. Opened June 28, 1977; see note. (Closed July 28, 1977). **Agamemnon** (24). By Aeschylus; conceived by Andrei Serban and Elizabeth Swados using fragments of the original Greek and Edith Hamilton's translation. Opened August 2, 1977; see note. (Closed August 28, 1977). Produced by New York Shakespeare Festival, Joseph Papp producer, Bernard Gersten associate producer, at the Delacorte Theater in Central Park.

BOTH PLAYS: Scenery, Douglas W. Schmidt; press, Merle Debuskey, Bob Ullman. Previously presented in these productions by New York Shakespeare Festival Lincoln Center, *Threepenny Opera* 5/1/76 for 307 performances when it received a special Best Plays citation, and *Agamemnon* 5/1/77 for 38 performances.

THREEPENNY OPERA

Ballad Singer	Roy Brocksmith	Jake	William Duell
Mack the Knife	Philip Bosco	Bob	K.C. Wilson
Jenny Towler	Ellen Greene	Ned	Paul Ukena Jr.
Jonathan Peachum	Jerome Dempsey	Jimmy	Robert Schlee
Samuel	Tony Azito	Walt	John Ridge
Charles Filch	Ed Zang	Tiger Brown	David Sabin
Mrs. Peachum	Gretel Cummings	Smith	Marc Jordan
Matthew	Ralph Drischell	Lucy Brown	Penelope Bodry
Polly Peachum	Caroline Kava	Messenger	Jack Eric Williams

Directed by Richard Foreman; costumes, Theoni V. Aldredge; lighting, Pat Collins; sound, Roger Jay; musical direction, Stanley Silverman; production stage manager, Michael Chambers; production supervisor, Jason Steven Cohen.

AGAMEMNON

Clytemnestra	Gloria Foster	Chorus Leader	Earle Hyman
Cassandra	Dianne Wiest	Iphigenia	Suelain Moy
Agamemnon	Jamil Zakkai	Watchman	Jon De Vries
Aegisthus	Ron O'Neal	Herald	William Parry

Directed by Andrei Serban; music, Elizabeth Swados; costumes, Santo Loquasto; lighting, Jennifer Tipton; production stage manager, Louis Rackoff.

Note: Press date for *Threepenny Opera* was 7/6/77, for *Agamemnon* 8/10/77.

*The Light Opera of Manhattan. Repertory of thirteen operetta revival programs. **H.M.S. Pinafore** (42). Book and lyrics by W.S. Gilbert; music by Arthur Sullivan. Opened June 29, 1977. **The Pirates of Penzance** (35). Book and lyrics by W.S. Gilbert; music by Arthur Sullivan. Opened July 6, 1977. **The Merry Widow** (49). Book by Victor Leon and Leo Stein; music by Franz Lehar; English lyrics by Adrian Ross. Opened July 13, 1977. **Naughty Marietta** (14). Book and lyrics by Rida Johnson Young; music by Victor Herbert. Opened August 3, 1977. **The Vagabond King** (14). Book and lyrics by W.H. Post and Brian Hooker; music by Rudolf Friml. Opened August 17, 1977. **Ruddigore** (21). Book and lyrics by W.S. Gilbert; music by Arthur Sullivan. Opened September 14, 1977. ***The Mikado** (50). Book and lyrics by W.S. Gilbert; music by Arthur Sullivan. Opened September 28, 1977.

Also **The Sorcerer** and **Trial by Jury** (21). Book and lyrics by W.S. Gilbert; music by Arthur Sullivan. Opened October 5, 1977. **Iolanthe** (14). Book and lyrics by W.S. Gilbert;

music by Arthur Sullivan. Opened November 23, 1977. **Mlle. Modiste** (35). Book and lyrics by Henry Blossom; music by Victor Herbert. Opened January 11, 1978. **The Grand Duchess of Gerolstein** (28). Libretto by Henri Meilhac and Ludovic Halevy; English translation by Charles Lamb Kenney; music by Jacques Offenbach. Opened February 8, 1978. **Patience** (14). Book and lyrics by W.S. Gilbert; lyrics by Arthur Sullivan. Opened March 29, 1978. **The Gondoliers** (14). Book and lyrics by W.S. Gilbert; music by Arthur Sullivan. Opened April 19, 1978. Produced by The Light Opera of Manhattan, Inc. (LOOM), William Mount-Burke producer-director, at the Eastside Playhouse.

ALL PLAYS — Directed by William Mount-Burke; musical director and conductor, William Mount-Burke; associate director, Raymond Allen; assistant musical director, Brian Molloy; assistant conductor, J. Michael Bart; stage manager, Jerry Gotham; press, Jean Dalrymple, Todd Pearthree.

H.M.S. Pinafore, The Mikado, The Pirates of Penzance, Ruddigore, The Merry Widow, Naughty Marietta and *The Vagabond King* were last produced last season, and *Iolanthe, The Gondoliers* and *Patience* in the 1976-77 season, in LOOM repertory.

Choristers in various productions: Constance Little, Mary Miller, Jo Shelnutt, Ed Harrison, Rob Main, Calvin Selfridge, Joseph Smith, Sheleigh Grube, Karen Kruger, Linda Plona, Michael Barnett, David Besch, Gail Elizabeth Evans, Maeve Gyenes, Marilyn Kaeshian, Francine Katz, Miki Newmark, Janice Papdos, Steve Brown, Steve Kluger, James Lawer, Walter Richardson, Richard Weston, Randa Ball, Nancy Breece, Robert Bauckham, Dan Bernstein, Robert Urbanowicz, Corina Hall, Sara Taubman, Dianne Simmons.

PERFORMER	"H.M.S. PINAFORE"	"THE PIRATES OF PENZANCE"	"RUDDI-GORE"	"THE MIKADO"
Raymond Allen	Joseph Porter	Maj.-Gen. Stanley	Robin Oakapple	Ko-Ko
Diane Armistead	(Buttercup)	(Ruth)		(Katisha)
Alida Augen			(Rose Maybud)	
Jeanne Beauvais		(Ruth)	Dame Hannah	
Sandy Burnard	(Josephine)			
Andrew Callahan			(Sir Despard); Old Adam	
Elizabeth Devine		(Kate)	Ruth	Peep-Bo
Jan Downing		(Edith)	(Zorah)	
Elizabeth Harr				(Katisha)
Michael Harrison				(Nanki-Poo)
Michael Harvey	(Rackstraw)			
Paul Huck	(Carpenter)			
Nancy Hoffman	(Josephine)	(Mabel)	(Rose Maybud)	(Yum-Yum)
Joan Lader	Hebe	(Isabel)	Mad Margaret	Pitti-Sing
Ethel Mae Mason	(Buttercup)			
Georgia McEver	(Josephine)	(Mabel)		(Yum-Yum)
Valerie Mondini		(Edith)	(Zorah)	
John Palmore	(Boatswain)	(Samuel)		
Nancy Papale	(Josephine)			(Yum-Tum)
Kristin Paulus		(Isabel)		
Vashek Pazdera	Dick Deadeye	Sergeant	(Sir Roderic)	Mikado
Gary Pitts	(Rackstraw)			(Nanki-Poo)
Steven Polcek	(Carpenter)			
Lawrence Raiken	(Rackstraw)			
Walter Richardson	(Carpenter)			
Gary Ridley	(Boatswain)	Frederic	Dauntless	(Pish-Tush)
Julio Rosario	Capt. Corcoran	Pirate King	(Sir Despard); (Sir Roderic)	Pooh-Bah
Mary Lee Rubens	(Josephine)			(Yum-Yum)

PERFORMER	"H.M.S. PINAFORE"	"THE PIRATES OF PENZANCE"	"RUDDI-GORE"	"THE MIKADO"
William Walsh				(Pish-Tush)
Mary Wolff		(Samuel)		
Rosemarie Wright		(Kate)		

(Parentheses indicate role in which the performer alternated during the season)

PERFORMER	"THE MERRY WIDOW"	"NAUGHTY MARIETTA"	"THE VAGABOND KING"
Raymond Allen	Popoff	Silas Slick	Louis XI
Jeanne Beauvais	Sonia	Adah	Huguette DuHamel
Sandy Burnard	(Natalie)		
Andrew Callahan	(Nova Kovich)		
Dennis Curran	(Khadja)		Rene DeMontigny
Elizabeth Devine	Praskovia	Fanchon	
Peggy Dufour	(Natalie)	(Marietta)	
Dennis English		Sir Harry Blake	
Michael Harrison	(Prince Danilo)	Capt. Warrington	
Michael Harvey	(Camille de Jolidon)		
Paul Huck		Rudolfo	
Edward Hustwit			Casin
Joanne Jamieson		Felice	
Joan Lader	Olga	Lizette	Lady Mary
Georgia McEver		(Marietta)	Katherine DeVaucelles
James Nadeaux	Nish	Florenze	Tristan
Tom Olmstead	(Khadja)		
Kristin Paulus		Nanette	Margot
Steven Polcek	(Nova Kovich)		
Lawrence Raiken	(Camille de Jolidon)		
Gary Ridley	Raoul de St. Brioche	Lt.-Gov. Grandet	Francois Villon
Julio Rosario	(Pince Danilo)	Etienne Grandet	Tabarie
Kenneth Sieger	(Marquis de Cascada)		
William Walsh	(Marquis de Cascada)		
Mark Wolff	(Marquis de Cascada)		

(Parentheses indicate role in which the performer alternated during the season)

PERFORMER	"THE SORCERER" AND "TRIAL BY JURY"	"IOLANTHE"	"PATIENCE"	"THE GONDOLIERS"
Raymond Allen	John Wells	Lord Chancellor	Bunthorne	Plaza-Toro
Alida Augen	(Constance)			
Diane Armistead	Lady Sangazure	Fairy Queen	Lady Jane	
Robert Berlott				Annibale
Bronwen Brown			Lady Ella	
Paul Bufano	(Jury Foreman)			
Sandy Burnard		Celia		Fiametta
Andrew Callahan	(Notary); Usher			
Katherine Cuba				(Giulia)
Elizabeth Devine		Fleta	(Lady Saphir)	(Vittoria)
Elizabeth Harr				Duchess Plaza-Toro
Michael Harrison	Alexis			

PERFORMER	"THE SORCERER" AND "TRIAL BY JURY"	"IOLANTHE"	"PATIENCE"	"THE GONDOLIERS"
Joan Lader	Mrs. Partlet	Iolanthe	Lady Angela	Tessa
Georgia McEver	(Aline); (Plaintiff)		Patience	Casilda
Valerie Mondini	(Constance)			
James Nadeaux	Judge			
Katherine Neville				(Giulia); (Inez)
Tom Olmstead				(Giorgio)
John Palmore	Counsel		Maj. Murgatroyd	Francesco
Nancy Papale		(Phyllis)		
Kristin Paulus		Leila	(Lady Saphir)	(Inez)
Vashek Pazdera		Pvt. Willis	Col. Calverly	Don Alahambra
Gary Pitts	Defendant	Lord Tollolier	Dunstable	Marco
Frank Prieto			Solicitor	
Walter Richardson	(Notary); (Jury Foreman)			(Giorgio)
Gary Ridley	Dr. Daly	Strephon	(Grosvenor)	Luiz
Kathy Rogers				(Vittoria)
Julio Rosario	Sir Pointdextre	Lord Mountararat	(Grosvenor)	Giuseppe
Mary Lee Rubens	(Aline); (Plaintiff)	(Phyllis)		Gianetta
William Walsh				Antonio

(Parentheses indicate role in which the actor alternated during the season)

The Pirates of Penzance, Naughty Marietta, The Vagabond King, Ruddigore, The Mikado, The Gondoliers scenery, William Schroder; *The Merry Widow, The Sorcerer* scenery, Elouise Meyer; *H.M.S. Pinafore, The Pirates of Penzance, The Merry Widow, Naughty Marietta, The Mikado, Patience* costumes, George Stinson; *The Vagabond King, The Gondoliers* costumes, William Schroder; *The Sorcerer* wardrobe donated by Huntington Hartford; *Trial by Jury* costumes, Elouise Meyer; *The Merry Widow* lighting, Peggy Clark; *The Merry Widow, Naughty Marietta, The Vagabond King* choreography, Jerry Gotham.

THE SORCERER — Act I: Exterior of Sir Marmaduke's mansion, mid-day. Act II: The same, midnight.

The first New York Production of record of *The Sorcerer* was by the William A. Brady company in repertory beginning 4/19/15. It was subsequently presented off Broadway by the Light Opera Theater in the seasons of 1943-44, 1945-46 and 1946-47, its last professional New York revival.

TRIAL BY JURY — Place: A court of Justice

The last professional New York production of *Trial by Jury* was by The American Savoyards off Broadway 6/7/66 for 28 performances.

MLLE. MODISTE

Fifi	Georgia McEver	Comte de St. Mar	Lloyd Harris
Mme. Cecile	Jeanne Beauvais	Capt. Etienne De Bouvray	Gary Ridley
Franchette	Sandy Burnard	Gaston	Julio Rosario
Nanette	Elizabeth Devine	Francois	Andrew Callahan
Mrs. Hiram Bent	Joan Lader	Lt. Rene	John Palmore
Bebe	Kristin Paulus	Hiram Bent	Raymond Allen

Milliners, Guests, Dancers, Soldiers, Servants: Kathy Rogers, Katherine Cuba, Joanne Jamieson, Robert Berlott, William Walsh, Walter Richardson, Tom Olstead.

Scenery, Louise Krozek; costumes, James Nadeaux; lighting, Peggy Clark; choreography, Jerry Gotham; special consultant, Alfred Simon.

Time: Circa 1906. Act I: Mme. Cecile's Hat Shop, Rue de la Paix, Paris. Act II, Scene I: Comte

de St. Mar's chateau, a year later. Scene 2: "The Charity Bazaar" in the garden of the chateau.
Mlle. Modiste was first produced by Charles Dillingham 12/25/05 for 202 performances. It was revived 5/26/13 for 24 performances and 10/7/29 for 48 performances, its last professional New York production of record.
Tom Boyd replaced Lloyd Harris 3/8/78.

ACT I

"Furs and Feathers" .... Hat Shop Girls
"Here Is a Pretty Hat" .... Fanchette, Nanette
"When the Cat's Away" .... Fanchette, Nanette, Mme. Cecile
"The Mascot of the Troop" .... Fifi, Ensemble
"The Time, the Place and the Girl" .... Etienne, Ensemble
"Hats Make the Woman" .... Mme. Cecile, Gaston
"Walks" .... Hiram, Fifi
"If I Were on the Stage" ("Kiss Me Again") .... Fifi
"Love Me, Love My Dog" .... Gaston
Finale .... Ensemble

ACT II

Scene 1
Prelude
"Starlight, Star Bright" .... Etienne
"I Want What I Want When I Want It" .... Count
Scene 2
"The Charity Bazaar" .... Ensemble
"Ze English Language" .... Mme. Cecile
"Kiss Me Again" (Reprise) .... Fifi, Etienne
"The Keokuk Culture Club" .... Mrs. Brent
"The Absinthe Frappe" .... Hiram, Ensemble
"The Nightingale and the Star" .... Fifi
Finale .... Ensemble

THE GRAND DUCHESS OF GEROLSTEIN

Grand Duchess	Diane Armistead	Baron Grog	Andrew Callahan
Wanda	Sandy Burnard	Ladies in Waiting:	
Fritz	Larry Raiken	Iza	Kathy Rogers
General Boum	Julio Rosario	Olga	Bronwen Brown
Baron Puck	Raymond Allen	Amelie	Katherine Cuba
Prince Paul	Gary Ridley	Charlotte	Kristin Paulus
Nepomuc	James Nadeaux		

Scenery, Louise Krozek; costumes, Marianne Powell-Parker; lighting, Peggy Clark; choreography, Jerry Gotham; special consultant, Louise Hayden Granbery.
Time: Circa 1860. Place: The Grand Duchy of Gerolstein. Act I: A military camp. Act II: A room in the palace. Act III, Scene 1: The bedchamber. Scene 2: A room in the palace.
A spoof of war and court intrigues first produced in the U.S.A. in 1867 and celebrated for its "Sabre Song." It has never been revived in New York under this title, though an Offenbach work *The Grand Duchess* was presented in 1890 and 1894.

Stage Blood (15). Revival of the play by Charles Ludlam. Produced by the Ridiculous Theatrical Company, Charles Ludlam artistic director, at the Truck and Warehouse Theater in repertory with *Der Ring Gott Farblonjet*. Opened July 1, 1977. (Repertory closed August 14, 1977)

Carleton Stone;			
Gilbert Fey	Ethyl Eichelberger	Helga Vain	Lola Pashalinski
Carleton Stone Jr.	Charles Ludlam	Jenkins	John D. Brockmeyer

Edmund Dundreary .... Bill Vehr   Elfie Fay .... Black-Eyed Susan

Directed by Charles Ludlam; scenery, Bobjack Collejo; costumes and graphics, Arthur Brady; lighting, Richard Currie; production stage manager, Richard Gibbs; press, Alan Eichler.

This *Hamlet* parody was previously produced by the Ridiculous Theatrical Company 12/8/74 for 45 performances.

*New York Shakespeare Festival Public Theater. Schedule of fourteen programs. **Miss Margarida's Way** (30). By Roberto Athayde. Opened July 31, 1977 matinee. (Closed September 4, 1977 and transferred to Broadway; see its entry in the "Plays Produced on Broadway" section of this volume). **Landscape of the Body** (64). By John Guare. Opened September 27, 1977; see note. (Closed November 20, 1977) **The Misanthrope** (63). Musical adaptation of the play by Molière; adaptation and lyrics by Richard Wilbur; music and songs by Jobriath Boone; additional songs by Margaret Pine and Arthur Bienstock. Opened October 5, 1977; see note. (Closed November 27, 1977) **Tales of the Hasidim** (20). Adapted by Paul Sills from Martin Buber in the Improvisational Theater Company production. Opened November 18, 1977; see note. (Closed December 3, 1977) **The Mandrake** (165). Revival of the play by Niccolo Machiavelli; new translation by Wallace Shawn. Opened December 7, 1977. (Closed April 30, 1978) **A Photograph** (62). By Ntozake Shangé. Opened December 1, 1977; see note. (Closed January 22, 1978) **The Dybbuk** (62). Revival of the play by S. Ansky; translated by Mira Rafalowicz; new version developed by Mira Rafalowicz and Joseph Chaikin. Opened December 6, 1977; see note. (Closed January 29, 1978).

Also **The Water Engine** (63). By David Mamet. Opened December 20, 1977; see note. (Closed February 11, 1978 and transferred to Broadway; see its entry in the "Plays Produced on Broadway" section of this volume) **A Prayer for My Daughter** (127). By Thomas Babe. Opened December 27, 1977; see note. (Closed April 16, 1978) **Museum** (78). By Tina Howe. Opened February 7, 1978: see note. (Closed April 16, 1978) **Curse of the Starving Class** (62). By Sam Shepard. Opened February 14, 1978; see note. (Closed April 9, 1978) **Runaways** (80). Musical written and composed by Elizabeth Swados. Opened February 21, 1978; see note. (Closed April 30, 1978 and transferred to Broadway; see its entry in the "Plays Produced on Broadway" section of this volume) ***I'm Getting My Act Together and Taking It On the Road** (14). Musical with book and lyrics by Gretchen Cryer; music by Nancy Ford. Opened May 16, 1978; see note. ***Mango Tango** (3). By Jessica Hagedorn. Opened May 28, 1978. Produced by the New York Shakespeare Festival, Joseph Papp producer, Bernard Gersten associate producer, at the Public Theater.

ALL PLAYS — Production supervisor, Jason Steven Cohen; press, Merle Debuskey, Bob Ullman, Richard Kornberg.

MISS MARGARIDA'S WAY

Miss Margarida .... Estelle Parsons   Rest of Her Students .... The Audience
One of Her Students .... Colin Garrey

Directed by Roberto Athayde; scenery and costumes, Santo Loquasto; lighting, Martin Tudor.

Domineering, emotionally twisted teacher harangues her "class," which includes the members of the audience, in a metaphor of fascistic oppression. A foreign play previously produced in Brazil, Argentina, Europe and San Francisco. The play was presented in two parts.

LANDSCAPE OF THE BODY

Betty .... Shirley Knight   Raulito .... Richard Bauer
Capt. Marvin Holohan   F. Murray Abraham   Bert .... Paul McCrane
Rosalie .... Peg Murray   Donny .... Anthony Marciona

Joanne	Alexa Kenin	Masked Man; Dope King;	
Margie	Bonnie Deroski	Bank Teller	Raymond J. Barry
Durwood Peach	Remak Ramsay		

Standby: Misses Knight, Murray — Barbara Andres. Understudies: Misses Deroski, Kenin — Laura Dean; Messrs. McCrane, Marciona — Rob De Rosa; Messrs. Ramsay, Abraham — Tom Klunis.

Directed by John Pasquin; music and lyrics, John Guare; scenery and costumes, Santo Loquasto; lighting, Jennifer Tipton; arrangements and incidental music, Wally Harper; pianist, Rod Derefinko; production stage manager, Stephen McCorkle; stage manager, Trey Altemose.

Place: A ferry to Nantucket and Greenwich Village. The play was presented in two parts.

Young woman from Maine finds murder and madness in the big city. Previously presented at Academy Festival Theater, Lake Forest, Ill.

THE MISANTHROPE

Alceste	John McMartin	Clitandre	Edward Zang
Philinte	John Bottoms	Acaste	Seth Allen
Oronte	Arthur Burghardt	Guard	Walt Gorney
Celimene	Virginia Vestoff	Arsinoe	Helen Gallagher
Basque	William Parry	Dubois	Joshua Mostel
Eliante	Deborah Rush		

Musicians: Allen Shawn piano; Billy Kerr woodwinds; Anca Cismaru 1st violin; Miles Hoffman 2d violin, viola; Byron Duckwall cello, Dean Crandall bass.

Understudies: Misses Rush, Gallagher — Mimi Turque; Messrs. Zang, Mostel — William Parry; Messrs. McMartin, Burghardt — Paul Richards. Standby: Messrs. Bottoms, Allen — Robert Jackson.

Directed by Bill Gile; scenery, Bill Stabile; costumes, Carrie F. Robbins; lighting, Arden Fingerhut; musical direction, Allen Shawn; dance sequences, Rachel Lampert; orchestrations, Robert Rodgers, Bill Brohn; production stage manager, D.W. Koehler; stage manager, Jason LaPadura.

Place: Celimene's house in Paris. The play was presented in two parts.

The last professional New York production of *The Misanthrope* took place on Broadway 3/12/75 for 94 performances (and the last production of the Richard Wilbur version was by APA 10/9/68 for 86 performances).

TALES OF THE HASIDIM

Joshua Broder	Mina Kolb
Severn Darden	Paul Sand
Anthony Holland	Eugene Troobnick

Directed by Paul Sills; lighting, Victor En Yu Tan; music, Fred Kaz; production stage manager, Peter Reed Glazer; stage manager, Nancy Golladay.

Act I: Levi Yitzhak of Berditcher. Act II: Zusya of Hanipol.

Dramatizations of Martin Buber's Hasidic tales, followed by a series of improvisational theater skits and acts. This program opened the Public Theater Cabaret, a new setup for cabaret productions in Martinson Hall.

THE MANDRAKE

Singer	Thelma Nevitt	Waiter	Paca Thomas
Prologue; Siro	Wallace Shawn	Madonna Sostrata; Woman	
Callimaco	James Lally	at church	Angela Pietropinto
Ligurio	John Ferraro	Brother Timothy	Larry Pine
Prof. Nicia	Tom Costello	Lucrezia	Corinne Fischer

Musicians: Dan Carillo guitar, mandolin; Charley Gerard woodwinds; Richard Weinstock keyboards.

Directed by Wilford Leach; music, Richard Weinstock: scenery, Wilford Leach; costumes, Patricia McGourty; lighting, Victor En Yu Tan; production stage manager, Bill McComb.

Place: In and around the Piazza della Signoria, at the Trotteria Primavera, at the house of Callimaco and Prof. Nicia and at Il Duomo. The play was presented without intermission.

This Machiavelli comedy was previously produced as *Mandragola* by Equity Library Theater in the 1945-46 season and by The Extension in the 1967-68 season. This production first appeared in Public Theater workshop 11/18/77.

John Bottoms replaced Larry Pine 1/24/78. Larry Pine replaced John Bottoms 2/21/78.

A PHOTOGRAPH

Michael	Michele Shay	Earl	Count Stovall
Sean David	Avery Brooks	Claire	Hattie Winston
Nevada	Petronia Paley		

Dancer — Charlisse Drakeford.

Understudies: Misses Paley, Winston — Carol Lynn Maillard; Messrs. Stovall, Brooks — Tucker Smallwood; Miss Shay — Linda Thomas Wright.

Directed by Oz Scott; choreography, Marsha Blanc; music composed by David Murray; scenery, David Mitchell; costumes, Beverly Parks; lighting, Victor En Yu Tan; visuals, Collis Davis, David Mitchell; production stage manager, Richard S. Viola; stage manager, Leanna Lenhart.

Act I: Silence is too much for a poem. Act II: Music is the least love she'd bring you.

Subtitled *A Study of Cruelty,* a "poemplay" collection of short comments on a variety of contemporary subjects.

THE DYBBUK

Rabbi Azriel	Richard Bauer	Musician	Ellen Maddow
Osher	Robert Blumenfeld	Chanon	Bruce Myers
Chana-Esther	Shami Chaikin	Student Bridegroom	Mark Nelson
Woman in Town;		Woman in Town;	
Musician	Alice Eve Cohen	Rich Woman	Marcell Rosenblatt
Wedding Guest; Judge	Joseph Davidson	Man in Synagogue;	
Henoch; Beggar	Bernard Duffy	Bridegroom's Father	Mark Samuels
Maggid	Corey Fischer	Rabbi's Wife; Beggar	Margo Lee Sherman
Pregnant Woman; Beggar	Jenn Hamburg	Michol; Musician	Arthur Strimling
Leah	Marcia Jean Kurtz	Sender	Jamil Zakkai
Student Beggar	Hal Lehrman Jr.	Shimshon; Musician	Paul Zimet
Woman in Town; Basia;		Freyda	Sonia Zomina

Understudies: Miss Chaikin — Jenn Hamburg; Messrs. Fischer, Zimet — Robert Blumenfeld; Mr. Myers — Bernard Duffy; Messrs. Duffy, Nelson, Blumfeld, Strimling — Hal Lehrman Jr.; Miss Kurtz — Marcell Rosenblatt; Miss Zomina — Anne Barclay; Mr. Bauer — Steven Gilborn; Messrs. Zakkai, Samuels — Arthur Strimling.

Directed by Joseph Chaikin; scenery, Woods Mackintosh; costumes, Mary Brecht; lighting, Beverly Emmons; *The Heart and the Spring* story adapted by Corey Fischer: production stage manager, Louis Rackoff; stage manager, Frank DiFilia.

The Dybbuk's last professional New York productions were by The National Theater of the Deaf 4/8/75 for 8 performances and in Yiddish by the Jewish State Theater of Bucharest 9/19/72 for 8 performances. This production was presented without intermission.

THE WATER ENGINE

Charles Lang	Dwight Schultz	Bernie	Michael Miller Jr.
Rita	Penelope Allen	Dave Murray	Colin Stinton
Morton Gross	David Sabin	Sound Effects Man	Eric Loeb
Lawrence Oberman	Bill Moor	Announcer	Paul Millikin
Mrs. Varec	Barbara Tarbuck	Musician	Alaric Jans
Mr. Wallace	Dominic Chianese	Miss Annie Hat	Herself

Directed by Steven Schachter; scenery, John Lee Beatty; costumes, Laura Crow; lighting, Dennis Parichy; music, Alaric Jans; production stage manager, Jason La Padura; stage manager, Harold Apter.

Understudies: Messrs. Schultz, Stinton — Eric Loeb; Messrs. Chianese, Moor, Sabin — Paul Milikin; Mr. Miller — Dominic Chianese Jr.; Misses Allen, Tarbuck — JoAnne Belanger.

Time: 1934, the second year of "The Century of Progress Exposition." Place: Various Chicago locations. The play was performed without intermission.

Subtitled *An American Fable,* a radio play-within-a-play about an inventor violently suppressed by industrial interests when he invents an engine that will run on water.

Patti LuPone replaced Penelope Allen 2/7/78. Michael Miller Jr. changed his name to Michael J. Miller when the production transferred to Broadway.

A PRAYER FOR MY DAUGHTER

Kelly .... George Dzundza   Jimmy .... Alan Rosenberg
Jack ....Jeffrey De Munn   Simon .... Laurence Luckinbill

Understudies: Mr. Dzundza — Ron McLarty; Mr. Rosenberg — John Joseph Cali; Messrs. De-Munn, Luckinbill — Ronald Hunter.

Directed by Robert Allan Ackerman; scenery, Bil Mikulewicz; costumes, Bob Wojewodski; lighting, Arden Fingerhut; production stage manager, Kitzi Becker; stage manager, Andy Lopata.

Time: The present. Place: A New York City police station house. The play was presented in two parts.

The night's work of two policemen interrogating a pair of suspected killers.

A Best Play; see page 189.

MUSEUM

CAST: Guard — Larry Bryggman; Michael Wall — Bruce McGill; Jean-Claude, 2d Man Passing, Mr. Gregory — Jean-Pierre Stewart; Francoise, Ada Bilditsky, Lillian — Frederikke Meister; Annette Frebel, Chloe Trapp — Kaiulani Lee; Liz; Mira Zadal, Kate Siv — Robyn Goodman; Carol, Gilda Norris — Kathryn Grody; Blakey, Julie Jenkins — Kathleen Tolan; Mr. Hollingsford, 1st Man Passing, Giorgio — Gerry Bamman; Elizabeth Sorrow, Tink Solheim — Dianne Wiest; Peter Ziff, 2d Guard — Dan Hedaya; Mr. Salt, 1st Guard, Elderly Man — Steven Gilborn; Mrs. Salt, Zoe — Jane Hallaren; Maggie Snow, Barbara Castle, Harriet — Lynn Milgrim; Bob Lamb, Bill Plaid — Jeffrey David Pomerantz; Will Willard, Steve Williams — Joel Brooks; Fred Izumi — Calvin Jung; Barbara Zimmer, May, Elderly Woman — Karen Ludwig.

Understudies not in cast: Elaine Bromka, Peter Craig, Jerry Cunliffe, Donna Isaacson, Michael Medeiros.

Directed by Max Stafford-Clark; scenery, Robert Yodice; costumes, Patricia McGourty; lighting, Jennifer Tipton; production stage manager, Alan Fox; stage manager, Robert J. Mooney.

Three paintings in a gallery observe the stream of human beings passing before them. The play was presented without intermission. Previously produced in workshop at the Public Theater during the 1976-77 season.

CURSE OF THE STARVING CLASS

Wesley .... Ebbe Roe Smith   Ellis .... Eddie Jones
Ella .... Olympia Dukakis   Malcolm .... John Aquino
Emma .... Pamela Reed   Emerson .... Michael J. Pollard
Taylor .... Kenneth Welsh   Slater .... Raymond J. Barry
Weston ....James Gammon

Understudies: Messrs. Pollard, Barry, Welsh, Aquino — Charles Dean; Miss Dukakis — Marsha Haufrecht; Mr. Smith — Raynor Scheine; Messrs. Jones, Gammon — Arlen Dean Snyder, Miss Reed — Kathy Danzer.

Directed by Robert Woodruff; scenery and costumes, Santo Loquasto; lighting, Martin Tudor; music written and performed by Bob Feldman; production stage manager, Zane Weiner; stage manager, Patricia M. Morinelli.

Hunger of all kinds, moral and physical, stimulated and used by the exploiters to dominate and strip the exploited. The play was presented in three parts.

RUNAWAYS

Hubbell .... Bruce Hlibok   A.J. ....Anthony Imperato

Ebbe Roe Smith and co-player in *Curse of the Starving Class*

Jackie ....Diane Lane	Eric .... Evan Miranda
Lidia .... Jossie De Guzman	Iggy .... Jonathan Feig
Melinda ....Trini Alvardo	Deidre ....Karen Evans
Nikki Kay Kane .... Nan-Lynn Nelson	EZ .... Leonard (Duke) Brown
Manny .... Randy Ruiz	Luis ....Ray Contreras
Eddie .... Jon Matthews	Mex-Mongo ....Mark Anthony Butler
Sundar .... Bernie Allison	Jane ....Kate Schellenbach
Roby .... Venustra K. Robinson	Interpreter for Hubbell .... Lorie Robinson
Lazar .... David Schechter	Chorus .... Sheila Gibbs, Toby Parker

Musicians: Judith Fleisher piano, toy piano; John Schimmel string bass; Leopoldo F. Fleming congas, timbales, bongos, bells, siren, others; David Sawyer triangle, trap set, glass, ratchet; Patience Higgins saxophones, flutes; Elizabeth Swados guitar.

Understudies: Michelle Dagarvarian, Katherine Diamond, C.S. Hayward, Rachael Kelly, Michael Laylor, Timmy Michaels, Jaime Perry.

Directed by Elizabeth Swados; scenery, Douglas W. Schmidt, Woods Mackintosh; costumes, Hilary Rosenfeld; lighting, Jennifer Tipton; English-Spanish translations, Jossie De Guzman;

arrangements improvised by the musicians; production stage manager, Gregory Meeh; stage manager, Peter Glazer.

In the words of Elizabeth Swados, "a collage around the profound effects of deteriorating families" extensively researched and partially improvised, with several actual runaways in the cast.

ACT I SONGS AND SPEECHES

You Don't Understand ....Hubbell
(with improvisation by Bruce Hlibok)
I Had to Go .... A.J., Schimmel
Parent/Kid Dance .... Company
"Appendectomy" .... Jackie
"Where Do People Go" .... Company
Footstep .... Nikki, Schimmel, Lidia, Manny
(Spanish argument by Jossie De Guzman and Randy Ruiz)
"Once Upon a Time" .... Lidia, Company
Current Events ....Eddie
"Every Now and Then" ....Sundar, Company
Out on the Street ....Hubbell, Lorie
(with improvisation by Bruce Hlibok)
Minnesota Strip .... Roby
"Song of a Child Prostitute" ....Jackie, Lidia, Manny, Luis
Christmas Puppies ....Nikki
Lazar's Heroes ....Lazar
"Find Me a Hero" .... Lazar, Company
Scrynatchkielooaw ....Nikki
"The Undiscovered Son" .... Eric, Fleisher, Schimmel
I Went Back Home .... Iggy, Jackie
This Is What I Do When I'm Angry ....Deidre
"The Basketball Song" .... EZ, Company
(Dance — Luis)
Spoons .... Manny
"Lullaby for Luis" .... Lidia, Luis, Higgins, Company
"We Are Not Strangers" .... Eric, Company

ACT II SONGS AND SPEECHES

In the Sleeping Line .... Company
(A.J.'s Dream — Anthony Imperato; Roby's Dream — Venustra K. Robinson; Jackie's Dream — Diane Lane; Lazar's Dream — David Schechter; Eddie's Dream — Vincent Stewart; Nightmares in Spanish — Jossie De Guzman, Randy Ruiz, Ray Contreras)
"Lullaby From Baby to Baby" .... Melinda, Hubbell, Deidre
Tra Gog in Dein Whole (I Will Not Tell a Soul) .... Lazar, Hubbell
"Revenge Song" .... Company
Enterprise .... Deidre, Nikki, Mex-Mongo, Company
Mr. Graffiti .... Mex-Mongo
"Sometimes" .... Roby, Lazar, Company
Clothes ....Iggy
"Where Are Those People Who Did *Hair*" ....Lazar, Deidre
"The Untrue Pigeon" ....Nikki
"Senoras de la Noche" .... Lidia, Manny, Nikki
We Have to Die? ....Deidre
Appendectomy II ....Jackie, Melinda
"Let Me Be a Kid" .... Company
To the Dead of Family Wars ....Deidre
Problem After Problem ....Hubbell, Lorie
"Lonesome of the Road" .... Luis, Sundar, Company

I'M GETTING MY ACT TOGETHER
AND TAKING IT ON THE ROAD

Heather	Gretchen Cryer	Cheryl	Betty Aberlin
Joe	Joel Fabiani	Jake	Don Scardino
Alice	Margot Rose		

Band: Scott Berry piano, Lee Grayson guitar, Bob George drums, Dean Swenson bass, flute.
Understudies: Misses Rose, Aberlin — Nadine Connors; Mr. Fabiani — Gene Lindsey; Mr. Scardino — Michael Ayr; Miss Cryer — Betty Aberlin.

Directed by Word Baker; costumes, Pearl Somner; lighting, Martin Tudor; orchestrations by the band with the composer; orchestration for "Strong Woman Number" by Elliot Weiss; production stage manager, Marjorie Horne; stage manager, Andy Lopata.

Women's lib in the life of a cabaret performer. Musical numbers in this show were not separately listed.

MANGO TANGO

With Jessica Hagedorn; Ota Paul Pheeroan Aklaff drums; Cisse Michael Gregory Jackson vocals, guitars, keyboards; Leonard Jones bass, vocals.

Directed by Regge Life; music composed and arranged by Cisse Michael Gregory Jackson; costumes, Beverly Parks; lighting, Victor En Yu Tan; stage manager, Shawn King.

Recitation of poems by Jessica Hagedorn about her Manila childhood and arrival in the United States, with a musical background.

The season's special events in the New York Shakespeare Festival Public Theater complex included workshop productions, *A Month of Sundays* special events, guest productions, etc. See their entries in the "Plays Produced Off Off Broadway" section of this volume.

Note: Press date for *Landscape of the Body* was 10/12/77, for *The Misanthrope* 11/22/77, for *Tales of the Hasidim* 11/30/77, for *A Photograph* 12/21/77, for *The Dybbuk* 12/22/77, for *The Water Engine* 1/5/78, for *A Prayer for My Daughter* 1/17/78, for *Museum* 2/26/78, for *Curse of the Starving Class* 3/2/78, for *Runaways* 3/9/78, for *I'm Getting My Act Together and Taking It On the Road* 6/14/78.

In Joseph Papp's Public Theater there are many separate auditoriums. *Miss Margarida's Way, Landscape of the Body, The Dybbuk* and *Curse of the Starving Class* played the Estelle R. Newman Theater; *The Misanthrope, A Prayer for My Daughter* and *I'm Getting My Act Together and Taking It On the Road* played the Florence S. Anspacher Theater; *Tales of the Hasidim, The Water Engine* and *Runaways* played the Public Theater Cabaret in Martinson Hall, *A Photograph* and *Museum* played LuEsther Hall; *The Mandrake* and *Mango Tango* played The Other Stage.

Children of Adam (69). Musical revue with words and music by Stan Satlin. Produced by John A. Vaccaro and James J. Wisner in association with R. Anthony Zeiger at the Chelsea Westside Cabaret Theater. Opened August 17, 1977. (Closed October 9, 1977)

Gene Bua	Robert Polenz
Elizabeth Lathram	Roger Rathburn
Karen Philipp	Carole Schweid

Band: Jimmy Wisner keyboards, Warren Nichols bass, Jeremy Harris drums.

Conceived and directed by John Driver; choreography, Ruella Frank; musical direction and vocal arrangements, Jimmy Wisner; scenery, Ernest Allen Smith; costumes, Polly P. Smith; lighting, Robert F. Strohmeier; assistant producer, Bert Stratford; production stage manager, Sari E. Weisman; stage manager, Robert I. Cohen; press, Jeffrey Richards Associates.

Time and Place: The span of a lifetime. The show was presented without intermission.

Collection of more than two dozen musical numbers varying in style, frequently sentimental.

MUSICAL NUMBERS: "Dreams" — Company; "Mr. & Mrs. Myth" — Company; "What's Your Name?" — Company; "Move Along" — Band; "Sex Is Animal" — Company; "It's Really You" — Robert Polenz; "Walkin' " — Company; "You've Got to Die to Be Born Again" — Gene Bua; "Rise in Love" — Company; "The Wedding" — Company; "The Flowers and the Rainbow"

— Company; "Life" — Company; "It Ain't Easy/Equilib" — Company; "Sleep My Child" — Elizabeth Lathram.

Also "I Must Go Now" — Karen Philipp; "Like a Park on Sunday" — Roger Rathburn; "Part of the Plan" — Bua, Philipp, Rathburn, Carole Schweid; "I Can Feel" — Schweid; "Sleepin' Around" — Company; "The Wooden People" — Company; "Cacophony" — Company; "Maybe You Can See Yourself" — Lathram, Company; "Just a Feeling (My Spirit Awakening)" — Company; "The Flowers and the Rainbow" (Reprise) — Lathram, Polenz; "No More Games" — Schweid, Rathburn; "I Can Make It/Song Song" — Philipp, Bua; "The Sweetest Songs Remain to Be Sung" — Company; "Children of Adam" — Company.

The Grand Kabuki National Theater of Japan (13). Program of two Kabuki plays: **Yoshitsune Senbonzakura** by Takeda Izumo, Miyoshi Shoraku and Namiki Senryu and **Kurozuka** by Kimura Tomiko. Produced by Kazuko Hillyer, with the gracious assistance of the Japan Foundation, at the Beacon Theater. Opened August 31, 1977; suspended performances September 4, 1977 and reopened September 13, 1977. (Closed September 18, 1977)

YOSHITSUNE SENBONZAKURA

Prince Kuro Hogen;	Kawazura Hogen .... Dan-En Ichikawa
Yoshitsune .... Danshiro Ichikawa IV	Azuka ....Tokicho Nakamura
Lady Shizuka	Retainer ....O-Ishi Hirotsugu
Gozen ....Mon-no-suke Ichikawa VII	Tadnaobu;
Shigekiyo .... Ju-en Ichikawa	Genkuro .... En-no-suke Ichikawa III

Waiting Maids — Hideju Katacka, Hikaru Kusanagi, Hirokazu Kihara, Takajiro Ichikawa; Ruffian Priests — Dan-en Ichikawa, Ju-en Ichikawa, Hikaru Kusanagi, Hirokazu Kihara, Takijiro Ichikawa, O-Ishi Hirotsugu.

Written in 1747, one of the three great classical Kabuki plays, it lasts ten hours of which this production is merely the episode *Shi No Kiri* about Yoshitsune and an enchanted white fox.

KUROZUKA

Yukei ....Mon-no-suke Ichikawa VII	Tarogo .... Danshiro Ichikawa IV
Yamato ....Yonekichi Nakamura IV	Iwate .... En-no-suke Ichikawa III
Sanuki .... Ju-en Ichikawa	

Noh dance-drama, written in 1939, about a struggle between priests and demons.

BOTH PLAYS — Singers and Musicians: Choshi Imafuji, Rokuzo Kineya, Shunjyuro Kineya, Tetsujiro Matsunaga, Katsuroku Kineya, Katsutoshiharu Kineya, Rokunobu Kineya, Sukesaburo Kineya, Toshihiro Kineya, Roshu Tosha, Tsurujiro Fukuhara, Kanshiro Tanaka, Chojyuro Tanaka, Takisaku Mochizuki, Kazuo Nakai, Yukio Miyahara, Masataka Sugino, Suizan Sakai, Fujitayu Takemoto, Genjiro Tsurusawa, Shigematsu Toyosawa.

Directed by Norio Takeshiba; produced by Shockiku Co.; presented by Maison Des Arts; simultaneous translation, Faubion Bowers; stage manager, Toshi Ogawa; press, Gurtman & Murtha.

Counsellor-at-Law (62). Revival of the play by Elmer Rice. Produced by Michael Gardner in association with Jayne Wolf and the Hotel Diplomat in the Quaigh Theater production at the Quaigh Theater. Opened September 6, 1977. (Closed October 16, 1977)

Bessie Green ....Kent Wilson	John P. Tedesco ....Leonard Di Sesa
Henry Susskind ....Raymond Faber	Regina Gordon ....Claudine Catania
Sarah Becker ....Madeline Shaw	Herbert Howard
Moreti; Bootblack ....Charles Lutz	Weinberg ....Robert Nersesian
Zedorah Chapman ..Maxine Taylor-Morris	Arthur Sandler ....Jay Diamond
Goldie Rindskopf ....Ann Saxman	Lillian LaRue ....Kristen Christopher
Charles McFadden ....John Neary	Messenger ....Hart Faber

Roy Darwin ....Douglas Popper
George Simon ....George Guidall
Rigby Crayfield ....George Spelvin
Cora Simon ....Carolyn Lenz
Lena Simon ....Joan Turetzky
Peter J. Malone ....Mel Jurdem
Hirschberg ....Ian Ehrlich

Johann Breitstein ....Richard Spore
David Simon ....Glenn Alterman
Harry Becker ....Dennis Lieberson
Richard Dwight Jr. ....Mike Shari
Dorothy Dwight ....Valentina Fratti
Francis Clark Barid ......Glen McClaskey

Directed by Will Lieberson; scenery and costumes, Christina Giannini; lighting, Bill McComb; sound, George Jacobs; production stage manager, Ted Mornel; press, Max Eisen, Judy Jacksina.

Time: The 1930s. Place: A suite of law offices in midtown New York City. The play was presented in three parts.

Counsellor-at-Law was first produced on Broadway 11/6/31 for 292 performances and played two return engagements the following season, 9/12/32 for 104 performances and 5/15/33 for 16 performances. It was revived on Broadway 11/24/42 for 258 performances.

*Roundabout Theater Company. Schedule of six revivals. **Naked** (129). By Luigi Pirandello; translated by William Murray. Opened September 6, 1977; see note. (Closed December 31, 1977). **You Never Can Tell** (31). By George Bernard Shaw. Opened October 4, 1977; see note. (Closed October 30, 1977). **Othello** (76). By William Shakespeare. Opened January 3, 1978; see note. (Closed April 9, 1978) **The Promise** (91). By Aleksei Arbuzov; translated by Ariadne Nicolaeff. Opened January 21, 1978; see note. (Closed April 9, 1978) ***The Show-Off** (43). By George Kelly. Opened April 25, 1978; see note. ***Pins and Needles** (3). Musical revue with music and lyrics by Harold Rome. Opened May 30, 1978; see note. Produced by Roundabout Theater Company, Gene Feist and Michael Fried producing directors, at Roundabout Stage One *(You Never Can Tell, Othello, Pins and Needles)* and Stage Two *(Naked, The Promise, The Show-Off).*

NAKED

Ersilia Drei ....Marie Puma
Ludovico Nota ....Larkin Ford
Signora Onoria ....Nina Dova

Alfredo Cantavalle ......Philip Campanella
Franco Laspiga ....Lucien Zabielski
Grotto ....Richard Sterne

Directed by Gene Feist; scenery, Ron Antone; costumes, Nancy L. Johnson; lighting, Robert Strohmeier; sound, Philip Campanella; production stage manager, Paul Moser; press, Mark Arnold.

Time: Late 1920s. Place: Rome, the combination study and living room of the writer Ludovico Nota. Act I: Afternoon. Act II: The following morning. Act III: Later that afternoon. The play was presented in two parts with the intermission following Act I.

Naked, the drama of a young girl's disillusionment, was first produced in New York by Mme. Simone in French-language repertory 10/20/25. Subsequent productions took place on Broadway 11/8/26 for 32 performances and off Broadway in the seasons of 1950-51 and 1953-54 and as *To Clothe the Naked* 5/27/67 for 30 performances.

YOU NEVER CAN TELL

Dolly ....Kristie Thatcher
Valentine ....Curt Dawson
Philip ....Richard Niles
Mrs. Clandon ....Rachel Gurney
Gloria ....Sarah-Jane Gwillim
Mr. Crampton ....Ralph Clanton

Walter (William) ....Norman Barrs
M'Comas ....Richard Neilson
Bohun ....David Sabin
1st Waiter ....Jeff Passero
2d Waiter ....John Savage

Directed by Tony Tanner; scenery, Timothy Galvin; costumes, V. Jane Suttell; lighting, Richard Butler; score, Philip Campanella; production stage manager, Tom Gould.

The first New York professional performance of record of Shaw's 1897 play was 1/9/05 for 129 performances. It has been revived on Broadway 4/5/15 and 3/16/48 for 39 performances and off Broadway in the 1952-53 season.

OTHELLO

Othello	Earle Hyman	Bianca	Elizabeth Owens
Iago	Nicholas Kepros	Duke; Lodovico	John Straub
Desdemona	Mary Carney	Montano; Senator	Craig Dudley
Emilia	Carmen de Lavallade	Officer; Gentleman	Kale Brown
Cassio	Edmund Davys	Gentleman; Officer	Wesley Stevens
Roderigo	Powers Boothe	Senator; Officer	Thomas Brooks
Brabantio; Gratiano	Wyman Pendleton		

Attendants: Michael Arabian, James Scott Bell, Jane Milne, Mary Grace Pizzullo, Thomas M. Ries.

Directed by Gene Feist; scenery, Jeff Fiala; costumes, Christina Giannini; lighting, John McKernon; original score, Philip Campanella; production stage manager, Holley Jack Horner.

The Scenes — Venice: A street, night; Brabantio's palace, that night; before the Sagittary, an inn, the same night; a chamber in the Senate House, late the same night. Cyprus: A seaport, an open place near the harbor, a week later; before Othello's Citadel, evening; within the Citadel, night; before the Citadel, morning of the next day; within the Citadel, that day; the garden of the Citadel, later that day; before the Citadel, day; within the Citadel, night; a street, the same night; a bedchamber in the Citadel, later that night.

Othello played in a bare setting. Its last professional New York production was on Broadway by American Shakespeare Festival 9/14/70 for 16 performances.

THE PROMISE

Marat	Christopher Goutman	Leonidik	Davis Hall
Lika	Marilyn McIntyre		

Directed by Michael Fried; scenery, Ron Antone; costumes, Nancy L. Johnson; lighting, Robert Strohmeier; sound, Philip Campanella; production stage manager, Paul Moser.

This Russian play was originally produced on Broadway 12/2/67 for 23 performances. This is its first professional New York revival.

THE SHOW-OFF

Clara Hyland	Ellen Tovatt	Joe Fisher	Terence Marinan
Mrs. Fisher	Polly Rowles	Aubrey Piper	Paul Rudd
Amy Fisher	Kit LeFever	Mr. Gill	Joseph Warren
Frank Hyland	Joseph Costa	Mr. Rogers	Ken Costigan
Mr. Fisher	Harry Ellerbe		

Directed by John Ulmer; scenery, Ron Antone; costumes, Nancy L. Johnson; lighting, Robert Strohmeier; sound, Philip Campanella; production stage manager, Paul Moser.

Time: 1924. Place: The Fisher living room, North Philadelphia. Act I, Scene 1: Evening, May. Scene 2: The same, three hours later. Act II: Six months later, 5:30 p.m. Act III: The following Monday, 4 p.m.

The last professional New York production of *The Show-Off* was in APA repertory on Broadway 19/13/68 for 19 performances.

PINS AND NEEDLES

Phyllis Bash	Randy Graff
Trudy Bayne	Robin Hoff
David Berman	Tom Offt
Richard Casper	Dennis Perren
Daniel Fortus	Elaine Petricoff

Twin Pianos: Philip Campanella, Marc Segan.

Directed by Milton Lyon; choreography, Haila Strauss; scenery and lighting, Scott Johnson; costumes, Donna Meyer; musical direction, Philip Campanella; production stage manager, Holley Jack Horner.

Pins and Needles was originally produced by International Ladies' Garment Workers' Union Players at Labor Stage Theater 11/27/37 for 1,108 performances. It included material by Arthur

Paul Rudd and Polly Rowles in the Roundabout production of *The Show-Off*

Arent, Marc Blitzstein, Emanuel Eisenberg, Charles Friedman and David Gregory, in addition to the Harold Rome score. This is its first professional New York revival.

MUSICAL NUMBERS — ACT I: "Social Significance" — Company; "Not Cricket to Picket" — Elaine Petricoff; "I've Got the Nerve To Be in Love" — Trudy Bayne, David Berman; "Call It Un-American" — Richard Casper, Tom Offt, Daniel Fortus; "Papa Don't Love Mama Any More" — Randy Graff, Robin Hoff, Berman, William Green, Dennis Perren; "Oom for One" — Petricoff; "Sunday in the Park" — Berman (Papa), Graff (Mama), Offt (Son), Hoff (Daughter), Perren (Policeman), Phyllis Bash (Carriage Lady), Casper (Ice Cream Man), Bayne, Petricoff (Strolling Ladies), Fortus (Radical); "I'm Just Nuts About You!" — Bayne (Girl), Fortus (Stage Manager); "What Good Is Love" — Bash; "Doing the Reactionary" — Graff (Mrs. Eugene Delacroix Dalrymple III), Casper, Hoff, Offt, Bayne (Her Friends); "Chain Store Daisy" — Graff; "Back to Work" — Company.
ACT II: "It's Better With a Union Man" — Perren (Narrator), Petricoff (Girl), Berman (Hero), Offt (Villain); "When I Grow Up" (The G-Man Song) — Fortus; "F.D.R. Jones" — Perren

(Husband), Bash (Wife), Company (Neighbors); "Nobody Makes a Pass at Me" — Petricoff; "One Big Union for Two" — Bayne, Casper; "Mene, Mene, Tekel" — Bash, Berman, Graff, Hoff, Offt, Perren; "We're the Ads" — Fortus, Casper; "Status Quo" — Perren (Teacher), Casper, Offt, Hoff, Bayne (Students); "We Sing America" — Perren, Company.

Note: Press date for *Naked* was 10/24/77, for *You Never Can Tell* 10/17/77, for *Othello* 1/30/78, for *The Promise* 1/24/78, for *The Show-Off* 5/18/78, for *Pins and Needles* 7/6/78.

*The Passion of Dracula (246). By Bob Hall and David Richmond; based on the novel by Bram Stoker. Produced by The Dracula Company at the Cherry Lane Theater. Opened September 28, 1977.

Jameson	Brian Bell	Mr. Renfield	Elliott Vileen
Dr. Cedric Seward	K. Lype O'Dell	Wilhelmina Murray	Giulia Pagano
Prof. Van Helsing	Michael Burg	Jonathan Harker	Samuel Maupin
Dr. Helga Van Zandt	Alice White	Count Dracula	Christopher Bernau
Gordon Lord Godalming	K.C. Wilson		

Understudy: Miss Pagano — Sara Herrnstadt

Directed by Peter Bennett; scenery, Bob Hall, Allen Cornell; costumes, Jane Tschetter; lighting, Allen Cornell; produced by Bob Hall, David Richmond, Eric Krebs; production stage manager, Andrea Naier; press, Jeffrey Richards Associates, Bruce Lynn.

Time: Autumn 1911, Place: England, the study of Dr. Seward's home. Act I: Early evening. Act II: Three days later, just past sundown, Act III:A half hour later.

A new version of the Dracula story similar in tone and incidents to its predecessors, previously produced at George St. Playhouse, New Brunswick, N.J.

William Lyman replaced Christopher Bernau 2/78. Stefan Schnabel replaced Michale Burg 3/15/78.

The Present Tense (24). Musical revue written by Stephen Rosenfield, Haila Strauss, Ralph Buckley, Jeff Sweet (head writer) and the cast; music and lyrics by Allen Cohen, Bob Joseph, Alan Menken, Muriel Robinson, Don Siegel, Jeff Sweet and Lee S. Wilkof. Produced by Roger Ailes and John Fishback with The Comedy Club Company at the Park Royal Theater. Opened October 4, 1977. (Closed October 23, 1977)

Barbara Brummel	Lianne Kressin
Chris Carroll	Michael Nobel
Jim Cyrus	Lee S. Wilkof

Directed by Stephen Rosenfield; musical director, Skip Kennon; scenery and costumes, Paul DePass; lighting, John Fishback; assistant director, Haila Strauss; associate producer, Norma Ferrer; production stage manager, Haila Strauss; press, Jeffrey Richards Associates, Bruce Lynn.

Topical revue of skits and songs

MUSICAL NUMBERS: "Cautiously Optimistic" (by Alan Menken) — Company; "Yankee Man" (by Alan Menken) — Barbara Brummel, Jim Cyrus, Lee S. Wilkof, Chris Carroll, Michael Nobel; "Margaret" (by Alan Menken and Muriel Robinson) — Lianne Kressin; "Come to Cuba" (by Don Siegel) — Wilkof, Company; "Song for a Crowded Cabaret" (by Jeff Sweet) — Carroll; "The Carter Song" (by Allen Cohen) — Cyrus; "Love Me or Leave Me" (by Don Siegel) — Brummel; "Man on a Subway" (by Don Siegel and Bob Joseph) — Cyrus; "Possum Pie" (by Lee S. Wilkof) — Wilkof; "Sklip, Dat, Doobee" (by Don Siegel) — Company.

The Phoenix Theater. 25th anniversary season schedule of five programs. **Hot Grog** (22). Musical with book by Jim Wann; music and lyrics by Bland Simpson and Jim Wann. Opened October 6, 1977; see note. (Closed October 23, 1977). **Uncommon Women and Others** (22). By Wendy Wasserstein. Opened November 17, 1977; see note. (Closed December 4, 1977) **The Elusive Angel** (22). By Jack Gilhooley. Opened December 22,

Anna Levine and Cynthia Herman in the Phoenix production of *Uncommon Women and Others*

1977; see note. (Closed January 8, 1978). **One Crack Out** (22). By David French. Opened January 12, 1978; see note. (Closed January 29, 1978) And *City Sugar* by Stephen Poliakoff to open 6/5/78. Produced by The Phoenix Theater, T. Edward Hambleton managing director, Marilyn S. Miller executive director, Daniel Freudenberger artistic director, at the Marymount Manhattan Theater.

HOT GROG

Anne Bonney	Mimi Kennedy	Mr. Read	Mary Bracken Phillips
Gov. Charles Eden	Patrick Hines	Maj. Stede Bonnet	Homer Foil
Calico Jack Rackham	Terry O'Quinn	Savannah	Rebecca Gilchrist
Blackbeard (Edward Teach)	Louis Zorich	Jamaica	Kathi Moss
Caesar	John McCurry	Lt. William Rhett	Roger Howell
Israel Hands	Timothy Meyers		

Musicians: Jeff Waxman keyboards; Richard Grando winds; Larry Packer guitar, fiddle; John Schimmel bass; Paul Von Wageningen drums.

Directed by Edward Berkeley; musical staging, Patricia Birch; musical direction, Jeff Waxman; scenery and lighting, James Tilton; costumes, Hilary Rosenfeld; sound, R.S.D. Weeden; production manager, Tom Aberger; stage manager, James Harker; press, Gifford/Wallace, Inc. Eileen MacMahon, Michael Catalano.

Time: 1718. Place: Coastal Carolina. The play was presented in two parts.

Adventures of and with the pirate Blackbeard. Previously produced by the Musical Theater Lab, Washington, D.C.

ACT I

Overture .... The Band
"Seizure to Roam" .... Calico, Company

"Got a Notion" .... Anne, Calico
"Come on Down to the Sea" .... Anne, Company
"Hot Grog" .... Company
"The Pirates' Life" .... Anne, Company
"The Difference Is Me" .... Read
"Change in Direction" ....Read, Anne, Company

ACT II

"Heaven Must Have Been Smiling" ....Anne, Calico, Company
"Hack 'Em" ....Rhett
"Treasure to Bury"/ "One of Us" .... Blackbeard, Read, Stede, Caesar, Hands, Calico
"Sea Breeze" ....Anne, Governor
The Chase .... The Band
"Skye Boat Song" .... Anne, Read, Stede
"Marooned" .... Calico, Anne, Read, Stede
The Swordfight .... The Band
"The Head Song" ....Blackbeard, Caesar, Hands
"Drinking Fool" .... Calico, Company
"Bound Away" .... Anne, Company

UNCOMMON WOMEN AND OTHERS

Kate Quin	Jill Eikenberry	Mrs. Plumm	Josephine Nichols
Samantha Stewart	Ann McDonough	Susie Friend	Cynthia Herman
Holly Kaplan	Alma Cuervo	Carter	Anna Levine
Muffet DiNicola	Ellen Parker	Leilah	Glenn Close
Rita Altabel	Swoosie Kurtz		

Directed by Steven Robman; scenery and lighting, James Tilton; costumes, Jennifer Von Mayrhauser; production stage manager, Tom Aberger; stage manager, Madeline Mingino.

Place: A restaurant in the present, and six years earlier at a college for women. The play was presented in two parts.

Flashbacks to college years in a "Seven Sisters"-type institution.

THE ELUSIVE ANGEL

Carlton Pine	Brad Davis	"Bo-Peep" Braxton	Martha Gaylord
Mary Pine	Maureen Anderman	Ken Harrison	William Knight
"Slick" Jessup	Graham Beckel	Lucy	Alexa Kenin

Directed by Steven Robman; scenery and lighting, James Tilton; costumes, Jennifer Von Mayrhauser; songs, Arthur Miller, Jack Gilhooley; production stage manager, Tom Aberger; stage manager, Madeline Mingino.

Place: A major northern city. Act I: A living room in a modest apartment house, Act II: The same, the following Saturday.

Drama of a childless couple seeking to adopt a baby.

ONE CRACK OUT

Al	Jerry Zaks	Charlie Evans	Kenneth Welsh
Jack the Hat	Norman Snow	Suitcase Sam	James Greene
Earl	Ed Cambridge	Helen	Teri Garr
Bulldog	Al Freeman Jr.	McKee	John Aquino
Wanda	Christine Baranzki		

Directed by Daniel Freudenberger; scenery, James Tilton; costumes, Julie Weiss; lighting, Paul H. Everett; billiard consultant, Steve Mizerak; production stage manager, Tom Aberger; stage manager, Madeline Mingino.

Act I, Scene 1: A pool hall in Toronto, Monday, around noon. Scene 2: Charlie's apartment, Monday, 5:45 p.m. Scene 3: The pool hall, Monday, 6:10 p.m. Scene 4: Charlie's apartment, Monday, later. Scene 5: The pool hall, Tuesday afternoon. Act II, Scene 1: The pool hall, Wednesday, 5 p.m. Scene 2: Charlie's apartment, Wednesday, 11 p.m. Scene 3: The pool hall, Wednesday, 11:30 p.m.

A pool hustler in a tight spot with ruthless gamblers. A foreign (Canadian) play first presented in the U.S. in a staged reading at Phoenix Theater last season.

Note: Press date for *Hot Grog* was 10/10/77, for *Uncommon Women and Others* 11/21/77, for *The Elusive Angel* 12/26/77, for *One Crack Out* 1/16/78.

The American Place Theater. Schedule of four programs. **Cockfight** (28). By Elaine Jackson. Opened October 7, 1977; see note. (Closed October 30, 1977) **Passing Game** (28). By Steve Tesich. Opened November 18, 1977; see note. (Closed December 11, 1977) **Fefu and Her Friends** (44). By Maria Irene Fornes. Opened January 6, 1978; see note. (Closed February 12, 1978) **Conjuring an Event** (28). By Richard Nelson. Opened March 10, 1978 matinee; see note. (Closed April 2, 1978) Produced by The American Place Theater, Wynn Handman director, Julia Miles artistic director, at The American Place Theater.

ALL PLAYS — Literary advisor, Bonnie Marranca; stage manager, Jeffrey Rowland; press, Jeffrey Richard Associates, Bruce Lynn.

COCKFIGHT

Reba	Mary Alice	Jesse	Gylan Kain
Sampson	Morgan Freeman	Claudia	Cynthia McPherson
Carl	Charles Brown		

Understudy — George Lee Miles.

Directed by Woodie King Jr.; scenery, C. Richard Mills; costumes, Ruth Morley; lighting, Edward M. Greenberg; presented in association with Woodie King Jr.: production stage manager, Nancy Harrington.

Time: Mid-1970s. Place: Bay area near San Francisco, a converted chicken farm. Act I, Scene 1: Early evening. Scene 2: Next morning. Act II, Scene 1: Half hour later the same day. Scene 2: Evening of the following day.

A woman's frustration in the midst of men whose macho front is more pose than performance.

PASSING GAME

Debbie	Susan MacDonald	Andrew	Pat McNamara
Randy	Paul C. O'Keefe	Henry	Howard E. Rollins Jr.
Richard	William Atherton	Rachel	Novella Nelson
Julie	Margaret Ladd		

Standbys: Misses MacDonald, Ladd — Jacklyn Lee Bartone; Mr. Rollins — Dean Irby; Messrs. Atherton, McNamara — Barry Jenner; Miss Nelson — Cynthia McPherson.

Directed by Peter Yates; scenery, Kert Lundell; costumes, Ruth Morley; lighting, Neil Peter Jampolis; basketball sequences choreographed by Richard D. Morse; production stage manager, Nancy Harrington.

Two men, one black and one white, share antagonistic egos and a penchant for wife-abuse, with fatal consequences. The play was presented in two parts.

FEFU AND HER FRIENDS

Fefu	Rebecca Schull	Emma	Gordana Rashovich
Cindy	Dorothy Lyman	Paula	Connie LoCurto
Christina	Elizabeth Perry	Sue	Arleigh Richards
Julia	Margaret Harrington	Cecilia	Judith Roberts

Understudy — Kathleen Chalfant.

Directed by Maria Irene Fornes; scenery, Kert Lundell, Nancy Tobias; costumes, Theo Barnes; lighting, Edward M. Greenberg; production stage manager, Nancy Harrington.

Time: Spring 1935. Place: New England. Part I — Noon, the living room. Part II: Afternoon, the lawn, the study, the kitchen, the bedroom. Part III: Evening, the living room.

Vignettes of character and emotion expressed in a gathering of women, staged so that the audience is occasionally partitioned along with the action in different parts of the theater. Previously produced off off Broadway by New York Theater Strategy.

CONJURING AN EVENT

Charlie	.... Michael Cristofer	Man	.... MacIntyre Dixon
Annabella	.... Sigourney Weaver	Smitty	.... Dan Hedaya
Waiter	.... John Jellison	Sleeves	.... Frank Hamilton

Standby — John Jellison.

Directed by Douglas C. Wager; scenery, David Lloyd Gropman; costumes, William Ivey Long; lighting, Paul Gallo; sound design, Carol Waaser; production stage manager, Peggy Peterson.

Act I: Pen and Pencil Club. Act II: Charlie's apartment.

Journalism viewed in violent metaphor as action which can cause an event as well as reaction to it. Previously produced in workshop at the Mark Taper Forum.

Guest productions at American Place Theater included The Acting Company repertory (see its entry elsewhere in this section) and *Michael Hennessy Mime and Music Theater;* music composed and performed by Dan Biegen and Eric Sayer; lighting, Michael Pettee; production stage manager, Michael Pettee; with Dan Blegen, Michael Hennessy and Eric Sayer; 5/4/78-5/7/78 for 6 performances.

Note: Press date for *Cockfight* was 10/16/77, for *Passing Game* 11/18/77, for *Fefu and Her Friends* 1/13/78, for *Conjuring an Event* 3/19/78.

Survival (47). Play written by the cast and director; music by Selaelo Dan Maredi. Produced by Clyde Kuemmerle and The Negro Ensemble Company at the Astor Place Theater. Opened October 9, 1977. (Closed November 20, 1977)

Fana David Kekana	Selaelo Dan Maredi
Themba Ntinga	Seth Sibanda

Directed by Mshengu; additional staging for New York production, Dean Irby; design, Clyde Kuemmerle; stage manager, Harrison Avery; press, Lewis Harmon.

Political statements in episodes of prison life, presented in two parts. A foreign (South African) play previously presented by Workshop 71 Theater Company in that country.

I (7). By Frederic Baal. Produced by the Théâtre Laboratoire Vicinal of Belgium and Jack Temchin at the Leperq Space of the Brooklyn Academy of Music. Opened October 12, 1977. (Closed October 20, 1977)

Directed by Anne West; sculpture-properties and personae conceived by Olivier Strebelle; press, Jeffrey Richards, Bruce Lynn. With Anne West.

One-character theater piece, a series of effects of seemingly random words and gestures. A foreign play previously produced in Belgium and in New York at the Guggenheim Museum.

*Circle Repertory Company. Schedule of five programs. **Feedlot** (49). By Patrick Meyers. Opened October 13, 1977 (Closed November 27, 1977) **Ulysses in Traction** (47). By Albert Innaurato. Opened December 8, 1977. (Closed January 22, 1978) **Lulu** (20). Revival of a play by Frank Wedekind adapted from his *Earth Spirit* and *Pandora's Box.* Opened February 9, 1978. (Closed February 28, 1978) **Two From the Late Show** (21). Program of one-act plays: *Brontosaurus* by Lanford Wilson and *Cabin 12* by John Bishop. Opened March 9, 1978. (Closed April 9, 1978). ***The 5th of July** (35). By Lanford Wilson. Opened April 27, 1978. Produced by Circle Repertory Company, Marshall W. Mason artistic director, Jerry Arrow executive director, at the Circle Theater.

FEEDLOT

Gene Harris	.... Mark J. Soper	Wesley	.... Jeff Daniels

Billy Fred .... Joseph Ragno   Kelly .... Edward Seamon
John .... James Ray Weeks

Directed by Terry Schreiber; scenery, Hal Tine; costumes, Laura Crow; lighting, Dennis Parichy; sound, Charles London; production stage manager, Amy Schecter; press, Rima Corben.

Time: The present. Place: The control tower of a feedlot in Texas. Act I: 11 p.m. Act II, Scene 1: 3 a.m. Scene 2: 5 a.m.

The long lonely hours of the feedlot night shift put emotional burdens on some of the cowboys working there.

ULYSSES IN TRACTION

Bruce Garrick .... Michael Ayr   Dr. Steven Klipstader .... Ken Kliban
Emma Konichowski .... Trish Hawkins   Dr. Stuart Humphreys ...... Jack Davidson
John Morrisey, M.F.A. ...... William Hurt   Mae .... Joanna Featherstone
Doris Reinlos .... Sharon Madden   Leonard Kaufman, M.F.A. .... Jake Dengel

Directed by Marshall W. Mason; scenery, John Lee Beatty; costumes, Laura Crow; lighting Dennis Parichy; sound, Charles S. London, George Hansen; production stage manager, Fred Reinglas.

Time: Spring 1970. Place: The rehearsal hall in the arts complex of Chapel University, Detroit. Act I: Evening. Act II: Later that night.

Drama students and teachers are obsessed with a rehearsal while outside the building a riot is taking place.

LULU

Animal Tamer;   Prince Escerny; Heilmann;
  Roderigo Quast .... Ken Kliban   Dr. Hilti .... Burke Pearson
August; Escherich; Ferdinand;   Countess Geschwitz ... Jacqueline Bertrand
  Police Inspector .... Michael Ayr   Alfred Hugenberg; Bob ...... Danton Stone
Lulu .... Trish Hawkins   Marquis Casti-Piani .... Mark Soper
Dr. Schon .... Jack Davidson   Magelone .... Sharon Madden
Schwarz; Mr. Hunidei .... Jeff Daniels   Kadidja .... Mariellen Rokosny
Dr. Goll; Puntchu .... Gerard Russak   Bianetta Gazil .... Nancy Snyder
Alwa Schon .... William Hurt   Ludmilla Steinherz .... Joyce Reehling
Schigolch .... William Robertson   Kungu Poti .... Robert E. Barnes Jr.

Directed by Rob Thirkield; scenery, John Lee Beatty; costumes, David Murin; lighting, Ruth Roberts; original music, Norman L. Berman; sound, Charles S. London; production stage manager, Amy Schecter.

Time: Pre-World War I. Act I, Scene 1: Germany, Schwarz's studio. Scene 2: Drawing room of Dr. Goll's house, seven months later. Scene 3: Dressing room in Alwa's theater, six months later. Act II, Scene 1: Germany, Dr. Schon's house. Scene 2: Dr. Schon's house, a year and a half later. Act III, Scene 1: Paris, Casti-Piani's salon. Scene 2: London, an attic.

The life and death of a *femme fatale* as per two Wedekind plays which were also combined in an opera by Alban Berg. *Earth Spirit* was previously produced off Broadway in the season of 1950-51 and in a translation entitled *Lulu* 3/27/70 for 1 performance.

BRONTOSAURUS

Antique Dealer .... Tanya Berezin   Nephew .... Jeff Daniels
Assistant .... Sharon Madden

CABIN 12

Bob McCullough .... Jonathan Hogan   Girl .... Nancy Snyder
Harold McCullough ...... Edward Seamon   Man .... Michael Ayr

BOTH PLAYS — Scenery, Nina Friedman; lighting, Gary Seltzer; production stage manager, Amy Schechter.

BRONTOSAURUS — Directed by Daniel Irvine; costumes, Laura Crow.

Time: The present. Place: New York City, alternating between the shop of the antique dealer and her apartment.

Described as "an encounter between a searcher and a survivor" (an antique dealer and a young theologian), previously produced by Circle Repertory Company in its "Late Show" 10/25/77-11/27/77.

CABIN 12 — Directed by Marshall Oglesby; costumes, Irene Nolan.

Time: The present. Place: A motel cabin in western Virginia.

The effect of a young man's death on his family. Previously produced by Circle Repertory Company in its "Late Show" 1/5/78-1/20/78.

THE 5TH OF JULY

Kenneth Talley Jr.	William Hurt	June Talley	Joyce Reehling
John	Jonathan Hogan	Shirley	Amy Wright
Gwen	Nancy Snyder	Aunt Sally	Helen Stenborg
Jed	Jeff Daniels	Weston Hurley	Danton Stone

Directed by Marshall W. Mason; scenery, John Lee Beatty; costumes, Laura Crow; lighting, Marc B. Weiss; original song, Jonathan Hogan; sound, Chuck London; production stage manager, Fred Reinglas.

Place: The Talley Place, a farm near Lebanon, Mo. Act I: Early evening, Independence Day, 1977. Act II: The following morning.

Oddly-assorted group of 1960s survivors share their imperfections and find support in each other's common denominator of humanity.

A Best Play; see page 239.

Circle Repertory Company's special projects this season included a booking of *This Living Hand,* a dramatic recreation of the life of John Keats through his poetry and letters and memoirs of his friends, written, produced, directed, designed and performed by Mark Stevenson, for 2 performances 5/21 and 5/22.

Chelsea Theater Center. Schedule of three programs. **Rum an Coca Cola** (40). By Mustapha Matura. Opened October 18, 1977; see note. Closed in Brooklyn October 30, 1977 and transferred to Manhattan November 2, 1977. (Closed November 20, 1977). **Green Pond** (32). Musical with words by Robert Montgomery; music by Mel Marvin. Opened November 22, 1977; see note. Closed in Brooklyn December 4, 1977 and transferred to Manhattan December 7, 1977. (Closed December 18, 1977) **Old Man Joseph and His Family** (24). By Romulus Linney. Opened January 18, 1978 matinee. Closed January 22, 1978 and transferred to Manhattan January 25, 1978. (Closed February 5, 1978) Produced by Chelsea Theater Center, Robert Kalfin artistic director, Michael David executive director, at the Academy of Music in Brooklyn and the Westside Theater in Manhattan.

RUM AN COCA COLA

Creator	Leon Morenzie	Bird	Lou Ferguson

Steel Band: Kurt Nurse, Byron Griffith, Winston Phillips.

Standby: Messrs. Morenzie, Ferguson — Sullivan Walker.

Directed by Donald Howarth; produced by arrangement with Oscar Lewenstein; scenery, Wolfgang Roth; costumes, Debra J. Stein; lighting, William Mintzer; production stage manager, Bob Jaffe; stage manager, Jan Rugh; press, Susan Bloch, Doug Johnson.

Place: A beach in Trinidad. The play was presented without intermission.

U.S. premiere of Trinidadian play about a one-time Calypso king and his young disciple. A foreign play previously produced at Royal Court Theater, London.

GREEN POND

Liz	Stephanie Cotsirilos	Sam	Stephen James
Dana	Christine Ebersole	Frank	Richard Ryder

Musicians: Mel Marvin conductor, piano; Bryson Borgstedt woodwinds; David Erwin guitar; Jim Ferguson bass; Randy Oswalt percussion.

Directed by David Chambers; scenery and costumes, Marjorie Kellogg; lighting, Arden Fingerhut; vocal arrangements and orchestrations, Mel Marvin; production stage manager, Dorothy J. Maffei.

Time: Summer 1976. Place: Somewhere in the American South. The play was presented in two parts.

Attitudes of the 1970s expressed by two couples vacationing on the South Carolina coast. Previously produced at Stage South, S.C.

MUSICAL NUMBERS — ACT I: "Green Pond," "Pleasant Company," "Daughter," "I Live Alone," "The Eyes of Egypt," "How We Get Down." ACT II: "Alligator Meat," "Priceless Relics," "Woman to Woman," "Brother to Brother," "Hurricane," "Hard to Love," "On the Ground at Last."

OLD MAN JOSEPH AND HIS FAMILY

Cast: Chamberlain, Clothdyer, Father of Groom — Nesbitt Blaisdell; Mary — Jacqueline Cassel; Boy, Sheetspreader, Zeno — Louis Gambalvo; Joseph — Lou Gilbert; Midwife, Mother of Bride, Mother #2 — Donna Haley; Bride, Mother #1, Old Woman — Marcia Hyde; High Priest, Beggar, Zeno's Father — Peter Kingsley; Sad and Beautiful Lady, Zeno's Mother, Mother of Groom — Berit Lagerwall; Herald, Boy, Milo, Groom, Jesus — Peter Scolari; Boy, Schoolmaster, Father of Bride — Charlie Stavola.

Understudies: Mr. Gilbert — Nesbitt Blaisdell; Miss Cassel — Marcia Hyde; Others — Peter Kingsley, Bill E. Noone, Katherine Parks.

Directed by Robert Kalfin; produced in collaboration with the Colonnades Theater Lab, Michael Lessac artistic director; scenery and costumes, Carrie F. Robbins; lighting, Mark DiQuinzio; music, Ken Guilmartin; production stage manager, Arthur J. Schwartz.

Act I, Scene 1: Joseph the carpenter. Scene 2: The Temple at Jerusalem; Scene 3: Joseph and Mary at home. Scene 4: The miracle of the sad and beautiful lady. Scene 5: The miracle of the wedding. Scene 6: The miracle of the fish. Act II, Scene 1: The miracles of the children. Scene 2: The child terror. Scene 3: The boy on the roof. Scene 4: Old Man Joseph.

Jesus's childhood dramatized as a folk tale. Previously produced off off Broadway at Colonnades Theater Lab.

Note: Press date for *Rum an Coca Cola* was 10/26/77 matinee, for *Green Pond* 11/30/77.

Housewife! Superstar! (34). One-man show by and with Barry Humphries. Produced by Michael White and Arthur Cantor at Theater Four. Opened October 19, 1977. (Closed Nov. 20, 1977)

Staged by Ian Davidson; scenery, Brian Thompson; lighting, Andrea Wilson; accompanist, Iris Wilson; production stage manager, Larry Bussard; press, C. George Willard.

Single-handed comedy by the Australian comedian as a middle-aged housewife.

*A Life in the Theater (244). By David Mamet. Produced by Jane Harmon at Theater de Lys. Opened October 20, 1977.

John .... Peter Evans   Stage Manager ..... Benjamin Hendrickson
Robert .... Ellis Rabb

Understudies: Mr. Rabb — John Clarkson; Mr. Evans — Benjamin Hendrickson; Mr. Hendrickson — Michael Adkins.

Directed by Gerald Gutierrez; scenery, John Lee Beatty; costumes, John David Ridge; lighting, Pat Collins; incidental music, Robert Waldman; production stage manager, Frank Hartenstein; press, Hunt/Pucci Associates, Betty Lee Hunt, Maria Cristina Pucci, Fred Hoot.

Place: Various spots around a theater. The play was presented without intermission.

Young man's ambition, older man's sadness, in episodes with two actors conversing backstage and playing fragments of various plays they're in. Previously produced by the Goodman Theater, Chicago.

Jose Ferrer replaced Ellis Rabb and James McDonnell replaced Peter Evans 5/9/78. A Best Play; see page 155.

*Manhattan Theater Club. Schedule of five programs. **Chez Nous** (28). By Peter Nichols. Opened October 26, 1977; see note. (Closed November 27, 1977). **Play and Other Plays** (35). Program of three one-act plays by Samuel Beckett: *Play, That Time* and *Footfalls*. Opened December 14, 1977; see note. (Closed January 15, 1978) **Statements After an Arrest Under the Immorality Act** by Athol Fugard and **Scenes From Soweto** by Steve Wilmer (35). Opened February 1, 1978; see note. (Closed March 5, 1978) ***Catsplay** (37). By Istvan Orkeny; translated by Clara Gyorgyey; produced with the New York Shakespeare Festival, Joseph Papp producer. Opened April 5, 1978; see note. ***Strawberry Fields** (8). By Stephen Poliakoff. Opened May 24, 1978. Produced by Manhattan Theater Club, Lynne Meadow artistic director, Barry Grove managing director, at Manhattan Theater Club Downstage.

ALL PLAYS — Associate director, Thomas Bullard; associate artistic director, Stephen Pascal; press, Robert Pontarelli, Caryn Katkin.

CHEZ NOUS

Dick	John Tillinger	Le Français	Charles Mayer
Phil	Sam Waterston	Burt	Jim Jansen
Diana	Christina Pickles	Zoe	Linda Atkinson
Liz	Barbara Caruso		

Directed by Lynne Meadow; associate director, Richard Maltby Jr.; scenery, John Conklin; costumes, Nanzi Adzima; lighting, Dennis Parichy; sound, George Hansen; production stage manager, Maureen Lynett.

Time: July. Place: A converted barn in the South of France. Act I, Scene 1: Late morning. Scene 2: Afternoon; Scene 3; Evening. Scene 4: Late morning the next day. Act II, Scene 1: Early afternoon. Scene 2: Later that afternoon; Scene 3: Late morning the next day.

Two English couples adapting to unconventional sex and family lifestyles. A foreign play previously produced in London.

PLAY AND OTHER PLAYS

Play		*That Time*	
1st Woman	Sloane Shelton	Face and Voice	Donald Davis
2d Woman	Suzanne Costallos	*Footfalls*	
Man	Donald Davis	May	Suzanne Costallos
		Mother's Voice	Sloane Shelton

Directed by Alan Schneider; scenery and costumes, Zack Brown; lighting, William Mintzer; production stage manager, Jody Boese.

The first professional New York production of *Play* was by Theater 64 off Broadway 1/4/64 for 121 performances. In *That Time*, an elderly man listens to a soliloquy being piped at him. In *Footfalls*, an elderly woman paces up and down while her ancient mother waits in the wings.

That Time and *Footfalls* were first produced at the Royal Court Theater in London in May, 1976 and had their American premieres at the Arena Stage, Washington, D.C. in 1976. This is their first New York production.

STATEMENTS AFTER AN ARREST UNDER THE IMMORALITY ACT

Frieda Joubert	Veronica Castang	Detective-Sergeant	
Errol Philander	Robert Christian	J. DuPreez	John C. Vennema

Time: December 17, 1966. Place: The town of Nouport, Cape Province, South Africa.

SCENES FROM SOWETO

Black Actor	Robert Christian	White Actor	John C. Vennema

Time: Nov. 24, 1975-Dec. 10, 1976. Place: Oxford University, Great Britain and various locations in and around the city of Johannesburgh, South Africa.

Directed by Thomas Bullard; scenery, David Potts; costumes, Judy Dearing; lighting, Dennis Parichy; dialect coach, Gordon Jacoby; production stage manager, Jody Boese.

Statements After an Arrest Under the Immorality Act deals with South Africa's regulations on sexual apartheid, a foreign play previously produced at the Royal Court Theater in London and elsewhere. *Scenes From Soweto* depicts incidents in the life of Nelson Malubane, a foreign play previously produced in London.

CATSPLAY

Mrs. Bela Orban .... Helen Burns	Ilona .... Susan Sharkey
Giza .... Katherine Squire	Yoshka .... Peter Phillips
Paula Krausz .... Jane Cronin	Victor Vivelli .... Robert Gerringer
Yanos ....Charles Mayer	Mme. Adelaide Vivelli ..... Eleanor Phelps
Mrs. Mihaly Almasi .... Bette Henritze	

Directed by Lynne Meadow; scenery, John Lee Beatty; costumes, Jennifer Von Mayrhauser; lighting, Dennis Parichy; music, Robert Dennis; sound, Chuck London; dramaturge, Andy Wolk; associate producer, Bernard Gersten; production stage manager, David S. Rosenak.

Time: The mid-1960s. The Correspondents: Mrs. Bela Orban, 127 Csatarka St., Budapest, and her sister Giza, Luetberg Manor, Garmisch-Partenkirchen, Bavaria. The play was presented in two parts. A romantic triangle in the golden years. A foreign (Hungarian) play previously produced in Szolnok and Budapest, and elsewhere including the Arena Stage, Washington, D.C. and the Tyrone Guthrie Theater, Minneapolis. This production played 35 performances through 5/7/78 at Manhattan Theater Club, then was presented for an additional run by Eugene V. Wolsk and Frank Milton beginning 5/31/78 at the Promenade Theater.

Sherry Steiner replaced Susan Sharkey and I.M. Hobson replaced Robert Gerringer 5/31/78.

STRAWBERRY FIELDS

Charlotte ....Susan Sharkey	Mrs. Roberts;
Kevin .... Nicholas Woodeson	Cleaning Woman .... Geraldine Sherman
Nick .... Brad O'Hare	Kid; Police Constable ...... Ralph Seymour

Directed by Stephen Pascal; scenery, Robert Yodice; costumes, Judy Dearing; lighting, Dennis Parichy; music consultant, Dennis Douglas; sound, Gary Harris; dialect, Timothy Monich; fights, Jake Turner; production assistants, Lucky Rice, Laura Bemis; assistant director, Thomas Bullard; associate artistic director, Stephen Pascal; production stage manager, Paul Fitzmaurice.

Time: The present. Place: Various locations up an English motorway. The play was presented in seven scenes with an intermission following Scene 4.

Right-wing rebels on a mission in their van on a turnpike, vs. a hitchiker who opposes their ideas. A foreign play previously produced at the National Theater in London.

Note: Press date for *Chez Nous* was 11/6/77, for *Play and Other Plays* 12/18/77, for *Statements After an Arrest Under the Immorality Act* and *Scenes From Soweto* 1/5/78, for *Catsplay* 4/9/78, for *Strawberry Fields* 6/2/78.

A Man and His Women (71). One-man show with Craig Russell. Produced by Jonathan Scharer in association with Stephen Novick. Opened October 31, 1977. (Closed January 20, 1978)

Musical direction, Stephen Stucker; sound, Bob Casey; gowns, Tony Marando; lighting consultants, Consolidated Edification; stage manager, Nicholas Plain; Press, Elizabeth Rodman, Harold Lubin, Sharon Mear, Harriett Trachentenberg.

Act I: Blonde women. Act II: Women of color. Impressions of famous women.

Nightsong (35). Musical revue with words and music by Ron Eliren. Produced by Irwin Steiner at the Village Gate Downstairs. Opened November 1, 1977. (Closed December 4, 1977)

Ron Eliren	Holly T. Lipton
Joy Kohner	Dian Sorel

Directed by Dan Early; musical direction, Jaroslav (Yaron) Jakubovic; scenery, Harry Silverglat; costumes, Ron Whitehead, Margot Miller; lighting, Jo Mayer; sound, Alan Stieb; production stage manager, Karen Winer; press, Bruce Cohen.

Self-described "Musical Mosaic" program of songs.

Classic Stage Company (CSC). Repertory of six programs. **A Midsummer Night's Dream** (32). Revival of the play by William Shakespeare. Opened November 10, 1977; see note. **Rosmersholm** (28). Revival of the play by Henrik Ibsen; new English version by Christopher Martin. Opened November 17, 1977; see note. **Serjeant Musgrave's Dance** (20). Revival of the play by John Arden. Opened December 8, 1977; see note. **The Maids** (21). Revival of the play by Jean Genet; translated by Bernard Frechtman. Opened January 3, 1978. **The Running of the Deer** (20). By Karen Sunde. Opened February 2, 1978; see note. **The Madwoman of Chaillot** (29). Revival of the play by Jean Giraudoux; adapted by Maurice Valency. Opened March 2, 1978; see note. (Repertory closed April 2, 1978). Produced by Classic Stage Company, Christopher Martin artistic director, at the Abbey Theater.

ALL PLAYS: Directed by Christopher Martin (except *Serjeant Musgrave's Dance* directed by John Shannon); incidental music, *The Madwoman of Chaillot* mazurkas, musical direction, Noble Shropshire; production stage manager, John Shannon; stage manager, Christopher Barns.

PERFORMER	" A MID-SUMMER NIGHT'S DREAM"	"SERJEANT MUSGRAVE'S DANCE"	"THE RUNNING OF THE DEER"	"THE MAD-WOMAN OF CHAILLOT"
Barbara Blackledge	Hermia		Polly; Mistress White	Irma
Ted Britton	Demetrius	Earnest Collier	Adjutant Reed; James	Sergeant; Bertaut
Ray Dooley	Lysander	Pvt. Hurst	Tom	Pierre
Frank Dwyer	Quince	Bludgeon	Maj. Gen. Greene	Ragpicker
Patrick Egan	Bottom	Pvt. Attercliffe	Gen. Washington	President
Richard Kite			Adam	Waiter
Thomas Lenz			2d Poler	Peddler; Policeman
Christopher Martin	Theseus; Oberon	Musgrave	Gen. Lee; Rahl	Doctor
Christiane McKenna	Helena	Annie	Sara; Mistress Potts	Flower Girl; Mme. Josephine
Brian Muehl			1st Poler; Dragoon	Juggler
Frank Pita			McKonkey	
Brian Rose	Egeus; Snout; Cobweb	Parson	Gen. Alexander	Baron
Claude-Albert Saucier	Flute; Peaseblossom	Slow Collier	Ben	Deaf-Mute
Harlan Schneider	Starveling; Mustardseed	Mayor	Col. Glover	Broker
Noble Shropshire	Philostrate; Puck	Pvt. Sparky; Dragoon Officer	Maj. Gen. Sullivan; Honeyman	Prospector
Diana Stagner				Streetwalker; Mlle. Gabrielle

Christopher Martin, Patrick Egan and Karen Sunde in the CSC production of *Serjeant Musgrave's Dance*

PERFORMER	"A MID-SUMMER NIGHT'S DREAM"	"SERJEANT MUSGRAVE'S DANCE"	"THE RUNNING OF THE DEER"	"THE MADWOMAN OF CHAILLOT"
Karen Sunde	Hippolyta; Titania	Mrs. Hitchcock		Madwoman of Chaillot
Robert Todd			Deserter	Street Singer
Alberto Tore		Pugnacious Collier		
Andrew Traines	Snug; Moth	Constable	Mac	Little Man; Sewerman
Susan Varon				Mme. Constance

A MIDSUMMER NIGHT'S DREAM — Scenery and lighting, Clarke Dunham; costumes, Marianne Powell-Parker; masks, Joe Bigelow.

The play was presented in two parts. Its last professional New York production was by New

York Shakespeare Festival at the Mitzi E. Newhouse Theater in Lincoln Center 1/19/75 for 62 performances.

SERJEANT MUSGRAVE'S DANCE — Scenery and lighting, Philip Graneto; costumes, Joseph Bigelow; period weapons, Lowell Patton.

The play was presented in two parts. Its last professional New York production was its American premiere off Broadway 3/8/66 for 135 performances.

sTHE RUNNING OF THE DEER — Scenery, Christopher Martin; costumes, Rachel Kurland; mime supervision, Thomas Lenz, Brian Muehl.

A new play by a member of the CSC company, about the last few months of 1776 in America. The play was presented in two parts.

THE MADWOMAN OF CHAILLOT — Scenery, Christopher Martin; costumes, Rachel Kurland; textual advisor, Claude-Albert Saucier.

The play was presented in two parts. Its last professional New York production was off Broadway 3/22/70 for 7 performances.

ROSMERSHOLM

Rebekka West	Karen Sunde	Johannes Rosmer	Ray Dooley
Mrs. Helseth	Barbara Blackledge	Ulric Brendel	Christopher Martin
Dean Kroll	Frank Dwyer	Peder Mortensgaard	Noble Shropshire

Scenery and lighting, Clarke Dunham; costumes, Marianne Powell-Parker.

New English version of the Ibsen play by CSC's artistic director, Christopher Martin, presented in two parts. The last professional New York production of *Rosmersholm* was the Roundabout's off Broadway 12/3/74 for 32 performances.

THE MAIDS

Claire	Ted Britton	Madame	Noble Shropshire
Solange	Patrick Egan		

Scenery, Christopher Martin.

An all-male cast in performance of this Genet work, presented without intermission. The last professional New York production of *The Maids* was its American premiere off Broadway 11/14/63 for 62 performances. It was part of CSC's repertory as an off-off-Broadway group in the season of 1974-75.

Note: Press date for *A Midsummer Night's Dream* was 11/13/77, for *Rosmersholm* 11/27/77, for *Serjeant Musgrave's Dance* 12/11/77, for *The Running of the Deer* 2/5/78, for *The Madwoman of Chaillot* 3/5/78.

Esther (8). By C.K. Mack. Produced by Saul Novick and Jomeldin Productions at the Promenade Theater. Opened November 29, 1977. (Closed December 4, 1977)

Directed by Joel Zwick; scenery, Franco Colavecchia; costumes, David James; lighting, Ed Greenberg; incidental music, Bruce Coughlin; press, Hunt/Pucci Associates. With Dianne Weist, Stephen Keep, Charles Turner, John Milligan, Joel Kramer, Bruce Kornbluth.

Psychological drama about the legendary Jewish Queen of Persia.

The Negro Ensemble Company. Schedule of three programs. **The Offering** (59). By Gus Edwards. Opened November 26, 1977; see note. Closed January 1, 1978 and reopened in repertory February 7, 1978. (Closed February 28, 1978). **Black Body Blues** (40). By Gus Edwards. Opened in repertory with *The Offering* January 19, 1978; see note. (Closed March 5, 1978). **The Twilight Dinner** (27). By Lennox Brown. Opened April 14, 1978; see note. (Closed May 14, 1978) Produced by The Negro Ensemble Company, Douglas Turner Ward artistic director, Robert Hooks executive director, Frederick Garrett administrative director, at the St. Marks Playhouse.

THE OFFERING

Bob Tyrone	Douglas Turner Ward	Princess	Olivia Williams

Martin ....Charles Weldon   Ginny ....Katherine Knowles

Directed by Douglas Turner Ward; scenery, Raymond C. Recht; costumes, Arthur McGee; lighting, Paul Gallo; production stage manager, Horacena J. Taylor; press, Howard Atlee, Clarence Allsopp, Becky Flora.

Time: The present. Place: A basement apartment in West Side Manhattan. The play was presented in two parts.

An old man and a young one in confrontation.

BLACK BODY BLUES

Arthur .... Samm-Art Williams   Louis ....Frankie R. Faison
Andy .... Norman Bush   Fletcher .... Douglas Turner Ward
Joyce .... Catherine E. Slade

Directed by Douglas Turner Ward; scenery, Raymond C. Recht; costumes, Arthur McGee; lighting, Paul Gallo; production stage manager, Horacena J. Taylor.

Time: The present, the month of August. Place: New York City, an apartment in the Broadway-Times Square area. The play was presented in two parts.

Melodramatic clash of two brothers symbolic of differing black lifestyles. Previously produced in a staged reading at National Playwrights Conference, Waterford, Conn.

THE TWILIGHT DINNER

Jimmy .... Leon Morenzie   Ray .... Reuben Green
Elissa ....Karen Bernhard

Directed by Douglas Turner Ward; scenery, Samuel Gonzalez; lighting, James Fauvell.

Two blacks from different countries, who had been friends in the 1960s, confront each other in a New York restaurant in the present.

Note: Press date for *The Offering* was 11/26/77, for *Black Body Blues* 1/24/78, for *The Twilight Dinner* 4/18/78.

Joe Masiell Not at the Palace (23). Musical revue with special material by Jerry Herman, Will Holt, Fred Ebb and John Kander. Produced by Lily Turner at the Astor Place Theater. Opened December 11, 1977. (Closed January 8, 1978)

Debra Dickinson   Gena Ramsel
Anita Ehrler   Nancy Salis
Joe Masiell

Directed by James Coco; choreography, C. Tod Jackson; scenery and costumes, C. Tod Jackson; arranged and conducted by Christopher Bankey; lighting, James Nisbet Clark; production stage manager, James Nisbet Clark; press, Saul Richman.

Concert-style revue, a frame for Joe Masiell's performance as a singer and occasional narrator.

ACT I — "When I'm Playin' the Palace" (by Jerry Herman); "Everything" (by Holmes & Williams); "Two for the Road" (by Bricusse & Mancini); "You and I" (by Leslie Bricusse); "The Lady Is a Tramp" (by Rodgers & Hart); "Io E' Te" (by Morricone & Pace); "I Don't Want to Know" (by Jerry Herman); "In My Life" (by Lennon & McCartney); "We Were Young" (by Joe Masiell); "If You Like the Music" (by Pete McCann); "Here's That Rainy Day" (by Burke & Van Heusen); "Money, Money, Money" (by Anderson & Ulvaeus); "Money, Money" (by Kander & Ebb); "This Funny World" (by Rodgers & Hart); "But the World Goes 'Round" (by Kander & Ebb).

ACT II — "What Now My Love" (by Delance & Becaud, English lyric by Carl Sigman); "Who" (by Charles Aznavour, English lyric by Herbert Kretzmer); "It Will Be My Day" (by Charles Aznavour, English lyric by Bob Morrison); "Madeleine" (by Jacques Brel, English lyric by Shuman & Blau); "Crazy Melody" (by Varel & Bailly, English lyric by Will Holt); "Hey Poppa" (by Kander & Ebb).

Joseph and the Amazing Technicolor Dreamcoat (16). Revival of the musical based on the Old Testament story; book, music and lyrics by Tim Rice and Andrew Lloyd Webber. Produced by Brooklyn Academy of Music at Brooklyn Academy of Music. Opened December 13, 1977. (Closed December 25, 1977)

Directed and choreographed by Graciela Daniele; scenery supervision, John Pitts; costume supervision, Dona Granata; press, Louis Sica, John Howlett. With Alan Weeks, David-James Carroll, William Parry.

This musical was previously produced by Young Vic in London, and elsewhere including Brooklyn Academy of Music 12/30/76 for 23 performances. The list of musical numbers appears on pages 335-6 of *The Best Plays of 1976-77.*

The Contessa of Mulberry Street (13). By Nicholas D. Bellitto. Produced by Gene Frankel and Cleveden T. Kingston at the Frankel Theater. Opened January 4, 1978. (Closed January 15, 1978)

Directed by Gene Frankel; staging, Andrew Louca; scenery, Wilton Duckworth; costumes, Shelly Friedman; lighting, Candice Dunn; press, Max Eisen. With Lou Criscuolo, Willi Kirkham, George Igoe, Murray Shactman, James Sappho, Keren Liswood, Phillip Kraft.

Family life in Little Italy. Previously produced off off Broadway at Gene Frankel Workshop.

The Beard (13). Revival of the play by Michael McClure. Produced by John Jobe at the Quaigh Theater. Opened January 5, 1978. (Closed January 15, 1978)

Directed by Philip Minor; scenery, John Jobe; costumes, Arthur Connell; lighting, Michael Smith; press, Max Eisen. With Morris Lafon, Ruth Brandeis.

Previously produced off Broadway 10/24/67 for 100 performances.

My Astonishing Self (48). One-man performance by Donal Donnelly as George Bernard Shaw; devised by Michael Voysey from the writings of George Bernard Shaw. Produced by Arthur Cantor at the Astor Place Theater. Opened January 18, 1978. (Closed March 5, 1978)

Production stage manager, Larry Bussard; press, C. George Willard.

Excerpts from Shaw's letters, pamphlets, diaries, lectures, etc., putting forth his views on a variety of subjects. The play was presented in two parts. A foreign play previously produced at Dublin, Ireland Drama Festival and elsewhere including Loeb Drama Center, Cambridge, Mass.

By Strouse (156). Musical revue with music by Charles Strouse; lyrics by Lee Adams and Martin Charnin. Produced by Norman Kean at the Ballroom. Opened February 1, 1978. (Closed April 30, 1978)

Gary Beach	Maureen Moore
Donna Marshall	Gail Nelson

Directed by Charles Strouse; design, Connie and Peter Wexler; choreography, Mary Kyte; musical direction, Randy Barnett; press, Henry Luhrman associates, Anne Weinberg, Terry Lilly.

Collection of Charles Strouse theater songs from *Bye Bye Birdie, All American, Golden Boy, It's a Bird It's a Plane It's SUPERMAN, Applause, Annie* and the unproduced shows *Hunky Dory, Palm Beach, The Borrowers, Flowers for Algernon* and *Marjorie Morningstar,* plus other works. Previously produced off off Broadway at Manhattan Theater Club. The play was presented without intermission.

MUSICAL NUMBERS — "Stick Around," "A Lot of Livin' to Do," "The Immigration and Naturalization Rag," "This Is the Life," "Colorful," "What a Country," "N.Y.C.," "Don't Forget 127th Street," "I'm Not in Philadelphia," "Half of Life," "One Boy," "One Last Kiss," "We Love You Conrad," "Born Too Late," "Bye Bye Birdie," "How Lovely To Be a Woman,"

Donna Marshall, Maureen Moore, Gary Beach and Gail Nelson in
By Strouse

"Livin' Alone," "Some Bright Morning," "Marjorie Morningstar," "Welcome to the Theater," "But Alive," "In a Silly Mood," "One of a Kind," "Good Friends," "Everything's Great," "Hunky Dory," "You're Never Fully Dressed Without a Smile," "Put on a Happy Face," "Tomorrow," "Once Upon a Time," "Lorna's Here," "Night Song," "Those Were The Days," "Applause," "A Broadway Musical."

The BAM Theater Company. Schedule of four revivals. **The Devil's Disciple** (15). By George Bernard Shaw. Produced in association with The Center Theater Group/Ahmanson Theater. Opened February 8, 1978. (Closed February 19, 1978) **The Play's the Thing** (30). By Ferenc Molnar; adapted by P.G. Wodehouse. Opened February 26, 1978 matinee. (Closed March 19, 1978). **Julius Caesar** (31). By William Shakespeare. Opened April 7, 1978. (Closed April 23, 1978) ***Waiting for Godot** (1). By Samuel Beckett; produced in cooperation with Goethe House. Opened May 31, 1978. Produced by The BAM Theater Company. Frank Dunlop director, Berenice Weiler administrative director, at the Brooklyn Academy of Music.

THE DEVIL'S DISCIPLE

Annie Dudgeon	Margaret Hamilton	Dudgeon	Robert Cornthwaite
Essie	Louise Heath	Uncle William's Wife	Betty Ramey
Christy Dudgeon	Randy Pelish	Uncle Titus's Wife	Peggy Rea
Rev. Anthony Anderson	Barnard Hughes	Dick Dudgeon	Chris Sarandon
Judith Anderson	Carole Shelley	Sergeant	John Orchard
Lawyer Hawkins	Fred Stuthman	Maj. Swindon	Earl Boen
Uncle William Dudgeon	Allan Lurie	Gen. Burgoyne	George Rose
Uncle Titus		Chaplain Brudenell	Ken Letner

Townspeople, Soldiers: Norman Abrams, Timothy Askew, Jason Buzas, Paul Diaz, George McDaniel, Ron Perkins, Rudolf Ranier, Robert Rhys, Rex Stallings, Holly Villaire.

Musicians: Russel Detrick, Jay Leslie, David Levy.

Understudies: Messrs. Sarandon, Rose, Boen, Stuthman — George McDaniel; Misses Shelley, Heath — Holly Villaire; Mr. Hughes — Ken Letner; Miss Hamilton — Peggy Rea; Messrs. Pelish, Lurie — Ron Perkins; Mr. Cornthwaite — Rudolf Ranier; Mr. Orchard — Rex Stallings.

Directed by Frank Dunlop; scenery and costumes, Carl Toms; lighting, F. Mitchell Dana; production stage manager, Barbara-Mae Phillips; press, Louis Sica, John Howlett.

Time: Late autumn, 1777. Place: Websterbridge, N.H. Act I: Morning, the Dudgeon farmhouse. Act II: Evening the Rev. Anderson's house. Act III: The next day, inside and outside the Town Hall. The play was presented in two parts with the intermission following Act II.

The Devil's Disciple was first produced in New York by Richard Mansfield 10/4/97 for 56 performances. Professional revivals took place in Mansfield repertory 11/20/99; 4/23/23 in a Theater Guild production; and 1/25/50 for 127 performances in a New York City Theater Company production. The 1978 production was previously presented in Los Angeles.

THE PLAY'S THE THING

Mansky .... Kurt Kasznar	Ilona Szabo .... Carole Shelley
Sandor Turai .... Rene Auberjonois	Almady .... George Rose
Albert Adam .... Austin Pendleton	Mell .... Stephen Collins
Johann Dwornitschek .... Rex Robbins	Lackeys ...... Norman Abrams, Paul Diaz

Directed by Frank Dunlop; scenery, Santo Loquasto; costumes, Nancy Potts; lighting, F. Mitchell Dana; production stage manager, Frank Bayer.

The last New York professional production of *The Play's the Thing* was by the Roundabout 1/9/73 for 64 performances off Broadway and 5/7/73 for 87 more performances on Broadway.

JULIUS CAESAR

Julius Caesar .... George Rose	Metellus Cimber; Strato ...... Philip Kraus
Octavius Caesar .... Thomas Hulce	Cinna; 1st Soldier .... Terry Alexander
Marcus Antonius .... Austin Pendleton	Flavius; Artemidorus;
Lepidus .... Sheldon Epps	Volumnius .... Paul Perri
Cicero; Titinius .... Ken Letner	Soothsayer .... Sheldon Epps
Popilius Lena; Marullus;	Young Cato .... Rex Stallings
Messala .... George McDaniel	Lucius .... Michael Gennaro
Marcus Brutus .... Rene Auberjonois	Ceasar's Servant;
Cassius .... Richard Dreyfuss	2d Soldier .... Paul Diaz
Casca .... Rex Robbins	3d Soldier .... Norman Abrams
Trebonius; Lucilius .... Stephen Davies	Calpurnia .... Sloane Shelton
Decius Brutus; Pindarus ...... Justin Deas	Portia .... Holly Villaire

Directed by Frank Dunlop; scenery, Carole Lee Carroll; costumes, Dona Granata; lighting, F. Mitchell Dana; music, Frank Bennett; production stage manager, Barbara Mae Phillips.

The last professional New York productions of *Julius Caesar* were, off Broadway, Joseph Papp's at the Heckscher Theater 2/19/62 for 10 performances, the Edison Arena's 6/20/50 for 31 performances; and, on Broadway. Orson Welles's Mercury Theater production 11/11/37 for 157 performances.

WAITING FOR GODOT

Estragon .... Austin Pendleton	Pozzo .... Michael Egan
Vladimir .... Sam Waterston	Boy .... R.J. Murray Jr.
Lucky .... Milo O'Shea	

Directed by Walter D. Asmus; scenery, Carole Lee Carroll; costumes, Dona Granata; lighting, Shirley Prendergast; production stage manager, Frank Bayer.

This is Samuel Beckett's own English version of his play, based on the production he staged for the Schiller Theater in Berlin. The last professional New York production of the play was off Broadway last season in the Schiller Theater production, in German, 3/29/77 for 7 performances.

In the Brooklyn Academy of Music there are a number of separate auditoriums. *The Devil's Disciple* played the Opera House, *The Play's the Thing* played the Helen Carey Playhouse, *Julius Caesar* and *Waiting for Godot* played the Leperq Space.

*P.S. Your Cat Is Dead (81). Revival of the play by James Kirkwood. Produced by Haskell/Spiegel Productions at the Promenade Theater. Opened March 22, 1978.

| Vito | Vasili Bogazianos | Jimmy | Peter Simon |
| Kate | Claire Malis | Fred | John Shearin |

Standbys: Mr. Simon — John Shearin; Messrs. Bogazianos, Shearin — Stephen Burleigh; Miss Malis — Ruth Nerken.

Directed by Robert Nigro; scenery, Judie Juracek; lighting, Michael Orris Watson; production stage manager, H. Todd Iveson; press, Henry Luhrman Associates, Anne Obert Weinberg, Terry M. Lilly.

Time: New Year's Eve. Place: Jimmy Zoole's loft apartment, New York City. Act I, Scene 1: Late evening. Scene 2: Thirty minutes later. Act II: The same night.

Revised version of the play originally produced off Broadway 4/7/75 for 16 performances as a seven-character play.

A Bistro Car on the CNR (61). Musical with dialogue by D.R. Andersen, music by Patrick Rose, lyrics by Merv Campone and Richard Ouzounian. Produced by Jeff Britton and Bob Bisaccia at the Playhouse Theater. Opened March 23, 1978. (Closed May 14, 1978)

| Kathy | Marcia McClain | Jessica | Henrietta Valor |
| Ted | Patrick Rose | Dan | Tom Wopat |

Directed by Richard Ouzounian; choreography, Lynne Gannaway; musical direction, John Clifton; scenery and costumes, John Falabella; lighting, Ned Hallick; associate producer, Jimmy Merrill; stage manager, Craig Saeger; press, Gifford/Wallace, Inc.

Place: The converted baggage car of the "Rapido," making its final trip from Toronto to Montreal.

A baggage car of a Canadian train is converted into a cabaret/bistro where musical works in progress are put on for the entertainment of passengers during the five-hour trip (based on an actual situation a few years ago). A foreign play previously produced in Canada.

ACT I

Overture
"C.N.R." ... Company
"Twenty-five Miles" ... Kathy
"Guitarist" ... Ted
"Passing By" ... Dan, Kathy
"Madame La Chanson" ... Jessica
"Oh God I'm Thirty" ... Ted
"Ready or Not" ... Kathy, Jessica
"Sudden Death Overtime" ... Ted
"Bring Back Swing" ... Company
"Yesterday's Lover" ... Jessica
"Four Part Invention" ... Company
"Nocturne" ... Company

ACT II

"La Belle Province" ... Company
"Ensemble" ... Jessica, Ted
"Dewey and Sal" ... Dan, Kathy
"Here I Am Again" ... Ted
"Street Music" ... Company
"Other People's Houses" ... Kathy
"Genuine Grade A Canadian Superstar" ... Dan, Company
"I Don't Live Anywhere Anymore" ... Dan
"The Lady Who Loved to Sing" ... Company
"Somebody Write Me a Love Song" ... Jessica
Finale ... Company

The Acting Company. Repertory of three revivals. **Mother Courage and Her Children** (10). By Bertolt Brecht; translated by Ralph Manheim. Opened April 5, 1978. **King Lear** (9). By William Shakespeare. Opened April 9, 1978. **Duck Variations** (3). By David Mamet. Opened April 16, 1978 matinee. (Repertory closed April 23, 1978) Produced by The Acting Company, John Houseman producing artistic director, Alan Schneider and Michael Kahn artistic directors, Margo Harley executive producer, at the American Place Theater.

PERFORMER	"MOTHER COURAGE AND HER CHILDREN"	"KING LEAR"
Gregg Almquist		Gloucester
Dennis Bacigalupi		Fool
Brooks Baldwin		Oswald
Frances Conroy	Kattrin	Cordelia
Kevin Conroy	Ellif	Edgar
Daniel Corcoran		King of France
Tom Donaldson		Edmund
James Harper	Swedish General	Kent
Jeffrey Hayenga	Swiss Cheese	Captain
Patricia Hodges	Yvette	Regan
Ron Jacobson		Burgundy
Anderson Matthews	Chaplain	Albany
Tom Robbins		Cornwall
Mary Lou Rosato	Mother Courage	Goneril
David Schramm	Cook	Lear
Henry Stram		Doctor

MOTHER COURAGE — Additional cast members: Tom Donaldson, Tom Robbins, John Greenleaf, Henry Stram, Brooks Baldwin, Daniel Corcoran, Dennis Bacigalupi, Ron Jacobson, Gregg Almquist, Leslie Geraci, Harriet Harris.

Directed by Alan Schneider; music and lyrics, Paul Dessau; musical direction, Albert Hague; scenery, Ming Cho Lee; costumes, Jeanne Button; lighting, David F. Segal; production stage manager, Daniel Morris; press, The Merlin Group, Ltd.

The last professional New York porduction of *Mother Courage* was on Broadway in Yiddish by The Jewish State Theater of Poland 11/16/67 for 11 performances.

KING LEAR — Directed by John Houseman; fights, B.H. Barry; Fool's dance, Elizabeth Keen; conductor, Stephen Colvin; music, Marc Blitzstein; scenery, Ming Cho Lee; costumes, Nancy Potts; lighting, David F. Segal.

The last professional New York production of *King Lear* was off Broadway by Royal Shakespeare Company 2/25/75 for 16 performances.

DUCK VARIATIONS

With Richard Ooms, David Schramm.

Directed by Gerald Gutierrez; scenery, John Lee Beatty; costumes, John David Ridge; lighting David F. Segal.

The last professional New York production of *Duck Variations* was its New York premiere 6/16/76 for 273 performances.

The Acting Company also presented a work in progress, *The Other Half* by Elinor Jones, directed by Amy Saltz, musical staging by Elizabeth Keen, musical direction by Penna Rose, lighting by Skip Rapoport, 4/22 matinee for 3 performances.

Life of Galileo (20). Revival of the play by Bertolt Brecht; translated by Ralph Manheim and Wolfgang Sauerlander. Produced by Columbia University School of the Arts, Schuyler Chapin dean, Theater Division, Bernard Beckerman chairman, and The New York Actors' Theater, Laurence Luckinbill, Robin Strasser, Rudy Caringi artistic directors, in association with Penney and Ron Dante and Ilse and Henry Wolf at Havemeyer Hall of Columbia University. Opened April 5, 1978. (Closed April 23, 1978)

CAST: Galileo Galilei — Laurence Luckinbill; Andrea Sarti — Jack Magee; Mrs. Sarti — Mary Carver; Ludovico Marsili — Michael O'Hare; Priuli the Prosecutor, Very Old Cardinal — Joseph Davidson; Sagredo, Father Christopher Clavius, Vanni, Filippo Mucius — Richard Zavaglia; Virginia — Francesca James; Senator, Mathematician, Soldier, Monk, Secretary — Laurence Attile; Senator, Secretary, Shady Individual, Peasant — Alexander Wells; Doge, Lord Champberlain, Fat Prelate, Gaffone, Ballad Singer, Town Crier — Henry Grossman; Grand Duke Cosmo de Medici, Lackey, Monk, Manservant, Child — Joel Charap; Federzoni — Robert Mont; Philosopher, Cardinal Bellarmine, High Official, Border Guard — Bernie McInerney; Nun, Ballad Singer's Wife — Samantha Laine; Woman, Child — Lillian Jenkins; Little Monk — Rudy Caringi; Cardinal Inquisitor, Clerk — Gil Rogers; Cardinal Barberini (later Pope Urban VIII) — Peter White.

Directed by Rudy Caringi; scenery and lighting, James Tilton; costumes, Ursula Belden, Elizabeth P. Palmer; music composed and performed by Howard Harris; producer for The New York Actors' Theater, Robin Strasser; producer for Columbia University, Andrew Harris; production coordinated by John P. Fleming; "Chalktalker" graphics by Bob Gale; stage manager, Frederic H. Orner; press, Bob Ullman.

Brecht's play about Galileo in a new English translation, presented in two parts. Its last professional New York production was by The Repertory Theater of Lincoln Center 4/13/67 for 76 performances.

23 Skiddoo (10). Multimedia production with text by William S. Burroughs, Brion Gysin, Wilhelm Reich and the Marquis de Sade. Produced by Le Plan K at the Washington Square Methodist Church. Opened April 5, 1978. (Closed April 16, 1978)

Directed by Frederic Flamand; music written and performed by Yves Mousty; production coordinator, Sabrina Hamilton. With Baba, Daniel Beeson, Carlos de Ponte, Frederic Flamand, Bruno Garny.

Visiting Belgian troupe in an avant-garde display representing "a grim view of a future more repressive than 1984."

*Family Business (57). By Dick Goldberg. Produced by Honey Waldman at the Astor Place Theater. Opened April 12, 1978.

Isaiah Stein	Harold Gary	Bobby Stein	Richard Greene
Jerry Stein	Joel Polis	Phil Stein	David Rosenbaum
Norman Stein	David Garfield	Young Man	Richard Levine

Directed by John Stix; scenery, Don Jensen; stage manager, Richard Delehanty; press, Saul Richman.

Time: Late autumn, 1974. Place: The main room of Isaiah Stein's home in Beverly, Mass. Act I: Late afternoon. Act II: Seven days later, evening. Act III: Three weeks later, morning.

Sons fall out after their father's death. Previously produced at the Stockbridge, Mass. Festival. A Best Play; see page 321.

*The Neon Woman (44). By Tom Eyen. Produced by Bruce Mailman and Ina Meibach Minkin at the Hurrah Discotheque. Opened April 16, 1978.

Joni	Maria Duvall	Connie	Helen Hanft
Kitty LaRue	Sweet William Edgar	Kim	Brenda Bergman
Speed Gonzalez	George Patterson	District Attorney	Lee Corbet
Willy; Senator	William Duff-Griffin	Flash Storm	Divine
Rita	Debra Greenfield	Laura	Hope Stansbury

Directed by Ron Link; scenery and graphics, Herbert Nagle; lighting, Jack Ranson; costumes and makeup, Van Smith; production stage manager, Jack Kalman; press, Alan Eichler.

Murder among strip-tease artists, a burlesque of mystery plays.

*The Best Little Whorehouse in Texas (50). Musical with book by Larry L. King and Peter Masterson; music and lyrics by Carol Hall. Produced by Universal Pictures at the Entermedia Theater. Opened April 17, 1978.

Rio Grande Band	Eloise .... Marta Sanders
Leader .... Craig Chambers	Durla .... Debra Zalkind
Farmer; Melvin P.	Leroy Sliney;
Thorpe .... Clint Allmon	Aggie #77 .... Bradley Clayton King
Shy Kid; Aggie #7 .... Gerry Burkhardt	Stage Manager; Cameraman;
Miss Wulla Jean .... Edna Milton	Aggie #12 (Specialty
Traveling Salesman; Scruggs;	Dance) .... Tom Cashin
T.V. Colorman;	Sheriff Ed Earl
Governor .... Jay Garner	Dodd .... Henderson Forsythe
Slick Dude; Soundman;	Mayor Rufus Poindexter;
Ukranian Aggie #1	Senator Wingwoah ...... J. Frank Lucas
Placekicker .... Cameron Burke	Edsel Mackey .... Don Crabtree
Amber .... Pamela Blair	Doatsey May;
Shy .... Joan Ellis	Reporter #1 .... Susan Mansur
Jewel .... Delores Hall	TV Announcer .... Larry L. King
Mona Stangley .... Carlin Glynn	Angel Imogene Charlene .... Lisa Brown
Girls at Miss Mona's:	Aggie #21;
Linda Lou .... Donna King	Reporter #2 .... Paul Ukena Jr.
Dawn .... Lisa Brown	Aggie #71;
Ginger .... Louise Quick-Bowen	Reporter #3 .... Michael Scott
Beatrice .... Jan Merchant	Aggie #11;
Taddy Jo .... Carol Chambers	Governor's Aide .... Jay Bursky
Ruby Rae .... Becky Gelke	Aggie #17 .... James Rich

Girls: Lisa Brown, Carol Chambers, Donna King, Susan Mansur, Louise Quick-Bowen, Debra Zalkind. Cowboys: Jay Bursky, Bradley Clayton King, Michael Scott, Paul Ukena Jr. Choir: Jay Bursky, Becky Gelke, Delores Hall, Jan Merchant, James Rich, Marta Sanders. The Dogettes: Gerry Burkhardt, Jay Bursky, Michael Scott, Paul Ukena Jr. Melvin Thorpe Singers: Becky Gelke, Bradley Clayton King, Susan Mansur, Jan Merchant, James Rich, Marta Sanders. Townspeople: Carol Chambers, Bradley Clayton King, Edna Milton, James Rich, Marta Sanders. Angelettes: Louise Quick-Bowen, Becky Gelke, Donna King, Debra Zalkind, Jan Merchant. Photographers: Michael Scott, Paul Ukena Jr., James Rich, Jay Bursky.

Alternate Dancers: Monica Tiller, Jerry Yoder, Gena Ramsel.

Directed by Peter Masterson and Tommy Tune; musical numbers staged by Tommy Tune; musical direction and vocal arrangements, Robert Billig; scenery, Marjorie Kellogg; costumes, Ann Roth; lighting, Dennis Parichy; sound, John Venable; associate choreographer, Thommie Walsh; musicians, Rio Grande Band; production stage manager, Paul Phillips; stage manager, Jay Schlossberg-Cohen; press, Jeffrey Richards Associates, Maurice Turet, Jeanna Gallo.

Time: The present. Place: The State of Texas.

A cherished Texas institution comes under attack from moralistic do-gooders. Previously produced in workshop at the Actors Studio.

A Best Play; see page 261.

ACT I

Prologue .... Craig Chambers, Rio Grande Band
"20 Fans" .... Mona, Girls, Cowboys, Farmer,
                    Shy Kid, Miss Wulla Jean, Traveling Salesman, Slick Dude, Choir
"A Lil' Ole Bitty Pissant Country Place" .... Mona, Girls
"Girl You're a Woman" .... Mona, Shy, Jewel, Girls
"Watch Dog Theme" .... Melvin P. Thorpe, Dogettes

"Texas Has a Whorehouse in It" .... Thorpe, Thorpe Singers, Dogettes
"Twenty-Four Hours of Lovin" .... Jewel, Girls
"Watchdog Theme" (Reprise) .... Dogettes
"Texas Has a Whorehouse In It" (Reprise) .... Thorpe, Dogettes, Mayor, Scruggs,
Edsel, Doatsey Mae, Church Lady,
Lady Convent, Townspeople
"Doatsey Mae" .... Doatsey Mae
"Angelette March" .... Imogene Charlene, Angelettes
"The Aggie Song" .... Aggies
"Bus From Amarillo" .... Mona

ACT II

"The Sidestep" .... Governor, Governor's Aide, Sen. Wingwoah,
Thorpe, Dogettes, Thorpe Singers
"No Lies" .... Mona, Jewel, Girls
"Good Old Girl" .... Sheriff, Aggies
"Hard Candy Christmas" .... Amber, Linda Lou, Ginger, Dawn, Ruby Rae, Beatrice
"Hard Candy Christmas" (Reprise) .... Girls
Finale .... Company

The Proposition (24). Improvisational musical revue conceived by Allan Albert. Produced by The Proposition Workshop, Inc., Allan Albert artistic director, Carol Lawhon managing director, at the Actors' Playhouse. Opened May 3, 1978. (Closed May 21, 1978)

Raymond Baker	Timothy Hall
Anne Cohen	Deborah Reagan

Standby: Shelley Barre.

Directed by Allen Albert; musical direction, Robert Hirschhorn, John Lewis, Donald Sosin; lighting, Dick Williams; stage manager, Matthew Cohen; press, Howard Rogut, Marshall Ballou.

This improvised material based on suggestions from the audience was presented in two parts. The Proposition was formed in 1968 in Cambridge, Mass., is now based at the Berkshire Theater Festival in Stockbridge, Mass. and was previously presented off Broadway 3/4/71 for 1,109 performances in various editions.

*The Biko Inquest (17). By Norman Fenton and Jon Blair. Produced by Arthur Cantor by arrangement with Paddington Press, Ltd., Norman Fenton and Jon Blair at Theater Four. Opened May 17, 1978.

Sidney Kentridge	Fritz Weaver	Prof. Johann David Loubser	James Cook
Martinus Prins	David Gale	Prof. Proctor	William Myers
Jan van Rensburg	Bill Moor	Dr. Ivor Lang	Martin Shakar
Col. Pieter Goosen	Philip Bosco	Dr. Benjamin Tucker	Carl Low
Maj. Harold Snyman	Jess Osuna	Dr. Colin Hersch	Jonathan Moore
Lt. Eric Wilken	John Vennema		

Understudies: Messrs. Weaver, Bosco — David Gale; Messrs. Gale, Low — William Myers; Messrs. Moore, Osuna — Martin Shakar; Messrs. Vennema, Cook, Myers, Moore — Charles Helsley; Mr. Shakar — James Cook.

Directed by Norman Fenton and Jon Blair; prologue by Donald and Wendy Woods; scenery, Eric Head; costumes, Patricia McGourty; lighting, Clyde Kuemmerle; production stage manager, Christopher Kelly; stage mananger, Charles Helsley; press, C. George Willard.

Time: Nov. 14-Dec. 2, 1977. Place: The Old Synagogue in Pretoria, South Africa, now used as a courtroom. The play was presented in two parts.

Dramatization of transcripts of the inquest into the death of Stephen Biko in his jail cell Sept. 12, 1977, with all the character names those of real participants except that of van Rensburg, a composite of several state advocates. A foreign play previously produced in London.

*International Stud (10). By Harvey Fierstein. Produced by Players Theater at the Players Theater. Opened May 22, 1978.

Piano Man	Ned Levy	Arnold	Harvey Fierstein
Lady Blues	Diane Tarleton	Ed	Richard Dow

Directed by Eric Concklin; costumes, Mardi Philips; lighting, Joanna Schielke; musical direction and arrangements, Ned Levy; production stage manager, Lee Evans; press, Jeffrey Richards Associates, Maurice Turet, Bruce Lynn, Jeanna Gallo.

Scene 1: January, a night club dressing room. Scene 2: February, "The Stud" bar. Scene 3: June, Arnold's and Ed's apartments. Scene 4: September, "The Stud" bar. Scene 5: November, the dressing room. The play was presented without intermission.

The emotional complexities and sufferings of a drag queen. Previously produced off off Broadway at La Mama.

*Ridiculous Theatrical Company. Repertory of three plays by Charles Ludlam. ***Stage Blood** (4). Opened May 24, 1978. ***The Ventriloquist's Wife** (3). Opened May 25, 1978. ***Camille** (1). Opened May 27, 1978. Produced by Ridiculous Theatrical Company, Charles Ludlam artisitc director, at One Sheridan Square.

PERFORMER	"STAGE BLOOD"	"CAMILLE"
Black-Eyed Susan	Elfie Fey	Olympe de Taverney
Steve Borst		Joseph; Butler
John D. Brockmeyer	Jenkins	Baron de Varville
Robert Fuhrman		Duval Senior
Charles Ludlam	Carleton Stone Jr.	Marguerite Gautier
Adam McAdam	Carleton Stone; Gilbert Fey	Nanine
Lola Pashalinski	Helga Vain	Prudence de Duvernoy
Everett Quinton		Nichette
Bill Vehr	Edmund Dundreary	Armand Duval

THE VENTRILOQUIST'S WIFE — Conceived and executed by Charles Ludlam; lighting, Richard Currie; costumes, Steven Burdick, Tom Claypool; stage manager, Robert Fuhrman; press, Alan Eichler.

With Black-Eyed Susan, Charles Ludlam, Walter Ego.

Psychodrama, previously produced by this company off off Broadway.

STAGE BLOOD — Directed by Charles Ludlam; lighting, Richard Currie; costumes, Arthur Brady, Mary Brecht. Previously presented off Broadway this season 7/1/77 for 15 performances.

CAMILLE — Directed by Charles Ludlam; scenery, Bobjack Callejo; lighting, Richard Currie; costumes, Mary Brecht.

Time: 1848. Act I: Paris, Marguerite's drawing room. Act II, Scene 1: Country home at Auteuil. Scene 2: Olympe's house, six months later. Act III: Marguerite's bedroom, Paris, six months later on New Year's Day. Freely adapted by Ludlam from *La Dame Aux Camelias* and last presented 5/13/64 for 113 performances.

PLAYS PRODUCED
OFF OFF BROADWAY

AND ADDITIONAL PRODUCTIONS

Here is a comprehensive sampling of off-off-Broadway and other experimental or peripheral 1977-78 productions in New York, compiled by Camille Croce. There is no definitive "off-off-Broadway" area or qualification. To try to define or regiment it would be untrue to its fluid, exploratory purpose. The listing below of about 600 programs by 80 major OOB groups and another 200-plus programs by 120 or more miscellaneous groups is as inclusive as reliable sources will allow, however, and takes in almost all Manhattan-based, new-play-producing, English-language organizations listed by the Off Off Broadway Alliance and the Theater Development Fund — plus many others.

The more active and established producing groups are identified in **bold face type,** in alphabetical order, with artistic policies and the name of the managing director(s) given whenever these are a matter of record. Each group's 1977-78 schedule is listed with play titles in CAPITAL LETTERS. Often these are works in progress with changing scripts, casts and directors, usually without an engagement of record (but an opening or early performance date is included when available).

With increasing prominence, many of these off-off-Broadway productions are outgrowing a merely experimental status with special contractual arrangements like the Equity showcase code (allowing concessions in employing professional actors for a run limited to 12 performances), a letter of agreement (permitting even longer runs and higher admission prices in certain circumstances) and, closer to the edge of the commercial theater, a so-called "mini-contract" with provisions for even longer runs and higher ticket prices. Without going into the complicated specifics of these special arrangements, we have expanded our coverage of this middle ground of New York production between off-off and off Broadway, so that each showcase, mini-contract or other special-arrangement production of a new or seldom-revived script is identifiable, with its title in **bold face type,** and with all available data on opening dates, performance numbers and major production and acting credits.

A large selection of lesser-known groups and other shows that made appearances off off Broadway during the season appears under the "Miscellaneous" heading at the end of this listing.

Academy Arts Theater Company. Commitment to the community via major revivals, original works, theater for deaf audiences, children's theater. Robert Cusack, director.

THE LOVELIEST AFTERNOON OF THE YEAR by John Guare, directed by Jill Yager; I CAN'T IMAGINE TOMORROW by Tennessee Williams, directed by Michael Bright. August, 1977.
THE GRASS HARP (musical) based on Truman Capote's novel, book and lyrics by Kenward

Elmslie, music by Claibe Richardson. August 11, 1977. Directed by Loi Leabo and John W. Wilson; with Jean Richards, Larry Filiaci, Linda Jo Rauth, Deborah Meyers.
THE PATIENT and THE RATS (one-act plays) by Agatha Christie. September 9, 1977. Directed by Karen Hoffman and Robert Cusack.
THE BALLOONS by Kira Osarczuk. October, 1977.
A PERFECT ANALYSIS GIVEN BY A PARROT (one-act play). By Tennessee Williams, directed by Jill Yager; SOMETHING I'LL TELL YOU TUESDAY (one-act play) by John Guare, directed by Karen Hoffman. October 13, 1977.
IN CELEBRATION by David Storey. November, 1977. Directed by June Rovenger; with Frank Hamilton, Ruby Holbrook, Anthony Call.
THE RED BALLOON by Albert Lamorisse. December, 1977. Directed by Debbie Leonard.
THE LAST LEAF and GIFT OF THE MAGI by O. Henry. December, 1977. Directed by Jill Yager.
EAST LYNNE by Mrs. Henry Wood, directed by Dorothy Stuart; THE REAL INSPECTOR HOUND by Tom Stoppard, directed by Robert Pesola. January 13, 1978.
PRIVATE LIVES by Noel Coward. February, 1978. Directed by David McNitt.
WOMEN I HAVE KNOWN by M. Tulis Sessions. February, 1978. Directed by Michael T. Gregoric.
ARMS AND THE MAN by George Bernard Shaw. February, 1978. Directed by Loukas Skipitaris.
LUDLOW FAIR and BE WHO YOU ARE by Lanford Wilson. March 17, 1978. Directed by Thomas Ryan.
MIXED DOUBLES (two plays) by David Libman. March, 1978. Directed by June Rovenger.
CLARENCE DARROW by David Rintels. March 30, 1978. Directed by Kathy Reed.
SING MELANCHOLY BABY written and directed by Michael Deveraux. April 12, 1978.
SORRY, WRONG NUMBER by Lucille Fletcher and I CAN'T IMAGINE TOMORROW. April 14, 1978. Directed by Robert Cusack.
WHAT THE BUTLER SAW by Joe Orton, directed by Robert Cusack; THE GREAT NEBULA IN ORION by Lanford Wilson, directed by Robert Pesola; EX-MISS COPPER QUEEN ON A SET OF PILLS by Megan Terry, directed by Karen Hoffman. May, 1978.

Actors' Alliance. Dedicated to bringing actors and audiences together in a community of delight, understanding and humanity. William Arrigon, William Newman, Nina Polan, founding members.

AMERICAN HAMBURGER by Robert Heide and THE COMEBACK by Jack Gilhooley (7). December 22, 1977. Director, Tom Everett. With James Higgins, Doris Gramovat, Paul Lieber, Mark Simon, Jack Poggi.

THE WINNER GOES HOME (11). By Lyla Hay Owen. March 31, 1978. Director, William Arrigon; scenery and costumes, Kathe Berl. With Helen Breed, James Higgins, Liis Kailey, Paul Lieber, Jay McCormack, Tom Sminkey, Charmian Sorbello.

BEAUTY LIKE THE NIGHT (15). By Kathy Hurley. May 5, 1978. Director, Eda Reiss Merin; scenery and costumes, Kathe Berl. With Kathlyn Barnes, Kathy Hurley, Stephen Novelli, Jeanne Schlegel, Tom Sminkey, Diana Walker.

The Actors Studio. Development of talent in productions of old and new works. Lee Strasberg, artistic director.

PRIVATE OPENING by Norman Wexler. June 2, 1977.
THE BEST LITTLE WHOREHOUSE IN TEXAS (musical) by Larry L. King and Peter Masterson, music and lyrics by Carol Hall. November, 1977. Directed by Peter Masterson; with Henderson Forsythe, Liz Kemp, Larry L. King.
ALFRED THE GREAT by Israel Horovitz. February 1, 1978. Directed by Ben Levit.
1st Annual Festival of plays from the Playwrights' Unit of The Actors Studio (staged readings): INDIANHEAD by Nancy Fales; THE CONSOLING VIRGIN by Bruce Serlen; SURVIVORS by Herbert Liebman; ROCKAWAY BOULEVARD by Richard Vetere; THE LOUNGE PLAYER by Israel Horovitz; THE BIGGEST THIEF IN TOWN by Mario Frat-

ti; SPECTRE by Saul Zachary; SPEAKEASY by Linda Segal; HARD FEELINGS by Jeffrey Sweet; SORROWS OF STEPHEN by Peter Parnell. May 2-27, 1978.

Afro-American Studio. Stimulating an awareness of the black experience in terms of theater. Ernie McClintock, artistic director.

I'M BEING HIT by Clay Goss and THE SIRENS by Richard Wesley. March 17, 1978. Directed by Ernie McClintock.
THE ISLAND by Athol Fugard, John Kani and Winston Ntshona. March 18, 1978. Directed by Richard Gant.
CEREMONIES IN DARK OLD MEN by Lonne Elder III. March 19, 1978.
FREEMAN by Phillip Hayes Dean. April 15, 1978.

Amas Repertory Theater. Creative arts as a powerful instrument of peaceful change, towards healthier individuals. Rosetta LeNoire, founder and artistic director.

HELEN (12). Book by Lucia Victor; lyrics and music by Johnny Brandon. October 20, 1977. Director, Lucia Victor; music director, arranger, Danny Holgate; scenery, Michael Meadows; lighting, Paul Sullivan; choreography, costumes, Bernard Johnson. With Robert Barnes, Kevin John Gee, Jean Dushon, Evie Juster, Chuck Patterson.

BEOWULF (12). Book and lyrics by Betty Jane Wylie; music by Victor Davies. December 1, 1977. Director, choreographer, Voigt Kempson; music director, Clyde Williams; scenery, Michael Meadows; lighting, Paul Sullivan; costumes, Lindsay Davis. With Robert Anderson, Nora M. Cole, Joey Ginza, Susanne Montgomery, Michelle Stubbs.

BOSTON BOSTON (12). Book by William Michael Maher; music by Bill Brohn; lyrics by Bill Brohn and William Michael Maher; based on an idea by Rosetta LeNoire. April 27, 1978. Director, choreographer, William Michael Maher; music director, John Lenehan; scenery, Michael Meadows; lighting, Paul Sullivan; costumes, Sydney Brooks. With David Lile, Susan J. Baum, Diane Tarleton, Corliss Taylor-Dunn, Philip Shaw, Allen W. Lane.

COME LAUGH AND CRY WITH LANGSTON HUGHES conceived and directed by Rosetta LeNoire; music by Jobe Huntley; lyrics by Langston Hughes. February 9, 1978. With Bob Brooker, Roslyn Burrough, Richard Eber, Pat Palmer, Earl Rice, Autris Paige, Eugene Edwards.

The American Place Theater Subplot Cabaret. Work by American humorists. Wynn Handman, director.

WORD OF MOUTH (comedy revue) (12). By Young Humorists at the Subplot Cabaret (including pieces by David Rasche, Annette Kurek, Ted Tally); composer, arranger, John Lewis. April 22, 1978. Director, Denise A. Gordon; scenery and lighting, Craig Evans; costumes, Karen Perry. With Andrew Davis, Annette Kurek, Barry Press, David Rasche, Marcell Rosenblatt.

American Stanislavski Theater (AST). Development of the Stanislavski technique in the American theater. Sonia Moore, artistic director.

MY POOR MARAT by Aleksei Arbuzov; translated by Irene Moore. January 13, 1978. Directed by Sonia Moore; with Brian Wiley, Marian Brady, Dionis Enrique.
THE BOOR by Anton Chekhov, THE STRONGER by August Strindberg, and THE MAN WITH THE FLOWER IN HIS MOUTH by Luigi Pirandello. February 24, 1978. Directed by Sonia Moore; with David Herman, John Sheets, Frone Lund, Olga Frontino, Raisa Danilov, Laurel Thornby, Peter Sherayko.
LONG DAY'S JOURNEY INTO NIGHT by Eugene O'Neill. April 7, 1978. Directed by Sonia Moore; with David Herman, Darell Brown, Peter Sherayko, Dionis Enrique, Frone Lund.

Association of Theater Artists. Presents classical and modern plays, including new and experimental works. Roderick Nash, artistic director and director of all plays.

OTHELLO by William Shakespeare. November 19, 1977. With John Carrozza, Tom Mucciolo, Marcia Lee Merrill, Susan Kaslow.
SWEET BIRD OF YOUTH by Tennessee Williams. January 28, 1978. With Michael Morrows, Peg Osborne, Robert Frink, Marcia Lee Merrill, Maureen Barnes.
THE WOOD DEMON by Anton Chekhov. April 1, 1978. With Trish Johnson, Lee Evans, Robert Frink, Marcia Lee Merrill, Michael Morrows.

Bond Street Theater Coalition. Performing indoor and al fresco before a wide variety of audiences to make theater a socially relevant, environmentally conscious art form. Patrick Sciarratta, artistic director.

THE MYTH OF ERYSICHTHON (street theater) developed by Patrick Sciarratta and the Company. June, 1977.
PLUMS (cabaret) by Family Electric Theater. December, 1977. Directed by Nicholas Petron.
A GOD BEFORE OLYMPUS by Patrick Sciarratta. February, 1978.
A TALE OF VISION by Patrick Sciarratta. March, 1978.

Cherubs Guild Corporation. To present an exploration of human life through theater. Carol Avila, president.

PLAY WITH A TIGER by Doris Lessing. October 13, 1977. Directed by Hillary Wyler; with Carol David, James Goodwin Rice, Joseph McCaren, Sherill Price, Ken Bachtold, Viveca Parker.

The Classic Theater. Conceived and executed with the strictest artistic integrity and dramatic value. Maurice Edwards, artistic director.

BREMEN COFFEE (12). By Rainer Werner Fassbinder. January 27, 1978 (American premiere). Director, Manfred Bormann; production design, David Craven. With Cynthia Exline, Christopher Cooke, Helen Kelly, Angelynne Bruno, Ronald Wendschuh.

THE COUNTRY GENTLEMAN (12). By George Villiers and Sir Robert Howard. March 30, 1978. Director, Maurice Edwards; scenery, Ronald Daley; costumes, Ruth Thomason. With Edmund Williams, Bruce Bouchard, Mary Mims, Lee Owens, Chris Weatherhead.

CHARLES THE SECOND OR, THE MERRY MONARCH by John Howard Payne and Washington Irving. September 15, 1977. Directed by Warren Kliewer; with Don Atkinson, Alan Gilbert, Jonathan Chappell, Patricia Cray, Michele LaRue.
THE MALCONTENT by John Marston. November 4, 1977. Directed by Richard Bruno and Maurice Edwards; with Denise Assante, Robert Baines, Madlyn Cates, Dan Durning, John Michalski, Alex Reed, Maurice Edwards.
A VIENNESE EVENING (staged readings from translated works by Arthur Schnitzler and Karl Kraus.) February 1, 1978. Directed by Maurice Edwards; with Jonathan Chappell, Saylor Creswell, Ted Gargiulo, Richmond Hoxie, Lisa Milligan, Jeffrey Spolan.

Colonnades Theater Lab. Resident repertory company with an in-training program for actors. Michael Lessac, artistic director.

MOLIÈRE IN SPITE OF HIMSELF (100). Adapted and directed by Michael Lessac; based on Mikhail Bulgakov's *A Cabal of Hyprocrites.* March 9, 1978. Scenery, Robert U. Taylor; lighting, Randy Becker; costumes, Hillary A. Sherred. With Bill E. Noone, Tom Tammi, Nesbitt Blaisdell, Edward Edwards, Donna Haley, Louis Giambalvo, Berit Lagerwall.

Counterpoint Theater Company. Maintain high standards of excellence in the service of plays of distinction, through theatrical productions of enduring value. Howard Green, artistic director, Paulene Reynolds, managing director.

ARTHUR (12). By Ferenc Molnar. March 3, 1978 (N.Y. premiere). Director, Howard Green; scenery, Tony Giovanetti; lighting, Jesse Ira Berger; costumes, Deborah Shaw. With Morris Alpern, Charles Durand, Trudi Mathes, Ed Crowley, Anne C. Twomey.

THE HAPPY JOURNEY TO TRENTON AND CAMDEN and THE LONG
CHRISTMAS DINNER by Thornton Wilder. November 25, 1977. Directed by Terry
Walker; with Carol Grant, Lynn Polan, Michael Mantel, Mary Anisi, Hope Cameron.
EXIT THE KING by Eugene Ionesco. January 13, 1978. Directed by Howard Green; with
Ellen Bry, Charles Durand, Alice Emerick, Clement Fowler, Sanford Morris, Lynn Polan.
ARMS AND THE MAN by George Bernard Shaw. April 28, 1978. Directed by Isaac
Schambelan; with Jay Bonnell, Carol Grant, Ron Orbach, Lynn Polan, Stephanie Satie,
Stephen Stout.

The Cubiculo and Cubiculo III. Experiments in the use of theater, dance, music, etc.
housed in four studios and two performance spaces. Philip Meister, artistic director.

3rd Annual Festival of plays from Israel Horovitz's workshops for playwrights: THE MOM
AND POP STORE (one-act play) by Robert Lerner, directed by Jordon Hott; SHOWMAN
by Daniel Lyon; SCOOTER THOMAS MAKES IT TO THE TOP OF THE WORLD by
Peter Parnell (reading); THE REASON WE EAT by Israel Horovitz; THE 75TH by Israel
Horovitz and TEMPORARY TECHNICAL DIFFICULTY by Fred Zollo (readings); NOT
A THURSDAY AFTERNOON by Ellen Joan Pollack; NICOLE WILLING by Nancy
Fales; FLYING HORSES by Janet Neipris (reading). June 2-12, 1977.

THE LABORATORY (12). By June Daniels. November 18, 1977. Director, Ron Daley;
scenery and lighting, Preston Yarber; costumes, Margo La Zaro. With James Anderson, Kermit Brown, Margaret Donohue, Lee Kheel, Stephen Novelli, Andy Murphy.

Direct Theater. A professional company of actors and other stage artists exploring new
techniques. Allen R. Belknap, artistic director.

AN EVENING WITH RITA GARDNER (17). June, 1977. Musical director, Jim Litt; lighting,
Richard Winkler.

THE BEASTS (20). By H.N. Levitt. February 8, 1978. Director, Allen R. Belknap; scenery,
Ilse Kritzler; lighting, Richard Winkler; costumes, Richard Keshishian. With Bennes Mardenn,
Richard Leighton, Henson Keys, Terence Markovich, Ethan Phillips.

MODIGLIANI (47). By Dennis McIntyre. May 3, 1978. Director, Allen R. Belknap; scenery,
Bill Groom; lighting, Richard Winkler; costumes, Richard Keshishian. With Richard
Leighton, Ethan Phillips, William Mesnik, Joe Conti, Peggy Schoditsch, Richard Seff, Robert
Van den Berg.

Drama Committee Repertory Theater. Performs classics and adaptations of all nations
and new plays. Arthur Reel, artistic director.

ISLAND CAFE by Stephen Metcalfe, directed by Jim Arneman; MEMORY OF HARVEY
AND RICKY written and directed by Douglas Clark (12). March 20, 1978.

POSSESSION (12). Written and directed by Arthur Reel. April 26, 1978. Scenery and
lighting, A. Yacknowitz.

GETTING MARRIED by George Bernard Shaw. July 1, 1977. Directed by Arthur Reel.
OVERRULED by George Bernard Shaw, directed by John Bower; A POUND ON
DEMAND by Sean O'Casey, directed by Arthur Reel. July 20, 1977.
DON JUAN IN HELL by George Bernard Shaw. August 11, 1977. Directed by John Bower.
THE RED DEVIL and CAIN AND ARTYOM adapted and directed by Arthur Reel, from
stories by Maxim Gorky. August 14, 1977.
WARD SIX adapted and directed by Arthur Reel, from a story by Anton Chekhov. September
8, 1977.
LYSISTRATA by Aristophanes. September 17, 1977. Directed by James Prichard.
MISALLIANCE by George Bernard Shaw. October 13, 1977. Directed by Susan B. Ayers.
HEART OF DARKNESS by Joseph Conrad, adapted and directed by Arthur Reel.
November 26, 1977.

AN IDEAL HUSBAND by Oscar Wilde. December 23, 1977. Directed by Pamela Caren Billig.
CHICHIKOV'S JOURNEY adapted and directed by Arthur Reel, from story by Nikolai Gogol. March 24, 1978.
COMRADES by August Strindberg. April 25, 1978. Directed by Alan Lehrman.
MAN OF DESTINY by George Bernard Shaw, directed by James Cole Center; AUGUSTUS DOES HIS BIT by George Bernard Shaw, directed by Mel Barnard. May 28, 1978.

Drama Ensemble Company. New plays by new playwrights, ensemble work and a theater relevant to today. Peter Ehrman, artistic director.

THE HOLY SOCKS OF ST. SPASMUS (20). By Steve Lassoff. February 24, 1978.
THE WAGER by Mark Medoff. March 31, 1978. Directed by Robert Caprio; with Donald Biehn, Maggie Flanigan, Steve Vesce, Gregory Zittel.
THE BOOK OF EZEKIEL by Matthew Causey. April 22, 1978.

Dramatis Personae. Sexually oriented entertainment. Steven Baker, director.

LUNATICS AT LARGE by James Reach. May, 1978. Directed by Edmund W. Trust.
BOYS, BOYS, BOYS (revue) continued its run through April 27, 1978.

Encompass Theater. Dedicated to finding, developing and producing new playwrights and composers. Special emphasis on new and seldom-performed plays and musicals by and about women. Nancy Rhodes, artistic director, Roger Cunningham, producer.

SAINT JOAN OF THE STOCKYARDS (20). (Operetta) by Bertolt Brecht, translated by Naomi Replansky; music by Paul Kazanoff. May 24, 1978. Director, Jan P. Eliasberg; musical direction, Miriam Charney; scenery, Tracy Killam; costumes, Sally Lesser, Kathleen Smith. With Valda Aviks, Ron Faber, Will Patton, Joan MacIntosh, Christopher McCann. (Co-production with Epic Construction Company.)

PANTALOON, HE WHO GETS SLAPPED (opera) by Bernard Stambler, based on *He Who Gets Slapped* by Leonid Andreyev, music by Robert Ward. January 18, 1978.
HEAR THEIR VOICES: WOMEN FOUNDERS OF THE AMERICAN THEATER, 1910-1945: MISS LULU BETT by Zona Gale. March 9, 1978; CAN YOU HEAR THEIR VOICES by Hallie Flanagan. March 11, 1978; EXPRESSIN' WILLIE by Rachel Crothers. March 16, 1978; THE OLD MAID by Zoë Akins. March 18, 1978; ALISON'S HOUSE by Susan Glaspell. March 23, 1978; MACHINAL by Sophie Treadwell. March 25, 1978.

Ensemble Studio Theater. Nucleus of playwrights-in-residence dedicated to supporting individual theater artists and developing new works for the stage. 40-50 projects each season, initiated by E.S.T. members. Curt Dempster, artistic director, Marian Godfrey, associate director.

REFLECTIONS OF A CHINA DOLL (16). (One-woman show) by and with Susan Merson. October 20, 1977. Director, Barbara Tarbuck.

EULOGY FOR A SMALL-TIME THIEF (16). By Miguel Pinero. November 17, 1977. Director, Jack Gelber.

MAMA SANG THE BLUES (12). By Katherine Cortez. January 12, 1978. Director, Terese Hayden; scenery and lighting, Fred Kolouch; costumes, Sigrid Insull. With Paul Austin, Jacqueline Brookes, Margot Stevenson, Michael Wright, Barbara Covington.

INNOCENT PLEASURES (16). By Arthur Giron. March 9, 1978. Director, Harold Stone; scenery, Nancy Tobias; lighting, Geoffrey Dunbar; costumes, Sigrid Insull. With Pirie MacDonald, Nancy Franklin, Paul Gleason, Jack R. Marks, Daniel Ziskie.

Workshop Productions
ALL THE WAY HOME by Tad Mosel. November 3, 1977. Directed by Jim Seymour.
HISTORY by Tony Giardina. November 18, 1977. Directed by Barnet Kellman.

WHIMPERS written and directed by Marsha Haufrecht. December 15, 1977.
HOLY LAND by Lyle Kessler. January 16, 1978. Directed by Paul Austin.
JUNO'S SWANS by Elaine Kerr. January 26, 1978. Directed by Jack Going.
THE ATTIC (one-act play) by Katharine Long. February 4, 1978. Directed by Bill Cwikowski.
THE ONLY GAME IN TOWN by Frank D. Gilroy. February 17, 1978. Directed by Paula Marchese.
INDULGENCIES IN THE LOUISVILLE HAREM by John Orlock. March 24, 1978. Directed by Ellen Sandler.
MARATHON '78 (festival of new plays and pieces) schedule included: DEJA VU by Curt Dempster; THE NEXT CONTESTANT by Frank D. Gilroy, directed by Curt Dempster; WAITING FOR MICKEY AND AVA by Irene Dailey; A QUALIFICATION FOR ANABIOSIS by Charles Gordone; LEAVING HOME by Marcia Haufrecht, directed by Charles GORDONE: TRAVELING COMPANION by Anthony McKay; FOR WHOM IT MAY CONCERN by Conrad Bromberg; directed by Anthony McKay; DOTTY THE DRIBBLY DOODLIN' DAME by Dimos Condos; SPLIT by Michael Weller; PIECES by Bill Cwikowski; THE DAUGHTER OF HER COUNTRY by Vincent Canby; AUNTIE HAMLET by Dan Isaac; PLAYING DOLLS by Susan Nanus; LAST RITE FOR SNOW WHITE by Robin Wagner. April 13-23.
Welfare by Marcia Haufrecht. May 22, 1978. Directed by Don Blakely.
THE FAMILY PLAY by Wallace Shawn. May 24, 1978. Directed by Kathleen Tolan.

Equity Library Theater. Actors' Equity sponsors a series of revivals each season as show-cases for the work of its actor-members and an "informal series" of original, unproduced material. George Wojtasik, managing director.

GLAD TIDINGS by Edward H. Mabley. October 13, 1977. Directed by Bill Herndon; with Lucy Martin, Wayne A. Miller, Randall Robbins, Diane Linden, Sands Hall, Etain O'Malley, Kermit Brown, Kevin Bacon.
CARNIVAL (musical) book by Michael Stewart; based on material by Helen Deutsch; music and lyrics by Bob Merrill. November 3, 1977. Directed by Susan Schulman; with Jack Hoffman, Sue Anne Gershenson, Carl Don, Laura Kenyon, Joel Craig, Michael Murray, Jill Cook.
THE CRUCIBLE by Arthur Miller. December 8, 1977. Directed by David William Kitchen; with Ronald Wendschuh, Victor Caroli, Tara Loewenstern, William Pardue.
ALLEGRO (musical) book and lyrics by Oscar Hammerstein II; music by Richard Rodgers. January 12, 1978. Directed by William Koch; with Daniel D. Kruger, M. Lynn Wieneke, Sonja Anderson, Gordon Stanley, Richard Rossomme.
COUNT DRACULA by Ted Tiller. February 16, 1978. Directed by Robert Lanchester; with William Shust, John Peilmeier, Susan Vare, Frances Peter, Ian Stuart.
GAY DIVORCE (musical) book by Dwight Taylor, Kenneth Webb and Samuel Hoffenstein; adapted by Robert Brittan; music and lyrics by Cole Porter. March 9, 1978. Directed by Robert Brink; with Richard Sabellico, Sarilee Kahn, Paul Ames, Cynthia Meryl, Joseph Billone, Bob Ari.
THE TAMING OF THE SHREW by William Shakespeare. April 6, 1978. Directed by John Henry Davis; with Eric Booth, Stephanie Cotsirilos, Judith Townsend, William Daprato, Ed Van Nuys.
COMPANY (musical) book by George Furth, music and lyrics by Stephen Sondheim. May 4, 1978. Directed by Robert Nigro; with Albert Harris, Renee Roy, Valerie Beaman, Paige O'Hara, Lauren White, Richard Kevlin-Bell.
Informal Series (3 performances each)
JAZZ BABIES (musical revue). Conceived and directed by Marc Jordan Gass. September 12, 1977.
BLACK TUESDAY by Joan Stein and Ted Weiant. October 17, 1977. Directed by Ted Weiant.
CELEBRATE MY LOVE by Linda Nerine. November 21, 1977. Directed by Eric Uhler.
THE RABINOWITZ GAMBIT by Rose Leiman Goldemberg. December 12, 1977. Directed by June Plager.
2 (musical revue) by Julie Mandel. January 23, 1978. Directed by Clinton Atkinson.

HOW FAR IS IT TO BABYLON. Written and directed by Caryl Young. February 6, 1978.
THE DIVIDED BED by James V. Hatch and Victor Sullivan. March 20, 1978. Directed by
Warren Kliewer.
THE ADOPTED MOON by Jack Black. April 17, 1978. Directed by Gregory Macosko.
THE SPECIALIST (opera) libretto by Stuart Michaels, music and lyrics by Lou Rodgers.
May 15, 1978. Directed by Stuart Michaels.

4th Wall Repertory Company. Permanent ensemble company with an interest in
developing new plays by resident playwrights. Luba Elman, producer, Gary Palmer,
chairman.

DON'T STAND IN THE DOORWAY (102). By Ken Krauss. September 22, 1977. Scenery,
Linda Hacker; lighting, Paul Shafer, costumes, Phyllis Elkind. With Jocko Marcellino, Evie
Weitzer.

OFF THE WALL (comedy revue) (60). Staged by Gary Palmer. October 21, 1977.

Gene Frankel Theater. Development of new works and revivals for the theater. Gene
Frankel, artistic director, executive producer.

FRESHWATER by Virginia Woolf (N.Y. premiere) and AN EVENING IN BLOOMSBURY
by Victoria Sullivan (world premiere) (12). June 8, 1977. Director, Jon Fraser; lighting,
William Megalos; costumes, Joe Bigelow. With Connie Rock, J. Nisbet Clark, George Hall,
Katherine Rau, Denise Bissette, Paul Merrill, Thomas Sminkey.

KINGDOM and THE CEREMONY (12). By Ali Wadud. October 7, 1977. Director, Regge
Life; scenery, Adalberto Ortiz; lighting, Edward Currelley; costumes, Leslie Day. With Louise
Mike, Jay Moss, Victor Anthony Thomas, Diane Bivens, Bette Howard, Milton Grier, Dan
Cochran.

THE CONTESSA OF MULBERRY STREET (12). By N.D. Bellitto. November 11, 1977.
Director, Andrew Louca; scenery, Wilton Duckworth; lighting, Candice Dunn. With Willi
Kirkham, Richard de Faut, Keren Liswood, James Sappho, Philip Kroft, George Igoe, Murray
Schactman.

ZOYA'S APARTMENT (12). By Mikhail Bulgakov. February 10, 1978 (American premiere).
Director, Earl Ostroff; scenery, Sam Gonzalez; lighting, Dan Koetting; costumes, Judith
Fauvell. With Hava Kohav, Nancy LeBrun, Raf Michaels, Joseph Capone, Mark Cohen.

THE VERANDAH (12). Written and directed by Clifford Mason. May 5, 1978 (world
premiere). Scenery and lighting, Tony Castrigno; costumes, Pamela Lincoln. With Lee
Richardson, Juanita Mahone, Herb Downer, Rosanna Carter, Jodi Long, Lloyd Davis.

The Glines. Arts center committed to the creation, production, and exhibition of works
dealing with the gay experience. John Glines, producer.

WONDERFUL LIVES (musical) (32). Written, directed, choreographed, and designed by
James B. Ferguson. September 21, 1977. Lighting, Marcia Madeira. With Cynthia Cobey,
Timothy Gray, Rick Walsh.

FLESH FAILURES (12). Written, directed and designed by Dennis Embry. With Brynda Mattox, Vincent Burger. THE FREDDIE CORVO SHOW (12). By Emily L. Sisley. Director,
Peter Dowling; scenery, Jean Warfield. With Sarah Simpson, Dana Bate.

MIRACLE ON WEST BROADWAY (musical revue) (12). December 26, 1977. Director,
Lawrence Lane.

HAPPY NEW ERA (12). By Paul Hunter. Director, Dana Bate. With Jacque Dean, Dana
Bate. PRISONER OF LOVE (12). By Richard Hall. Director, Peter Dowling; scenery, Gus
Alicon. With John Archibald, Richard Voinché, Heikko Kerin. January 26, 1978.

CROSSING THE LINE (12). By John Hawkins. February 6, 1978. Director and designer, Dana Bate. With John Tansey.

THE WAR WIDOW (12). By Harvey Perr. April 20, 1978. Director, Fred Gorelick. With Noni Connor, Nick Kaplan, Lynnanne Zager, Carol Keefe, Lynn Weinstein.

JOURNEY by Ronn Tombaugh; CONSTRUCTIONS by Frank Lonabaugh; BIRTHDAY by Steven J. Myers; COMING OUT by Stephen J. Vogel; WAVES CLAPPING LIKE ANGELS by John Soldo; HAPPY NEW ERA by Paul Hunter (one-act plays in repertory). November, 1977.
HOT PEACHES. December 1, 1977.
LAWRENCE LANE AND TIM CAHILL (benefit cabaret). March 13, 1978.
THE DADDY OF US ALL by Tom Miller. March 15, 1978. Directed by Richard Voinche.
THE HEAT WAVE COMPANY (musical revue). March 29, 1978. With Michael Blaze, Jimmy Mello, Casey Wayne, Peter Shadow.
A SONG AT TWILIGHT by Noel Coward. April 6, 1978. Directed by Lester Malizia; with Susan Blommaert, Natalija Nogulich, Ronn Tombaugh.
GULP! reopened May 28, 1978.

Hudson Guild Theater. Original material and premieres performed. Craig Anderson, artistic director.

TREATS (24). By Christopher Hampton. October 5, 1977 (American premiere). Director, Michael Montel; scenery and lighting, Peter Wexler; costumes, Donald Brooks; associate designer, Tom Schwinn. With Suzanne Lederer, John Glover, Kenneth Welsh.

THE DODGE BOYS (24). By George Sibbald. November 23, 1977 (world premiere). Director, Craig Anderson; scenery, Douglas W. Schmidt; lighting, John Gleason; costumes, Sandra Nye. With Jane Lowry, William Le Massena, David Gale, Ben Slack, David Bowman.

MOLLY (30). By Simon Gray. January 11, 1978 (N.Y. premiere). Director, Stephen Hollis; scenery, Philipp Jung; lighting, John H. Paull; costumes, Patricia Adshead. With Tammy Grimes, Michael Higgins, Margaret Hilton, Josh Clark, Kenneth T. Scott, William A. Serow.

"DA" (24). By Hugh Leonard. March 8, 1978 (N.Y. premiere). Director, Melvin Bernhardt; scenery, Marjorie Kellogg; lighting, Arden Fingerhut; costumes, Jennifer Von Mayrhauser. With Barnard Hughes, Brian Murray, Lois de Banzie, Mia Dillon, Sylvia O'Brien, Lester Rawlins, Paul Rudd, Richard Seer.

MY MOTHER WAS A FORTUNE TELLER (24). May 5, 1978 (world premiere). Director, Arthur Laurents; scenery, Philipp Jung; lighting, Toni Goldin; costumes, Bill Kellard; musical staging, Elizabeth Keen; musical direction, Herbert Kaplan. With Phyllis Newman.

Impossible Ragtime Theater (IRT). Dedicated to exploration of the director's role in all aspects of theater. Ted Story, artistic director, George Ferencz, associate director.

WOMEN I HAVE KNOWN (18). Written and performed by M. Tulis Sessions. December 17, 1977. Director, Michael T. Gregoric; scenery, Larry Fulton; lighting, Jo Mayer.

WHERE'S THE BEER, FRITZ (5). Music by Dan Schreier and Michael Roth. January 20, 1978. Director, George Ferencz; lighting, John Gisondi; costumes, Sally J. Lesser and Kathleen Smith. With Eva Charney, Annette Kurek, Richard Leighton, Jack Eric Williams, Janice K. Young.

RUSTY AND RICO AND LENA AND LOUIE (18). By Leonard Melfi. May 5, 1978 (world premiere). Director, John Shearin; scenery, Tom Warren; lighting, Curt Ostermann; costumes, Margo La Zaro. With Zina Jasper, Justin Deas.

PLAY STRINDBERG by Friedrich Duerrenmatt, translated by James Kirkup. October 2, 1977. Directed by Ted Story; with Tom Bade, Anita Keal, Neil McKenzie.
SPIDER'S WEB by Agatha Christie. February 3, 1978. Directed by Penelope Hirsch; with Donald R. Klecak, Johanna Leister, John Lemley, Harold G. Meyer, Nan Wilson.

Margaret Hilton and Tammy Grimes in a scene from *Molly* at Hudson Guild Theater

CLASH BY NIGHT by Clifford Odets. March 17, 1978. Directed by Stephen Zuckerman; with Marie Cheatham, Jay Devlin, Erik Fredricksen, Annette Kurek, Don Perkins, William R. Riker.

Directors Lab Series
THE PROBLEM by A.R. Gurney Jr. Director, Penelope Hirsh. With Celia Weston, Ray Xifo; DREAMS OF FLIGHT by Brian Richard Mori. Director, Lawrence Harbison. With Mikell Pinkney, Earl Miller. (12 performances each) January 19, 1978. Lighting, Curt Ostermann; costumes, Margo La Zaro.

MIND GAMES (4). Written and directed by Roberto Monticello. January 2, 1978. Scenery and lighting, Chip Bullock. With Marcia Blau, Frank Cardo, Rosemary Child, George Dickerson, Vicki Eubank, Leigh Gilchrist, Suzanne Hartman, Mallory Hoover.

THE BEDROOM (4). By M.H. Appleman. April 28, 1978. Director, Anita Khanzadian; scenery, Marcie Begleiter; lighting, Chip Bullock; costumes, Margo La Zaro. With Etain O'Malley, James Zvanut.

BIRDBATH by Leonard Melfi. January 6, 1978. Directed by Alison Mackenzie; with Margaret A. Flanagan, Stephen Zettler.
CAME AND WENT: COME AND GO by Samuel Beckett and COMINGS AND GOINGS

by Megan Terry. February 17, 1978. Directed by Jon Fraser; with Judith Goldman, Zannie Lexow, Bonnie Max, Michael Bias, Joel Freedman, Sandy Weintraub.
MASTER CLASS and OLD BLUES (one-act plays) by Jonathan Levy. March 3, 1978. Directed by Ted Weiant; with Cheryl Green, Raina Toumanova, Kevin O'Leary, Bryce Holman, Jerry McGee, Orrin Reiley.
THE RIDE ACROSS LAKE CONSTANCE by Peter Handke, translated by Michael Roloff. April 21, 1978. Directed by Matthew Maguire.
OEDIPUS adapted from Sophocles. May 5, 1978. Directed by John Sumakis; with Donald Smith, Christy Max Williams, Anne Collins.

INTAR. Innovative culture center for the Hispanic American community of New York City focusing on the art of theater. Max Ferra, artistic director.

CARMENCITA (24). Book and lyrics by Manuel Martin Jr.; music by Tania Leon and Coleridge T. Perkinson. May 19, 1978. Director, Manuel Martin Jr.; scenery, Sally Locke; lighting, Jenny Ball; costumes, Manuel Yesckas. With Brenda Feliciano, Walter Valentino, Giovanni Cotto, Liz Rosner, Adriane Maura.

Interart Theater. Showcase opportunities which provide a professional environment for women playwrights, directors, designers and performers to participate in theatrical activity. Margot Lewitin, coordinator.

NEVER WASTE A VIRGIN (work-in-progress). Conceived and performed by The Cutting Edge. October 20, 1977.

BECCA (24). Book, lyrics and music by Wendy Kesselman. December 2, 1977. Director, Barbara Rosoff; music director, arranger, Jerome Leonard Isaacs; choreographer, Dalienne Majors; scenery, Linda Conaway; lighting, Geoffrey T. Cunningham; costumes, Jane Stein. With Trini Alvarado, John Bucek, Karen Stefko, William Wagner, Tom Corbett.

WHERE MEMORIES ARE MAGIC AND DREAMS INVENTED (16+). By Susan Nanus. January 18, 1978. Director, Susan Einhorn; scenery, Ursula Belden; lighting, Pat Stern; costumes, Jean Steinlein. With Sylvia Gassell, Kay Medford, Lenore Lovemen, Michael Kaufman, Allen Swift, Laura Copland.

WHO'S A LADY (5). Conceived and performed by Annette Miller and Naomi Thornton. March 30, 1978.

SISTER/SISTER (work-in-progress) (15+). By Clare Coss, Sondra Segal and Roberta Sklar. May 5, 1978. Lighting, Annie Wrightson; costumes, Florence Rutherford. With Barbara George, Mary Lum, Mary Lyon, Debbie Nitzberg, Sondra Segal.

HEY, RUBE (16). By Janet McReynolds. May 5, 1978. Director, Vickie Rue; scenery and lighting, Barbara Ling; costumes, Nanzi Adzima. With Rosemary Moore, Avra Petrides, Kathleen Roland, Jess Osuna.

The Irish Rebel Theater (An Claidheamh Soluis). Dedicated to establishing an awareness among people of all ethnic backgrounds of the artistic expression of the Irish people. Michael McQuaid, coordinator.

AT THE HAWK'S WELL, THE ONLY JEALOUSY OF EMER and THE DEATH OF CUCHULAIN by William Butler Yeats. June 2, 1977. Directed by Michael McQuaid.
THE FREEDOM OF THE CITY by Brian Friel. January 28, 1978. Directed by Jim Olwell.
DID YEZ SEE THAT? written and directed by Nye Heron; FULL MOON IN MARCH by William Butler Yeats, directed by Michael McQuaid; GUESTS OF THE NATION by Neil McKenzie, directed by Dennis McKenna (one-act plays). May 19, 1978.

Jean Cocteau Repertory. Located in the historic Bouwerie Lane Theater, the Jean Cocteau Repertory presents vintage and modern classics on a rotating repertory schedule. Eve Adamson, artistic director.

OVERREACHED!! OR A NEW WAY TO PAY OLD DEBTS by Philip Massinger. September 16, 1977. Directed by Christopher Martin; with Craig Smith, James S. Payne, Steve Randolph, Michele Farr, Tom Keever, Amy K. Posner.
HAMLET by William Shakespeare. September 30, 1977. Directed by Eve Adamson; with Tom Keever, Harris Berlinsky, Craig Smith, Barbara Schofield, Michele Farr.
THE COCKTAIL PARTY by T.S. Eliot. November 4, 1977. Directed by Eve Adamson; with Craig Smith, Michele Farr, Barbara Schofield, Coral S. Potter, Steve Randolph.
NO EXIT by Jean-Paul Sartre. February 3, 1978. Directed by Eve Adamson; with Michael F. Clarke, Tom Keever, Amy K. Posner, Barbara Schofield.
VOLPONE by Ben Jonson. March 3, 1978. Directed by Eve Adamson; with Coral S. Potter, Craig Smith, Michael F. Clarke, Harris Berlinsky, Michele Farr, Andy MacCracken.
'TIS PITY SHE'S A WHORE by John Ford. April 14, 1978. Directed by Eve Adamson; with Craig Smith, Coral S. Potter, Steve Randolph, Harris Berlinsky, Amy K. Posner.

Jewish Repertory Theater (JRT). Presents English-speaking plays relating to the Jewish experience. Ran Avni, artistic director.

DANCING IN NEW YORK CITY (12). By Julius Landau. December 1, 1977. Director, Ran Avni; scenery and lighting, Howard Kessler. With Herb Duncan, Carol Rosenfeld, Rod Bladel, Frank Biancamano, Marilyn Robbins.

ANNA KLIEBER (12). By Alfonso Sastre, translated by Ray J. Smith. March 16, 1978 (N.Y. premiere). Director, Don Marlette; scenery, Adalberto Ortiz; lighting, Vince Abramson; costumes, Dennis O'Connor. With Jennifer Sternberg, Jay Bonnell, Robert Coe, Jonas McCord, David Schall, David Zucker.

IVANOV by Anton Chekhov, translated by Alex Szogyi. June 2, 1977. Directed by Don Marlette, with James Goodwin Rice, Paul Espel, Rosalind Greer, Jay Bonnell, Marjorie Austrian, Lynn Polan.
THE COLD WIND AND THE WARM by S.N. Behrman. October 27, 1977. Directed by Edward M. Cohen; with Tobias Haller, Daniel Pollack, Nathan Habib, Shelley Rogers, Michael John Slade, Fanchon Miller, Peter Reznikoff.
THE MERCHANT OF VENICE by William Shakespeare. February 2, 1978. Directed by Jonathan Foster; with Shelly Desai, Linda Barnhurst, Eloise Watt, Gideon Davis, David Krasner, Terence Marinan.
I AM A CAMERA by John van Druten. May 4, 1978. Directed by Jeff Epstein; with Bradley Boyer, Denise Lute, Olga Druce, Frances Peter.

Jones Beach Marine Theater. Each summer a musical classic is presented in this huge outdoor theater on Long Island. Guy Lombardo, 1977 producer; Lee Guber and Shelly Gross, 1978 producers.

FINIAN'S RAINBOW (musical) book by E.Y. Harburg and Fred Saidy, music by Burton Lane, lyrics by E.Y. Harburg. June 30, 1977. Directed by John Fearnley; with Christopher Hewett, Beth Fowler, Stanley Grover, Charles Repole.

Joseph Jefferson Theater Company. Performs solely American plays, both revivals and new works, largely drawn from their Playwrights' Workshop; houses Theater for Older People. Cathy Roskam, founder.

LYRICAL AND SATIRICAL: THE MUSIC OF HAROLD ROME (12). Conceived and directed by Julianne Boyd; music director, Vicki H. Carter; choreographer, Jeff Veazey; scenery, Lee Mayman; lighting, Boyd Masten; costumes, Rachel Kurland. With Cris Groenendaal, Sophie Schwab, Gordon Stanley, Susan Waldman.

BED & BREAKFAST (12). By Marion Fredi Towbin. February 23, 1978. Director, John Desmond; scenery, Richard B. Williams; lighting, Frances Aronson; costumes, Harry Curtis. With Beatrice Ballance, Donald Gantry.

Cynthia Exline, Nada Rowand and Gwendolyn Brown in *Moon Cries* at Joseph Jefferson Theater

MOON CRIES (12). By Midge Maroni. April 26, 1978. Director, Cathy Roskam; scenery, Vittorio Capecce; lighting, Norman Coates; costumes, Polly Lee. With Cynthia Exline, Nada Rowland, Gwendolyn Brown, David MacEnulty.

THE SECOND MAN by S.N. Behrman. June 1, 1977. Directed by Marvin Einhorn; with Anne C. Twomey, Doug Stender, Roger Chapman, Nita Novy.
INHERIT THE WIND by Jerome Lawrence and Robert E. Lee. October 26, 1977. Directed by John Henry Davis; with Sherry Rooney, Peter Van Norden, Humbert Allen Astredo, Ian Martin, Richmond Hoxie, Sam Blackwell.

Theater for Older People
GAMES by Howard Webber, adapted by B.J. Davis and Susan Miller. June 14, 1977. Directed by John Henry Davis and Cathy Roskam; with Eleanor Cody Gould, Marilyn Redfield, Paul Meacham, John Craven.
NEVER TOO OLD written and directed by George Romaine. April 25, 1978. With Julie Denny, Estelle Gettleman, Sabine Herts, David Kerman.

Staged Reading
FAMILY FRIENDS by Harvey Zuckerman. January 26, 1978. Directed by Ellen Sandler; with Nancy Franklin, Barbara Spiegel.

The Judson Poets' Theater. The theater arm of Judson Memorial Church and its pastor, Al Carmines, who creates a series of new, unconventional musicals which are sometimes transferred to the commercial theater. Al Carmines, director.

CAMP MEETING (musical; new version). By Al Carmines. August 5, 1977. Director, Bob Herget; scenery, John Pitts; lighting, Edward I. Byers; costumes, Michele Edwards, Blae Hannahan. With Joel Higgins, Essie Borden, Lee Guilliatt, Tony Clark, Trisha Long.

TATYANA REPINA (12). By Anton Chekhov; translated by John Racin. March 31, 1978 (American premiere). Director, Arne Zaslove; musical director, Al Carmines; scenery, Richard B. Williams; lighting, Victor En Yu Tan; costumes, A. Christina Giannini. With Essie Borden, Alver Rongstad, James Carruthers, Pamela Burrell, Margaret Wright.

CHRISTMAS RAPPINGS (annual production) by Al Carmines. December 15, 1977. With Theo Barnes, Essie Borden, Margaret Wright, Lee Guilliatt, David Vaughan, Ira Siff.

La Mama Experimental Theater Club (ETC). A busy workshop for experimental theater of all kinds. Ellen Stewart, director.

BETWEEN THE WARS. By Wilford Leach. June 2, 1977. With Manhattan Project.

THE SIXTY MINUTE QUEER SHOW. By Kenneth Bernard; composer, John Braden. June 2, 1977. Director, John Vaccaro.

CALIGULA. By Albert Camus; translated by Justin O'Brien; music and direction, Tom O'Horgan. June 4, 1977. Scenery, Bill Stabile; lighting, Jo Mayer; costumes, Randy Barcelo; sound, David Congdon. With Seth Allen, Patrick Farrelly, Thomas Kopache, Barbara Montgomery, Marybeth Ward.

THE LEGEND OF WU CHANG. Adapted from Hazelton and Benrimo's *The Yellow Jacket* and directed by Tisa Chang. October 6, 1977. Scenery, Sam Gonzalez; lighting, Larry Steckman; costumes, Susan Sigrist; choreographer, Hseuh-Tung Chen. With Pan Asian Repertory Theater.

THE LYSISTRATA NUMBAH!. By Spiderwoman Theater. October 20, 1977. Director, Muriel Miguel.

THUNDERSTORM. By Tsao Yu. November 3, 1977. Director, Tisa Chang; scenery, John Slavin; lighting, Larry Steckman; costumes, Susan Sigrist. With Pan Asian Repertory Theater.

THE SEVEN DEADLY ELEMENTS. Adapted from Max Ernst's *Une Semaine de Bonte,* by Creation. December 9, 1977. With Maurice Blanc, Terry Barrell, Karen Feinberg, Susan Mosakowski, Robert Todd.

BEDTIME STORY and A POUND ON DEMAND. By Sean O'Casey. January 12, 1978. With Irish Traveling Theater.

FAR FROM HARRISBURG. By Jean-Paul Wenzel, translated by Francoise Kourilsky and Nicholas Kepros. January 5, 1978. Director, Francoise Kourilsky; scenery, Alain Chambon. With Maurine Holbert, Pablo Vela, Gaynor Coté.

INTERNATIONAL STUD. By Harvey Fierstein. February 2, 1978. Director, Eric Concklin; lighting, Joanna Schielke; costumes, Mardi Phillips; music director, Ned Levy. With Harvey Fierstein, Steve Spiegel, Diane Tarleton. (Reopened March 17, March 31, 1978.)

THE TEMPEST. By William Shakespeare; music and direction by Tom O'Horgan. February 14, 1978. Scenery, Bill Stabile; lighting, Laura Rambaldi; costumes, Randy Barcelo. With Tom Kopache, Robin Karfo, Raymond Patterson, Patrick Burke, Robert Stocking. (La Mama Ceta).

SLOW POISON and SMALL FIRES. By Ruis Woertendyke and Paul Felix Montez. February 14, 1978. (La Mama Ceta).

THE COOLEST CAT IN TOWN. Book and lyrics by William Gleason; music by Diane Leslie. February 23, 1978. Director, Frank Carucci.

JUBA (musical). By Laurence Holder, John Braden, William Elliott, Richard Weinstock. March 2, 1978. Director, John Vaccaro. (La Mama Ceta).

ROSE MOON March 17, 1978. Written and composed by Pauline Oliveros.

CARMILLA (operetta). By J.S. LeFanu; music by Ben Johnston. March 27, 1978. Director, Wilford Leach.

HUMBOLDT'S CURRENT. By Ping Chong and The Fiji Company. March 30, 1978. (new edition).

FRAGMENTS OF A TRILOGY. THE TROJAN WOMEN, ELECTRA and **MEDEA.** Conceived and directed by Andrei Serban; music by Elizabeth Swados. May 3, 1978.

FAUST: PART ONE (mini-contract). By Johann Wolfgang von Goethe, translated by Walter Kaufman. May 4, 1978. Director, Fritz Bennewitz; composer and music director, Ada Janik; scenery, Wes Cronk; costumes, Karen Miller; choreographer, Lia Meletopoulo. With Jamil Zakkai, James Leon, Christine Campbell. (La Mama Ceta).

THE GOOD WOMAN OF SETZUAN. By Bertolt Brecht; music by Elizabeth Swados. May 19, 1978. Director, Andrei Serban.

MOMENTS IN THE LIFE OF THE PRODIGAL SON conceived and directed by Marianne Macellin. November 20, 1977. With Attic Theater.
PHAEDRA and OEDIPUS adapted and directed by Ethyl Eichelberger, music by Richard Cumming, Roger Aaronson. November 30, 1977.
HERBERT AND EVA NELSON (cabaret). November 30, 1977.
SHUKO NADAOKA WORKSHOP. January 10, 1978.
THE BOND OF POISON by Thom Sokoloski with Lynn Greenblat. February 9, 1978.
DWIGHT NIGHT (one-man show). April 3, 1978. With Dwight Marfield.
THREE SOLO PIECES written and performed by Winston Tong. April 20, 1978.
'TIS PITY SHE'S A WHORE by John Ford. May 8, 1978. Directed by Radu Penciulescu.
EXPUBIDENT by Perkin Barnes, Dwight Carson and Sary Guinier, music by Perkin Barnes. May 31, 1978. Directed by Gloria Zelaya. (La Mama Ceta).
BROTHERS AND SISTERS by Ruis Woertendyke. May 31, 1978. Directed by Arthur Rodriguez. (La Mama Ceta).

Labor Theater. Committed to bring to the working class dramatic works that relate to their lives or delve into the roots of their heritage. C.R. Portz, artistic director.

NIGHT SHIFT (24). By Martin Goldsmith. October 21, 1977. Director, C.R. Portz; scenery and lighting, Joe Riley; costumes, Alicia Rogue. With Rip Torn, Amy Wright, Barbara Spiegel, John D. Swain, Jean Barker.

I JUST WANTED SOMEONE TO KNOW (12). By Bette Craig and Joyce Kornbluh. May 12, 1978. Director, C.R. Portz; scenery, Richard Hoover, lighting, Richard Ellis; costumes, Kathy Fredericks. With Valerie Morrell, Phyllis Look, Dorothy Lancaster, Jahne Bell, Margay Whitlock, Hortensia Colorado.

Lion Theater Company. Actors' company with an eclectic repertory. Gene Nye, producing director, Larry Carpenter, managing director.

K (61). Devised by Lion Theater Company; based on *The Trial* by Franz Kafka. November 25, 1977. Director, Garland Wright; scenery and lighting, Garland Wright, John Arnone; costumes, David James. With Tony Campisi, Janice Fuller, Kim Ameen, Mary E. Baird, Jim McClure, Greg Grove.

THE DEATH AND LIFE OF JESSE JAMES (24). By Len Jenkin. May 11, 1978. Director, Gene Nye; choreographer, Kathy Kramer; scenery, Henry Millman; lighting, Frances Aronson; costumes, Bob Wojewodski; music, John McKinney. With Allan Carlsen, John Ingle, James McLure, William Brenner, Patrick Hughes, Peter Noel-Duhamel, Jerry Lazarus.

Workshop Four Series (5 performances each)
FATIMA BOOGIE. Conceived and directed by John Guerrasio. March 8, 1978. Choreographer, Kathy Kramer; scenery, Randi Frank; costumes, Bessie Ballantine.
STARS. Written and directed by Jim McClure. March 15, 1978.
PAGEANT IN EXILE (musical). By Randy Wilson. March 22, 1978. Director, Larry Carpenter; musical director, David Mettee.
THE NIGHTINGALE AND THE ROSE (and other fables). By Oscar Wilde, adapted by Richard Holm. March 29, 1978. Director, Kathy Arlt.

Mabou Mines. Theater collaborative whose work is a synthesis of motivational acting, narrative acting and mixed-media performance. Collective artistic leadership (produced in cooperation with New York Shakespeare Festival).

THE LOST ONES. By Samuel Beckett, adapted and directed by Lee Breuer; music composed and performed by Philip Glass. October 4, 1977. Environment, Thom Cathcart. With David Warrilow, Lynn Spano. (Reopened January 18, 1978.)

THE SHAGGY DOG ANIMATION. Written and directed by Lee Breuer. November 19, 1977. Scenery, Linda Wolfe, Don and Rebecca Christensen, Allison Yerxa, Julie Archer; lighting and sound, Robin Thomas; costumes, Jeanne Button. With Ruth Maleczech, William Raymond, JoAnne Akalaitis, Frederick Neumann, Linda Wolfe, Terry O'Reilly, Clover Breuer. (Reopened January 6, 1978; April 28, 1978.)

DRESSED LIKE AN EGG based on Colette's writing, designed and directed by JoAnne Akalaitis. October 1, 1977. With JoAnne Akalaitis, Ruth Maleczech, Ellen McElduff, William Raymond, David Warrilow.

Manhattan Project. A theater company in its ninth year whose experiments include Lewis Carroll and Molière as well as original writers. Andre Gregory, artistic director.

BETWEEN THE WARS written and directed by Wilford Leach. June 2, 1977.

Manhattan Theater Club. A producing organization with three stages for fully-mounted off-Broadway productions, readings, workshop activities and cabaret. Lynne Meadow, artistic director.

Upstage
THE WAYSIDE MOTOR INN (20). By A.R. Gurney Jr. November 2, 1977 (world premiere). Director, Tony Giordano; scenery, David Potts; lighting, Spencer Mosse; costumes, Kenneth M. Yount. With Jill Andre, Margaret Barker, John Braden, Jill O'Hara, Gary Cookson, Wayne Tippit.

FRANKIE AND ANNIE (20). By Diane Simkin. December 28, 1977. Director, Paul Schneider; scenery, David Potts; lighting, Jeff Davis; costumes, Anne Wolff. With Robin Bartlett, Sarah Chodoff, Shelby Brammer, Mario Carlo Mariani, Wendie Beth Marks, Sherry Steiner, Daniel Stern.

RED FOX/SECOND HANGIN' (28). By Roadside Theater; written by Don Baker and Dudley Cocke. March 1, 1978. Director, Michael Posnick; scenery, David Potts; lighting, Curt Ostermann. With Don Baker, Gary Slemp, Frankie Taylor.

SAFE HOUSE (20). By Nicholas Kazan. April 5, 1978. Director, Jonathan Alper; scenery, David Potts; lighting, Bennet Averyt; costumes, Flo Rutherford. With Deborah Hedwall, Kaiulani Lee, Paul Schierhorn, John Shea, Lisabeth Shean.

RIB CAGE (20). By Larry Ketron. May 17, 1978. Director, Andy Wolk; scenery, David Potts; lighting, Dennis Parichy; costumes, Linda Fisher. With David Selby, Kristin Griffith, J.T. Walsh, Lynn Milgrim, Grayson Hall, I.M. Hobson.

Cabaret (28 performances each)
BY STROUSE conceived, composed and directed by Charles Strouse. November 9, 1977. With Gary Beach, Kim Fedena, Maureen Moore, Gail Nelson.
MARTIN CHARNIN. November 18, 1977.
DORY PREVIN: LADY WITH A BRAID (words and music of Dory Previn). December 28, 1977. Directed by Caymichael Patten; with Bob Gunton, Lynne Lipton, Jill O'Hara.
AIN'T MISBEHAVIN' (musical tribute to Fats Waller). February 8, 1978. Directed by Richard Maltby Jr.; with Irene Cara, Nell Carter, Andre De Shields, Armelia McQueen, Ken Page.
HAS ANYBODY HERE FOUND LOVE? Lyrics by Lois Wyse, music by Carol Frankel. March 8, 1978. Directed by Miriam Fond; with Marilyn Caskey, Rosalind Harris, Judith Anna Roberts.
JIM WANN'S COUNTRY CABARET. April 5, 1978. Directed by John Haber; with Cass Morgan, Kathi Moss, Guy Strobel, Jim Wann.
HAPPY WITH THE BLUES (music of Harold Arlen). May 3, 1978. Directed by Julianne Boyd; with Jean Andalman, Barbara Andres, Stephen James, Sarilee Kahn, Orrin Reiley.

Medicine Show Theater Ensemble. Developmental ensemble to discover unconfined levels of thought and potential for more expansive action. James Barbosa, Barbara Vann, artistic directors.

DON JUAN IN HELL (40). By George Bernard Shaw (company developed). December 8, 1977. Design elements, Antoni Miralda; costumes, Robert Hines; music, Jalalu Kalvert Nelson; dances, Margot Colbert. With James Barbosa, Chris Brandt, Katherine Burger, Peter Green, Patience Pierce, Gretchen Van Ryper, Barbara Vann.
MUMMERS' PLAY (12). (Traditional, expanded by the company). December 27, 1977. Director, Barbara Vann; music, Donald Johnston. With James Barbosa, John Bower, Chris Brandt, Katherine Burger, Gerry Goodman, Jill Goldstein, Peter Green, Patience Pierce, Morrisa Schwartz.

Nat Horne Theater. Purpose is to train dancers to be actors and singers as well; as a result, all types of plays are produced. Nat Horne, Albert Reyes, artistic directors.

42ND STREET (mixed media musical revue). By Albert Reyes. June 20, 1977. Director, choreographer, Nat Horne. With Nat Horne, Freda Scott, Milledge Mosley, Jay Montreal, Tim Elliott.

WAR OF THE WORLDS (19). Adapted, directed and designed by Albert Reyes. October 14, 1977. Sound, Mark Kalman; lighting and special effects, Gail Kennison. With Steve Abbruscato, Jean Brown, Richard Kay, John Swayze, Michael Howard.

GAMEPLAN (12). By Dan Lauria. November 30, 1977. Director, Vincent Gugleotti; scenery, Joseph Long; lighting, Gary Seltzer; costumes, Dottie Saliski. With Bruce Connelly, Dan Lauria, Sam Locante, Neal Mandell, Bill Marcus, Fred J. Scollay.

THE PHANTOM (16). Musical adapted from *The Phantom of the Opera* and directed by Albert Reyes. March 17, 1978. Scenery, F. Wesley Dixon; lighting, Pam Belyea; costumes, Zahra and Marcia Payne. With Nat Horne, Tim Elliott, Fred Lazarus, Charmion Clark, Eduardo Silva.

GARDEN/PARK (12). Book by Joseph George Caruso; music by Anthony Manno; lyrics by Anthony Manno and Harmon Dresner. April 13, 1978. Director, George Bunt; musical director, Robert Brown; scenery and costumes, Michael Bottari, Ronald Case; lighting, Ray Dooley. With Jacquie Ullendorf, Bill Nabel.

THE PHANTOM (12). Musical adapted from *The Phantom of the Opera* and directed by Edward Brown. May 12, 1978. Scenery, Don Warshaw; lighting, Pam Belyea; costumes, Zahra and Marcia Payne. With Nat Horne, Eve Marlowe, Brian O'Reilly, Lee Shepherd, Diane Baldassari, Beverly Shelton, Scott Groves.

BECKETT by Jean Anouilh and THE LION IN WINTER by James Goldman; adapted and directed by Edward Brown. November 11, 1977. With Michael Burton, Michael Finnerty, Randolph Walker, Suzanne Gilbert.
KASPAR by Peter Handke; translated by Michael Rolloff. January 4, 1978. Directed by David Yakir; with Anthony-Joseph Piazza.

The New Dramatists. An organization devoted to playwrights; member writers may use the facilities for anything from private cold readings of their material to workshop stagings. Stephen Harty, administrative director, Peter Kozik, workshop coordinator.

Workshop Stagings (5 performances each)
LOSERS. By Donald Wollner. October 11, 1977. Director, Ellen Sandler; scenery, Nancy Tobias; lighting, Jo Mayer. With Barnes Miller, Mitchell McGuire, Peter Boyden, Alan North, J. Kevin Scannell, Joan Grant.

FILIGREE PEOPLE. By Peter Dee. April 18, 1978. Director, David Kerry Heefner; scenery, Phillip Jung; lighting, Patricia Moeser. With Robin Howard, William Perley, Josephine Nichols, Tom Jarus, Celia Weston.

Readings
WINDCHIMES by Anna Marie Barlow. June 16, 1977. With Mia Heidi, Lois Battle, Augusta Dabney, Bob Shrewsbury, Dan Ziskie.
TWO MARYS by Warren Kliewer. June 20, 1977. With Ruth Baker, Ed Crowley, Michele LaRue, John Wyeth.
BURNING BRIGHT by Lyle Kessler. June 24, 1977. With Rudy Bond, Sully Boyar, Demo DiMartile, Peter Weller, Pamela Reed.
FILIGREE PEOPLE by Peter Dee. June 28, 1977. With Henry Tunney, Linda Russell, Pat Podell, Glenn Zeitler.
AMAZING GRACE by Peter Maloney. September 19, 1977. With Bill Wiley, Fred Morsell, Cortez Nance.
THE UNDRESSING OF A NUDE by William Andrews. October 20, 1977. Directed by William Rhys; with J.J. Lewis, Ingrid Sonnichsen, Joel Simon, Eric Conger, Dan Desmond.
CASANOVA (musical) book and lyrics by John Wolfson, music by Ralph Affoumado. October 28, 1977. With Irwin Pearl, Faith Catlin, Ruth Jaroslow, Richard Dahlia, William Starrett.
CARNIVAL DREAMS by Conn Fleming. November 1, 1977. With Elizabeth Ashley, Austin Pendleton, John Cullum, Robert Earl Jones.
VOODOO TRILOGY by Frank Gagliano. November 3, 1977. Directed by Bill Martin; with Barbara Montgomery, Stephanie Cotsirilos, Rosemary De Angelis, Peter Saputo.
WRITERS CAMP by Peter Dee and Albert Lynch. November 7, 1977. Directed by Jim Goss; with Don Howard, David Kerry Heefner, Kathleen Turner, Henson Keys.
MOTHER RYAN by Maurice Noel. November 10, 1977. Directed by Paul Schneider; with Polly Adams, Matthew Coles, Leora Dana, Robert McFarland.
DANCIN' TO CALLIOPE by Jack Gilhooley. November 14, 1977. With Graham Beckel, Rosemary DeAngelis, Martina Degnan.
BIERCE TAKES ON THE RAILROADS! by Phil Bosakowski. November 17, 1977. Directed by Jim Kramer; with Humbert Allen Astredo, Tom Bade, Dolores Kenan, Terry O'Quinn, Miles Chapin, Maris Hasen.
TORNADO by Pat Kolt Staten. November 22, 1977. Directed by B.J. Whiting; with Sue Lawless, Edmund Williams, Steven Gilborn, Susan McVeigh, Suzanne Ford.
THE BEACH CHILDREN by John von Hartz. December 8, 1977. Directed by Mark Silverstein; with Bill Randolph, Susan Porretto, Jackie Blue, Mark Margolis, Larry Ross.
JUST OFF PARK by Stuart Vaughan. January 11, 1978. With Katherine Manning, Henderson Forsythe, Earl Trussell, Anne Murray.
THE BOOTH BROTHERS by Warren Kliewer. January 20, 1978. With Michael Levin, Hal Davis.
THE AMERICAN OASIS by Steven Somkin. January 30, 1978. Directed by Will Maitland

Weiss; with Jack McClure, Jess Adkins, Jerry Rockwood, Fern Howell.

THE MAN WHO DREW CIRCLES by Barry Berg. February 10, 1978. Directed by Cliff Goodwin; with Richard Fancy, Richard DeFabees, Robert Chamberlain, Anita Keal, Ruth Klinger.

A DISTURBANCE OF MIRRORS by Pat Kolt Staten. February 24, 1978. Directed by Ellen Sandler; with Carol Quinn, David Rasche, Scott Sparks, Laure Mattos.

THE VERANDAH written and directed by Clifford Mason. March 3, 1978. With Herb Downer, Loretta Devine, Richard Ward, Lee K. Richardson, Leila Danette.

MOTHERS AND DAUGHTERS by John von Hartz. March 8, 1978. With Ilene Kristen, Lynn Milgrim, Anna Minot.

A SMALL WINTER CRISIS by Warren Kliewer. March 15, 1978. With Marvyn Haines Jr., Ellen Novack, Jonathan Chappell.

THE SUGAR BOWL by Stanley Taikeff. March 17, 1978. Directed by Thomas Gruenewald; with Clarence Felder, Jerry Zaks, Maurice Copeland, Peter DeLaurier, Lynn Cohen.

THREE MILLION ROSEBUDS by Peter Cookson. March 21, 1978. Directed by Tony Giordano; with David Rasche, Carolyn Lagerfelt, Laure Mattos, John Horton.

AVENUE B by Jack Gilhooley. April 6, 1978. Directed by Pamela Singer; with Carlos Cestero, Alma Cuervo, Jim DeMarse, Ilene Kristen.

MARVELOUS BROWN by Diane Kagan. April 27, 1978. With Rudy Hornish, Edward Seamon, Doug Higgins.

THE PRIVATE EYE OF HIRAM BODONI by Frank Gagliano. May 3, 1978. With Roger Morden, Edward Seamon, Judith Reagan.

NAPKIN NOTES by Philip A. Bosakowski, directed by Jim Kramer; FREDERICK JORDAN'S DREAM by Peter Dee, directed by Scott Redman; IN THE MODERN STYLE by Stanley Taikeff (one-act plays). May 3, 1978.

UNTITLED PLAY by Conn Fleming. May 23, 1978. With John Mintun, William Andrews, Polly Holliday, Suzanne Marley, Chandra Oppenheim.

New Federal Theater. The Henry Street Settlement's training and showcase unit for new playwrights, mostly black and Puerto Rican. Woodie King Jr., director.

DADDY (18). By Ed Bullins. June 9, 1977. Director, Woodie King Jr.; scenery, Karl Eigsti; lighting, Shirley Prendergast; costumes, Judy Dearing; music, Carolyn Franklin. With Todd Davis, Nick Smith, Elizabeth Van Dyke, Dana Manno, Jewel Brimage, Nathan George.

SEASON'S REASONS (18). Written and directed by Ron Milner; music by Charles Mason. July 14, 1977. Scenery, C. Richard Mills; lighting, George Greczylo; costumes, Anita Ellis; choreographer, Gail Kaleem. With Chris Campbell, Tommy Hicks, Barbara Stephenson, Leon Thomas.

NIGHT SONG (12). By Patricia Lea; music by Walter Davis. October 20, 1977. Director, Walter Jones; scenery, Joseph Gandy; lighting, Ernest Baxter; costumes and choreography, Judy Dearing. With Mimi Ayers, James Whitten, Mary Jay, Ronnie Rayford, Sam Singleton.

THE BLOCK PARTY (12). Written and directed by Joseph Lizardi. January 12, 1978. Scenery, Jose M. Feliciano; lighting, Sandra Ross; costumes, Edna Watson. With James Turner Brown, Julie Carmen, Charles Grant, Lou Miranda, Larry Ramos, Gail Smith.

AFRICAN INTERLUDE (18). By Marti Evans-Charles. March 2, 1978. Director, Shauneille Perry; scenery, C. Richard Mills; lighting, Sandra Ross; costumes, Judy Dearing.

DO LORD REMEMBER ME (12). By James DeJongh. March 30, 1978. Director, Regge Life; scenery, C. Richard Mills; lighting, Sandra Ross; costumes, Beverly Parks. With Frances Foster, Louise Stubbs, Joe Attles, Barbara Clarke, Chuck Patterson.

RUN'ERS (12). By Ivey McCray. April 27, 1978. Director, Novella Nelson; scenery, C. Richard Mills; lighting, Victor En Yu Tan; costumes, Ellen Lee; mime, Rick Wexsler. With Kuumbha Alouba, Pamela Poitier.

New York Shakespeare Festival Public Theater. Schedule of experimental workshop of work-in-progress productions and guest residencies, in addition to its regular productions. Joseph Papp, producer.

UNFINISHED WOMEN CRY IN NO MAN'S LAND WHILE A BIRD DIES IN A GILDED CAGE (18). By Aishah Rahman. June 10, 1977. Director, Bill Duke; music, Stanley A. Cowell and Bill Duke; lyrics, Aishah Rahman; scenery, Linda Conaway; lighting, Curt Ostermann; costumes, Judy Dearing. With Kirk Kirksey, Arthur Burghardt.
MISS MARGARIDA'S WAY (16). By Roberto Athayde. June 21, 1977. With Estelle Parsons, Daniel Hugh-Kelly.
IN THE WELL OF THE HOUSE (12). By Charles C. Mark. July 1, 1977. Director, Davey Marlin-Jones; scenery, Jerry Rojo; lighting, Arden Fingerhut; costumes, Judy Dearing. With James Noble, Jack Collard, Henson Keys, Clarence Felder.
INTIMATIONS (11). Written and directed by Crispin Larangeira. July 15, 1977. Lighting, Jerry Bloom; costumes, Mary Brecht. With Frank Adu, Ellis Williams, Lauren Taylor.
FLUX (12). By Susan Miller. August 23, 1977. Annabel Leventon, scenery and lighting, Scott Johnson; costumes, Hilary Rosenfeld. With Robyn Goodman, Ron Faber, Jane Hallaren, Joel Brooks, Mark Baker, Kathleen Tolan.
A PRAYER FOR MY DAUGHTER (18). By Thomas Babe. September 30, 1977. Director, Robert Allan Ackerman; scenery, Bil Mikulewicz; lighting, Arden Fingerhut; costumes, Bob Wojewodski. With Jeffrey De Munn, Clifton James, Alan Rosenberg, Chris Sarandon.

WHERE THE MISSISSIPPI MEETS THE AMAZON cabaret (15). Written and performed by Jessica Hagedorn, Thulani (Davis) Nkabinde, Ntozake Shangé. December 4, 1977. Director, Oz Scott; lighting, Victor En Yu Tan; costumes, Beverly Parks.

THE QUANNAPOWITT QUARTET PART ONE: HOPSCOTCH (4). By Israel Horovitz. March 3, 1978. Director, Jack Hofsiss; scenery, Woods Mackintosh; lighting, Victor En Yu Tan; costumes, Jennifer Von Mayrhauser. With John Heard, Marybeth Hurt.
GUM (5). By Walter Corwin. April 3, 1978. Director, Susan Gregg; with Milburn Mehlhop, Irene O'Brien, John Pielmeier. (Lunchtime Theater).
THE QUANNAPOWITT QUARTET PART TWO: THE 75TH (8). By Israel Horovitz. April 22, 1978. Director, Jack Hofsiss; scenery, Woods Mackintosh; lighting, Victor En Yu Tan; costumes, Jennifer Von Mayrhauser. With Tom Aldredge, Elizabeth Wilson.
TAUDshow, a play for one actor, from the life and works of Antonin Artaud, devised and performed by Jerry Mayer, directed by John Pynchon Holms. April 18, 1978.

New York Stage Works. Dedicated to development and exposure of new American playwrights and theater artists. Craig LaPlount, producing director.

AMERICAN VERMILION. By Gary Copeland. November 26, 1977. Director, Craig LaPlount; scenery and costumes, Harry Lines; lighting, Terry Alan Smith. With Bob Ari, Robert Ramer, Nick Roberts.
Directors' Festival (one-act plays in repertory, 2 performances each): TURNING by Jim Inman, directed by Robert Ravan; KING OF TROY written and directed by Robert Pesola; HOLMES AND MORIARTY by Allen Sternfield, directed by Will Maitland Weiss; DOORMAN by Oakley Hall III, directed by William L. Partlan; DIGGERS LAMENT by Dan Bianchi, directed by Robert Mantione; INSIDE by Norman Beim, directed by Duke Kant; BRECHT IN EXILE by Bertolt Brecht, directed by Chris Silva; LOOKOUT by Robert D. Hoeft, directed by Richard Gershman; WAX MUSEUM by John Hawkes, directed by Andy Foster; MOZART AND SALIERI by Alexander Pushkin, directed by Mary Robinson. December 8-19, 1977.
THE ELEPHANT CALF and IN SEARCH OF JUSTICE (one-act plays) by Bertolt Brecht. March 10, 1978. Directed by Chris Silva; with Richard Patrick-Warner, John Ingle, Allan Wasserman.

New York Theater Ensemble. Provides an opportunity for the development of theater artists. Lucille Talayco, artistic director.

Joe Attles, Chuck Patterson, Louise Stubbs, Frances Foster, Tomas Brimm and Barbara Clarke in *Do Lord Remember Me* at New Federal Theater

TWELFTH NIGHT by William Shakespeare. July 7, 1977. Directed by Joseph B. Garren.
TRANSITIONS FOR A MIME POEM and THAT ALL DEPENDS ON HOW THE DROP FALLS by Owa. August 4, 1977. Directed by Stephen D. Agins.
WHAT POPPA WANTS adapted from *The Merchant* by Plautus. September, 1977. Directed by Jeanette Cocci.
THE WHITE WHORE AND THE BIT PLAYER by Tom Eyen., October 13, 1977. Directed by Ruth Evans.
THE REVENGER'S TRAGEDY by Cyril Tourneur. November, 1977. Directed by Carol Poster.
ROSMERSHOLM by Henrik Ibsen. December, 1977. Directed by Daniel Literas.
THE WAY OF THE WORLD by William Congreve. January 12, 1978. Directed by Steven Keim.
THE DANCE OF DEATH by August Strindberg. February, 1978. Directed by Kip Rosser.
THE MISER by Molière. March 2, 1978. Directed by Elizabeth Grossman.
DON JUAN by Molière. May 19, 1978. Directed by David Willinger.

New York Theater Strategy. Organization of playwrights for the production of their works. Maria Irene Fornes, president.

12 performances each:
THE SIXTY MINUTE QUEER SHOW. By Kenneth Bernard; music by John Braden. June 2, 1977. Director, John Vaccaro.

KONTRAPTION. By Rochelle Owens. February 9, 1978. Director, Barbara Rosoff; scenery, Mitchell Greenberg; lighting, Geoffrey T. Cunningham; costumes, Bernard Roth. With Ernest Wiggins, Karen Elise Swanson, Mary Jay, Larry Fishman.

THE NEON WOMAN. By Tom Eyen. February 2, 1978. Director, Ron Link. With Divine.

THE OVENS OF ANITA ORANGEJUICE, A HISTORY OF MODERN FLORIDA. By Ronald Tavel. March 9, 1978. Director, Harvey Tavel; scenery, Harvey Fierstein; lighting, Joanna Schielke; costumes, Lohr Wilson; incidental music and choreography, Ned Levy. With Sharon Barr, Hortensia Colorado, Robert Fowlkes, Joris Stuyck.

SUBURBAN TREMENS and INCREASED OCCUPANCY. By Robert Heide. April 6, 1978. Scenery and costumes, Ted Barnes; lighting, Carol Graebner. With Mark Simon.

TOO LATE FOR YOGURT. Written and directed by H.M. Koutoukas. April 7, 1978. Scenery, Peter Hulit; lighting, Carol Graebner. With Mary Boylan, Ronnie Cooper, Bruce Eyster, Peter Hulit, Rissell Krum, Viva Welles.

New York Theater Studio. Dedicated to producing contemporary plays new to this country and seldom-seen classics. Richard V. Romagnoli, artistic director, Cheryl Faraone, managing director.

THE BEAST (11). By Snoo Wilson. September 20, 1977 (American premiere). Director, Richard V. Romagnoli; scenery, Larry Brodsky; lighting, Gerald Dellasala; costumes, Kenneth Yount. With Peter Vogt, Susan Sharkey, Susan Greenhill, Richard Harmel, Walker Hicklin, Steven Smith.

No Smoking Playhouse. Eclectic producing policy. Norman Thomas Marshall, artistic director.

FESTIVAL OF ONE-ACT PLAYS: THE ANGEL OF DEATH by Ron W. DeFord, directed by George Wolf Reily, with Nancy Mainguy, Dempster Leech, Sturgis Warner, Norman Thomas Marshall; BREADBASKET by Jeannine O'Reilly, directed by George Wolf Reily, with Amy Lerner, Nancy Mainguy; DAVID AND BATHSHEBA (opera) libretto by Ronald Sarno, music by William Schimmel, directed by William Schimmel, with Keith King, Marleen Schussler; KANGAROO by Thomas Hischak, directed by Eelin Stewart Harrison, with Rod Bladel, Toby Clark, Jessica Hull; WAITING FOR THE BUS by Ramon Delgado, directed by Eelin Stewart Harrison, with Jane Cook, Patricia Mertens; YOU DON'T KNOW ME, I'M NOT FAMOUS written and directed by Diane Kornblatt and Amy Lerner, with David Kern, Amy Lerner. June 8-27, 1977.
WALDEN POND (20). By Joe Renard. February 24, 1978. Director, Norman Thomas Marshall; designer, Don Jensen; lighting, Gerald Bloom. With Diana Buckhantz, Peter Jolly, Maggie Tucker, JR Horne, Stanley Zawatsky.
THE ANNUAL SEDUCTION OF EMERSON FITZGERALD MCWADD. By Jeannine O'Reilly. February 26, 1978. Director, George Wolf Reily. With F. Murray Abraham, Malcolm Gray.
ISADORA (one-woman show) (20). By Jerry James, Ann Beigel and Catherine Harris. Designer, Joe McGrath. With Ann Beigel.

Off Center Theater. Provide free or low-cost theater to those who cannot afford Broadway and to whom established commercial fare is neither appealing nor relevant. Abigail Rosen, producer.

A SMALL DISTURBANCE (12). By Richard W. Bruner. December 7, 1977. Director, Marvin Kahan; scenery and lighting, Peter Mainguy; costumes, Karen Christeson. With Tony McGrath, Abigail Rosen.

CAPPELLA (18). By David Boorstin and Israel Horovitz, adapted from Israel Horovitz's novel. January 6, 1978. Director, David Boorstin; scenery and lighting, Daniel Thomas Field. With Davida Bloom, Katia Howard, Allan Wasserman, Sol Frieder, Gisela Caldwell.

THE LIARS (12). By Walter Beakel. February 9, 1978. Director, Tony McGrath; scenery and lighting, Daniel Thomas Field. With Jerry Chase, Harold Herbstman, John Rothman, Barbara Worthington, Renaldo De Silva.

THE LAST VAUDEVILLE SHOW AT RADIO CITY MUSIC HALL (12). By Stanley Seidman. April 27, 1978. Director, Abigail Rosen; designer, Daniel Thomas Field; composer, lyricist, Peter Wright.

Ontological-Hysteric Theater. Avant-garde theater productions written, directed and designed by the group's founder, Richard Formean.

BLVD. DE PARIS (I'VE GOT THE SHAKES) OR TORTURE ON A TRAIN (BRAIN-MECHANISMS OF THE RE-DISTRIBUTED FRENCH VIRGIN) OR CERTAINLY NOT (A TORTUOUS TRAIN OF THOUGHT) (89). December 21, 1977. With Kate Manheim, John Erdman, Robert Schlee, Peyton, Cynthia Pattison.

The Open Space in Soho. Focus on presenting new plays and developing new playwrights; also experimental programs. Lynn Michaels, Harry Baum, directors.

PHOTOGRAPH (18). By Gertrude Stein. September 15, 1977. Director, James Lapine; scenery and costumes, Maureen Connor; lighting, Paul Gallo. With Gwendolen Hardwick, Elaine Hartnett, Gabrielle Olejniczak, Gloria Pilot, Robert Rood.

VIVA REVIVA (11). (Musical) by Eve Merriam; music by Amy D. Rubin. October 13, 1977. Director, Graciela Daniele; scenery and costumes, Kate Carmel; lighting, Rick Shannin. With Kathryn Boule, Lynn Gerb, Laura Layva, Deborah Dotson.

THEATER EXPERIMENTS IN SOHO — FESTIVAL I: STUART SHERMAN'S TENTH SPECTACLE (PORTRAITS OF PLACES); SLIGHT by Richard Foreman; **WORK SONG** by The Talking Band; **PASSAGE** by Richard Peaslee; **AN ACTRESS (FROM IOWA)** by Sue Sheehy; **KOMACHI** by Solaris; **IDENTITY CONTROL** by Michael Kirby and **THEATER FILTERS** by Robb Creese, both with Structuralist Workshop; **CORNET** by Facets Performance Ensemble. November 3-27, 1977.

THE WHALE SHOW (12). Compiled and directed by Allan Albert. December 1, 1977. Scenery, Michael Sharp; lighting, Dick Williams; costumes, Hilary M. Rosenfeld. With The Proposition Workshop.

TWO BY MISHIMA: THE LADY AOI and **KANTAN** (12). By Yukio Mishima, translated by Donald Keene. January 19, 1978. Director, Jon Teta; scenery and costumes, Jane Coleman; lighting, Harry Baum. With Kitty Chen, Gerrie Lani Miyazaki.

THEATER EXPERIMENTS IN SOHO — FESTIVAL 2: LUMINOUS BODIES by Mathew Causey; **PUBLICITY STUNT** by James Leo; **HARLEQUIN** by Bill Simmer, with Structuralist Workshop; **LIVE COMEDY: LET'S SEE WHAT'S IN THE REGRIGERATOR** and **A DAY WITH MIKE** by Michael Smith; **FUNERAL RITE FOR JEAN GENET** by Ron Smith; **A MYTHOGYNOUS JOURNEY** by Sandra Stewart. March 2-19, 1978.

People Performing, Inc. New, socially significant musicals. Peter Copani, playwright-in-residence, Joseph Tiraco, producer.

THE ITALIAN AMERICANS (4). Songs by Peter Copani. April 15, 1978. Director, Don Signore; music director, John Spalla. With Beth Bloom, Laura Maruzzella, Patty Quinn, Dominick Pallatto, Bob Kazanowitz, Jay Kirsch, Vicki Casella.

The Performance Group. Experiments with new, collaborative and non-verbal creative techniques. Richard Schechner, director.

OEDIPUS (62, including open rehearsals). By Seneca; adapted by Ted Hughes. October 13, 1977. Director, Richard Schechner; environment and lighting, Jim Clayburgh; costumes, Theodora Skipitares; music, Paul Epstein; music director, Peter Zummo. With Stephen Borst, Caroline Ducrocq, Ron Guttman, John Holms, Joan MacIntosh, Leeny Sack.

COPS (54, including open rehearsals). By Terry Curtis Fox. March 16, 1978. Director, Richard

Schechner; environment and lighting, Jim Clayburgh; costumes, Sigrid Insull. With Elizabeth LeCompte, Willem Dafoe, Timothy Shelton, Ron Vawter, Stephen Borst.

NAYATT SCHOOL (30, including open rehearsals). By Spalding Gray and Elizabeth LeCompte in collaboration with Libby Howes, Bruce Porter and Ron Vawter. April 21, 1978. Director, Elizabeth LeCompte; scenery, Bruce Porter and Elizabeth LeCompte; lighting, Jim Clayburgh. With Joan Jonas, Ursula Easton, Tena Cohen, Michael Rivkin, Erik Moskowitz, Spalding Gray, Ron Vawter, Libby Howes.

RUMSTICK ROAD composed and directed by Spalding Gray and Elizabeth LeCompte. December 1, 1977.

Perry Street Theater. Dual emphasis placed on producing scripts by new playwrights and on experimentation with other contemporary and classical scripts. Vasek Simek, producer and artistic director.

COWBOY JACK STREET (16). Written and directed by Joan Tewkesbury; music and lyrics by Tony Berg and Ted Neely; additional music by Michael Barry Greer. November 25, 1977. Scenery and costumes, Judie Juracek; lighting, Paul Everett. With Scott Glenn, Rodney Hudson, Doug Handy, Victoria Boothby.

SCENES FROM COUNTRY LIFE (12). By Norman Plotkin; music by Michael S. Roth; lyrics by Norman Plotkin and Michael S. Roth. March 8, 1978. Director, Carl Weber; scenery, Jonathan Arkin; lighting, Will Morrison; costumes, Perry McLamb. With Kevin O'Connor, Will Patton, Jerry Cunliffe, Marilyn Meyers.

NATIVE SON (16). By Richard Wright and Paul Green. March 7, 1978. Director, Dick Gaffield; scenery, Scott Moore; lighting, William Plachy; costumes, Walker Hicklin, Gayle Everhart; music director, Greg Gilford. With Bo Rucker, Erma Campbell, Ceal Coleman, Terrance Wendell Harris, Harvey Pierce.

THE MARRIAGE OF MISSISSIPPI by Friedrich Duerrenmatt. October 27, 1977. Directed by Vasek Simek; with Jordan Myers, Dino Laudicina.

Playwrights Horizons. Give playwrights the opportunity to see their work produced by professionals in an atmosphere devoid of commercial pressure. Robert Moss, artistic director, Jane Moss, managing director.

Manhattan Full Productions (asterisk indicates also performed at Queens Festival Theater)
CRACKS (12). By Martin Sherman. June 16, 1977. Director, Larry Carpenter; scenery, Ruth A. Wells; lighting, Frances Aronson; costumes, Jean Steinlein. With Holly Barron, Robert Brian Berger, Elizabeth Ruscio, William Sadler, Joel Brooks.

GOGOL (12). By Len Jenkin. October 20, 1977. Director, David Schweizer; scenery, Charles Stone; lighting, Marty Kapell; costumes, Khorshid Panthaky. With Michael Arabian, Sharon Barr, Lori DeVito, Peter Harris, Lisa Sloan, Jeffrey Ware. (In association with The Second Company of the Williamstown Theater Festival.)

ANGEL CITY (15). By Sam Shepard. October 21, 1977. Director, Marty Kapell; scenery, Charles Stone; lighting, Marty Kapell; costumes, Khorshid Panthaky. With Gregory T. Daniel, Peter Harris, Randle Mell, Charles Shaw-Robinson, Jeffrey Ware. (In association with The Second Company of the Williamstown Theater Festival.)*

BACK COUNTY CRIMES (13). By Lanie Robertson. Director, Harold DeFelice; scenery and lighting, Marty Kapell; costumes, Khorshid Panthaky. With Beverly Barbieri, Gregory T. Daniel, Kathy Danzer, Anthony Pasqualini, Charles Shaw-Robinson. (In association with The Second Company of the Williamstown Theater Festival.)*

TWO SMALL BODIES (12). By Neal Bell. December 1, 1977. Director, Thomas Babe; scenery, Richard Kerry; lighting, James Chaleff; costumes, William Ivey Long. With Catherine Burns, Larry Bryggman.

THREE SONS (20). By Richard Lortz. January 12, 1978. Director, Robert O'Rourke; scenery, Jimmy Cuomo; lighting, Marilyn Rennagel; costumes, Susan Denison. With Richard Cox, Joseph Giardina, David Little, Rita Lloyd, Jerry Matz.*

SHAY (20). By Anne Commire. February 23, 1978. Director, Elinor Renfield; scenery, Jane Thurn, lighting, Pat Stern; costumes, Michel J. Cesario; sound, Philip Campanella. With Marge Redmond, Jack Gilpin, Marvin Chatinover, Avril Gentles, Dallas Greer, Pat Lysinger, Conrad McLaren, Shirley Richards.*

HOOTERS (30+). By Ted Tally. April 18, 1978. Director, Gary Pearle; scenery, Charles McCarry; lighting, Frances Aronson; costumes, Elizabeth Palmer. With Victor Bevine, Michael Kaufman, Christine Lahti, Erika Petersen.*

Manhattan Workshops (2 performances each)
S.W.A.K.. By Sally Ordway. November 3, 1977. Director, Elinor Renfield. With Alix Elias, Quincy Long, Lane Sanford, Virginia Stephens, D. Victor Truro, Barbara Spiegel.
LIBBY AND THE GIANTS. By Stephen Hanan. November 18, 1977. Director, David Boorstin. With Michael Cooke, Miller Lide, Virginia Morris.
DECEMBER TO MAY. By Jane Staab. December 8, 1977. Director, Anthony Hancock. With Malcolm Groome, Bump Heeter, Penny White, Gina Sisk, Jessica Hull.

Queens Festival Theater
THE GINGERBREAD LADY by Neil Simon. June 11, 1977. Directed by Rae Allen; with Thomas Dillon, Helen Gallagher, Dorrie Kavanaugh.
THE PLAYBOY OF THE WESTERN WORLD by John Millington Synge. July 16, 1977. Directed by Michael Montel; with Jon Peter Benson, Sarah Chodoff, Kaiulani Lee, David Selby, Pat McNamara.
ANYTHING GOES (musical) book by Guy Bolton, P.G. Wodehouse, Howard Lindsay and Russel Crouse, music and lyrics by Cole Porter. October 15, 1977. Directed by Larry Carpenter; with Justine Johnson, Henrietta Valor, Terry Byrne, Edmond Dante.
A CHRISTMAS CAROL by Charles Dickens, adapted and directed by Christopher Cox. November 26, 1977. With Christopher Hewett, Michael Arabian, Sara Birtman-Fox, C.S. Hayward, Court Miller.
THE MEMBER OF THE WEDDING by Carson McCullers. January 7, 1978. Directed by Philip Himberg; with Frank Adu, Beverly Barbieri, Reathel Bean, Mark Hattan, Cynthia Frost, Beatrice Winde.
DIAL M FOR MURDER by Frederick Knott. February 18, 1978. Directed by Robert Moss; with Robert Baines, Maria Cellario, Drew Keil, William Perley, William Sadler.
A MIDSUMMER NIGHT'S DREAM by William Shakespeare. April 18, 1978. Directed by Robert Moss; with Catherine Burns, William Carden, Gilbert Cole, Mark Hattan, Olgalyn Jolly, Victoria Boothby.
AWAKE AND SING! by Clifford Odets. May 13, 1978. Directed by Alfred Gingold; with Jack Aaron, Nancy Marchand, Paul Sparer, Reuben Schafer, David Little, Fredric Stone, Kim Ameen.

Puerto Rican Traveling Theater. Professional company presenting bilingual productions primarily of Puerto Rican and Hispanic playwrights, emphasizing subjects of relevance today. Miriam Colon, founder and producer.

THE FM SAFE (10+). By Jaime Carrero. April 11, 1978. Director, Alba Oms; scenery, Robert F. Strohmeier; lighting, Larry Johnson; costumes, Maria Ferreira. With Miriam. Colon, Luis Avalos, Norberto Kerner, Chino Vega, Freddy Valle, Ray Muniz.

Quaigh Theater. Primarily a playwrights' theater, devoted to the new playwright, the established contemporary playwright and the modern (post-1920) playwright. William H. Lieberson, artistic director.

DRY SHERRY: THE ICING and THE ADMISSIONS CHAIRMAN (8). By John Sherry. November 14, 1977. Director, Martin Oltarsh; scenery, John Macgregor; lighting, Bartlett Bigelow. With Helen Breed, Dorothy Farrell, Ron Foster, Rudy Hornish, Nancy Berg.

THE THIRD DAUGHTER (12). By Mario Fratti. January 18, 1978 (American premiere). Director, Harry F. Thompson. With the Austin College Theater Company.

THE EXORCISM OF VIOLENCE (9). Written and directed by Sidney Morris. March 31, 1978. With Matty Selman, Amy Whitman, Frank Nastasi, Kay Williams, Lawrence James, Ira Lee Collings, Mona Sands.

COUNSELLOR-AT-LAW by Elmer Rice. July 26, 1977. Directed by Will Lieberson; with George Guidall, Carolyn Lenz, Kent Wilson, Claudine Catania, Joan Turetzky.

3 SMALL PLAYS BY BIG PLAYWRIGHTS: AT LIBERTY by Tennessee Williams, directed by Ted Mornel; EPISODE ON AN AUTUMN EVENING by Friedrich Duerrenmatt, directed by Bill Lentsch; THE SWEETSHOPPE MYRIAM by Ivan Klima, directed by Ted Mornel, March 7, 1978.

DEAD END by Sidney Kingsley. April 25, 1978. Directed by Will Lieberson; with Craig Alfano, Stephen Berenson, Fred Ivory, Peter Jeffries-Ferrara, Hal Muchnick, Michael Stumm.

Lunchtime Theater

HOME FREE by Lanford Wilson. June 31, 1977. Directed by Ted Mornel; with Peter Jack, Cam Kornman.

THE SMELL OF FLOWERS by George Stiles. July 11, 1977. Directed by Douglas Popper.

STEINBERG by David Feldman. July 25, 1977. Directed by Albert Brower; with Sal Carollo, Richard Greaker, Frank Meyer, Madeline Rockower, Richard Spore.

LUNCH WITH FRATTI: THE LETTER, HER VOICE and THE PIGGYBANK by Mario Fratti. January 16, 1978. Directed by Viktor Allen; with Susan Levine, Alan Clement, Stephan Morrow, Maxine Taylor-Morris.

TRUE GREATNESS by Valerie Owen, directed by Viktor Allen; AT LIBERTY by Tennessee Williams, directed by Ted Mornel. January 30, 1978. With Henry Vartanian, Mimi Weddell, Cam Kornman, Ann Saxman.

SECOND CHANCE by Elyse Nass. February 14, 1978. Directed by Kathleen Huber; with Elizabeth Abbassi, Ruby Payne.

LUNCHTIME by Leonard Melfi. March 6, 1978. Directed by Bob McAndrew; with Lin Kosy, Richard Leonard.

LA BAKHAIR conceived and performed by Jessie Hill. March 20, 1978.

WHEN THE SUN GOES DOWN by Michael Shurtleff. April 3, 1978. Directed by John Cacciatore; with Judith Kercheval, Rusti Moon, Jane Roberts.

CAPPERS by Stuart Silver and READY FOR TEDDY by Joel Ensana. April 17, 1978. Directed by Bill McComb; with Jo-Ann Marshall, Debbie Novak, Paca Thomas, Christopher Culkin, Louise Larabee.

CHANGES: A LOVE STORY by George Hammer. May 1, 1978. Directed by Ann Raychel; with Gerry Lou, John A. Murray.

ON WITH THE STUFF: FOUR WHORES IN OUTER SPACE by Jessie Hill. May 15, 1978. Directed by Tanden Peyton.

Richard Morse Mime Theater. To create a home for a permanent mime repertory theater in America. Richard Morse, artistic director.

THE ARTS AND LEISURE SECTION OF THE NY TIMES. September, 1977. With Rasa Allen, Byam Stevens, Charles Penn, Kristin Sakai, Gjertine Johansen.

GIFTS. December 21, 1977.

TINTINNABULA. Conceived and directed by Richard Morse. March 3, 1978. With Richard Morse, Rasa Allen, Gabriel Barre.

Shelter West. Aims to bring the community challenging theater based on artistic integrity. Judith Joseph, executive director, Dan Mason, artistic director.

THE RELUCTANT VAMPIRE (12). By Malcolm Marmorstein. June 10, 1977. Director, Larry Conroy; scenery, James Conway; lighting, Marsha Imhof. With Bob Levine, Gerrianne Raphael.

DANCERS (12). By Brendan Ward. July 6, 1977. Director, Dan Mason; scenery, Tom

Schwinn; lighting, Paul Mathiesen; costumes, Annick Leymarie. With Michael Detmold, Kathy Flanagan, Dan Hayes, Judith Joseph, Laurie Lathem.

CONSIDER THE ROACHES (12). By Len Seaberg. August 3, 1977. Director, Beverly Brumm; scenery, John Argento; lighting, Paul Mathieson; costumes, Annick Leymarie. With Leo Creed, Vicki Harris, William Mesnik, Carol Tenley, Deborah Tiernan.

RATS NEST (12). By Neil and Joel Cohen. October 12, 1977. (Reopened January 26, 1978, 12 performances.) Director, Michael Murphy; scenery, Steve Shadley; lighting, Marsha Imhof. With Susan Lange, Kenneth Larsen, Tom Nardini, Bobby Pickett.

DOWNFALL OF THE EGOTIST JOHANN FATZER (12). By Bertolt Brecht. November 9, 1977 (American premiere). Director, W. Stuart McDowell; scenery, W. Stuart McDowell; lighting, Marsha Imhof; costumes, Annick Leymarie. With Michael Detmold. Alexander Duncan, Jim Maxson, William Mesnik, Peter Siiteri.

AGNES BERNELLE — BLACK CHAMPAGNE (12). One-woman cabaret.

HENRY'S DAUGHTER (12). One-woman show by Cavada Humphrey. December 11, 1977. Director, Sarah Sanders; scenery and lighting, Tom Schwinn; costumes, Edwin Weaver.

WOMEN I HAVE KNOWN (12). Written and performed by M. Tulis Sessions. January 9, 1978. Director, Michael T. Gregoric; scenery, Doug Terranova; lighting, Fran Miksits.

THE BRIGHT AND GOLDEN LAND (12). By Harry Granick. March 29, 1978. Director, Len Gochman; scenery, James Conway, Michael Holm; lighting, Lee Amon; music, David Freeman. With Chip Zien, Pierre Epstein, Estelle Omens, Rueben Schafer, Stephen Mark Weyte, Darlene Wasko.

THE COMRADES (12). By August Strindberg; translated and directed by Katrin Tralongo. May 8, 1978 (American premiere). Scenery, Adam Kurtzman, Katrin Tralongo; lighting, James Joseph. With Michael Kolba, Ira Rubin, James Vann, Trudi Mathes, Eleanore Auer, Constance Stellas.

THE AFFAIRS OF ANATOL by Arthur Schnitzler. December 7, 1977. Directed by Janet Sarno; with Dan Mason, Jeffrey McLaughlin, Linda Geiser, Anita Keal, Leah Kreutzer, David Louden.

Shirtsleeve Theater. Full productions of new works. John A. Vaccaro, James J. Wisner, artistic directors.

PIANO BAR (12). Music by Rob Fremont; lyrics by Doris Willens. February 9, 1978. Director, Albert Takazauckas; music director and arranger, Jimmy Roberts; choreographer, Nora Peterson; scenery and costumes, Michael Massee; lighting, Robert F. Strohmeier. With Christopher Callan, Karen De Vito, Steve Elmore, James McMahon, Dan Ruskin, Richard Ryder.

DEAR LIAR by Jerome Kilty. May 12, 1978. Directed by John Driver; with Lois Kibee, Louis Turenne.

Soho Rep. To make the classics, old and new, theatrical, accessible and fun. Marlene Swartz, Jerry Engelbach, artistic directors.

MISTER T (12). By Michael Zettler. November 4, 1977. Director, Stephen Zuckerman; scenery, Trueman Kelley; lighting, Gary Seltzer; costumes, Margo La Zaro. With Jonathan Frakes, Kathleen Turner, David Forsyth.

THE FOUR LITTLE GIRLS (12). By Pablo Picasso. January 7, 1978 (N.Y. premiere). Director, Richard Gershman; scenery, Rosaria Sinisi; lighting, D. Schweppe; costumes, Donato Moreno. With Deborah Johnson, Lily Knight, Tricia Metz, Diane Johnson.

SOHO THEATER OF THE AIR (12). Conceived, compiled and directed by Carol Corwen.

March 6, 1978. Scenery, Mark Haack; costumes, Sue Cox; composer, music director, Tom Shelton. With Suzanne Toren, Stephen Mellor, Randy Knolle, Anne Gartlan.

FAMOUS FRENCH FARCES: THE CHAIRS by Eugene Ionesco; director, Jon Fraser; **BETTER DEAD** by Georges Feydeau, adapted and directed by Jude Schanzer and Michael Wells (12; *Better Dead* N.Y. premiere). March 25, 1978. Scenery, Nanette Reynolds; lighting, Carol Corwen; costumes, Susan Cox. With Ray Xifo, Michael Basile, Penelope Hirsch, Marie Rice.

BILLY LIAR by Willis Hall and Keith Waterhouse. June 11, 1977. Directed by Jerry Engelbach.

THE KILLING OF SISTER GEORGE by Frank Marcus. August 5, 1977. Directed by Marlene Swartz.

THE REAL INSPECTOR HOUND by Tom Stoppard. August 13, 1977. Directed by Tim Brennan.

MISALLIANCE by George Bernard Shaw. September 17, 1977. Directed by Trueman Kelley.

THE MISER by Molière, adapted and directed by Moshe Yassur. October 1, 1977.

PEER GYNT by Henrik Ibsen. October 23, 1977. Directed by Carol Corwen.

THE PLAY'S THE THING by Ferenc Molnar, adapted by P.G. Wodehouse. November 25, 1977. Directed by Jack Cunningham.

ABELARD AND HELOISE by Ronald Duncan. December 10, 1977. Directed by Trueman Kelley.

PHILADELPHIA, HERE I COME! by Brian Friel. January 28, 1978. Directed by Ron Daley.

THE MAGISTRATE by Arthur Wing Pinero. February 17, 1978. Directed by James Milton.

POE IN PERSON (one-man show). April 14, 1978. Directed by Marilyn Vale; with Conrad Pomerleau.

CYRANO DE BERGERAC by Rostand, translated by Brian Hooker. April 28, 1978. Directed by Jerry Engelbach.

South Street Theater Company. Developing an outdoor environmental theater at South Street Seaport Museum; also year-round indoor theater on Theater Row. Michael Fischetti, artistic director, Jean Sullivan, director.

Lunchtime Theater

EAST LYNNE by Mrs. Henry Wood, adapted by Brian Burton. July 5, 1977. Directed by Michael Fischetti and Jean Sullivan.

THE FORCED MARRIAGE (one-act play) by Molière. July, 1977. Directed by Jack Eddleman.

A VIEW FROM THE BRIDGE by Arthur Miller. March 14, 1978. Directed by Paul McCarren.

ANDROCLES AND THE LION by George Bernard Shaw. May 5, 1978. Directed by Alan Simpson.

Stage Directors and Choreographers Workshop Foundation. Experimental showcase. Marty Jacobs, executive director.

3 performances each

THE LIFE & WORLD OF KAHLIL GIBRAN. By Robert Haddad. January 9, 1978. Director, Madolin Cervantes.

WHEN THE OLD MAN DIED. By Keith Aldrich. April 3, 1978. Director, Rina Elisha.

COCTEAU. By Roy Finamore. May 22, 1978. Director, Rosemary Foley.

Theater at St. Clement's. Concerned with the development of new plays in workshop, experimental and showcase situations. Michael Hadge, program director, Jeffrey M. Jones, administrator.

THE SPONSOR (12). Written and directed by Ira Lewis. September 15, 1977. Scenery, Oldson Holmes; lighting, Will Morrison; costumes, Margo La Zaro. With Michael Strong, Paul Sparer, Olga Druce, David Patch.

FENDERS (12). By Bruce Serlen. October 7, 1977. Director, Stephen Roylance; scenery, Patricia Healy; lighting, Marilyn Reed, Wayne Schrengohst; costumes, Margo La Zaro. With David Dean, Deborah Offner, J.T. Walsh.

BIG MAGGIE (12). By John B. Keane. December 15, 1977. Director, Larry Spiegel; scenery Stephen J. Cramer; lighting, Will Morrison; costumes, Margo La Zaro. With Robin Howard, Chris Keeley, Megan Hunt, Faith Catlin, Bill Severs.

SELF-ACCUSATION by Peter Handke, translated by Michael Roloff; THE SALIVA MILKSHAKE by Howard Brenton (12 performances each). January 12, 1978. Director, Robert Gainer; lighting, Stephen J. Cramer. With McLin Crowell, Y York, John Neary, James Wilson, Roby Brown. (Presented by the Brooklyn Bridge Theater Company).

OF MEN AND ANGELS: TOTAL RECALL and WHAT THE BABE SAID (12). By Martin Halpern. April 13, 1978. Director, Paul Austen; scenery and lighting, Stephen J. Cramer; costumes, Margo La Zaro. With Mitchell Jason, Nancy Burke, Edmond Genest.

VOICES (12). By Susan Griffin. May 18, 1978. Director, Estelle Parsons; scenery and lighting, Stephen J. Cramer; costumes, Margo La Zaro. With Catherine Burns, Anne Shropshire, Susan Greenhill, Rochelle Oliver, Janet Ward.

Theater for the New City. Specializing in serious, dramatic musical form. George Bartenieff, Crystal Field, artistic directors.

TURTLES DON'T DREAM (12). Written and directed by H.M. Koutoukas. June 20, 1977. Music, Cosmos; environmental music, Tom O'Horgan; choreographer, Gino de Fulgentiis; scenery, Mario Rivoli; lighting, Don McConnell; costumes, Bruce Eyster. With Illa Howe, Gino de Fulgentiis, Mary Boylan, Joy Hatton.

LEONA IS A FUNNY NAME (12). By Donald Kvares. August 25, 1977. Director, Ted Mornel; scenery, Brian Evans. With Maxine Albert, Steven Hart, James Howley, Viktor Allen.

DRY SHERRY: THE ICING and THE ADMISSIONS CHAIRMAN (12). By John Sherry. September 22, 1977. Director, Martin Oltarsh; scenery, Stephen Edelstein; lighting, Barbara J. Schwartz. With Nancy Berg, Bob Clarke, Rudy Hornish, Linda Spector, Ron Foster, Helen Breed.

THE ROOM (6). November 3, 1977. Director, Saskia Noordhoek Hegt; music, Andrew Schloss; words, Earlene Smith. With Hillary Hurst, Epp Kotkas, Joseph Mydell, Earlene Smith. (Reopened January 19, 1978, 12 performances.)

THE GUILLOTINE (11). By Helen Duberstein. November 10, 1977. Director, Michael McGrinder; lighting, Barbara Tulliver; costumes, Michael Arian. With Sherry H. Arell, Sharon Pierson, Cathy Cevoli, Michael Long, Mary Lee Kellerman.

ANTONEMENTS (12). By Israel Eliraz, translated by David Zinder. December 22, 1977. Director, Rina Elisha; music, Haim Elisha; lyrics, Lynn Ahrens; scenery, Michael Greenberg; lighting, Craig Kennedy; costumes, Edmond Felix; choreographer, Haila Strauss. With Bruce Kent, Claudia Zahn, Roberta Reardon, Leslie Middlebrook, Beth Bloom, Jerri Lines.

JUST FOLKS (12). By Romulus Linney. January 22, 1978. Director, John Olon-Scrymgeour; scenery, Jane Thurn; lighting, Willard Shaffar; costumes, Sigrid Insull; music, Lee Scott Goldstein. With William McIntyre.

WORK SONG (16). By Mark Kaminsky and The Talking Band. February 9, 1978. Scenery, Jeremy Lebensohn; lighting, Beverly Emmons; costumes, Mary Brecht; music, The Company and Elizabeth Swados. With Sybille Hayn, Ellen Maddow, Tina Shepard, Margo Lee Sherman, Arthur Strimling, Paul Zimet.

THE LIARS (9). By Ron Lampkin. February 10, 1978. Director, Ken Buckshi; scenery and costumes, Jane Przybysz; music director and arranger, David Tice. With Bill Daniels, John De Tommaso, Martha MacMahon, Bill Maloney, Patrick Stack.

CLARA BOW LOVES GARY COOPER (12). By Robert Dahdah and Mary Boylan. February 16, 1978. Director, Robert Dahdah; scenery, Steve Edelstein; lighting, John Dodd; costumes, Gene Galvin. With Jeryll Adler, Kurt Schlesinger, Anna Ratafia.

OIL! (12). By Neil Tucker. March 9, 1978. Director, Seth Allen; scenery and costumes, Saint-Amant. With Ron Ballard, Denise Davis, Jewel Hickman, Irma Sandrey, Richard Spore, Kathy Helmer.

WINO ROSE (cabaret) by Andy Laurie. Match 17, 1978. Director, Willis Alexander; scenery, Bruce Arzig, Trevor Hoteler; lighting, Matt Baylor; costumes, Patty Paul; choreographer, Charles Mayer Karp.

BOAT, SUN, CAVERN (24). By Arthur Sainer. April 20, 1978. Director, Crystal Field; scenery and lighting, Stephen Edelstein; costumes, Halyna Kuzman; music, George Prideaux and Mark Hardwick. With George Bartenieff, Nancy Haffner, Ken Buckshi, Mary McDonnell, Crystal Field, Paul Tumbleson.

THE BASS FIDDLE (16). Written and directed by Avram Patt, from a story by I.L. Peretz. April 27, 1978. Scenery, Peter Cunneen, Avram Patt; music, Alice Eve Cohen; masks, Amy Trompetter. With The Barking Rooster Theater.

COSMICOMICS by Italo Calvino, translated by William Weaver, adapted and directed by Gordon Rogoff and **THE TORRENTS OF SPRING** by Turgenev, adapted and directed by Donald Sanders (14). May 17, 1978. Design, Vanessa James; lighting, Ken Tabachnik; music, Timothy LuBell. With the BBC Project.

THE PLEBIANS REHEARSE THE UPRISING. By Gunter Grass; translated by Ralph Manheim. June 6, 1977. Director, Ruis Woertendyke.
THE BALLAD OF THE SEVEN SLEEPING BROTHERS IN CHINA (12). By Tadeusz Micinski. July 14, 1977. Director, Viola Stephan.
"?" (4). (Multi-media production) by Michael Kushner. July 18, 1977. With Michael Anthony, John Farrell, Betsy Quint, Mona Robson, Edward Yankee.
THE TIME THEY TURNED THE WATER OFF by Crystal Field, George Bartenieff and TNC Company and THE RICH MAN, POOR MAN PLAY by Arthur Sainer. August 6, 1977. Director and composer, Crystal Field; scenery, Donald L. Brooks; costumes, Edmond Felix; music director, arranger, Mark Hardwick. (Street plays in repertory.)
FACE STOOL: Henry Gruvman (mime). September 8, 1977.
THE SHOPPING BAG MADONNA (4) by Mary Julia Karoly. October 3, 1977. Director, Anthony De Vito. With Ruth Brandeis, Steven Burch, Glenn Czako, Ann Whiteside, Kay Worthington.
WALLS (improvisational piece) by Radio Free Theater. November, 1977. Director, Susan Jenks Dudley, A.W. Brunn; lighting, Barbara Tulliver, Linnaea Tillett. With Susan-Heide Arbitter, Mary Beth Casper, Gary Richards, Jeremy Stuart.
MASQUERADES (5). Written and directed by Melisande Potter. January 20, 1978. (Mime and dance.)
LIVES (3). One-act pieces by Edmond Felix, Roberta N. Rude, Marc Powers. February 20, 1978. With PAF In-School Troupe.
REALISM IN OUR TIME (8). Written and directed by Daryl Chin. March 10, 1978. With Denis Cleary, Kathleen Gittel.
THE CANCER OF AMBITION (4). By Richard Levine. March 30, 1978. With Hali Breindel, Ben Chase.
SPIDERWOMAN THEATER FESTIVAL: THREE WORKS-IN-PROGRESS, THE LYSISTRATA NUMBAH! and I CELEBRATE THE WOMAN by Nina Miller (16). March 30, 1978.
ROUND TRIP TICKET (12). By Bruce Jones. May 5, 1978. Director, John Simonetti.
THE LOVES OF A WOMAN (3). (Cabaret) with Kathy Wells. May 11, 1978.
KING RICHARD III. By William Shakespeare, adapted and directed by Michael Stuart Long. April 6, 1978.

Theater Genesis. Writers' theater; production of new American plays. Walter Hadler, artistic director.

> THE DAY ROOSEVELT DIED by Barry Pritchard, directed by Kevin O'Connor; THE RUFFIAN ON THE STAIR by Joe Orton, directed by Harry Schultz (12). February 16, 1978. With the Workshop Theater.
>
> CONTRIBUTIONS (12). By Ted Shine. March 10, 1978. Director, Edmund Cambridge. With Sarallen, Laurence Fishburne III, Arthur French, Phillip Lindsay, Barbara Montgomery.
>
> THE TRUTH ABOUT THE TRUTH (8). By Harold Stuart. April 6, 1978. Director, Norman Jacob; scenery, Joe Stephenson; lighting, John Dodd; costumes, Edna Watson. With Keith Archie, Adolph Caesar, Carl Gordon, Les Roberts, Rony Clanton, Gregory T. Daniel.
>
> ONCE UPON A TIME A MAN CAME OUT OF THE DARK (8). (Theater pieces) written and directed by Richard Ploetz. April 27, 1978. With Jacklyn Maddox, John Ellis, Anne Paul, Larry C. Lott.
>
> WHEN PETULIA COMES. By Caroline Emmons. May 4, 1978. Director, Edward M. Cohen; lighting, DiDi Salzman. With Lisa Sloan, Kathleen Chalfant, Tom Leo, Tobias Haller, Kathy Danzer.
>
> THE IMMEDIATE FAMILY (3). By Mitchell Redman. May 13, 1978. Director, Charles Shain; lighting, Patrick O'Rourke. With Gregory Salata, Kurt Feuer, Joseph Jamrog, Jennie Ventriss.
>
> ANGEL CITY by Sam Shepard. May 18, 1978. Directed by Lawrence Sacharow. With The Theater Project.

Theater of the Open Eye. Total theater involving actors, dancers, musicians and designers working together, each bringing his own talents into a single project; also children's programs. Jean Erdman, Eric Bass, artistic directors.

> MOON ON SNOW (one-act plays) (12). By Ken Gaertner. April 6, 1978. Director and designer, Trueman Kelley.

> THE SHINING HOUSE (12). Conceived, directed and choreographed by Jean Erdman; music by Michael Czajkowski. May 25, 1978.

> HECUBA by Euripides. November 17, 1977. Directed by Ketti Melonas.
>
> DARK OF THE MOON by Howard Richardson and William Berney. December 15, 1977. Directed by Alan Wynroth; with Sturgis Warner.
>
> RAVEN'S DANCE. April 27, 1978. Directed by Eric Bass.
>
> TWILIGHT CRANE (dance drama). May 19, 1978. Directed by Eric Bass; with Muna Tseng, John Tatlock.

Theater of the Riverside Church. To combine the best of the professional world with the management of a community-run theater. Anita L. Thomas, artistic director.

> OUT OF OUR FATHER'S HOUSE (12). Adapted by Eve Merriam, Jack Hofsiss, and Paula Wagner from *Growing Up Female in America* by Eve Merriam. October 25, 1977. Director, Jack Hofsiss; scenery, John Lee Beatty; lighting, Cheryl Thacker; costumes, Maureen Connor. With Maureen Anderman, Charlotte Moore, Laura Esterman.

> FIXED (28). Book by Robert Maurice Riley; conceived by Anita L. Thomas and George Faison; music and lyrics by Gene Bone and Howard Fenton; additional lyrics by Langston Hughes. November 26, 1977. Director, George Faison; music director, Thom Edlun; scenery, David Chapman; lighting, Chenault Spence; costumes, Victor Capecce. With J. Edward Adams, Miriam Burton, Ray Anthony Jones, Patricia Hyling, Urylee Leonardos, Ilene Lewis, Barbara Montgomery.

> CORRAL (12). Compiled and directed by Allan Albert. February 1, 1978. Scenery, Woods MacKintosh; lighting, Dick Williams; costumes, Hilary M. Rosenfeld; music arranger, John Guth; music director, Peter Kairo. With The Proposition Workshop.

THE HEALERS (12). By Ava Jacobs. March 10, 1978. Director, Scott Reiniger; scenery, Chip Mulberger; lighting, R.F. Strohmeier; costumes, Laurence Mercier. With Georgia Southcotte, David Emge, Gary Cookson, Sharron Shayne, Lissa Bell.

THE STAR WITHOUT A NAME (12). By Mihail Sebastian; translated by Hermania Vlasopolos. April 13, 1978. Director, Al Asermely; scenery, Thom Edlun; lighting, Al Sayers; costumes, Jeffrey Ullman. With Jayne Bentzen, Steven Hart, Mark Russel, Clyde Burton, Ada Rodriguez, Carol Thompson, Peter Reznikoff, Matthew Sakolsky, Herbert DuVal.

THE LOVELIEST AFTERNOON OF THE YEAR by John Guare. With Roger Chapman, Nancy Lawson; I LOVE MY VOICE (one-woman show) by Stephen Holt and Don Arrington. Directed by Calvin Churchill; with Lynn Marie Oliver. May 18, 1978.

Theater Off Park. Theater for the community, attempting to reach as wide an audience as possible through as wide a variety of productions as possible. Patricia Flynn Peate, director.

SACRAMENTS (12). By Jo Ann Tedesco. June 2, 1977. Director, Mel Winkler. With Mimi Cecchini, Bob Costanzo, Peter Gatto, Ray Serra, Karen Shallo, Laura Julian.

SHUFFLE ALONG (12). Music and lyrics by Noble Sissle and Eubie Blake. February 2, 1978. Director, Julianne Boyd; music director and accompanist, Vicki Carter; choreographer, Dana Manno; scenery, and costumes, Lee Mayman; lighting, Boyd Masten. With Dabriah Chapman, Lynnie Godfrey, Roger Lawson, Vernon Spencer.

THREE ON THE LIGHT SIDE: MODERN MANNERS, TOMORROW I'LL BE FIFTY and **ANCIENT GRUDGES** (12). By Leila Blake. May 12, 1978. (American premiere). Director, June Plager; scenery, Bil Mikulewicz; lighting, Lori Masterton.

THE PHYSICIAN IN SPITE OF HIMSELF by Molière, translated by Morris Bishop. October 6, 1977. Directed by Harry Shifman; with Ross Quint, Dennis Eichelberger, Dean Gardner, Tara Lowenstern, Howard Shalwitz.
THE SECOND SHEPHERDS' PLAY. December 15, 1977. Directed by Elaine Kanas; with Neil Napolitan, Daniel Ziskie, Nancy Foy, Sheldon Silver, Y. York, Dennis Douglas, Frederikke Borge.

Thirteenth Street Repertory Company. Musical company focusing on new work; also children's programs. Edith O'Hara, artistic director.

THREE FAIR TALES (one-act plays) by Tom Millott. June, 1977.

RATTLE OF A SIMPLE MAN (12). By Charles Dyer. July, 1977. Director, Robert Dorfman. With Renee Zevon, Bill Shuman, Robert Engels.

SWAMP FOX (comedy revue) written and performed by Duffy Magesis, Michael Sklaroff. July, 1977.
THE VILLAIN STILL PURSUED HER by Actors Cabaret Theater. August 19, 1977.
SHEILA, A WOMAN UNCOVERED (one-woman show) by Charles Swindell. September, 1977.

STYX BORDER (12). By David E. Rappoport. Director, Joseph Garren; lighting, Bruce J. Kraemer. With Deborah Dolnansky, Carol London, Vickie Usher, Nette Reynolds. **THE OPERATION** (12). By L.M. Vincent. Director, Donato Colucci; scenery, Robin Kantor. With Jack Ross, Mel Minter, Janet Bailey Rosenberg. October 2, 1977.

MAGIC AFTERNOON (12). By Wolfgang Bauer, translated by Herb Greer. October, 1977. Director Philip Gushee. With Jim Staskel, Joan Harris, Suzanne Love, Steven Pinsler.

GRAY SPADES (12). By William T. O'Neill. October 15, 1977. Director, Julie Cesari.

LOVE MATCH by Richard Hall. October, 1977.
POGEY BAIT by George Birimisa. November, 1977. Directed by Don Enoch.

AFTERMATH OF AN EAGLE by Alan L. Reed. November, 1977. Directed by Loren Liebling.

JOAN AND THE DEVIL (musical) book and lyrics by Seymour Reiter, music by Dick Hyman. February 25, 1978. Directed by Brandy Rabin.

NEW YORK CITY IS CLOSED (12). Written and directed by Walter Cotton. April, 1978.

FOR THE ONE I LOVE WITH REGRETS TO THOSE I LIED TO (12). Book and lyrics by Forbes J. Candlish; music by Richard O'Donnell. May 17, 1978. Director, Forbes J. Candlish and Steven Harris.

Time and Space, Ltd. Express theater in terms of form and process; to express the word and the idea as a priority via the actor. Linda Mussman, artistic director (and director of all productions).

THE MOMENT by Virginia Woolf, adapted by Linda Mussman. September 14, 1977. With Claudia Bruce, Ron Harrington.

THE BANDIT PRINCESS by Kikue Tashiro. January 18, 1978. With Robert Balderson, Maggie Brown, Claudia Bruce, Ron Harrington.

TRG Repertory Company. Theater revival group, presenting original and professional revivals of seldom-seen plays. Marvin Kahan, artistic director (and director of all productions).

LITTLE MURDERS by Jules Feiffer. November 18, 1977.

THE GINGERBREAD LADY by Neil Simon. March 8, 1978.

Urban Arts Corps. Dedicated to the development of theater arts and craft skills in the black community. Vinnette Carroll, artistic director.

12 performances each

THE INCARNATIONS OF REVEREND GOODE BLACQUE DRESSE. Written and directed by Garland Lee Thompson. April, 1978. Scenery, Jane Angus; costumes, Edna Watson; choreography, Rita Marquez.

SATURDAY NIGHT AT THE WAR. By John Patrick Shanley. April, 1978. Director, Charles Turner; lighting, Sandra Ross; costumes, Leslie Boyce.

ARCHIBALD & BASIL. Written and directed by Chip Keyes. May, 1978. Lighting, Jim Fauvell.

THE SEA AT DAUPHIN. By Derek Walcott. May, 1978. Director, Leon Morenzie; scenery, Jane Angus; lighting, Sandra Ross.

THE GINGHAM DOG by Lanford Wilson. December, 1977. Directed by Vinnette Carroll.

Walden Theater. Eclectic producing policy; in association with Walden School. Bruce Cornwell, producing director.

FASHION by Anna Cora Mowatt. October 21, 1977. Directed by Allen Schoer.

THE CHALK GARDEN by Enid Bagnold. March 1, 1978. Directed by Bruce Cornwell.

'TIS PITY SHE'S A WHORE by John Ford. April 5, 1978. Directed by Allen Schoer.

West Park Theater. Cooperative, accessible laboratory theater founded in 1975. Clark Kee, artistic director.

THE GREAT AMERICAN SINGING COMMERCIAL (12). By Clark Kee; music composed and directed by Alpha Walker. October 19, 1977. Director, Rachel Hockett; scenery, Harvey R. Denkin; lighting, Bruce A. Kraemer. With Mark Peters, Alaina Warren, Nancy T. Diaz, Daniel D. Kruger.

VOICES: I HAVE A WHITE HORSE and **A PORTRAIT OF TWO MEN DYING** (12). By

Martin Meyers. November 30, 1977. Director, Richard Kagey; lighting, Pam Coutilish. With Joan Maniscalco, Steve Spiegel, Robert Edward Bridges, Martin Treat.

THE YELLOW SOUND (12). By Vassily Kandinsky, translated by Clark Kee. January 18, 1978. Director, Harvey Denkin; scenery, Vicki Paul; lighting, Adam Gross; costumes, Debbie VanWetering; choreographer, Ariella Shapiro.

"... WHO?" ALAINA WARREN IN CONCERT (12). Concept and staging by William Rippner; material by Alaina Warren. February 16, 1978. Scenery, Cletus Johnson; lighting, Bruce A. Kraemer; costumes, Karen Magee.

LACKLAND (12). By Bill Bozzone. March 29, 1978. Director, Nancy Alexander; scenery, Gerard Bourcier; lighting, Margaret Giusto; costumes, Ann Sehrt. With Randall Forsythe, Adam LeFevre, Jack McClure, James Rebhorn, Richard W. Spore, Richard Vernon.

RITUAL (12). By Clark Kee. May 3, 1978. Directors, Clark Kee, Harvey Denkin; production design, Barry Shils. With Stephen de Pietri, Mark Peters, Sherrill Smith, Dana Evans, Rachel Hockett.

West Side Community Repertory Theater. Contemporary approaches to classical plays. Andres Castro, director (and director of all productions).

THE PLAYBOY OF THE WESTERN WORLD by John Millington Synge. June 16, 1977. With Thomas O'Mahoney, Ken Bush.
LADY WINDERMERE'S FAN by Oscar Wilde. September 30, 1977.
THE MILLIONAIRESS by George Bernard Shaw. February 17, 1978. With Jennifer Underwood, Samantha Louca.

WPA Theater. New plays and revivals of neglected works, all in the intimate, humanistic tradition; an ongoing experiment in American realism. R. Stuart White, Howard Ashman, artistic directors, Kyle Renick, managing director.

THE BALLAD OF THE SAD CAFE (16). Adapted by Edward Albee from Carson McCullers's novel. October 13, 1977. Director, R. Stuart White; scenery, Edward T. Gianfresco; lighting, Craig Evans; music, William Flanagan. With Alan Mixon, Kaiulani Lee, John E. Allen, Richard Alexander Millholland, Don Welch, Ron Welch.

GOREY STORIES (12). From works by Edward Gorey, adapted by Stephen Currens. December 8, 1977. Director, Tony Tanner; scenery Edward Gianfresco; lighting, Craig Evans; costumes, Clifford Capone; music, David Aldrich. With Liz Sheridan, Gemze de Lappe, Susan Marchand, Dennis McGovern, John Michalski, Leon Shaw, June Squibb.

IF YOU CAN'T SING, THEY'LL MAKE YOU DANCE (7). Written and directed by Phillip Hayes Dean. January 27, 1978. Scenery, Judie Juracek; lighting, Craig Evans; costumes, Judy Dearing. With Marge Eliot, Patricia O'Toole, Frank Adu.

THE DAY THE BLANCHARDVILLE, NORTH CAROLINA POLITICAL ACTION AND POKER CLUB GOT THE BOMB (12). By Nicholas Kazan. March 2, 1978. Director, Douglas Johnson; scenery, Vincent Ashbahian; lighting, Kathy Giebler; costumes, David Menkes. With Dann Florek, Bill Nunnery, Harry Orzello, Don Reeves, J.T. Walsh, Ilene Kristen, Rebecca Gilchrist.

EARLY DARK (16). By Reynolds Price. April 13, 1978. Director, R. Stuart White; scenery, Edward T. Gianfresco; lighting, Craig Evans; costumes, Marcia Cox; music, H. Ross Levy. With Corabel Alexander, Anne Gerety, James Remar, Estelle Evans, Rod Houts, Kathy McKenna, J.R. Horne.

The York Players. Each season, five productions of classics are mounted with professional casts; concerned with bringing classics to neighborhood residents. Janet Hayes Walker, artistic director.

BON VOYAGE (12). Book and lyrics by Edward Mabley; from *Le Voyage de Monsieur Perrichon* by Eugene Labiche and Eduard Martin; music by Jacques Offenbach; adapted by Vera Brodsky Lawrence. November 18, 1977 (world premiere). Director, Edward Mabley; scenery, James Morgan; lighting, Charles F. Morgan, Jesse Ira Berger; costumes, Judy Gillespie. With John Newton, Janet Hayes, Kathleen McKearney, Harry Danner, Michael D. Wickenheiser.

JOHN BROWN'S BODY by Stephen Vincent Benet. October 14, 1977. Directed by Janet Hayes Walker; with Celeste Holm, Wesley Addy, James Pritchett.
EXILES by James Joyce. March 3, 1978. Directed by Vincent Dowling; with Helen Breed, Susan Stevens, Owen Sullivan, Ken Costigan, Christopher Smith, Drina Rigan.
GALLOWS HUMOR by Jack Richardson. April 7, 1978. Directed by Stuart Howard; with John Newton, Barbara Gaines, Jim Jansen, Ron McLarty, Mary Carter.
CYRANO DE BERGERAC by Edmond Rostand. May 12, 1978. Directed by Janet Hayes Walker; with John Newton, Viveca Parker, Gary Poe, Charles Berendt, Douglas Barden, Kale Brown.

Miscellaneous

In the additional listing of 1977-78 off-off-Broadway productions below, the names of the producing groups or theaters appear in CAPITAL LETTERS and the titles of the works in *italics*. This list consists largely of new or reconstituted works and excludes most revivals, especially of classics. It includes a few productions staged by groups which rented space from the more established organizations listed previously.

A BUNCH OF EXPERIMENTAL THEATERS: THE BUNCH FESTIVAL '77. Schedule included: *Preface* by Joseph Dunn and Irja Koljonen, with American Contemporary Theater; *Fearful Symmetry* by Ken Jacobs, with Apparition Theater of New York; *Never Waste a Virgin* conceived and directed by Andrea Balis in collaboration with Elizabeth Levy; *The Initiate* (theaterdance work) by and with Joan Evans; *Catskill Dervish,* directed by Ric Zank, with Iowa Theater Lab; *The Shaggy Dog Animation* with Mabou Mines; *A Celebration of Winter Solstice* with Manhattan Project; *Blvd. de Paris* with Ontological Hysteric Theater; *Oedipus* and *Rumstick Road* with The Performance Group; *Punch and Judy* and *The Ventriloquist's Wife* with Ridiculous Theatrical Company; *People and Places: Stuart Sherman Spectacles; Pig, Child, Fire!* with Squat. November 24-December 19, 1977.

ACTORS AND DIRECTORS LAB. *May I Have the Pleasure of This Dance* (one-man show) by Robert Lloyd. May, 1978.

ACTORS' CONSORT. *Alchemy da Vinci* by Louis Phillips. August, 1977. *Izshe Izzy or Izhe Ain'tze or Iz They Both?* by Lonnie Carter. September, 1977. *Push the Button* by Robert Nason. September, 1977. *The Square Roots of Toby Handman* (one-woman show). September, 1977.

ACTORS GROUP THEATER. *Dance of Departure* and *Woman . . . Alive* by James Jennings. September, 1977. *Going Home* by James Jennings. December, 1977. *Chart Busters* and *How to Cope* by Bruce Serlen. February 1, 1978. Directed by James Jennings.

ACTORS' PLAYHOUSE. *Journey to Eldorado* by Robert Minford. February 21, 1978.

AFRO-AMERICAN TOTAL THEATER. *Karma* (musical) book and lyrics by John Scott, music by Stan Cowell. December 8, 1977. Directed by Elaine Head. *The Estate* by Ray Aranha. January, 1978. Directed by Duane Jones.

AMDA. *A Sound of Silence* by Harold Willis. September 23, 1977. Directed by Carol Kastendieck. *A Day's Grace* by John Fazakerley. February, 1978. Directed by Warren Robertson. *Enemy* by Robin Maugham. April 19, 1978. Directed by Michael Diamond; with Richard Abernathy, Kenneth Gray, Hugo Napier. *The Conversion* by David Ives. May, 1978. Directed by Lynn M. Thompson.

AMERICAN CONTEMPORARY THEATER. *Preface* by Joseph Dunn and Irja Koljonen. March 3, 1978.

AMERICAN RENAISSANCE THEATER. *Women in Concert: Ethel Smith.* September, 1977. *The Poetry of Gene Conlon.* September 20, 1977. Directed by Robert Elston. *Women in Concert: Elizabeth Perry.* October, 1977. *An Act of Kindness* by Joseph Julian. April 27, 1978. Directed by Robert Elston; with Scotty Bloch, Tony Call.

AMERICAN THEATER ALLIANCE. *Baal* by Bertolt Brecht, translated by William E. Smith and Ralph Manheim. February 22, 1978. Directed by Aaron Levin.

AMERICAN WRITERS THEATER FOUNDATION. *Nonsense* (poetry) by Lewis Carroll, adapted by Marilyn Esper, conceived and directed by Thomas Fontana. August, 1977. *Commonplays: True Love (Will Never Die)* and *Last Days of the Dixie Girl Cafe* by Robin Swicord. April 27, 1978. Directed by Lynn M. Thomson.

ARTURO'S. *Comings and Goings* by Megan Terry. September, 1977. Directed by Tom Waites. *Harold Arlen: Harlem, Hollywood and Broadway* (revue). February, 1978.

ASTOR PLACE THEATER. *Love, Love, Love!* (musical revue) by Johnny Brandon. June, 1977. Directed by Buck Heller; with Michael Calkins, Mel Johnson Jr., Pat Lundy, Neva Rae Powers, Glory Van Scott.

BACKSTREET EMPORIUM COMPANY. *The Cat's Pajamas* by Ralph Carideo. December 1, 1977. Directed by Bob Kazmayer.

BEALS'S THEATER IN THE LOFT. *Stings* based on Sylvia Plath's works, created and directed by Margaret Beals and Lee Nagrin. March, 1978.

BELGRAVE STUDIO. *About Midnight* by Ernestine Cook. November, 1977. Directed by Cynthia Belgrave.

BIJOU THEATER. *A Condition of Shadow* (one-man show) by and with Jerry Rockwood. November, 1977.

BILLIE HOLIDAY THEATER. *Young, Gifted and Broke* (musical) by Weldon Irvine. June, 1977. Directed by Marjorie Moon.

BMT. *This House* by Barbara de La Cuesta. March, 1978. Directed by Ellis Santone.

BREAD AND PUPPET THEATER. *Masaniello.* September 6, 1977.

THE BROOK. *My Imaginary Lover* (musical) by Constance Brooks. July 14, 1977. *Yangsville* by Lisa Lehman and Charles T. Kivette. October 28, 1977. *I Celebrate the Woman* (one-woman show) by and with Nina Miller. *On the Plains and in the Jungle* (solo piece) by Lanny Harrison, music by Frank Ferrucci. March, 1978.

BROWN SHOE GUILD THEATER. *Between the Ax* and *Vigil* by Michael Macharet. April 27, 1978. Directed by Kevin Marshall.

CENTURY THEATER. *Patio/Porch* (two plays) by Jack Heifner. April 13, 1978. Directed by Garland Wright; with Fannie Flagg, Ronnie Claire Edwards.

CHRIST METHODIST CHURCH. *Fisticuffs at Snitchfrog Manor* written and directed by Larry O'Connel. December 16, 1977.

CITHAERON. *The Hungerers* by William Saroyan, *Halloween* by Leonard Melfi and *Orange and Red on Red* by Bruce Serlen. November 2, 1977. Directed by Ellis Santone and Anthony Watts. *Judith — A Ballad* adapted and directed by Steven Brant. January, 1978. *Eyn-Sof* (one-woman show) by Caralyn Shapiro and Deborah Nitzberg. January, 1978. With Deborah Nitzberg.

CLINTON EXPERIMENTAL THEATER. *Mohawk* by Donald Kvares and *Mongols* by Robert Heide. June 1, 1977. Directed by James Jennings. *No Honey, or One More Life Saved* written and directed by Nicholas B. Daddazio and *Sins of the Father* by Gerry Holland. July, 1977. Directed by Dale DeGroff.

COLONNADES THEATER LAB SPACE. *Zinnia* by Emily Frankel. November, 1977. Directed by John Cullum; with Carol Mayo Jenkins, Emily Frankel.

CORNER LOFT THEATER. *A Fine Summer Night* written and directed by Michael Shurtleff. December 27, 1977. With Hugo Napier, Anne Gerety, Suzannah Knight, James Congdon.

CREATIVE TIME. *Butler's Lives of the Saints.* December, 1977. Directed by Ann Wilson.

THE CUBICULO SPACE. *On Reflection, Maybe* conceived by Jane Stein, written and directed by Peter Lobdell, music by William Schimmel. April 13, 1978. *Reunion* (musical) book and lyrics by Melvin H. Freedman and Robert Kornfeld, music by Ron Roullier, additional songs by Carly and Lucy Simon. May 12, 1978. Directed by Jeffery K. Neill.

DOUBLE IMAGE THEATER. *Insufficient Evidence* by Eliezer Lipsky. February 17, 1978. Directed by Helen W. Mayer.

DRAMATIC WORKSHOP. *The Sleep Walkers* written and directed by Charlotte Durham. August 19, 1977. *Close One Eye* by Dulce Mann. October 28, 1977. Directed by Joe Donovan. *Defy Surrender!* (three plays) by Charles Ruhl and Targenou. December, 1977. Directed by Ron Wentz. *Help Wanted* by Betzie Parker White. May 12, 1978. Directed by Helen Scourby; with John J.J. Clark, Carolyn Geer, Evie Juster, David Sigel.

EDEN'S EXPRESSWAY. *A Girl Starts Out . . .* texts by George Eliot and Andrea Dworkin, conceived and directed by Eleanor Johnson, Judah Kataloni and Michele Manenti. April 14, 1978. With Michele Manenti.

18TH STREET PLAYHOUSE. *Reuben Rein* by Sookie Stambler. September 22, 1977. Directed by Joseph Ditrinco; with the Poker Flat Players. *Transit: The One A.M. Collection* and *Night of the Chocolate Bear* by Tony Mazzadra. December 7, 1977. *The Rabinowitz Gambit* by Rose Leiman Goldemberg. December 15, 1977. *Fool's Passage* by Randy Neale. March 8, 1978. With Brown Ledge Theater Company. *Mr. Mother* written and directed by Jose Alcarez. April 21, 1978. *Diet Theater* by Erik Brogger. May, 1978. Directed by Robert Engels.

FIRST AMENDMENT COMEDY TROUPE. *Comedy Faces of '78* (cabaret). January 26, 1978.

FOUNDATION THEATER. *Let's Talk about It Later* by Bonnie Kessler Clarin. June, 1977. *Only a Woman* (musical) by Morna Murphy and Ralph Martell. October, 1977. Directed by Morna Murphy.

FOURTH FRIDAY PLAYWRIGHTS. *The Dividing Line* by Sal Coppola and *The Vacation* by John Kneilings (readings). October 14, 1977.

FRANKLIN THOMAS LITTLE THEATER. *Shadows* by Gertrude Greenridge. June 10, 1977. Directed by Franklin Thomas. *Two in the Back, Swan Song* and *South of Atlanta.* October, 1977. Directed by Franklin Thomas and Charles McRae.

FREDERICK DOUGLASS CREATIVE ARTS CENTER. *Crucificado* by Edgar White. March 23, 1978. Directed by Basil Wallace; with Mimi Ayers, Sam Singleton, Edythe Jason, Morton Banks.

G.A.P. THEATER COMPANY. *Desperado* by Richard Vetere. April 30, 1978. Directed by James Furlong; with Nick Mariano, Steven Edwards, Roberto Monticello, Liza Vann, Stacie Linardakis.

GATHERING PLACE. *Room* by Sharon Dennis. April, 1978.

GLUCK SANDOR ENSEMBLE COMPANY. *White Swans* by Philip Lanza. May, 1978.

GOETHE HOUSE. *Merz* (one-man show) by Peter Froelich, writings of Kurt Schwitters. October 13, 1977.

GRAMERCY ARTS THEATER. *The Passionate Men* by Keith Winter and Hattie May Pavlov. September 29, 1978. Directed by Edward Townley.

GREENWICH MEWS THEATER. *Come on Strong* by Garson Kanin. November, 1977. Directed by David Graubert.

HARLEM PERFORMANCE CENTER. *Gods at War* by Frank W. James. May 18, 1978.

HARTLEY HOUSE. *Monsieur de Pourceaugnac* by Molière. March, 1978. Directed by Jerry Heymann.

HIGH STAR PLAYHOUSE. *Future Memories* (one-act play) by Christopher Cross. March 16, 1978.

HENRY STREET SETTLEMENT HOUSE. *Choices* by Sidney Grimsley. June, 1977. Directed by Nancy Gabor. *The Phantom Tollbooth* adapted by Susan Nanus from Norton Juster's work. November 19, 1977. Directed by Susan Einhorn. *About Iris Berman* by Arnold Rabin. December 2, 1977. Directed by Stanley Brechner. *Be My Valentine* written and directed by Karl Friedman. February 11, 1978. *Onury* by Shauneille Perry. March 11, 1978. Directed by Irving Vincent. *In the Beginning* by Aharon Megged. March 17, 1978. Directed by Stanley Brechner; with Carol Case. *Sammy and Cleo* (musical) book by Robert S. Reiser, music by Margaret Pine, lyrics by Steve Brown. April 13, 1978. Directed by Andrea Balis. *Umschlagplatz: A Place of Transfer* (staged reading) works by Marek Edelman. April 19, 1978. Latino Playwrights Reading Series: *One Lousy Sunday* by Osvaldo Dragun. April 3, 1978. *Desecration* by Ray Flores. April 24, 1978. *Looking for Tomorrow* by Ringo Reyes. May 22, 1978. Directed by Marvin Camillo.

HOTEL SUTTON EAST. *Be Who You Are* (musical revue). March 17, 1978. With Kersten Anderson, Kathleen Cullen, Maureen Hopkins.

HUNTER PLAYWRIGHTS. *Angel Face* by Susan Horowitz. February 1, 1978. Directed by Susan Schulman; with Martha Schlamme, Court Miller. *Movie of the Month* and *I.C.U.* by Daniel Meltzer. May 12, 1978. Directed by Marc Gass; with Thomas Barbour, David Brand, Richard Portnow, Jay Thomas, Audrie Zerul.

THE KITCHEN. *Modern Love* and *The Lucy Amarillo Stories* by Constance De Jong, music by Phil Glass. October 21, 1977.

KUKU RYKU THEATER LAB. *Mr. Cripple Kicks the Bucket* by Constance Wilkinson and *Watchmaker* by Allan Havis. November, 1977. *Sacco and Vanzetti Meet Julius and Ethel Rosenberg* by C.E. Wilkinson. February 7, 1978. Directed by William Finley.

LONE STAR CAFE. *Prairie Passion* by Bob Jewett and Stephen Zuckerman, music by Chenango. July, 1977.

MANHATTAN LAMBDA PRODUCTIONS. *Gay Lunacy.* June 3, 1977. Directed by Edmund W. Trust.

MEDUSA'S REVENGE. *Bayou* by A.M. Simo. September, 1977.

MODERN TIMES THEATER. *Tell Me a Riddle* by Tillie Olsen, adapted and directed by Denny Partridge. February, 1978. With Steve Friedman, Linda Donald, Jackie Stern, Joan Rosenfels, Gerard Mercurio.

MORGAN'S OLD N.Y. TAVERN. *See-Saw-Sea* (musical) by T.P. McCann and Lionel Kilberg. November, 1977.

MUSIC-THEATER PERFORMING GROUP OF THE LENOX ARTS CENTER. *The Tennis Game* by George W.S. Trow. February 1, 1978. Directed by Timothy Mayer; with Leora Dana, Linda Atkinson, Linda Hunt, Donald Symington, Jon Huberth. *Twelve Dreams* conceived and directed by James Lapine. March 8, 1978. *The American Imagination* by Stanley Silverman and Richard Foreman. April 30, 1978.

NATIONAL BLACK THEATER. *Women in the Wilderness* (one-act play) by Alice Childress and *Seven Comes Up-Seven Comes Down* (one-act play) by Lonne Elder III.

NETTLE CREEK PLAYERS. *For the Snark Was a Boojum, You See* (musical revue) by Jeff Duteill and Stan Smith. August 20, 1977.

NEW HERITAGE REPERTORY THEATER. *Man-Wo-Man: Michael* by Ed Bullins, directed by Pat Golden; *Passion Without Reason* by Neil Harris, directed by Ernestine Johnson. May, 1978.

NEW LIBERTY VAUDEVILLE. *Fathertime Waltz* by Karen Abarbanel. October 14, 1977.

N.Y. MIME DRAMA COMPANY. *The Last Romance of Miss Cheese* (mime plays and dances) by Gabriel Oshen. June 7, 1977.

N.Y. PUBLIC LIBRARY. *Hotel for Brokenhearted Grandmothers* by Mildred Trencher and

Take the First Subway to Siberia by David Toll. October 26, 1977. Directed by Edward Rubin. *Stoop* by Stephen Holt. December 12, 1977. *Judy: a Garland of Songs.* December 19, 1977. Directed by Jeffery K. Neill. *Visitation* by Albert Evans and *Where Have All the Stars Gone?* by Henry Merz. April 3, 1978. *Mother of the Year* written and directed by Ed Rubin. April 10, 1978.

N.Y. STUDIO THEATER. *Cannibals* by Michael Warner. November, 1977.

OKC THEATER. *The Two Tigers* by Brian McNeill. November, 1977. *A Meaningful Relationship* by Don Flynn. April, 1978.

THE OPEN EYE SPACE. *Natures* by Richard Howard. June 1, 1977. Directed by Michael Feingold.

PERFORMANCES STAGED. *Striptease/A Brooklyn Fantasy* by Uzi Parnes. October 21, 1977.

PERFORMING GALLERY. *Annie and Arthur* by Michael Schulman. January, 1977.

PERFORMING GARAGE. *The Initiate* by and with Joan Evans, music by Matthew Greenbaum. November, 1977. *Stuart Sherman's Tenth Spectacle* and *3=1*. February 17, 1978. *TAUDshow* based on Antonin Artaud's work and life, devised and performed by Jerry Mayer. March, 1978. Directed by John Pynchon Holms. (Also performed at the Public Theater.) *The Folon Expedition* by Robert Dunn. April, 1978. Directed by Caroline Ducrocq. *An Evening of Faggot Theater* by Pink Satin Bombers. April 13, 1978. *Bleacher Bums* conceived by Joe Mantegna, created by Roberta Custer, Richard Fire, Dennis Franz, Jack Wallace, Josephine Paoletti, Carolyn Purdy-Gordon, Michael Saad, Keith Szarabajka, Ian Williams. April 19, 1978. Directed by Stuart Gordon; with the Organic Theater Company.

POTATO PLAYERS. *Sooner or Later* by George Naylor, directed by Sharon Carnicke; *Stars and Usherettes* by Doug Fallon, directed by Jim Harris (one-act plays). July, 1977.

THE PRIORY. *Putting Them to Pasture* by Vito Gentile Jr. March 10, 1978. *What's New?* (revue). March, 1978. Directed by Jason McAuliffe.

PRISM THEATER. *Saturday Adoption* by Ron Cowen. May 4, 1978. Directed by Tom Aberger; with Joseph Adams, Anthony Griffin, Kathy Wells, Randall Robbins, Michael Wiles.

PROCESS STUDIO. *Where Is the Genius Who Could Take My Place* (musical) by Gloria Broide, Robin Leroy Ellis, Elizabeth Meyers, Joseph F. Leonardo. July 7, 1977. Directed by Richard Simson. *The Haunting of Dowd's Landing* by Larry O'Connel, directed by Mickey Elias; *Cassandra and Aaron* by Abigail Quart, directed by John Camera. October 13, 1977.

PRODUCTION COMPANY. *Disgustingly Rich* (cabaret). December, 1977. Directed by Sheldon Epps. *Trial of the Moke* by Daniel Stein. January, 1978. *My Great Dead Sister* by Arthur Bicknell. April 20, 1978.

PRODUCTION UNIT. *Fences and Faded Love* by A.N. McCloskey. May 12, 1978. Directed by Susan McCosker.

RIVERSIDE THEATER WORKSHOP. *The Crocodile* by Luigia Miller, music by Franca Sparacio. March, 1978.

QUOG MUSIC THEATER. *Noah* (musical) written and directed by Eric Salzman and Michael Sahl. February 23, 1978.

RAFT THEATER. *The Enchanted Journey* adapted and directed by Anna Antaramian. January 19, 1978.

THE RED ROBINS PROJECT. *The Red Robins* by Kenneth Koch, based on his novel. January 17, 1978. Directed by Donald Sanders; with Kate Farrell, Lynn Bowman, Donald Sanders, Taylor Mead, Brian Glover.

ROYAL COURT REPERTORY. *World's First Country Western Women's Lib Musical Comedy* (musical) by Lu Ann Horstman. February, 1978. Directed by Phyllis Craig. *Auditions for the Last Roundup* by James Crafford. May 29, 1978. Directed by Phyllis Craig.

ROYAL PLAYHOUSE. *The Laundry* by David Guerdon, adapted by Howard Richardson. April, 1978. Directed by Steve Chernak.

R.P.M. PLAYERS. *Rainbows for Sale* by John Ford Noonan, directed by Ronald Maccone; *Concerning the Effects of Trimethylchloride* by John Ford Noonan, directed by Ray Fitzgerald. May 4, 1978.

ST. CLEMENT'S SPACE. *Throne of Straw* by Harold Lieberman. November 12, 1977. Directed by Peter Micka. *Simon Says* by John Stimson. November, 1977. Directed by Barbara Messing. *Final Twist* by Bob Barry. February 2, 1978. With Peter Galman, Don Howard, Jack LoGiudice, Thomas MacGreevy, Holland Taylor. *Travellers* by Ilsa Gilbert, music by Jim Green. May 8, 1978. Directed by Maurice Edwards. *Rosa* by William Archibald, music by Baldwin Bergersen. May 10, 1978.

S.A.M. REPERTORY. *Killing "The Murder Game", Out With the Crowd* and *The Way Out* (one-act plays) by Ronald N. Galluccio. July, 1977. Directed by Robert S. Pace.

SHANDOL COMPANY. *Ah! That Widow* adapted by Jerry Edwards. June, 1977. Directed by Ted Tiller. *The Bridge at Belharbour* by Janet Neipris. February, 1978. Directed by Frank Girardeau.

SHINBONE ALLEY THEATER. *Our Lady of Shinbone Alley* by Bill Bly. May, 1978.

SIDEWALKS OF N.Y. *The Sins of Scaramouche* (improvisation). April, 1978. Directed by Gary Beck.

SOHO BOOKS. *Sandra and the Janitor* by William Packard. November, 1977. Directed by Michael Herring. *The Ectasy of St. Zero, Retold* written and directed by Matthew Causey; *Lady in Sanger's Woods* by Charles Frederick, directed by Rachel Barr. December, 1977.

SQUAT. *Pig, Child, Fire!* written, directed and performed by Squat Theater. November, 1977.

STAGE DOOR PRODUCTIONS. *Simon Says* by John Stimson. October, 1977.

STAGE MAXIMUS. *A Barbershop in Pittsburgh* by Jasper Oddo. June 10, 1977. Directed by Gary Robertson. With Frank Cardo, Kevin Browne, Joan Conrad, Susan Oakey, Kevin Gilmartin.

STAGE 73. *Under the Gaslight* by Augustin Daly. June 28, 1977. Directed by Michael Bavar; with Peter Siiteri, Christine Kelly, Marianne Burke, Eric Hoffman. *A Son Come Home* by Ed Bullins; *On Being Hit* by Clay Goss; *Getting It Together* by Richard Wesley (one-act plays). July, 1977. Directed by George Lee Miles. *Sepia Star* (musical) by Ed Bullins and Mildred Kayden. August 11, 1977. *Second Wind* written and directed by Terry Gregory. October 26, 1977. *King of the Castle* by Eugene McCabe. February 9, 1978. Directed by John Tallman Bissell; with Michael M. Ryan, Terrence O'Hara, Molly Scoville, W.B. Brydon.

STAGELIGHTS THEATER. *About Time!: Manhattan Transference* by William Tucker, directed by Calvin Holt; *The Guys in the Truck* by Howard Reifsnyder, directed by Amielle Zemach; *The Blackpool Thing* and *The Interview* by John Patrick Hart, directed by R.B. Naar. January 20-29, 1978. *The Straight Man* by Paul Sambo and *At Crazy Jane's* by Steven Otfinoski. March 24, 1978. Directed by Michael Lange.

STEINWAY ST. PRODUCTIONS. *Rhythms in Light Blue* written and directed by Joe Sharkey. September 15, 1977. With John Del Regno, Erika Fox.

STONEWALL THEATER. *A Crime* (musical) book and lyrics by Stewart H. Benedict, music by Linder Chlarson. June, 1977. Directed by William Eff.

STOREFRONT STUDIO THEATER. *The Ashes of Mrs. Reasoner* by Enid Rudd. September, 1977. Directed by Joan Udell.

STUART SHERMAN'S NINTH SPECTACLE. October 14, 1977.

STUDIO 13. *Toy Room* by Bob Angelica. February 26, 1978. Directed by Kevin Marshall; with Lorraine Barrett, Alan Safier.

STUDIO 407. *4 Thunder of Silence* written and directed by Frank Oates. March, 1978.

TEN TEN PLAYERS. *Shadow of My Fathers* by Scot Paxton. March 31, 1978.

THEATER LAB OF N.Y. *Us and Them* by Tony Schwab. April, 1978.

THEATER MATRIX. *Cannibals* written and directed by Michael Warner. October, 1977. *The Story of an Hour* by Kate Chopin, adapted by The Actress Company. May 18, 1978.

THEATER THREE. *Toys in the Attic* by Lillian Hellman. May, 1978.

THREE MUSES. *One Summer* (musical) by Philip M. Smith. November, 1977. Directed by Edwin Norman Illiano. *The Eternal Circle* by Nomi Rubel. February, 1978. Directed by Dennis Thread. *The Reception* by L.M. Vincent. May 23, 1978.

TITLE THEATER. *More Than a Boy's Game* by Dan Lauria. June 1, 1977. Directed by Kevin W. Dowling. *Poker Ltd.* by Tsipi Keller. September 15, 1977. Directed by Martin Zurla. *Stripes* by Bill Simmer. January, 1978. Directed by Maria Mitchell Owen.

T.O.M.I. *Light Sings* (musical) conceived and directed by Keith Levenson, music by Gary William Friedman. March 3, 1978.

TOP OF THE GATE. *The Alice B. Toklas Hashish Fudge Revue* by William Russo. January, 1978.

TOSOS. *The West Street Gang* written and directed by Doric Wilson. June 5, 1977.

TOUSSAINT GROUP. *Cages* written and directed by Gordon Watkins. March 2, 1978.

TRINITY PLAYERS. *Richelieu* by Edward Bulwer-Lytton. February 9, 1978. Directed by Tom Borasy. *Evening of One-Acts* including *Shenanigans* by James A. Barone, directed by Steve Zimmer; *Why I'm a Bachelor* by Conrad Seiler, directed by Michael McConkey. April 14, 1978.

THE TROLLEY COMPANY. *The Nut Farm* by John C. Brownell. June 15, 1977. Directed by Mark J. Roth.

THE TROUPE. *The Bitch* written and directed by Andy Milligan. October 7, 1977. *World War Zero* written and directed by Joe Renard; *Black Mirror* by Jackie Skarvellis, directed by Andy Milligan. December 2, 1977. *The Comeback* by Jack Gilhooley, directed by Tom Everett; *American Hamburger* by Robert Heide. February 1, 1978. *Dracula, a Modern Fable* by Norman Beim. February 3, 1978. Directed by Andy Milligan. *No Time for Sorrow* by James Jennings; *The Sailor and the Siren* by Daniel Haben Clark. February, 1978. Directed by Andy Milligan. *Smoking Pistols* and *Mohawk Point* by Donald Kvares. February, 1978. Directed by Dan Devere Handley. *It Looks Like a Lovely Day* by Antoinette Kray. February 27, 1978. *Moods: Lanterns* and *Silences* (one-act plays) by Tanden Peyton. March 27, 1978. Directed by Andy Milligan. *Woman to Woman* (three plays) by Michael Shurtleff. March, 1978. Directed by Richard Futch, Anthony Giamo, Susan Rosenstock; with Cheri Couture, Elizabeth Page, Shellen Lubin, Jacqueline Kroschell. *Lover's Choice Tonight* written and directed by Ron Maker. April, 1978. *A Queen's Revenge* (one-act plays) by Norman Beim. April, 1978. *The Bagman* and *A Woman and Her Dog* by Peter Schmideg. April 17, 1978. Directed by Dan Devere Handley. *The Peony Lantern* by Don Ferguson. May, 1978. *Chalk It Up* (one-act plays) written and directed by Daniel Haben Clark. May 8, 1978. *Locusts* written and directed by Ed Evans. May, 1978.

TRUCK & WAREHOUSE THEATER. *Jabberwock.* June 9, 1977. Directed by Matt Chait; with Gabriel Barre, Michael Lynch, Priscilla Manning, Richard Pierce. *Gay?* by Hot Peaches. September 13, 1978. *The T.V. Show* by Hot Peaches, book and lyrics by Ian McKay, music by Jan Robijns. March 23, 1978. Directed by Ian McKay. *Electric Spaghetti* (festival). April 21-May 13, 1978.

2 PERCENT REPERTORY THEATER. *Bombs Away* written and directed by Lou Alphonse Poppe. January 11, 1978.

WARD NASSE GALLERY. *Pickers* by Richard Taylor, directed by Virginia Barrie; *The Last Rose of Summer* written and directed by Wayne Mahler. December 1, 1977. *Womansong* (revue). May 5, 1978. Directed by Vincent Napoli.

WASHINGTON SQUARE METHODIST CHURCH. *Cenci/Bardo* by Antonin Artaud, adapted from S.W. Taylor's translation and directed by Peter Rose. September, 1977.

WESTBETH THEATER CENTER. *War and Peace of Common Folk* written and directed by Soon-Teck Oh. June, 1977. *Der Apfel* and *Mrs. Carson's Palm and Tarot Class* (one-act plays) written and directed by Edgar Grana. June 26, 1978. *Essential Shepard: Icarus's Mother, Cowboy Mouth* (co-written by Patti Smith), *Hawk Moon #1* by Sam Shepard. July, 1977. Directed by Ian McColl and Bill Hoffman. *10 Sideway Walkers* by Tom Brockland and Bent Hagestad. January, 1978. Directed by Tom Brockland. *The Phil Stein Show.* February 2, 1978. With Phil Stein. *R* by C.V. Peters. February 16, 1978. Directed by David McKenna. *The Abyssinia Projections* by Odd Vark. March 2, 1978. *A History of Modern Florida* by Ronald Tavel. April, 1978. Directed by Harvey Tavel. *Funeral March for a One-Man Band* by Ron Whyte. May, 1978. Directed by Leonard Peters; with Ellen Barber, Dwight Schultz, Rob DeRosa, June Squibb, Thomas Toner, Dennis Boutsikaris.

WHITE MASK THEATER. *Springtime for Mahler* written and directed by Donald Kvares. October 14, 1977. *Si Kabayan* (one-act play) by Utay Sontani. May 3, 1978.

WONDERHORSE THEATER. *Scenes from an Almost Socialist Marriage* developed and performed by Susan Cooper and Chris Kraus. March, 1978.

CAST REPLACEMENTS AND
TOURING COMPANIES

Compiled by Stanley Green

The following is a list of the more important cast replacements in productions which opened in previous years, but were still playing in New York during a substantial part of the 1977-78 season; or were still on a first-class tour in 1977-78; or opened in New York in 1977-78 and went on tour during the season (casts of first-class touring companies of previous seasons which were no longer playing in 1977-78 appear in previous *Best Plays* volumes of appropriate years).

The name of each major role is listed in *italics* beneath the title of the play in the first column. In the second column directly opposite appears the name of the actor who created the role in the original New York production (whose opening date appears in *italics* at the top of the column). Indented immediately beneath the original actor's name are the names of subsequent New York replacements, together with the date of replacement when available.

The third column gives information about first-class touring companies, including London companies (produced under the auspices of their original New York managements). When there is more than one roadshow company, #1, #2, etc., appear before the name of the performer who created the role in each company (and the city and date of each company's first performance appears in *italics* at the top of the column). Their subsequent replacements are also listed beneath their names, with dates when available.

A note on split-week touring companies appears at the end of this section.

ANNIE

	New York 4/21/77	*#1 Toronto 3/23/78* *#2 London 5/3/78*
Oliver Warbucks	Reid Shelton Keene Curtis 2/6/78 Reid Shelton 2/27/78	#1 Norwood Smith #2 Stratford Johns
Annie	Andrea McArdle Shelley Bruce 3/7/78	#1 Kathy-Joe Kelly #2 Andrea McArdle
Miss Hannigan	Dorothy Loudon	#1 Grace Connell #2 Sheila Hancock
Grace Farrell	Sandy Faison	#1 Kathryn Boulé #2 Judith Paris
FDR	Raymond Thorne	#1 Sam Stoneburner #2 Damon Sanders
Rooster Hannigan	Robert Fitch	#1 Gary Beach #2 Kenneth Nelson
Lily	Barbara Erwin	#1 Lisa Raggio #2 Clovissa Newcombe

ASHES

New York 1/25/77

Colin	Brian Murray Joel Fabiani 6/8/77
Anne	Roberta Maxwell Dianne Wiest 6/8/77
Man	John Tillinger Gavin Reed 6/8/77
Woman	Penelope Allen Veronica Castang

BUBBLING BROWN SUGAR

New York 3/2/76 — #1 Chicago 6/22/76 — #2 London 9/28/77

	New York 3/2/76	*#1 Chicago 6/22/76* / *#2 London 9/28/77*
John Sage; Rusty	Avon Long Charles "Honi" Coles 6/20/77 Avon Long 7/4/77	#1 Vernon Washington Charles "Honi" Coles 8/77 #2 Billy Daniels
Irene Paige	Josephine Premice	#1 Mable Lee Marilyn Johnson 8/77 #2 Elaine Delmar
Checkers; Dusty	Joseph Attles Jay Flash Riley 6/20/77 Joseph Attles 7/4/77	#1 Jay Flash Riley #2 Lon Satton
Marsha; Young Irene	Vivian Reed Ursuline Kairson 2/15/77	#1 Ursuline Kairson Vivian Reed 2/15/77 Bettye Lavette 8/77 #2 Helen Gelzer
Bill; Time Man	Vernon Washington David Bryant 6/22/76 Stanley Ramsey	#1 Charles "Honi" Coles Ronald "Smokey" Stevens 8/77 #2 Charles Augins

CALIFORNIA SUITE

	New York 6/10/76	*#1 Palm Beach 3/7/77* / *#2 Baltimore 11/7/77*
Hannah; Diana; Gert	Tammy Grimes Rue McClanahan 4/4/77 Tammy Grimes 4/11/77	#1 Penny Fuller #2 Elizabeth Allen
William; Sidney; Stu	George Grizzard Kenneth Haigh 2/28/77 David McCallum 5/2/77	#1 David McCallum #2 Robert Reed
Millie; Beth	Barbara Barrie Marge Redmond 1/17/77	#1 Rosemary Prinz #2 Patti Karr
Marvin; Mort	Jack Weston Joseph Leon 5/77 Vincent Gardenia 6/13/77	#1 Vincent Gardenia #2 Warren Berlinger

CHICAGO

	New York 6/3/75	St. Louis 8/29/77
Roxie Hart	Gwen Verdon Lenora Nemetz 7/30/75 Liza Minnelli 8/8/75 Gwen Verdon 9/15/75 Ann Reinking 2/7/77	Penny Worth Gwen Verdon 4/4/78
Velma Kelly	Chita Rivera Lenora Nemetz 7/28/76	Carolyn Kirsch Chita Rivera 4/4/78
Billy Flynn	Jerry Orbach	Jerry Orbach
Matron	Mary McCarthy Alaina Reed 1/10/77 Georgia Creighton 7/77	Edye Byrde
Amos Hart	Barney Martin Rex Everhart 2/20/76 Barney Martin 3/1/76 Rex Everhart 9/76 Richard Korthaze 8/77	Haskell Gordon
Annie	Michon Peacock Joan Bell 5/10/76	Susan Streater
Go-to-Hell Kitty	Charlene Ryan Fern Fitzgerald 3/76 Gena Ramsel	Karen Tamburrelli
Mona	Pamela Sousa Debra Lyman 12/76	Clara Leach
Mary Sunshine	M. O'Haughey	M. O'Haughey

A CHORUS LINE

	N.Y. Off-Bway 4/15/75 N.Y. Bway 7/25/75	#1 Toronto 5/3/76 London 7/22/76 #2 San Francisco 5/11/76 #3 Baltimore 2/9/77
Kristine	Renee Baughman Cookie Vazquez 4/26/76 Deborah Geffner 10/76	#1 Christine Barker Vicki Spencer 2/77 #2 Renee Baughman Cookie Vazquez 10/76 #3 Christine Barker
Sheila	Carole Bishop (name changed to Kelly Bishop 3/76) Kathrynann Wright 8/76	#1 Jane Summerhays Geraldine Gardner 2/77 #2 Charlene Ryan Fern Fitzgerald #3 Jane Summerhays
Val	Pamela Blair Barbara Monte-Britton 4/26/76 Karen Jablons 10/76 Mitzi Hamilton 3/1/77	#1 Mitzi Hamilton Linda Williams 2/77 #2 Pamela Blair Mitzi Hamilton 12/77

Karen Jablons 12/77
Mitzi Hamilton 3/78

#3 Mitzi Hamilton
   Karen Jablons 3/1/77
   Pamela Blair 11/77

Mike

Wayne Cilento
Jim Litten 6/77

#1 Don Correia
   Jeff Hyslop 7/10/76
   Michael Howe 2/77
#2 Don Correia
#3 Jeff Hyslop
   Troy Garza

Larry

Clive Clerk
Jeff Weinberg 10/76
Clive Clerk 1/77
Adam Grammis 2/77
Paul Charles 12/77

#1 T. Michael Reed
   Jack Gunn 2/77
#2 Roy Smith
   Keith Keen
#3 T. Michael Reed
   John Fogarty

Maggie

Kay Cole
Lauree Berger 4/26/76
Donna Drake 2/77
Christina Saffran 3/78

#1 Jean Fraser
   Veronica Page 2/77
#2 Kay Cole
   Donna Drake 10/76
   Lisa Donaldson 2/77
#3 Betty Lynd

Richie

Ronald Dennis
Winston DeWitt Hemsley
   4/26/76
Edward Love 6/77
A. William Perkins 12/77

#1 A. William Perkins
   Roy Gayle 2/77
#2 Ronald Dennis
   Larry G. Bailey 1/78
#3 A. William Perkins
   Millard Hurley 12/77

Judy

Patricia Garland
Sandahl Bergman 4/26/76
Murphy Cross 12/77

#1 Yvette Mathews
   Judy Gridley 2/77
#2 Patricia Garland
   Victoria Tabaka
#3 Murphy Cross

Don

Ron Kuhlman
David Thomé 4/26/76

#1 Ronald Young
   Lance Aston 2/77
#2 Ron Kuhlman
   Dennis Edenfield 10/76
#3 Brandt Edwards
   Barry Thomas

Bebe

Nancy Lane
Gillian Scalici 4/26/76
René Ceballos 9/77
Karen Meister 1/78

#1 Miriam Welch
   Susan Claire 2/77
#2 Nancy Lane
   Trudy Bayne
#3 Miriam Welch

Connie

Baayork Lee
Lauren Kayahara 4/26/76
Janet Wong 2/77

#1 Jennifer Ann Lee
   Cherry Gillespie 2/77
#2 Baayork Lee
   Lauren Kayahara 2/77
   Sachi Shimizu
#3 Jennifer Ann Lee
   Cherylene Lee

Diana

Priscilla Lopez

#1 Loida Iglesias

Barbara Luna 4/26/76
Carole Schweid 5/7/76
Rebecca York 8/76
Loida Iglesias 12/76

Diane Langton 2/77
#2 Priscilla Lopez
Chris Bocchino 10/76
#3 Gina Paglia
Diane Fratantoni

Zach

Robert LuPone
Joe Bennett 4/26/76
Eivind Harum 10/76
Robert LuPone 1/31/77
Kurt Johnson 5/77
Clive Clerk 7/77
Kurt Johnson 8/77

#1 Eivind Harum
Jean-Pierre Cassel 10/76
#2 Robert LuPone
Joe Bennett 10/76
Anthony S. Teague
#3 Eivind Harum
Clive Clerk 8/77

Mark

Cameron Mason
Paul Charles 10/76
Timothy Scott 12/77

#1 Timothy Scott
Peter Barry 2/77
#2 Paul Charles
Jimmy Roddy 10/76
R. J. Peters
#3 Timothy Scott
Scott Geralds

Cassie

Donna McKechnie
Ann Reinking 4/26/76
Donna McKechnie 9/27/76
Ann Reinking 11/29/76
Pamela Sousa 1/77
Vicki Frederick 2/9/77
Pamela Sousa 11/14/77
Candace Tovar 1/78
Pamela Sousa 3/78

#1 Sandy Roveta
Petra Siniawski 2/77
#2 Donna McKechnie
Ann Reinking 9/27/76
Vicki Frederick 11/29/76
Pamela Peadon 2/9/77
Pamela Sousa 1/78
#3 Pamela Sousa
Deborah Henry 11/77

Al

Don Percassi
Bill Nabel 4/26/76
John Mineo 2/77
Ben Lokey 4/77
Don Percassi 7/77

#1 Steve Baumann
Jeffrey Shankley 2/77
#2 Don Percassi
Jack Karcher
#3 Steve Baumann
Donn Simione

Greg

Michel Stuart
Justin Ross 4/26/76

#1 Andy Keyser
Mark Dovey
Stephen Tate 2/77
#2 Michel Stuart
Andy Keyser 10/76
#3 Mark Dovey
Ronald Stafford

Bobby

Thomas J. Walsh
Christopher Chadman 6/77
Ron Kurowski 1/78

#1 Ron Kurowski
Leslie Meadows 2/77
#2 Scott Pearson
Michael Austin 4/77
#3 Ron Kurowski

Paul

Sammy Williams
George Pesaturo 4/26/76
René Clemente 2/78

#1 Tommy Aguilar
Michael Staniforth 2/77
#2 Sammy Williams
Tommy Aguilar
#3 Tommy Aguilar
René Clemente

DRACULA

	New York 10/20/77	*Baltimore 5/19/78*
Count Dracula	Frank Langella	Raul Julia
		Jean LeClerc 7/17/78

EQUUS

New York 10/24/74

Dr. Martin Dysart Anthony Hopkins
   Anthony Perkins 6/30/75
   Richard Burton 2/16/76
   Anthony Perkins 5/11/76
   Douglas Campbell 8/6/76
   Anthony Perkins 10/5/76
   Alec McCowen 2/15/77
   Anthony Perkins 3/15/77
   Leonard Nimoy 6/13/77

Note: For complete list of other casting in the New York and road companies, see *The Best Plays of 1976-77*.

THE FANTASTICKS

New York 5/3/60

El Gallo Jerry Orbach
   Gene Rupert
   Bert Convy
   John Cunningham
   Don Stewart 1/63
   David Cryer
   Keith Charles 10/63
   John Boni 1/13/65
   Jack Metter 9/14/65
   George Ogee
   Keith Charles
   Tom Urich 8/30/66
   John Boni 10/5/66
   Jack Crowder 6/13/67
   Nils Hedrick 9/19/67
   Keith Charles 10/9/67
   Robert Goss 11/7/67
   Joe Bellomo 3/11/68
   Michael Tartel 7/8/69
   Donald Billett 6/70
   Joe Bellomo 2/15/72
   David Rexroad 6/73
   David Snell 12/73
   Hal Robinson 4/2/74
   Chapman Roberts 7/30/74
   David Brummel 2/18/75
   David Rexroad 8/31/75
   Roger Brown 9/30/75
   David Rexroad 9/1/76
   Joseph Galiano 10/14/76
   Keith Charles 3/22/77
   Joseph Galiano 4/5/77

Raul Julia as Count Dracula in
Dracula

Douglas Clark 5/2/78
Joseph Galiano 5/23/78

Luisa Rita Gardner
 Carla Huston
 Liza Stuart 12/61
 Eileen Fulton
 Alice Cannon 9/62
 Royce Lenelle
 B. J. Ward 12/1/64
 Leta Anderson 7/13/65
 Carole Demas 11/22/66
 Leta Anderson 8/7/67
 Carole Demas 9/4/67
 Anne Kaye 5/28/68
 Carolyn Magnini 7/29/69
 Virginia Gregory 7/27/70
 Leta Anderson
 Marty Morris 3/7/72
 Sharon Werner 8/1/72
 Leilani Johnson 7/73
 Sharon Werner 12/73
 Sarah Rice 6/24/74
 Cheryl Horne 7/1/75
 Sarah Rice 7/29/75
 Betsy Joslyn 3/23/76

Matt Kenneth Nelson
 Gino Conforti
 Jack Blackton 10/63

Paul Giovanni
Ty McConnell
Richard Rothbard
Gary Krawford
Bob Spencer 9/5/64
Erik Howell 6/28/66
Gary Krawford 12/12/67
Steve Skiles 2/6/68
Craig Carnelia 1/69
Erik Howell 7/18/69
Samuel D. Ratcliffe 8/5/69
Michael Glenn-Smith
   5/26/70
Jimmy Dodge 9/20/70
Geoffrey Taylor 8/31/71
Erik Howell 3/14/72
Michael Glenn-Smith
   6/13/72
Phil Killian 7/4/72
Richard Lincoln 9/72
Bruce Cryer 7/24/73
Phil Killian 9/11/73
Michael Glenn-Smith
   6/17/74
Ralph Bruneau 10/29/74
Bruce Cryer 9/30/75
Jeff Knight 7/19/77

Note: As of May 31, 1978, 26 actors had played the role of El Gallo, 18 actresses had played Luisa, and 20 actors had played Matt.

FOR COLORED GIRLS WHO HAVE CONSIDERED SUICIDE/WHEN THE RAINBOW IS ENUF

	N.Y. Off Bway 5/17/76 *N.Y. Bway 9/15/76*	*Washington 10/13/77*
*Lady in Brown**	Janet League Roxanne Reese 3/8/77	Beverly Anne
Lady in Yellow	Aku Kadogo Leona Johnson	Jonette Kelley
Lady in Red	Trazana Beverley Saundra McClain	Latanya Richardson
Lady in Green	Paula Moss Jonette Kelley 2/15/77 Saundra McPherson 10/10/77	Brenda J. Davis
Lady in Purple	Risë Collins	Gloria Calomee
Lady in Blue	Laurie Carlos	Paula Larke
Lady in Orange	Ntozake Shangé Seret Scott 10/16/76 Sharita Hunt 4/5/77	Barbara Alston

*For tour, character known as *Lady in Pink*.

GEMINI

N.Y. Off Bway 3/13/77
N.Y. Bway 5/21/77

Fran Geminiani   Danny Aiello

Lucille Grande*   Anne DeSalvo
                         Stephanie Gordon 11/22/77
                         Anne DeSalvo 4/10/78

Francis Geminiani   Robert Picardo
                         Dennis Bailey 2/27/78

Marshall Lowenstein*   Jonathan Hadary

*Character names changed to Lucille Pompi and Herschel Weinberger for the Broadway engagement

GREASE

	New York 2/14/72	Millburn, N.J. 9/1/76
Danny Zuko	Barry Bostwick Jeff Conaway 6/73 John Lansing 11/74 Treat Williams 12/75 Lloyd Alann 6/14/76 Treat Williams Adrian Zmed Patrick Swayze	Adrian Zmed
Sandy Dumbrowski	Carole Demas Ilene Graff 3/73 Candice Earley 6/17/75 Robin Lamont Forbesy Russell Andrea Walters 11/77	Andrea Walters
Betty Rizzo	Adrienne Barbeau Elaine Petrikoff 3/73 Randee Heller 5/74 Karren Dille 12/1/75 Livia Genise Judy Kaye 5/10/77 Lorelle Brina	Lorelle Brina
Kenicke	Timothy Meyers John Fennessy Jerry Zaks Timothy Meyers Danny Jacobson Michael Tucci Matt Landers Danny Jacobson	Paul Regina Jr.
Vince Fontaine	Don Billett Gardner Hayes Jim Weston John Holly Walter Charles	Douglas Barden

	Jim Weston 1/76 Walter Charles Stephen M. Groff	
Marty	Katie Hanley Meg Bennett Denise Nettleton Marilu Henner Char Fontanne Diane Stilwell 8/76 Sandra Zeeman	Char Fontanne Sandra Zeeman

HAPPY END

	Brooklyn 3/8/77 *New York 5/7/77*
Lt. Lillian Holiday	Shirley Knight Meryl Streep 4/12/77 Janie Sell 6/27/77
Bill Cracker	Christopher Lloyd Bob Gunton Christopher Lloyd 5/7/77
Dr. Nakamura	Tony Azito Victor Pappas

I LOVE MY WIFE

	New York 4/17/77	*London 10/6/77*
Alvin	Lenny Baker James Brennan 2/27/78	Richard Beckinsale
Cleo	Ilene Graff	Deborah Fallender
Monica	Joanna Gleason Virginia Sandifur 5/1/78	Liz Robertson
Wally	James Naughton	Ben Cross

THE KING AND I

	New York 5/2/77
The King	Yul Brynner Michael Kermoyan 4/11/78 Yul Brynner 5/2/78
Anna Leonowens	Constance Towers Angela Lansbury 4/11/78 Constance Towers 5/2/78
The Kralahome	Michael Kermoyan Jae Woo Lee 4/11/78 Michael Kermoyan 5/2/78

Angela Lansbury as Anna with two of her Royal Siamese Children in *The King and I*

THE MAGIC SHOW

New York 5/28/74

Doug*   Doug Henning
                              Joe Abaldo 3/30/76
                              Doug Henning 7/21/76
                              Joe Abaldo 11/3/76

Cal   Dale Soules
                              Dara Norman 10/29/75
                              Dale Soules

Charmin   Anita Morris
                              Loni Ackerman 8/75
                              Louisa Flaningam 3/76
                              Natalie Mosco 9/12/77

Feldman   David Ogden Stiers
                              Kenneth Kimmins 12/29/74
                              Timothy Jerome 7/25/75
                              Stephen Vinovich 4/14/76
                              Rex Robbins 5/23/76
                              Kenneth Kimmins 10/27/76

*Name of character changed to Joe when Mr. Abaldo played role.

MAN OF LA MANCHA

	New York 9/15/77	*San Francisco 2/14/78*
Don Quixote	Richard Kiley	Richard Kiley
Aldonza	Emily Yancy	Emily Yancy
Sancho	Tony Martinez	Tony Martinez
Innkeeper	Bob Wright	Bob Wright

OTHERWISE ENGAGED

	New York 2/2/77
Simon	Tom Courtenay
	Dick Cavett 7/21/77
	Steven Sutherland 9/12/77
	(Wed. mats only)

PIPPIN

	New York 10/23/72	*Washington 8/3/77*
Pippin	John Rubinstein	Michael Rupert
Charles	Eric Berry	Eric Berry
Catherine	Jill Clayburgh	Alexandra Borrie
Fastrada	Leland Palmer	Carole Schweid
Berthe	Irene Ryan	Thelma Carpenter
Leading Player	Ben Vereen	Larry Riley

Note: For complete list of cast changes in New York, see *The Best Plays of 1976-77*.

SAME TIME, NEXT YEAR

	New York 3/13/75	*Toronto 12/1/75*
Doris	Ellen Burstyn	Joyce Van Patten
	Joyce Van Patten 10/20/75	Barbara Rush 8/3/76
	Loretta Swit 12/1/75	
	Sandy Dennis 6/21/76	
	Hope Lange 5/31/77	
	Betsy Palmer 10/24/77	
George	Charles Grodin	Conrad Janis
	Conrad Janis 10/20/75	Tom Troupe 8/3/76
	Ted Bessell 12/1/75	
	Don Murray 3/8/77	
	Monte Markham 1/3/78	

THE SHADOW BOX

	New York 3/31/77
Joe	Simon Oakland
	Clifton James 5/23/77

Brian   Laurence Luckinbill
                           Josef Sommer 8/77

Felicity   Geraldine Fitzgerald
                           Mary Carver 4/30/77

Beverly   Patricia Elliott
                           Gwyda Donhowe 8/77

SHENANDOAH

	New York 1/7/75	*Chicago 10/5/77*

Charlie Anderson	John Cullum
	  William Chapman 11/1/76
	  John Cullum 6/7/77
		John Cullum
		  John Raitt 10/25/77

Jenny	Penelope Milford
	  Maureen Silliman 9/8/75
	  Emily Bindiger 5/17/77
		Suzy Brabeau

Anne	Donna Theodore Leslie Denniston	Jana Schneider

James	Joel Higgins
	  Wayne Hudgins 2/76
	  Paul Myrvold 4/77
		Paul Myrvold

Jacob	Ted Agress Roger Berdahl 9/76	Dean Russell
Sam	Gordon Halliday	Gordon Halliday

Gabriel	Chip Ford
	  Brent Carter
	  David Vann 4/76
	  Donny Cooper 7/76
	  Tony Holmes 11/76
		Tony Holmes

Robert	Joseph Shapiro
	  Mark Perman
	  Steve Grober
		Steve Grober

SIDE BY SIDE BY SONDHEIM

	New York 4/18/77	*#1 Chicago 10/27/77* *#2 Hollywood 4/7/78*

	Millicent Martin
	  Nancy Dussault 9/19/77
		#1 Carol Swarbrick
		  Marina MacNeal
		  11/11/77
		  Carol Swarbrick 12/1/77
		#2 Millicent Martin

	David Kernan
	  Larry Kert 8/1/77
	  Jack Blackton 2/17/78
		#1 David Chaney
		  J. T. Cromwell 12/2/77
		  David Chaney 12/10/77
		#2 Larry Kert

Julie N. McKenzie
   Bonnie Schon 9/12/77

   Georgia Brown 10/17/77
   Carol Swarbrick 2/17/78

Ned Sherrin
   Hermione Gingold 10/17/77
   Burr Tillstrom 2/27/78

#1 Bonnie Schon
   Marina MacNeal
   12/2/77
   Bonnie Schon 12/15/77
#2 Barbara Heuman

#1 Cyril Ritchard
   Brenda Forbes 11/25/77
   Burr Tillstrom 12/4/77
#2 Hermione Gingold

SLY FOX

	New York 12/14/76	*San Diego 3/4/78*

Foxwell J. Sly	George C. Scott
	   Robert Preston 5/10/77
	   Vincent Gardenia 1/2/78
		Jackie Gleason

Mrs. Truckle	Trish Van Devere Beth Austin 5/10/77	Patty Dworkin
Jethro Crouch	Jack Gilford	Irwin Corey
Simon Able	Hector Elizondo Jeffrey Tambor 8/77	Cleavon Little
Miss Fancy	Gretchen Wyler	Marie Wallace
Abner Truckle	Bob Dishy James Gallery	Bob Levine
Lawyer Craven	John Heffernan	Edward Zang

VANITIES

		#1 Washington 10/21/76 *#2 Chicago 3/19/77* *#3 Detroit 4/20/77*
	New York 3/22/76	

Joanne	Kathy Bates
	   Sally Sockwell 12/76
		#1 Lucie Arnaz
		   Priscilla Lopez 1/4/77
		#2 Barbara Sharma
		   Kathy Bates 8/10/77
		   Nancy New 10/3/77
		   Bennye Gettyes 12/7/77
		   Joyce Bulifant 1/22/78
		#3 Joyce Bulifant

Kathy	Jane Galloway
	   Cordis Heard 12/77
		#1 Stockard Channing
		   Valorie Armstrong
		   1/4/77
		#2 Lesley Ann Warren
		   Mary Ann Chinn 6/14/77
		   Deanna Deignan 9/21/77
		#3 Carrie Snodgress
		   April Shawhan 7/77

Mary	Susan Merson	#1 Sandy Duncan
	Monica Merryman 2/78	Kathy Bates 1/4/77
		#2 Elizabeth Ashley
		Elizabeth Farley 6/28/77
		Elizabeth Ashley 7/17/77
		Kelly Bishop 9/21/77
		Camilla Carr 11/9/77
		#3 Barbara Anderson

THE WIZ

	New York 1/5/75	*Los Angeles 6/15/76*
Tinman	Tiger Haynes	Ben Harney
Lion	Ted Ross	Ted Ross
	James Wigfall 5/11/76	Ken Prymus
	Ken Page 6/6/77	
	James Wigfall 10/31/77	
	L. Michael Gray 2/7/78	
Scarecrow	Hinton Battle	Charles Valentino
	Gregg Burge 12/76	
Dorothy	Stephanie Mills	Ren Woods
		Renée Harris 10/76
Glinda	DeeDee Bridgewater	DeeDee Bridgewater
	Deborah Burrell 4/12/76	Roz Clark 10/76
		Peggy Blue
Evillene	Mabel King	Ella Mitchell
	Irene Reid	Carolyn Miller
	Theresa Merritt 4/12/76	
	Ruth Brisbane 9/76	
	Ella Mitchell 7/77	
The Wiz	Andre De Shields	Andre De Shields
	Alan Weeks 5/4/76	Kenneth Scott (a/k/a Kamal)
	Andre De Shields 1/25/77	1/25/77
	Carl Hall 7/17/77	
Addaperle	Clarice Taylor	Vivian Bonnell
	Jozella Reed	
	Clarice Taylor	
Aunt Em	Tash Thomas	DeeDee Bridgewater
	Esther Marrow	Roz Clark 10/76
		Peggy Blue

FACTS AND
FIGURES

LONG RUNS ON BROADWAY

The following shows have run 500 or more continuous performances in a single production, usually the first, not including previews or extra non-profit performances, allowing for vacation layoffs and special one-booking engagements, but not including return engagements after a show has gone on tour. In all cases the numbers were obtained directly from the shows' production offices. Where there are title similarities, the production is identified as follows: (p) straight play version, (m) musical version, (r) revival.

THROUGH MAY 31, 1978

(PLAYS MARKED WITH ASTERISK WERE STILL PLAYING JUNE 1, 1978)

Plays	Number Performances	Plays	Number Performances
Fiddler on the Roof	3,242	The King and I	1,246
Life With Father	3,224	Cactus Flower	1,234
Tobacco Road	3,182	Sleuth	1,222
Hello, Dolly!	2,844	1776	1,217
My Fair Lady	2,717	Equus	1,209
*Grease	2,600	Guys and Dolls	1,200
Man of La Mancha	2,328	Cabaret	1,165
Abie's Irish Rose	2,327	*A Chorus Line	1,157
Oklahoma!	2,212	Mister Roberts	1,157
Pippin	1,944	Annie Get Your Gun	1,147
South Pacific	1,925	The Seven Year Itch	1,141
Harvey	1,775	Butterflies Are Free	1,128
Hair	1,750	Pins and Needles	1,108
*The Magic Show	1,643	Plaza Suite	1,097
Born Yesterday	1,642	Kiss Me, Kate	1,070
Mary, Mary	1,572	Don't Bother Me, I Can't Cope	1,065
The Voice of the Turtle	1,557	The Pajama Game	1,063
Barefoot in the Park	1,530	Shenandoah	1,050
Mame (m)	1,508	The Teahouse of the August	
Arsenic and Old Lace	1,444	Moon	1,027
The Sound of Music	1,443	Damn Yankees	1,019
How To Succeed in Business		Never Too Late	1,007
Without Really Trying	1,417	Any Wednesday	982
Hellzapoppin	1,404	A Funny Thing Happened on	
*The Wiz	1,380	the Way to the Forum	964
The Music Man	1,375	The Odd Couple	964
Funny Girl	1,348	Anna Lucasta	957
*Same Time, Next Year	1,344	Kiss and Tell	956
Oh! Calcutta!	1,314	Bells Are Ringing	924
Angel Street	1,295	The Moon Is Blue	924
Lightnin'	1,291	Luv	901
Promises, Promises	1,281	Chicago	898

Plays	*Number Performances*	*Plays*	*Number Performances*
Applause	896	Tea and Sympathy	712
Can-Can	892	Junior Miss	710
Carousel	890	*Oh! Calcutta! (r)	710
Hats Off to Ice	889	Last of the Red Hot Lovers	706
Fanny	888	Company	705
Follow the Girls	882	Seventh Heaven	704
Camelot	873	Gypsy (m)	702
The Bat	867	The Miracle Worker	700
My Sister Eileen	864	Cat on a Hot Tin Roof	694
No, No, Nanette (r)	861	Li'l Abner	693
Song of Norway	860	Peg o' My Heart	692
A Streetcar Named Desire	855	The Children's Hour	691
Comedy in Music	849	*For Colored Girls, etc.	688
Raisin	847	Purlie	688
That Championship Season	844	Dead End	687
You Can't Take It With You	837	The Lion and the Mouse	686
La Plume de Ma Tante	835	White Cargo	686
Three Men on a Horse	835	Dear Ruth	683
The Subject Was Roses	832	East Is West	680
Inherit the Wind	806	Come Blow Your Horn	677
No Time for Sergeants	796	The Most Happy Fella	676
Fiorello!	795	The Doughgirls	671
Where's Charley?	792	The Impossible Years	670
The Ladder	789	Irene	670
Forty Carats	780	Boy Meets Girl	669
The Prisoner of Second Avenue	780	Beyond the Fringe	667
Oliver	774	Who's Afraid of Virginia Woolf?	664
Bubbling Brown Sugar	766	Blithe Spirit	657
State of the Union	765	A Trip to Chinatown	657
The First Year	760	The Women	657
You Know I Can't Hear You When the Water's Running	755	Bloomer Girl	654
Two for the Seesaw	750	The Fifth Season	654
Death of a Salesman	742	Rain	648
Sons o' Fun	742	Witness for the Prosecution	645
Candide (mr)	740	Call Me Madam	644
Gentlemen Prefer Blondes	740	Janie	642
The Man Who Came to Dinner	739	The Green Pastures	640
Call Me Mister	734	Auntie Mame (p)	639
West Side Story	732	A Man for All Seasons	637
High Button Shoes	727	The Fourposter	632
Finian's Rainbow	725	Two Gentlemen of Verona (m)	627
Claudia	722	The Tenth Man	623
The Gold Diggers	720	Is Zat So?	618
Jesus Christ Superstar	720	Anniversary Waltz	615
Carnival	719	The Happy Time (p)	614
The Diary of Anne Frank	717	Separate Rooms	613
I Remember Mama	714		

Plays	Number Performances	Plays	Number Performances
Affairs of State	610	Florodora	553
Star and Garter	609	Ziegfeld Follies (1943)	553
The Student Prince	608	Dial "M" for Murder	552
Sweet Charity	608	Good News	551
Bye Bye Birdie	607	Let's Face It	547
Irene (r)	604	Milk and Honey	543
Broadway	603	Within the Law	541
Adonis	603	The Music Master	540
Street Scene (p)	601	Pal Joey (r)	540
Kiki	600	What Makes Sammy Run?	540
Flower Drum Song	600	The Sunshine Boys	538
A Little Night Music	600	What a Life	538
Don't Drink the Water	598	The Unsinkable Molly Brown	532
Wish You Were Here	598	The Red Mill (r)	531
A Society Circus	596	A Raisin in the Sun	530
Absurd Person Singular	592	Godspell	527
Blossom Time	592	The Solid Gold Cadillac	526
The Me Nobody Knows	586	Irma La Douce	524
The Two Mrs. Carrolls	585	The Boomerang	522
Kismet	583	Follies	521
Detective Story	581	Rosalinda	521
Brigadoon	581	The Best Man	520
No Strings	580	Chauve-Souris	520
Brother Rat	577	Blackbirds of 1928	518
Show Boat	572	Sunny	517
The Show-Off	571	Victoria Regina	517
Sally	570	Half a Sixpence	511
Golden Boy (m)	568	The Vagabond King	511
One Touch of Venus	567	The New Moon	509
Happy Birthday	564	The World of Suzie Wong	508
Look Homeward, Angel	564	The Rothschilds	507
The Glass Menagerie	561	Sugar	505
I Do! I Do!	560	Shuffle Along	504
Wonderful Town	559	Up in Central Park	504
Rose Marie	557	Carmen Jones	503
Strictly Dishonorable	557	The Member of the Wedding	501
A Majority of One	556	Panama Hattie	501
The Great White Hope	556	Personal Appearance	501
Toys in the Attic	556	Bird in Hand	500
Sunrise at Campobello	556	Room Service	500
Jamaica	555	Sailor, Beware!	500
Stop the World — I Want to Get Off	555	Tomorrow the World	500

LONG RUNS OFF BROADWAY

Plays	Number Performances	Plays	Number Performances
*The Fantasticks	7,514	The Connection	722
The Threepenny Opera	2,611	Adaptation & Next	707
Godspell	2,124	Oh! Calcutta!	704
Jacques Brel	1,847	Scuba Duba	692
You're a Good Man		The Knack	685
Charlie Brown	1,547	The Club	674
The Blacks	1,408	The Balcony	672
Let My People Come	1,327	America Hurrah	634
The Hot l Baltimore	1,166	Hogan's Goat	607
Little Mary Sunshine	1,143	The Trojan Women (r)	600
El Grande de Coca-Cola	1,114	Krapp's Last Tape &	
One Flew Over the		The Zoo Story	582
Cuckoo's Nest (r)	1,025	The Dumbwaiter &	
The Boys in the Band	1,000	The Collection	578
*Vanities	959	Dames at Sea	575
Your Own Thing	933	The Crucible (r)	571
Curley McDimple	931	The Iceman Cometh (r)	565
Leave It to Jane (r)	928	The Hostage (r)	545
The Mad Show	871	Six Characters in Search of an	
The Effect of Gamma Rays on		Author (r)	529
Man-in-the-Moon Marigolds	819	The Dirtiest Show in Town	509
A View From the Bridge (r)	780	Happy Ending & Day of	
The Boy Friend (r)	763	Absence	504
The Pocket Watch	725	The Boys From Syracuse (r)	500

DRAMA CRITICS CIRCLE VOTING, 1977-78

The New York Drama Critics Circle voted the Irish play *"Da"* by Hugh Leonard the best play of the season on the first ballot, with a majority of 12 votes of the 18 critics present and voting (2 by proxy). These 18 votes for a single best play were distributed as follows: *"Da"* 12 (Clive Barnes, John Beaufort, Glenne Currie, William Glover, Ted Kalem, Walter Kerr, Emory Lewis, Julius Novick, William Raidy by proxy, John Simon, Allan Wallach, Douglas Watt), *The Curse of the Starving Class* 2 (Harold Clurman, Edith Oliver), *Cold Storage* 1 (Howard Kissel), *Molière in Spite of Himself* 1 (Richard Eder by proxy), *The Water Engine* 1 (Martin Gottfried), with one abstention (Jack Kroll).

Having named a foreign play best of bests, the Critics then voted to attempt to select a best American play, but on the first ballot none received a majority, with the 18 first-choice votes distributed as follows: *The Curse of the Starving Class* 6 (Barnes, Clurman, Glover, Kalem, Kroll, Oliver), *The Water Engine* 3 (Eder, Gottfried, Watt), *Chapter Two* 2 (Beaufort, Wallach), *Cold Storage* 2 (Currie, Kissel), *The Gin Game* 2 (Kerr, Lewis) and 1 each for *Bleacher Bums* (Novick), *A Life in the Theater* (Raidy) and *A Prayer for My Daughter* (Simon).

According to its voting rules, the Circle then proceeded to a second, multiple-choice ballot weighted to produce a point consensus with 3 points given to a critic's first choice, 2 for second and 1 for third, with proxy voting now ceasing. In order to win, a play must receive a point total of three times the number of those voting (now 16 without the proxies) divided by two, plus one, i.e. 25 points.

On this second ballot *The Curse of the Starving Class* was still on top, but with a point total of only 20. Now the Circle could have followed the precedent it set last year by asking the critics to vote a third ballot restricted to candidates which had received 10 points or more on the second ballot. William Glover made a motion, however, that the Circle discontinue the voting and not name a best American play this season. The motion carried 8 to 7, with one abstention.

In the best-musical category, *Ain't Misbehavin'* won on the first ballot with a majority of 9 votes (Clurman, Currie, Glover, Kerr, Lewis, Oliver, Simon, Wallach, Watt), with other votes distributed as follows: *Runaways* 4 (Beaufort, Eder by proxy, Kroll, Raidy by proxy), *On the Twentieth Century* 3 (Barnes, Gottfried, Kissel) *The Best Little Whorehouse in Texas* 1 (Kalem). Julius Novick abstained because he had not seen all the contending musicals and Norman Nadel was present but not voting for the same reason. Brendan Gill, Hobe Morrison and Edwin Wilson were absent and not voting.

SECOND BALLOT FOR BEST AMERICAN PLAY

Critic	1st Choice (3 pts.)	2d Choice (2 pts.)	3d Choice (1 pt.)
Clive Barnes *Post*	The Curse of the Starving Class	Chapter Two	A Prayer for My Daughter
John Beaufort *Monitor*	Chapter Two	The Gin Game	A Life in the Theater
Harold Clurman *The Nation*	Curse Starving Class	The Mighty Gents*	Prayer for Daughter
Glenne Currie UPI	Cold Storage	Prayer for Daughter	The Gin Game
William Glover AP	Curse Starving Class	A Life in the Theater	The Gin Game
Martin Gottfried	The Water Engine	The Mighty Gents*	Chapter Two
Ted Kalem *Time*	Curse Starving Class	Cold Storage	Prayer for Daughter
Walter Kerr *Times*	The Gin Game	Family Business	Deathtrap
Howard Kissel *Women's Wear*	Cold Storage	The Gin Game	The Water Engine
Jack Kroll *Newsweek*	Curse Starving Class	The Water Engine	Landscape of the Body
Emory Lewis Bergen *Record*	The Gin Game	Chapter Two	The 5th of July
Julius Novick *Village Voice*	Bleacher Bums	A History of the American Film	The Water Engine
Edith Oliver *New Yorker*	Curse Starving Class	Prayer for Daughter	The Gin Game
John Simon *New York*	Prayer for Daughter	Cold Storage	Curse Starving Class
Allan Wallach *Newsday*	Chapter Two	A Life in the Theater	Curse Starving Class

Douglas Watt   The Water Engine   A Life in the Theater   The Last Street Play*
  Daily News

The Last Street Play was a previous title and version of *The Mighty Gents*

CHOICES OF SOME OTHER CRITICS

Critic	Best Play	Best Musical
Judith Crist	"Da"	Ain't Misbehavin'
Brendan Gill	"Da"	Ain't Misbehavin'
New Yorker		
Stewart Klein	"Da"	Ain't Misbehavin'
WNEW-TV		
Hobe Morrison	"Da"	Abstain
Variety		
Leonard Probst	"Da"	Ain't Misbehavin'
WNBC Radio		

NEW YORK DRAMA CRITICS CIRCLE AWARDS

Listed below are the New York Drama Critics Circle Awards from 1935-36 through 1977-78 classified as follows: (1) Best American Play, (2) Best Foreign Play, (3) Best Musical, (4) Best, regardless of category (this category was established by new voting rules in 1962-63 and did not exist prior to that year).

1935-36—(1) Winterset
1936-37—(1) High Tor
1937-38—(1) Of Mice and Men, (2) Shadow and Substance
1938-39—(1) No award, (2) The White Steed
1939-40—(1) The Time of Your Life
1940-41—(1) Watch on the Rhine, (2) The Corn Is Green
1941-42—(1) No award, (2) Blithe Spirit
1942-43—(1) The Patriots
1943-44—(2) Jacobowsky and the Colonel
1944-45—(1) The Glass Menagerie
1945-46—(3) Carousel
1946-47—(1) All My Sons, (2) No Exit, (3) Brigadoon
1947-48—(1) A Streetcar Named Desire, (2) The Winslow Boy
1948-49—(1) Death of a Salesman, (2) The Madwoman of Chaillot, (3) South Pacific
1949-50—(1) The Member of the Wedding (2) The Cocktail Party, (3) The Consul
1950-51—(1) Darkness at Noon, (2) The Lady's Not for Burning, (3) Guys and Dolls
1951-52—(1) I Am a Camera, (2) Venus Observed, (3) Pal Joey (Special citation to Don Juan in Hell)
1952-53—(1) Picnic, (2) The Love of Four Colonels, (3) Wonderful Town

1953-54—(1) Teahouse of the August Moon, (2) Ondine, (3) The Golden Apple
1954-55—(1) Cat on a Hot Tin Roof, (2) Witness for the Prosecution, (3) The Saint of Bleecker Street
1955-56—(1) The Diary of Anne Frank, (2) Tiger at the Gates, (3) My Fair Lady
1956-57—(1) Long Day's Journey Into Night, (2) The Waltz of the Toreadors, (3) The Most Happy Fella
1957-58—(1) Look Homeward, Angel, (2) Look Back in Anger, (3) The Music Man
1958-59—(1) A Raisin in the Sun, (2) The Visit, (3) La Plume de Ma Tante
1959-60—(1) Toys in the Attic, (2) Five Finger Exercise, (3) Fiorello!
1960-61—(1) All the Way Home, (2) A Taste of Honey, (3) Carnival
1961-62—(1) The Night of the Iguana, (2) A Man for All Seasons, (3) How to Succeed in Business Without Really Trying
1962-63—(4) Who's Afraid of Virginia Woolf? (Special citation to Beyond the Fringe)
1963-64—(4) Luther, (3) Hello, Dolly! (Special citation to The Trojan Women)
1964-65—(4) The Subject Was Roses, (3) Fiddler on the Roof

1965-66—(4) The Persecution and Assassination of Marat as Performed by the Inmates of the Asylum of Charenton Under the Direction of the Marquis de Sade, (3) Man of La Mancha

1966-67—(4) The Homecoming, (3) Cabaret

1967-68—(4) Rosencrantz and Guildenstern Are Dead, (3) Your Own Thing

1968-69—(4) The Great White Hope, (3) 1776

1969-70—(4) Borstal Boy, (1) The Effect of Gamma Rays on Man-in-the-Moon Marigolds, (3) Company

1970-71—(4) Home, (1) The House of Blue Leaves, (3) Follies

1971-72—(4) That Championship Season, (2) The Screens, (3) Two Gentlemen of Verona (Special citations to Sticks and Bones and Old Times)

1972-73—(4) The Changing Room, (1) The Hot l Baltimore, (3) A Little Night Music

1973-74—(4) The Contractor, (1) Short Eyes, (3) Candide

1974-75—(4) Equus, (1) The Taking of Miss Janie, (3) A Chorus Line

1975-76—(4) Travesties, (1) Streamers, (3) Pacific Overtures

1976-77—(4) Otherwise Engaged, (1) American Buffalo, (3) Annie

1977-78—(4) "Da", (3) Ain't Misbehavin'

PULITZER PRIZE WINNERS, 1916-17 to 1977-78

1916-17—No award

1917-18—Why Marry?, by Jesse Lynch Williams

1918-19—No award

1919-20—Beyond the Horizon, by Eugene O'Neill

1920-21—Miss Lulu Bett, by Zona Gale

1921-22—Anna Christie, by Eugene O'Neill

1922-23—Icebound, by Owen Davis

1923-24—Hell-Bent fer Heaven, by Hatcher Hughes

1924-25—They Knew What They Wanted, by Sidney Howard

1925-26—Craig's Wife, by George Kelly

1926-27—In Abraham's Bosom, by Paul Green

1927-28—Strange Interlude, by Eugene O'Neill

1928-29—Street Scene, by Elmer Rice

1929-30—The Green Pastures, by Marc Connelly

1930-31—Alison's House, by Susan Glaspell

1931-32—Of Thee I Sing, by George S. Kaufman, Morrie Ryskind, Ira and George Gershwin

1932-33—Both Your Houses, by Maxwell Anderson

1933-34—Men in White, by Sidney Kingsley

1934-35—The Old Maid, by Zoë Akins

1935-36—Idiot's Delight, by Robert E. Sherwood

1936-37—You Can't Take It With You, by Moss Hart and George S. Kaufman

1937-38—Our Town, by Thornton Wilder

1938-39—Abe Lincoln in Illinois, by Robert E. Sherwood

1939-40—The Time of Your Life, by William Saroyan

1940-41—There Shall Be No Night, by Robert E. Sherwood

1941-42—No award

1942-43—The Skin of Our Teeth, by Thornton Wilder

1943-44—No award

1944-45—Harvey, by Mary Chase

1945-46—State of the Union, by Howard Lindsay and Russel Crouse

1946-47—No award

1947-48—A Streetcar Named Desire, by Tennessee Williams

1948-49—Death of a Salesman, by Arthur Miller

1949-50—South Pacific, by Richard Rodgers, Oscar Hammerstein II and Joshua Logan

1950-51—No award

1951-52—The Shrike, by Joseph Kramm

1952-53—Picnic, by William Inge

1953-54—The Teahouse of the August Moon, by John Patrick

1954-55—Cat on a Hot Tin Roof, by Tennessee Williams

1955-56—The Diary of Anne Frank, by Frances Goodrich and Albert Hackett

1956-57—Long Day's Journey Into Night, by Eugene O'Neill

1957-58—Look Homeward, Angel, by Ketti Frings

1958-59—J. B., by Archibald MacLeish

1959-60—Fiorello!, by Jerome Weidman,

George Abbott, Sheldon Harnick
and Jerry Bock
1960–61—All the Way Home, by Tad Mosel
1961–62—How to Succeed in Business Without
Really Trying, by Abe Burrows,
Willie Gilbert, Jack Weinstock and
Frank Loesser
1962–63—No award
1963–64—No award
1964–65—The Subject Was Roses, by Frank
D. Gilroy
1965–66—No award
1966–67—A Delicate Balance, by Edward
Albee
1967–68—No award
1968–69—The Great White Hope, by Howard
Sackler

1969–70—No Place to Be Somebody, by
Charles Gordone
1970–71—The Effect of Gamma Rays on Man-
in-the-Moon Marigolds, by Paul
Zindel
1971–72—No award
1972–73—That Championship Season, by
Jason Miller
1973–74—No award
1974–75—Seascape, by Edward Albee
1975–76—A Chorus Line, by Michael Bennett,
James Kirkwood, Nicholas Dante,
Marvin Hamlisch and Edward
Kleban
1976–77—The Shadow Box, by Michael
Cristofer
1977–78—The Gin Game, by D.L. Coburn

THE TONY AWARDS

1976-77

The musical revue *Side by Side by Sondheim* was inadvertently omitted from the list of best-musical Tony Award nominees in *The Best Plays of 1976-77*. It was produced by Harold Prince in association with Ruth Mitchell, by arrangement with The Incomes Company, Ltd., was nominated for best musical together with *Annie* (the eventual Tony winner in this category), *Happy End* and *I Love My Wife* and should have been listed with them.

1977-78

The Antoinette Perry (Tony) Awards are voted by members of the League of New York Theaters and Producers, the governing bodies of the Dramatists Guild, Actors' Equity, the American Theater Wing, the Society of Stage Directors and Choreographers, the United Scenic Artists Union and members of the first-night and second-night press, from a list of four nominees in each category.

The list of shows eligible (Broadway shows only; off Broadway excluded) is provided by the Tony administration's Eligibility Committee, consisting this year of Jesse Gross, Stuart W. Little, Joan A. Rubin and Susan Harley. Nominations of four in each category are made by a committee of critics whose personnel changes annually at the invitation of the abovementioned League, which administers the Tony Awards under an agreement with the American Theater Wing. The 1977-78 Nominating Committee was composed of William Glover of the Associated Press, Paul Myers of the Library and Museum of the Performing Arts at Lincoln Center, Elliot Norton of the Boston *Herald American,* Seymour Peck of the New York *Times* and Robert Wahls of the New York *Daily News*.

The list of 1977-78 nominees follows, with winners in each category listed in **bold face type**.

BEST PLAY (award goes to both producer and author). *Chapter Two* by Neil Simon, produced by Emanuel Azenberg; **"Da"** by **Hugh Leonard,** produced by **Lester Osterman, Marilyn Strauss** and **Marc Howard;** *Deathtrap* by Ira Levin, produced by Alfred de Liagre Jr. and Roger L. Stevens; *The Gin Game* by D.L. Coburn, produced by The Shubert Organization, Hume Cronyn and Mike Nichols.

BEST MUSICAL PLAY. **Ain't Misbehavin'** produced by **The Shubert Organization, Emanuel Azenberg, Dasha Epstein, Jane Gaynor** and **Ron Dante;** *Dancin'* produced by Jules Fisher, The Shubert Organization and Columbia Pictures; *On the Twentieth Century* produced by The Producers Circle 2 (Robert Fryer, James Cresson, Mary Lea Johnson, Martin Richards); *Runaways* produced by Joseph Papp.

BEST BOOK OF A MUSICAL PLAY. *A History of the American Film* by Christopher Durang; **On the Twentieth Century** by **Betty Comden** and **Adolph Green;** *Runaways* by Elizabeth Swados; *Working* by Stephen Schwartz.

BEST SCORE OF A MUSICAL PLAY. *The Act,* music by John Kander, lyrics by Fred Ebb; **On the Twentieth Century,** music by **Cy Coleman,** lyrics by **Betty Comden** and **Adolph Green;** *Runaways,* music and lyrics by Elizabeth Swados; *Working,* music and lyrics by Craig Carnelia, Micki Grant, Mary Rodgers, Susan Birkenhead, Stephen Schwartz and James Taylor.

OUTSTANDING PERFORMANCE BY AN ACTOR IN A PLAY. Hume Cronyn in *The Gin Game,* **Barnard Hughes** in *"Da",* Frank Langella in *Dracula,* Jason Robards in *A Touch of the Poet.*

OUTSTANDING PERFORMANCE BY AN ACTRESS IN A PLAY. Anne Bancroft in *Golda,* Anita Gillette in *Chapter Two,* Estelle Parsons in *Miss Margarida's Way,* **Jessica Tandy** in *The Gin Game.*

OUTSTANDING PERFORMANCE BY AN ACTOR IN A MUSICAL. Eddie Bracken in *Hello, Dolly!,* **John Cullum** in *On the Twentieth Century,* Barry Nelson in *The Act,* Gilbert Price in *Timbuktu!*

OUTSTANDING PERFORMANCE BY AN ACTRESS IN A MUSICAL. Madeline Kahn in *On the Twentieth Century,* Eartha Kitt in *Timbuktu!,* **Liza Minnelli** in *The Act,* Frances Sternhagen in *Angel.*

OUTSTANDING PERFORMANCE BY A FEATURED ACTOR IN A PLAY. Morgan Freeman in *The Mighty Gents,* Victor Garber in *Deathtrap,* Cliff Gorman in *Chapter Two,* **Lester Rawlins** in *"Da"*

OUTSTANDING PERFORMANCE BY A FEATURED ACTRESS IN A PLAY. Starletta DuPois in *The Mighty Gents,* Swoosie Kurtz in *Tartuffe,* Marian Seldes in *Deathtrap,* **Ann Wedgeworth** in *Chapter Two.*

OUTSTANDING PERFORMANCE BY A FEATURED ACTOR IN A MUSICAL. Steven Boockvor and Rex Everhart in *Working,* Wayne Cilento in *Dancin',* **Kevin Kline** in *On the Twentieth Century.*

OUTSTANDING PERFORMANCE BY A FEATURED ACTRESS IN A MUSICAL. **Nell Carter** and Charlaine Woodard in *Ain't Misbehavin',* Imogene Coca in *On the Twentieth Century,* Ann Reinking in *Dancin'.*

OUTSTANDING DIRECTION OF A PLAY. **Melvin Bernhardt** for *"Da,"* Robert Moore for *Deathtrap,* Mike Nichols for *The Gin Game,* Dennis Rosa for *Dracula.*

OUTSTANDING DIRECTION OF A MUSICAL. Bob Fosse for *Dancin',* **Richard Maltby Jr.** for *Ain't Misbehavin',* Harold Prince for *On the Twentieth Century,* Elizabeth Swados for *Runaways.*

OUTSTANDING SCENIC DESIGN. Zack Brown for *The Importance of Being Earnest,* Edward Gorey for *Dracula,* David Mitchell for *Working,* **Robin Wagner** for *On the Twentieth Century.*

OUTSTANDING COSTUME DESIGN. **Edward Gorey** for *Dracula,* Halston for *The Act,* Geoffrey Holder for *Timbuktu!,* Willa Kim for *Dancin'.*

OUTSTANDING LIGHTING DESIGN. **Jules Fisher** for *Beatlemania* and **Dancin',** Tharon Musser for *The Act,* Ken Billington for *Working.*

OUTSTANDING CHOREOGRAPHY. Arthur Faria for *Ain't Misbehavin',* **Bob Fosse** for *Dancin',* Ron Lewis for *The Act,* Elizabeth Swados for *Runaways.*

MOST INNOVATIVE PRODUCTION OF A REVIVAL. **Dracula** produced by **Jujamcyn**

1977-78 TONY BEST-PERFORMANCE WINNERS: John Cullum in *On the Twentieth Century*, Jessica Tandy in *The Gin Game*, Barnard Hughes in *"Da,"* Liza Minnelli in *The Act*

Theaters, Elizabeth I. McCann, John Wulp, Victor Lurie, Nelle Nugent and Max Weitzenhoffer; *Tartuffe* produced by Circle in the Square; *Timbuktu!* produced by Luther Davis; *A Touch of the Poet* produced by Elliot Martin.

SPECIAL AWARDS (voted by the Tony Administration Committee). Third annual Lawrence Langner Award for lifetime achievement to **Irving Berlin**. Special Award to the **Long Wharf Theater**, New Haven, Conn. as an outstanding regional theater (designated and recommended by vote of the American Theater Critics Association). Theater Award '78 to **Charles Moss** and **Stan Dragoti** for their "I Love New York Broadway Show Tours" TV advertising campaign.

THE OBIE AWARDS

The *Village Voice* Off-Broadway (Obie) Awards are given each year for excellence in various categories of off-Broadway shows — and frequently off-off-Broadway shows, as close distinctions between these two areas are ignored in Obie Award-giving. The Obies are voted by a committee of *Village Voice* critics and others, whose 1977-78 members were Richard Eder, Michael Feingold, Terry Curtis Fox, Erika Munk, Julius Novick, Gordon Rogoff, Arthur Sainer and Ross Wetzsteon.

LIFETIME ACHIEVEMENT. Peter Schumann's **Bread & Puppet Theater.**

BEST PLAY. **The Shaggy Dog Animation** by Lee Breuer.

DISTINGUISHED PERFORMANCES. **Richard Bauer** in *Landscape of the Body* and *The Dybbuk;* **Nell Carter** in *Ain't Misbehavin';* **Alma Cuervo** and **Swoosie Kurtz** in *Uncommon Women and Others;* **Kaiulanu Lee** in *Safe House;* **Bruce Myers** in *The Dybbuk;* **Lee S. Wilkof** in *The Present Tense.*

DISTINGUISHED DIRECTORS. **Robert Allan Ackerman** for *A Prayer for My Daughter;* **Thomas Bullard** for *Statements After an Arrest Under the Immorality Act;* **Elizabeth Swados** for *Runaways.*

DISTINGUISHED DESIGN. **Garland Wright** and **John Arnone** for *K;* **Robert Yodice** for *Museum.*

SPECIAL CITATIONS. **Ain't Misbehavin';** **Eric Bentley; Joseph Dunn** and **Irja Koljonen** for *Preface;* **James Lapine** for *A Photograph;* **Jerry Mayer** for *TAUDshow;* **Stuart Sherman;** **Squat; Winston Tong.**

ADDITIONAL PRIZES AND AWARDS 1977-78

The following is a list of major prizes and awards for achievement in the New York theater this season. In all cases the names of winners appear in **bold face type.**

1977 MARGO JONES AWARD to a professional producer and theater for the encouragement of new playwrights through a continuing policy of producing new plays. **Marshall W. Mason** and **Circle Repertory Company.**

1977-78 JOSEPH MAHARAM FOUNDATION AWARDS for outstanding New York theatrical design by American designers. Scenery design — **Edward Gorey** and **Lynn Pecktal** for *Dracula* and **John Lee Beatty** for *A Life in the Theater.* Costume design — **Jules Fisher** for *Dancin'.* Honorable mention: scenery design — Robin Wagner for *On the Twentieth Century,* Edward Gianfrancesco for *The Ballad of the Sad Cafe,* David Mitchell and Collis Davis for *A Photograph,* JoAnne Akalaitis for *Dressed Like an Egg,* Robert Yodice for *Museum;* costume design — Willa Kim for *Dancin',* Randy Barcelo for *Ain't Misbehavin',* Edward Gorey and John David

Ridge for *Dracula;* lighting design — Pat Collins for *A Life in the Theater,* Craig Evans for *The Ballad of the Sad Cafe,* Victor En Yu Tan for *A Photograph.* Judges were Harold Clurman, Mel Gussow, Henry Hewes, Edward F. Kook.

ELIZABETH HULL-KATE WARRINER AWARD to the playwright whose work produced within the 1976-77 season dealt with controversial subjects involving the fields of political, religious or social mores of the time, selected by the Dramatists Guild Council. **Ronald Ribman** for *Cold Storage.*

BRANDEIS AWARDS IN THEATER ARTS. **Long Wharf Theater. Hume Cronyn and Jessica Tandy.**

1977 GEORGE FREEDLEY MEMORIAL BOOK AWARD to the book on live theater which best demonstrates outstanding scholarship, readability and contribution to knowledge during the preceding year, voted by a jury of the Theater Library Association, to **Theater Design** by George C. Izenour.

JAMES N. VAUGHAN MEMORIAL AWARD established and presented by The Shubert Foundation to a non-profit performing arts group. **Manhattan Theater Club.**

ROSAMUND GILDER AWARD for creative achievement, voted by the New Drama Forum. **Michael Lessac,** founder and director of Colonnades Theater Lab.

OUTER CRITICS' CIRCLE AWARDS for distinguished achievement in the New York theater, voted by critics of out-of-town and foreign periodicals. Play — **"Da"** by Hugh Leonard. Musical — **Ain't Misbehavin'.** Performances — **Barnard Hughes** in *"Da,"* Martin Balsam in *Cold Storage,* **John Wood** in, *Deathtrap,* **Vicki Frederick** in *Dancin',* **Nancy Snyder** in *The 5th of July.* Direction — **Melvin Bernhardt** for *"Da."*

CLARENCE DERWENT AWARDS for the most promising female and male actors on the metropolitan scene. **Margaret Hilton** in *Molly.* **Morgan Freeman** in *The Mighty Gents.*

34TH ANNUAL THEATER WORLD AWARDS for the outstanding new performers in Broadway and off-Broadway productions during the 1977-78 season. **Vasili Bogazianos** in *Ain't Misbehavin'.* **Carlin Glynn** in *The Best Little Whorehouse in Texas.* **Christopher Goutman** in *The Promise.* **William Hurt** in Circle Repertory Theater productions. **Judy Kaye** in *On the Twentieth Century.* **Florence Lacey** in *Hello, Dolly!.* **Gordana Rashovich** in *Fefu and Her Friends.* **Bo Rucker** in *Native Son.* **Richard Seer** in *"Da".* **Colin Stinton** in *The Water Engine.* Special award to **Joseph Papp** and **New York Shakespeare Festival** for an unprecedented record in discovering and encouraging unknown talent.

DRAMA DESK AWARDS for outstanding achievement. Director of a play — **Melvin Bernhardt** for *"Da."* New play — **"Da"** by Hugh Leonard. Director of a musical — **Stephen Schwartz** for *Working;* Peter Masterson and **Tommy Tune** for *The Best Little Whorehouse in Texas.* Choreography — **Bob Fosse** for *Dancin'.* Lyrics — **Carol Hall** for *The Best Little Whorehouse in Texas.* Score — **Cy Coleman** for *On the Twentieth Century;* **Carol Hall** for *The Best Little Whorehouse in Texas.* Actress in a play — **Jessica Tandy** in *The Gin Game.* Actor in a play — **Barnard Hughes** in *"Da."* Featured actress, play — **Eileen Atkins** in *The Night of the Tribades.* Featured actor, play — **Morgan Freeman** in *The Mighty Gents.* Production of a musical — **Emanuel Azenberg, Dasha Epstein, The Shubert Organization, Jane Gaynor** and **Ron Dante** for *Ain't Misbehavin'.* Female performance, musical — **Bobo Lewis** in *Working;* **Swoosie Kurtz** in *A History of the American Film.* Featured male performance, musical — **Kevin Kline** in *On the Twentieth Century.* Scene design — **Robin Wagner** for *On the Twentieth Century.* Costumes — **Florence Klotz** for *On the Twentieth Century.* Lighting design — **Jules Fisher** for *Dancin'.* Unique theatrical experience — **Estelle Parsons** in *Miss Margarida's Way.* Special award for outstanding contribution to the professional theater — **the off-off-Broadway theater movement.** Drama Desk Nominating Committee: Debbi Wasserman, Alvin Klein, Ira J. Bilowit, John Madden, Tom McMorrow, Sam Norkin.

1977-1978 PUBLICATION
OF RECENTLY-PRODUCED PLAYS

Alphabetical Order/Donkey's Years. Michael Frayn. Methuen (paperback).
American Buffalo. David Mamet. Grove Press (paperback).
Bonjour la Bonjour. Michel Tremblay. Talonbooks (paperback).
Bridget's House. Hull Truck Theater Company. TQ Publications (paperback).
Butterfingers Angel, The. William Gibson and Ellen Keusch. Paulist Press (also paperback).
Cherry Orchard, The. Jean-Claude van Itallie's translation of the play by Anton Chekhov. Grove
    Press (paperback).
Clouds. Michael Frayn. Methuen (paperback)
Counting the Ways/Listening. Edward Albee. Atheneum.
Destiny. David Edgar. Methuen (paperback).
Dog Days. Simon Gray. Methuen (paperback).
Double Standard. John Fenn. Playswest Press (paperback).
Gemini. Albert Innaurato. James T. White.
Gimme Shelter. Barrie Keeffe. Methuen (paperback.
Jo Ann in the White House. Irving Stettner (paperback).
Jolly GreenTrack, The. Louis Phillips. CTL Plays (paperback).
Last Jew, The. Yaffa Eliach and Uri Assaf. Alef-Alef Theater Publications (paperback).
Life in the Theater, A. David Mamet. Grove Press (also paperback).
Man With Bags. Eugene Ionesco, adapted by Israel Horovitz from a translation by Mari-France
    Ionesco. Grove Press (paperback).
Mecca. Ted Whitehead. Faber & Faber (paperback).
Misanthrope, The. Tony Harrison's version of the play by Molière. Rex Collings (paperback).
Motion of History, The. Imamu Amiri Baraka. Morrow.
Night of the Tribades, The. Per Olov Enquist, translated by Ross Shideler. Hill and Wang (also
    paperback).
Poor Murderer. Pavel Kohout, translated by Herbert Berghof and Laurence Luckinbill. Viking.
    Penguin (paperback).
Poor Tom/Tina. David Cregan. Methuen (paperback).
Privates on Parade. Peter Nichols. Faber & Faber (paperback).
Salem's Daughters. John Fenn. Playswest Press (paperback).
Saturday Night Women. Michael Judge. Proscenium Press (paperback).
Sea Anchor, The. E. A. Whitehead. Theater Arts (paperback)
Sea Gull, The. Jean-Claude van Itallie's translation of the play by Anton Chekhov. Harper & Row
    (paperback).
Secrets of the Rich. Arthur Kopit. Farrar, Straus.
Sexual Perversity in Chicago/Duck Variations. David Mamet. Grove Press (paperback).
Shadow Box, The. Michael Cristofer. Drama Book Specialists. Avon (paperback).
Sherlock Holmes. Tim Kelly. Pioneer Drama Service (paperback).
Transfiguration of Benno Blimpie, The. Albert Innaurato. James T. White.
Visions of Kerouac. Martin Duberman. Little, Brown (also paperback).
Weapons of Happiness. Howard Brenton. Methuen (paperback).
Wreckers. David Edgar. Methuen (paperback).

A SELECTED LIST OF OTHER PLAYS
PUBLISHED IN 1977-1978

Alcestiad, The. Thornton Wilder, Harper & Row.
America Hurrah and Other Plays. Jean- Claude van Itallie. Grove Press (paperback).
Best Short Plays of 1977, The. Stanley Richards, editor. Chilton.
Black Girl: From Genesis to Revelations. J.E. Franklin. Howard University.
Collected Plays: Volume Two. Bertolt Brecht. Vintage Books (paperback).
Complete Plays of Joe Orton, The. Grove Press (paperback).
Complete Works: One. Harold Pinter. Grove Press (paperback).

Complete Works: Two. Harold Pinter. Grove Press (paperback).
East Lynne: A Musical. Robert Neil Porter and Jack Perry. Pioneer Drama Service.
Enemy of the People, An. Arthur Miller. Penguin (paperback). Reprint.
Iphigenia at Aulis. New translation of Euripides's play by W. S. Merwin and George E. Dimock. Oxford.
Madras House, The. Harley Granville-Barker. Methuen (paperback).
Oedipus the King. New translation of Sophocles's play by Stephen Berg and Diskin Clay. Oxford.
Pinter: Plays — One. Harold Pinter. Methuen (paperback).
Nine Plays of Eugene O'Neill. Eugene O'Neill. Modern Library.
Pirandello's One-Act Plays. Luigi Pirandello. Samuel French. (paperback).
Portable Arthur Miller, The. Arthur Miller. Penguin (paperback).
Portable Bernard Shaw, The. George Bernard Shaw. Penguin (paperback).
Portable Shakespeare, The. William Shakespeare. Penguin (paperback).
Rhesos. New translation of Euripides's play by Richard Emil Braun. Oxford.
Rise and Fall of the City of Mahagonny, The. Bertolt Brecht and Kurt Weill. David R. Godine (paperback).
Sherlock Holmes. William Gillette and Arthur Conan Doyle. Pioneer Drama Service (paperback).
Tarry Flynn. Patrick Kavanagh's novel adapted by P. J. O'Connor. Proscenium Press (paperback).
Three Plays. Eduardo De Filippo. Hamish Hamilton.
Three Plays by John Osborne. John Osborne. Bantam (paperback).
Three Plays. Emmanuel Robles, translated by James A. Kilker. Southern Illinois University Press.
Threepenny Opera, The. Bertolt Brecht. Translation by Hugh MacDiarmid. Methuen (paperback).
View from the Bridge, A. Arthur Miller. Penguin (paperback). Reprint.
Wild Oats. John O'Keeffe. Theater Arts (paperback).
Women of Trachis. New translation of Sophocles's play by C. K. Williams and Gregory Dickerson. Oxford.

MUSICAL AND DRAMATIC RECORDINGS OF NEW YORK SHOWS

Title and publishing company are listed below. Each record is an original cast album unless otherwise indicated. An asterisk (*) indicates recording is also available on cassettes. Two asterisks (**) indicate it is available on eight-track cartridges.

Act, The. DRG. (RCA). (*) (**)
Baker's Wife, The. Take Home Tunes.
Best Little Whorehouse in Texas, The. MCA/Universal.
Flora, the Red Menace (re-issue). RCA.
Golden Boy (reissue). Capitol.
Greenwillow (reissue). Columbia Special Projects.
Hostage, The (reissue). Columbia Special Projects.
I Love My Wife. Atlantic. (*) (**)
King and I, The (1977 cast). (*) (**)
Merry Widow, The (New York City Opera Production; electronically simulated stereo record). Angel. (*)
On the Twentieth Century. Columbia. (*) (**)
Party With Comden and Green, A. Stet.
Porgy and Bess (three-record complete recording of Houston Grand Opera production). RCA.
Rodgers & Hart Revisited (Vols. 3 and 4). Painted Smiles.
Starting Here, Starting Now. RCA. (*) (**)
Tovarich (reissue). Capitol.
Unpublished Cole Porter. Painted Smiles.
Very Good Eddie. DRG (RCA).

NECROLOGY

MAY 1977-MAY 1978

PERFORMERS

Abbott, Merriel (84) — November 6, 1977
Aber, Marlene (60) — September 21, 1977
Abdun-Nur, Virginia (59) — October 13, 1977
Ahn, Philip (72) — February 28, 1978
Alberg, Somar (69) — May 31, 1977
Alden, Hortense (76) — April 2, 1978
Ames, Vic (51) — January 23, 1978
Andreasen, Anna Lisa (67) — May 29, 1977
Anspach, Frederic (60) — August 19, 1977
Armstrong, R.L. — March 10, 1978
Ashley, Barbara (50) — March 1, 1978
Ashley, Sylvia (73) — June 30, 1977
Astor, Gertrude (90) — November 9, 1977
Banks, Sally (77) — August 13, 1977
Barnett, Vince (75) — August 10, 1977
Barres, Madeleine (70) — April 10, 1978
Barrie, Wendy (65) — February 2, 1978
Barris, Herbie (68) — December 28, 1977
Bates, Michael (57) — January 11, 1978
Ben-Ami, Jacob (86) — July 2, 1977
Benson, Roy (63) — December 6, 1977
Berenson, Abe (68) — December 7, 1977
Bern, Maria (77) — September 27, 1977
Betz, Carl (56) — January 18, 1978
Bianchi, Marilyn Broth (45) — July 14, 1977
Biberman, Abner (69) — June 20, 1977
Blackman, Don (65) — September 11, 1977
Blunt, Paul F. — January 2, 1978
Bolan, Marc (29) — September 16, 1977
Bonomo, Joe (76) — March 28, 1978
Bontsema, Peter H. (80) — February 4, 1978
Bouchey, Willis (70) — September 28, 1977
Bourbon, Diana (78) — March 19, 1978
Boyd, Bill (67) — December 7, 1977
Boyd, Stephen (48) — June 2, 1977
Breeden, John (73) — September 9, 1977
Brennen, Claire (43) — November 27, 1977
Brickley, Shirley (33) — October 13, 1977
Brooks, Geraldine (52) — June 19, 1977
Brown, Alfred C. (80) — January 28, 1978
Brown, Zara Cully (86) — February 28, 1978
Bryan, Adelaide (82) — July 25, 1977
Bunn, Alden (52) — August 21, 1977
Burke, Hilda (73) — April 6, 1978
Cabot, Sebastian (59) — August 23, 1977
Callas, Maria (53) — September 16, 1977
Calley, Robert S. (88) — May 8, 1977
Cannon, Raymond (84) — June 7, 1977
Carlisle, Elsie (70's) — September 6, 1977
Carlson, Richard (65) — November 25, 1977

Carrier, Ada Boyd (87) — March 25, 1978
Carson, Eldridge (69) — February 11, 1978
Cazale, John (42) — March 12, 1978
Chaplin, Charles (88) — December 25, 1977
Chapman, Edward (75) — August 9, 1977
Claney, Elizabeth (71) — July 12, 1977
Collins, Laura (26) — September 1977
Coontz, Williard (62) — April 7, 1978
Cooper, Wyatt (50) — January 5, 1978
Corbett, Jean (66) — February 1978
Craven, Robin (71) — May 15, 1978
Crosby, Bing (76) — October 14, 1977
Crowe, Eileen (79) — May 8, 1978
Cummin, Marguerite (78) — Dec. 29, 1977
D'Albie, Julian (86) — April 6, 1978
Damien, Mary-Louise (88) — January 31, 1978
Darvas, Nicholas (57) — June 3, 1977
Dean, Basil (89) — April 22, 1978
De Haven, Carter (90) — July 20, 1977
Del Rio, Jack (66) — March 8, 1978
De Marney, Derrick (71) — February 18, 1978
Denny, Sandy (31) — April 21, 1978
DeWitt, Paul (50) — March 19, 1978
Dominico, Michael (48) — July 5, 1977
DuBois, Louis-Alexis (44) — January 11, 1978
Dudley, Frank — July 13, 1977
Dulac, Anto (76) — Summer 1977
Dwyer, Ruth (80) — March 2, 1978
Echols, J. Kermit (56) — January 5, 1978
Eglevsky, Andre (60) — December 4, 1977
Eilers, Sally (69) — January 5, 1978
Elder, Ruth (73) — October 9, 1977
Eliot, Jean (45) — April 20, 1978
Fenton, Leslie C. (76) — March 25, 1978
Finn, Adelaide Raine (84) — January 20, 1978
Fishman, Duke M. (71) — December 22, 1977
Flenn, Karl (47) — April 9, 1978
Flickenschild, Elisabeth (72) — October 1977
Ford, Mary (53) — September 30, 1977
Francen, Victor (68) — Winter 1977
Frazier, Beulah (64) — January 27, 1978
Fussell, Sara E. (61) — Spring 1978
Gage, Ben (63) — April 28, 1978
Gaillard, Lucille (88) — August 11, 1977
Geer, Will (76) — April 22, 1978
Genn, Leo (72) — January 26, 1978
Gerard, Rolf (84) — April 17, 1978
Gifford, Ross (49) — November 5, 1977
Givney, Kathryn (81) — March 16, 1978
Gluckman, Leon (55) — February 21, 1978
Godsey, James F. (63) — January 17, 1978
Gordon, Glen (63) — September 16, 1977

501

Gordon, Leona (49) — November 13, 1977
Gorman, Madeleine (61) — June 10, 1977
Graham, Lee E. (64) — September 6, 1977
Gray, Billy (73) — January 4, 1978
Grayson, Larry (46) — January 14, 1978
Greene, Angela (55) — February 9, 1978
Greenstein, Joseph L. (84) — October 8, 1977
Greenwood, Charlotte (87) — January 18, 1978
Greer, David (65) — November 17, 1977
Grund, Leo (77) — March 8, 1978
Guerriero, William (61) — March 4, 1978
Hacha, Robert (54) — October 9, 1977
Hagen, Jean (54) — August 29, 1977
Hall, Arch (69) — April 28, 1978
Halliday, Hildegarde (75) — October 10, 1977
Harbin, Robert (68) — January 12, 1978
Harrison, James (69) — November 9, 1977
Hart, Winifred (78) — March 19, 1978
Haupt, David (81) — August 27, 1977
Haydock, Ron (37) — August 14, 1977
Hayes, Frances X. "Jack" (76) — Spring 1978
Heap, Jimmy (55) — Winter 1977
Herreros, Enrique (73) — September 17, 1977
Hewins, Nancy (75) — January 18, 1978
Hill, Thelma (53) — December 21, 1977
Hinnant, Bill (42) — February 17, 1978
Hoctor, Harriet (74) — June 9, 1977
Holden, Michael (31) — September 23, 1977
Holmes, Edward (66) — July 12, 1977
Holmes-Gore, Dorothy (81) — Oct. 14, 1977
Homolka, Oscar (79) — January 27, 1978
Hood, Gail (81) — May 11, 1978
Hood, Gretchen (91) — May 2, 1978
Hoskins, Troy (66) — April 6, 1978
Hughes, Lysbeth — March 28, 1978
Hugo, Emmons H. (81) — July 19, 1977
Huisman, Jacqueline (56) — March 28, 1978
Hulbert, Jack (85) — March 25, 1978
Hyams, Leila (72) — December 4, 1977
Jacobsen, Mae (72) — March 28, 1978
Jagendorf, Sophie S. (83) — June 20, 1977
Jamis, Bill (52) — July 10, 1977
Johnson, Jason — November 24, 1977
Jones, Kenneth (32) — September 20, 1977
Kallos, Nellie Knight (80) — October 10, 1977
Kane, Linda Carole (25) — August 1, 1977
Karasavina, Tamara (93) — May 26, 1978
Kath, Terry (31) — January 23, 1978
Keffer, Charles Henderson Jr. — Winter 1977
Keller, Greta (70) — November 4, 1977
Kelly, Lloyd B. (81) — December 25, 1978
Kenny, Bill (63) — March 23, 1978
Keppel, Joe (82) — Fall 1977
Kimball, Florence (87) — November 24, 1977
King, Teddi (48) — November 18, 1977
Kipness, Alexander (87) — May 14, 1978
Kurzer, Leon Diegfried (77) — March 5, 1978

Lane, Jane (72) — Winter 1978
La Verne, Francis (72) — October 28, 1977
Lawson, Stan (68) — July 17, 1977
LeBlanc, Fernand A. (75) — March 9, 1978
Lochary, David (31) — July 29, 1977
Lockhard, Kathleen (84) — February 17, 1978
Lockin, Daniel (34) — August 21, 1977
Loper, Mary Stuart (84) — March 16, 1978
Lucas, Paul (73) — October 26, 1977
Lunt, Alfred (84) — August 3, 1977
Mackie, Eddie (89) — January 2, 1978
Manetta, Joseph (79) — October 15, 1977
Mann, Cato (90) — December 14, 1977
Mann, George (72) — November 23, 1977
Marais, Josef (72) — April 27, 1978
Marlowe, Nora — December 31, 1977
Marx, Groucho (86) — August 19, 1977
Matthews, Altonell H. (72) — August 6, 1977
McCallan, Clement (64) — Summer 1977
McCoy, Tim (86) — January 29, 1978
McGrath, Paul (74) — April 13, 1978
McNamara, Maggie (48) — February 18, 1978
Meehan, Danny (47) — March 29, 1978
Mell, Joseph (62) — August 31, 1977
Merritt, George (86) — Fall 1977
Middleton, Robert (66) — June 14, 1977
Miller, Alice Bradford (82) — June 12, 1977
Morrison, Ann (62) — April 18, 1978
Mostel, Zero (62) — September 8, 1977
Murdoch, Bryden (53) — May 1, 1978
Myers, Jess D. (72) — October 9, 1977
Naramore, Charles (55) — October 21, 1977
Nebel, Long John (66) — April 10, 1978
Nesbitt, Ann Greenway (78) — June 26, 1977
Nielson-Terry, Phyllis (84) — Sept. 25, 1977
Novack, Shelly (30) — May 27, 1978
Oakie, Jack (74) — January 23, 1978
Oberman, Jack (70) — July 21, 1977
O'Brien, Seamus (41) — May 14, 1977
O'Duffy, Dave — Winter 1977
O'Neill, James L. (93) — July 18, 1977
Osburne, Marg (49) — July 16, 1977
Oxenar, Elizabeth (66) — March 28, 1978
Papkin, Irving (77) — March 13, 1978
Parrish, Laura (96) — August 15, 1977
Paulson, John W. (77) — August 7, 1977
Pearson, Mack (75) — June 19, 1977
Pelt, Timothy (31) — September 6, 1977
Perkins, Voltaire (80) — October 10, 1977
Phipps, Sally (67) — March 17, 1978
Pickering, Sara (39) — December 11, 1977
Porter, Mary — March 23, 1978
Porter, Dick (46) — January 6, 1978
Powell, Robert (38) — October 24, 1977
Powell, William Jr. (35) — May 26, 1977
Presley, Elvis (42) — August 16, 1977
Rasser, Alfred (71) — August 18, 1977

Reed, Alan (69) — June 14, 1977
Reese, Eleanor (84) — June 20, 1977
Reid, Dorothy (81) — October 12, 1977
Rhein, Mitchell (77) — September 23, 1977
Riccardo, Rick Jr. (47) — June 3, 1977
Ridgway, Patricia (53) — February 8, 1978
Risson, Barbara (57) — August 2, 1977
Rissoni, Gidita (81) — May 31, 1977
Ritchard, Cyril (79) — December 18, 1977
Rivers, Victor (29) — July 8, 1977
Rizzuto, Ginger (57) — December 3, 1977
Robbins, Jean (73) — June 20, 1977
Rock, Edith Blossom — January 14, 1978
Rockwell, George I. (89) — March 2, 1978
Rose, Howard (95) — March 28, 1978
Rose, Irving (81) — September 9, 1977
Roy, Jahar (58) — August 11, 1977
Rueff, Annette H. (87) — April 24, 1978
Russell, George Robert (72) — March 13, 1978
Salkin, Lucien (50) — October 1, 1977
Sandor, Gluck — March 11, 1978
Scannell, Phyllis (63) — September 16, 1977
Schoenffler, Paul (80) — November 21, 1977
Schone, Lotte (86) — December 22, 1977
Shankar, Uday (76) — September 26, 1977
Shaw, Lillian (92) — February 6, 1978
Sheppard, Jim (40's) — August 18, 1977
Shindo, Eitaro (78) — December 24, 1977
Simpson, Ryllis G. (79) — February 18, 1978
Sinclair, Edward (63) — August 29, 1977
Smiley, Ralph (62) — September 14, 1977
Smith, Sydney G. (68) — March 4, 1978
Speaks, Margaret (72) — July 16, 1977
Stanley, Charles (38) — October 1977
Stephens, Lewis (77) — March 7, 1978
Stevenson, Mary — August 8, 1977
Steward, Sophie (69) — Summer 1977
Stuart, Gil (58) — June 8, 1977
Stueckgold, Grete (82) — September 13, 1977
Tagliabue, Carol (80) — April 5, 1978
Takada, Minoru (78) — December 28, 1977
Tallman, Frank (59) — April 16, 1978
Tannahill, Myrtle (91) — Summer 1977
Teshima, Yazaemon (78) — January 3, 1977
Tetzel, Joan (56) — October 31, 1977
Thomas, Powys (51) — June 22, 1977
Thordsen, Kelly (61) — January 23, 1978
Toutain, Roland (72) — October 1977
Trevor, Austin (80) — January 22, 1978
Truman, Ralph (77) — October 16, 1977
Urquhart, Molly (71) — October 6, 1977
Valente, Maria (80) — October 29, 1977
Vidor, Florence (82) — November 3, 1977
Villepontreau, William H. (71) — April 1, 1978
Wallace, Regina (86) — February 13, 1978
Wallenda, Karl (73) — March 22, 1978
Ward, Harold F. (44) — January 28, 1978

Warner, Rae (80) — January 15, 1978
Waters, Ethel (80) — September 1, 1977
Wayne, Frances (60's) — February 6, 1978
Weeks, Ada May (80) — April 25, 1978
Weiss, Rudolph (77) — April 5, 1978
White, Alice (75) — June 26, 1977
Wiley, Charles A. (67) — July 25, 1977
Williams, Berl (59) — March 11, 1978
Wilson, Dwayne E.S. (40) — March 27, 1978
Wilson, Gwenda (55) — August 18, 1977
Wood, Peggy (86) — March 18, 1978
Wyner, Billie (76) — Fall 1977
Yegros, Lina (65) — May 1978

PLAYWRIGHTS

Abrams, Leon (84) — July 5, 1977
Batson, George D. (61) — July 25, 1977
Baumer, Marie (76) — July 31, 1977
Biddle, Katherine (87) — December 30, 1977
Boardman, Thelma — April 21, 1978
Box, H. Oldfield (73) — February 21, 1978
Carney, Frank (73) — September 11, 1977
Chase, Ilka (72) — February 15, 1978
Clay, Buriel II (34) — May 22, 1978
Dlaznowsky, Moshe (71) — July 30, 1977
Emanuel, Ken (34) — January 7, 1978
Heuvers, Herman (86) — June 9, 1977
Higham, David (82) — April 1, 1978
Horwitt, Arnold B. (59) — October 20, 1977
Lawson, John Howard (82) — August 12, 1977
Levitt, Saul (66) — September 30, 1977
Lowell, Robert (60) — September 12, 1977
MacLiammoir, Micheal (78) — March 6, 1978
Mallin, Tom (50) — Winter 1978
McGowan, John P. (81) — May 28, 1977
Mihura, Miguel (72) — October 28, 1977
Packard Elon E. (54) — December 17, 1977
Pearlman, Ronny (35) — October 6, 1977
Petrova, Olga (93) — November 30, 1977
Rattigan, Terence (66) — November 30, 1977
Reed, Daniel (86) — February 9, 1978
Sheekman, Arthur (76) — January 12, 1978
Truax, James — June 26, 1977
Underhill, Geoff (51) — May 9, 1978
Ure, Joan (58) — Winter 1978
Williamson, Hugh (76) — January 13, 1978

COMPOSERS, LYRICISTS

Addinsell, Richard (73) — November 15, 1977
Bernstein, Alan (37) — May 1, 1978
Bixio, Cesare Andrea (82) — March 5, 1978
Bradford, Alex (51) — February 15, 1978
Branscombe, Gena (95) — July 26, 1977
Brent, Earl K. (63) — July 8, 1977
Bruce, Donald (60) — July 16, 1977

Burkhard, Paul (65) — September 6, 1977
Byfield, Jack (75) — June 27, 1977
Cory, George (55) — April 11, 1978
Cuclin, Dimitrie (92) — Winter 1978
Evans, Tolchard (77) — March 12, 1978
Gensler, Lewis (81) — January 15, 1978
Gilger, Adam (86) — November 4, 1977
Gillis, Don (65) — January 10, 1978
Grossman, Edward (86) — January 10, 1978
Hall, Arthur E. (77) — March 4, 1978
Igelhoff, Peter (73) — April 8, 1978
Joyce, Randolph P. (25) — November 11, 1977
Khachaturian, Aram (74) — May 1, 1978
Le Caine, Hugh — July 2, 1977
Marrone, John (77) — November 5, 1977
Nabokov, Nicholas (75) — April 6, 1978
Newman, Charles (76) — January 9, 1978
Purcell, Harold (69) — May 28, 1977
Raskin, Milt (61) — October 16, 1977
Reynolds, Malvine (77) — March 17, 1978
Roetter, Guido (64) — November 9, 1977
Satterfield, LaVonne (56) — January 18, 1978
Satterwhite, Collen (57) — February 6, 1978
Shand, Terry — November 11, 1977
Tcherepnin, Alexander (78) — Sept. 29, 1977
Waslon, Alvin E. (51) — June 23, 1977
Wright, Ken (70) — March 13, 1978

PRODUCERS, DIRECTORS, CHOREOGRAPHERS

Albrecht, Joseph (84) — October 1977
Allvine, Glendon (84) — November 5, 1977
Ayres, Bert (79) — March 16, 1978
Bailey, Edwin (50's) — July 17, 1977
Baird, John — April 5, 1978
Balcon, Michael (81) — October 16, 1977
Ballen, Ivan (69) — February 18, 1978
Binyon, Claude (72) — February 14, 1978
Bresler, Jerry (65) — August 23, 1977
Brickman, Miriam (45) — July 2, 1977
Brill, Leighton (84) — July 26, 1977
Buchman, Larry (35) — September 23, 1977
Bunetta, Frank (62) — March 30, 1978
Burleigh, Fred — July 12, 1977
Carter, Richard (58) — April 9, 1978
Cassidy, Frank (57) — March 7, 1978
Castle, William (63) — May 31, 1977
Citarella, Jean G. (79) — October 9, 1977
Coats, Gordon T. (48) — September 14, 1977
Cochran, Gifford A. (71) — January 3, 1978
Cohan, Mitchell (63) — January 30, 1978
Cohen, Emanuel (85) — September 9, 1977
Cramer, Joseph I. (63) — September 27, 1977
Culp, Louis J. — October 15, 1977
Dalton, Emmet (80) — March 4, 1978
Darro, Jack (76) — December 7, 1977

Daves, Delmer (73) — August 17, 1977
Dickstein, Solomon (87) — December 13, 1977
Doran, D.A. (80) — March 5, 1978
Edwards, Herbert T. (76) — June 21, 1977
Edwards, Webley (71) — October 5, 1977
Eguchi, Takaya (77) — December 25, 1977
Ezekiel, Margaret U. (63) — August 14, 1977
Finklehoffe, Fred F. (67) — October 5, 1977
Fokine, Bitale (72) — December 29, 1977
Fournier, Maurice (61) — April 9, 1978
Garnett, Tay (83) — October 3, 1977
Geller, Bruce (47) — May 21, 1978
Girdler, William (30) — January 21, 1978
Godfrey, Isidore (76) — September 12, 1977
Goel, Devendra (59) — February 26, 1978
Hartford-Davis, Robert (54) — June 12, 1977
Hawks, Howard (81) — December 19, 1977
Infascelli, Roberto (37) — August 18, 1977
Jaffe, Saul (63) — November 1, 1977
Jayne, David W. (40) — September 23, 1977
Kersken, Herman (79) — June 11, 1977
King, Maurice (62) — September 2, 1977
Koenig, Lester (58) — November 20, 1977
Kolt, Heiko (75) — October 2, 1977
Lamb, Judy — December 21, 1977
Lenzi, Joseph (54) — February 15, 1978
Lewis, Albert (93) — April 5, 1978
Lian, David (42) — February 14, 1978
Loew, Arthur M. (79) — September 6, 1977
Lorch, Chester A. (77) — January 20, 1978
MacCallum, William A. (54) — Jan. 18, 1978
Mammarella, Anthony (53) — Nov. 27, 1977
Mandell, Harry L. (64) — September 1977
McCann, William (84) — November 15, 1977
McKimson, Robert (66) — September 27, 1977
Mirell, Leon I. (54) — December 7, 1977
Mohr, Robert (67) — May 29, 1977
Morey, Edward (84) — July 14, 1977
Nathan, Paul (64) — November 16, 1977
Neumann, Mathias (56) — May 31, 1977
Nichols, Sam Clatie (33) — December 7, 1977
O'Malley, David P. (81) — September 27, 1977
Potter, H.C. (73) — August 31, 1977
Raset, Val (67) — July 26, 1977
Reizner, Lou (44) — June 25, 1977
Robinson, Maurice L. (61) — October 12, 1977
Rossellini, Roberto (71) — June 3, 1977
Schneider, Benno (79) — August 13, 1977
Schouten, Richard (47) — July 3, 1977
Schwartz, Samuel H. (69) — July 1, 1977
Segal, Alex (62) — August 22, 1977
Spieker, Franz-Josef (44) — March 18, 1978
Taylor, Vernon R. (48) — March 31, 1978
Tourneur, Jacques (73) — December 19, 1977
Tourtellot, Arthur (64) — October 18, 1977
Vercammen, Jules C. (56) — Nov. 12, 1977
Waldman, Ronald (63) — March 10, 1978

Wilson, Lou (68) — March 18, 1978
Wychodzki, Phillip — January 31, 1978
Young, Harry (66) — October 16, 1977
Zollo, Carmen F. (54) — December 16, 1977

DESIGNERS

Bracher, Gordon (55) — July 5, 1977
Coffin, Gene (72) — October 18, 1977
Day, Bruce (36) — September 4, 1977
Finch, Helen (83) — March 16, 1978
Lawson, Kate (83) — November 14, 1977
Luthardt, Robert (69) — October 1, 1977
Poindexter, H.R. (41) — September 24, 1977
Sahlin, Don (49) — February 19, 1978
Shafer, Hal (57) — January 14, 1978
Thompson, Eric G. (76) — January 1978
Thompson, Frank (57) — June 4, 1977

CRITICS

Bone, Harold M. (80) — September 6, 1977
Byram, John (76) — November 29, 1977
Cann, Alexander (74) — December 21, 1977
Findlay, Richard (47) — October 12, 1977
Goddard, Robert (65) — May 15, 1978
Gray, Bert (54) — December 29, 1977
Greenberg, Eliezer (80) — June 2, 1977
Haskins, John (59) — September 16, 1977
Jacobs, J. Edwin (75) — April 18, 1978
McCullough, Donald (76) — January 19, 1978
Oppenheimer, George (77) — August 14, 1977
Rogers, William G. (82) — March 1, 1978
Schneider, Isidor (80) — August 3, 1977
Schorer, Mark (69) — August 11, 1977
Sherwin, Louis (96) — May 11, 1978
Slonimsky, Yuri (76) — April 2, 1978
Tarran, Geoffrey — Winter 1978
Untermeyer, Louis (92) — December 18, 1977
Verrill, Addison (36) — September 14, 1977
Williard, Charlotte (71) — October 20, 1977
Wilson, Ivy Crane (90) — December 7, 1977
Wyatt, Euphemia (93) — January 31, 1978

CONDUCTORS

Adler, Kurt (70) — September 21, 1977
Alliger, John B. (76) — September 18, 1977
Baldi, Joe (73) — September 2, 1977
Becker, Louis (79) — August 2, 1977
Black, Norman (69) — July 9, 1977
Brandwynne, Nat (67) — Winter 1978
Charninsky, Hyman (78) — July 11, 1977
Cottrell, Louis Jr. (67) — March 21, 1978
DeSimone, Robert (66) — July 6, 1977
Dowdy, Paul (36) — March 23, 1978

Firstman, Samuel (78) — September 15, 1977
French, Albert (66) — September 28, 1977
Fuhrman, Clarence (82) — November 1, 1977
Funk, Larry (71) — July 15, 1977
Garber, Jan (82) — October 5, 1977
Gregory, Bill (65) — May 1978
Grigaitis, Walter (65) — November 20, 1977
Harvey, Bob (64) — January 10, 1978
Harvey, Ned (60) — December 5, 1977
Jones, Ev (83) — April 19, 1978
Khaikin, Boris (73) — May 10, 1978
Littau, Joseph (86) — September 29, 1977
Lombardo, Guy (75) — November 5, 1977
McCall, Fred W. Jr. (72) — Nov. 17, 1977
Novak, George E. (53) — February 23, 1978
McAuley, Ray (33) — April 11, 1978
Miller, Max (60) — September 5, 1977
Minovich, Jack (66) — October 3, 1977
Noble, Ray (71) — April 3, 1978
Parillo, Nicklos (90) — January 25, 1978
Pederson, Bert (56) — August 23, 1977
Powers, Thomas — June 4, 1977
Re, Payson — April 1, 1978
Ringwall, Randolph (88) — January 26, 1978
Rose, Albert P. (68) — August 18, 1977
Schippers, Thomas (47) — December 16, 1977
Steinberg, William (78) — May 16, 1978
Stokowski, Leopold (95) — Sept. 13, 1977
Uber, Harry R. Jr. (62) — July 23, 1977

MUSICIANS

Anderson, Johnny F. (63) — October 13, 1977
Arndt, Nola (88) — July 20, 1977
Ball, Desiree (84) — July 20, 1977
Barnes, George (56) — September 4, 1977
Bartlett, Ethel (82) — April 17, 1978
Black, Joe (52) — June 30, 1977
Bochco, Rudolph (77) — October 6, 1977
Bolognini, Remo (78) — August 8, 1977
Brown, Hazen H. (68) — November 19, 1977
Brussells, Iris (77) — September 5, 1977
Buckner, Milt (62) — July 27, 1977
Butler, Jerry (20) — July 29, 1977
Calimahoa, Lambros (66) — October 28, 1977
Camdon, Gerry (29) — February 2, 1978
Churchey, Victor N. (63) — January 24, 1978
Clemo, Alice (79) — September 2, 1977
Cohen, Sidney (62) — January 26, 1978
Cook, Roderick V. (74) — October 11, 1977
Criss, Sonny (50) — November 19, 1977
Cullen, Thomas V. (67) — October 22, 1977
Dalton, William (78) — August 11, 1977
Edwards, Sidney (68) — February 3, 1978
Emerson, Charles R. (51) — August 14, 1977
Foley, Warren A. (75) — February 18, 1978
Fosshage, George (82) — February 21, 1978

French, Pete (63) — December 1, 1977
Gaines, Cassie — October 20, 1977
Gaines, Steve — October 20, 1977
Giglia, Feliz (56) — November 30, 1977
Goldmark, Aaron (66) — June 11, 1977
Hanley, Myron (62) — January 16, 1978
Haverbeck, Joseph A. (80) — April 23, 1978
Hechter, Colman (42) — January 23, 1978
Herbert, Gregory (30) — January 31, 1978
Hubinon, Paul J. (35) — May 24, 1977
Hyman, John (78) — October 9, 1977
Jackson, Albert (70) — March 1, 1978
Jackson, Jack (71) — January 14, 1978
Johnson, Harold (60) — March 28, 1978
Kamuca, Richie (46) — July 22, 1977
Kirk, Rahsaan (41) — December 5, 1977
Lee, Jackie (51) — May 6, 1978
Levin, Joseph (74) — September 19, 1977
Lieber, Olga (81) — May 9, 1977
Lindner, J. James (81) — September 23, 1977
Malcuzynski, Witold (62) — July 17, 1977
Mardigan, Art — June 6, 1977
Marsala, Joe (71) — March 3, 1978
Matera, Angelo J. (73) — September 1, 1977
Matthews, William A. (85) — May 4, 1978
Mazzari, Fred (66) — January 27, 1978
McAdam, William J. (23) — June 17, 1977
Miles, Don (67) — August 25, 1977
Mills, Gladys (55) — February 25, 1978
Nallin, Walter E. (60) — April 26, 1978
Neill, Everett H. Jr. (28) — May 28, 1977
Oster, Ernst (69) — June 30, 1977
Paris, Norman (51) — July 10, 1977
Peterson, Charles (62) — January 21, 1978
Richardson, Alexander D. (81) — Jan. 6, 1978
Rivera, Mon (53) — March 12, 1978
Rose, Wolfgang (70) — September 6, 1977
Russell, Bill (54) — January 16, 1978
Russotto, Leo (81) — January 29, 1978
Serebryakov, Pavel (68) — Summer 1977
Shanks, Albert (71) — December 7, 1977
Sherman, Harry (73) — June 3, 1977
Shewell, Lennington (68) — January 27, 1978
Spivakovsky, Issy (75) — August 8, 1977
Steele, Billy (46) — Winter 1977
Taylor, Billy Jr. (51) — November 15, 1977
Taylor, Gertrude Monk (87) — April 13, 1978
Thone, John E. (45) — January 25, 1978
Van Zant, Ronnie — October 20, 1977
Verdi, Thelma (81) — December 25, 1977
Vetere, Joseph (69) — November 24, 1977
Wilhousky, Peter (75) — January 4, 1978
Williams, Joe (79) — June 13, 1977
Willis, Joseph Ernest (65) — October 19, 1977
Wolf, Loraine (57) — February 28, 1978
Wummer, John (78) — September 6, 1977
Yancy, Clyde A. (68) — January 22, 1978

OTHERS

Ackerman, Paul (69) — December 31, 1977
  Editor, *Billboard*
Adleman, Meyer (79) — March 23, 1978
  Chief barker, Philadelphia Variety Club
Baer, Raymond (61) — January 2, 1978
  Stage electrician
Bailey, Maurice M. (83) — December 29, 1977
  Theater manager
Baldwin, Faith (84) — March 18, 1978
  Novelist
Baranoff, Abe M. (73) — March 26, 1978
  Manager, Broadhurst Theater
Barrere, Jean (59) — August 29, 1977
  Broadway stage manager
Beck, Louise Heims (89) — March 16, 1978
  Widow of Martin Beck
Bennett, Bernard (76) — June 21, 1977
  Show business attorney
Bernstein, Lillian Coogan (85) — Oct. 23, 1977
  Mother of Jackie Coogan
Bohrer, Seymour H. (51) — October 1, 1977
  Entertainment accountant
Bowles, Heloise (58) — December 28, 1977
  Columnist
Braunsweg, Julian (80) — March 27, 1978
  Founder, London's Festival Ballet Company
Brecher, Louis J. (79) — July 8, 1977
  Founder, Roseland Ballroom
Cain, James M. (85) — October 27, 1977
  Novelist
Capparelli, Joseph D. (83) — July 17, 1977
  Head carpenter, Philadelphia Shubert
Connell, Thomas J. (77) — November 23, 1977
  Chief electrician
Cooper, Doug (56) — August 1, 1977
  Talent agent
Dallas, Hugh Nicholas (43) — July 16, 1977
  Owner Palm Theater, San Diego
Davis, Hal C. (63) — January 11, 1978
  President, Amer. Federation of Musicians
Deegan, Thomas J. Jr. (67) — Nov. 16, 1977
  Public relations consultant
Deering, Vaughan (87) — March 19, 1978
  Professor of theater, Fordham
Deutsch, Lawrence E. (57) — Nov. 12, 1977
  Theater executive
Diston, Leo (70) — February 16, 1978
  Song plugger
Dorfman, Nat N. (82) — July 3, 1977
  Publicist
Edelson, Alan (67) — April 3, 1978
  Publicist
Engle, George S. — June 25, 1977
  Theater executive
Fagan, Kathleen A. — October 8, 1977
  Script supervisor

Fields, Dorothy (36) — July 5, 1977
Manager and publicist
Foster, John Daniel (70) — April 2, 1978
Spartanburg Little Theater
Freeman, Don (69) — February 1, 1978
Theatrical illustrator
Gaines, Blanche (88) — October 29, 1977
Agent
Garamoni, Daniel A. (75) — Sept. 17, 1977
President, Chicago Federation of Musicians
Garber, Jack (62) — May 31, 1977
Road publicist
Golden, Jay (86) — May 19, 1977
Theater manager
Goodman, Alice H. (72) — February 4, 1978
Wife of Benny Goodman
Greeley, Horace W. (56) — June 24, 1977
Assistant radio-TV editor, *Variety*
Gross, Irving (62) — June 21, 1977
Manager director, Loew's State
Gross, Phyllis (44) — August 27, 1977
Hayes Registry and Actors Exchange
Hastings, Sue (93) — June 30, 1977
Puppeteer
Herman, Lilla (80) — January 12, 1978
Theater party organizer
Herrmann, Ottomar (69) — Summer 1977
Trainer of Lippizan stallions
Hope, Constance (69) — June 13, 1977
Opera, concert publicist
Hughes, Alice (78) — June 20, 1977
Columnist, *World-Telegram*
Kaminstein, Abraham L. (65) — September 10, 1977
Registrar of Copyrights
Kantor, MacKinlay (73) — October 11, 1977
Novelist, poet
Kaplan, Jordan (47) — November 18, 1977
House manager
Karlweis, Ninon T. (68) — September 9, 1977
Agent
Kelly, Billy (46) — July 13, 1977
Agent
Kiernan, Walter (75) — January 8, 1978
Newspaper reporter
Koussevitsky, Olga (76) — January 5, 1978
Widow of Serge Koussevitsky
Kramer, Abe (76) — February 28, 1978
Theater executive
Kuchuk, Ben (72) — July 16, 1977
Agent
Lacy, Madison (79) — April 26, 1978
Film pioneer
Lemmer, Ruby Ada (93) — June 27, 1977
Tiller Girls dance line
Lieb, Jack H. (71) — January 6, 1978
Newsreel cameraman

Lippmann, Walter (85) — December 14, 1977
Columnist, author
Malino, Jerome E. (83) — December 7, 1977
Theater attorney
Marouani, Daniel (79) — November 1977
Agent
Marcus, Eli (77) — August 8, 1977
Photographer
Martin, Al (73) — January 25, 1978
Showgirl manager
Martus, Leo K. (82) — September 7, 1977
Theater attorney
May, Waldo R. (75) — June 17, 1977
Theater executive
McCarroll, Marion C. (84) — August 1, 1977
Columnist "Beatrice Fairfax"
McClellan, John (81) — November 28, 1977
Chairman, Copyright Subcommittee
McGaw, Charles (67) — April 8, 1978
Dean, Goodman School, Chicago
McGinley, Phyllis (72) — February 22, 1978
Poet, essayist
Mean, Phyllis Read (79) — March 1, 1978
Translater of operas
Mintz, Charles F. — January 12, 1978
Theater restaurant attorney
Moriarty, Patrick John (68) — Dec. 29, 1977
Restaurateur
Morrison, Eleanor (49) — February 18, 1978
Publicist
Moshlak, Milton (54) — November 25, 1977
Lighting technician
Nabokov, Vladimir (78) — July 2, 1977
Author
Newman, Howard (64) — September 8, 1977
Publicist
Norman, Ruth (74) — December 26, 1977
With Civic Repertory Theater
Oestreicher, Fred P. (69) — May 31, 1977
Publicist
Olivere, Peter C. (87) — March 18, 1978
Entrepreneur
O'Morrison, Janet — August 7, 1977
Administrative assistant
O'Neill, Shane (57) — June 22, 1977
Son of Eugene O'Neill
Opperman, Anne (73) — June 2, 1977
Principal aide to Sol Hurok
Payne, Earl Hall (76) — February 8, 1978
Theater manager
Perlman, Phyllis (81) — August 11, 1977
Publicist
Phillips, Benjamin F. (90) — Sept. 15, 1977
Maker of stringed instruments
Pierce, Eddie (57) — July 21, 1977
Manager, Ice Capades West

Powers, John Robert (84) — July 19, 1977
Founder, the Powers Agency
Randolph, Popsie (57) — January 6, 1978
Road manager
Raymer, Alvin S. (63) — November 26, 1977
Theater manager
Reese, Gustave (77) — September 7, 1977
Music teacher
Rosenthal, David (98) — April 5, 1978
Stage manager
Salusse, Jean (46) — July 23, 1977
Chairman, Paris Opera Board
Scharper, Albert (66) — September 25, 1977
Managing editor, *Daily Variety*
Schulberg, Adeline (83) — July 15, 1977
Agent
Shapiro, Herman (80) — March 28, 1978
Stage manager
Sherry, Jane (41) — June 1977
Agent, personal manager
Siegfried, William P. — February 9, 1978
Assistant Register of Copyrights
Simon, Bernard (75) — June 25, 1977
Publicist and editor
Sinnot, Howard (77) — February 24, 1978
General Artists Corp.
Smadback, Arthur (90) — September 6, 1977
Operator, New York Coliseum

Smith, Irwin (85) — August 24, 1977
Expert on Shakespearean playhouses
Spear, Richard D. (53) — January 22, 1978
Teacher, Wayne State University
Tracey, Hugh (74) — October 23, 1977
Authority on African music
Vaughan, James (74) — September 2, 1977
Theater attorney
Walters, Lou (81) — August 15, 1977
Operator, Latin Quarter
Warembud, Norman H. — February 16, 1978
President, Ethnic Music
Warner, Frank (74) — February 27, 1978
Folklorist
Wharton, John F. (83) — November 24, 1977
Theater attorney
Wilson, Michael (63) — April 9, 1978
Screen writer
Withington, Whitney (59) — January 22, 1978
Cape Cod Caper magazine
Wolfson, Arthur M. (65) — July 26, 1977
Emanu-El cantor
Zarky, Norma G. (60) — October 24, 1977
Specialist in entertainment law
Zellerback, Harold L. (83) — January 29, 1978
Theater executive

THE BEST PLAYS, 1894–1977

Listed in alphabetical order below are all those works selected as Best Plays in previous volumes in the *Best Plays* series. Opposite each title is given the volume in which the play appears, its opening date and its total number of performances. Those plays marked with an asterisk (*) were still playing on June 1, 1978 and their number of performances was figured through May 31, 1978. Adaptors and translators are indicated by (ad) and (tr), the symbols (b), (m) and (l) stand for the author of the book, music and lyrics in the cast of musicals and (c) signifies the credit for the show's conception.

NOTE: A season-by-season listing, rather than an alphabetical one, of the 500 Best Plays in the first 50 volumes, starting with the yearbook for the season of 1919–1920, appears in *The Best Plays of 1968–69.*

PLAY	VOLUME	OPENED	PERFS.
ABE LINCOLN IN ILLINOIS—Robert E. Sherwood	38–39.	.Oct. 15, 1938.	. 472
ABRAHAM LINCOLN—John Drinkwater	19–20.	.Dec. 15, 1919.	. 193
ACCENT ON YOUTH—Samson Raphaelson	34–35.	.Dec. 25, 1934.	. 229
ADAM AND EVA—Guy Bolton, George Middleton	19–20.	.Sept. 13, 1919.	. 312
ADAPTATION—Elaine May; and NEXT—Terrence McNally	68–69.	.Feb. 10, 1969.	. 707
AFFAIRS OF STATE—Louis Verneuil	50–51.	.Sept. 25, 1950.	. 610
AFTER THE FALL—Arthur Miller	63–64.	.Jan. 23, 1964.	. 208
AFTER THE RAIN—John Bowen	67–68.	.Oct. 9, 1967.	. 64
AH, WILDERNESS!—Eugene O'Neill	33–34.	.Oct. 2, 1933.	. 289
AIN'T SUPPOSED TO DIE A NATURAL DEATH—(b,m,l) Melvin Van Peebles	71–72.	.Oct. 7, 1971.	. 325
ALIEN CORN—Sidney Howard	32–33.	.Feb. 20, 1933.	. 98
ALISON'S HOUSE—Susan Glaspell	30–31.	.Dec. 1, 1930.	. 41
ALL MY SONS—Arthur Miller	46–47.	.Jan. 29, 1947.	. 328
ALL OVER TOWN—Murray Schisgal	74–75.	.Dec. 12, 1974.	. 233
ALL THE WAY HOME—Tad Mosel, based on James Agee's novel *A Death in the Family*	60–61.	.Nov. 30, 1960.	. 333
ALLEGRO—(b,l) Oscar Hammerstein II, (m) Richard Rodgers	47–48.	.Oct. 10, 1947.	. 315
AMBUSH—Arthur Richman	21–22.	.Oct. 10, 1921.	. 98
AMERICA HURRAH—Jean-Claude van Itallie	66–67.	.Nov. 6, 1966.	. 634
AMERICAN BUFFALO—David Mamet	76–77.	.Feb. 16, 1977.	. 135
AMERICAN WAY, THE—George S. Kaufman, Moss Hart	38–39.	.Jan. 21, 1939.	.. 164
AMPHITRYON 38—Jean Giraudoux, (ad) S. N. Behrman	37–38.	.Nov. 1, 1937.	. 153
ANDERSONVILLE TRIAL, THE—Saul Levitt	59–60.	.Dec. 29, 1959.	. 179
ANDORRA—Max Frisch, (ad) George Tabori	62–63.	.Feb. 9, 1963.	. 9
ANGEL STREET—Patrick Hamilton	41–42.	.Dec. 5, 1941.	. 1,295
ANIMAL KINGDOM, THE—Philip Barry	31–32.	.Jan. 12, 1932.	. 183
ANNA CHRISTIE—Eugene O'Neill	21–22.	.Nov. 2, 1921.	. 177
ANNA LUCASTA—Philip Yordan	44–45.	.Aug. 30, 1944.	. 957
ANNE OF THE THOUSAND DAYS—Maxwell Anderson	48–49.	.Dec. 8, 1948.	. 286
*ANNIE—(b) Thomas Meehan, (m) Charles Strouse, (l) Martin Charnin, based on Harold Gray's comic strip "Little Orphan Annie"	76–77.	.Apr. 21, 1977.	. 464
ANOTHER LANGUAGE—Rose Franken	31–32.	.Apr. 25, 1932.	. 344
ANOTHER PART OF THE FOREST—Lillian Hellman	46–47.	.Nov. 20, 1946.	. 182
ANTIGONE—Jean Anouilh, (ad) Lewis Galantière	45–46.	.Feb. 18, 1946.	. 64
APPLAUSE—(b) Betty Comden and Adolph Green, (m) Charles Strouse, (l) Lee Adams, based on the film *All About Eve* and the original story by Mary Orr	69–70.	.Mar. 30, 1970.	. 896

PLAY   VOLUME OPENED PERFS.

PLAY	VOLUME	OPENED	PERFS.

HOMECOMING, THE—Harold Pinter .... 66–67. .Jan.   5, 1967. .   324
HOME OF THE BRAVE—Arthur Laurents .... 45–46. .Dec.   27, 1945. .   69
HOPE FOR A HARVEST—Sophie Treadwell .... 41–42. .Nov.   26, 1941. .   38
HOSTAGE, THE—Brendan Behan .... 60–61. .Sept.   20, 1960. .   127
HOT L BALTIMORE, THE—Lanford Wilson .... 72–73. .Mar.   22, 1973. .   1,166
HOUSE OF BLUE LEAVES, THE—John Guare .... 70–71. .Feb.   10, 1971. .   337
HOUSE OF CONNELLY, THE—Paul Green .... 31–32. .Sept.   28, 1931. .   91
HOW TO SUCCEED IN BUSINESS WITHOUT REALLY TRYING
—(b) Abe Burrows, Jack Weinstock, Willie Gilbert
based on Shepherd Mead's novel, (l, m)
Frank Loesser .... 61–62. .Oct.   14, 1961. .   1,417

I AM A CAMERA—John van Druten, based on
Christopher Isherwood's Berlin stories .... 51–52. .Nov.   28, 1951. .   214
I KNOW MY LOVE—S. N. Behrman, based on
Marcel Achard's *Auprès de ma Blonde* .... 49–50. .Nov.   2, 1949. .   246
I NEVER SANG FOR MY FATHER—Robert Anderson .... 67–68. .Jan.   25, 1968. .   124
I REMEMBER MAMA—John van Druten, based on
Kathryn Forbes's book *Mama's Bank Account* .... 44–45. .Oct.   19, 1944. .   714
ICEBOUND—Owen Davis .... 22–23. .Feb.   10, 1923. .   171
ICEMAN COMETH, THE—Eugene O'Neill .... 46–47. .Oct.   9, 1946. .   136
IDIOT'S DELIGHT—Robert E. Sherwood .... 35–36. .Mar.   24, 1936. .   300
IF I WERE KING—Justin Huntly McCarthy .... 99–09. .Oct.   14, 1901. .   56
IMMORALIST, THE—Ruth and Augustus Goetz, based on
André Gide's novel . . .   53–54. .Feb.   8, 1954. .   96
IN ABRAHAM'S BOSOM—Paul Green .... 26–27. .Dec.   30, 1926. .   116
IN THE MATTER OF J. ROBERT OPPENHEIMER—
Heinar Kipphardt, (tr) Ruth Speirs .... 68–69. .Mar.   6, 1969. .   64
IN THE SUMMER HOUSE—Jane Bowles .... 53–54. .Dec.   29, 1953. .   55
IN TIME TO COME—Howard Koch, John Huston .... 41–42. .Dec.   28, 1941. .   40
INADMISSIBLE EVIDENCE—John Osborne .... 65–66. .Nov.   30, 1965. .   166
INCIDENT AT VICHY—Arthur Miller .... 64–65. .Dec.   3, 1964. .   99
INDIANS—Arthur L. Kopit .... 69–70. .Oct.   13, 1969. .   96
IHERIT THE WIND—Jerome Lawrence, Robert E. Lee .... 54–55. .Apr.   21, 1955. .   806
INNOCENTS, THE—William Archibald, based on
Henry James's *The Turn of the Screw* .... 49–50. .Feb.   1, 1950. .   141
INNOCENT VOYAGE, THE—Paul Osborn, based on
Richard Hughes's novel *A High Wind in Jamaica* .... 43–44. .Nov.   15, 1943. .   40
INSPECTOR CALLS, AN—J. B. Priestley .... 47–48. .Oct.   21, 1947. .   95
ISLAND, THE—Athol Fugard, John Kani, Winston Ntshona ... 74–75. .Nov.   24, 1974. .   52
"IT'S A BIRD IT'S A PLANE IT'S SUPERMAN"—(b)
David Newman and Robert Benton, (l) Lee Adams,
(m) Charles Strouse, based on the comic
strip "Superman" .... 65–66. .Mar.   29, 1966. .   129

J. B.—Archibald MacLeish .... 58–59. .Dec.   11, 1958. .   364
JACOBOWSKY AND THE COLONEL—S. N. Behrman,
based on Franz Werfel's play .... 43–44. .Mar.   14, 1944. .   417
JANE—S. N. Behrman, suggested by W. Somerset
Maugham's story .... 51–52. .Feb.   1, 1952. .   100
JANE CLEGG—St. John Ervine .... 19–20. .Feb.   23, 1920. .   158
JASON—Samson Raphaelson .... 41–42. .Jan.   21, 1942. .   125
JESSE AND THE BANDIT QUEEN—David Freeman .... 75–76. .Oct.   17, 1975. .   155
JEST, THE—Sem Benelli, (ad) Edward Sheldon .... 19–20. .Sept.   19, 1919. .   197
JOAN OF LORRAINE—Maxwell Anderson .... 46–47. .Nov.   18, 1946. .   199
JOE EGG (see *A Day in the Death of Joe Egg*)

PLAY	VOLUME	OPENED	PERFS.

MR. AND MRS. NORTH—Owen Davis, based on
Frances and Richard Lockridge's stories .... 40–41. .Jan.   12, 1941. .   163
MRS. BUMSTEAD-LEIGH—Harry James Smith .... 09–19. .Apr.   3, 1911. .   64
MRS. MCTHING—Mary Chase .... 51–52. .Feb.   20, 1952. .   350
MRS. PARTRIDGE PRESENTS—Mary Kennedy,
Ruth Hawthorne .... 24–25. .Jan.   5, 1925. .   144
MY FAIR LADY—(b, l) Alan Jay Lerner, based on
Bernard Shaw's *Pygmalion,* (m) Frederick Loewe .... 55–56. .Mar.   15, 1956. . 2,717
MY SISTER EILEEN—Joseph Fields, Jerome Chodorov,
based on Ruth McKenney's stories .... 40–41. .Dec.   26, 1940. .   864
MY 3 ANGELS—Samuel and Bella Spewack, based on
Albert Huston's play *La Cuisine des Anges* .... 52–53. .Mar.   11, 1953. .   344

NATIONAL HEALTH, THE—Peter Nichols .... 74–75. .Oct.   10, 1974. .   53
NATIVE SON—Paul Green, Richard Wright, based on
Mr. Wright's novel .... 40–41. .Mar.   24, 1941. .   114
NEST, THE—(ad) Grace George, from Paul Geraldy's
Les Noces d'Argent .... 21–22. .Jan.   28, 1922. .   152
NEXT—(see *Adaptation*)
NEXT TIME I'LL SING TO YOU—James Saunders .... 63–64. .Nov.   27, 1963. .   23
NICE PEOPLE—Rachel Crothers .... 20–21. .Mar.   2, 1921. .   247
NIGHT OF THE IGUANA, THE—Tennessee Williams .... 61–62. .Dec.   28, 1961. .   316
NO MORE LADIES—A. E. Thomas .... 33–34. .Jan.   23, 1934. .   162
NO PLACE TO BE SOMEBODY—Charles Gordone .... 68–69. .May   4, 1969. .   250
NO TIME FOR COMEDY—S. N. Berhman .... 38–39. .Aprl.   17, 1939. .   185
NO TIME FOR SERGEANTS—Ira Levin, based on
Mac Hyman's novel .... 55–56. .Oct.   20, 1955. .   796
NOEL COWARD IN TWO KEYS—Noel Coward *(Come
Into the Garden Maud* and *A Song at Twilight)* .... 73–74. .Feb.   28, 1974. .   140
NORMAN CONQUESTS, THE—(see *Living Together,
Round and Round the Garden* and *Table Manners*)

O MISTRESS MINE—Terence Rattigan .... 45–46. .Jan.   23, 1946. .   452
ODD COUPLE, THE—Neil Simon .... 64–65. .Mar.   10, 1965. .   964
OF MICE AND MEN—John Steinbeck .... 37–38. .Nov.   23, 1937. .   207
OF THEE I SING—(b) George S. Kaufman, Morrie
Ryskind, (l) Ira Gershwin, (m) George Gershwin .... 31–32. .Dec.   26, 1931. .   441
OH DAD, POOR DAD, MAMA'S HUNG YOU IN THE
CLOSET AND I'M FEELIN' SO SAD—Arthur L. Kopit .... 61–62. .Feb.   26, 1962. .   454
OKLAHOMA!—(b, l) Oscar Hammerstein II, based on
Lynn Riggs's play *Green Grow the Lilacs,* (m)
Richard Rodgers .... 42–43. .Mar.   31, 1943. . 2,212
OLD MAID, THE—Zoë Akins, based on Edith Wharton's
novel .... 34–35. .Jan.   7, 1935. .   305
OLD SOAK, THE—Don Marquis .... 22–23. .Aug.   22, 1922. .   423
OLD TIMES—Harold Pinter .... 71–72. .Nov.   16, 1971. .   119
OLDEST LIVING GRADUATE, THE—Preston Jones .... 76–77. .Sept.   23, 1976. .   20
ON BORROWED TIME—Paul Osborn, based on
Lawrence Edward Watkin's novel .... 37–38. .Feb.   3, 1938. .   321
ON TRIAL—Elmer Rice .... 09–19. .Aug.   19, 1914. .   365
ONCE IN A LIFETIME—Moss Hart, George S. Kaufman ...... 30–31. .Sept.   24, 1930. .   406
ONE SUNDAY AFTERNOON—James Hagan .... 32–33. .Feb.   15, 1933. .   322
ORPHEUS DESCENDING—Tennessee Williams .... 56–57. .Mar.   1, 1957. .   68
OTHERWISE ENGAGED—Simon Gray .... 76–77. .Feb.   2, 1977. .   309
OUTRAGEOUS FORTUNE—Rose Franken .... 43–44. .Nov.   3, 1943. .   77
OUR TOWN—Thornton Wilder .... 37–38. .Feb.   4, 1938. .   336

PLAY	VOLUME	OPENED	PERFS.
OUTWARD BOUND—Sutton Vane	23–24.	.Jan. 7, 1924. .	144
OVER 21—Ruth Gordon	43–44.	.Jan. 3, 1944. .	221
OVERTURE—William Bolitho	30–31.	.Dec. 5, 1962. .	41
P.S. 193—David Rayfiel	62–63.	.Oct. 30, 1962. .	48
PACIFIC OVERTURES—(b) John Weidman, (m, l) Stephen Sondheim, additional material by Hugh Wheeler	75–76.	.Jan. 11, 1976. .	193
PARIS BOUND—Philip Barry	27–28.	.Dec. 27, 1927. .	234
PASSION OF JOSEPH D., THE—Paddy Chayefsky	63–64.	.Feb. 11, 1964. .	15
PATRIOTS, THE—Sidney Kingsley	42–43.	.Jan. 29, 1943. .	173
PERIOD OF ADJUSTMENT—Tennessee Williams	60–61.	.Nov. 10, 1960. .	132
PERSECUTION AND ASSASSINATION OF MARAT AS PERFORMED BY THE INMATES OF THE ASYLUM OF CHARENTON UNDER THE DIRECTION OF THE MARQUIS DE SADE, THE—Peter Weiss, English version by Geoffrey Skelton, verse (ad) Adrian Mitchell	65–66.	.Dec. 27, 1965. .	144
PETRIFIED FOREST, THE—Robert E. Sherwood	34–35.	.Jan. 7, 1935. .	197
PHILADELPHIA, HERE I COME!—Brian Friel	65–66.	.Feb. 16, 1966. .	326
PHILADELPHIA STORY, THE—Philip Barry	38–39.	.Mar. 28, 1939. .	417
PHILANTHROPIST, THE—Christopher Hampton	70–71.	.Mar. 15, 1971. .	72
PHYSICISTS, THE—Friedrich Duerrenmatt, (ad) James Kirkup	64–65.	.Oct. 13, 1964. .	55
PICK-UP GIRL—Elsa Shelley	43–44.	.May 3, 1944. .	198
PICNIC—William Inge	52–53.	.Feb. 19, 1953. .	477
PIGEONS AND PEOPLE—George M. Cohan	32–33.	.Jan. 16, 1933. .	70
PLAY'S THE THING, THE—Ferenc Molnar, (ad) P. G. Wodehouse	26–27.	.Nov. 3, 1926. .	326
PLAZA SUITE—Neil Simon	67–68.	.Feb. 14, 1968. .	1,097
PLEASURE OF HIS COMPANY, THE—Samuel Taylor, Cornelia Otis Skinner	58–59.	.Oct. 22, 1958. .	474
PLOUGH AND THE STARS, THE—Sean O'Casey	27–28.	.Nov. 28, 1927. .	32
POINT OF NO RETURN—Paul Osborn, based on John P. Marquand's novel	51–52.	.Dec. 13, 1951. .	364
PONDER HEART, THE—Joseph Fields, Jerome Chodorov, based on Eudora Welty's story	55–56.	.Feb. 16, 1956. .	149
POOR BITOS—Jean Anouilh, (tr) Lucienne Hill	64–65.	.Nov. 14, 1964. .	17
PORGY—Dorothy and DuBose Heyward	27–28.	.Oct. 10, 1927. .	367
POTTING SHED, THE—Graham Greene	56–57.	.Jan. 29, 1957. .	143
PRICE, THE—Arthur Miller	67–68.	.Feb. 7, 1968. .	429
PRIDE AND PREJUDICE—Helen Jerome, based on Jane Austen's novel	35–36.	.Nov. 5, 1935. .	219
PRISONER OF SECOND AVENUE, THE—Neil Simon	71–72.	.Nov. 11, 1971. .	780
PROLOGUE TO GLORY—E. P. Conkle	37–38.	.Mar. 17, 1938. .	70
R.U.R.—Karel Capek	22–23.	.Oct. 9, 1922. .	184
RACKET, THE—Bartlett Cormack	27–28.	.Nov. 22, 1927. .	119
RAIN—John Colton, Clemence Randolph, based on the story by W. Somerset Maugham	22–23.	.Nov. 7, 1922. .	648
RAISIN IN THE SUN, A—Lorraine Hansberry	58–59.	.Mar. 11, 1959. .	530
RATTLE OF A SIMPLE MAN—Charles Dyer	62–63.	.Apr. 17, 1963. .	94
REBEL WOMEN—Thomas Babe	75–76.	.May 6, 1976. .	40
REBOUND—Donald Ogden Stewart	29–30.	.Feb. 3, 1930. .	114
REHEARSAL, THE—Jean Anouilh, (ad) Pamela Hansford Johnson and Kitty Black	63–64.	.Sept. 23, 1963. .	110
REMAINS TO BE SEEN—Howard Lindsay, Russel Crouse	51–52.	.Oct 3, 1951. .	199

PLAY	VOLUME	OPENED	PERFS.

SLEUTH—Anthony Shaffer .... 70–71. .Nov. 12, 1970. . 1,222
SLOW DANCE ON THE KILLING GROUND—William Hanley .... 64–65. .Nov. 30, 1964. . 88
SLY FOX—Larry Gelbart, based on *Volpone* by
    Ben Jonson .... 76–77. .Dec. 14, 1976. . 495
SMALL CRAFT WARNINGS—Tennessee Williams .... 71–72. .Apr. 2, 1972. . 192
SOLDIER'S WIFE—Rose Franken .... 44–45. .Oct. 4, 1944. . 253
SQUAW MAN, THE—Edwin Milton Royle .... 99–09. .Oct. 23, 1905. . 222
STAGE DOOR—George S. Kaufman, Edna Ferber .... 36–37. .Oct. 22, 1936. . 169
STAIRCASE—Charles Dyer .... 67–68. .Jan. 10, 1968. . 61
STAR-WAGON, THE—Maxwell Anderson .... 37–38. .Sept. 29, 1937. . 223
STATE OF THE UNION—Howard Lindsay, Russel Crouse ...... 45–46. .Nov. 14, 1945. . 765
STEAMBATH—Bruce Jay Friedman .... 70–71. .June 30, 1970. . 128
STICKS AND BONES—David Rabe .... 71–72. .Nov. 7, 1971. . 367
STONE AND STAR—Robert Ardrey, also called
    Shadow of Heroes .... 61–62. .Dec. 5, 1961. . 20
STOP THE WORLD—I WANT TO GET OFF—(b, l, m)
    Leslie Bricusse, Anthony Newley .... 62–63. .Oct. 3, 1962. . 555
STORM OPERATION—Maxwell Anderson .... 43–44. .Jan. 11, 1944. . 23
STORY OF MARY SURRATT, THE—John Patrick .... 46–47. .Feb. 8, 1947. . 11
STRANGE INTERLUDE—Eugene O'Neill .... 27–28. .Jan. 30, 1928. . 426
STREAMERS—David Rabe .... 75–76. .Apr. 21, 1976. . 478
STREET SCENE—Elmer Rice .... 28–29. .Jan. 10, 1929. . 601
STREETCAR NAMED DESIRE, A—Tennessee Williams .... 47–48. .Dec. 3, 1947. . 855
STRICTLY DISHONORABLE—Preston Sturges .... 29–30. .Sept. 18, 1929. . 557
SUBJECT WAS ROSES, THE—Frank D. Gilroy .... 64–65. .May 25, 1964. . 832
SUMMER OF THE 17TH DOLL—Ray Lawler .... 57–58. .Jan. 22, 1958. . 29
SUNRISE AT CAMPOBELLO—Dore Schary .... 57–58. .Jan. 30, 1958. . 556
SUNSHINE BOYS, THE—Neil Simon .... 72–73. .Dec. 20, 1972. . 538
SUN-UP—Lula Vollmer .... 22–23. .May 25, 1923. . 356
SUSAN AND GOD—Rachel Crothers .... 37–38. .Oct. 7, 1937. . 288
SWAN, THE—Ferenc Molnar, (tr) Melville Baker .... 23–24. .Oct. 23, 1923. . 255
SWEET BIRD OF YOUTH—Tennessee Williams .... 58–59. .Mar. 10, 1959. . 375

TABLE MANNERS—Alan Ayckbourn .... 75–76. .Dec. 7, 1976. . 76
TAKE A GIANT STEP—Louis Peterson .... 53–54. .Sept. 24, 1953. . 76
TAKING OF MISS JANIE, THE—Ed Bullins .... 74–75. .May 4, 1975. . 42
TARNISH—Gilbert Emery .... 23–24. .Oct. 1, 1923. . 248
TASTE OF HONEY, A—Shelagh Delaney .... 60–61. .Oct. 4, 1960. . 376
TCHIN-TCHIN—Sidney Michaels, based on François
    Billetdoux's play .... 62–63. .Oct. 25, 1962. . 222
TEA AND SYMPATHY—Robert Anderson .... 53–54. .Sept. 30, 1953. . 712
TEAHOUSE OF THE AUGUST MOON, THE—
    John Patrick, based on Vern Sneider's novel .... 53–54. .Oct. 15, 1953. . 1,027
TENTH MAN, THE—Paddy Chayefsky .... 59–60. .Nov. 5, 1959. . 623
THAT CHAMPIONSHIP SEASON—Jason Miller .... 71–72. .May 2, 1972. . 844
THERE SHALL BE NO NIGHT—Robert E. Sherwood .... 39–40. .Apr. 29, 1940. . 181
THEY KNEW WHAT THEY WANTED—Sidney Howard .... 24–25. .Nov. 24, 1924. . 414
THEY SHALL NOT DIE—John Wexley .... 33–34. .Feb. 21, 1934. . 62
THOUSAND CLOWNS, A—Herb Gardner .... 61–62. .Apr. 5, 1962. . 428
THREEPENNY OPERA—(b, l) Bertolt Brecht, (m)
    Kurt Weill, (tr) Ralph Manheim, John Willett
    (special citation as best revival) .... 75–76. .Mar. 1, 1976. . 307
THURBER CARNIVAL, A—James Thurber .... 59–60. .Feb. 26, 1960. . 127
TIGER AT THE GATES—Jean Giraudoux's *La Guerre de*
    Troie n'aura pas lieu, (tr) Christopher Fry .... 55–56. .Oct. 3, 1955. . 217
TIME OF THE CUCKOO, THE—Arthur Laurents .... 52–53. .Oct. 15, 1952. . 263

INDEX

Play titles appear in **bold face**. *Bold face italic* page numbers refer to those pages where complete cast and credit listings for New York productions may be found.

Baker, Word, 399
Bakkom, James, 138, 139
Bal, Henry "Kaimu," 124
Balaban, Bob, 355, 356
Balcena, Anthony, 379
Balcon, Michael, 504
Baldaro, Barrie, 133
Baldassari, Diane, 443
Balderson, Robert, 459
Balderston, John L., 24, 33, 355
Baldi, Joe, 505
Baldridge, Harold G., 132, 133
Bald Soprano, The, 110
Baldwin, Brooks, 422
Baldwin, Faith, 506
Baldwin, Nigel, 98
Balis, Andrea, 461, 464
Ball, David, 115
Ball, Desiree, 505
Ball, Jenny, 437
Ball, Lani, 370
Ball, Michael, 132
Ball, Patricia, 119
Ball, Randa, 389
Ball, William, 112
Ballad of the Sad Cafe, The, 460, 497, 498
Ballad of the Seven Sleeping Brothers In China, The, 456
Ballance, Beatrice, 438
Ballantine, Bessie, 442
Ballantyne, Paul, 100
Ballard, John W., 354
Ballard, Larry R., 69
Ballard, Ron, 456
Ballard, Stephanie, 139
Ballen, Ivan, 504
Ballet, Arthur, 41, 131
Balloons, Buffoons and Bubbles, 68
Balloons, The, 428
Ballou, Marshall, 425
Balsam, Martin, 16, 34, 360, 498
Baltzell, Deborah, 73, 122
Balyasnikov, 105
Bamman, Gerry, 350, 396
BAM Theater Company, The, 30, 38, 419-420
Bancroft, Anne, 10, 19, 20, 358, 495
Bandit Princess, The, 459
Banham, Russ, 358
Bank, Danny, 354
Bankey, Christopher, 417

Banks, Jonathan, 88
Banks, Morton, 463
Banks, Sally, 501
Bannerman, Guy, 138
Banninger, Carole, 365
Baptiste, Nicole, 70, 71
Bara, Frank, 142
Baranoff, Abe M., 506
Baranski, Christine, 78, 406
Barbeau, Adrienne, 477
Barbeau, Francois, 135, 136
Barber, Ellen, 468
Barbershop in Pittsburgh, A, 466
Barbieri, Beverly, 450, 451
Barbosa, James, 443
Barbour, Thomas, 464
Barcelo, Randy, 372, 440, 497
Barclay, Anne, 395
Barclay, Remi, 101
Barcone, Eugene, 112
Barden, Douglas, 461, 477
Barker, Christine, 471
Barker, Jean, 441
Barker, Margaret, 442
Barker, Stephen, 120
Barkhouse, Janet, 134
Barking Rooster Theater, The, 456
Barkla, Jack, 101
Barlow, Anna Marie, 444
Barnaby Sweet, 74-75
Barnard, Mel, 432
Barnes, Clive, 39, 490, 491
Barnes, George, 505
Barnes, Kathlyn, 428
Barnes, Marjorie, 88
Barnes, Perkin, 441
Barnes, Peter, 93
Barnes, Robert, 429
Barnes, Robert C., 115
Barnes, Robert E., Jr., 409
Barnes, Ted, 448
Barnes, Theo, 407, 440
Barnett, Daniel, 86, 87
Barnett, Jayne, 373
Barnett, June, 79
Barnett, Michael, 389
Barnett, Nate, 383
Barnett, Randy, 418
Barnett, Vince, 501
Barnhurst, Linda, 438
Barns, Christopher, 414
Baron, Roger, 129
Barone, James A., 467
Barr, Rachel, 466
Barr, Richard, 72

Barr, Sharon, 448, 450
Barre, Gabriel, 452, 467
Barre, Shelley, 425
Barrell, Terry, 440
Barrere, Jean, 506
Barres, Madeleine, 501
Barrett, Christopher, 356
Barrett, James Lee, 347
Barrett, Leslie, 71
Barrett, Lorraine, 466
Barrie, Barbara, 470
Barrie, Virginia, 467
Barrie, Wendy, 501
Barrington, Diana, 83
Barris, Herbie, 501
Barron, Holly, 106, 450
Barrs, Norman, 401
Barry, B. H., 422
Barry, Betty Claire, 141
Barry, Bob, 466
Barry, Ellen, 97
Barry, Gene, 129, 141, 381
Barry, Ivor, 120
Barry, Mary, 112
Barry, Paul, 97, 114
Barry, Peter, 473
Barry, Philip, 18, 66, 82, 86, 102, 117-118
Barry, Raymond J., 394, 396
Bart, J. Michael, 389
Bartenieff, George, 455, 456
Barter Theater, 67-68
Bartlett, D'Jamin, 129, 381
Bartlett, Ethel, 505
Bartlett, Peter, 116, 380
Bartlett, Robin, 442
Barton, Daniel, 364
Barton, Donald, 116
Barton, John, 77
Barton, Karen Lamb, 95
Barton, Ken, Jr., 95
Bartone, Jacklyn Lee, 407
Bartos, Lorlee, 81
Barulich, Maryann, 115
Basch, Harry, 91
Bash, Phyllis, 402, 403, 404
Basic Training of Pavlo Hummel, The, 348
Basile, Michael, 454
Bass, Eric, 457
Bass, Liz, 120
Bassett, Clyde, 82
Bassett, Paul R., 79, 80
Bass Fiddle, The, 456
Basso, Bob, 89
Bate, Dana, 434, 435
Bateman, Bill, 365

564   INDEX

Rice, Elmer, 38, 44, 452
Rice, James Goodwin, 430, 438
Rice, Joel Key, 356
Rice, Lucky, 413
Rice, Marie, 454
Rice, Sarah, 475
Rice, Tim, 38, 358, 418
Rich, Alan, 39
Rich, James, 354, 424
Richard Morse Mime Theater, 452
Richards, Arleigh, 407
Richards, David, vii, 16, 64, 124
Richards, Gary, 456
Richards, Gerald, 72, 78
Richards, James, 77
Richards, Jean, 428
Richards, Jeffrey, 408, 424
Richards, Lloyd, 130, 361
Richards, Martin, 362, 495
Richards, Paul, 394
Richards, Scott, 121
Richards, Shirley, 451
Richards, Thom, 100
Richardson, Alexander D., 506
Richardson, Claibe, 428
Richardson, Howard, 457, 465
Richardson, Jack, 461
Richardson, James G., 90
Richardson, Latanya, 476
Richardson, Lee, 104, 379, 434, 445
Richardson, Ronald, 364
Richardson, Sally, 116
Richardson, Walter, 389, 391
Richard III, 66, 97, 114, 115, 124, 137
Richelieu, 467
Rich Man, Poor Man Play, The, 456
Richman, Saul, 417, 423
Richmond, Brian, 134
Richmond, David, 32, 404
Richmond, Fred, 42
Rickert, Steven, 68
Ride Across Lake Constance, The, 437
Ridge, John David, 355, 388, 411, 422, 497-498
Ridgway, Patricia, 503
Ridiculous Theatrical Company, 31, 38, 392-393, 426, 461

Ridley, Gary, 389, 390, 391, 392
Ridley, Jane, 67
Riegert, Peter, 90, 91
Rield, Ron, 127
Ries, Thomas M., 402
Riesel, Robert, 380
Rieser, Terry, 71
Rigan, Drina, 461
Riggin, Patricia, 121
Riker, William R., 436
Riley, Jay Flash, 73, 470
Riley, Joe, 441
Riley, Larry, 480
Riley, Maggie, 96
Riley, Robert Maurice, 457
Riner, Richard, 89
Ring Gott Farblonjet, Der, 386, 392
Ringwall, Randolph, 505
Rinklin, Ruth E., 377
Rintels, David, 428
Rintoul, Brian, 132
Rio Grande Band, 424
Rippner, William, 460
Riscol, Randolph, 365
Rissel, Robert, 107
Risson, Barbara, 503
Rissoni, Gidita, 503
Ritchard, Cyril, 86, 482, 503
Ritchie, Lynn, 76
Ritman, William, 72, 88, 359, 363, 378
Ritual, 460
Rivals, The, 69, 70
Rivera, Chita, 471
Rivera, Mon, 506
Rivera, Ruth, 360
Rivers, Victor, 503
Riverside Theater Workshop, 465
Rivkin, Michael, 450
Rivoli, Mario, 455
Rizley, Martin, 83
Rizzuto, Giner, 503
Roadside Theater, 442
Robards, Jason, 10, 24, 34, 35, 359, 495
Robber Bridegroom, The, 127, 128
Robbins, Carrie F., 384, 394, 411
Robbins, Ellen, 121
Robbins, Everett, 373
Robbins, Jana, 76
Robbins, Jean, 503
Robbins, Marilyn, 438

Robbins, Randall, 433, 465
Robbins, Rex, 72, 356, 420, 479
Robbins, Sanford, 98, 99
Robbins, Tom, 422
Robelo, Mike, 91
Robert, Denise, 135
Robert, Philippe, 134
Roberts, Arthur H., 108
Roberts, Chapman, 474
Roberts, Doris, 362
Roberts, Douglas, 69
Roberts, Eve, 116
Roberts, Howard, 382, 383
Roberts, Jack, 74
Roberts, Jane, 452
Roberts, Jimmy, 453
Roberts, Judith, 407, 443
Roberts, Les, 116, 457
Roberts, Nick, 446
Roberts, Richard, 133
Roberts, Ruth, 409
Roberts, Ted, 133
Roberts, William, 104
Robertson, Barbara E., 74, 75
Robertson, Gary, 466
Robertson, Lanie, 450
Robertson, Liz, 478
Robertson, Margaret, 138
Robertson, Pat, 101
Robertson, Warren, 461
Robertson, William, 350, 409
Robijns, Jan, 467
Robin, Gil, 367, 368
Robinson, Hal, 474
Robinson, Lorie, 375, 397
Robinson, Marguerite, 95
Robinson, Mary, 446
Robinson, Maurice L., 504
Robinson, Muriel, 404
Robinson, Venustra K., 375, 376, 397, 398
Robison, Barry, 74, 99, 100, 101
Robman, Steven, 123, 131, 406
Robson, Mona, 456
Robson, Wayne, 134, 139
Roby, John, 133
Roche, Con, 67
Rock, Connie, 434
Rock, Edith Blossom, 503
Rockaway Boulevard, 428
Rockower, Madeline, 452
Rockwell, George I., 503
Rockwood, Jerry, 445, 462
Rodd, Marcia, 69, 70

594   INDEX